Come
Spring

Ben   Ames   Williams

ISBN: 0-9678716-0-3

Library of Congress Catalog Card Number: 00-130579

THIS 2000 EDITION BY ARRANGEMENT WITH THE ESTATE OF
BEN AMES WILLIAMS IN CARE OF HAROLD OBER ASSOCIATES
NEW YORK, NEW YORK

Printed by Versa Press, Incorporated
East Peoria, Illinois

Cover by Tim Seymour Designs
Camden, Maine

UNION HISTORICAL SOCIETY
P.O. Box 154, Union, Maine 04862
207-785-5444
www.midcoast.com/comespring

Lish Partridge's later home

Phin Butler

To Sunnyback Pond

Col Wheaton's Camp (Partridge's first house)

Rapids

FOREST

Phin Butler's Path

Matt Hawes

Jason Ware Beaver Dam Maple Tree

Royal Mess

Carry 160 FT. EL.

Josiah Robbins

Steep Bank

ROUND POND

The Swimming Tree

Tree Bridge

SEVEN TREE POND

Johnny Butler

200 Acres

FOREST

Philip Robbins 1776 250 FT. EL.

Cleared 1777

SEVEN TREE ISLAND

Mill

dams

KY HILLSIDE

Jess Robbins 100 FT. EL.

Moses Hawes

700 Acres

FOREST

PATH

Richard Comings 1776

Detail of
STERLINGTOWN
Incorporated as Union
in 1780

David Robbins 1776

PATH

¼   ½   ¾
Scale of Mile

Ezra Bowen   Abijah Hawes

Introductory Notes

When Ben Ames Williams decided to write about the lives of ordinary people during a war, he researched records of the settlers along the Georges River in what became the town of Union, Maine. In the same year the Declaration of Independence was signed, Philip Robbins brought his family up this river. They cleared the land, built cabins, weathered the hardships of cold, hunger and backbreaking work and created a community in the wilderness.

Come Spring is the fictionalized account of those first settlers. The story follows eight years of struggles and joys, providing accurate pictures of their daily lives. Williams had walked their land, traveled from pond to pond by canoe, noted conditions in all seasons to give his characters authenticity of voice and behavior.

The Union Historical Society has identified the sites of the original cabins, the graves of the settlers and the depression marking the site of the small windowless cabin in which 14 of them lived during their first winter.

A. Carman Clark
Union, Maine
Spring, 2000

The cover was done by Bernadette N. Lynch, a self-taught artist of Brunswick, Maine. "Ben" was captivated by *Come Spring*; she painted what she felt the setting might have been. Her original was presented at Union's 1998 Founders Day to the Union Historical Society, in recognition of its work to maintain and promote the historical sites depicted in this book.

The Publisher

Contents

I

The River

The attempt in this book has been to tell the story of the founding of a small Maine town, by ordinary people, in what was then an ordinary way. It was the way in which towns were founded from the Atlantic seaboard west to the great plains, by stripping off the forest and putting the land to work. The people in this book were not individually as important as George Washington; the town they founded was not as important as New York. But people like them made this country, and towns like this one were and are the soil in which this country's roots are grounded.

1

MIMA woke before day. The sky above the open hatch was spangled with stars, not yet paled by coming dawn. The Sally sloop was almost motionless, seeming strangely stable after the steady tumble and the creaking drive of these days on the passage from the westward. The night sky was cloudless; and lying with wide eyes, staring up through the hatch, Mima saw the stars swing to and fro, as though they were attached to the little vessel, their motion thus determined. Were the stars watching? Were they as far away as they seemed? Were there people on those stars, men and women, young men and girls, children? Did they too strive and plan and hope? Did they too feel within themselves, as she did, something deep and sure and powerful that day by day unfolded; that grew within her as her babies would one day grow and ripen in her womb? Her eyes were deep with wonder, but they were unafraid. This was life, this swelling strength in her; this was her life, here in her body, waiting to be lived, waiting to be shared, waiting to be passed on into other bodies, into the bodies of fine straight sons and of brave and loyal daughters.

She folded her arms across her breasts, lying warm and still, treasuring and guarding the rich stores of life which were her treasure to preserve and to bestow. To bestow that life was the only certain way to preserve it. The preachers spoke of immortality as though it were as far away as the stars; but was it not immortality to pass on a part of your life to make another one? Yet before your life was fit to be passed on, it must be kept fine and clean. Perhaps life was like the one talent in the parable in the Bible; perhaps you earned the right to an eternal life by the brave use you made of this one.

She was for a while alone with her thoughts; but then she became conscious again of the others here close around her. The Sally sloop had carried a load of cordwood to the westward; but it was a human freight which now she bore. In her hold, here under the open hatch, sleeping every which way among the bales and bundles of their household goods, there were seven people. Mima as she lay held close against her side her eight-year-old sister Susie; and beyond Susie was Bet, Mima's older sister, who had married Richard Comings two years ago, and whose boy baby lay now in her arms. Mima's mother and her two younger brothers were together in the forward part of the hold; and Mima wondered whether her mother too was awake, lying quietly, watching the stars, trying to imagine what this day and the days and years that were to come would bring. Her father and Richard Comings were sleeping on deck, leaving to the womenfolks and the younger children the relative privacy and shelter of the hold.

Mima saw suddenly that the stars were paler now; so day was near. Her heart began to pound, with slow deep beats; and a strong excitement shook her. They had anchored at full dark last night to wait for dawn and a landward breeze and a tide to help them up the river; but Mima had wished that even in the darkness they might go on, till Captain Watson laughed at her eagerness, and pinched her cheek and told her there was time enough.

'The land has always been there, waiting for you, Mima,' he said. 'It'll wait till you come!'

* * * * *

This Captain James Watson had for some years commanded coasters, carrying cordwood or lime to the westward, coming home to St. George's in ballast or with some small cargo of supplies for the settlement here; and he had had a part in many things. Mima from the day they sailed out of Boston asked him many questions; and he was glad to answer her, watching her while he talked. She was nineteen, lean and fine-drawn, with a look about her as though she faced a strong and steady wind. He thought she was like the figureheads some vessels carried, with her fine brow and her clean-molded cheeks and chin and the round breasts firm under her tight gown which she had a little outgrown. They had spent long hours together since the Sally sloop sailed, and he talked while she listened. He told her that he and Ben Burton had had a part in that famous tea party in Boston three years before.

'I'd come in with a load of cordwood,' he explained, 'and Ben and me heard the talk and saw the broadsides; so we crowded into the Old South Meeting-House with the rest of them, not knowing at all what it was about till we heard the speeches; and when there was the rush for the wharves after, why, we followed on.'

'Were you painted up like Indians?' she asked.

'Not us. Maybe we were brown enough from sea and sun and wind; but none in Boston town were like to know us anyway. I rubbed a smear of kettle soot across my face; but Ben did not even that. He was in the hold fixing the slings, and me on deck to break the chests open with a nigger-hoe. Tide was fair low, and going; and before we finished there was tea like seaweed on the flats, and it was piled up deck-high by the gangway, so we had to shovel it out of the way to keep it from sliding and blowing back on board.'

'Didn't the soldiers try to stop you?'

'Not them!' He chuckled at the memory. 'The King's Admiral came walking along the wharf to see the fun, and there were heads out of every window near.'

'Why didn't they keep the tea and drink it? Seems like it was a shame to waste it so.'

'Well, you'll mind the ones that started the whole thing were them that had tea to sell and didn't want more of it coming in; so if anyone tried to save a bit, down on him they came. I put a handful in the pocket of my pea jacket, to show to the folks here to prove what we'd done.'

'Was it all right to drink?'

'It might have been if there hadn't been a packet of snuff that opened up in that pocket.' He chuckled at a sudden memory. 'Speaking of tea, they tell a tale up where we're heading, Mima, how Marm Alexander, the Captain's missus, the time he was elected to captain the militia here twenty-five years ago, set out to cook some tea for the womenfolks. It was the first she ever had seen; so she boiled it and poured off the broth and buttered the leaves — and the old folks that tried it will tell you to this day even hogs wouldn't eat it.'

He liked the way her laughter rang; and he liked talking to her so that he might watch her color come and go as her pulse quickened at his tales, or slowed again. He showed her his 'Lett Pass', dated in Salem in December two years before, which allowed him to take a load of wood into Boston after the Port Bill had closed the port to all vessels.

'I was the first to take a cargo in after the Port Bill,' he said. 'Thirty cords of oak and beech I had aboard.'

She was interested in his navigation of the sloop. The forested coastline looked all alike to her, and she asked him how he would be sure to know their destination when he came to it. He said he could make into George's River blindfolded, on the darkest night and in the thickest fog; and yesterday as they approached their destination he had pointed out their marks and courses. They kept south of Damiscove Island and then made up for Pemaquid Point, and brought it west-southwest, and laid their course for the river mouth. She recognized Egg Rock from his description while they were still two or three leagues away. They drew in among the islands with the sun low and lower in the west; and the shores dark with spruce and pine put on robes of purple shadow. They passed between two islands scarce half a mile apart, and the one on their starboard hand was no more than a few rods long. Captain Watson told her the larger islands, some two miles off to the eastward, bore the same name as the river into which they would presently be making; but the river's actual mouth was still miles away. The faint breeze held long enough to let them anchor in a cove on the larboard side of the passage, within the embrace of a sheltering point of land, as night came down. She asked whether this was mainland or an island which gave them shelter now.

'An island,' he said, 'right off the end of the main. We're no more than a mile below Tom Henderson's fort. You'll see it first thing in the morning. Be sure you wake. We'll catch the tide at sunup, and ride it all the way.'

* * * * *

Mima, in this dawning as the stars began to fade, could no longer bear to stay below. Susie's head was heavy on her shoulder, but she freed herself without waking the child, and caught the hatch coaming and climbed out on deck. It was cold, and despite her warm shawl she shivered and her teeth chattered faintly. Her father and Rich were rolled in their blankets on the decks aft; and they did not rouse. She lowered a wooden bucket overside and splashed the icy water in her face and caught her breath at the shock of it; but on the heels of that chill, warmth ran through her everywhere. The shore close aboard was a black wall of dark spruces towering among the stars, seeming to lean toward her when she looked up at

them. She heard a stir aft as Captain Watson came up from
the small cabin; and then her father woke, and he and Captain
Watson spoke a moment together and then moved toward
where Mima stood scrubbing her face dry with her petticoats.
Captain Watson laughed and said she must like to be frozen
if she washed in such water. He went forward to rouse Reuben
Hall to make sail, and Mima and her father were left together
in the waist.

Philip Robbins was at the time forty-six years old. His half-
brother, Oliver, had come from Attleboro fourteen years ago
to build the first frame dwelling house in the lower plantation
of St. George's; and another half-brother, Ebenezer, settled on
the Fox Islands, in the great bay a little to the northward.
Philip's own son David had come one summer to visit Oliver;
and he brought back glowing reports of the fine timber on the
land, the fertile soil when the trees were cleared away. Two
years ago he moved his wife and their two babies up here and
bought a farm in the upper town.

What Philip heard from David and from Oliver led him to
come to see for himself; and what he saw fired his imagination
and fused his determination to remove all his family here and
make a new home in the untouched wilderness. He negotiated
the purchase of a vast tract of land west of Seven-Tree Pond,
some seven miles up the river from tidewater; and he and his
older sons had come in the spring and worked all this summer
clearing the land and making a crop. Philip left his sons here
when he went home to bring on his family. Richard Comings
had come with him in May, stayed long enough to clear land
and sow a crop and build a cabin, and then returned to Stough-
ton to close out his affairs there. He and Bet and the baby
joined his father-in-law in this removal now.

When Philip woke this morning, his sleep-clouded thoughts
cleared as the sky clears when the west wind blows. He felt the
nearness of all these who were his blood and bone, aboard the
little sloop. To them this was an adventure which they faced

eagerly; but it was he who had brought them here, and upon his strength and wisdom all their lives depended. The sober weight of that grave responsibility was heavy on the man. When he came to where his daughter stood, he drew Mima close against his side, his arm around her waist.

'Well, we're this far, Mima,' he said. 'It's not like we'll be troubled by the King's ships now.'

'Have you been worried, Father?'

'Some,' he admitted; and he said: 'I've not told your mother about this. There was no need to trouble her. But when I came before — you know I had to go to Salem to find a passage — there were ships about. The British had just moved out of Boston; but they were still lying off the harbor, so we had to dodge them. There was one of our privateers convoyed us for two hours or so; but then she went off to chase a sail she saw, and we were uneasy all the way after.'

'You'd have beat them if they'd chased us,' she said, and smiled up at him teasingly. 'Remember what you said yourself — three years ago, to the British officers that were bragging so — that one of us could beat any two of them and eat them before breakfast, if they came out into the country? You did it, too, driving them all the way from Concord back to Boston town.'

He chuckled. 'I did no driving, that day. We were too late — except to help eat the vittles other men took off of them, when we got to Cambridge. All my big talk got me was a look at the inside of a jail. No, one of their fleet tenders could have gobbled us any time this side of Boston, and no help for it — and all I own in the world here aboard.' His eyes clouded at his own thoughts. 'D'ye think we'll manage, Mima?' he asked, wanting to be reassured.

'We will,' she said steadily. 'David and Eben and Jess will have all ready for us, sure. We'll do fine.'

'Ye've not seen it yet,' he reminded her. 'There's nought but great trees all around, that have to be falled and burned before there's any room for farming. There's a main of work ahead for all of us, these next years.'

She said slowly: 'It's the job we have to do, all of us that live in all the colonies. Here's new country everywhere, and it's not the King's any more. We've said it's ours; but it's not ours just for the saying. We have to use it before it's ours; clear the land and make it bear, and bear children to live on it.' Her voice was still and quiet in the dawn. 'Talking won't make it ours, nor signing declarations that we're independent. We've got to use the land everywhere. Use it, and live on it.' She looked up at him. 'That's work enough for our lifetimes, Father, and for more lifetimes to come. We can't do it all, but we can do what we can, and we can have children and raise them to work at it after us.'

His arm tightened around her; and there was a teasing tenderness in his tones. 'You can't have children just by wanting them, Mima. You'd have been sooner wedded if we'd stayed to home.'

'There will be men here.'

'Your brothers, yes; and Rich Comings, and me. That's all!'

'There'll be men coming. There's a big work to do, and big men will come to do it. Fine men.' She smiled up at him. 'Never be afraid, Father, I'll have a-plenty to choose from.'

'Them that come here will be too tired, by night, for any bundling and dandling with the girls.'

She tossed her head, laughing, yet with a ringing in her tones like the sound of bells. 'When I've seen the one I want,' she said, 'I'll not wait for all that.' And she whispered: 'He and I will have too much to do to be wasting any time.'

2

DAY was on them, seeming to
come suddenly. At one moment, the islands and the main were
low dark shadows between dark sea and darker sky. At the
next, they began to assume form and definition. Philip woke
Rich Comings to help them get the anchor up; and Rich came,
blinking sleepily, along the deck past where Mima stood. He
stumbled, as though he were walking in his sleep. He was a
stocky, fair-haired man with a round face, and there was a little
white scar not half an inch long in his left cheek below the eye
around which the skin puckered faintly, so that he seemed
sometimes to be squinting against the sun. He nodded to her
in the dawn dusk, but without speaking. He was always inclined to silence; and Mima sometimes thought he might be almost lonely, surrounded as he was by the whole Robbins clan.
They were a vocal lot, all of them ready talkers; and Bet, whom
he had married, talked more than any of them. Rich had
never seemed to be one of them, as Dave's wife, Bess Chapman,
had so readily become. Perhaps sons-in-law were always a
little more like outsiders, whom you resented because your

sister belonged to them and no longer to you. Mima herself liked Rich, and Bet loved him; there was no doubt of that. He was devoted to Bet, and he was a worker. Even Philip said Rich was worth two of Dave.

Rich went forward now with her father to raise the anchor, while Reuben Hall and Captain Watson hoisted the sails. Mima added her young strength to theirs, swaying her weight with Reuben Hall on the lift of the mainsail. He was a big young man who when there were no tasks to do aboard the sloop could always drop off to sleep as readily as a dog, though he woke more hardly. Mima had seen him sleep like a dead man, flat on his back in the sun, with his mouth open, snoring faintly. He did not look at her as she helped him now; but when their hands touched, she saw his ears burn red. She had seen him sometimes watching her when he thought she did not know.

The mainsail caught the first dawn breeze; the anchor thumped the deck; the sloop gathered way, and suddenly it came to life, as those below waked and began to throng on deck. Young Philip, Mima's five-year-old brother, was first. He was principally distinguished by a fine crop of freckles left over from the summer, and a tremendous pride in his clubbed hair caught with a twist of eelskin so that he was a small replica of his elders. He was missing one tooth, and the resulting lisp made him nowadays self-conscious and silent. Jacob came on his heels. Jacob was fourteen, lean and gawkish, with big hands and feet and an Adam's apple that pumped wildly when he was even silently excited. It had been a source of shame and incipient revolt in him all summer that he had been left behind when Philip brought his two older sons to Maine in May; but he was reconciled now in the imminence of his own arrival in the promised land. Susie was only a minute behind Jacob, and Mrs. Robbins lifted her head out of the hold and considered the November dawn and said grudgingly:

'Well, by the looks, it won't snow this morning anyway.

Mima, give Susie's hair a lick and a promise, will you. And don't let Phil fall overboard. Jake, you keep an eye on him too. I won't be easy till he's ashore.'

Mima said reassuringly: 'He'll be all right.' Mrs. Robbins was dubious about this adventuring into the wilderness at her age. She disappeared, and Mima hauled water from overside and washed Sue's face and Philip's. Jacob might have hauled the water, but he had gone to watch Reuben Hall steer. Mima handed a full pail down to her mother, and saw Bet lying in her blankets, looking up, her countenance serene in peace and rich content, so that Mima knew she was nursing little David, now almost a year old. Mima smiled down at her sister, feeling herself warm and happy as she always did when she watched Bet nurse the baby; and Bet said whisperingly, careful not to disturb her son:

'I'll come as soon as he's et, Mima. Can you see the river?'

'Yes. We're making into it now.'

Bet made a low laughing sound, a murmur of faint pain, and looked down where her baby lay hidden under the blanket and said happily:

'He's fierce as a colt for his breakfast.'

'Don't let him hurt you,' her mother warned her.

'Bless his heart, I love it when he does. He's so big and strong.'

Mima, turning away, felt herself tingling with a fierce desire for that bliss which Bet already had. She brushed out Susie's fine fair hair, and sent Philip to be in Jacob's charge aft, and she and Susie went forward. She stood in the bow, her arms clasped, her eyes glowing, watching while they opened out ahead of them the wide welcome of the river. She did not hear Captain Watson approach till he said beside her:

'You can see Captain Henderson's house and fort now, inside that point ahead, if you know where to look. It'll be all plain in a minute. Light's coming fast.'

'Was the fort built to fight the Indians?'

He chuckled. 'Scared of Indians, Mima?'

'I don't know. I don't think so. Do they come here now?'

'Not to bother us; not lately. Thirty years ago all the settlers down here packed into Tom Henderson's place during the troubles. The Indians didn't come much on that west bank. Oliver Robbins was about the only settler on the east bank in the early days, only there were some over Wessaweskeag way. Eb Thorndike took up six hundred acres there; but he never brought his family. Used to net salmon in the river, and make salt, and trade up the Bay. He had a pet moose once, a calf his son Josh caught, but it died.' Then he said with an excessive gravity: 'But you'll have to look out for Indians up where you're going. Ben Burton's been working up there building houses for Doc Taylor, and he was telling me there was some around.'

His tone was jocular, so she was not disturbed. 'We're going to live in Packard's house this winter,' she said. 'It came to Father when he bought from Doctor Taylor. My brothers are there now, getting ready for us.'

'Well, it's a good house if Ben Burton built it,' he assured her. 'But don't forget about the Indians. The King may turn 'em loose on us. Maybe you'd better shave your hair, to be real safe.'

She laughed. 'You're making fun of me!'

'Dunno's I am,' he said, too seriously to deceive her. 'Ben ought to know about Indians if anyone does.' Susie clung to Mima's skirt, and Mima pressed the girl's head affectionately against her side; and little Phil came running to join them as Captain Watson went on: 'Ben's old man was in the thick of it, in the trouble twenty years ago. He had a blockhouse up ahead, stone so's they couldn't burn it; but they killed two of his men and lifted the hair of another that wa'n't quite dead, twenty years ago last March.'

Mima felt Susie trembling; and she said reassuringly: 'That was ever so long ago — before I was born.'

'Well, they had quite a time around here for two-three years,' he insisted. 'The Hendley boys was ambushed on Mill River. They'd gone after frost-fish. The red devils killed Henry, but Joe managed to get back to the fort after they'd gone. He was minus his hair, and his insides was dragging on the ground where one of 'em had socked a tomahawk into his stomach.' He grinned in a dry way. 'The thing on Joe's mind, he'd hid his silver sleeve-buttons in a stump on the way home, in case the Indians got him again, and he wanted to tell his folks where to find them. Soon's he told them, he died. He set a heap of store by those buttons, I sh'd judge.'

Philip clung tight to Mima's hand, and Captain Watson said: 'Oh, I could tell you stories enough! They jumped out on some of the womenfolks one day, carried Mis' Thompson off, and it cost Thompson forty dollars to get her back. He 'lowed it was worth it, but he's kind of kept her reminded of it ever sence.' He chuckled. 'There was Miss Lamb, she'd just finished milking when they come. She run like a good one. Had a piece to go, and a set of bars to climb, but she made it, and fetched her pail full of milk all the way and never spilled a drop. She claimed she didn't know she had it.'

He added, in a different tone: 'A woman gets a thing in her mind to do, she's apt to do it. Down here' — he nodded toward the western shore — 'in '55, some Indians got into Joe Bradford's house before he saw 'em. It was right handy to the fort, but the Indians butchered Joe and Mis' Bradford. She had her baby in her arms when one of them put his hatchet into her head. When she dropped the baby, their young one, a girl about fourteen, grabbed it and run. One of the Indians threw his tomahawk after her and cut her side open, and she held her insides in with one hand and the baby in the other and made it to the fort. She got over it, too. Moved to Vermont. I heard she's married and raising children of her own now.' He spat in hearty approval. 'I'll bet she'll raise 'em too. She'd be a hard one to stop anything she set out to do, it looks to me.'

Mima's eyes were glowing as she watched the wooded shores they passed. 'Did you ever fight them yourself?' she asked.

He said, his lips suddenly tightening: 'Never had to, but I owe them something I'd like to pay. See that tall tree ahead, this side the point?'

'The one that's higher than the others around it?'

'Yes. There was others the same size; but they've been cut off for lumber. Cutting lumber along there, they never bothered with anything unless it was so big two men couldn't reach around it. They left all the sapling stuff. But that tree you see, they didn't cut that account of it's rotten part way up on one side; and there's a spring about two rods below it. Cap'n John Watson, my half-brother, was killed there. He was coming down river in his sloop and sent his brother Bill and a man named Larrabee ashore to fetch water from the spring. Indians grabbed them in the woods, and when they didn't come back, Cap'n John put off to see what had happened to them. A Frenchman hailed him and told him to come ashore, but John tried to row away, so they shot him, cut his insides out, and hung him on a tree.' He added: 'Mis' Gamble and an old man name of Jameson was all that was left on the sloop. Indians tried to grab 'em that night; but with her loading the guns and him shooting, they kep' 'em off! Only it upset Mis' Gamble so she had her baby — it was stillborn — before morning, with nobody but Jameson to 'tend to her.' He flung up his hand, pointing. 'There, you can see Henderson's now; all plain.' And he added: 'That was in '57.'

'The year I was born.' Mima's eyes were on the low red buildings, the small clearing ringed with forest. She asked:

'Was Bill — John's brother — your half-brother too?'

'Yes. He got clear of them after, came back from Canada, and him and me took up land on the high ground opposite the fort at St. George's. Watson's Point, they call it. You'll see it right off, now.'

'Is Tom Henderson's fort the beginning of the town?'

'Well, you might say the lower town runs along all the way from the broad cove up. You can see some of the houses ahead, and time you get opposite the cove you can see St. George's Fort. The river runs right straight at it, the last few miles.' The wind was freshening, a fine southeaster to help them on their way. He added: 'We're getting the first of the flood now. I like to run up river on low water. You can see the channel, the flats out of water on both sides. There's quite a lot of trouble you can get into if you don't know your way. Soon's we pass the point here, we'll keep over't starboard till we get opposite the broad cove. There's ledges to larboard two-thirds of the way across the river, this side the cove.' He added: 'You can see the fort in town from there, what there is left of it.'

He went aft to relieve Reuben Hall at the helm, and Susie tugged at Mima's skirt and asked: 'Mima, will the Indians hurt me?'

Mima hugged her, laughing proudly. The child's tone was as remote and unshaken as though she spoke of breakfast, without fear. But young Philip was more disturbed, and Mima saw his lip quivering; so she said gaily: 'Phil and I won't let them, Susie. Of course Phil will have to do the fighting, because he's a man; but you and I will load the guns for him and he can just shoot them bang, bang, bang; like knocking apples off a fence!'

Little Phil laughed delightedly at the prospect. Then Mrs. Robbins called them and there was breakfast to be eaten; corn-meal mush with pork scraps in it, and hot sugared tea. They were all too excited to be hungry; but Mrs. Robbins held them to it. 'Eat it up!' she insisted. 'You, Jake, clean your dish. Pa, you're as bad as the rest of 'em. Eat every scrap. Some day you'll be hungry and wish you had it.'

Her husband grinned amiably. 'Like to know how many times I've heard you say that, Ma! "Clean your dish! Eat it up!"'

'Well, if there's anything I hate to see it's good vittles wasted.'

'A sparrow'd starve to death if he tried to live on what we waste.' He said, in a lower tone, with a deep tenderness: 'You've done with mighty little, Ma, bringing up these young ones. We'd all have gone hungry, sometimes, if it warn't for you. And one pair of britches goes right down the line from me to Phil.'

'Well, I never did see the sense of getting new when we could make the old ones do.'

'And you never throwed a thing away that warn't plumb wore out.'

She said fiercely: 'Folks would be better off half the time to make things do — or else do without.'

While they were still eating, they passed the point where Tom Henderson's fort and building stood. A man came to watch them and Captain Watson whooped a greeting. Then the shores receded into deep coves on either hand. The hardwoods were bare, their leaves gone except where oaks still showed a dull russet brown; but the forests of pine and spruce were dark and gleaming in the risen sun. Above the fort, along both banks, Mima saw small clearings, usually dotted with stumps, a log house in each clearing; and once or twice trees had been felled over acres of ground and left to lie, as though a great wind had thrust them down. Above the coves, they entered narrower waters, where the river bed was not half a mile from shore to shore; and she felt the land begin to embrace them welcomingly. Henderson's was near two miles behind. Beyond the narrows, Captain Watson hauled toward the eastern shore.

'Have to keep Henderson's in sight till we pass the ledges,' he explained. 'If you let the point shut in the fort too soon, you're heading right for trouble.' Above the narrows the river widened again, and she saw him now and then look aft to make his course good. Presently the river narrowed once more, and she could see ahead of them a straight reach two or three miles long, and a rising hill beyond. 'That's Madambettox,' he told her. 'The hill. And you can see the old fort now, if your eyes are good enough.'

'I see it. It's big, isn't it?'

'The main part's all of a hundred feet on a side, laid up of logs twenty inches square, and loopholes and flankers on the corners. They had cohorns in the fort, and some iron guns in a blockhouse down by the water, with a covered way up to the fort. Then there were barracks for soldiers, and places for the folks to live when the Indians drove them in, all built around against the walls inside, and storehouses for food, and to keep powder and shot in, and a well in the middle that never went dry.'

'Did everyone go there when the Indians came?'

'There or to the blockhouses. Tom Kilpatrick had his own blockhouse when he was Captain, up't the head of the narrows; and Ben Burton had his, stone, down below. Burton's Fort, they called that. And you saw Henderson's as we came by.'

'But I mean, did everyone go into the forts somewhere? Didn't anyone stay at home?'

'It weren't safe,' Captain Watson assured her. 'It weren't any too safe even handy t'the fort. Man named Dave Creighton was killed and scalped in '47 right above where Fort Wharf is now.' His eyes were on his marks. The flooding tide had almost covered the flats; but the channel was straight enough. He said: 'I didn't go to scare the children with my Indian talk, a while ago. I was maybe funning with you a little. What I said was true enough; but that was all of twenty years ago.'

Mima's head lifted strongly. 'You didn't scare them. If we were easy scared, we wouldn't be coming here.'

'There ain't a thing to hurt you,' he assured her. 'Wolves are around some; but they're easy drove off. Bears are all right. Mostly you'll be living on bear meat, and moose meat maybe. Bears are handiest. They come around the clearings, so you don't have so far to lug the meat. Moose, mostly you have to go after and pack home, or maybe sled it in the wintertime. But none of them'll hurt you. Nothing will, long as you don't fall in the river and drown, or get lost in a blizzard in the winter, or get in the way of a tree when it's on the way down.'

Mima said, her eyes steady on the shores ahead of them: 'Cap'n, you talk a lot about Ben Burton. I guess you're pretty good friends with him?'

He nodded. 'Yes, we be. Ben's all right.' He grinned. 'Of course I like my flip once in a while, or a noggin of rum on a cold day; and Ben don't ever touch it. But he's man-size, just the same.'

'How old is he?'

He looked at her quickly, a shrewd amusement in his eyes. 'Well, now, let me see,' he said. 'He was thirteen when his pa died, and that was in '63. That'd make Ben twenty-six now, the way I figger it.'

'Did the Indians kill his father?'

He laughed robustly. 'Cap Burton? He was worth twenty Indians. No, he had a row with Cap'n North one night, in March it was. They was cronies; but they got into an argument, maybe had just a drop too much. It was at Cap'n North's house. When it come time for Cap'n Burton to start home — he had to paddle acrost the river — Cap'n North said he might full as well stay; but he was mad enough to be stubborn, so he started. But he couldn't make it to shore, 'count of new ice; and it wouldn't bear his weight, so he froze to death.'

She made a pitying sound, and he went on: 'He'd brought Ben up to be pretty rugged. Ben and his sisters used to stand guard on top of the fort when they was young ones. Then when his father died, Ben promised his ma he'd never touch a drop of liquor, and he never has. He's a first-rate ship carpenter. Doc Taylor hired him to help build the buildings up in Taylortown where you're going.'

'We bought our land from Doctor Taylor,' she said; and she asked, her eyes straight ahead: 'Is Ben Burton up there now?'

'Was, last I heard; but he figured on getting a commission in the army if he could. Doc Taylor was trying to put it through. If Ben's got that, he'll be gone up t'the westward by now.'

She asked: 'Is he married?'

Captain Watson chuckled wisely, and Mima's cheek was bright. She laughed with him, rubbing her hot cheeks with her hands. 'I'll tell him you was asking,' he warned her. He touched the helm, called: 'Rube!' Reuben Hall, asleep on deck amidships, roused and came toward him and he said: 'Stand by. We'll get the sails off her, sweep her in.' He told Mima: 'I want to stop here at Fort Wharf a minute, give Major Wheaton the dispatches I brought.'

She did not answer, watching the nearing shore.

3

EVERYONE helped with the sweeps as the Sally sloop moved slowly in to Fort Wharf, but Mima while she worked studied the wharf ahead of them, the rising slopes behind it, the dark mass of the fort, the houses — log and frame — visible here and there, and the men and women who came trooping down to meet the sloop. The upper and the lower plantations of St. George's had close to two hundred inhabitants, scattered along twenty miles of river; and the arrival of any vessel from the westward brought everyone to hear the news she brought.

Mima pushed at a sweep beside her father, and he too scanned the crowd ahead. 'Don't see Oliver,' he said. 'Or any of the boys. I thought they might be down — but they didn't know for sure when we'd come.'

'There's more folks coming,' she pointed out. 'Down the path past the fort.'

The sloop came near the wharf. When she touched, Major Mason Wheaton was the first to step foot on board; and Mima found her eye drawn to him instantly, and held. Since the Colonies had signed their Declaration of Independence at Philadelphia four months before, the militia companies had been reorganized, and the scattered settlements put in some order for defense against whatever was to come. Major Wheaton was locally in command, and there was a bold force in his eye and in the jut of his jaw. He seemed taller than the men about him, towering over them not so much physically as by something strong in him and almost violent. Captain Watson clasped his hand and gave him a packet and introduced Mima's father.

'Philip Robbins, Major,' he said. 'Oliver's half-brother. He's bought land up at Seven-Tree Pond from Doc Taylor.'

'Your servant, Robbins,' the Major agreed. 'Oliver's on his way here to meet you.' And he asked: 'Dealt with Taylor, did you? Then hold on to your eye teeth! That God-damned politician will have them if you don't.' He slapped the packet of letters across his palm. 'What's the news, Cap'n?' he demanded.

Mima came nearer where they stood and he watched her with a lively eye. Mason Wheaton had come to St. George's a dozen or fifteen years ago, and he had at once assumed — and been accorded — a position of leadership in the settlement. His wife's death had left him with two children, a boy not yet ten, and a daughter younger. He was no more than forty years old, and he paid more attention to Mima now than to what Captain Watson had to tell him. The news was bad. The British had destroyed the American fleet hastily constructed by Arnold on Champlain, and now commanded the lake and held Crown Point.

'But they'll not move this winter,' Captain Watson predicted. 'There'll be time to get men together to meet them and to beat them another year.'

'What about General Washington?' Major Wheaton asked, still watching Mima.

'You've heard Howe got New York away from him,' Captain Watson said. 'Washington will back off into New Jersey, they say, and make Howe come after him.'

Wheaton nodded indifferently. He spoke to Philip. 'You've got a handsome family.'

Philip turned and saw Mima at his shoulder and drew her forward. 'This is about the best I've got, Major,' he said, smiling. 'My daughter Mima.'

'Your servant, ma'am,' Major Wheaton told her. 'Robbins, I'll be coming up to Seven-Tree Pond to pay you a call, one day. You'll have all the sprigs in town beating a track to your door. Any more to match her?'

His tone made Mima smile; and her father said in a dry amusement: 'Why, no. My Bet is married a'ready; and Susie's just passed eight years old. The other five are boys.'

Wheaton laughed. 'Well, with five sons you won't have to hire help. Bought from Taylor, did you?'

Philip nodded. 'Seventy-five hundred acres — more or less.'

'Papers passed? Money paid?'

'Not yet.'

'Buy on time,' Wheaton advised. 'We'll see paper money go to pot before we're through. Buy now and pay paper later and you'll have your land for nothing.'

Before Philip could answer, a cry from her mother made Mima turn. 'Here's Dave, Pa,' Mrs. Robbins called, and Mima saw her brother elbow through the crowd on the wharf and spring aboard. An instant later she was in his arms.

'Oh, Dave!' she cried. 'You did come to meet us. I knew you would. Did Jess? Did Eben?'

He hugged her hard. 'Ho, Mima, you're a woman grown, in these two years!' he exclaimed, and kissed her roundly. 'Why, I thought you'd be a long-leg still!' He held her off to look at her; and then his mother caught him, and the others came clamoring around, and he had to answer a dozen questions at once. David was a tremendous man, taller than his father, with something comic in his tones, and mirth in his eyes; and he laughed at their clamoring inquiries and answered them all at once. 'Yes, Bess is fine; but she'll be glad to see you

She's lonesome for the sight of a white woman. Only woman she's seen since May was a squaw. The young ones are fine, too. Bess is expecting in February.' He said Jess and Eben had not come down-river. 'We didn't know for sure when you'd be here. I be'n waiting three days. They've got plenty to do up-river.' To his father, he said: 'I'm getting rid of my land in the upper town, selling out any day now, to Dave Kelso.'

Then someone hailed them from the wharf, and they all turned, and Philip called calmly: 'Morning, Oliver.' Mima remembered her uncle only vaguely. He had come to St. George's a dozen or fifteen years ago, when she was four or five years old. He was a bearded man in linsey-woolsey trousers and a sheepskin frock; and there was something stern and sombre in his bearing and in his wintry eye. He stepped aboard the sloop and shook Philip's hand, and greeted Mrs. Robbins; and he said: 'This is my Mily.'

Mily, beside him, was a lovely, golden-haired child of twelve or so, with eyes like a kitten's, who promptly kissed all her cousins; and Jake's Adam's apple worked like a churn handle in his embarrassment. Mima thought she had never seen anyone so pretty. Then Susie suddenly screamed with delight: 'Uncle Will! Oh, Uncle Will!' Mima turned to see her throw herself into the arms of the newcomer. He was Will Gregory, who had married Philip's sister, and lived now in Camden; and Mima ran to meet him. She had always liked him. He had a way of pleasing children, as he pleased Susie now, holding her in his arms while he greeted Mima and then her mother.

'Guess I'll steal Susie here,' he told Mrs. Robbins. Susie giggled, her arms around his neck. 'Always did want one like her.' He added more seriously: 'Say I do take her home with me till you're settled. I'll fetch her safe and sound in a week or so, before winter sets in.'

'You're welcome to her,' Mrs. Robbins assured him. 'It'd be a load off my mind if you'd take Phil, too. They're a nuisance when a body's trying to get anything done; underfoot all the time, into everything.'

He chuckled. 'Don't know as I want another man along when I go off with a gal as pretty as Susie here,' he said. Philip and Oliver, Mason Wheaton, and Captain Watson were talking together; and Mima went to rescue Jake from Mily, who was dazzling him with her friendliness.

'How's Lucy?' she asked. 'I remember her, and Otie, and Lois and all of them.' Uncle Oliver's wife had died three or four years before, leaving him with a houseful of children. He had come home a year ago to marry again, a widow woman in Attleboro. 'How does your new mama like here?'

Mily said demurely: 'She don't like it much. There's no Baptist minister here, and she wants one awful.' Mima remembered that Uncle Oliver's new wife was famous for her devotion to the church. 'Lucy's home,' Mily added. 'She's sick abed.' She watched Jake skulking away toward the bow, and David came to put his arm around Mima and Mily escaped to pursue Jake. Dave asked teasingly:

'How come you didn't bring a husband along, Mima? Men back home must be blind! You're pretty enough to set fire to wet hay.'

'Didn't see one to suit,' she said, tossing her head, smiling. 'I'm some particular.'

'We'll find a man for you,' he promised.

Major Wheaton, coming to say good-bye to Mima, heard David. 'Hold on, there!' he protested. 'I've took up this piece of new land myself. No trespassers!' He told Mima: 'Got to go ashore now. Cap'n Watson has to keep the tide to carry you up to the lower ripples; but I don't aim to forget you, miss. I'll be up there on the prowl.'

Mima smiled, confused and happy too; and David warned her: 'Look out for him, Mima. He runs a regular track up and down the river, smelling around everybody's doorstep like an old dog.'

The Major clapped him on the shoulder. 'You keep the pups away till the old dog comes,' he said. 'I'll hold you responsible.' He bowed to Mima and turned away.

Captain Watson shouted: 'All right, everybody off!' He spoke to Mima's father. 'I'll fetch you as far as Miller's landing, come down on the tide myself, so let's move.'

Susie, but not Phil, went with Uncle Will. Mily tried to persuade Jake to stay and visit a while with them in the lower town; but he refused, red to the ears. Uncle Oliver said a sober farewell and went ashore. When he was gone, the lines were loosed, and those left aboard the Sally manned the sweeps again. The sloop moved slowly from the wharf out into deeper water and away.

* * * * *

Once they began to move, Mima did not look back. She helped with the sweeps till tide and wind took the sloop in hand. Then she and little Phil went forward to the bows to watch the channel ahead of them. Almost at once the river, turning sharply westward, narrowed till it became a proper stream, and no longer — as it had been till now — more like an arm of the sea that pierced the land. As they entered this narrower reach with the village on their right and the high land of Watson's Point on their left, the surging tide caught them and bore them on. They rounded a sharp bend and ran for a while southwesterly. The sail, when Watson's Point cut off their breeze, shivered and flapped; but the tide gave them way enough till they emerged from the narrows into a wider reach of river that turned northwesterly. Here tide flats showed again on either hand, and there were salt marshes between the river and the rising ground, and Mima saw a smaller river come in from the right, and a mill and a shipyard there with a sloop framed on the ways. Beyond, on either bank, houses were strung like beads along the stream. The upper town had been settled forty years before, but Indian wars had since then more

than once driven all the dwellers to the shelter of the fort; and
houses had been burned and never rebuilt, fields cleared and
then abandoned, so that the pressing wilderness sometimes
crowded down to the river's edge.

They had five or six miles to go to reach Miller's landing at
the lower ripples; and during that whole journey Mima and
Philip stayed together in the bow to watch the gently winding
stream up which they sailed. Sometimes Mima could see only
a short distance, but at others long reaches opened out before
her; and from the log houses along the banks men and women
and children came out to wave and call as the sloop stole
softly by.

David joined them after a while, happy in pointing out to
her this and that along the way. He asked whether she had
seen the limekiln on the eastern bank as they left the town behind, and the Lermond mill and shipyards at Oyster River;
and whether she had noticed the shipways on Packard's rock in
the lower town.

'It's Ben Packard's house we'll live in this winter,' he explained. 'There was a sloop built down there six years ago;
and Packard's wife and baby started to Boston on her and she
was lost off Cape Ann in a snow squall. Dave Patterson was
her captain. Every soul aboard was drowned; and they say
Ben Packard's not the same since. He's a sober, dry man. He
took it hard, him building a house up here and then Taylor
selling it to us over his head.'

Mima listened, still and attentive, hearing, remembering,
absorbing all this new world as a sponge absorbs water. As
they went on, he told her the names of those whose stump-dotted
clearings they passed.

'They bought from General Waldo,' he said. 'But they have
to pay a peppercorn for rent every year if it's asked for.' And
he began to tease her about how hard it would be for her to find
a husband in Taylortown. 'There'll be just our three families
there, this winter,' he warned her. 'So you'll not know where
to look for a man.'

She laughed, her head high. The day, even thus late in the fall, was sunny and warm; and though there might be a chill in the breeze, they rode with it, borne on by wind and tide, so it did not touch them hard.

'It'll not be me doing the looking,' she reminded him. 'That will be for him to do!'

He wagged his head. 'Don't look for too much,' he warned her. 'It takes a man that's half-wolf, half-otter to come a-courting up where we're going.' And he said with a chuckle: 'Joe Coombs down at Wessaweskeag, when he kept company with Bess Gamble in that second house ahead there on the west bank, every time he wanted to come a-bundling with her it meant ten or fifteen miles of woods-running and bog-trotting to get up here; and then he had to cross the river. That meant finding a float or a wherry, and half the time they'd be all on the wrong side, so he'd have to load his clothes on a log and swim over and dress himself after. He did it last April when the ice war'n't any more than out.'

'Did she have him?'

David grinned. 'After that she did,' he said. 'She 'lowed she'd have to sleep with him to warm him up enough so the icicles would thaw off of him. So she married him and he took her home.' He added: 'But anyone wants to come sparking you, Mima, he'll have a ways to go to get up to where we'll be.'

'Is it beautiful, Dave?'

'Why, likely 'tis,' he admitted. 'I never noticed. Too busy working, or killing bears, or netting pigeons or something.'

'Does Bess like it? And the babies?'

'Certain,' he assured her. 'Jason's already practising cutting down trees, and he's not five yet.' He added in a different tone: 'Chloe's a beauty, Mima, and Joe's a whopper, and I told you Bess is expecting in February?'

Mima's eyes were glowing. 'Yes.' Her hand touched his arm. 'Dave, it's fine, isn't it, when men and women go into the woods together, and work together, and raise their children and make their homes and do everything together. Women have always stayed in the house and been weak and sickly and delicate and made men wait on them. But this is different, isn't it? Women are as strong as men, really, aren't they?'

He laughed and clapped his arm around her shoulders. 'I'll teach you to drop a tree as quick as a man,' he promised. 'Get you so you can swing an axe and you'll make a good wife for a lazy man!'

'It's going to be different,' she insisted, smiling at his foolery, but holding to her point. 'It'll be a different kind of world after we women have helped our men take this country, and make homes in it. It's a long time in the world since women have had a chance to build homes, Dave; but that's what they're for. It's what they're best at.' She watched the silver river between forested banks ahead of them. 'It's a long time since women had a big job like this to do. All this' — she opened her arms with an embracing gesture — 'it isn't the King's any more, Dave. It's ours.'

He grinned, half amused, half indulgent. 'Don't look for too much,' he warned her. Then, remembering: 'But you always were one to think big, see a lot in a little. I can knock down a few trees and build a house out of them and move in; and when it's done, it's just a house to keep off the rain, keep out the cold. But you'd make a game out of it, or a story to tell.'

She smiled at her own thoughts. 'I don't know how to say it, Dave,' she said. 'But women know. Women do more thinking ahead than men do, I guess. Men, all they want is to work till they're tired, and eat, and go to bed; but women like to plan things out, get them settled. A man, he thinks about his own job, what he's doing; but women always know that women all over the world are doing the same things she's doing.'

'Bess is different since we came up here,' he reflected. 'In Walpole she worked hard, but she was tired all the time. I never thought she could do all she does up here. When the other babies were coming, she was sick a lot of the time; but this one she's been fine.'

'When's it coming, Dave? February?'

He nodded, and he added: 'I'm glad Ma'll be there. Bess hasn't seen a woman's face — not a white woman's — since we went up to Taylortown last May.'

Mima looked at him quickly. 'Were there really Indians there this summer?'

'Yes. Two-three families.'

'Did they bother you?'

'Sho, no. They're right enough — only if maybe one of 'em gets a little rum in him.' He indicated the angle of the river which they were approaching. 'That's Andrews Point,' he said. 'Hugh McLean tried shipbuilding there; but he never did more than put up one frame that rotted on the ways. Alex Kellock lives there now. He's a rum seller, the first in the town.'

'Is it an inn?'

'No, John McIntyre keeps an inn; but likely we'll put up with old Sam Boggs tonight.'

'Can't we go on, go home?'

'No. We'll land our stuff at Miller's and get Boggs to haul it across the carry.' He chuckled and added: 'Sam Boggs is quite a man. When he come here, forty years ago, nobody else wanted the upper lots. Too many Indians around. But he took 'em, and he raises sheep and cattle, and hunts, and farms. The last Indian trouble in '59, he wanted to stay up there. They say his daughter burned their house down so he'd have to move to the fort. His is the last place this side Seven-Tree Pond.'

There were long pauses in their talk. After a while she asked: 'Dave — if you and Bess already had a house here — why did you go on up there?'

'Well,' he said, 'Father offered to give me land if I'd move, a hundred and fifty acres for me, and fifty acres for Bess, to pay her for cooking and taking care of us all while we worked up there this summer. It's better land than I had here.'

Mrs. Robbins called to them to come and eat if they were hungry. The wind was light, and tide more than wind helped them on, pressing them sometimes so near the banks that the men had to take poles and set them clear again. Mima returned to the bow, and the forested shores fell back a few rods and the river meandered through salt marshes. David, ready in the bow with a setting pole, said: 'It's a scant mile from here to the landing.'

'There are houses all along.'

He nodded. 'It's quite a town here already; a store, and mills and all. They've asked to incorporate and call it Warren, after Doctor Warren that the redcoats killed at Bunker Hill.'

'I wish we could go on tonight. I want to get there.'

He chuckled at her eagerness. 'You may not like it the way you look to, Mima. There's a pile needs doing and a long job to get it done.'

'I don't know as it matters whether you get a thing done or not,' she confessed. 'I think the fun's in working at it.'

'I don't know. I like getting a thing done.'

She argued: 'But Dave, if a man does finish a thing, he don't just set. He starts right in doing something else. It's the doing that keeps folks contented, I think.' She asked quickly, pointing ahead: 'Is that the landing?'

'That's Miller's, yes,' he said. 'I'll go help Pa get the goods up out of the hold. Cap'n Watson won't want to tie up longer than he has to.'

He turned away; but Mima and Phil stayed where they were, and Mrs. Robbins came presently to join them. The older woman did not speak, and when Mima looked at her, she saw that her mother was white and tense, with brimming eyes. She said reassuringly:

'Now, Mother, we'll be fine.'

'Like enough,' her mother assented. 'But I'm old for it,

The River

Mima; old to start new things.' Her eyes rested gently on the girl. 'You're young and new. You'll grow up to it. But it's hard for a woman like me, that always knew where to lay her hand on everything, to have to see it all packed up and carted off two weeks' journey and put down somewheres else.'

Mima urged: 'We'll help, Mother. We'll all help.' She said: 'See, we're here.'

The sails came down, the sweeps went out. Two or three men came from Miller's house to meet them, and as the Sally glided in with way enough, David came to stand with Mima and her mother, and he said:

'Miller, here, he's a nice old coot; but he believes in a lot of foolishness. Take it along this time of year in the fall and he'll claim he can hear the fairies cooking dinner — says they fry their meat on the white frost. Mrs. Miller walks to church barefoot every Sunday to save shoe leather, puts her shoes on when she gets there.'

The sloop touched, and he vaulted overside to help ease her in, the men ashore stepping into the water to lend a hand. Captain Watson and old Miller both gave orders, shouting together till the Sally was secure against the landing stage of great logs made fast to the bank at their upstream ends, hanging in the current with boards across to make a platform.

The work of unloading began. Everything they owned in the world was aboard the Sally sloop; but with a dozen pairs of hands to help, the task went quickly, and on the bank the pile grew. There was the little cherrywood table which was Mrs. Robbins' particular pride, and her pewterware packed in chests, and a dozen red-cedar kids of assorted sizes, and the huge high-backed settle which Philip had warned her was too big to go into the house where they would live this winter. There were boxes of odds and ends; a coals carrier, the spice grinder, the tinderbox with the steel rattling around inside. There were cooking dishes, kettles for boiling, kettles for baking, the long-handled skillet, the iron spider. There were four fine feather beds, the ticking woven of cotton and tow; and there was the loom on which that web of ticking had been woven, and the small spinning wheel and the big one. There were piggins and ewers and wooden trenchers and pewter porringers and basins and canisters. There were farming tools; axes and scythes and brush hooks and pitchforks and stave splitters. Mima, standing with her mother, said:

'I didn't know we had so much. What's that bale of stuff wrapped up in the quilt, Mother?'

'Old clothes,' Mrs. Robbins told her. 'Your pa's and all. Some warn't wore out, and some I can make do with a little mending.'

Mima said, half to herself, smiling: 'Wear it out. Make it do. You're always saying that.'

'Well, you may laugh,' Mrs. Robbins retorted. 'But you'll find that's one sure way to get along.'

The sloop continued to give up its cargo; bedsteads, and chairs, and stools, and bags of corn to feed them through the winter, and salt pork, and barrels of potatoes, and muskets, and a keg of powder, and a keg of rum. The men worked at top speed, and Mima saw some of them watch her with sidelong glances. One in particular, who seemed not much more than a boy, was forever looking toward her. Once she caught his eye, and his cheek burned red.

David presently lifted her ashore, and the children with her; and she helped her mother tally every bale and box and parcel. When at last their belongings were all unloaded, and the sloop cast off to go down-river with the tide, Mima stayed to see it out of sight. It disappeared around Andrews Point, and she turned with a sense of finality toward the scattered houses of the town. The sloop had brought them. Now it was gone; but they were come to stay. They would never need it again. She faced serenely the years that lay ahead.

4

MILLER'S landing, where their goods had been put ashore, was at the lower ripples. The men attacked at once the task of carrying everything by hand up to the Boggs farm to be put in the barn overnight. Mima would have helped, but David said:

'We can manage.' He told her cheerfully: 'You get more work out of the men just by standing around and watching them than all you could carry. They're strutting at it like a lot of turkeys!' He added: 'And there's time enough. We can't go on tonight, anyhow. Ez Bowen just set out to walk it — he's working for Taylor up there — and I sent word by him to have Phin Butler bring down Taylor's big ferry tomorrow morning early. We'll have to take two-three loads, even with that.' And he explained: 'River makes a bend north of here, comes down till it ain't two miles from Boggs' place. He'll haul us over. That way we get around the falls and just have dead water from there up to Seven-Tree Pond.'

He loaded himself and tramped away. Mrs. Robbins had gone ahead to see her goods bestowed. Mrs. Miller, a comfortable, motherly little old woman, came to speak to Mima.

'You step up to the house and keep warm,' she said hospitably. 'You'll have to stay the night somewhere, and I'll be real glad to put you up.'

Mima thanked her. 'You're good to take us in,' she said. 'But I don't know what my father aims to do.'

'Well, he'll have to stay somewhere,' Mrs. Miller assured her. 'And it's a comfort to see new folks coming, and to know there'll be some living up-river from us. Only for Boggs, we're the farthest, and with the war, and Indians around and all, there's times I get real nervous.'

Mima and Jacob, as things turned out, lodged with the Millers that night. Philip and Mrs. Robbins and little Phil slept in the Boggs house, and the others at McIntyre's. But when the goods had all been moved, David came to Miller's with a young man in tow. Mima recognized the youngster as the one who had blushed under her glance, and worked twice as hard afterward, that afternoon.

'Want to make you acquainted with Bill Dicke, Mima,' David said with utmost gravity. 'He's got pop-eyed and twisty-necked this afternoon, trying to watch you and work at the same time. He's going off to the war, now, but don't you worry. He'll be back.' He winked, and Mima colored brightly, and Dave said: 'We're going to be short of young blades around here, with Bill going, and Jim Anderson, and Andy Malcolm, and Frank Young.' Bill Dicke was staring at Mima open-mouthed. 'They're going off day after tomorrow down Machias way,' David explained. 'But after he comes back, Bill 'lows he'll spend most of his time up at our place. He was about the first ever went up-river that far. He can tell you what it's like.'

Mima saw that David was making sport of this youngster who was more like a shy boy than a man. She said gently: 'I'm happy to make your acquaintance, Mr. Dicke.'

Bill blushed and mumbled; and David said: 'Tell her about your comet, Bill, and how you knew this war was coming.'

'Well, I did so!' the young man retorted, forgetting his embarrassment, his color rising in anger at David's tone; and he told Mima: 'I was hunting. I'd gone up to Seven-Tree Pond in my float; and when it come night, I set out to sleep on th' island, 'count of Indians mebbe. There's an old Indian tomb there, so they don't ever come on the island. It 'uz raining frogs and pitchforks, so I drug the float ashore and turned it up on its side and kind of scrooged in under it till it quit raining; and then I woke up and it had cleared off, and burn me if there warn't a star on fire, with the flames shooting out two-three rod. "God," I says to myself. "What's that?" I was skeered some and no mistake; and I tell't folks from then on that there was big trouble coming. I be'n saying so for seven years now. They laughed for a while; but they're all over laughing now.'

'You were right, weren't you,' Mima agreed; and under her kindness, Bill was tongue-tied with bliss again. Dave asked him questions, trying to lead him to further speech; but the more Dave asked, the less Bill Dicke said.

In the end, they returned to McIntyre's. Dave invited Miller to come for a bowl of flip with them; but the old man said gently:

'Nay, I'll have none of the heathenish brew. 'Tis as bad as rum, and worse maybe, stealing up on you before you're looking.'

So Dave and Bill departed; but Mima and Jake sat long that night before the dying fire while Mima asked Miller a thousand questions. He had come from Scotland a dozen years before and taken up a vacant lot here on the western side of the river. 'And it was a wild land then, ma'am,' he told her. 'Nought but the woods around, and things crying in the night; aye, and in the forest and on the river and in the black sky above. There was more than humans around too, you'll mind, and I've seen more than one cow that had been elf-shot in my time.'

Jacob drew closer to Mima's side, his Adam's apple pumping, and old Mrs. Miller said devoutly: 'Aye, indeed it was so.'

Mima asked whether he had been up to Seven-Tree Pond, and Miller said: 'Many's the time.' He told her that it was no more than four years since the first axe had been laid to a tree up there. 'In the fall of '72, it was,' he said. 'The Andersons, from the Sterling neighborhood, with Jim Malcolm from the lower town and young John Crawford from the village here, bargained with Thomas Flucker to bring some land there under the plow if he'd give them the land for their trouble. They built a camp on a knoll thirty rods north of the Mill Stream, and cleared some land and ran a possession fence across from the pond to George's River. Flucker was acting for the Waldo heirs, mind. But he's a Loyalist, and there's no place for such here. He's gone now, and he's sold off his land. He sold their land from under them, and more too, to Doctor Taylor. The Andersons had a survey, but they had just cut staves and lumber, done no planting at all, so Flucker would never give them a deed.'

'Father bought from Doctor Taylor,' Mima said, and the old man nodded.

'Taylor bought it all from Flucker,' he assented. 'The whole township for a thousand pounds. That's no more than nine-pence an acre. Taylor came from Lunenburg with his two bound men, John and Phinehas Butler, and three others, to begin to clear the land. That was two years ago.'

He talked on and on, diverging into byways of reminiscence, till the fire burned low. Mima slept in the loft bed that night. The last flames sent a flickering light along the roof beams as her eyes closed; and she woke early, and helped Mrs. Miller with breakfast, and then David came to fetch her away.

He brought with him young Phinehas Butler. Butler was not yet nineteen years old, younger than Mima, bound out to Doctor Taylor to serve till he should be twenty-one.

'He fetched Doc Taylor's big ferry down, to take our gear up,' David explained, grinning. 'He's another that can tell you all about up there, Mima.' And he warned the young man: 'She'll

ask you so many questions she'll have you tongue-tied, Phin.
She had Bill Dicke gawping yesterday. Don't let her wear
you down.'

Butler grinned in a shy way. 'Well, I dunno as there's much
to tell,' he said. He spoke with a faint hesitation, jerking his
head forward as though he threw out the words with a physical
effort. His neck was long and thin, so that she thought of a
turkey's neck, pumping back and forth when the bird walks.
His right eyelid had a nervous twitch in it, as though he were
winking at her.

'Mr. Miller says you've worked up there these two years,'
she suggested.

Phin's head pumped as though he were about to speak, and
David said, imitating the movement and exaggerating it: 'I
dunno how much he worked, but he was there!' Phin grinned
in red embarrassment, and Mima thought Dave's gift of
mimicry might sometimes leave wounds. She wished to reassure Phin, and she said:

'I'm glad we're going to be neighbors. You must have
started early this morning, to get here this soon.'

'I dunno'm,' he said. 'Sun warn't up.'

Dave led him away to help with the work of moving their
belongings. Philip Robbins had hired Sam Boggs to freight
their household goods across the neck to the foot of the long
reach of river that came down from the pond; and most of the
morning was spent in this laborious business. There was no
road, not much more than a trail; and instead of a cart, Boggs
had a sort of drag, made of cedar poles framed together, one
end suspended from the yoke the oxen wore, the other dragging
on the ground. This vehicle would carry only a small load, so
there were several trips to be made. Boggs supervised the
loading and put his oxen in motion with hoarse cries, prodding
them with the tickler. For the first trip, Mima — carrying a
burden of bedding on her back — walked beside him, full of
questions; and the old man expanded under her interest.

'Been here forty year,' he told her. 'Here or hereabouts. Yes, ma'am, they was plenty Indians, them days. Never bothered me. I'd have stayed here, but one time they riz and my gal Annie was skeered. She was bent and determined we'd go to the fort and I said I'd be dummed if I would. What did she do?' He bellowed at one of the oxen that reached for a tuft of dead grass. 'Burnt the house down; that's what! I larruped her plenty; give her a good whop on the backside every jump from here to the fort. I was half a mind to scalp her, too. I taught her to be more skeered of me than Indians, and next trouble we stayed right here.'

'Did the Indians ever bother you?' Mima asked.

'Not what I'd call bother. There was one time I was up't Crawford's Pond with Steve Hart, hunting, and seven of 'em chased us back to the fort; but that didn't bother me — as long as they didn't catch us.' Indians were all right, he assured her. They got mad sometimes, with whites coming in and killing off the moose. You couldn't blame them. But treat them right and they would treat you right, he said.

While the oxen went to and fro, so did they all, carrying what they could, except that Mrs. Robbins stayed by the river with her increasing pile of possessions, and Jake and little Phil, Bet and the baby stayed with her. After the second trip, Sam Boggs turned over the business to his son.

'Here's Young Sam,' he told Philip. 'He'll look after you.' Young Sam, Mima judged, was almost as old as her father; a lean, bold man with a strong mouth and a merry eye. 'I'll be up along to see how you manage,' Old Sam promised. 'I'm one likes to hit for the woods once in so often. Getting crowded around here. Any time you want stock — sheep, oxen, hogs, neat cattle — I'm your man. I've always raised more critters than crops.' He chuckled. 'They do their own seeding,' he explained. 'All you have to do is give the old bull a chance and he'll tend to it. I'll be stopping by.'

He stayed behind while they started across the carry for the third time, Dave and Rich and Phin Butler and Philip following the drag, Mima walking with Young Sam. She found him not so full of talk as his father; but there was a calm precision about him; and it was he who when they arrived at the river supervised the first loading of the ferry.

'That's all it's safe to take, one trip,' he said at last, 'but you can leave the rest of your gear right here till you're ready to come for it. Cover it against the weather and there'll be nobody bother it if you left it here till spring. I'll haul the rest of it over today — there ain't but one more load — so you can get it any time.'

He stayed to see them start. Philip made sure the load was secure and turned to Mrs. Robbins.

'Well, we're ready, Ma,' he said. 'But it's loaded pretty deep. We can't all ride in it and be safe. It will take Rich and me to row, and you womenfolks can ride; but we'll have to take it easy. Phin Butler and Dave are going to walk it, and I guess Jake can leg it with them.'

Mrs. Robbins assented, and came to get into the ferry; but Dave said:

'Hold on, Ma. Someone will have to set us across first. The best walking's up the east side the river. There's bog up the west side till you get to the foot of the pond.'

Mima said: 'I'd choose to walk up, with Dave and Jake. It'll make the barge safer, that much less weight.'

'Can as well as not,' Dave assured her. 'There's just a spotted trail, but them long legs of yours will do it.'

Philip Robbins agreed, and the boat was deep-laden when they all got in. Mrs. Robbins called warnings while they crossed, and they alighted on the north bank and stayed to see the others take their places in the ferry and set out. When it was gone, Young Sam Boggs swung his oxen away and they turned to the trail, but David was eager to come home, and he told Mima:

'I'm going to hustle along. Jake can come with me, if he

Come Spring

can keep up; but Phin will take it easy, Mima.' He chuckled. 'He always does. You stay with him.'

'I want to get there quick as I can,' she admitted. 'But I can walk better than I can run.'

So when David went off at a jog, with Jake trotting behind him, she came more slowly after them, following on Phin Butler's heels; and she began at once to lead Phin into talk. He was at first silent and embarrassed, shy and ill at ease; but there was a steadiness in Mima of a sort to reassure a man, and he responded to it. She asked whether he had helped clear the trail they would follow.

'I dunno as it's cleared to mention,' he confessed, jerking out the words with that spasmodic motion of his head. 'It's just spotted trees.'

'Will we see any bears or anything, do you think?'

'I dunno,' he repeated doubtfully. She thought Phin was uncertain about most things. 'First time I come up here, we rowed up the river and the pond and landed nigh the mouth of Crawford's River, looking for the Anderson camp. Couldn't find it in the dark, but we started a moose and he nigh skeered the back teeth out of me, busting off through the brush when we didn't know what it was.'

'Was that this year?'

'No, ma'am, two years ago, the eighteenth day of July. Next day we found the Anderson camp and moved in. It warn't but a hole in the ground with boards over it. They come about a week after and tried to put us out, but Doc Taylor had bought the land out from under them, you might say.'

'Have you been there ever since?'

'Why, no, ma'am,' he said, in an apologetic tone. 'The first year we cleared a few acres, and then come fall Doc Taylor hired me and John out in Thomaston and went back t'the west'ard.' She saw that once he began to talk, the words came more easily. 'Then last summer John and me — he's my brother — cleared all the way from Seven-Tree Pond to

Crawford's. Taylor hired us out to Ben Packard for last winter.'

'We're going to live in Packard's house.'

He nodded. 'We lived there last winter, getting out lumber.'

'Was it cold?'

'The cold didn't bother; but Packard didn't feed us good. I run into a b'ar asleep under a log over't Crawford's Pond and kilt it with an axe or we'd have starved. After that we lived high, long as the meat lasted.'

'Killed it with an axe?'

'Why, yes, ma'am,' he assented, as though not sure what he said was true. 'It was asleep, all but, the way they are in winter. It was easy kilt.' He went on: 'Then come spring, your pa bought all that land off of Doc Taylor, so Packard had to get off. Dave moved into Packard's log house, fetched his wife and young ones, and your pa and your brothers come with him.' He said admiringly: 'That Jess is a great one! He's going to make a man. Eben, too.' These were Mima's brothers. He went on: 'We've had quite a lot doing up here this summer. Your pa had five-six men working, besides the boys.' Jess was seventeen, Eben two years younger. 'Dave's wife cooked for them. Rich Comings planted some ground thaᵗ he'd cleared before he went back t' the west'ard. Your brothers have harvested his corn for him. Then Ben Burton and Nat Fales have be'n building a frame house for Doc Taylor; and Taylor put up a big barn, about thirty by forty. It took all we had in us to git the frame up. Lugging and a-h'isting them big timbers would rip the meat right off'n your arms. We was all so done in, we didn't work to mention for a week after.'

Mima, trudging at his heels, watching his sure feet pick their way, asked: 'Does Doctor Taylor pay good wages?'

'John and me are bound out,' Phin reminded her humbly. 'We're due to get an ordinary suit of clothes and a good suit and a hundred acres of Taylor's land when our time's done.'

'Will you come to live up here?'

'I dunno. I aim to,' he confessed. She thought him a curiously uncertain young man, humble and mild.

'Is Doctor Taylor here now? Father expected to sign the papers for the land before he went home to get us. Doctor Fales had them all drawn up, but Doctor Taylor was gone when my father got there.'

'No, ma'am, he's not. I dunno as he's likely to be, this winter.' He asked in a different tone: 'Has your father got a writing?'

'I don't know.' She smiled to hear herself echoing Phin's doubtful phrase. 'Why? Do you think Doctor Taylor will make any trouble?'

'I dunno, ma'am. Only, he's in politics. My pa always said if a politician tells you he'll do something, make him write it down.' He added: 'Taylor's slippery sometimes. If it was me, I'd want a writing. I dunno.'

They were moving through the hardwood growth on the east shore of the pond, following the high land, too far back from the water to catch more than an occasional glimpse of it through the leafless trees. The November day was overcast, and the stark branches over their heads were gaunt against a leaden sky. Mima thought her mother must be cold, in the boat on the open lake, with no exertion to keep her warm. The forest about them was majestic; the tall oaks and beeches and maples arched above their heads; the underbrush plucked at their garments as they passed. They walked a while in silence, till she saw Phin's long neck move as his head jerked forward, and knew he was about to speak. He said it felt like snow, and she assented, and she said:

'My father and my brothers got out a barn frame this summer, but he didn't put it up.'

'Yes, ma'am. Ben Burton hewed the timbers for him. Your pa's got a log house built too, a storehouse. No doors nor windows, just a place to pack your gear in till he gets time to build a proper house for you.'

'Are you going to be up here this winter?'

'No, ma'am, not right along. I might go in the army if Ben Burton gets his commission that he's looking for. Doc Taylor's working to get it for him. If I do go,' he added hopefully, 'I might get out of being bound.'

She asked: 'Do you think the King will set the Indians on us, up here?'

'I dunno.' He said: 'We're nigh there. We'll be to the Mill Stream in a little now.'

Mima felt herself suddenly breathless; she was so near journey's end. She spoke no more, afraid her voice would betray her. She trod lightly at his heels, scarce feeling the ground under her feet. Phin trudged on, never hurrying, never slackening his gait; and she watched the set of his head, the breadth of his shoulders, the easy play of his waist, the firm flow of muscles in his hips and thighs. But he would go into the army, go away to fight. She could not hold him back from that. Men had to win this land as well as use it. Women could not fight; but they could do their part in the greater, longer task that must be done.

When they emerged at last from the forest, Mima was forewarned by the thinning of the trees ahead, and she hurried her steps till she was by Phin's side. 'Is that it ahead?' she asked.

'Yes, ma'am. We've cleared some this side the stream. We'll come out opposite the mill, only a little below. We have to go down to the pond to cross. No boat on the millpond.' And he said, as the trees opened out before them: 'There's the mill.'

They emerged from the forest upon an outcropping of ledge below which the ground fell away steeply for a rod or two and then sloped more easily to the pond some fifteen or twenty rods away. Mima stopped still, her eyes swinging in a slow survey. She could look down across a narrow strip of burnt-land where charred trunks lay to the pond, and across to the farther shore. Directly opposite, there was a dip in the distant hills, and a corresponding nearer dip in the lower hills along the shore of the pond; and in this dip, half screened by trees still standing by the water's edge, she saw a cabin from which smoke ascended. Phin, following her eyes, said:

'That's Packard's, where you'll live. The river comes in a little above. There's another pond half a mile up-river toward that notch in the hills.'

She nodded, her throat too full for speech. She could see well up toward the head of the pond, since the land across the Mill Stream had been cleared. Her eye followed up the stream from where it flowed into the lake below them till it was lost to view in a rocky gorge a few rods from where she stood. Some oaks stood along that gorge, and she could hear the play of water; and beyond, at a little distance, there stood a small framed house, and a barn, and nearer, by the stream, the unfinished frame of the mill.

Phin explained: 'That's the barn we raised, and the house Taylor built. We hauled the boards up from Lermond's on the ice. The mill will work when there's enough water. We'll hail them, get a float to set us across the stream down't the pond.' He added, looking right and left over the burned land dotted with charred stumps: 'We cleared all that, this last two years, mostly John and me.'

She nodded, and he lifted his voice in a long halloo. Out of the barn two or three men appeared, and one of them whooped and began to run toward them, the others following more slowly. Even at this distance, Mima recognized her brother Jess. She went to meet him. Phin said: 'Down this way,' but Mima went straight forward till she came to the lip of the gorge. Below her, the little river ran dancing to the pond. It had cut a bed for itself — with the help of frost — through solid rock. The walls were ten or fifteen or twenty feet high, sometimes flat as boards where great slabs had been flaked off, sometimes broken down into smaller fragments that lay tumbled in disorder by the water side.

Jess, racing toward her, still fifty yards away, shouted: 'Come down to the pond.' She followed Phin that way, her feet padding in the ashes of the recent burning here. Jess was ahead of her, running down the farther bank of the stream to launch a dugout float at its mouth and cross to their side. She reached the shore as his craft touched, and he jumped out and came bounding toward her; a compact youngster rather short than tall, already formed and strong. He kissed her roundly, and asked how they all were; and she asked how Eben was, and Bess.

'Fine as frog hairs,' he assured her. 'Only Bess is scared how she'll act when she sees you, not seeing a woman since May. She's afraid when she does see one, she'll play the fool!' Two or three men had followed him down to the pond. He left Mima where she was while he ferried Phin across, and one of the men came back with him. 'This is Ben Burton, Mima,' he said. 'He's going down-river.'

Burton shook her hand. He had strength and poise in his glance, and a cheerful easiness. She said readily: 'Cap'n Watson told me a lot about you, the tea party and all.'

'Jim's a talker,' Burton agreed. 'But he's a liar too. I'll come back sometime and tell you the straight of it. Jess, you better go around the shore, 'stead of crossing over to your place. This float of yours is crank in a wind, and it's blowing some.'

'It's a durned good float,' Jess protested. 'I made it myself.'

'It looks more like a hog trough than a boat, Jess!' Mima protested.

'Well, it won't sink,' he assured her. 'You get in and set easy and I'll get you there.'

Burton stood by to see Mima take her place; and the men beyond the stream watched this embarkation. Mima found the rude craft remarkably unstable, and she sat still, hardly breathing, as Jess pushed out from the shore and took his paddle. She tried to look back; but he said sharply:

'Easy, Mima, or she'll pitch us out. She's like a colt, clever enough but a mite nervous. Just you leave the navigating to me.'

So Mima sat motionless, and the shore fell behind. 'There's our house,' he said. 'See the smoke, kind of blue in among the pines? And we've cleared that land along the shore. You can't tell much about it from here, but it's level enough for nigh onto a mile along the pond, real easy land to work.'

'I see the island!' she cried. 'Father told me about it. With seven trees on it. That's why they call this Seven-Tree Pond.'

'Yup! Then there's where the river comes in, north of where our house is. It comes out of another little pond about a mile in back. Sam Boggs says there's a pond, two-three miles north, as big as this one; and the river runs through it.' His voice was eager with young dreams. 'Some day I'm going to go all the way up river, as far as it goes.'

'I see the ferry coming up the other side.'

'Yup, but they're coming slow. I could see it before you got here. We'll be home before they are.' He had struck boldly across the pond, heading a little north of the island, paddling strongly. The float seemed to prefer to ride with a decided list to the right, and Mima's neck ached from her instinctive effort to balance the craft and keep it on an even keel. The shores toward which they drew were dark with spruce and pine, though she and Phin had come up through hardwoods on the east side of the pond. She spoke of this, and Jess said:

'Yup! Pop got the best side. The pine falls easy and it burns easy. That saves a heap of work, clearing the land.'

She thought he had changed, this summer, from boy to man. His way of saying 'Yup' was something new, curt and decisive. She suspected he might be imitating someone he admired. He was no taller than he had been in May, but he began to wear some of the erect aggressiveness small men so often defensively affect. They heard a dog bark ahead; and Jess chuckled. 'Listen to Tuner. He sure was glad to see Dave. You ought to hear him tune up on a b'ar's track. Say, he sings.' And he said: 'Used to be an Indian grave on the island there, Mima. All built out of stones. They took 'em to use for foundations over at Taylor's. And there's a pair of geese nest there on the island every year. They've took their goslings and gone south now.'

A slop of water came aboard, so that she sat in a puddle. 'Jess, do people ever get drowned in a boat like this?' she asked.

He chuckled. 'Skeered?'

'Yes.'

'Y' know, you're funny,' he said. 'You say you're skeered, but you don't sound so.'

'Part of me is,' she said. 'The talking part isn't, maybe; but I'm scared inside.'

'A man wouldn't let on.'

'There's no harm in being scared as long as you do what you'd ought to, scared or not scared.'

'I don't skeer easy,' he declared, and answered her question. 'Folks do get drowned, certain. I don't know as ever anyone did up here, but they do down below. Two years ago, Dave says, there was four people waiting to be buried all't the same time, and two of them had drowned. Bill James, and a girl name of Anna Young. She fell out of a float. She'd had a dream the night before that she would get drowned, dreamed who'd pick her body up afterward and all, and it come just like in her dream. She worked for Sam Boggs, doing washing. Somebody asked her to set 'em across the river, and she done it and fell out of the float on the way back.'

Mima said: 'I'm going to learn to swim.'

'Well, you'll have to wait a spell. Pond'll freeze over pretty soon now.' They were passing the head of the island; and he said: 'You can see where that Indian grave used to be. Indians won't ever go on the island. There was a family of them here this summer when Packard and Ben Burton took the stones, and they covered their faces and howled like good ones.'

They drew in toward the shore, angling northward. The ferry loaded with household goods was still half a mile below them, progressing laboriously under the striving oars; but Mima in the unstable float dared not turn to look back. Ahead she saw the house, on a knoll a few rods from the water, and a dog came bounding down the shore, and Jess cried: 'Here's Tuner, come to meet us.' He shouted: 'Ho, Tuner, b'ar!' The hound bayed with excitement and Jess said: 'All you've got to do is holler "b'ar" and Tuner goes crazy. Nothing tickles him as much as getting his nose full of b'ar smell. There's Dave and Bess now!'

Mima saw them on the shore ahead, Dave and his wife; and Bess was big with the baby that would come in February. Mima's eyes filled so that for a moment she could not see; and she hugged her arms across her breasts in that gesture so apt to be provoked by any strong deep emotion in her heart. Jess said behind her:

'Ain't Bess a sight? I tell her it's twins sure.'

'She's beautiful,' Mima whispered. 'Jess, you hadn't ought to talk so. That's our job, us women, having babies, men babies to do the work and girl babies to marry them and have more babies. You hadn't ought to make fun of Bess.'

'Sho, she likes it. She's as proud as wax.' Then he exclaimed: 'Say, where's she gone? What's wrong with her?'

For Bess, as they came within two or three rods, had turned with a movement like flight, slipping back up to the house, disappearing inside. Mima saw Dave try to call her back, and go after her; and then young Jake and Eben came racing from the woods beyond the house. Eben had been here with Jess and their father since May, helping clear the land. He was fifteen, two years younger than Jess and a year older than Jake; but he and Jake had always been as close as twins. On their heels trotted David's two older children. Jason was almost five, and Chloe was three. Little Joe was still a baby, so Mima thought he was doubtless asleep in the cabin. She had never seen him. He had been born since David moved up here. The float touched; and Mima stepped eagerly ashore and Eben kissed her, gently, as he did everything. Mima sometimes thought Eben was as tender as a woman. The two little children —

their fingers in their mouths, shy, withdrawn — watched doubt-fully, as though this strange newcomer might do something alarming.

David came down the path from the house, grinning with the embarrassment a man feels when he encounters one of those feminine reactions which are so completely beyond mas-culine comprehension. 'Bess run and hid,' he said helplessly. 'She says she don't want to see you.' He tried to explain. 'I guess she's woods queer. She ain't seen a woman for six months, and she 'lows you'll think she's a sight.'

Mima nodded understandingly. 'I'll find her,' she said. 'You all stay here.'

She started up the path, then paused and turned to look out across the lake again. To the southward, now not far away, the deep-laden barge with her father and Rich Comings rowing crept slowly toward them. Across the pond, she could see the clearing by the Mill Stream and the two or three buildings there. The rest of the farther shore was unbroken wilderness. After she and Phin left the river, they had seen no clearing till they came to the Mill Stream. Only the rough track from Boggs' landing across the carry, and the spotted trees that marked the trail up the east side of the pond, were works of man. Jake and Eben trotted off down the shore to meet the barge; and David was here with his two babies, waiting for the ferry to arrive. Mima turned and followed the path up toward the house.

She walked the short distance slowly. The excitement of this arrival at last at journey's end had produced in her a deep, sure peace and calmness; an insensibility to emotion that was coupled with an intense capacity for perception. Once clear of the fringe of trees close to the water, she saw down along the shore the clearing where their first planting had been done; a tract surprisingly small, with great trunks half burned lying at length, some of them no more than a line of ashes, some the skeletons of trees. Beyond the clearing, further from the pond, along the base of a low rocky hill, the pines had been felled and now lay brown and lifeless, waiting to be burned in the spring when the wood should have had time to dry. These down trees were in a narrow strip eight or ten rods wide, running some distance to the southward. She thought proudly that her father and her brothers had felled all those trees.

The house was built of the very trees which had been cut to give it room. It stood some thirty feet above the water, four or five rods from the shore, the door facing the pond. Down the shore along the pond she could hear Tuner barking, and the children shouting in shrill hail and welcome. Mima reached the door, made of hewed slabs, hung on wooden hinges. It hung half-closed. She pushed it open and went in.

The inside of the cabin was so dark that at first she could see nothing except the leaping flames on the hearth; but then she saw Bess sitting on a shingle block by the fireside, little Joe in her arms, hugged jealously to her breast. Bess's eyes seemed to glare and flicker whitely in the firelight. Mima crossed to her, and on her knees she held the other woman close and tenderly, kissing her, comforting her. She was thinking with a faint envy that Bess, only three or four years older than herself, already had three babies and another coming. Mima felt the other trembling in her arms; heard Bess's teeth chatter, stroked her shoulders soothingly, thought what to say. Everyone was better off with a job to do, to keep them from thinking about themselves, so she said:

'You've got everything mighty fine here, Bess. I'm glad, because it will make it easier for Mother. She's awful upset about moving, and worried, and dead sure things are going to go hard for us; and she's having change of life and that makes it harder for her. So we're going to have a time getting her settled and happy and all. We'll have to joke her about things.' She touched the baby's head. 'My, but Joe's big now! How old is he? Sixteen months? He'll be walking and everything in no time.'

She talked on, quietly and easily, till she felt the strained figure in her arms relax, and presently Bess even laughed in a breathless way and said:

'I knew I'd make a fool of myself when you all came, Mima. My, but you've grown up sence I saw you, and filled out and all. I don't know what got into me today; but I've be'n awful cranky and notional with this baby, right along. There's been times when it seemed as if, if I didn't get a chance to eat some real sour cucumber pickles and all I wanted of 'em, I'd just screech and holler — and we ain't even had any vinegar sence Pa went to fetch you all.'

Mima said reassuringly: 'Mother brought a barrel of it, made out of our own cider. Father didn't want to, but she said she wouldn't come if he didn't.' She heard voices near; and she said: 'Here they come. You mind, Bess, and kind of humor Mother. She's all right most times; but when she gets upset, no telling what she'll say. Just don't pay any heed, and she comes around all right.'

'The only thing,' Bess wretchedly confessed, 'I'm so tired, cooking and tending for them all summer, and it's been real hot, and no other woman even to talk to.'

'We're here now,' Mima told her warmly. 'You won't have to lift a hand.' And she said quickly: 'Hush, now. Here they are.' The ferry had landed. The others came trooping to the door.

II

Seven-Tree Pond

1

THE house on Seven-Tree
Pond to which Philip Robbins brought his family was about
eighteen by twenty feet, built of round logs notched together
at the corners and caulked with moss. At one end was the fireplace, open on both sides, with a chimney-back of flat stones
laid up against the logs. The cat-and-clay chimney, built of
sticks plastered with clay in which chopped straw had been
mixed, rested on wooden bars laid crosswise in crotched posts.
It had no jambs, and it was high enough above the floor so that
heavy back logs could be slipped in from either side. The fire
thus threw heat freely in three directions. The house had a floor
of loose boards. There was a cellar hole at the left of the door,
with a trap in the floor. Above the door, there was a garret, its
floor just high enough so that a tall man could walk under it
without bumping his head. A notched log served as stairway
to the garret. The shutter on the one small window slid in a
groove. There was no glass in the window. It was either open,
admitting light, or it was closed and dark.

Here, during the days after their arrival, Mrs. Robbins

established her household. Rich had his own cabin down the pond, where he and Bet and the baby made themselves at home; and Bet, with Rich silently assenting, said some of them must come and live there. 'You can't all crowd into this one room,' she protested. 'There'll be ...' She counted rapidly, naming them off, tallying them on her fingers: 'Pa and Ma is two; and Dave and Bess is four; and their three is seven; and Mima and Jess and Eben and Jake and Susie, when Uncle Will brings her home from Camden, is twelve, and Phil is thirteen. You'll be sleeping three deep! Besides, thirteen is bad luck!'

Dave protested: 'Whoa back! There's fourteen of us, counting the new one you're carrying.' He drew Bess against his side. 'And anyway, it won't be long. I'm building right away.'

'You never did anything right away in your life,' Bet told him sharply. 'You'll be all winter at it. Rich says we've got as much room as you have here.' She looked at Rich and he nodded. Mima thought the little scar on his cheek made him seem to smile, puckering his eye, as though it were twinkling at Bet's urgency; and Bet insisted: 'So we might full as well divide up, half and half, till Dave does get his house built — if he ever does.'

But Mrs. Robbins said the final word. 'No, you and Rich have got a right to be by yourselves,' she told Bet. 'Rich built his house, and it's his and yours. Dave'll get at the job and build his own. Till he does, we'll manage fine.'

But it needed managing. In preparation for the arrival of these others, David and Bess had already moved their own cord bed into the garret, and had set up there another bed which Dave made of cedar poles strung with strips of moose hide. There was not time the first day to do more than lay straw ticks on the floor; but next day another cord bed went into the garret, and the high poster was set up in the corner over the cellar, with a trundle bed beneath it. That second night, Philip and Mrs. Robbins had the poster, David and Bess with the baby slept in their bed in the garret, and their two older children in the bed David had built, beside it. Jacob and Jess took the other garret bed, and Eben slept on a straw tick on the garret floor. Mima and young Philip shared the trundle bed till Sue came home a week later. After that Sue slept with Mima, and Philip with Jacob; and Jess rolled in his blankets anywhere, with a bearskin for mattress.

Except for the beds, and two of her chairs, all of Mrs. Robbins' furniture went into the storehouse. There would be no room for it in the house so long as they were so many there. Even the loom and spinning wheel were for the present stowed away.

'I'll have enough to do, cooking for the whole of you, this winter,' she told Philip, 'without trying to do any weaving — even if I had the wool to do with.' He promised to get sheep next year and see to it thereafter that she had wool enough.

When Uncle Will brought Sue home from Camden, he stayed with them a day or two, lending a hand with the business of preparing for the winter, which even thus early in November began to grip the land. Mrs. Robbins already fretted at the cold; but he told her to be thankful for it.

'There'll be times next summer you'll wish you were freezing,' he said. 'The flies will rod you so. Little ones you can't hardly see, and when they bite you it's like a hot needle, and then it keeps you scratching for a week after.'

She said she could stand the flies better than being cold all the time; and Philip brought a huge log and laid it on the fire, and said cheerfully: 'There, Ma, that'll warm ye!'

'I didn't say I wanted to be roasted,' she assured him, and made a whistling sound. 'Whew! It's hot enough in here to fry eggs. Open the door!'

They laughed at her sudden swing from being cold to being hot, till she laughed with them. In the vigorous business of settling into the small quarters here, she was more cheerful than she had been on the voyage from the westward, with no tasks to do.

Mima was more concerned for Bess than for her mother.
Bess seemed, even after they were settled, drained and frail
and tired; and Mima was careful to relieve her of household
duties. But Susie could take care of the babies, and Mrs.
Robbins worked tirelessly and the house was small, so there
were hours when Mima was free, and she began to go abroad,
wandering alone through the forest, exploring this scene that
they must make their own. The land already cleared lay south
of the house, along the shore of the pond; and around the house
itself all the trees had been felled and either burned or used in
the construction of the cabin, except for a few left standing along
the pond. The cleared land was rich and well drained, and it
was almost free of stones. When they got the stumps out of it,
it would take the plow. Directly west of the house, over a low
rise, there was more land just as good, which Philip proposed
to clear and put under cultivation when he could. The soil was
clay on gravel, the clay well overlaid with rich loam. The
house itself stood near enough the water so that it was no chore
to carry all they needed. The knoll on which it had been built
sloped away in three directions, and they were on a point
which projected far enough into the pond so that they could
see from the door down past where Rich's house was located
to another point a mile away where David meant to build.

But though there was an open outlook to the south along the
clearing, and out across the pond, on the north and west
the forest was a wall, spruce and pine towering to the sky with
shadowed aisles between their great trunks and a floor so thick-
carpeted with fallen needles that scarce a bush grew. The
clearing was a fresh wound, the stumps still bleeding sap, the
earth dark with the ashes of the fire that had consumed the
fallen trees, as though the wound had been cauterized. But the
untouched forest all around was like a maze of many-shadowed
secret paths, inviting exploration; and Mima was eager to enter
them. From the house, over the tops of the nearer trees, she
could see that a wooded hill rose some two hundred feet above

the pond, half a mile southwest; and one day she climbed to its crest. There were on the northeast face open ledges which bore only scattered trees; and from these ledges she saw mountains ten or twelve miles away to the eastward, and the pond bright below.

But there was no outlook to the west at all. Jess had said a smaller pond lay in that direction and she planned soon to go seeking it, but for the present she was content to explore the nearer scene. It was a week before she had her first glimpse of that pond, and then it was from some distance. North of the house, the forest was untouched. She went one day along the shore as far as the river, twenty or thirty rods, and found that as the river approached Seven-Tree Pond it was forced to make half a circle around a high knoll that rose fifty or sixty feet above the water. She came there first at sunset, and when she rounded the knoll the sun, piercing the trees, laid dazzling spots of light on the river and on the waters of a deeply indented cove below her. The river came toward her in lazy meanderings, with shores that were sometimes low and marshy, sometimes projecting in points on which low brush or tall trees grew. Looking up this marshy vista, herself high enough to see over the opposing points of land dry enough to sustain trees, she saw a wider reach of water in the distance and knew it for an angle of the pond. In the sunset light it seemed to shine, and beyond, the farther shores were sullen blue in this November dusk.

She wished to go that way, feeling herself drawn to that further mystery, to that untouched solitude; and on the first occasion she did so. The river was her guide, but she could not follow it closely because of the marshy coves, flooded by high water every spring, which probed into the forest from its banks. So she paralleled the stream at a little distance; till she saw through the pines on her left a glint of water and swung that way. She came out on the shore of the pond opposite an island, half ledge, half wooded, a few rods offshore. Reeds grew between it and the shore so that she thought she could wade out to it if the water were not so cold.

She stayed a while there, content for the present to fill her eyes with this new prospect; but she extended her explorations on other days, devouring new experiences, full of a feeling like hunger which made her want to know every tree and rock, every hill and meadow, every spring and stream in this which was to be her world.

*   *   *   *   *

The house was the focus of their life, and Rich and Bet down the pond were their neighbors. Doctor Taylor had some men at work finishing the mill, and they could sometimes be seen moving to and fro, but they were strangers and transients, coming and going. After her first arrival Mima did not cross the pond that fall. She was more interested in their animal neighbors in the forest. They killed one bear in November. David's Tuner treed it in a tall spruce on the hill southwest of the cabin, and Jess and David and Philip caught up their guns and ran that way when the barking warned them. Jess outstripped the older men, while Mima raced by her father's side. Philip called to the boy already drawing ahead:

'Don't start shooting till we get there, Jess.'

But Jess was eight or ten rods ahead of them when he reached the foot of the tree. He threw up his gun and fired and the bear came tumbling down, stone dead. Philip said in a dry reprobation:

'I told you to wait, Jess.'

But Jess retorted: 'Yup! Heard ye; but I was skeered you'd miss it, Pa!' Jess was always apt to seize the better part, though Mima thought this was often as much from zeal as selfishness.

They killed two moose that fall. Mima had a part in each occasion. One day with the big hound for a companion she went up-river through the tall pines. In the faint stirring winds their tops moved and whispered together as though they compared notes on this newcomer. A scant mile from the house she came out upon the bank of the little pond, and followed around the south shore. On the opposite side of the pond she crossed a brook with a boggy meadow at its mouth. She had to swing inland to go around this obstacle, then returned to the shore again and pushed on. She found easy walking among great pines, some of them three or four feet through, and she came presently to the margin of the meadow at the head of the pond.

The meadow was dotted with moose bush and alder and willow shoots, and matted with long grass which frost had killed, and wet underfoot; so she stopped by its border, standing with her shoulders against one of the trees, her arms folded as though to embrace all that she saw. She remembered that Sam Boggs had said the beaver dam touched the shore here, and she found it and made her way out along it. She passed a reedy little pond where a brook was backed up by the dam, and went on till the willow shoots growing on either side of the dam interlaced across it and made walking difficult. The dam was high enough to give her a vantage from which she could see out across the meadows, her head higher than any but the tallest bushes; and she planned to bring an axe some day and clear a way so that she could walk along the length of the dam to the river.

But there was time enough for that. She would live here all her life. Moving back toward the higher ground again, she thought that some day there would be houses all around this little pond. Sam Boggs said it was called Round Pond because of its shape. She wondered where the houses would be, and then she saw a trickle of water in the soft ground near the end of the dam, and found a clogged spring, and dug it out with a stick and let the mud settle, and drank deep of the cold water that skimmed with ice so quickly on this stark November day. She wished there were a spring near her father's house, and she thought someone would build near this spring some day. She discovered a well-drained knoll among the pines a dozen rods away that would do for a house site, and the land all down

this western shore of the pond to the brook was, except for an occasional ledge, clear of boulders and easily brought under cultivation once the trees were felled. She extended her explorations,
pleased as a child with her discovery, picturing a snug house
on the knoll, a path down to the spring, another to a boat landing by the pond shore, where floats could be slid up on the
boggy border of the meadows out of harm's way. The path she
meant to cut along the beaver dam would be a short cut to her
father's house. It was true that to go that way meant twice
crossing the river, but there would be bridges, some day. She
erected, in her imagination, a cabin here of which she would
be the mistress; she saw herself busy at her tasks, carrying water
from the spring, watching her husband working the fields he
would clear south of the cabin, welcoming him when his toil
was done.

She was reluctant to leave this place. She turned back to
the beaver dam to look out once more across the meadows before starting home, and heard a sudden thrashing in the young
willows and heard Tuner's excited baying that receded
toward the forest northwestward, and she caught a glimpse of
something black in trotting flight before him. She thought it
might have been a bear. Tuner's song went farther and farther
away; and when at last Mima turned homeward she could no
longer hear him.

She expected him to overtake her, but he did not. When
she returned to the house, it was within an hour of dark. Old
Sam Boggs was there, bound up-river on a hunt for winter
meat; and when he heard her report, he thought it must have
been a moose Tuner had chased.

'If 'twas, it might circle back,' he said. 'Dave, say we go see.'

Mima went with them, feeling in some way responsible, and
concerned for Tuner. They went in Sam's big float, and when
they came to the little pond, Dave fired his gun.

'That will bring him if he hears it,' he predicted. Frost was
falling, and the November dusk was icy still. They waited, and

shouted, and David fired again; and in the hush that clapped down upon them when the echoes of the shot had died, Mima was intensely conscious of the boundless wilderness around them, and she seemed to feel it alert and listening, crouching like an animal frightened by the roar of the gun.

Sam paddled the float past where the river flowed into the pond; and he said, pointing with his paddle: 'I done that; let the river through there. It's a beaver dam runs clear across from the high ground, all of forty rod. I broke the dam there, shot one of them when he come to mend it. High water, the river always used to boil over the dam more t' the west'ard; but it's dug itself a channel here now. Guess 't'll always run through here.'

Mima asked whether there were still beaver about; and he said: 'Yes, ma'am; but they've kind of give it up, right here. That dam of theirs used to flow the hull meadow back to the high ground. That's why it's all growed up to grass and brush and no trees on it. But they've been bothered so much here by the Indians and the Anderson boys and me, and then the Butlers pestered 'em some, till they've scattered. Some of 'em have banked up, but mostly they've took to the brooks. Any brook any size and you'll likely find a dam or two on it; sometimes more.'

His voice droned on. He paddled across the north end of the pond and rammed the nose of the float ashore where the forest came down to the water, and suddenly Mima heard, faint and far off, a distant sound. She whispered: 'I hear him.'

After a moment David said: 'I don't! You, Sam?'

'Not yit.'

'You get to imagining you hear things, in the woods at night, Mima,' David told her.

Mima said: 'Sh! Listen.' And after a minute she insisted: 'I hear him all plain.'

David could hear nothing; nor could Sam. But Boggs said:

'Let off your piece again, Dave.' And a few minutes later, he said: ''Y Cracky, she's right! I can hear him now.'

David began to whistle and to shout, but it was minutes more before Tuner came to them. He was panting hard, and David felt him over and found a bruised gash on his shoulder. He scolded the great dog good-humoredly, and told him to come along, and left him to follow along the bank as the float turned homeward. The moon rose to touch with silver the tree-tops high above their heads, and a ghostly illumination lay across the pond.

But Tuner did not follow them. He barked and bounded on the bank and hung back till Sam Boggs said:

'Dave, he's got su'thing he wants to show ye.'

'Probably got a b'ar treed, the dumb fool.'

'I wouldn't say so. Say we go along, see what 'tis.'

Mima wished to go with them; but David dissuaded her. 'If it's far, we'll likely sleep out,' he said. They landed her on the east side of the pond where no river barred her way. 'You go along home,' he said. 'Keep down the river and you can't miss it.' He added, half in jest, half in wonder because she had heard Tuner before they did, a while ago: 'If you get lost, just listen. You'll hear Ma talking, with them ears of yours!'

She went back through the moonlit pines alone, thinking remotely that she ought to be afraid; the forest was so still, the trees tall above her head, the stealthy cold twining everywhere. But she was not afraid. This already was her home.

Sam and Dave returned an hour after light next day, burdened with the carcass of a yearling moose slung on a pole between them, its head and hooves and useless parts removed and thrown away. Tuner was praised for that exploit, but so was Mima too.

'She heard Tuner coming all of five minutes before Sam did,' Dave said, proud of his sister. 'And Sam heard him five minutes before me.' He laughed. 'Why, say, I guess Mima could hear a mouse kiss his wife a quarter of a mile off. She's got ears like an owl!'

Mima said: 'Likely I didn't hear him at all — only just thought I did. I sort of felt as if I knew he was coming, more'n hearing him.'

She had a more direct part in the killing of the other moose. November was mild, and though there might be skim ice in the coves, the ponds stayed open. Susie tagged along one afternoon toward the end of the month when Mima walked up to Round Pond; and when they came to the shore, Mima looked toward the meadows and saw the black bulk of a tremendous moose, just wading into the water. She left Sue to watch it from this distance, herself ran headlong to fetch someone to kill it, and heard an axe by the river and found Jess setting a squat trap for mink and told him to summon Philip. Jess raced for the cabin, and Mima returned to Susie; but when Jess came he was alone.

'Pa was busy,' he said. 'I'll kill it for you.'

She protested doubtfully, said maybe this business needed a wiser, or at least an older, head; but he saw the moose feeding on the moose bush along the beaver dam, and without waiting to argue the point loped away around the pond to begin the circuitous stalk. They saw no more of him for a while; but Philip came up through the woods to join them and to ask:

'Where'd Jess go?'

'After the moose,' Mima told him, and pointed to the black bulk yonder. 'I sent him to get you, but he said you were busy.'

Her father chuckled. 'He snuck in the house and got the gun and out again,' he said. 'I knew he was up to something. Jess'll never miss a chance to hog the fun.'

'He must be almost to it by now, the way he started.'

They watched, till by and by the moose yonder flung up its head in sharp alarm, and Jess rose out of the bushes almost beside it. The great black beast, its neck broken, went down before the sound of the shot could reach them; and Jess waved his arms and shouted in his triumph.

The moose proved to be a tremendous animal. Not even

Philip Robbins could span its horns from tip to tip with his extended arms. He estimated that it dressed over seven hundred pounds of meat and bone. As much of the meat as could not be immediately eaten was stripped off the bones and hung to freeze against a later use. The bones themselves were roasted and then broken and the marrow scraped out. Well salted, it would serve as a substitute for butter. Every bit of the carcass was used that could be, and Jess proudly brought home the great head and cleaned the skull and spiked it to the logs above the cabin door. The horns had thirteen prongs.

*   *   *   *   *

With December came the first snows, and ice closed the pond and the river and winter clamped hard down. Their winter tasks were few. They had as yet no stock to tend. Philip had chosen to sell out everything at home. David owned a yoke of oxen and two cows, as well as a brood sow and some fowl; but he had left them all on his farm in Warren to be brought up to Seven-Tree Pond in the spring. They had no concern about food. Philip had brought barrels of potatoes and flour and salt pork and other staples, and the crop they had made on the burned land here this summer supplemented what they brought. So there was food enough stored away in the cellar under the house; and the game they occasionally killed supplemented this. For the rest, they had only the daily chore of supplying wood for the fire, and of helping Dave build his cabin. Dave himself was an easy-going man, ready enough to spend the winter as they were; but Bess, as the time for her baby to be born drew near, was as eager to be in her own home as Mrs. Robbins was to have their room instead of their company, and she kept him at the task.

With so little to do, Philip had time for thought and for concern. He was worried because he and Doctor Taylor had as yet signed no papers covering his purchase of this land.

'I wouldn't put it past Taylor to make trouble,' he declared

'Flucker threw the Andersons off after he sold to Taylor, and Taylor might try the same trick on me. He can go ahead and let me clear all the land around here, and then go back on his word and I'll have my work for nothing. I ain't paid him anything yet, till the deal is closed. He can go back on it any time.'

He was uneasy too at the fact that in these hushed solitudes they could not know how the war was going. Once during the winter they had news from outside. In February, Ben Burton came to collect his bill for the barn frame he had hewed and sized the summer before. Across the pond at the Taylor clearing, Phin Butler and Ezra Bowen and two or three other men had spent much of the winter falling trees; and the day Burton on snowshoes crossed to the Robbins place, Phin came with him. Mima saw them coming and she and her father met them at the lake shore. Burton saw the moose head spiked above the cabin door and admired its size. 'Don't know as I ever saw bigger,' he said; and Jess, who had come down to meet them, glowed with pride. They went up toward the house together; but Phin stayed uncertainly by the shore and Mima turned back to him.

'I didn't know as you'd still be here,' she said. 'You talked about going in the army.'

'I'm going with Major Burton,' he explained. 'Any time now.'

'Is your brother going?' she asked, trying to put him at his ease.

'I dunno as he will,' he said, jerking the words out with that turkey-like motion of his head and neck, his eyelid flickering nervously. 'He's working down in the lower town this winter.' He added: 'He's keeping company with kin of yours. Lucy Robbins, Oliver Robbins' gal. Oliver's yore uncle, ain't he?'

Mima said he was her father's half-brother. 'I haven't seen Lucy since we were children.'

'Johnny says she'll have him soon's his time's out,' Phin assured her. 'He'll be twenty-one the tenth o' this month, so I dunno as he'll do any soldiering.' He added: 'Taylor's due to give him a piece of land up here, so you'll have 'em for neighbors.'

'We need neighbors,' Mima agreed. She said: 'Come up and set. It's cold, standing here.'

He followed her doubtfully, and they came into the dark, crowded cabin, where with door and window closed the great fire gave the only light. Burton was saying: 'I made a trip t' the west'ard, carried a petition to Boston for the folks in the lower town. Left here the twenty-sixth day of last November and come into Boston the first day of December. I went horseback. Safer than going by water, and quicker too. With a horse, you don't have to wait for no wind. There's eight ferries from here to Boston, not counting rivers I waded or swum the horse over. I turned over the petition and went to see Taylor about the commission he was trying to get for me; but things was so upset, with Howe chasing Washington through Jersey, that you couldn't tell who from which. Taylor had got my commission last September, it turned out, but it had to be approved or the like.'

Mima watched him while he talked, more interested in him than in what he said. He spoke with a quick and lively animation, with many gestures, and a constant play of expressions across his countenance. He was so tall that he had to stoop to clear the garret floor under which her father could pass erect; and he had a fair skin and fair hair and a sparkling blue eye. As though he felt her regard upon him he looked at her now and then, seemed sometimes to speak to her more than to the others. He said:

'The lower town's petition's due to come up in General Court next month. They want to name it after General Thomas that died of smallpox up't Chamblee, when they sent him to back off from Quebec. But I set out to tell you about what

Washington did t'the Hessians. He caught 'em at Trenton, crossed the river and caught 'em drunk and asleep, and handled 'em as easy as yarded moose, killed half of 'em and captured the rest. Then when Howe came down on him, Washington backed off and hit the lobsterbacks another lick at a place name of Princeton. That give Howe his bellyful for this winter. He went back to New York, and Washington's at Morristown. My papers got approved there. I'm taking Phin Butler here back with me. Phin 'lows he'd as soon serve out his bound time in the army as working for Taylor.' His eyes twinkled at Mima. 'Don't see why he'd want to leave here with some of the neighbors he's got, but he does.'

Phin blushed and Mima smiled, and Philip Robbins asked questions, about the army, about the fighting. 'I told some of the redbacks last year that one of us could handle two of them,' he said stoutly. 'They'll find it's so.'

When the war talk ended, Philip said: 'I been wanting a chance to pay you for that barn frame, Ben.'

'I 'lowed you would,' Burton agreed. 'Fetched my bill along. Money ain't worth what it was, but we won't argue about it. I made the bill out last November, before I set out for Boston, but I've had no chance to get up here before.' He said: 'See here, Robbins, I've got a heifer over across the pond that'll be ready to serve in July. You'll want critters up here, and with me going t'the army, I'll sell her cheap.'

'I haven't got no place to put her this winter.'

'I'll turn her over to Sam Boggs till she's served. You can get her, come spring. Say twelve dollars?'

After some discussion, they agreed to trade; and Ben said: 'I 'lowed you'd want her. I put her down on the bill. Here it is. It comes to a hundred, sixteen, and six all told.'

He handed Philip the bill and Philip passed it to Mima. 'See if it adds up, Mima,' he directed. 'I ain't got my specs.' She looked at the little slip:

Nov^br 22   1776 St Georges
Philip Robins Dr

To Hughing of a fraim for a Barn O. T....................	£22	10 0
To 9 Days work of Myself and Brother at 3£ per Day......	27	00 0
To one Heffer at 12 Dollars...........................	27	00 0
To 13 Days Work at 37/6..............................	24	6 6
	£100	16 6

'That's right,' she assented.

'I'll give you an order on Boston if that's satisfactory,' Philip told Burton. 'I'm selling my farm down there, getting ready to pay Taylor. We ain't signed the papers yet, but he agreed on seventy-five hundred acres at fifty cents.'

'Well, he might want more, with money worth less all the time,' Burton reflected. 'But I won't change my bill on you.'

Business done, Burton and Phin Butler stayed to talk a while. Philip offered them rum. Phin accepted, but Burton declined; and Mima remembered that Captain Watson had said he never drank liquor. He asked Mima how she stood the wilderness. She said she liked it fine; and he asked teasingly: 'Wolves scare you, do they?'

'We ain't heard them only two-three times,' her father told him. 'Over Madomock way. They come up after the moose over there, likely.'

Phin Butler, taking courage from the rum, entered the conversation. 'We don't hardly ever hear 'em east of the river,' he said.

Eben, Mima's younger brother, spoke up proudly. 'Mima can hear 'em farther'n anybody. She's got ears like an owl. She heard 'em night before last going on an hour, and nobody else did at all; but Sam Boggs come back past here yesterday, said they was howling plenty.' Mima's keen sense of hearing already began to be a legend. 'Jess says Mima can hear a rabbit scratch his ear a mile away.'

Ben Burton said: 'So? Well, next to eyes, I'll take ears.' He chuckled. 'A nose like a dog's would be handy, too.'

Jess spoke. 'Sam Boggs says we can go over on the Madomock and kill moose any time. I aim to go.'

Burton chuckled. 'Well, you'll never kill one bigger than your first one,' he said. 'But you want to be careful, hunting. It comes on to storm real sudden up here sometimes. Here five-six years ago there come on a blizzard in October, right on top of warm weather. Jim Dicke and John Anderson, down Sterling way, got caught out in it and got lost and froze t' death, and two women over by Lermond's cove.' He said gravely: 'Thing to do if it comes on sudden and catches you, don't get excited, and don't wear yourself out bucking it. Get out of the wind somewhere, bury yourself in the snow maybe. When you get cold, move around till you're warm and then lie down again. You can last two-three days, that way; and by that time it'll clear off and you can see where you are. Long as you ain't scared and don't wear yourself out, you'll be all right in the long run.'

When he and Phin departed, Mima and Eben stayed together on the lake shore to watch them slog away across the snow-covered pond; and Eben said: 'Say, he's a great man, ain't he, Mima? I'm apt to go fight in the war myself soon's I get my growth.'

Mima dropped her arm around him. 'Don't you, Eben,' she said. 'I don't want you to go fighting in any war. I don't want ever anything to happen to you.'

2

WINTER laid so firm a grasp upon them that it seemed a permanent condition, like a wakeful night when the hours are endless till the reluctant dawn. They filled as they could the long and weary days. David had traded with Indians who camped near the house during the summer just gone for two pairs of snowshoes, and they tried their hands at making duplicates. Rich as a boy had been apprenticed to a tanner, and he cured moose hide for webs and thongs; but these their first attempts were clumsy ones. Sam Boggs proposed to Philip to go with him to the Madomock after moose meat; but Philip, since there was this winter no shortage of provisions, decided to stay at home. Jess went instead, snatching at the chance to escape the work on David's cabin, and Tuner went with them.

Before they returned, with a hand sled well loaded, and packing meat besides, the new cabin was finished. It was half a mile beyond Rich's, down the pond. The chimney could not be built properly when clay froze while they worked it, so that the cabin was always this winter half full of smoke that curled along the roof. Nevertheless David and Bess and the three children moved in. The removal was accomplished before Jess and Sam Boggs came home, everyone helping to carry or to haul Dave's beds and belongings down the pond; and Mima stayed the first two nights to help Bess settle. Bess was still too tired to do much work. All summer she had cooked for the men, and with her own children needing her attention too; and when the arrival of the others might have taken some burden off her shoulders, her increasing weight made it hard for her to move around. Mima put everything in order in the new cabin, and she warned Dave secretly to do as much as he could, to save Bess in every way.

'You menfolks worked hard all summer clearing the land,' she admitted. 'But she worked full as hard as if she'd been falling trees. A woman carrying a baby needs some chance to rest, Dave.'

Dave nodded sober agreement. 'But the hardest thing of all for her was not having womenfolks for company,' he confessed. 'That's what wore her down. I helped with the work all I could, but she wanted a woman.'

Mima stayed with Bess till the hunters returned. Bess relished the fresh meat they brought, finding it welcome after the salt pork which was their staple fare; and she seemed stronger afterward. Mima went home, hoping to find that her mother was happier with more room in the small cabin; but Mrs. Robbins protested that having so much room was worse than not having enough.

'Before, a body knowed they couldn't do things right and didn't wear theirselves out trying,' she declared. 'But now't there's a chance to do something, there's nought to do with.'

Mima laughed at her, and Philip promised to put a proper oven in the fireplace, come spring, and to swing an iron crane that wouldn't be always charring through, and to make things more handy every way.

He was diligent to make her days easier; but for her this first winter was a long one and a tedious. She was used to having neighbors within reach in time of need — even if that need was no greater than a mere hunger for conversation — but Rich and Bet were three-quarters of a mile away down the pond, and Dave and Bess in the new cabin were beyond them. Mrs. Robbins was awkward on snowshoes, and fussed and fumed at the necessity of wearing them, so she seldom went that far. Jess and Eben one day produced a hand sled and bundled her on it and took her for a ride as far as Rich's and back; but Mrs. Robbins froze her nose in the wind and vowed never to go again.

A day or two later, however, her concern about Bess, whose time was near, overcame her fears. 'She worked too hard for any sense, last summer,' she reminded Philip. 'On her feet all the time from day to dark warn't good for her.' The day was for February mild enough, though snow lay deep everywhere. 'I dunno but I could stand it to go see her,' she declared. 'If some of you would haul me down.'

They made an occasion of that expedition, seizing the opportunity for some break in the monotony of their lives. All of them went along, with snowshoes or without; and Jess and Eben hauled the sled with Mrs. Robbins as a passenger while the rest broke trail ahead. The cavalcade came whooping and laughing down the pond.

They found Bess weary; but she was merry at the sight of them, and Dave, worried about Bess, was so glad to see them that a sort of intoxication took possession of him. He had always a comic gift for mimicry and clowning; and he convulsed them all by imitating Bess and her unwieldy movements as she went about her tasks. Even Bess laughed at him; but Mrs. Robbins laughed least of all, and Mima saw her brother Eben watching Bess with a sort of wonder in his eyes and a deep affection.

Mima's own concern for Bess went deeper, so when the cavalcade started back up the pond, she stayed behind to take all the household tasks off the other's hands. There was room for her in the garret with the two older children. Little Joe slept in a crib near the big bed below. Mima stayed, and Bess was glad to have her; and Mima saw how Dave tried every day to find ludicrous tricks and devices which would make Bess smile.

'She's had a mean time with this one, these last two months,' he admitted to Mima one day when they were out-of-doors together. 'I'll be glad when it's here. Her legs never swoll up like this before.'

Mima was not versed in the lore of childbirth; but she had heard older women talking, and she was sure Bess would be all right after the baby came. She told Dave so; and he nodded and said:

'I guess likely; but it's hard on her now, all the same. I play the fool all I can, to kind of keep her cheered up.'

He humored her in every way. Bess wanted fresh meat to eat, and David and Jess hunted steadily to bring it in; but the nearest moose were now yarded over on the Madomock, and that meant a three- or four-day trip, even if the men were lucky enough to kill quickly. The bears were all hibernating, and the snow lay deep so that finding their dens was hopeless. The men saw partridges budding; but powder was too expensive to waste on small game. They set snares, and sometimes caught a partridge, or a rabbit; but one rabbit was no more than one meal.

Mrs. Robbins thought the baby was due about February 27. Bess was sure if it did not come before that she could not endure the waiting. Mima had no opinion and no time to form one; she was too busy taking care of Bess and the children; and she found a completely satisfying happiness in having even a small share in this miracle of birth. The baby was very active, and Mima liked to feel it; so Bess called her on every occasion, and Mima with her hand pressed to Bess's abdomen could follow the continuous motion of a heel or a head as the baby turned in the womb. Sometimes it kicked against her pressing hand, and she laughed with delight, and Bess might laugh at Mima's laughter. They agreed that the baby must be a boy, it was so vigorous; and they called it 'David' and chuckled over its antics, and Mima said:

'Are they all like this?'

'No. They're different even before they're born, seems like. You can tell the difference, the way they feel.'

'You really have them to love and all before you ever see them, don't you?'

Bess said: 'Well, you don't get to love them much till toward the end. First off when you know they're coming, you're scared; and then you get to kind of liking them, and then they start making you up-chuck in the morning and you'd like to smack them, and then they start bulging you out till you're a sight, and you hate that. But towards the end, like now, when you know they're almost here, you get to thinking how sweet they're going to be till you can't hardly bear it.'

Sometimes Dave shared with them this game of feeling his prospective namesake's antics; and always he strove to keep Bess cheerful and content. Mima had never seen this side of her brother before. He might be argumentative, or loud in laughter as he ridiculed someone, and he had always teased Mima unmercifully since she was a little girl. But he was infinitely patient with Bess now; and although Mima found Bess sometimes unreasonable and irritating, David never seemed to think so. When her appetite for fresh meat became more and more insistent, and he could not satisfy it nearer home, he decided to go over to the Madomock and get a moose for her. Mima knew he would have preferred to stay at home till the baby came; but when he suggested going, Bess said:

'Go ahead. A piece of moose would go good.'

'I kind of hate to leave you.'

'I'm all right. You'll have time to get back.' Her tone was resentful. 'The way I feel, the baby's not coming till fall.'

So he made his plans. Jess would go with him, and Tuner, of course. They departed on the twentieth of February.

Next day, Mima felt herself oppressed by a deep restless foreboding. She was forever going out-of-doors to look at the weather; and though the sky was cold blue above the white blaze of the sunned snow, Mima thought she could hear a far, high howl of bitter winds in presage of a storm. February had been a month of storm, and drifts were deep. She put on her snowshoes and went up the pond to ask her mother to come and lodge that night with Bess; but Mrs. Robbins was sure that Bess was still a week short of her time. She would not come; but she sent Eben back with Mima, to summon her if Bess began her pains.

The snow that night at first came soundlessly, small flakes dropping straight down; but Mima heard hissings in the fire, and when she opened the door, snow was already inches deep outside the threshold. Bess stirred in her bed and asked:

'Snowing, Mima?'

'Some,' Mima said. Eben was snoring on the floor, little Joe in his crib, the two older children soundlessly asleep in the garret overhead. Mima heard more clearly now that far sound like the roar of a great wind overhead. She said: 'It won't last, Bess.' She came to sit beside the other. 'Is he moving?' she asked. 'Can I feel him kick?'

'He did a while ago, pretty hard,' Bess said. 'But he hasn't since. He's gone to sleep, prob'ly.'

Mima laughed. 'Bless his heart! We'd best do the same. Don't worry about the snow, Bess.' She slipped into bed with Bess, holding her close, pretending to sleep so that Bess might be reassured.

The wind came suddenly, pouncing like a great beast, so violent even in its first thrust that a tree somewhere near, stiff with frost, came crashing down. Eben and the children slept without waking; but Mima rose and went to tend the fire. When she turned, in the light from the flames she saw Bess awake and watching her; and Bess seemed like one listening to a faint, far sound. Mima went quickly to her side, whispering a wordless question.

Bess said: 'Yes — I think. There've been three pains.' She shivered. 'Mima, I'm cold!'

Mima woke Eben, bade him build up the fire. 'And put snow in the pot, Eb, to melt for water,' she said. She knelt beside Bess, holding the other's hand. A stronger pressure of the wind rattled the boards that covered the roof. She felt Bess's clasp tighten on her fingers, tight and tighter. Eben, still half asleep, stumbled out-of-doors to fetch wood. In the moment that the door was open, Mima heard a wolf's far howl, borne on the wind. Then Eben returned with an armful of billets and chunked the fire, his eyes carefully averted from Bess and Mima.

Bess said: 'It's coming, Mima.' She asked: 'What time is it?'

'Towards morning, I guess. You're all right, Bess.'

'I'll walk up and down. I always do.' She sat up on the edge of the bed.

'Eb,' Mima directed, 'you go get Mother. Tell her the pains have begun.'

Eben hesitated. 'Gorry,' he said, 'Ma'll have a time to get here. It's a-blowing out, and drifting deep.'

Yet he reached for his heavy shag jacket. Mima had a moment's doubt. Eben was only fifteen years old, and yet this was a gale that blew. The tramp through the woods in the darkness had its perils. But — she needed her mother here. Eben could make it. She said: 'You go along. You follow up the shore so you won't get lost.'

Eben nodded; but before departing he went to Bess, sitting on the bed. He touched her shoulder gingerly; and she looked up at him, and he said in a husky voice: 'You're all right, Bess. Dave was real smart, marrying you. He got a good one. I'll fetch Ma. You'll be fine.'

Then he bolted, embarrassed at his own emotion; and Bess began to cry, and Mima caught her and asked whether it hurt terribly and Bess whispered: 'No, it don't. But you're all so good to me.'

Mima laughed tenderly at her tears. 'Why wouldn't we be!'

'I was so scared last summer,' Bess confessed. 'I was scared something would happen before you all got here. I'd be so tired, some days, with the men to do for and them hungry all the time.'

'We're here now, Bess.' The wind blew harder. They walked arm in arm a while, stopping when Bess had to stop, talking when she could, talking steadily, because if they were silent the storm seemed to roar close about them.

But Mima did not notice what Bess said, or what she herself answered. She was thinking of Eben, following him in her thoughts, sharing his battle with the storm.

* * * * *

When Eben left the house that night, he did as Mima had advised. He descended to the pond and headed northward along the shore, trying to keep under the lee of the bank. But the gale came out of the north, roaring down the pond to meet him; so the bank, though it served as a guide, gave him no shelter. The boy struggled on; he shut his eyes to protect them against the driving flakes, but when he opened them again, the line of underbrush that marked the shore had disappeared. He knew he had wandered out on the pond; so he took the wind on his right shoulder and came back to the land again. Among the trees there was some shelter from the wind. He swung inland to avoid the sweep of wind down the clearing, but presently he reached the foot of the fell-piece where the pines he and Jess and David had cut during the summer lay waiting to be burned; and that obstacle of tree-tops in a vast entanglement stopped him. His strength was failing, and he could not go on. He remembered Ben Burton's advice not to be afraid; to lie down and rest; so he crawled under the interlacing boughs and found a sort of cave and scraped away the snow and piled it up in walls around him.

Day came dimly through the snow, but the blizzard blew

harder with dawn. He tried to go on; but the wind blinded him and he could not see his way. He crept into shelter again, emerging now and then to flog warmth back into his arms and legs, crawling back into his shelter when the howling gale beat him down.

He stayed there all day. At dark the wind eased, the snow ceased to fall, and he could go on. He plodded through snow knee-deep, and came to his father's house and stumbled in.

'I guess I'm too late, Ma,' he said apologetically. 'Mima sent me before day this morning, but I couldn't make it. I be'n lying up all day, in the cut-down, the way Ben Burton said I could.' And before Mrs. Robbins could catch him in her arms he was on the floor, already asleep from exhaustion and long aching cold.

They put him to bed and warmed him, and rubbed the frost out of cheeks and nose. Then Mrs. Robbins said: 'Now I'll start.'

Philip told her sensibly: 'If the baby was on the way this morning, Ma, it's here by now.' But Mrs. Robbins was already putting on her heavy garb.

'I'm a-going,' she said. 'Them two girls alone, they'll need me anyway. You can suit yourself.'

He nodded. 'Well, I 'lowed you would,' he said. 'I'll go along. I guess me and Jake can haul you.'

'I can walk.'

'Too bad Dave weren't here,' he reflected.

'Bess craved fresh meat,' she reminded him. 'Dave went to fetch it for her.' She added fretfully: 'Don't talk to me about Dave. Him and Jess out in this storm! I guess I've got enough on my mind.' She knotted her shawl. 'I'm ready,' she said decisively. 'You come on.'

Jacob offered to help haul her on the sled, but Mrs. Robbins said she could walk. She bade him stay and take care of Eben and the young ones. She and Philip trudged down to the pond and followed the shore. The wind was gone; the night was still and cold, with bleak stars shining. On their right hand the shore marched, and on their left the starlit surface of the pond lay dim and shadowed. The seven tall trees on the island were black between them and the sky, then fell behind. Now and then Philip looked over his shoulder to see how she fared; but always she said indomitably:

'I'm all right. You go on.'

Yet despite her courage, the snowshoes wearied her till at last she had to rest. He came back to her; and they stood together while she caught her breath, and he said:

'Boy or girl, I wonder?'

She said: 'Come on. I won't be easy till we're there.'

* * * * *

Mima and Bess, after Eben was gone, heard the wind howl and the dry slash of driven snow against the solid log walls which sheltered them, and time dragged itself away, and Mima hoped Eben was all right, hoped her mother would come. Once after pain had made her stand still a moment, Bess said breathlessly: 'I don't take long, Mima. With Joe it was short of two hours. Ma'd better hurry.'

'I know what all to do,' Mima bravely assured her, 'if she don't come in time.'

'I hope she don't come,' Bess said. 'I always did love you, Mima.' Her eyes glazed, and her voice had a curious, metallic tone.

Mima whispered: 'Was that one bad?'

Bess's fingers tightened hard on her arm. She laughed breathlessly. 'Mima — if you know what all to do — you'd better do it! He's right handy! He's coming!' And she whispered: 'I'd better lie down. He wouldn't like being born on the floor.'

Mima helped her to the bed. Bess whispered: 'He's coming, Mima! He's coming!' She cried: 'Dave! Dave! Dave!'

Mima pleaded desperately: 'Hold back, Bess. Don't let him come till Mother gets here!'

'I can't help it, Mima! I can't help it!' Bess's voice rose in something that was almost a scream.

Mima stared at the other woman, lying helpless there; and Bess tried to smile up at her. She said brokenly: 'I can't hold back, Mima. You wait and try to hold back yourself sometime.' Then her face twisted; and her lips drew tight, and after that passed she said apologetically: 'You'll have — to do for me, Mima. I can't wait!'

Mima said: 'It's all right. I'll take care of you.' She tried to remember what to do. This and that and that and this. She found composure, calm, serenity. She was suddenly miraculously efficient and complete in all her parts, in all her actions. This and that and this.

'He's here,' she said presently.

'Is he beautiful?' Bess whispered.

'Sh!' Mima told her. Then she cried softly: 'Bess darling, it isn't a boy! It's a girl!'

Bess said in a sudden, fierce tone, terrible with fear: 'Mima! Why doesn't she cry?'

* * * * *

For Mima the day was long. She had Bess here to tend; but when no one came and the blizzard still blew, she knew Eben had not reached home. He could not even have come safe to Rich's house; for if he had, Rich would have gone to bring Mrs. Robbins, or Bet would have come to help here. So Eben must be lost in the storm, half-frozen, perhaps dead. She thought of Eben; and Bess remembered Dave somewhere off toward the Madomock, and she wept because she had sent him away to die.

The day passed and night came; and the children were asleep before Mima heard the clack of snowshoes coming up from the pond. She snatched a shawl and ran out-of-doors, and her first word was to ask:

'Is Eb all right?'

Her father said: 'Yes. But he had to lay up through the storm, didn't git to us till just now.'

Mima spoke to her mother. 'The baby came awful fast,' she said in a low tone. 'But it was dead. There was a knot in the cord, Mother, pulled tight. It was a little girl. Bess knew before I did. She knew when it didn't cry.'

For a moment no one spoke. The hushed wilderness, the deathly stillness of lifeless winter pressed upon them hard. Then Mrs. Robbins said: 'There warn't a thing I c'd have done, even if I'd be'n here.'

'No.'

'How's Bess?'

'She didn't take on,' Mima confessed. 'But she wants Dave.' Her tone was warm with pride. 'She wants to have another one, soon's ever they can.'

Mrs. Robbins made an assenting sound. 'Bess is fine.' She spoke with no bitterness. 'She worked too hard last summer, Philip. She paid her baby for the land you got cleared.'

Philip said: 'It's bad, Ma. But men have to work, and women too.'

She touched his arm. 'Don't blame yourself. Bess wouldn't. It's the way it is, is all.'

She moved on toward the cabin and they followed her. Bess was awake when they came in. The children stirred in the garret, and firelight showed their small heads looking down.

'I'll do for Bess, Mima,' Mrs. Robbins said. 'You're wore out. You go up with the young ones, get some rest now. I'll do for her. You go along.'

3

EARLY in March, overnight, the weather changed. The wind came southerly and the drifts began to shrink, and by the middle of the month there was open water around the edges of the ponds. Sam Boggs said March was the best time to kill moose, when they floundered helplessly in deep snow while a crust supported the hunters; but a warm rain thinned the snow blanket so rapidly that the favorable season was gone almost before it began. Jess and Rich Comings tried their luck to the eastward, beyond Crawford's Pond. They found no moose, but they came back with a cat-fawn which they had treed and killed. Powder was a dollar a pound, and hard to come by, so they did not waste a shot on it; but Jess climbed the tree with a club and drove the creature out on a long limb and shook it off. Rich and the dogs — his Lion and David's Tuner — killed it; but the skin was spoiled.

March sped, and by early April, the brooks were open; and the ice went out of the river and then the pond cleared, and there were alewives running at the falls in Warren. Mima heard a robin's morning song; and a day or two later Mrs.

Robbins stepped out of the door and saw the bright flash of a bluebird's wing in the warm sun. All one day a flight of pigeons passed, high overhead, hurrying northward in what seemed an unending river of birds; and Mima caught the whisper of their wings. Her father came to watch them go, and he said: 'They'll be back. They nested over back of Crawford's Pond on the hardwood ridges last year, miles of them, so thick they'd break down the trees. The squabs eat good, fat as butter.'

He and David went down to Warren to drive home Dave's oxen and his two cows and his brood sow. On that same trip, Philip dickered with Sam Boggs for a fresh cow and a sow and boar, and he bought four ewes and penned them by the pond below the house. The pen was built of cedar posts seven or eight feet high, set close, their tops bound together to make a solid barricade against the danger of marauding wolves. That was at Boggs' advice.

'Let one wolf get in at them and you won't have no sheep the next morning,' he said. 'They don't bother so much in the summertime; but you might as well build for the winter whilst you're building.'

The snow, by mid-April, was almost gone. When the wind was right, they could hear the river roar over rapids somewhere north of them; and Mima, listening to that far sound in the night, planned to go some day and see where it came from. There must be a fall, she thought, or a narrow gorge, constricting the water so that it came plunging through with tossing plumes of spray. Once she walked up to Round Pond, and the willows in the meadows at the head of the pond showed a mist of green, and the swamp maples were blazing, and the high water lapped against the old beaver dam. Frogs were shrill in every little puddle she passed. Beaver were building a dam across the little brook on the west side of the pond, and they had dropped a poplar tree that was fully eighteen inches in diameter. Returning, she saw in a low flat where the water had begun to recede, the uncurling sprouts of ferns. They looked exactly like the head of a fiddle, and she stripped off the transparent skin which covered them and found them tender and delicately flavored. She took home as many as she could find and cooked them for greens. Her mother could not stomach them, said they looked too much like little green worms to suit her; but the others liked them, found them doubly welcome after a long winter of bread and potatoes, turnips and pork, and such dull fare.

Philip's four ewes dropped five lambs. The sheep storm came two days later, and spread three or four inches of fresh wet snow over everything; but the lambs survived it without taking any harm. After that, spring came with a rush, and there were ducks in the pond and in the river. Another flight of pigeons passed; and once Mima thought she heard a turkey gobble. Her father said it was possible.

'There might be a few around,' he told her. 'Used to be plenty back home when my father was a boy; but they move out when the land is cleared.'

David agreed that there were some in the region. 'But they're scarce,' he admitted. 'Turkeys and deer. There hasn't been a deer killed that I know of since we moved up here, and not many turkeys.'

Frost came out of the ground and for days it was impossible to walk anywhere without sinking deep in soft mud. Then May brought warm sun and fair, dry weather; and in the middle of the month Philip and his sons burned off the fell-piece they had cut over the year before. For the burning, they chose a late afternoon when the wind was settled from the west, and started fires along the west side of the cutting. In an astonishingly short space of time the whole tract was ablaze, flames leaping to the skies as dusk fell and night came down, clouds of smoke and burning embers blowing out across the lake. Myriads of small creatures took to the water to escape the fire. Squirrels and rabbits swam up the shore or down, seeking a safe landing; and the children killed them with clubs. The fire blazed up fiercely till night's damps somewhat hushed it; but it burned all night with a crackling, steady roar. Mima was full of a strong, fierce exultation at this wholesale victory over the forest that was their enemy; that must be destroyed before they could make this land their own. In the gray dawn of the next day, she went with her father along the burned tract. The foliage, the underbrush, the smaller branches all were gone to ashes now; but the great trunks still held flames that played along their lengths like red flowers blooming.

'Them big logs will burn for days,' her father told her. 'They'll burn clear up, some of them. We'll have to watch the fire, make sure it don't start up and get away. When they're cooled off enough so's we can get at 'em, we'll get the oxen in and drag what's left into piles and burn 'em again. With luck, we'll be rid of the heft of it in another week.'

Mima nodded, standing with her arms folded across her breast. She felt like a victor who sets his foot upon his enemy's neck. Here was their mark upon the land. Till now it had belonged to no one; had gone its own way, untended, uncontrolled. Now its subjection was begun; it lay helpless, submitting to their mastery.

The wind, holding from the west, scoured away the ashes and spread them on the pond so that its clear waters were gray with them for days and would hold all summer tiny particles of ash in suspension. But also, as though the heat of the fire had brought them to life, the flies came. They appeared almost overnight and in clouds and swarms. One day there were none; the next you noticed them; the next they were everywhere, alighting on faces and hands, drawing blood wherever they bit. The children, too young to fight them off, too absorbed in their own interests of the moment to notice their annoyers, were the worst sufferers. Ten minutes out-of-doors left them streaming blood from countless bites. The bites became swollen and inflamed and itched for days; and in this

first summer before they had acquired even a slight measure
of immunity to the poison, they all — children and adults —
wore lumpy foreheads, eyes swollen half shut, throats puffed
as though they suffered from mumps. Mima tried a dozen
balms and unguents to keep the flies from biting the children.
The gummy sap that exuded from the evergreens, spruce,
balsam, fir, and pine offered some protection. Anything was
better than naked endurance of the torment. Men and women
adopted any expedient, hoping it might give some relief from
the perpetual attacks. A heavy smudge was useful to discourage the insects; so there was always a small fire kept going
just outside the door of the house, and green stuff was heaped
upon it to produce great clouds of smoke like a screen. The
smoke poured into the cabins, setting everyone coughing there,
yet it was better than the flies.

Late in May, Philip sowed summer rye on the burnt-land,
and harrowed it in with a drag made of young birches which
the oxen drew slowly to and fro. The planting was begun.

*   *   *   *   *

Toward the end of May, Ezra Bowen came across the pond
to see Philip on business. Mima remembered him from that
first day of her coming up the pond with Phin Butler. He was a
stocky young man, with shoulders so broad and heavy that
even from a distance he was easily recognized, sandy-haired,
with a broad face and skin that stayed white through any
exposure to the sun; and he had a quiet way of talking that
inspired confidence. Mima and Jess and Philip met him when
he landed, and he told Philip his errand.

'I've been working for Taylor for two years,' he explained.
'Figured to buy from him; but he's selling the place over there
to Johnny Butler. Johnny's married Lucy Robbins and they
aim to move up here this summer. So I'll have to start fresh
I've an idee I'd ruther be this side the pond.'

Jess exclaimed: 'Johnny married, is he? Phin said he was

bundling with Lucy last winter. Say, I'm glad they're moving up here!' They discussed this news with a lively satisfaction; but Philip came back to Bowen's business. He welcomed the chance to sell part of his holdings.

'Did you have any piece in mind?' he asked.

'Down the pond,' Bowen said. 'I'll show you.' So he and Philip walked down the shore path past the burnt-land; and Mima went with them. Bowen, on the way, confessed: 'I couldn't pay you right off, but I'm good for it. I'm married, and I'm responsible. My wife's down't Thomaston. She was Experience Tolman. Your brother Oliver'll tell you the Tolmans are good stock.' He added apologetically: 'We hain't any children. Had a little girl named Polly, just gone a year ago; but she died. I thought I'd start clearing this summer, if I could make a dicker with you.'

Robbins said frankly: 'We can dicker, but I can't pass title yet. The papers are all drawn in Doctor Fales' office; but Taylor and me ain't signed and sealed. You can start working and take your own chances.'

Bowen was satisfied with that much. Mima stopped at Dave's to tell the news of their cousin's marriage. Bess was glad to hear it, but Dave laughed and said:

'Lucy'll liven things up some around here. She's pretty as a squirrel.'

Mima said: 'I haven't seen her since they moved up here from home. She didn't come to the wharf the day we got here.' She asked: 'Is Johnny like Phin?'

'Not to mention,' Dave told her. 'Not so big, for one thing; and he's livelier. Phin don't know his own mind, but if there's anything Johnny don't know — and say — I never found out what it is. He's a talker. Stutters some. I always figured that was because he tries to say everything at once. He's a lean, loping young jump-over-the-fence. Black hair, and some gray in it a'ready, and always ready for any hell!' He laughed and clapped his knee. 'He's a great hand to brag and blow,' he

said. 'And get him to arguing and you can't down him. He
can run like a rabbit. Jumped a moose one day and tried to
run it down. It run right away from him, and we kind of
rodded him about it, and he says: "W-well," he says, "it got
away from me, b-but it's got four legs to my t-two, and every
leg t-twicet as long as m-mine. If it'd b-be'n a b-b'ar I'd have
c-cotched it," he says. "I c-c'n outrun any b-b'ar!" '

He roared with mirth at his own words. Mima stayed till
her father and Bowen returned, then walked back up the pond
with them, and when Bowen had put off in his float she asked
her father: 'Did you trade?' He nodded. 'What piece does he
want?'

'Down past Dave's,' he said. 'Bowen's a good man, I've
heard.' He clapped his fist into his hand. 'Mima, I've got to
get Taylor to sign, soon's he comes, get this thing straight. I've
talked up this place to more'n one. There's apt to be strangers
coming in, this summer, wanting to buy, and me not knowing
is the land mine to sell.'

She reminded him that Doctor Taylor might not come to
Seven-Tree Pond this summer. 'Mr. Bowen said he was selling
the house and the mill to Johnny Butler.'

'Likely Oliver put in some money on that trade,' her father
reflected. 'With Lucy marrying Johnny. But if Taylor don't
come, I'll go down, first chance, and see Doc Fales.' He
clapped his arm around her. 'We'll make a town here, Taylor
or no Taylor!' he cried.

*   *   *   *   *

As summer began to flow across the land, Mima found herself
spending much time with Bess and David. Bess had risen
bravely from the blow of her baby's death, and her head was
high. As soon as the frost was out of the ground, the baby had
been buried on a knoll above the cabin, and David split and
smoothed a spruce slab and lettered on it: 'Silence Robbins,
Feb. 22, 1777.' Bess and Mima planned to bring wild flowers

to plant around the spot, and in June they began to do this. The children went with them, and they watched the process with a lively interest even though the black flies kept small faces and hands always itching and swollen.

Working over the little grave, the first in the new settlement, Mima remembered that Indian tomb which had been on the island. The island with its seven tall trees was the most conspicuous natural object in their lives, confronting them whenever they came out of the cabin door. The geese had returned to raise their brood there again this year, and eagles had a nest in one of the tall pines, and Mima sometimes watched the great birds flapping heavily along the shore or soaring high above the pond. She had landed on the island once, and found where the Indian grave had been; and working today to make this small grave where the baby lay a place of beauty, she wondered whether it too would some day be profaned.

She and Bess presently undertook another task. David in building his cabin had been hampered by cold weather in the work on the chimney; so it needed now to be rebuilt. With him doing the heavier work, Bess and Mima built a cat-and-clay chimney that would bake hard and last long. They repaired the calking between the logs, of moss gathered and pounded in, and plastered that with clay; and Bess decided they could build an oven as easily. It could be out-of-doors; she could more handily do her baking there than in reflector pans before the fire or in the covered kettles. Without telling Dave her real intent, she asked him to drive stakes and set a stout platform at a suitable height; and she and Mima laid on this a floor of crossed sticks plastered with clay. Dave asked questions and was told that this would be a playhouse for the children; but one day, when he went down-river with his father to see Doctor Fales in Thomaston about that matter of the deed from Taylor, they attacked the task with a rush to finish it and surprise Dave when he should return. They cut willow withes and wove them into a dome that would be plastered with clay baked hard. Bet Comings came down to watch the work; and she came again the next day to help apply the clay and mould it into place. She was to have a baby in October, and she and Bess talked of that and of the plans Bess and David made for their next. Bet was always a chatterbox, with a rattling tongue. Mima, listening to them, felt herself excluded from all that was important in the world.

'You make me mad,' she protested. 'Having babies all the time and me with never a husband to my name nor any man that's like to want me!' Her envy of their happy plans was in her tones. Bet laughed.

'You won't be so hot for it when your time comes,' she predicted. 'I'm always mad as a wet hen when I first find out. Rich says I ain't fit to live with, but I tell him he'd ought to think of that sooner. It's like buying on time. A man don't stop to figure he'll have to pay up for his fun after.'

When she presently started home, Bess walked part way with her, leaving little Joe to play at Mima's feet. Mima worked steadily on the oven; but she was thinking of these two whose lives were so full, and of herself with neither babe, nor home, nor husband, nor any fruitful task to do. She said ruefully aloud:

'I'll probably just go on helping other women take care of their babies and never see one of my own'; and she smacked the unoffending clay on the oven, and young Joseph whimpered at her feet. She thought he was startled by the sound, and she stooped to drive away the tiny black gnats that swarmed around his head and to murmur: 'There! Did Mima scare him?'

But then she saw that the baby was looking at something behind her, leaning sidewise to look past her, still whimpering with faint alarm, his thumb deep in his mouth. She looked up over her shoulder and then she came whirling to her feet, conscious of the clay on her hands and her arms, on her skirts, between her toes, on her bare feet and legs, in her very hair.

For she saw, coming toward her, a young man. He wore a

three-cornered hat, a ragged blue coat with long tails, white petticoat breeches sadly torn and stained, leggings and moccasins of skins. His long black hair was loose and untended. He was tremendously tall, and his chin was blue with beard, and he carried a musket in one hand, an axe in the other. There was a pack on his back, and all his person was hung with odds and ends of powder horns, cooking dishes, shot pouches. They were tied to his pack strap, to his sash, anywhere. Mima thought that he looked mighty tired and footsore. He came stumbling toward her, and the baby at her knee, finding itself forgotten, clung to her skirts and hid behind them. The man came on till they were only a few yards apart before he stopped. He stopped slowly and carefully. He grinned at Mima in an apologetic way, and carefully leaned his musket and his axe against a tree and slipped his pack. Then he sat down, and then he lay down on his back, his arms spread, and pushed his feet up against the tree where his weapon leaned, till they were well above the ground. He spoke without looking at her.

'It lets the blood drain out of them,' he said, wiggling his toes in the moccasins. 'They're tired.' He added: 'They've got a right to be. I've come a ways.'

She said: 'I'll fetch you a drink.' She brought bucket and cup from the cabin. 'It ain't real fresh, if you'd ruther wait till I can go down to the pond?'

He said: 'Thanks, ma'am, I ain't thirsty. Let me just lay here.'

'Where did you come from?'

'Boston,' he told her. 'Five days. That's quite a walk, it you're in a hurry.'

'Why did you hurry?'

'I've been in the army. Got Continental bills for my pay. I want to buy me a piece of land with 'em, so I hurried to get here while the bills was still worth a little something.' He said: 'My name's 'Bijah Hawes, from Franklin. There's others coming up here from there when they get through being soldiers.

I heard Philip Robbins was selling land here. Who're you?'

'His daughter.'

'Is that your young one? Say, the flies have rodded him awful.'

'They're pretty bad. No, he's my brother Dave's. This is their house.'

Still flat on his back, 'Bijah Hawes said: 'See here, I'm not choosey. I'll take the land right next to this, that I just come over, as much as I can pay for.'

She told him: 'Ez Bowen that works for Taylor, he's buying down below. I guess there's some land between him and Dave here, but Father and Dave have gone to see David Fales in Thomaston about the title. You'll have to wait till they come home.'

His eyes twinkled. 'Shucks, we can deal, you and me. I'll give you my bills, and you see to it that your pa deeds me as much land as they'll buy.' He crammed a roll of paper into her hands. 'Now I'm going to sleep till sometime. I been travelling mostly night and day.'

'Did you send your alls by the coasters?'

'You're looking at the whole thing; my money, and my alls, and me!' His feet slid down off the tree; and before she could speak again, she saw his limbs slacken as he drowned in sleep.

She stood a moment looking down at him, not sure whether she liked him or not. She felt, despite his weariness, a bold assurance in him, and none of that deference most men paid her; yet he was tired, and perhaps hungry, and a stranger. She went down to the pond to fill the water pail and saw a dugout skirting the shore of the pond, coming toward her from the south. Here were her father and David returning home.

Mima waited, brushing automatically at the little black gnats which tormented her ceaselessly, till the float came near. She remembered to wash the clay off her hands and feet and legs, and then David stepped out beside her.

'Where's Bess?' he asked, looking all around in a sharp solicitude.

'She walked home with Bet,' Mima told him. She remembered the oven, almost completed now, which David must admire; and she hoped Bess would be at the house in time to see his surprise and pride when he first saw it. 'She'll be back any time.'

David unloaded from the float a few parcels, supplies from the towns down-river. Her father said: 'Step in, Mima, and I'll ride you home.'

She shook her head. 'There's a man here to see you, Father,' she said. 'About buying land. He gave me his money. I put it in the house.' She pointed up the bank behind her. 'He's asleep.'

'Asleep?' Dave echoed, and saw her bright cheek, and chuckled. 'Sa-ay, Mima, couldn't you keep him int'rested?' He laughed aloud as her color blazed; but Philip asked:

'Where is he, Mima? Doc Fales says the land's as much mine as if the papers was already signed, so I'm ready to sell to anyone that wants to buy.'

'Up here,' Mima said. 'You come along.'

Before they reached the house, Bess appeared, the older children on her heels. They came almost to the spot where the oven stood, before David — with a youngster on each shoulder, clinging for balance to his hair — saw it. He stopped then, spilling children; and he cried:

'Say, what's that? Gor Rye! Bess, it's an oven, ain't it?' He caught her proudly. 'Say, that's what you and Mima were up to when I left!'

Bess was beaming with pride, and he hugged her, and Mima said: 'He's around here, Pa. See here.'

The young man was still asleep, flat on his back, his arms extended, his head lolling on one side, his legs spread, with the tree against which his feet had been propped between them. Mima explained in a low tone: 'His name's 'Bijah Hawes.

He's walked all the way from Boston, in five days. He comes
from Franklin; and he says some other men from there are
coming when they can.'

Her father nodded. 'Well, that suits me,' he said. 'We
want 'em.' He looked down at his daughter with twinkling
eyes. 'Guess you'll have plenty to pick from, yet, Mima.
Don't go taking the first one that heaves his grapples at
you.'

She saw that the young man's eyes were open and she said
hurriedly: 'He's awake.' 'Bijah sat up, unwrapping his legs
from around the tree; and he grinned at Philip in a flashing
way which showed all his fine teeth; and he surveyed Philip
and then Mima.

'Say, how'd you ever happen to have a gal as handsome as
this one?' he demanded. 'She must take after her ma!'

Philip said amiably: 'I hear you walked from Boston.'

'So my feet say.' 'Bijah looked at his worn moccasins. 'But
soon as I saw her I was glad of it. I'd have crawled if I had to,
if I'd known you raised them like that up here.' He told Mima:
'Wait till Joel Adams hears about you. He'll come a-running.
He'll walk ten miles any day to clip a pretty girl.' He rose and
grasped Philip's hand. 'I've come to stay. I turned my money
over to her here to keep for me. She can keep anything of mine.
Where's my land?'

Mima wondered who Joel Adams was. Dave said hospitably ·
'Come in and set. I'll strike up a fire, get a smudge going to
drive off these flies.'

So they turned indoors, and before Mima and her father
presently departed, the business was done. Young Hawes
would take the land between David and Ezra Bowen, a hundred
acres more or less. Philip had agreed to pay Taylor fifty cents
an acre; he thought himself entitled to a profit, asked seventy-
five dollars for the tract between Bowen and Dave. Hawes
had not quite that much, but Philip agreed to take what he had.

'I ain't so much in it for the money,' he admitted. 'I bought myself because I wanted to come up here and live; bought more than I wanted, calculated to sell off some. But I want neighbors, too. I'd rather have a good neighbor than his money.'

'Bijah said frankly: 'I don't know how good a neighbor I'll be; but I want to start clearing right off, this summer. I've had my bellyful of the war. There's others in Franklin talk of coming. My brother Matt, for one; and Mose Hawes, my cousin. Matt's trying to get Joel Adams and Jason Ware to come with him.' He grinned. 'I don't know as he can talk Joel into it. Joel ain't ready to settle down. They're in the army now. But if I give them a good report — you'll have a dozen like me here next fall or next spring.'

They made their trade on that basis. Philip would give title to the land in return for what script 'Bijah had, and for 'Bijah's good word to the others who might be persuaded to join him here.

He would lodge that night with David. Mima and Philip paddled homeward up the pond, and Philip said:

'Well, there's another neighbor, Mima. There'll be a fine clack of axes along this side the pond this summer. I didn't get my price, but he didn't get real good land either. Dave and Bowen have all the best low land, both sides of him. All he gets is a strip along the shore. The rest is rough and rocky.' He added with a dry amusement in his tones: 'I sh'd judge you'll have a chance to set up housekeeping with him if you're a mind to. He ain't slow to speak up about his druthers. Take to him, did ye?'

Sitting in the bow, her back to him, she said: 'I liked him all right; but I'd like anybody that came here to live.'

'Better go easy,' he advised. 'I doubt if he'll stick it. Anybody that'd be satisfied with the land he took never will make a farmer.'

'He kept talking about Joel Adams,' she said, half to herself, wondering why that name stayed in her mind. Its very syllables were somehow satisfying. She asked: 'Did you get straightened out about Doctor Taylor?'

'Fales is going to tend to it,' he said. 'He tells me we can quit fretting. The land's ours. It's our job to make it work for us, that's all.'

They paddled on in silence, and her thoughts returned again to that Joel Adams. 'Bijah Hawes had said the other man would come in a hurry if he knew she were here; he had said that Joel was not ready to settle down. Beyond that she knew nothing of this man who was only a name to her; but she tried to shape him in her thoughts, to imagine what he would be like when he came. The sun was low so that here on this west side of the pond they were in shadow; but the seven tall trees on the island ahead were still bright at the top; and across the pond the eastern shore lay all sunned and beautiful in the new green of early summer. Mima saw the old gander of the pair of wild geese that nested on the island, his head high and watchful, moving off as they came near, and her father said:

'They were there last summer, raised their goslings. We never bothered to try a shot at them. Powder costs too much to waste it on birds.' And he added quietly: 'We might need all the powder we've got. They say down-river that the King might turn loose the Indians on us.'

The sun dropped swiftly, and color began to overshoot the sky. 'They won't come here,' she predicted. 'Sam Boggs went up through to Sunnyback Pond four days ago to get out some trunnels He wouldn't go if there was Indians to be scared of.'

Her father chuckled. 'Boggs never took stock in Indians.' He added: 'But I guess if they was headed this way they'd hit Sam first, if he's up-river. He'd come a-h'isting home, give us a warning, maybe.' He said: 'I bought a yoke of oxen from Will Boggs, the old man's son. I figure to drive 'em up next week. Jess and Eben can go get 'em, and our heifer that I bought from Ben Burton.'

They could see the house ahead, through occasional breaks

in the fringe of trees and bushes along the shore, and Mima saw Jacob running to meet them. She asked curiously: 'What's Jake in such a hurry for?'

'Dunno,' her father said; but a moment later Jacob came near enough to call to them in a panting whisper:

'Pa! Pa, there's Injuns come!'

Mima saw Jake's Adam's apple jumping with excitement. Her father asked sharply: 'Have they done any hurt?'

'No, they just come a while ago. They're making a birch-bark hovel up nigh the river. Jess and Eben are watching them, with their guns and all. Ma and Sue and Phil are inside the house. They ain't come nigh us at all.'

Philip drove the float quietly on toward the landing. The skies were bright with sunset hues. Jacob said, keeping pace with them: 'There's an old man and two young ones, and a squaw and two babies, Pa. The men are just setting. The squaw's building the camp and got a fire going and cooking and all. Say, she's a hustler! Mima, why don't you ever hustle some, so Pa and Jess and Eben and me can set around?' He rattled on: 'Oh, and there's a man named Dunbar, says he lives at Ducktrap, come with a lot of wooden dishes, bowls and all, to sell. He's up t'the house.'

They were near the landing now; and a long hail came from the forest to the west, toward Round Pond. Jacob at that sound gasped: 'Gor Rye! What's that?'

His father spat with relief. 'Sam Boggs, I sh'd judge,' he said. 'Sounds like him.' And he added: 'Well, Indians or no Indians, we're home.'

He nosed the float ashore, and Jess and Eben, their guns in their arms, came toward the landing from the knoll beyond the house. Philip asked: 'What they doing, Jess?'

'Making camp, just this side the river,' Jess said. 'They act all right, Pa. Dave said the ones here last summer behaved theirselves. Maybe these here are the same ones.'

Philip nodded, going on up to the house, a little uneasy at

these new neighbors. As they approached the door, a lean, cadaverous old man stepped out to meet them. He was tall and gaunt to the point of emaciation, and his wide mouth curved in a placating grin, his lips working nervously. He said in a thin voice:

'Guess you're Robbins. I'm Dunbar of Ducktrap. I come to see if you wanted any wooden dishes, bowls or trenchers or such. I make 'em myself, bass wood, or red cedar for buckets and piggins, or some I make out of birch and pine. Depends on what you'd druther.'

'Ma's the one to talk to,' Philip told him.

'A fine woman,' Dunbar agreed. 'A mighty fine woman. She bid me stay to sup and sleep. I told her I'd do; but I might take a bite, at that.'

Then the clap of hooves made them turn as Sam Boggs rode out of the woods into the clearing. He bestrode one horse and led another, its panniers heavily loaded with treenails already in the round; and at the door he swung down to greet them. Young Jacob cried at once:

'Mister Boggs, there's Indians here!'

Sam saw the boy's excitement, saw them all a little uneasy. 'Sho,' he said. 'That's just old Jimbuck, and his two sons, and one of their squaws, and her kids. They range down here 'most every summer. It's always been a good place for moose.' He added with a grin: 'They'd have be'n here before now; but they came to my camp up't Sunnyback Pond the day my mare died foaling; so they set right down and et the mare. 'Lowed she beat any moose meat he ever hooked a tooth into, old Jimbuck did. They et pretty steady for three days, so's t' finish her before she spoiled. Then by that time the colt was done for, so I give it to them. They cut it up and fetched it along down here. Time they've got that et, they'll have killed a moose, or a b'ar.'

Philip said hospitably: 'Come in and set, Sam. Jess and Eben killed a cow moose over in the meadows at sunsetting last night, and we'll need help to eat it before it turns. Stay the night, the both of you.' He included Dunbar in the invitation. 'Jake, you take care of the horses.'

'Guess your old woman don't want two more to feed,' Sam suggested; but Mrs. Robbins called from her cooking by the fire indoors:

'Come on in! The more the merrier. I'd feed an army if they'd stay here, and them Indians around. We'll all wake up scalped some morning, sure's you're born.'

Sam laughed, stepping indoors. 'Sho, don't you fret. Jimbuck won't let them two young bucks start any war. He keeps them busy hunting for him.' He said admiringly: 'It takes two of 'em, just to keep him fed. I've seen that old boy set down with a fawn about a month old, and eat every mite of it. Yes, and crack the bones and suck the marrow too; and all he did, he belched and licked his fingers and looked around for more.'

Mrs. Robbins had served them promptly. He gnawed the last gobbet off the chop-bone in his hand and reached for another, and she set a fresh spider full to sizzle over the fire. Dunbar of Ducktrap said:

'That's so, old Jimbuck can eat, sure.'

Mima smiled; for Dunbar had already proved himself no mean trencherman. She said: 'You'll have another chop, I guess.'

'Oh, I guess I'll do,' he told her; but he took the chop, loosened his girdle, and fell to. The talk ran on. Sam Boggs could talk and eat at the same time, and Philip prompted him, and Jess listened to his every word; for Sam was a famous hunter, and the boy had a bent that way. Mima, in a rising curiosity to see just how much he would eat, offered Dunbar another handsome collop of moose meat; and he sighed and said he guessed he would do, but he took it. This Dunbar was a frail man to look at; but there was nothing frail about his capacity for eating. He said at each fresh proffer: 'I guess I'll do'; but that, she found, was only a qualified refusal. She saw Sam Boggs watching her with a lively eye; so she persisted in offering Dunbar more and more meat. The others were finished, even Sam; but Dunbar ate on and on. His only sign of distress was to loosen his sash now and then.

But at last the limit came. 'I guess I'll do,' he said, more forcibly than before. 'Enough's enough and too much is plenty!' And as though at the sound of a sudden alarm, he rose and bolted out-of-doors.

Sam Boggs slapped his knee. ''Y Godfrey's lights, young woman, you filled him up for once!' he cried. 'I never seen it done before.' He chuckled. 'Must be he et hearty at noon,' he declared. 'Or you'd never have done it. Old Jimbuck is a hand to eat; but they say Dunbar can eat a moose, and then eat its calf for pie, if he's real hungry.'

The little cabin was crowded that night. Mima and Sue, who usually slept together in the trundle bed, went into the garret with Jess and Eben and Jacob, and Philip slept with his mother below. Mima, half awake, heard her father and Sam Boggs and Dunbar in long talk by the dying fire, before they rolled up in blankets on the floor.

4

SAM BOGGS took so casually the arrival of Jimbuck and his family that Mima forgot any anxiety their coming had provoked; and her dreams that night were untroubled. She woke, as she often did, at first birdsong, just before day, and lay listening to the chorus outside the cabin — and to the antiphonal snores of Sam Boggs and Dunbar on the floor below; and she marked with amusement that Dunbar, whose voice was a squeaky tenor, snored in a fine bass, even and rhythmic, while Sam Boggs was more given to snorts and gurgles and dry smackings of the lips, with no orderly pattern in his snores at all. She lay a while content with her thoughts, trying to recognize the songs of the birds outside the cabin. The bobolink she knew; two regular notes and then a rapturous cascade of liquid beauty. There was a sparrow whose song-pattern was much the same; two notes whistled slowly and followed by a quicker measure. She heard the crackle of one of the blackbirds with red-and-orange shoulder bars like epaulets, which nested in the nearest reedy cove along the shore, and there were many chirpings and whistlings she did not know.

Light came presently, showing itself through cracks in the roof or between the logs, and she slipped into her dress. When she crept down the ladder, the sleepers were not disturbed; but the door creaked as she opened it, and her father sat up to look at her as she went out. It was still short of sunrise; and Mima, turning down toward the pond, felt the cool dew on her bare feet. When she reached the water she stepped into it; and it was warm and soft, and she thought it would be delicious to wade into it till she was all covered to her neck, and she remembered her intent to learn to swim. The night had been warm, and a thick mist lay above the water, rising as high as the house so that when she came down toward the pond it curled and eddied about her. She knew when the sun rose by the way this white mist turned to gold as it began to thin and disappear. She washed her hands and face, lifting the water and letting it trickle back into the pond with silvery, tinkling sounds. She dried her face on her petticoat and loosed her hair to braid it.

But as she let the long locks go, she turned and saw a young Indian standing by the shore a rod away, between her and the cabin, looking at her with unwinking eyes. He was, it seemed to her, very tall; and he was slender, almost thin. His nose was bold and straight, his cheekbones high, his black eyes even while they watched her were forever darting this way and that without any motion of his head. He wore a small blanket thrown over his left shoulder and held at the waist by a girdle of moose hide loosely knotted, a clout of woven horsehair, and moccasins. His right side and shoulder, and his legs below the blanket, were red as fine-tanned leather may be red, a color curiously sombre and disturbing. He carried in his right hand a gun, the barrel and the stock bound together with a neat wrapping of sinew, as though they had threatened to part company and had been thus repaired.

Mima was startled at the sight of him. She had forgotten their new neighbors; and standing so completely motionless there beside a tall birch near the water, he was sufficiently alarming.

He moved no more than the tree, except for the continual watchful turning of his eyes; and after a moment her courage returned. If he meant harm, fear would not protect her. Her hair was about her shoulders. She left it so and moved up the path. She would have to pass within three paces of him, and she tried to think of something to say to him; but it seemed absurd to say that this was a fine morning, and she could think of nothing else. A robin discovered them there and clucked in alarm or in disapproval, like an old woman saying 'Tut-tut-tut' at the sight of young lovers who think themselves alone. Mima as she drew near where the Indian stood began to smell him. He or his blanket smelled of smoke, and of hot fat cooking, and of spoiled meat, and of sweat, and of something else she could not recognize, yet which filled her with a sick abhorrence. She passed where he stood, and he made no move. She went on up the path to the house, not looking back, wanting to run, holding her pace steady, imagining at every moment that she felt his hand suddenly entwined in her long hair to pull her backward, that she felt the knife circle her scalp, grating on the bone. She was drenched with sweat before she came safe to the house a hundred feet away, to find the others stirring there. When from the door she looked toward where he had stood, he had disappeared; and she tried to smile at her own alarm. But she did not speak to anyone of this encounter at dawn beside the pond.

That day the Indians came seemed to Mima a turning-point. They had climbed laboriously out of winter into spring, and the days had gone slowly; but now suddenly they began to speed. So much was happening. They were all hard at work, and down the pond 'Bijah Hawes and Ezra Bowen had built a hut for a temporary camp together and were clearing their land. Mima looked for the possible arrival of Matt Hawes, 'Bijah's brother, and of that Joel Adams of whom 'Bijah had spoken; but they did not come, and in July 'Bijah had word that they were gone to fight Burgoyne.

'Had a letter from Matt,' he told Philip. 'He claims Burgoyne's got to be stopped, or he'll meet Howe's army, and once
they hold the Hudson they'll have the country cut in two.'

He and Philip discussed the strategic situation as wisely as
two generals; but Mima felt only a personal disappointment
because the men 'Bijah expected did not come. Settlers were
needed here. Her father had hoped for new arrivals before
now. But June passed and the Indians were their only near
neighbors; and Mima could see that her father watched them
always with an uneasy eye. On the surface they were friendly
enough. Old Jimbuck and her father might have long talks
together, hindered by the limitations in Jimbuck's knowledge
of Philip's tongue; and Jess might go off on a hunt with the
younger buck, whose squaw worked tirelessly to take care of
them all. But the other, who had watched Mima by the pond
that morning, never showed even a surface friendliness. Several
times Mima discovered him watching her as she went about
her work at the house or just outside it. Sometimes he disappeared for days at a time; and the fact that he was in the
neighborhood prevented Mima from going for long walks alone
up toward Round Pond. He never spoke to her, never molested
her; but he might. Now and then he came boldly up to the
cabin and — using Philip Robbins' stone — ground his tomahawk to a razor edge; and when the children came near him
thus engaged, he scowled so ferociously that they might be
alarmed. Mima began to suspect that he played a part; that
he enjoyed the impression he created.

She liked the young squaw, and the Indian woman proved
to be astonishingly companionable. Though they never broke
down in any great degree the barrier of tongues between them,
the squaw taught Mima the art of bending and shaping bows
for snowshoes, and of weaving the webs, and how to dress skins
for use, and how to sew them into garments and moccasins.
Jess and Jacob wished to share these lessons; but the squaw
made it clear that this was not work for men.

June passed, and the ferocious black flies began to disappear; but their place was taken by a lesser insect, so small and transparent as scarcely to be visible, whose bite was like a hot needle's sting. The mosquitoes were always with them, worst of all at night when the black flies and other pests seemed to withdraw to muster their resources for a new assault.

In July, through Doctor Fales, Taylor and Philip Robbins settled their differences. The original agreement had been for the purchase of seventy-five hundred acres at about fifty cents an acre; but currency had so far depreciated that Taylor now demanded a dollar an acre. Robbins had not funds — nor could he find them — to finance the purchase of the original tract at that price; but he had already discovered that less land would satisfy him.

So a price was fixed, the deed drawn. Twelve hundred pounds lawful money was the price; and the deed described the tract of some four thousand acres as: 'Beginning at a hemlock-tree marked, by Seven-Tree Pond, so called, which is part of St. George's River; thence running west, by the line of the town of Warren 596 rods to a hemlock-tree, marked, at Waldoborough line; then north 7° west, two miles and a half by said line to a birch-tree, marked, at the north-east corner of said Waldoborough; thence east, two miles and ninety-six rods to St. George's River, near the mouth of Bowker Brook, so called; thence southerly, by said St. George's River as it runneth, and by Round Pond and Seven-Tree Pond as they lie, to the bound first mentioned.'

In the preamble to this deed, the settlement on Seven-Tree Pond acquired a name. Doctor Taylor wanted it called Taylortown; but Philip refused to agree to that. Doctor Fales suggested the compromise. The Andersons, the first to fell any timber north of the pond, had come from the Sterling neighborhood in Warren; so at Fales' suggestion the new settlement was referred to in the deed as Sterlingtown.

* * * * *

During the summer of 1777, the war affected them only in-
directly. The King's ships made hazardous any traffic from
the westward except in small craft that could dodge in and out
among the islands; and these coasters found themselves harassed
by their old neighbors who now, whether for loot or from
principle, avowed themselves loyal to the King. The effect was
to push the price of provisions extravagantly high. Tales came
up the river of grain at two and three dollars the bushel, of
families that went thirty and forty days without bread or even
potatoes. John Lermond's rye — over in the Burnt Lands at
the head of Oyster River — ripened early; and he flailed it out
on a flat ledge of rock and sold it by small quantities, no more
than half a bushel to a family, to those who might otherwise
have starved. Men were forced to live on flesh and fish; and in
Warren and Thomaston, where farms were close together, it
was not easy to kill game near at hand.

But in Sterlingtown, except for a lack of some things which
could only be had from Boston, there were no privations. The
rye sowed the year before had yielded well; and the rye and
corn planted this summer promised a plentiful harvest. Meat
could be killed — if you were lucky — at your very door. Not
only moose and bear were plentiful, but ducks too; and great
flocks of pigeons came to feed on the ripening grain. Dave had
a net; and Mima and Bet Comings, who now grew heavy with
her child, made another like it. With small spindles whittled
out of spruce, they tied the knots so fast that the net seemed to
flow across their knees. To attract the birds, Dave used a stool
pigeon; a captive tied to a low stake so that when a flock passed,
his efforts to rise and join them would attract their attention.
When great numbers of the flock alighted around the hoverer,
the net was sprung; and the watchers leaped to pinch the birds'
skulls till all those caught were dead. There was one famous day
this summer when Dave sprung his net three times, dawn, and
afternoon, and dark, and each time counted his catch by dozens,
three-score dozens for the day. The Indians used for a hoverer

a pigeon whose eyelids had been sewed together, so that when he was released he flew straight up till he reached the end of his tether, and his flutterings there might attract a flock a mile or more away. There was this summer no known nesting near, and Dave regretted that. The squabs, he said, were fat as butter and much to be preferred to the old birds. He knew how to net pigeons by wholesale; but he knew little of their habits except that acorns and beechnuts were their principal feed. Old Sam Boggs told Mima that they might feed during the day a hundred miles from their roost. 'When they come piling in to roost,' he assured her, 'they light so many in a tree it'll break off sometimes and kill the lot of 'em.' They netted hundreds of birds that summer. The pigeons they could not eat at once were cooked in their own fat and packed in vessels and the fat poured over them to cover them so that they would keep sweet and rich for weeks. Mima and her mother tried smoking them against a time of need, but this was not successful.

'Bijah Hawes had a particular enthusiasm for the sport of trapping pigeons. He early cleared a patch of land and planted corn as soon as he had done his burning. The green wood was not consumed by the fire, and charred carcasses of trees lay everywhere; but he did his planting among them, poking a hole in the ground with a sharpened stick, dropping in two or three kernels, brushing earth into the hole with his foot. He and Bowen worked together and they worked well; and after their corn was in, each helped the other build a cabin. But also 'Bijah came up to David's to help him trap the pigeons, and when the net was sprung he would shout his triumph so loudly that he might be heard at Philip's a mile away; and he would go racing from where he and David lay concealed to pinch the heads of the trapped birds, his great hands flying among the fluttering creatures whose heads came up through the meshes of the net, till he might be blood-smeared to the elbow.

'It's a sight to see him,' Dave told Mima. 'I kind of hate to kill the things, get my fun out of trapping them; but seems like he likes it. He'll get himself all gormed up with blood and feathers till it's a sight to sicken ye.'

Mima said: 'Well, they have to be killed, and I guess the sooner the quicker.'

'He wants to take one and sew up its eyelids the way the Indians do,' David said. 'But I wouldn't let him. No sense to it. We get a plenty the way we do it now.'

Mima defended 'Bijah — even thus mildly — more from a sense of fairness than from any partisanship. She had helped Dave trap the birds, had done her share in killing them and dressing them, and helping her mother put them down for later use. It had to be done. If 'Bijah could make a sport of it, so much the better. She saw him frequently that summer. He was a tireless young man; and after a day of hard work he was still ready to come up the shore for a visit with them, or to jog-trot down through the woods to Warren, six or seven miles away, returning at dawn next day. Mima liked him well enough, laughing at his audacious flatteries, amused by his bold tongue; and Philip said he was a worker, for all his fooling around. Mrs. Robbins had no use for him at all, and said so to his face. 'You'd ought to have something better to do than go loping through the woods all night like a bull moose in rutting time,' she told him stoutly. 'Chasing every girl in twenty miles. You can't fool me, you long, lean limb of Satan. There's the devil in you and well I know it.'

But 'Bijah laughed at her. 'Now ma'am, if you're the hand-somest woman in this neck of Hell you've got to expect the men to hang around,' he told her; and she snorted in scornful fury, and Philip laughed at her heat.

'I know how you feel, young fellow,' he told 'Bijah. 'I used to come twelve miles every Saturday night to bundle with Ma over Sunday. Kep' it up two years before she'd have me — and fit half the young men in town besides.'

'If I'd been there, I'd have combed your beard for you,' 'Bijah declared. 'I may yet, if she'll have me.'

Between them they plagued Mrs. Robbins without mercy, and Mima thought her mother began to enjoy this foolery, but she would never admit it. 'All he comes for is a free meal,' she said. 'So he won't have to cook his own and clean up after. You take notice he always gets here in time for supper, eating us out of house and home.'

'Let him come,' Philip insisted comfortably. 'There's plenty. We can turn him out when the good eating's over.'

* * * * *

Toward the end of July, Johnny Butler and Lucy moved into the Mill Farm across the pond. Under the terms which bound him to work for Taylor till he was twenty-one, Johnny was entitled to a tract of land; and he bought the buildings and all the furniture. Doctor Taylor had lost interest in the settlement, was ready to sell all his holdings here, no longer thought of coming to the Mill Farm to live; and Johnny profited by that fact, acquired a house and a farm already cleared, with crops ripening on the ground.

The day Johnny and Lucy came up the river was an occasion. Lucy's father, Oliver, Philip's half-brother, helped Johnny transport his few possessions; and Mrs. Robbins and Mily came to see Lucy settled. Philip Robbins and most of his clan crossed the pond to make the newcomers welcome. Oliver Robbins even on this occasion seemed to Mima a sober, silent man with an icy eye. His wife, that widow woman whom he had married, was as austere as he. But Mily, whom Mima remembered from the wharf below the fort at the time of their first arrival, was sunny enough to compensate for their gravity. Her hair was bright, her eyes that rare blue which is usually left behind with babyhood; and since last fall she was changed, ripening even at thirteen into an early maturity. She embarrassed Jake at once by pouring out on him that lavish

affection which a girl just coming to first womanhood is so apt
to offer some boy or man. She stood near him when he stood
or sat, she put her arm through his, and when they all came out
of the small house to sit a while on the river bank below the mill
and Jake sprawled on the ground, she took his head on her knee
and amused herself by loosing his hair and clubbing it again,
while Jake wriggled in a sort of wretched bliss, at once embarrassed and delighted by her adoration; till her stepmother,
coming belatedly out of the house, rated her and bade her
leave Jake be, and told her she should be ashamed of herself for
such carryings on. Mily obeyed, but with a defiant toss of her
head; and Mima saw her whisper something to Jake that made
him blush all the more. She was not near enough to be sure,
but her ears were keen; she thought Mily had promised Jake
always to love him best of everyone.

Lucy was like her younger sister in this capacity for affection.
She watched Johnny adoringly, was forever catching at his
hand or his arm when he passed near her, plumped herself on
his knee when he sat down. Mima liked her, liked to see her
fondness. She liked Johnny too. He was a lean young man, his
hair already sprinkled with gray, with that trick of stammering
a little of which David had spoken; and he was deferential to
Oliver and to Oliver's wife, seeming a little subdued till they
took Mily and started home. Mily insisted on kissing Jake
good-bye; and Jake at first held back till Jess said: 'Go on, Jake,
give her a good one.' Jake did, with a sudden violence in his
embrace, Mily's arms tight around his neck, till Oliver caught
Mily's arm and drew her sternly away.

After they were gone, there was a change in both Johnny
and Lucy, as though a restraining bond had been loosed; and
when Mrs. Robbins and Mima and Jess started back across the
pond in the last float, Johnny and Lucy stood arm in arm to
watch them go. Before they turned away toward the house,
Lucy kissed Johnny again. Mrs. Robbins happened to look
back, and saw them.

'Well!' she said sharply. 'She can't keep her hands off him, can she?'

Mima laughed. 'Why should she?' And she added more seriously: 'I guess she and Mily are just naturally kissers. And Uncle Oliver and his wife are so strict, probably it makes the girls worse that way. Mrs. Robbins acted as if there was something wrong about Mily's fixing Jake's hair. She's just a baby. They hadn't ought to take any notice of it. She'll outgrow it.'

'Lucy ain't outgrown it,' Mrs. Robbins reminded her. 'And if there's anything sickens me, it's to see folks carry on in the face and eyes of anyone that's around to see! Their ma was just the same. She was a Shepard; Elioenai, her name was. Ellie we called her. They married three-four years before Pa and me did, and it was a scandal to see them. They had their first in no time at all, and they had ten altogether, every two-three years, regular as if she was a cow, till she wore out and died. Now it's plain to be seen Oliver's starting a new batch with that widow woman he married. Lucy won't be much behind them, if you ask me.'

'Johnny's pretty happy about it,' Mima suggested. 'I guess he's suited.'

Mrs. Robbins made a scornful sound. 'He'll find out being married ain't all kissing and clipping,' she predicted. 'Ellie Robbins had a temper, and so has Lucy if I'm any judge. She'll take a broom handle to him, first time she feels like it. I know the blood. Sweet enough to sicken ye as long as they get their own way, and squalling like a cat when they don't.' She added honestly: 'Not but what Ellie settled down and made Oliver a good wife when she made up her mind to it. Maybe Lucy'll do the same.'

Jess said with a chuckle: 'Well, I like Lucy — and Mily too. She's grown up for her age. I'm glad they've come to live here, anyway. Johnny was up here some, last summer. He likes to hunt. Him and me get along.'

Mima thought she and Lucy would get along, and she expected to see much of the other girl; but the pond was an obstacle. She did not like to take the cranky dugouts across alone, and it was an impossible walk around the shore, boggy meadow to be crossed, and a tangled cedar swamp along its border. So their encounters were not as frequent as she had hoped, though she took every opportunity that offered to go across the pond.

One day late in August, Philip started for Warren. He had his barn to raise, and he went to see what men could be found to help him. Ben Burton had hewed the timbers the year before; but there had not yet been time to do the job. Philip went afoot, starting early. After he was gone, Jess heard a hail from across the pond and went down to the landing; and he made out Johnny Butler, over by the mouth of Mill River. Johnny bawled: 'Fi-i-ire!' So Jess, as an easier procedure than packing coals and taking them across, fetched flintlock and powder horn and paddled over.

Mima went with him to have a visit with Lucy; and after Johnny's fire was relighted, they all walked together down to where Jess had left the float. Johnny exclaimed: 'Say, w-what's that?' He pointed to a dark object on the water, swimming toward the Robbins landing.

'Ain't that Lion?' Jess suggested. Then his voice quickened. 'No 'tain't, Johnny. It's a b'ar! Fetch a club or something and jump in.'

Johnny's axe was at the landing, so he took that, and the two young men made the float leap. Jess bawled across the pond to whoever might hear him at the cabin: 'B'ar! B'ar! B'ar!' Eben came running down to the landing; and old Jimbuck emerged from his lodge among the trees. The dugout overtook the bear off the north end of the island, and Jess shouted:

'Bust him, Johnny!'

Johnny reached for the axe; but as he did so, the bear swerved savagely toward them, and Johnny caught up his paddle again.

'N-Not me, Jess!' he cried. 'I'll w-wait till he lands. I don't
want to go swimming with no b-b'ar!'

'Hit him in the head,' Jess urged.

'He can't get away,' Johnny argued. 'I'll run him down and
chop his head off soon's he lands. I c-can run down any b'ar!'

They turned the bear so that it landed on the island. The
beast picked a tree, squatted for a moment at its base, then
embraced it and began with teeth and claws to climb. It took
half a dozen shots to bring it down. Eben fetched another
musket, and balls for Jess's weapon; and they took turns firing
at the creature high above them. When the animal fell at last
it was slowly, catching weakly at one branch and another till
its grip failed and it came crashing through the lower branches
to thump heavily upon the ground, and move no more.

Once the bear was down, they started to butcher it on the
spot. Mima went ashore with Eben. It was some time before
Jess and Johnny loaded the dressed carcass, still smoking hot,
and the bloody pelt into the dugout and started ashore. As
they approached, Mima heard the sound of a runner racing
toward them up the border of the cleared land; and she made
a sharp sound for silence; said in a hushed voice:

'Someone's coming, running.'

The others could hear nothing; but old Jimbuck looked at
her in sharp attention. They listened, and Jess said: 'I don't
hear . . .'

But Jimbuck made a grunting sound of assent, and his eyes
on Mima had a new respect. She said softly: 'Jimbuck hears
them now.' Then Jess too caught the distant sound.

The runners, when presently they arrived, proved to be
Philip Robbins and Rich and David. They came at a loping
bound, their primed muskets ready; they burst down the bank,
turning tautly toward Jimbuck and his sons; and Philip was
pale with concern. But then he saw the carcass in the float and
understood; and still panting, with heaving lungs, he began to
grin.

'Pfoo!' he gasped. 'I'm blowed! I was halfway to Warren, heard them shots, thought sure the Indians had started trouble. I came at a dead run all the way. Yelled to Dave and Rich as I came by.'

He chuckled at the joke at his own expense, and the young people laughed with him; but Mima saw her mother at his side, smiling, yet comforting him with understanding too. The girl guessed some of the fierce anxieties which tormented her father day by day.

5

THE barn was raised in mid-September. Philip and his sons at odd times during the summer had cleared and levelled the spot behind the house where it would stand and had set stones to support the sills, and made all ready. Mima, watching their preparations, remembered what Phin Butler had said about the back-breaking work involved in raising Taylor's barn, and she spoke of this to her father. He said assentingly:

'It's hard for a few; but many hands make easy work. I'll get men to help.'

He could count under his own roof himself and Jess. Jess was only eighteen; but he was compact and strong. Eben, two years younger, was nimble enough, and sturdy and willing, but lacking a man's fibre for heavy lifting. David and Rich would help, and young 'Bijah Hawes and Ez Bowen, and Johnny Butler. Sam Boggs promised to bring his sons and three or four others. 'There's enough ready to come anywhere they'll get free rum,' he assured Philip. Nat Fales of Thomaston had helped Ben Burton hew the timbers; so Philip arranged with him to arrive ahead of time, and to supervise the actual raising. Fales laid and levelled and pinned the floor timbers and boarded them over, before the set day. Sam Boggs and the others from Warren arrived the night before, to feast like old Romans on broiled bear meat, spare ribs from the hog Philip Robbins had butchered for the occasion, and salmon which Eben and Jimbuck's married son had speared under a birch-bark flare the night before. They slept rolled in blankets and attacked the task at dawn.

Fales, a perplexed man in his fifties, whose shabby wig was forever slipping to one side or the other of his shiny bald head, had decided the sides of the barn might prove too heavy a lift for the men available; so he chose instead to raise first an end, and then the bays one by one. He framed the rear end first, laying the heavy posts in position on the barn floor, pinning them together with cross timbers and braces. When this was ready, the first lift was from the floor to shoulder high. The end was propped there, and then with pike poles they raised it the rest of the way. Once the framed end passed an angle of sixty degrees from the horizontal, the weight yielded to control. It rose easily to the perpendicular where the men held it poised while Fales saw it well braced with stay-laths. Then there was a respite while the rum went around before the work of framing the first bay began, and there were other intermissions afterward.

The work began at first light. At dusk, since there were so few hands, the rafters and purlines and the ridgepole remained still to be put in place, but they could be managed by Philip and his sons alone. When it was too dark to do more, a great fire lighted the barn frame gaunt against the stars, and Mima and her mother had mountains of victuals ready on a table made of boards laid on logs, and there was rum, and they turned to eat and drink and their voices rose as much from the relief that toil was ended as from the rum.

Mima helped to serve them, watching the men as she moved

to and fro, thinking how each one was, under the expanding influence of the rum they drank, himself yet different too. Her father was intoxicated as much by the fact that the barn frame was up as by his potations. David played the clown as he was likely to do, telling some tale about one of the German settlers over at Broad Bay.

'He heard a cow bawling,' Dave explained, 'and he run to see what was the matter and there was a b'ar killing it. He didn't have nothing only his axe. Well, he looked at the b'ar and the b'ar looked at him.' David imitated first the man and then the bear; and Mima thought he was exactly like a bear when he stood with his legs spread and his hands hanging like paws. 'So he hit his axe on a log to scare the b'ar away,' Dave explained, and clapped his hand down on his thigh. 'But the b'ar came for him. So he swung up into a little tree there was there, too small for the b'ar to get his arms around it, so he couldn't climb it. But the b'ar kep' trying. He'd go 'round and 'round the tree, looking for a way up!' Dave went around and around a stump, moving so like a bear that the men roared with laughter. 'He'd snuff and he'd snort and he'd growl,' said Dave; and he himself snuffed and snorted and growled, his teeth showing in a ferocious grin. 'And this man up the tree pulled his feet as high as he could; and he kep' howling for the bear to go away!' David clambered on the stump and stood above them, picking up one foot and then another, looking down with terror, screaming in a high falsetto: ' "Go 'way, Mister B'ar! Go 'way!" ' Howls of appreciative mirth drowned him out, till he had a chance to finish; and he said then: 'He was so scared he went dry for a week after, like a cow before she comes in. That bear scared the dog water out of him!'

Old Sam Boggs laughed at that tale till he cried. Mima noticed that of his two sons — they were not much younger than her father — William did not laugh; but Young Sam rolled on the ground and held his sides, and then he told a story in his turn, about another barn-raising where someone tried to stand on his head on the ridgepole and fell and broke his leg, and Old Sam said they were lucky to be through this one with no trouble.

'Things can go mighty wrong,' he declared; and he told about a house-raising he had seen as a young man, when they lacked men enough to do it right. 'They had to lean the end out to get the side timbers in,' he said, 'and one end got away from them, came down on a man named Perry that was helping hold it. It smashed his head on a rock, smashed it so hard they had to dig pieces of his skull out of the post with a gimlet!' He added with a great guffaw: 'No need of doing that, either. He never had no use for the pieces after they dug 'em out.'

Mrs. Robbins said irascibly: 'Sam Boggs, if you can't think of something a mite more cheerful to talk about, you'd better eat more and talk less! You turn my stummick.' She saw young Phil dip a piece of bread into the wooden bowl full of honey, and boxed his ears and told him it was full time he was abed; and Ez Bowen grinned and said:

'I can tell you how to learn him, Mis' Robbins. Had an old mare once that was always getting into the cornfield. Pa tried everything he knowed, and finally old Furman, lived next farm to us, 'lowed he could cure her. He fetched up three-four rifted shingles and tied them to her tail and give her a slap. She started off on a trot and they banged her on the rump and she began to run and the harder she run, the more they spanked her. She run all of a mile before she got rid of 'em, and she wouldn't ever eat corn — no, nor fodder either — from that day then and on.'

They were all served and replete; and Mima withdrew to a little distance, happy to watch the scene; the leaping flames, the laughing, talking, eating men, the naked frame of the barn built to last a century, gleaming in the firelight. Since September came, the summer pest of flies was done, even mosquitoes appearing only on the warmest nights; and there was after dusk had fallen a crisp chill in the air. The stars seemed bright and near. From the lake a loon called; and a heron flying down from Round Pond croaked high above her, and she looked up to try to see the great bird, but it was lost in the darkness of the sky. She thought that all across the lake and in the forest roundabout wild things must be watching this fire with wonder and with fear, yet curiously too; and she remembered with a sudden amusement how Jimbuck and his sons had watched all day, with a sort of startled impassivity, this extraordinary spectacle of men working till they were near dropping with exhaustion — and driving on to work some more. The unmarried son, the one whom Mima had first seen that morning by the pond, glowered morosely as he watched them; but Mima had long ago decided that his scowl was no more than a defensive gesture. So far as his actions went, he was friendly enough. A week ago he had brought a haunch of moose meat and thrown it into the house and stalked away without waiting for a word of thanks; and to show her appreciation she had taken down to the lodge a loaf of bread fresh-baked and given it to the squaw. From where she stood now she could see Jimbuck and his sons standing by the frame of the barn watching the men at their drinking and she was faintly sorry for them, excluded from this merrymaking.

Someone said beside her: 'Wondered where you'd got to, so I scouted around and here you was.' 'Bijah Hawes had come around through the shadows outside the circle lighted by the fire; and he seemed taller than ever when she looked up at him.

'I like to watch them all having a good time,' she told him. 'It's kind of pretty from here, with the stars on the water shining through the trees.'

''Tis so,' he agreed, and chuckled. 'But I'd rather have a good time myself than watch other folks have one. Too much of a crowd down there for me.' His arm clipped her around the waist. 'Let's you and me walk up to Round Pond and wait for moonrise.'

She put his hand down, or tried to, fumbling with it against her side. 'I'll be helping Mother clean up after them,' she said.

'They'll sit and swap lies all night,' he told her; and he grinned, still holding her, and said: 'I never went to a raising yet where there weren't a chance to take a girl walking in the dark after. A night like this and a girl like you and a raising, all coming together, we'd ought to do something about it. You come along.'

'Don't you, 'Bijah,' she said strongly; but he held her. She could only turn her head away and take his kiss on her hair above the ear, her head bowed. He laughed as he kissed her, and she got one hand free and cuffed him hard on the side of his head. The blow made a sharp, slapping sound; but a burst of laughter around the fire prevented anyone's hearing. 'Bijah said admiringly:

'Say, you'd give a man a mauling if you were a mind to!'

'Then stop your foolishness,' she told him, agreeably enough.

He chuckled and sat down, leaning against a stump beside her. 'There's points in foolishness,' he assured her good-humoredly. 'But it takes two to find 'em. No harm meant, Mima. Set down.'

She did not sit down, but she stood beside him. The flames leaped high, and she could hear Johnny Butler's excited, stammering voice, and a gust of laughter rose. 'Bijah said: 'Last barn-raising I was to, it was some livelier than this. Joel Adams and me went together. There was a threshing floor and a fiddle and gals enough to go 'round. Rain had held us up some; but it let up at dark, and we et and drunk and sung and danced all night and went at the job again in the morning. Joel's a great hand to sing.' She heard a ripple of mirth in his tones. 'Only some of his songs, you ain't likely to hear.'

'You talk a lot about him.'

'Most do that knows him,' he assured her. 'Specially the womenfolks. You go anywhere he's ever been, and the first thing you know, some mopsy's talking about Joel Adams to you.' She watched the fire, listened to the voices, felt the weight of the forest silence all around them. 'Joel and me have seen some times,' he declared. 'I'd hate to tell you.' He said lazily: 'Come on, set down. No one's going to bite you.' She did not move to obey and he said: 'I'd like to see the moon.'

'It comes late,' she reminded him.

'Say we set and wait for it.' He looked up at her, teeth flashing as he grinned. 'You're a sight to see, Mima,' he told her. 'With the firelight shining on you. You look as if your cheeks would be hot to touch. Let me wet my finger and see.'

She pressed her hands to her face. 'They're cool enough,' she said; but there was a still excitement in her. 'Bijah may have felt it in her tones. He rose on his knees, and then to his feet. She took a step away from him toward the fire, poised to run. He could so easily clap his hand across her mouth and carry her helpless away into the forest toward Round Pond. He said some husky word, laughing; he was not six paces off. She saw her father and Nat Fales withdrawn a little from the crowd, not far away; and she moved toward them, looking back at 'Bijah, her heart beat shaking her.

'Here's Father!' she said breathlessly.

'Bijah stopped, and she saw his teeth gleam in that wide grin like a dog's snarl that was always a little disturbing. She heard Fales, speaking to her father. 'Dave wanted me to tell you; but there wasn't no sense in telling you before. You had plenty on your mind.'

She went toward them, came beside her father as Philip said: 'Speak up, man. You don't have to break bad news to me as if I was a woman.'

'Well, there's trouble with Taylor,' Fales explained. 'Thurston, that went to pay him your money, a storm held him up with the last of it. He was a day late. Now Taylor says he'll take specie or nothing. Thurston told him he'd take paper or get nothing; and Taylor says he'll have specie or he'll sue.'

Philip Robbins laughed, and Mima saw his shoulders lift as though freed of some burden. He said: 'Nat, I've lallygagged with Taylor over a year now. He's gone back on his word, squirmed like a fish on a hook. He's got too much politics in him for my taste. But Nat — we've cleared right on to forty acres here — me and mine, right out of the woods. I've got me a house, and a barn now, and between us we've got three yokes of oxen, and four cows, and some hogs, and the sheep down in the pen. I've got this land under me. I put it to work. It's mine from now on.

'I've got the land, and Taylor's got the money — or it's be'n offered to him. That's the end of it. You tell Dave Fales to send word to Taylor that he can sue me to hell and get the devil for his lawyer, and much good may it do him!'

He laughed, his head thrown back. He hugged Mima against his side till her ribs cracked. He said: 'To hell with Taylor. Come back to the fire, Nat. There's more rum!'

Mima went with them. She saw 'Bijah join the crowd as they drew near. He must have circled through the shadows when she left him. He grinned at her, and she stopped between her father and Sam Boggs, and Philip said:

'Sam, I'm a mind to give them Indians one drink apiece. I feel pretty good tonight.'

'Don't you,' Sam warned him. 'If you did, they'd give all three drinks to Jimbuck, enough to get him drunk. He'd make 'em. An Indian don't see no sense in one drink. He don't like the taste of it. His idee is to drink enough to get drunk. They ain't like a white man — can drink enough and then stop.' He hiccoughed loudly. 'Getting drunk is all they know. You can't get an Indian to take one drink. He'll keep it on hand till he's got enough to go with it to fill him up. But they're all right sober,' he added fairly.

Philip chuckled. 'Did you hear about the Indian scare we had here?' he asked. He told the story of the bear Jess and Johnny had killed, and how he heard the guns and came running through the woods. 'I was some haired up,' he declared. 'Felt like a fool when I got here and see what it was.'

'A man that ain't used to them, it gives him the fidgets having them around,' Sam agreed.

'They're real friendly,' Mima said. 'The one that isn't married gave me a haunch of moose meat last week.'

Sam looked at her, suddenly serious. 'How'd he come to do that?'

'Why I was in the house — Mother had gone down to see Bet — and he just walked up to the door and threw it in.'

He grunted. 'You give him anything, did you?'

'I took them down a loaf of bread.'

'Throw it in the lodge?'

'Why no,' she said, puzzled by his tone. 'I gave it to the squaw.'

Sam said in an obvious relief: 'Well, that's something, anyway. I'll talk to Jimbuck, see to't they don't get any wrong idees. Don't you feed the critters, ma'am. That's their way when a young buck has got his eye on a squaw. He'll throw a haunch of venison in her wigwam, and then if she goes and throws an ear of corn into his, why that means they're married.' He looked at her gravely. 'You been carrying on with him, have you?'

Mima said strongly: 'No I've not!'

'No offense, ma'am.' He spoke soberly to Philip. 'I'll talk to Jimbuck,' he promised. 'Let an Indian get an idee into his head and sometimes you have to scalp him to get it out.' He told Mima: 'If you don't want to go off to Canada with him, you be careful how you go throwing ears of corn around.' She smiled; but he said: 'It's no joke. I'm telling you.'

* * * * *

Long after she was abed, Mima heard the talk go on around the fire. She lay awake, thinking of what Sam had said, and his obvious seriousness; thinking of 'Bijah; thinking persistently of Joel Adams whose name was so often on 'Bijah's tongue. Her pulse beat quick and hard, loud in her ear on the pillow.

In the garret above her, Phil was already asleep, and Sue lay
here in her arms. Her mother came in and went to bed; and
afterward one by one the boys followed, her father last of all.
Not till the last murmur of voices outside had ceased did Mima
herself fall asleep.

In the morning she was early awake. It was still full dark;
but presently she began to see faint light here and there
through cracks in the walls and around the door. Those chinks
would need to be well stuffed with moss before another winter.
She lay a while thinking of the night before; of 'Bijah who had
kissed her, and who might have kissed her again. She had been
surprised to find how strong he was. She had always thought
of herself as strong enough, but his arm around her had been
like an iron band, not tight enough to crush her, but too firm
for her easily to push aside till she slapped him and he let her go.

But that was the rum in him. She was not afraid of him; not
so long as her father and her brothers and Rich were here. She
realized with a faint surprise that thinking of Rich was deeply
reassuring. He was so quiet, seldom speaking at all in any
company, that it was easy to forget him; but Mima thought
now that there was stability in him. Bet was lucky to have such
a husband. Rich would take care of her. If 'Bijah ever really
became troublesome, she thought she might go to Rich as
quickly as to anyone.

Or if the young Indian seemed likely to be dangerous, she
thought Rich, better than any of them, could handle him without violence. But that would not be necessary. Sam Boggs was
going to speak to Jimbuck this morning; and thinking of Jimbuck and his sons, Mima was wide awake, anxious to be out-
of-doors.

While she was putting on her dress, her father stirred and
looked at her and slept again; and when Mima opened the
heavy door, her mother roused with a sharp movement, rising
on one elbow. But they did not speak to her, and when she
came out-of-doors, the men — Sam Boggs, and Nat Fales, and

the others from down the river — were no more than rolls of bedding on the ground.

As day came, a faint mist almost always rose from the surface of the pond; and it was all about the house now. She was intensely curious about the Indians, and she slipped cautiously through the pines to the knoll above their encampment. When she came near enough, she saw that they were gone. They must have left at first dawn. The squaw had stripped off of their narrow lodge the birch-bark slabs which roofed and sided it, doubtless taking the slabs with her against their night's encampment. Already the spot where the lodge had stood seemed a part of the forest again. It was no more marked than if a troop of animals had slept there for a while and then moved on. The Indians must have departed up the river, in that birch-bark canoe which was at once so much lighter and so much less stable than the heavy dugouts which Philip and her brothers had made. Mima wondered whether Sam Boggs had talked to Jimbuck last night, whether they were surely gone, or had merely withdrawn to some secret place up the river from which they might at any time come back here.

Returning to where over a pit dug into the side of the knoll she and her mother had cooked yesterday for the hungry men, she stirred up the coals and brought the fire to life; and 'Bijah Hawes woke at the sound of her movements and lifted his hand in silent salute and then went down to the pond and up along the shore toward the river. She heard presently a puffing and a splashing, and thought he must have startled a moose which now fled along the shore; and she ran that way to see it.

She saw instead 'Bijah himself, his body pale in the water, swimming boldly two or three rods offshore; and she watched him for a moment enviously, remembering that she had meant to learn to swim during this summer that now was gone. She did not know how to begin to try to learn; but 'Bijah seemed to swim so easily. She watched him from the shelter of the trees till he turned back toward the shore. Then, unseen, she re-

turned to tend the fire and start breakfast cooking. Sam Boggs
rolled over and sat up, bleary with the rum he had drunk the
night before. He grunted something and stumbled past her
down toward the pond, and 'Bijah Hawes came back, pink and
shining, his hair slicked down, and stopped beside her.

'Hoo!' he exclaimed. 'Now I feel better. Had a swim. Felt
good.'

She asked, busy with her tasks: 'How'd you learn to swim?'

'I've always paddled around, since I was a young one. Joel
Adams and me used to run together. He'll swim like an otter,
under water half the time. I never can open my eyes under
water; but he'll find a white pebble for you ten feet down.'
He warmed his hands and puffed and blew. 'I wrote him about
you,' he said with his audacious smile. 'He says he's coming
to see for himself. He'll be here before snow, if he can. He's
fighting Burgoyne now, but after they gobble Burgoyne, he's
coming.'

'Burgoyne might gobble them!'

'Not him. Not Joel. He's a man!'

Ezra Bowen roused at the sound of their voices and warmed
himself before departing toward the pond; and Sam Boggs returned, unwashed, rubbing his eyes. Philip Robbins came out
of the house, and then Jess, and the sun rose and tinted with
gold the light dawn fog which hung above the lake. The sky
above was blue, pink fog skeins dissipating as they rose.

'I see Jimbuck's gone,' Sam told Philip. 'I talked to him last
night.' He looked toward Mima, his eyes twinkling. 'The
young buck did have idees,' he assured her. 'But Jimbuck had
already set out to talk him out of them. He'll keep him in hand.
You don't have to give it a thought from now on.'

'Bijah asked curiously: 'What's that?'

'Why, Jimbuck's son had his eye on Mima,' Sam explained.
'Guess he figured he needed a squaw in his lodge.'

'Bijah's cheek reddened with slow anger. 'Why, God damn
his liver and lights!' he said. 'The red skunk! Where is he?'

He turned toward the lodge; but Sam said sharply: 'They're gone! Let 'em go! Don't ever go looking for trouble with an Indian, son!'

'I'll climb his frame!'

'He's gone, Sam said. 'Let him go.' And he said wisely: 'When you get ready to argue with an Indian, young Hawes, get ready to kill him. It's the only argument he knows. Anything less than that, he'll get his hatchet in your head before he's through.'

'Bijah grinned and sat down again. 'Leave it so,' he assented. 'Long as he's gone. But he'd better not come back again.' He looked at Mima, his eyes twinkling. 'He might not be the only one has ideas,' he told her with a cheerful audacity.

She said quietly: 'Some ideas, it takes two people.' He chuckled, slapped his knee.

Mrs. Robbins appeared, and breakfast presently was ready. Afterward Sam and the Warren men and 'Bijah and Ez departed. Nat Fales stayed a few days to help raise the rafters, and within the week the barn was sheathed, the roof on, rough bins built to store the corn and rye till it could be milled, stalls set off for the oxen and a tie-up for the cows. During the summer some hay had been cut in the meadows at the head of the pond and stacked there. Jess and Eben and Jacob now began to float it home. An occasional night brought frost, and across the pond the hardwoods put on the brilliant hues of fall.

* * * * *

Mrs. Robbins walked down one day to see Bet and came home in a fuming wrath at Rich. 'He's bound he'll take Bet down-river to have her baby,' she said. 'They aim to go to Thomaston, stay at Oliver's. I told him he was a fool. I can handle a baby, well as any midwife, and I told him so!'

Mima said: 'Rich takes care of Bet the best he knows.'

'You always have to stand up for him!'

'Bet's married to him,' Mima reminded her mother. 'You

might as well make up your mind you'll either have to get along with Rich or get along without Bet.'

'You don't have to remind me,' her mother told her sharply. 'Bet already did, more'n once. So they're going down-river; but I told them I was going along, and I am too.' Her voice was suddenly husky. 'You'll find out some day, Mima, when your daughter's having a baby, maybe you can't do a bit of good, but you want to be there!'

'Did Rich say you could go?'

Mrs. Robbins said stoutly: 'I didn't ask his say-so. I'm a-going, and that's all there is to that.'

So when the time came, she went with them. They took little David, and the bright hues of autumn were coming to their greatest beauty when they departed. Three days later Rich brought Mrs. Robbins happily home and she reported that the baby was a girl, named Esther, and that Bet was fine, even though she was not yet ready to return.

The glory of the foliage passed, the leaves began to fall. There was a sort of frenzy of work upon them all, so much still to be done against the winter that was near. Johnny Butler had tried to operate the mill across the pond, but the stones were small and poor, and the water that fall was low. To take corn to the mills at Oyster River was a tedious business; but Rich planned to take a load when he went to bring Bet and the baby home. When he set out, Jess went with him.

The day they would return, Mima and Mrs. Robbins went after dinner to make the cabin ready for their coming. They carried fire and Jake brought wood. Mima and her mother worked hard most of the afternoon while Jake wondered aloud what they found to do that kept them here so long. They scrubbed and scoured till Mrs. Robbins at last was satisfied; and they walked down to David's house to see Bess and the children there and to watch for the homecomers. Jake went on down the shore to meet the barge; and he came racing back to them at last, bursting with news.

'They're coming!' he cried. 'And there's a man with them come to buy some land, and he helped capture Burgoyne and his whole army two weeks ago and the war's as good as won!' And to their cloud of questions: 'No, he ain't coming to stay. Not now. Not till he's finished winning the war. His name's Joel Adams.'

Mima's heart began to thump against her ribs. She said, careful to hold her voice steady: ''Bijah Hawes told me about him.'

'Yes, he stopped at 'Bijah's,' Jake agreed, his Adam's apple working. 'He's going to live there. Ma, I'm going back and hear him tell about the war. He says they gave Burgoyne a good hiding. I'll come home in the morning, Ma.'

He turned, but Mrs. Robbins said sharply: 'You, Jake! You stay right here. I'll have Dave fetch him up to the house. If he's land-looking, he'll have to come to Pa anyway.'

The boy groaned. 'Gor ram it, Ma!' he exclaimed. 'I wish't I'd just have stayed, 'stead of coming and telling you.'

'You better be glad you didn't,' she assured him. 'I'd have tanned your hide.' She cried: 'There they be, now!'

They all raced for the shore as the barge came slowly in to the landing. Bet, the new baby at her breast, two-year-old David by her knee, sat proudly among the heaped sacks of cornmeal. Jess and Rich put the bow ashore, and Mima lifted little David out, and her mother cried: 'Get the baby, Mima! Give her here to me!' Mima obeyed, and Rich helped Bet, and he stood quietly by while the others all talked at once. Jess called to his brother:

'Come on, Jake! We'll row the barge home.' The meal would all be stowed in the new barn. He told his mother: 'There's a man coming to see Pa in the morning. Jake, did you tell them about Burgoyne?'

''Course I did. Ma won't let me go back down there. I want to hear Mr. Adams tell about the fighting.'

Mrs. Robbins said: 'You go along home, Jake! You'll have time enough to hear him tomorrow.'

He looked at her scornfully. 'I will not. He'll be talking to Pa, or making love to Mima. He says 'Bijah wrote to him about Mima. He says a pretty girl's what he's got to see up here before he buys any land. I guess he won't talk to anyone but her!'

Mima blazed crimson, and Jess chuckled and said: 'He's a talker, Mima.' His eyes twinkled. 'And a looker, too. You watch out you don't play the fool. It's be'n so long since you've had a feller make love to you, it'll make you flighty.'

She cried in mock ferocity: 'Go on, the both of you, or I'll flighty you!' Jake grudgingly took his place in the boat, and she watched them move away. When they were gone, she pressed her palms hard against her cheeks and wondered why they were not burned.

6

JOEL came to Philip's house next morning, a year to the day after their first arrival at Seven-Tree Pond. Mima was in the house when he arrived; but she heard voices at the new barn and went out. Her father was showing Joel and 'Bijah the bins of rye and corn, the summer's harvest; and Jake was watching the newcomer with goggling eyes, his long neck taut as a stretched line. They did not at once hear Mima behind them; but then her mother and Susie and Phil came out of the house and Jess and Eben were with them, and 'Bijah turned and saw her.

'Here she is, Joel,' he said, with his wide grin. 'Now call me a liar! Didn't I tell you?'

Mrs. Robbins said briskly: 'Hush your foolishness, 'Bijah.' She greeted Joel, and he said a word to them all, looking at Mima with a calm scrutiny. They all gathered around him, and Mima thought he might be the centre of any gathering. He sat down cross-legged on the sill in the barn door, and Philip nodded toward the filled bins again.

'That's what we've done with two years' work from the time we put the first axe into a tree on the land,' he said. 'We

cleared twenty acres last year, and we've cleared as much more
this summer, and burned it, and made a crop besides. A man
that's ready to work and knows farming can do himself good
here.'

Joel's eyes touched Mima, standing near him, listening. She
leaned against the jamb of the barn door, her hands behind
her, her head tipped back till it rested against the solid timber;
and her eyes were turned to watch him. For him she was in
profile and in silhouette against the morning sky, her face somewhat shadowed. It was as though she lay beside him, her head
on the pillow turned, her eyes in his.

'I think as much,' he said, assentingly. Mima thought he
had a golden way of speaking. His hair was long and not
clubbed; just now it lay loose on his shoulders. He had apolo-
gized for this when he greeted her mother, had said that he and
'Bijah had been swimming, scrubbing clean. He had been too
busy whipping Burgoyne, these last weeks, to have time for
bathing — but now his hair must dry and be stagged off to a
handier length. Mima was glad it was loose. It waved and
wished to curl. It was soft brown with golden lights, the sort
of hair a girl might cry for. 'I think he could,' Joel Adams told
her father, watching her. 'A kindness, certain.' When he
smiled, his left eyebrow had a way of lifting, teasingly, as
though there were a jest in everything he said. He must have
shaved this morning, for his cheek shone smooth; and when the
sun struck him sidewise, it made visible the faint soft down on
his cheekbones above the shaven line.

'Never mind the farm talk,' Mrs. Robbins told him sharply.
'I've lived with farm talk all summer till I'm sick of it. I want
to hear the news.'

'Why, we copped Johnny Burgoyne,' Joel said cheerfully
'For a while there weren't enough of us to do more than peck
at him and run; but Howe stayed in New York, and after
Burgoyne's Indians killed Jennie Macrae, we had men coming in from all over to have a shot at him.

'And he gave us time enough,' he added, laughing. 'He was like any soldier, ready to put off a battle for the chance to dance Sallinger's round with a wench — and he had his doxy along so he could always tumble her.'

Mima thought there were curious, unfamiliar words on his tongue; supposed they were a part of the common language of soldiers. She was attentive to everything about him, to his gestures, the way he smiled. He answered all their questions; but at last the talk turned again to the business which had brought him to Seven-Tree Pond.

'I don't know as I want to be a farmer myself,' he confessed, his glance for a moment touching Mima, his brow lifted in that quizzical way he had. 'I don't know as I can English it. I'll know better later. But Matt Hawes, 'Bijah's brother, is all for it. He wants Jason Ware and me to come up here with him and try it. Matt and Jason and me have stuck together from egg to bird. If we can dicker for the land?'

'We can dicker,' Philip promised him.

'How many of you are there here?' Joel asked.

'Three families this side the pond,' Philip told him. 'Mine, and David's, and Rich Comings'. And across the pond, there ...' He pointed. 'There's Johnny Butler, and Ez Bowen is married and making a farm to bring his wife to, and your friend here is hard at it.' He looked at 'Bijah Hawes. 'Four families a'ready, and another to come, and 'Bijah of an age for marrying.'

Joel Adams laughed and his glance met Mima's again. "'Bijah might not be a marrying man,' he said frankly. 'Nor me.'

Philip Robbins said amiably: 'I'm thinking you're one will know how to find a wife if you're a mind.'

Joel nodded cheerfully. 'If I was for it, I might be satisfied and not look farther than my eyes can see,' he agreed. 'But marrying and soldiering don't mix, and I'm not through soldiering. Johnny Burgoyne is beat, and he's the King's best. We

were put to our trumps to handle him, but there's more to do.
I've had my turn at the hard of it; but now I'll try the easy.
Last winter was Trenton and Princeton, and I froze a toe at
Morristown. I had my discharge then, and all my back pay in
a handful; but it was no more than enough to buy me a new
pair of pants and a fair meal. So I went back to the soldiering
again, to gobble Johnny Burgoyne.'

'I told the King's men to their face how't would be, a week
before that day at Lexington,' Philip Robbins declared; and
Joel asked politely:

'How was that?'

'Why, 'twas in a tavern in Boston town,' Philip explained,
always pleased to find a new audience for his story. 'I was
lieutenant of the Walpole company and I went to town and in
this tavern there were three or four of them, the redcoats,
bragging what they'd do to us if ever any fighting started; so
"Will you then?" says I. "I'm lieutenant of my company."
So they laughed at the notion of me being an officer; and they
said it was such officers as me that would beat us. That fetched
my dander up. "Hark'e," I says. "If ever you stick your noses
outside of Boston town in the line of fighting, you'll find we'll
fight better without officers than you'll ever fight with them."
I was in a wax by then. "Any one of us," I says, "will kill one
man and cripple another and take a third one prisoner home
to breakfast." ' Joel clapped his hand on his thigh, laughing
in high appreciation, and Philip added: 'They gave me a taste of
jail for my talk — but a week after that they went out to Lexington, and they're finding ever since that I said no lie.' He
added apologetically: 'But I've no mind to keep you talking
war. Ye came looking for land?'

'I did so,' Joel assented. 'Matt was bound I should. If I say
so, they'll come see, and we'll buy — if you'll wait till we've
the money in hand.'

'You can be suited here,' Philip assured him, 'and I want
neighbors more than I want money. I want to see a town here.
We'll look out a piece of land you'll like.'

Joel spoke directly to Mima. 'Ma'am,' he said, with that teasing lift of his brow, 'do you think we can be suited here? Say I was your husband and bade you pick out the land you'd buy for a house for the two of us, where would it be?' He spoke gravely. 'You've a running look to you, long legs and a searching eye. I'll lay you've scanned the land; and likely there's one place you've seen you'd rather have than another.'

Her eyes, without her knowledge, closed. 'There is so,' she said, then opened her eyes again and spoke to her father. 'Up by Round Pond, Father? The meadow's good to cut hay, and there's good land for the clearing, and a fine spring, and a knoll handy by to build a house.' She looked at Joel. 'And it's a master place for moose in the meadows.'

Joel stood up resolutely. 'We'll have a look at it,' he declared. 'How far away?'

'Not far,' Philip told him. 'Mima's right. There's two-three hundred acres there that'll clear clean, with no more stones on it than on my land here. Loam on clay and gravel, so it holds the water long enough, but it drains good too. I'll show you.'

'I'll go,' said Joel, speaking to Mima smilingly, 'if you'll come along to mark out the very spot you mean. I want to know we start on the right foot, you and me!'

'Bijah chuckled, but Mima said calmly: 'I'll come along.'

'Bijah and Joel had walked up from 'Bijah's hovel, and there was only one float at the landing, so they chose to walk; Philip and Jess and Eben and Mima, 'Bijah and Joel Adams. Jake came too, and he and Eben hung at the young soldier's elbow. Mima said little, but there was a quiet peace in her. She moved serenely, her cheeks bright with the crisp November air. They circled Round Pond and came to the spot she had found the year before, where she had dreamed that dream; but this was better than her dreams. When Joel a while ago asked her advice as to what land he should consider, he admitted her by that question to a secret partnership. She showed him proudly the spot she had found; the spring at the border of the meadow, the dry knoll a few rods away and handy to the pond, the great pines which grew in a clean-floored forest north and south, bordering pond and meadow.

'The ground's clean,' she said proudly. 'Not hardly a stone on it too big to pick up and throw away.'

Joel said he was satisfied. 'It would suit me to a trifle,' he declared, 'if I was a farmer. Maybe I'll turn out to be one. Matt's bound I should, and he's a hard man to talk down.' He told Mima: 'You'll like Matt. He's a steady, gentle man, as mild as they come — but I saw him kill three men with his gun butt one day when we were in a hobble!' He chuckled. ''Bijah and me, and Jason too, we're a trouble to him sometimes.'

They were walking homeward together, Joel and Mima, Jake and Eben at their heels, the others ahead. He watched her as he talked. Jake demanded to hear more about the time Matt Hawes killed three men with his gun butt, and Joel told that tale and others too. Mima paid no heed to his words, content to listen to his warm, golden tones like the sunlight through leafless trees in spring.

When they came to the house, Mrs. Robbins made Joel and 'Bijah stay to dinner; and Joel talked business with Philip.

'I'll make terms to suit you,' Philip told him. 'With paper money the way it is, a price means nothing. I want neighbors.'

'An easy buy is a hard bargain,' Joel commented shrewdly. 'Buy cheap and be sorry, they always tell me. Light come, light go.'

'Well, work's the only coin that buys for keeps,' Philip agreed. 'But you couldn't stay now, anyway, with nothing on hand to carry you through the winter. Come spring when you're ready to settle, I'll satisfy you.' He chuckled. 'I'll drive a hard bargain if you want it so.'

'Matt figures we'll be up here in May.'

'The ice will be out by then,' Philip agreed.

'I'll need to tell Matt and Jason a price.'

Philip scratched his head, and Mima, busy with dinner

preparations, listened intently. 'Well,' her father said, 'you'll want all that good land west of the pond and the meadows. It's right on to a mile from the foot of the pond up to my line. I own on to the west to the Waldoborough line; but it's hills and rocks. There might be a thousand acres, all told, with say two hundred that you can clear and plant easy. You pay me two dollars an acre for the nigh land — four hundred dollars hard — and I'll give you the rest of it to the west of you.'

'Hard money's hard to come by,' Joel reminded him.

'You can pay down what you can raise, and owe the rest. I won't push you. I'll be here the rest of my life, and so will you. There's no hurry.'

Joel laughed. 'The rest of my life's a lorg time, I hope,' he protested. 'If I buy — and a man offers me a price — I might sell. I'd like the fun of knocking over those big pines, but farming might be different.' He confessed, with a chuckle: 'I'm a man likes to move around, but I'll tell Matt and Jason what you say. If you see us in May, we'll deal. I can't say yes or no without I talk to them.'

When he left them that day, he expected to start for Boston within a day or two. After he and 'Bijah were gone, Mrs. Robbins said: 'Well, I like that young man. He's got an eye that'd give any girl the cold shivers — but he'd know how to warm her again. Safe to say he's tumbled a-plenty in his time. But I took note that when it come to talking business there warn't no fiddle-faddle about him.'

Philip agreed with her estimate. ''Bijah ain't much of a worker, Ez tells me,' he said. 'But from what this one says, this Matt Hawes will make a man. And Adams is all right. We get them up here, I guess they'll stay.'

Mima said nothing, but she lay awake that night thinking of Joel. He was gone now, but he would return, come spring. She heard from Dave next morning that he had gone down-river to wait for a boat bound to the westward, and her world was empty, but she filled it with thoughts of him. Then on the third day afterward he returned, appearing at the cabin, and her breath caught to see him.

'I had word from Matt in Thomaston,' he explained. 'He and Jason are getting a furlough next week, coming up here to see what there is; so I'll wait for them.' He spoke to Jess. 'You were telling me about that meadow by the other pond being a moose pasture. I never had a chance to kill a moose. Say we try.'

'We could, easy,' Jess assured him. 'We'll go watch this evening.' He added guardedly: 'They might not come out this time of year. Summer time you'd be sure to see one. They get out in the open to get away from the flies; but now the flies don't bother them so it's a chance is all.'

Joel looked across at Mima. 'Come along?' he proposed, his brow lifting in that quizzical way which suggested he meant more than he said.

Mima said: 'I could watch from the old maple, Jess.'

'Come, yes,' he agreed. He told Joel proudly: 'She can hear a moose a mile away, where I can't hear him forty rod. She's worth two men, listening.'

So Mima went with them. They took a float and Jess poled them up the river to the pond. He put them ashore at the foot of a big maple which grew close by the river mouth, on the east side, opposite the end of the old beaver dam. 'You can climb up in the tree and see all across the meadow,' he said. 'I'll go over opposite. If one comes out to feed, you signalize me — I'll be watching — and I'll come a-h'isting; or if I see one, I'll come carry you over.'

So Mima and Joel were left alone together. She had often climbed the great tree before. It made a good watchtower. Its boughs were low and hospitable; and now its leaves were fallen so that they could see out through the bare branches. She swung up to the perch she liked, the soft moccasins she wore since frost had come gripping and holding as surely as her bare feet clung in summer. Joel laid his flintlock on the ground and climbed up beside her. They stood with the trunk of the tree between them, he with his left arm around it, she with her right. Joel said: 'I judge you've done this before?' And she nodded.

'I come walking sometimes, and it's a good place to watch from. You can see where Jess has cut away some branches so even when the leaves are on we can look out.'

He said nothing, watching her, and she raised speech like a barrier between them, saying hurriedly: 'Only there's so much to see. There's a pool here in the river, right below what's left of the dam, and salmon in it, so you see them when the sun strikes right, or when they rub their sides on the bottom you can see their bellies flash and shine; and times they jump high out of the water. Only this time of year they're gone up-river somewhere. And if you stay quiet you see foxes sometimes, and once I saw a coon, and last summer there were otters had a slide on that clay bank over there. And bears come sometimes, if you're still.'

She had spoken softly, scanning the meadows. He found his own voice hushed to match hers. 'You like seeing things like that, I guess.'

'I like it, yes, all of it,' she assented. 'I like the river sliding by. The water keeps going by, but always there's more comes. A river's alive, I guess. Before anybody came here at all, the river was right here, running just the same; and after we're all dead and gone, it still will be. Maybe after all the people in the world are dead and gone it will still be here.' He watched her, saw her eyes deep and still, her cheeks glowing at her own thoughts. 'It's like people were water in a river,' she said. 'We keep going on, out of sight, dying; but babies keep coming along after us.'

He smiled, falling into her mood. 'And the little baby brooks are born up in the hills, and little spring-babies come bubbling up through pin gravel in the ponds till there's enough of them, and they grow up and make a river.'

'But when there are enough of them,' she amended, 'or
enough people, the water rises, overflows its banks. Like —
Father and the rest of us coming up here. We're like when a
pond gets bank-full, and it runs over and spreads into places
where there never was any water before, just the way there
never were any people here before.'

He said, watching her: 'But when the pond gets low, the
floods drain off and the water runs out again.'

'We won't do that,' she said. 'We've come to stay. By and
by there'll be more of us here, and when we've got enough
people we'll make a town; and then the young ones, the boys,
they'll go on up-river and make a new town, and their young
ones will make a new one beyond that; till the woods are all
gone and there's farms and people living and working and
saving everywhere.'

They were silent a while, their eyes sweeping the meadows.
Frost had killed the grass and it was broken down, lying in
swaths and swatches here and there, upright in other places.
'We can see good today,' she said. 'Take it in summer, the
grass is too tall, higher than a man's head, sometimes. But now
it's mostly down, and the leaves off the moose bush and the
willows. You can see all over. There's Jess, on the far end of
the beaver dam.'

Joel could not at first make Jess out, since only the other's
head showed above the leafless underbrush between; but she
made him see. The sun was low, in their eyes, about to drop
behind the wooded crest of the hills that rose five or six hundred
feet above the pond southwesterly, and there was already a
hint of purple dusk in the shadows along the southwest side of
the pond. The wind was light, faint airs from the south hardly
stirring. They talked in low tones, feeling the hush of approaching night, forgetting what they watched for here.

Till suddenly Mima realized that Jess had left his vantage
on the beaver dam and had descended to his float pulled
up among the reeds and was paddling toward them. She said:

'He's seen something. He's coming to fetch you.' She looked off up the meadows and discovered the moose, half a mile away, feeding out from the point of woods that ran down into the meadow from the northwest.

'There it is,' she said softly.

'It's black,' Joel protested. 'That's a bear!'

She shook her head. 'No. A duck looks black against grass, but not in your hand. It's the same with moose. They're kind of brown.' Jess was paddling fast, hurrying toward them; and she said: 'Slip down behind the trunk. Hide all you can.'

When Jess arrived, he explained what to do. The moose might be expected to feed from the woods up-wind to the pond. 'You go up this side, along the river,' he told Joel. 'I'll go back and go up the other. We'll get him between us, and toward the pond from us. Then we'll both work in nigh him across the meadows, get between him and the woods where he come out. He won't scent us that side of him; but if he does, we'll maybe get a shot when he heads for the woods again.' And he said: 'We've time enough. He'll move slow.'

Mima stayed where she was to watch what followed, and to signal to them any unexpected movement by the moose. When they were gone, she drew her skirts around her so that they might not flutter in any stir of air and so alarm the great beast. Joel had crawled away along the west bank of the river, keeping down out of sight, while Jess returned across the pond to the forest on the west. She saw with a quick satisfaction that the moose had somewhat changed its direction, angling toward the river and so toward Joel. She hoped Joel would get the shot, knew Jess would take it if he could.

The moose worked almost directly toward her, browsing quietly. 'Just like a cow,' she thought. 'Not paying any attention to anything.' She caught a distant glimpse of Jess working across the meadow toward the point of woods from which the moose had emerged. 'He's figuring Joel will scare the moose and it'll put back toward him and give him the shot,' she decided, and tried to locate Joel and presently caught a glimpse of him, hiding behind an elm that grew beside the river twenty rods above her. There were twin trees there, one on either bank, tremendous, with graceful spreading branches. Joel was erect, peering around the tree, trying to locate the moose, which was between him and the pond. She saw him suddenly crouch, and knew that he had seen it. It could not be far from where he hid, moving between him and her. Then suddenly she heard the heavy roar of his musket, and the moose leaped into a rocking trot, plunged down into the river and across, and raced away toward the woods east of the meadows.

She thought Joel had missed! The great creature showed no sign of faltering. Joel had sprung out of his concealment on the shot, and for a dozen paces pursued; but the river blocked his way and he stopped, uncertain what to do. Then she saw Jess coming at a lope across the meadows. He shouted, and Joel answered him, and Jess came to where the other stood.

Mima saw Joel pointing to traces on the ground. So the moose was hit! She knew Jess would follow the wounded creature till it fell. She saw Joel point toward her; but Jess led him away at a run, up the river. She watched till she saw them wade the river, a few rods above the elms, and come back and pick up the moose's track and plunge into the woods.

She dropped out of the tree and started for home, knowing herself forgotten. Jess would track that moose till he got it. They might not return till tomorrow or the day after.

She walked along the pond and down the north side of the river, keeping back on the high land to avoid the soft footing in the grassy coves, till she came to Seven-Tree Pond; and she hailed, and Eben presently heard and came to set her over the river, and she told him what had happened.

Jess and Joel returned late next day, each of them heavy laden with meat, and Joel was full of talk of their hunt. They had trailed the moose till dark, slept hungry, and resumed the trail in the morning. They found him dead far up the river, and dined off the carcass, and then they drew the beast and dressed it out. What they could pack, they brought home, and sprung the rest up in birch trees out of the reach of foxes or other marauders, with long white splinters stuck into it to frighten off marauding crows till someone could bring it home.

* * * * *

Next afternoon Mima walked down as far as Rich's house to see Bet and the new baby. Bet said Joel and 'Bijah Hawes had gone to Thomaston to await the arrival of his friends. 'Ez Bowen went with them,' Bet explained. 'He's trying to get his wife to come up and winter here.' She added: 'I doubt she will. She came to see me while I was at Uncle Oliver's having Esther. I don't guess she'll like here. Pretty hoity toity. "Prance" they call her, short for "Experience". She kind of prances, 'stead of walking.'

Mima remembered something Bowen had told her father, the day he came to talk about buying land. 'She had a baby die, didn't she?'

Bet sobered. 'I didn't know that.' She hugged her own small daughter closer with an unconscious gesture. 'Did she so? Poor thing!'

'He told Father so.'

'She carries a high head,' Bet reflected. 'Maybe it's so she won't let people see how bad she feels. Lucy don't like her, says she henpecks Ez and all. But Lucy's kind of a hard talker her own self.'

'I take to Ez,' Mima said. 'He's like Rich. You always know where to find him.'

She stayed all afternoon with Bet, walked home through the sharp November dusk; and she thought there was a feel of snow in the air. Winter presently would settle down upon them; they faced the long months of snow and cold, the long and weary wait for spring. Joel would go away to the westward presently, to the army again. He would return in the spring; but spring

would be long in coming. She remembered how they had
watched for the first signs of last winter's ending, six or eight
months ago. Even in March, open water had begun to show in
the river; but that was only an aggravation. Not till mid-May
did the first flood of new life begin to flow across the land.
She shivered a little, thinking of the long winter ahead of them,
as she walked slowly home.

* * * * *

November was half gone before Joel and his partners and
'Bijah appeared again at Philip's house. 'We aimed to get here
last night,' Joel said. 'But we stopped for a toddy at McIntyre's
Tavern, and the company was good.' His eyes were twinkling
audaciously. 'So we stayed the night there.' He made introductions. 'This is Matt Hawes, 'Bijah's brother; and this is
Jason Ware.'

Mima liked Matt Hawes from the first, as Joel had said she
would. He was inches shorter than 'Bijah; and he was fair
where 'Bijah was dark, and gentle of speech and of eye where
'Bijah was bold and heedless in his ways. Of Jason Ware she
was not so sure. He appeared to be a grumbler, with no enthusiasm for anything he saw; but she thought shyness might be
the source of his rough way of speech. When they all departed
afoot to walk up to Round Pond and look over the land Joel
had selected, Mima stayed behind; but she waited in a sharp
anxiety for their decision.

They returned in time for dinner and Matt was quietly enthusiastic about what he had seen; and Joel told them, as they
all stood in talk together:

'It was Mima here picked out the place for us. She said it
would be what we wanted.' He added, a mirthful light in his
eyes and a jest in his tones: 'I think she's one would know better
than most what would please a man — and how to give it to
him, if she was a mind to. When I wanted to know where to
look for land, I said she was to think herself wed to me and

picking out our home site, and she burned red as roses and showed me the land you saw today.' He laughed and warned them: 'So mind, when it comes time for weddings, our plans are made, Mima's and mine.'

Mima's cheeks were bright, but she said no word. There was something serene in her quietness which made Matt Hawes watch her gravely. 'You've done us a good turn, ma'am,' he said. 'It's a sightly place for sure.'

They had with Philip some talk of terms, and he said they must stay for dinner, and there was rum to drink to bind the bargain. Mima went out-of-doors and down to the waterside, standing there alone, her back against a birch tree, her hands behind her, looking off across the pond. She heard a step behind her and turned and saw Matt Hawes.

'It's a sightly place,' he said. 'Even with winter coming on.'

She nodded. 'It was fine a month ago,' she told him. 'With the leaves all red and gold.' She asked: 'Will you come in the spring?'

'We aim to,' he said. 'But there's no telling. Joel's a hard one to pin down. The latest thing in his mind is the one he wants to do. Right now he's bent to come, but that might not last till spring.'

'I guess you wouldn't come without him.'

He smiled. 'Well, him and Jason and me always have got along, done the same things.' He added: 'And there's no telling about the war.' She felt cold, thinking of what might happen. Men were killed in war. 'It looks now as though we had the King by the tail, and a downhill pull,' he said. 'But you can't tell.'

She said: 'Jason Ware don't say much. Did he like it?'

Matt chuckled. 'Jason's all right,' he assured her. 'He grumbles some — but Jason and me in the long run usually turn out to do what Joel decides. Only sometimes I help Joel do his deciding.'

She smiled a little. 'I can see how you'd all three get along — spite of being so different.'

'Joel'd make a good captain,' he told her. 'When he says "come along", men will go after him anywhere.'

He hesitated, as though about to add some word; but before he could do so, Philip hailed them from the house and they went back to the heaping board.

* * * * *

The three young men stayed two days. Philip Robbins would go with them to Thomaston where David Fales was to draw the plan and the deed covering their purchase. He decided to take advantage of the opportunity to have another grist of corn ground, before ice closed the pond; so the barge which Taylor had built was loaded the night before. Ice formed during the night in the coves and along the shore. Her father proposed to pick them up at 'Bijah's landing on his way down the pond; and Mima did not expect to see Joel again, but he arrived at daybreak to help row the barge.

'And I came to say good-bye to you, ma'am,' he told Mima. 'I'll be back, you know.'

'You'll be back,' she assented. 'Come spring?'

'I mean to.' He chuckled. 'But no man ever saw you without meaning to come back to you. I might say I'm coming now, and change my mind after.'

She was silent for a moment. 'I'll always be here,' she said then.

He moved uneasily at that, like a horse under the curb. 'I've made some jokes, some laughing talk to you,' he confessed in a faint embarrassment. 'It might have bothered you. I didn't mean to. Rough talk's easy caught in the army.'

'You've not hurt me, Joel.'

'I'll never,' he promised, and laughed and added audaciously: 'Except it be in love!'

Her cheeks warmed, but then her father came to say the barge was loaded, and they must go. When they were afloat,

Joel looked back and saw her to remember; saw her standing as she had stood that first day, leaning against the birch by the shore instead of against the barn door; but her head was tipped back in the same way, and it was turned to watch him. He raised his hand, and then took the oars. The barge moved away down the pond, but she stood where she was as long as she could see them.

Mrs. Robbins came to Mima then, and when Mima looked at her, she asked gently:

'What did you think of him, Mima?'

Mima said: 'He's the one.'

Mrs. Robbins nodded. 'Aye, yes. I thought so. It was all plain in your eyes.'

7

WINTER was a time when you waited for spring to come, and the weeks and months might be tedious and long; but for Mima this winter when spring meant Joel would return seemed to speed away. They were secure and comfortable. The great barn was the storehouse on which they drew for all their needs except fresh meat. Even the cattle were plentifully supplied. Not all the hay cut on the meadows at the upper end of Seven-Tree Pond had been ferried home; but the stacks there could be drawn upon when needed, and the pond, deep in snow atop the heavy ice, furnished easy travelling for the heavy pung Philip and his sons built in December. The barn, warmed by the bodies of the oxen and the cows, was snug against all weathers. Mima and Eben usually did the milking. On cold mornings the muzzles of the cows and their flanks might be touched with rime; but the teats were warm in Mima's hands and the warm milk steamed in the pails. They had other food in plentiful supply. There were potatoes in the cellar, and turnips and even cabbages buried in the pit beside the house, covered with hay;

there were rye and corn and a little wheat in the barn. They killed four pigs in December and saved every ounce of meat, smoking the hams in the bark wigwam Philip had built; they had smoked some great salmon which Jess and Eben speared in late summer when the great fish lay sluggish in deep pools waiting for a spate; they had even some alewives from the spring run, smoked and dried and stacked away in the barn. Sometimes they loaded corn on the hand sled and made the long journey down to Mill River to have it ground, a day to come, a day to go. They took turns at this chore, going by twos, except that David did not go. Bess was to have a new baby in February to take the place of Silence; and she kept Dave with her. His own anxiety took the form of bringing Mrs. James, the midwife, from Warren to live with Bess and await her time. Mrs. James was a voluble woman, and Mrs. Robbins and Mima might spend much time at David's listening to her tales. She thought highly of Mr. Urquhart, the minister in Warren, whose courtship of Miss McIntyre that winter engaged every clacking tongue in the upper town. He had come from Scotland a few years before, built a house, spoke of bringing his wife to join him; but after a while he spoke less of his wife and more of the young women of Warren.

'Now the poor good man's wife has died in Scotland,' Mrs. James explained. 'And the letter with the black border came to break his poor good heart for him; and because he turns an eye to the McIntyres for comfort, the friends of Ike Wyllie are saying maybe his wife is not dead at all.'

Mrs. Robbins asked, hungry for talk, why Isaac Wyllie's friends should say such things; and Mrs. James said stoutly: 'Sure and Ike wanted the McIntyre lass to wed with him, till Mr. Urquhart showed what a one for drink he was and always after the wenches in the lower town, so she would have no more to do with him at all. So now Ike, and Moses Copeland and a pack like them, are saying they'd like to see the letter that said Mrs. Urquhart died, and the poor good man lost it crossing the

river one day so how can he show it anyhow? And the Wyllies
are saying they'd like to know who fetched it and how did it
come, and stirring up the town to take the whole business before the Presbytery, and maybe not pay Mr. Urquhart his
salary, and him saving souls everywhere he turns till the town
would be a honeypot of wickedness if it wasn't for the poor
good man.'

'D'ye think he will marry Miss McIntyre?' Bess asked.

'Why wouldn't he, and her drooping with loving him?'

'But if his wife is alive? Would he lie, maybe?'

'Would he lie? He would not! I'd as soon call him a liar as
George Washington his own self.' Mrs. James filled her pipe
and plucked a coal and lit it. 'For a good poor man he is, and
as pure as George Washington.'

She recounted all the talk of Warren and of Thomaston too.
Dan Rokes, the hog-reeve, who had hired out to Oliver Robbins
these two years, would take over John Lermond's Number Four
farm this year. There was talk of building roads so men could
work out their taxes. Continental currency was down till it
was predicted that thirty dollars of paper would be needed to
buy one of specie before the year was done. It was said two
men would have to be furnished by the town for soldiers. Mrs.
James herself had no patience with soldiering nor with the war.
They were all good loyal subjects of the King, or should be.
Nevertheless it was said that all Tom Flucker's lands would be
confiscated, and it served him right for moving away. Dave
Kelso was doing well with David's old farm. Thomas McLellan
was coming from Falmouth to settle in Thomaston; and it was
said he was so near that he tied hay around the clapper of his
cowbells to keep them from wearing out. Jonathan Smith was
talking of taking up land in the eastern part of the old lower
town; and Oliver Robbins had told him he would starve to
death if he tried it. It was reported that David Fales would be
dropped as a town officer because of his Tory views; and Captain Gregg and Lieutenant Kellock and some other rowdies

calling themselves patriots had told him he'd ride a rail unless he abjured the King. David Fales told them he would do neither and to hell with them; but Mrs. Fales gave them a bucket of flip and the patriots got drunk and forgot their grievances. One John Sullivan talked of teaching a school in Thomaston if he could find pupils. The old woman's tongue rattled on and on. There was little she did not know and tell.

She came days before the baby was due, and sometimes they all gathered at Dave's house to hear her talk. The winter was so severe, the snow so deep, that beyond the necessary chores — hauling firewood and tending the animals — there was not much the men could do. Sometimes they felled trees, widening their clearings; and Jess built a line of squat traps up the river; and he went hunting when the signs were right, using this activity as a reason why he should not be expected to make the laborious trip down-river with corn to be ground. To cross to the Madomock, sleeping wherever night caught him, to kill moose and haul home as much of the meat as he could drag was quite as strenuous as hauling corn down-river and meal home with a good bed to sleep in on the way; and Mima, laughing at him for dodging the trip to the mill, told him so one day.

Jess laughed at her ignorance. 'There's all the difference,' he protested. 'One's work and t'other's fun!' They argued the point so long that in the end he challenged her to come with him after moose and see for herself, and she agreed to go. Mrs. Robbins protested, but they overruled her; and Philip was on their side.

'Let the girl go, Ma,' he urged. 'She'll take no harm. She's long-legged as a moose herself.' He added with twinkling eyes: 'And if she goes, here's once Jess will have to do his share of the work, anyway.' Jess was famous among them for dodging the heaviest tasks; they laughed tolerantly at his evasions.

He and Mima set out one day at first light. Snow was deep, but the crust was good. They hauled a hand sled, loaded with the scant provision they would require and two or three bearskins which would make their beds. Tuner went with them. They went up the river and across Round Pond, and on up the brook which flowed into it from the west till they surmounted the high land and came down into the Madomock valley.

They were all day on the way; and when they stopped at dusk, Jess set Mima to dig away snow till she had made a pit deep enough to give them some shelter from the wind. While she shovelled out the snow with her snowshoes, he cut hemlock boughs to insulate them against the icy ground; and he gathered firewood. When the hole suited him, he snapped a spark into a pinch of powder and lighted threads of birch bark and had presently a great fire roaring. He drew out coals and boiled the kettle and fried fat pork and they had tea and pork and cornbread. He spread one of the bearskins on the boughs, and he and Mima lay on it, spoon fashion, Mima in his arms, the other skins for covering. He called Tuner to curl up against Mima's stomach; and thus sandwiched between them, she was warm enough; and she thought it might have been Joel in whose arms she lay, and thinking of him fell asleep; but during the night Jess reversed the arrangement, so that he was between her and the big hound, and in his sleep he drew the bearskins more closely around him till her back was cold enough to wake her, and she fought some share of the skins away from him and called Tuner to her side again to warm her, while Jess pretended to sleep on, unconscious of her discomfort.

In the morning they found deep trails in the cedar swamps where the moose were yarded, and Jess posted himself in a likely place, and sent Mima, with Tuner on a leash, by a roundabout course to drive them toward his hidden stand. When she loosed Tuner, the great dog started a young bull, and bayed it, and Jess came near enough to shoot it while Tuner kept it engaged. It was no sooner down and his gun reloaded than a yearling blundered along the trails almost upon him. He killed that, not two rods from where the bull lay; and when Mima came to where he was, she found him butchering the great beasts, a cloud of steam rising from their hot entrails about him as he worked.

He packed a saddle and two haunches and the livers on the hand sled. Mima helped him bend down birch trees and spring the rest of the meat high out of the reach of marauding animals to wait till he could come another trip to fetch it. Then they harnessed Tuner to the sled, and each shouldered a towrope, and they started the long trip home. They were another night on the homeward way, feasting on broiled meat, sleeping like gorged wolves. When they came home, Philip asked amiably:

'Well, Mima, Jess take good care of you, did he?'

Mima laughed. 'He struck up the fire and did the cooking and shot the moose,' she said. 'I dug the bed hole and drove the moose and hauled the sled.'

Jess said with a grin: 'I kep' her busy. Figured that was the only way to keep her warm.'

'You didn't worry about me sleeping warm, I noticed!'

Jess winked at his father. 'Well, I aimed to,' he told her. 'But minute I put my arms around you, you started calling me Joel in your sleep. I figured dreaming about him would keep you warm!'

They laughed, and Mima's cheeks blazed, and she leaped at him and caught him and they wrestled like two bear cubs, rolling on the cabin floor.

*　*　*　*　*

The new baby was born on the nineteenth of February. The day was warm, water dripping from the eaves, the drifts shrinking in the sun. The baby was a girl, and David and Bess named her Lucy, to please Lucy Butler across the pond. When the baby was four days old, David took Mrs. James home to Warren, hauling her in state on a hand sled, Tuner helping him pull it; and Mima stayed the night with Bess till his return.

The warm days made her think of spring, and she said
happily:

'There'll be five families here, this summer, with Ezra Bowen
bringing his wife as soon as their baby comes.' She did not
speak of Joel; but she was thinking of him too.

Bess hugged little Lucy against her breast. 'She didn't dast
have her baby here,' she said proudly. 'Our Silence was the
first ever born here, and now our Lucy's the second. Even
Bet went down-river to have hers, but babies can be born here
as well as anywhere!'

Mima asked, after a moment: 'Bess, did you ever think maybe
I could have done something for Silence, if I'd known what to
do?'

'No, Mima,' Bess said quietly. 'Nor don't you ever think
that. I know now that she died a while before, when she
stopped moving. You mind she always was so busy twisting
and kicking me? Remember how you liked to feel her?'

Mima crossed her arms across her breasts. 'I want one of
my own,' she whispered; and Bess laughed and said:

'You'll not be long waiting after Joel Adams comes back.
Maybe he'll be here in May.'

Mima's cheeks were hot because Bess had read her thoughts;
but she protested defensively: 'He's not the only man!'

'I'm thinking he is for you,' Bess told her, and she added
mischievously: 'Me oh my, child, you were telling him so every
time you looked at him. David and I would laugh at it and
say he'd better go back to the war if he was going.'

'D'ye think the war will be over this summer?'

Bess shook her head. 'David says it's no more than begun.
He says the King won't give up till we go over and march
right into London town.' Bess smiled at her baby, asleep now,
its open mouth still half-touching her breast. 'But Mima,
we're a long way off from wars and everything here. We're
just maybe six or seven miles from tidewater, but we've heard
not much news for weeks now, except from Mrs. James. Gen-

eral Washington could be dead, and Philadelphia taken, and Sam Adams hung and we'd not know.'

Mima nodded. 'It doesn't make any difference to us here, either. All we can do is work and save and get ready for winter and have children and love each other. But Bess, I'm happier than I was in Walpole. There I was always fretted about something, the Stamp Acts, or tea, or what Boston folk were doing, or the people down the street. I was always in a stew about things that didn't touch me at all if I didn't know about them. Sometimes I think we're better off not knowing what's happening in the world. Hearing Mrs. James talk, half the people she talked about, I didn't even know their names; but I was all stirred up about Mr. Urquhart's wife in Scotland, and his lying or not, and his marrying or not; and Mother's talked of nothing else since. I wish I'd never heard of Mr. Urquhart. Our world here is no bigger than what I can walk over from our house; but everything I care about is in it. I wish I never had to hear anything about what's going on outside.'

'I know. I'm the same.' Bess's eyes were thoughtful. 'I wish it took us fourteen years to hear from Boston, even in summer, instead of fourteen days. Mima, if the King does win the war, we'll still have our farms here. We'll still work hard all our lives, and have children and raise them, and live and work and play and die. And if the King's beaten, it will be just the same. It's just the idea of winning or of being beaten that keeps us unhappy and fretting.'

'I wish my whole world was just no farther than I can walk and see and hear!'

Bess laughed. 'Tosh! If it was, where would Joel Adams be coming from?'

Mima's eyes were deep and warm. 'Oh, I can see him, hear him, all the time, even when I'm asleep. Wherever he is. He's in my world, Bess, never fear.'

Bess said: 'There, she needs to be changed!' They worked together over the baby; and Bess said in faint concern: 'Do

you suppose my milk is all right for her? She don't gain the
way she'd ought to.'

'Of course it is! Here's a fresh one. I'll wash that out.'

'Leave it for me to do.'

'Oh, I love to. It's like having a baby of my own.'

* * * * *

The baby, never strong, died toward daylight on the first of
March. From the first, it failed to thrive on Bess's milk; and
they had been able to find no food to agree with it. They tried
cow's milk diluted with water; they tried rye-water, and corn-
water; they tried in a quiet desperation everything they could
devise. Bess for days refused to let the baby leave her arms,
holding it tight as though by holding its body she could hold
its life too.

But when it died, there was no weakness in her. She said
steadily: 'Well, David, I'm not afraid. We love each other still.'

He held her, as she had held the baby. 'And we've three
young ones, anyway,' he said. 'And there'll be a baby we can
keep, by and by.'

Bess nodded. She pressed close to him. 'I hate winters,' she
whispered. 'Take care of me, Dave. I'll be all right, come
spring.'

* * * * *

After the baby died, this second spring, as though relenting,
came with a rush. Mima watched jealously for its forerunners,
and the first robin made her want to cry with thankfulness.
Early in April the river opened, and she could hear it roar as
lustily as a young bull, rioting in its strength in the still nights.
The days whirled past more and more swiftly; the frogs began
to pipe; the ice went out of the pond, and the ewes in their pen
dropped their lambs.

Joel would come in May. As April sped, Mima watched
down the pond day by day for any sign of him; and whenever

a float rounded the point a mile away and came toward their landing, she waited by the shore till she could recognize its occupants.

But it was mid-May before she had any word. Then one day she saw a man walking up the shore path toward the house; and even at a distance she recognized 'Bijah Hawes. His great height made him unmistakable. He was Matt's brother, and Matt was Joel's friend. She knew surely that he brought some news of Joel; and she guessed — since he came alone — it was not the news she waited to hear. Her father was at work on a stump in the clearing, preparing to make the oxen drag it from its bed in the still muddy ground; and she saw 'Bijah turn aside toward him. She hurried to join them, saw them meet as she drew near, heard 'Bijah say:

'Matt wanted me to tell you, Robbins. They're not coming this year.'

Mima's breath stopped and she felt her cheek drain, but 'Bijah called a greeting to her, and he came to meet her with his flashing grin, his teeth gleaming, his black hair glossy in the sun. 'Hear that, did you, Mima?' he asked. 'Matt and them ain't coming. I'll have you to myself this summer, any-way!' His hand grasped hers, and she said:

'We're glad to see you, 'Bijah.'

Her father asked: 'What happened to them?'

'Joel wanted more soldiering,' 'Bijah explained. 'And Jason and Matt stick with him. The three of them always did, since they was young ones.' He added: 'Joel's a hard one to tie down to anything. He never will say ahead of time what he aims to do. They didn't know for sure till the day before I come away.'

She nodded, understanding. She had felt that free strength in Joel that was impatient of any restraint, even if it were self-imposed. He would not readily turn his back on heedless days and accept the steady toil and the monotonously repeated tasks which making a farm in this wilderness involved.

But she knew well that on Joel all her life was centred now. 'Will he come next year?' she asked.

'Matt will bring him to it,' 'Bijah told her. There was a twinkle in his eye. He said: 'I think it was as much you as anything that kept him from coming now. He as good as said so; said he couldn't get you out of his head. He's afraid of you — or afraid what you'd do to him. Joel ain't one that will be in a hurry to settle down.'

She nodded, turning a little away. Philip asked some question about the progress of the war, and 'Bijah gave them news that seemed to make eventual victory sure. Ben Franklin had made a treaty with the French King; and the French would send an army and a fleet of great ships to help with the fighting.

'That will do it, give us time,' he said.

Philip Robbins protested stoutly: 'We didn't need French help. We can whip the English two to one before breakfast. I told them so. They put me in jail for saying it; but they let me out mighty quick.'

But Mima, listening, was glad the French would come to help. By that much was war's end brought nearer; and war's end would surely mean Joel's coming. Till Joel returned, her life would stand still.

8

THE frost came out of the ground, and Philip and his sons took advantage of mud time to pull stumps in the burned lands. Geese and ducks were flying, and twice great flocks of pigeons passed overhead. Bobolinks appeared and the black flies came. Planting time was on them with a rush, and the sows littered and the days were long and fine. Ezra Bowen brought Prance and the babies to their house down by the Warren town line, and 'Bijah Hawes was working at his clearing, building a house to replace the hovel that had served him till now. Philip Robbins expanded his farming operations, widened his clearings toward the west and down to the river, and increased his planting. He built a lean-to against the fine barn to increase its capacity; and he planned to add a room to the house, but work pressed so hard he never found the time.

Mima had long empty hours to fill, and she preferred to spend them out-of-doors. From the very doorstep there was much to see. The wild geese which lived on the island, made uneasy by their human neighbors, this summer sought new nesting ground;

but the eagles were still there. They lived by robbing the fish
hawks which were plenty around the pond, and Mima often
saw that piece of brigandage. Wherever a fish hawk hunted,
there was likely to be an eagle high above him; and the hawk's
dive on his quarry, his wings bowed forward to cut the water,
did not escape the eagle's watching eye. When the hawk rose,
turning his prey head to the wind, shaking the water off his
feathers like a wet dog, climbing heavily, the eagle would glide
nearer; and as soon as the hawk was high enough, the game
began. Usually when the hawk dropped its fish, the eagle was
quick enough to catch it before it struck the water. Mima
always hoped to see the hawk escape, but it never did.

There were always ducks in the pond and in the river, feeding
in the grassy bays along its shores; and there were loons, using
the river as a thoroughfare or moving in pairs along the shore
in shallow water, diving for their prey in the secret deeps,
calling in the lonely nights. Sometimes a chorus of them woke
Mima in the night with loud ululations. That was a seldom-
failing sign of storm.

From the shore, or from the ledgy summit of the hill southeast of her father's house, she liked to watch the birds on the
water or above it, but best of all, now that there were no
Indians near, she liked to walk up to Round Pond, sometimes
to stand on the very spot where Joel when he came would live.

But she did not always go so far, might be content to look from
a distance at the fine stand of pines where he would build some
day his house. The island in Round Pond near its eastern
shore was half ledge, half wooded. Between it and the mainland there was shallow water where reeds and rushes grew;
and Mima sometimes waded out to it. The bottom was clay,
firm enough to support her and yet soft and slippery underfoot,
so that once she fell flat in water three feet deep, and scrambled
to her feet, gasping and laughing at her own mishap. She
waded on to the island. The ledge was sunned and warm, and
she took off her dress and petticoats and laid them out to dry,

weighting them down with rocks so that they would not blow away; and in her shift she lay warm and sleepy in the sun. The wind and the sun had their way with her, and the sky was a blue sea across which sailed the clouds. Lying on her back, looking up at them, shading her eyes with her hands, she saw shapes among the clouds and forms of beauty like the beauty one may see in dreams; she thought the clouds were beautiful as God with His veil lifted. Perhaps He dwelt among them, watching happily this world of His. She lay so still that ducks fed among the reeds between her and the shore till when she moved their heads rose and they swam warily away, looking back over their shoulders to see if she meant them harm.

But Mima was not always content to come only to the island. Sometimes she walked around the south side of the pond; but she might have time only to go to the old maple where she and Joel had watched for the moose that day with Jess. To reach it she could go up-river in a float, or she could cross the river and go afoot. Jess likewise sometimes used the maple as a look-out, and to reach it more easily afoot he bridged the river. There was a spot where the stream narrowed between two rocky points till it was only fifteen or twenty feet wide, and at low water four or five feet deep. There he felled a tall pine in such a way that it lay across the stream, a few feet above the water; and he lopped off the branches on its top side to make crossing easier, and cut away enough of those which lay in the water so that a float could pass underneath. Mima might cross there and follow the high ground around the reedy marsh coves along the river to come to the old maple. Usually she went alone; but sometimes Susie or Phil kept her company; or even Eben. She liked having Eben go along. He understood her mind, knew why she always walked toward Round Pond, talked to her sometimes about Joel. A firm bond grew between them.

'Bijah Hawes would have kept her company on these excursions. Sometimes on Sunday he tramped up the pond to sit in talk with her father and Jess — but with his eyes on Mima in a twinkling speculation which disturbed her. Susie liked him, liked to perch on his knee and hear his talk; and on one such day she told him about a cow moose and her calf which she and Mima had watched from the maple tree the day before.

'I wanted to fetch someone to shoot it,' she said stoutly. 'But Mima wouldn't let me just because it had a baby.'

'Bijah said: 'Well! You two go tramping around the woods by yourselves, do you?'

'Yes, lots! There's nothing to hurt you. Mima goes by herself, too!'

'Bijah said: 'Does she so?' He grinned at Mima. 'Ain't you afraid of bears?' he asked her. 'You'd ought to have a man along to take care of ye. I can oblige ye, any time.'

'I guess you've got enough to do,' she told him. 'Without taking care of me.'

He did not argue the point; but a few days later he joined her at the lookout tree. She had gone up to Round Pond in the float, taking a brush hook along, and she landed at the end of the beaver dam and began to cut a path through young willows and underbrush along the top of it, toward the western shore. The bushes were for the most part small, and she worked steadily and surely, chopping them off near the roots, throwing them aside. The dam was broad and firm and in some places it rose a full six feet above the summer level of the pond. The beavers which built it had made a foundation of sticks and logs, and plastered it well, and in the scores or hundreds of years since it was begun it had caught silt from flood waters, and grasses had taken root on it and lived and died, so that it was like a firm embankment now. The path Mima cleared was not wide. It was often possible to pick a way without any cutting at all; but she lopped off the slender branches that met in her path, and cut down the more serious obstructions. She worked for an hour or two till she had cleared a way the length of the dam and came to where it ended as the meadows rose to merge into the higher wooded ground. There was water backed up above it where a smaller brook came down through the meadows. She drank at the spring and went on up to the knoll where some day Joel and the others would build their house, and stayed a while among the tall pines where sunlight made a pattern on the ground. She returned to the spring and cleaned it out again and thought to dig it deep some day and stone it up against Joel's coming. Then she retraced her way along the path she had cut, giving it another stroke here and there. The footing was still uncertain, with stubs sticking up where she had cut down clumps of moose bush or young willows or alder shoots; but it was easy in daylight to pick her way.

She returned to her float, and might have started home; but she was warm and the day was fine. She paddled up the river past the twin elms to the crossing, where spring floods had thrown up a shallow bar. It was here Joel and Jess had waded the river the day Joel killed the moose. She undressed and bathed, and when she came down toward the pond again she heard a sound in the woods on the east shore. It might be a moose or a bear, and she landed at the foot of the maple and climbed the tree to watch for the beast to emerge from the woods.

Nothing appeared, and the sounds ceased; but she stayed a while, watching the wind stir the grasses across the meadows in long waves of light and shadow. By and by she heard a sound below her; and 'Bijah came to the foot of the maple, grinning cheerfully. His black head was bare, his hair free.

'Coming down?' he challenged. 'Or am I a-coming up?'

'I heard you over on the other side of the river,' she remembered.

'I saw you,' he agreed. 'Went down and crossed and came to see what you were looking at.' He swung up to the branch below where she sat, standing on it, his head level with hers. 'You're a hard one to come by,' he told her cheerfully. 'I've come nights to fetch you out to see the moon, but the house is always shut tight.'

'We go early to bed — and up early. There's such a pile to do every day.'

'I could show you a heap of things to do at night,' he promised her audaciously. 'Or I could take you down some day and show you the house I'm building.'

She looked past him across the meadow. The new grass was already tall. In the river below them a musquash made a widening arrow of ripples as he swam downstream. Mima felt her heart pounding slowly in her breast, and she was confused and warm as though she had been hurrying on a hot summer day. She asked:

'Will you stay and live in it this winter?'

'Well, it's soon to know,' he confessed. 'I hate to sleep cold. Could a man come bundling up at your house — or you in his?'

She laughed, uneasy at his nearness. 'Send for your brother,' she advised. 'If you don't like alone.'

He shook his head. 'Matt won't come till Joel does!' His eyes were twinkling. 'I don't look for them to come at all. Joel's got too many friends where he is.' He was so near her that she moved back.

'It's a hot day,' she said defensively.

He laughed. 'I'm always hot when I'm nigh you.' Without warning he dropped his arm around her shoulders, drawing her toward him.

'Don't!' she said sharply, and with her hand against his chest pushed hard. Her left arm encircled the trunk of the maple, giving her some security; but he had only his hand on the branch on which she sat, his arm around her. Her thrust set him off balance, and when he tried to save himself, his foot in its wet moccasin slipped forward off the branch on which he stood. He fell backward — releasing her, or he must have pulled her with him — and hit his head against another branch and fell heavily to the ground ten feet below.

He lay there a moment, not moving; and Mima swung herself down, crying out his name, demanding to know whether he was hurt. He sat up, with a grimace of pain, and grinned at her. 'Not a bit,' he said. 'Just the breath jolted out of me — but looking at you would take the breath out of a man, anyway.' He made a long face. 'Would you break my neck for wanting a kiss?'

She nodded quietly. 'Yes,' she said. 'I might, if I didn't want to give it to you.'

Her tone sobered him. 'I meant no harm,' he said apologetically.

'I know.'

'What's against me?' he protested, almost sullenly. 'With Joel not around?'

She smiled. 'I guess a man is always surprised when a girl doesn't want to kiss him.'

He grinned, then, sitting at her feet. 'Never had it happen before,' he said. 'They mostly come asking for it.' He said: 'You'd know why they like it, maybe, if you tried me. Summer's a long time to go with no kissing in it.'

She asked: 'Did you come up here today to find me?'

'What if I did?'

'Don't come again, 'Bijah. You'll just have your trouble for your pains.' She stepped past him. 'I'm going home,' she said.

He did not speak. She went down to her float and looked back; but he had not moved. She asked doubtfully: 'Are you all right? Hurt at all?'

His wide grin flashed at her. 'What if my leg was broken — like my heart?'

'If it's no worse broke than your heart, you could outrun a moose,' she told him, laughing back at him, and stepped into the canoe.

*   *   *   *   *

The summer spun away like a spider's web drifting on an

August breeze. When the leaves began to turn, Dunbar of
Ducktrap came again, with his wooden wares; but this time
when Mima pressed him to eat more and more, he warily refused. He stayed a night with them; and he asked whether
Jimbuck had returned that summer. Philip said no, and Dunbar shook his head.

'I don't like the look of it,' he confessed. 'There were two
came to Belfast last week, friendly ones; and they say all the
Indians have gone to Canada for the winter, and they're coming down on us in the spring. Down the Kennebeck and the
Penobscot, thousands of them. They're due to get here about
the time the leaves are as big as a man's thumbnail, with the
British to set them on and wipe out every town this side Falmouth.'

'D'ye think there's truth in it?' Philip challenged, the others
silent and listening.

'I'd not know,' Dunbar admitted. Mima saw his Adam's
apple pump nervously. 'If they come, there'll be King's ships
in the Bay to meet them. I'll be taking a look out the last thing
at night and the first in the morning till the leaves are full size,
anyway.' He wagged his head. 'If old Jimbuck was around,
I'd feel better,' he said. 'He'd know the truth — and tell it.
His not coming makes it bad!'

He went on his way in the morning; and Mima remembered
his warning and Mrs. Robbins fretted about it. But Philip said:
'Ma, we're here to stay. No Indian's going to drive me out.
Not even if they come and try it.' He grinned. 'And one
thing's sure, I'm not going to get my tail down on anyone's
say-so. I've got too much to do to take time for worrying.'

Harvest time was on them and the days were too short for
all they wished to do. The leaves turned and began to fall,
and suddenly the trees were bare. The day after Lucy Butler's
baby was born, early in November, the pond skimmed over
with ice. Next day the ice was gone, but it would return, and
that first warning spurred 'hem to greater industry. Before

snow, they must be ready for the winter. Philip's was the only barn as yet built on this side of the pond. Dave and Rich had each built a low log stable to house their milk cows and their pigs; but their oxen would be stalled in Philip's barn with his. Hay, cut on the meadows above Seven-Tree Pond, had been rafted over and mowed in the barn and stacked on the poles which served as roof for the lean-to at one side; and there were bins in the barn to receive the corn after it was husked, and the rye after threshing. During the harvest Mima had helped, tying the grain into bundles after the scythes had passed, carrying the bundles to the drag on which oxen hauled them home. The ears of corn had been ripped from the stalks and hauled to the barn and piled on the floor in its further end, where the dunghill fowl not yet penned for the winter teased off the husks to get at the golden grains. Mrs. Robbins demanded that they be penned to put a stop to this, and Eben made slatted pens at one side of the barn and imprisoned them there.

They husked the corn themselves; but Philip decided to make of the threshing a sort of festival. 'As good a crop as we've had this year deserves a celebration,' he declared; and Mrs. Robbins agreed. Before the day set, he and Jess made flails out of staves hinged with moose hide, and the barn floor would serve for the threshing. Everyone came for the occasion except Lucy Butler, not yet able to be about. Even Johnny came to help with the work, though he went home at noon, and again at first dusk. Ez Bowen and Prance came up the pond, and 'Bijah, and Dave and Bess with their children, and Rich and Bet. The younger babies were put to bed in the house and Bess stayed with them, and Mima saw her hold one and then another close, crooning over them wistfully. The womenfolk cooked a mountain of victuals at noon, and Philip had a keg of rum ready for the thirsty ones. Mima saw that Prance Bowen held herself a little aloof. She worked as hard as any of them, but she seldom spoke except to call Ez, in a disturbingly shrill voice, and bid him do this or that. He obeyed her agreeably enough. Mima said once to her mother:

'She bosses Ez around, doesn't she?'

Mrs. Robbins made an exasperated sound. 'He'd ought to smack her one,' she said. 'If she looks down her nose at me a few more times, I'll do it myself.'

The men worked at the threshing tirelessly, spreading the bundles of rye on the floor, flailing it out, gathering up the straw. Mima and Jacob and Sue and even young Phil, seven years old now, swept the grain up and winnowed it and put it in the bins along the side of the barn floor.

It was full dark before the task was done. They turned to eat, gathering around a great fire built out-of-doors; and afterwards they danced, stamping and pounding, whistling or singing their own music, clapping their hands to keep the time, while Philip called the turns. The rum had circulated freely since before dinner in the middle of the day; and the men were flushed with it. 'Bijah Hawes seemed tremendous in the firelight, his head bare, his black hair tossing like a lion's mane. He swung his partners with such violence their feet might leave the ground, the sweat jerking off his brow with every stamp of his foot. Once he swung Mrs. Robbins till she was dizzy, and when he released her she would have fallen but he caught her and held her and kissed her for good measure, and she slapped his cheek resoundingly and he laughed, his head thrown back, and told her that was just sauce to the kiss. Then he saw Mima laughing and bounded to catch her.

'Your ma's given me a red ear!' he cried. 'A red ear always earns a kiss.' He kissed her before she could turn aside, fair on the mouth, while she twisted her head this way and that to escape him, and she heard their laughter all around, and fought to be free of him. As though her resistance set him on fire, he swept her up and bounded away from them all, toward the barn.

Eben leaped after him and caught 'Bijah and stopped him. 'Don't, 'Bijah,' he said. 'Mima doesn't want you to!'

'Bijah laughed at him. 'Grow up, young one!' he cried.

'How did you find out what a woman wants?' He tried to brush Eben aside; but so doing he loosed his grip on Mima, half-dropping her, and she got her feet on the ground, and then her father and David came toward them, and 'Bijah laughed and said: 'Why, there's no harm!' He released Mima and put his arm around Eben. 'You're a hot young rooster!' he said approvingly. 'You'll get a girl in a barn mow yourself some day — and not have to carry her to make her go.'

The moment that might have led to violence passed in laughter; but Mima was trembling as much with confusion as with anger, startled by some stirring in herself she did not know. A button was gone off her dress, lost somehow in 'Bijah's violence. She went into the house to fix it, and saw Bess with the children there, finding in them comfort for her own lost ones.

Mima stayed with Bess till the folk began to go; she went out then to bid them good-bye and found 'Bijah contritely waiting for a chance to speak to her. He met her as she approached the group around the dying fire, looking down at her, grinning and yet abashed.

'Glad you come out again,' he said. 'I was afraid you wouldn't. I didn't want to go off t'the west'ard with you maybe mad at me.'

She had not known he was going. 'Won't you winter here?'

He shook his head, chuckling. 'I told you, I don't like to sleep cold.' And when she drew away he touched her arm. 'Hold on,' he said. 'No harm meant, Mima. Get some rum in me and I play the fool — but I wouldn't go to scare you.'

'You didn't scare me.'

'Why, then, no harm's meant or done.'

'Will you be coming back in the spring?'

'Yes. It suits me, here, all but the notion of being all winter alone. I'm taking what I've raised to sell down-river.'

'I expect you'll see your brother.'

'Likely.' He told her: 'Mima, if Matt comes up here, you

marry him. He's worth Joel and Jason and me boiled down
to one. And he's the marrying kind.'

She laughed a little. 'I guess Matt will do his own picking
and choosing.'

'You'll suit him. You're the marrying kind yourself.'

'What makes you think that?'

He grinned. 'If you were the other kind, we'd have found it
out between us before now.'

There were others all about them; so she was secure. 'You
never said anything about marrying to me,' she reminded him,
smilingly; and before he could speak she called to Philip:
'Father, 'Bijah's selling his corn down-river, going to Boston.
Do you need more than you've raised?'

Philip came toward them. 'No, got enough in the bins to
feed an army,' he said. She left him with 'Bijah and turned
away.

* * * * *

Before the first of December there was snow on the ground;
and more fell day by day. Sam Boggs passed through on his
way to the Madomock swamps and said that Caleb Howard,
the blacksmith, was coming over from Broad Bay a few days
later to shoe his oxen. 'You might want to have him fix yours,'
he told Philip.

Robbins assented. 'They need it,' he agreed. 'I never got
around to it. Don't know as I could manage myself, anyway.
Fetch his own forge, does he?'

'No; if he has to bend a shoe a mite to fit it, he'll just build a
fire and heat it up in that. He'll fetch along as many shoes and
nails as he looks to need. I'm aiming to be home before he
comes. I can tell him you want him.'

Philip agreed, and Caleb Howard arrived a few days later.
He came up from Warren on snowshoes, packing his supplies.
By that time, their preparations for the winter were done, food
and forage and cattle all housed in the barn.

The barn stood southwest of the house and at about the same level, not far off. The stalls for the oxen, the tie-up for the cows where the gentle beasts rested with their necks between staves so that they could lie down or stand up without being released, and the pens where the three sows were housed were ranged along the south side, where the ground sloped away to accommodate the manure pile. The fowl were housed in a pen above the sows; but Philip planned next year to dig a pit under the tie-up for the pigs and make more room. Hay was mowed above the animals, on cedar poles laid across the timbers, and also above the grain chests on the opposite side of the barn, in which Philip's corn and rye and the surplus raised by Dave and Rich were stored. The lean-to was against the north wall. Its roof was a thatch of hay, six or eight feet thick, piled on cedar poles; but there were log walls at either end of the lean-to, and a yoke of oxen were stalled there, and gear could be stored there out of the weather, protected by the thatch — which served also as a reserve supply of feed for the cattle through the winter.

Caleb Howard arrived Thursday night. He was a ponderous giant of a man, and he smoked a great pipe which he himself had whittled out of an apple root, with a pierced cherry twig for a stem. He and Philip Robbins sat late, the night he arrived, in slow talk before the dying fire. Philip did most of the talking. Mima, in the trundle bed with Sue tight in her arms and sleeping warm as a puppy, listened to them and wondered why the blacksmith had not more to say. She thought him a stupid man, as slow of wit as he was of tongue. She fell asleep while they were still talking, and woke in the morning to find the man rolled in blankets on the floor at her feet. She scraped away the ashes that banked the coals and brought the fire to life and then went out-of-doors into a light fall of snow. The wind was from the pond, light and steady, the flakes coming down in evenly slanting lines.

When breakfast was done she stayed to help her mother clear

away; but presently she heard an ox bawl and went around to the barn to see what went forward. Jess and Eben had gone off up the river to run a line of traps from which this winter Jess hoped for great things. They would be gone overnight, swinging around Round Pond and up to the west side of Sunnyback, then returning tomorrow down the east side of the river. But David had come to help, and Mima found that the three men — her father and David and this Caleb Howard — had cast one of the oxen on the barn floor and secured him helpless there. The beast's feet were lashed, and David sat on his head, soothing him. Mima laughed to see David try to gentle the ox as she might have quieted a disturbed baby in the night. The cows rolled wide eyes, and one of them moo-ed dolorously; the fowl in their slatted pen clucked and crowed and cackled in a lively excitement at these goings on. The blacksmith knelt to try a shoe on the cast ox's foot and shook his head.

'Too wide,' he muttered. 'Got to bend it some.'

An open fire, he said, would not produce enough heat. He asked for a kettle, and Philip brought an iron pot big enough to contain a fire. He was afraid the heat might warp the pot; but Caleb said: 'No,' with the stubborn finality of a silent man. There was a great stump inside the lean-to, cut off just above the level of the ground, and he levelled this with an axe and set the kettle on top of it.

'Fire on the ground, cold air comes from all sides, so you don't get any heat,' he said. 'This way, the air comes down the sides of the pot, gets warm before it comes up through the fire, makes a better draught and a hotter fire.'

Philip brought a shovelful of coals from the house and dumped them into the kettle and fed them with chips, and while David still gentled the cast ox, the blacksmith took the axe to break up small stuff for a quick hot fire. Mima watched him build the fire to suit. When it was going, he fitted an S-curved iron pipe over the side of the pot, so that one end was on the bottom under the coals. Then he took the shoe and went to measure it against the hoof it must fit. He came back and marked the proper width on the oak sill of the lean-to.

He laid his light sledge ready there and then took the shoe with his tongs and thrust it into the pot. Mima peered into his pack basket made of hide stretched over a frame of bent spruce bows, surprised to see how much it contained; and he brushed her aside and drew out a small bellows and put the end of it into the upper end of that S-shaped iron pipe. The fire had burned down till there were coals. He began to blow air through the pipe. The blast came up through the coals, and a brisk fountain of sparks and flame spouted upward.

Mima's eyes followed these sparks as they rose; and she cried out in alarm. At the same moment her father uttered a great wordless shout and struck the bellows out of Caleb's hand. Mima too had seen the living spark blown up into the hay which hung down through the poles that roofed the lean-to; but before she could move, her father was snatching at it, trying to drag down the wisps that were afire.

The little flames spread like water across a floor, in all directions. Caleb looked stupidly at the damage he had done; and then David came running around the barn, summoned by his father's shout of dismay. He lent a hand for a moment, and Mima too; and their voices were clamorous and shouting. The blacksmith stood by, paralyzed by this emergency. Their efforts were hopeless. Already the fire was burrowing upward into the dry hay. The poles on which it rested were loose, laid at a moderate pitch, their inner ends which rested against the barn notched over a ridged log which supported them. David was the first to give over this fruitless plucking at the burning hay. He heaved upward on one of the poles, his shoulders buckling under that tremendous burden, and wrenched free its inner end and pulled it out of its place. Using it as a lever he began to try to pry the mass of burning hay away from the side of the barn. Philip helped, and Caleb Howard woke to a ponderous activity. The lean-to was some twenty feet long.

They succeeded in moving the hay at one end of it, heaving and sliding it till it toppled off the poles on the ground, while Mima began to throw snow on it, scooping it up with her hands, to try to drown or to smother the fire.

Then she heard her mother scream, and turned and saw Mrs. Robbins and Phil and Sue at the corner of the barn, calling for help. She ran past them to the barn door and looked in. The hay in the barn was afire. Flames had come through the cracks in the boarded walls and touched it off. Mrs. Robbins ran to catch her husband's arm and drag him away from his hopeless labors in the lean-to, to the more immediate necessity of saving the animals. Mima tried to free the cast ox, but he kicked her in his struggles, bruised her arm. The fowl were in a flurry, the animals bellowing, the three sows squealing in their pen. Stooping over — for already the upper part of the barn was a web of smoke and flame — she ran back to jerk open the door of the pigpen; and the sows bolted past her, one of them brushing her legs aside so that she fell. Flames curled down around the slatted pen where the fowl were housed, and when she tried to free them, the flames wreathed her hands and arms and drove her back.

Her father was between her and the door, wrenching loose the staves that held the cows. She helped him, helped drag one cow and then another over the cast ox to safety. David was busy with the stalled cattle, freeing them, clubbing them out of the stalls. They came at last with a rush through the smoke. She saw her father with an axe chopping free the ropes which bound the cast ox, and flames ran like mice along the hay that littered the barn floor, and a gout of burning hay fell off the east mow on the animal's rump. She saw little flames spread like ripples on a pool across the beast's flank, and she tried to beat out the fire with her hands, and then as the ropes let go the ox scrambled to its feet and, still hobbled, bounded like a rabbit over the doorsill to the open air, and tripped and fell and got up bawling and galloped on.

Philip turned to help David. The inside of the barn was a cave of fire. Mrs. Robbins had disappeared, and Mima ran to the house and met her mother at the door; and her mother cried: 'Help, quick, Mima!' Mima saw that the house, too, was afire. Either some spark from the barn, or some eccentricity of draught when the door was left open, sweeping flames that way, had set fire to the moss chinking between the logs at one end of the fireplace. Mima saw little flames in the narrow cracks between the logs. She looked for water, but the kettles were empty. Then Mrs. Robbins came with a rag on the end of a stick, the rag wetted with snow, and began to poke it between the logs. Mima ran to attack these flames from the outside, tearing strips off her petticoats, swabbing them in snow, pushing them into the cracks with a stick. Over her shoulder she saw that the barn now was all afire, flames breaking through the snow on the roof and spouting high. The barn was gone.

They damped out the flames between the logs. Over by the barn the three men were heaping snow on the hay off the lean-to roof, trying to save some of it. They worked in a desperate haste, and Mima thought David was a giant. Snow flew from his shovel in a steady stream, seemingly without pause. The burning hay disappeared in steam and then beneath a mound of snow before the heat of the burning barn drove them back.

Susie was crying. Mima took the little girl in her arms. 'Don't cry, Susie,' she whispered. She tried to laugh. 'Such big tears! If I could throw them on the fire it would go out splash!' Susie giggled through her tears. Mrs. Robbins beside them said hopelessly:

'I knew the barn was gone, first look. All we had to eat was in it. We'll starve this winter, Mima.'

Mima moved to reassure her, but before Mima could speak, her father came toward them. He was black and grimed, and his sleeve was charred away, and his arm was bright where live flame had touched him. He faced his wife almost shamedly.

'There goes all our corn and rye. We're licked, Ma,' he said. 'We're done!'

She put her arm around him, forgetting her own despair of a moment ago, since now he needed her. 'No **and** we're not,' she said stoutly. 'We'll do fine.'

9

THE barn burned on a Friday, with a rising rush of fury that at first drove them to a distance and at last charred the log walls of the house so that they needed to be wetted with snow to keep them from bursting into flame. Mima and her father and David and Caleb Howard all had burns that needed tending. Mrs. Robbins rubbed them with melted moose tallow to deaden the pain. The shelterless cattle bellowed hopelessly, trudging through deep snow. Except for the fowl, the stock had all come out alive; but Philip said the seared ox would doubtless die. 'He was burned half over,' he reminded them. They could not catch the beast. It hobbled off in awkward bounds, its forefeet still fast together, when they came near. While the burning barn, now a mass of embers, still gave up some flames, Rich arrived. At his advice, David shot the ox, as much to save it pain as for any other reason, and they butchered it that day.

Of the grain stored in the barn, Philip Robbins had saved one bushel of rye which happened to be sacked and ready to his hand. The rest was gone. But there were some potatoes in the cellar under the house, and turnips and cabbages in the pit. Food was not an immediate problem.

The immediate problem was the animals. They could not without shelter endure the winter's rigors; and they must be fed. Saturday morning Philip uncovered that small mound of hay off the lean-to which had been saved by heaping snow upon it; and the cattle came to it but would not eat, lowing mournfully. Philip thought the taste of smoke repelled them.

He and David put up that morning a shelter for them; a hurriedly constructed lean-to made by securing a ridgepole between two standing trees and leaning poles against it. They thatched it with spruce boughs, and banked boughs across the end; they shovelled out the snow inside and piled it against the base of the poles and watered it so that it would freeze and form a wind-tight wall. By noon they had something that would serve till better could be done.

But there was no feed for the hungry animals, and their complaints were monotonous and persisting. Jess and Eben came home early that afternoon with their pelts; an otter, a beaver from Round Pond, a few mink, and a sable. Philip discussed with them what must now be done. 'We'll have to go tomorrow, fetch a load of hay from Round Pond meadows,' he said. 'The beasts have to be fed.'

Jess said doubtfully: 'I dunno as the ice will hold, Pa. There's some black spots on the snow nigh the river.'

His father repeated doggedly: 'We've got to, Jess. The beasts have to be fed. I wish I'd cut more up there. There ain't but the one stack.'

'Guess't they'll have to eat browse the way a moose does,' Jess said ruefully. 'Nothing else for it, Pa.'

But Mrs. Robbins said strongly: 'You hush up, Jess. There's always some way. We'll manage, just you see.' She added, almost wistfully: 'But Pa, tomorrow's Sunday. I was thinking — there's no church to go to, and mostly so far Sunday's just been a day for visiting, since we came. I've missed it some. Say we all get together and have a kind of church meeting. It'd please me.'

Philip came to where she stood, put his arm around her. 'That's settled, then. We will.' He added with a wry grin: 'But the better the day, the better the deed. I figger we'll go first and haul home some hay for the critters. I can get into a more churchy frame of mind if they've got their bellies full. Their bawling kind of bothers me.'

She agreed to that, and Eben went down the pond to bid David and Eben come next day for dinner and for the meeting afterward. The butchered ox gave them a store of meat to make a feast for once; and Mrs. Robbins said: 'Tell them we'll make a time of it, Pa. I always say, when things are hard is the time to keep your head the highest.'

Mima went with Eben, tramping through the snow. She had a curious need for Rich, a feeling that to be with him would make her strong. There was no evasion in her. She knew well enough just how bitter this disaster must be in its consequences. They could feed themselves somehow, but the cattle were another matter. They had cut this summer the hummocky hay on the meadow north of Seven-Tree Pond and rafted home as much of it as they were likely for a while to need, mowing it in the big barn or stacking it on top of the lean-to. There was one big stack left in the meadow, and there was another on the meadows at Round Pond; but these would not feed the animals through the winter. Some other supply must be found. When she and Eben talked to Rich, she found him as ready as she was to face their situation realistically. Bet and Eben were more inclined to a vain optimism; but Rich, speaking slowly as he did when he spoke at all, said:

'We can't feed the cattle through. I aim to see Boggs, see if he can take some of 'em. If he can't, the thing to do is butcher some and keep just what we can feed.'

Bet urged: 'There's plenty of hay on Round Pond meadows you men didn't cut.'

'It's down and snowed down,' Rich reminded her. 'If there don't come too much snow, we can maybe turn the oxen in there, let them dig it up and eat it. But somebody would have to watch to keep the wolves off 'em — and the cows have to be here.' He and David had each a yoke of oxen — though one of Dave's had now been butchered to put it out of pain — and there were between them four fresh cows and two dry ones, besides a yearling heifer and a three-months-old heifer calf. 'If Boggs can't take 'em, best thing is butcher them we can't feed, or they'll all starve.'

He had not, as it proved, to go down to Warren to see Sam Boggs, for the man himself appeared at dusk at Philip's house, homeward bound from a hunt up the river. He stayed for supper and the night, telling tales of other barns that had burned.

'Queerest one ever I heard of,' he said, 'a woman over't Broad Bay, Mis' Himmel her name was, went to work one day to set a goose on some eggs, and she took some ashes to warm the nest. There was too much fire in the ashes and the nest caught and then the barn went!' He threw up his hands, in an expressive gesture; and Mrs. Robbins, watching her husband, fighting to distract him, said:

'Well, Pa, you mind Sol Millett, down home?' She told Sam Boggs: 'Sol had a cow come down with the horn distemper, so he set out to smoke its head. He put some live coals in a kettle, and some rags and old shoes on top of them. Smoke was so bad he couldn't stand it, so he went outside to get some fresh air, and the cow kicked the kettle over or something. Barn caught and burned right down, and Sol still a-coughing from the smoke.'

Sam said cheerfully: 'Well, that goose of Mis' Himmel's never would set from that day on. It got all the setting scared out of it when that nest caught fire. Guess it figured it was too hot in the seat to do anything to an egg but roast it.'

Philip reflected: 'Sol had four oxen and eight cows and four three-year-olds and two horses in his barn. He lost them all.

We all pitched in and built him a new barn.' He added: 'But that was in the summer time.'

'There's been barns struck by lightning, too, plenty of 'em,' Sam commented. 'I tell you, a barn's no place for a fire. I won't even take a lanthorn into mine. I milk by daylight, or else by the feel. No sir, it ain't nowise safe nor sensible to mix fire and hay.'

It was Mima who put to him the question she and Rich had discussed that afternoon, whether he could take any of their cattle to board for the winter. But he could not. 'My barns are full, for one thing,' he said regretfully. 'What with cattle and sheep and pigs. And I didn't make any too much hay, and I've bought three yoke of oxen this last month from folks that was moving back to the westward.' He said frankly: 'I'd advise you to butcher what you can eat, as fast as you can eat them. That will make that much more hay for the others and a better chance to bring them through.'

Philip did not speak; but Mima, watching his set face in the firelight, thought her father would not readily take this advice. If the beasts could be saved, they would be.

*   *   *   *   *

Sam Boggs stayed the night, but he left immediately after breakfast in the morning; and Jess and his father and Eben set out for Round Pond to get a pungload of hay. Mima went with them. The weather had turned bitter cold; the oxen hauling the pung moved in a cloud of steam. Philip Robbins walked beside them, driving them; the others followed behind. No wind had blown to drift the snow. It lay in an even blanket everywhere, or hung suspended in white clots on the boughs above them and sometimes fell in masses, or in thin streams sifted down. The sun was shining and there was a dazzling whiteness when it struck the snow. The day was all one shining glory, and even among the pines the glare was sometimes so bright it blinded them.

There were deep marshy bays on either side of the river, so that except at the bends where the stream touched hard ground they were not near it; but in the shallow narrows where Jess had dropped a pine to make a bridge, Mima saw a dark spot, and the snow was discolored around it where water had overflowed on the ice. She pointed this out to Jess, and he nodded.

'Ice hasn't made good where there's any current,' he said. 'But it's all right on the pond.'

Philip had this fact in mind; so when they came to the pond, he turned the oxen along the shore away from the river, clearing a path for them with his axe when it was necessary so to do, and he went halfway to the rocky little island before he swung them out on the surface of the pond. Now and then as they crossed, the ice cracked beneath them; but it held, and immunity lulled their fears.

They reached the meadows and came to the hay stacked there months before. They threw down a pile for the oxen to eat while they loaded the pung. Philip made the load, the others pitching on, Mima doing her full share; and in a short time they had as much aboard as Philip thought it safe to take at one time. They started home.

On that homeward journey, Mima and Eben lagged behind. Jess walked beside the pung, Philip by the oxen's heads. Eben had questions, misgivings.

'We're bad off, ain't we, Mima?'

She said honestly: 'Pretty bad, Eb, but we'll do. The trouble will be to bring the stock through the winter. We can manage for ourselves. You and Jess can shoot meat for us; and we can pack in corn from down-river, some.'

'They're short down-river, too,' he reminded her. 'They didn't make as good a crop as we did; and they'll need to carry over for seed. It'll be tight nipping, Mima.' He said in a boy's hot rage: 'The Tories down-river stopping the coasters have made it hard to get things from the westward.'

'We'll get along,' she insisted. The pung, loaded high, was a hundred yards ahead of them, the oxen plodding on. She smiled and said: 'We might be thinned down some, come spring; but we'll do the best we know how, Eb. That's all anybody can do; and if you do it, you have the fun of doing it — and nothing to be sorry for after, any way it comes.'

'I'd like to get a lick at them Tories,' Eben said hotly. 'I will some day!'

She laughed affectionately. 'I bet if they could hear you, they'd be scared.'

'They better be!' He said: 'Mima, Ma's great, isn't she. You watch her when Pa isn't looking and she's as scared as I am; but she don't let him see.'

'She's fine!' Mima touched his arm. 'Don't be worrying too far ahead, Eb. Take it a day at a time. No use worrying about March till we get December out of the way.'

Then suddenly her hand tightened on his arm; and her breath caught in a sharp dismay. He too had seen the pung ahead of them, halfway to the further shore, settle slowly sidewise and then tip forward. They heard their father shout, and saw Jess leap to help him; and they began to run to come up to the pung. What happened, happened slowly; yet with an inescapable precision and finality. Under the loaded pung, the ice settled, then gave way. Its front end went down; the ice broke under the hind feet of the oxen, and they scrabbled for footing, and Philip Robbins jumped to their heads, tugging vainly at the yoke to help them. Their clawing forefeet took the whole burden of their weight, their hindquarters already in the water. The ice let go, and a pan of it tipped, and Philip Robbins fell into the water between them, between their heads, facing them, clinging to the yoke. The pung slid forward almost on top of them, pressing their hindquarters under, pressing them down; and Philip fought free and caught the edge of the unbroken ice with snow a foot deep on top of it and tried to climb out. When Mima and Eben came near, Jess was on his stomach, reaching out with a pitchfork to give his father a handhold; and the oxen, dumbly struggling, were being pressed inexorably down.

Mima started toward her father to help him; but he shouted: 'Stay back!' She obeyed him. Eben crawled forward to hold Jess by the feet; and she pinned Eben's feet between her knees, holding his ankles with her hands. Philip gripped the pitchfork and hauled himself free. He crawled past Jess, dripping icy water, his lips already blue with cold. At the same time he gave orders.

'Scatter,' he said. 'Don't stay together. You might all break through. Get away from the pung. The oxen are gone.' He stood up, and the three obeyed him, separating, standing a rod or two apart, watching the floundering beasts. Then he said: 'No use watching. Nothing we can do.' He said grimly: 'Well, there's two we won't have to butcher, anyway. I'll hurry home, get warm.'

He had lost his snowshoes in the water, and Eben said: 'Take mine, Pa.' He kicked them loose, and Philip stooped and put them on. Then with no backward look he went clacking off at a shuffling trot across the snow.

Jess watched the drowning oxen with brimming eyes. 'Wish't I had a gun, Eb,' he said. 'Pore critters.'

Eben said: 'I don't want to look.' He turned away, began to plod through the knee-deep snow toward home. Mima and Jess came behind him. When from the shore they looked back, the pung had slid forward till only its rear end was supported by the ice. The fore end was in the water. Jess said: 'It's pushed them under by now.'

* * * * *

Philip Robbins seemed for an hour crushed by this new catastrophe. When he came home with chattering teeth, Mrs. Robbins made him drink off a huge measure of rum; she saw him in dry clothes and warm by the fire, where a huge cut of beef was spitted and roasting above a dripping-pan; she tried in every way to win him back to strength again.

But he was not easily heartened. He said hopelessly: 'It's

trouble on trouble. I had a good, well-stocked farm here day before yesterday morning. Now look at us!'

'We could be a sight worse off,' Mrs. Robbins reminded him. 'We might some of us have been hurt worse than a few blisters, for one thing. Or the house might have gone, too.' And she urged: 'We'll get along, Pa. We won't have much, but we can make it do; and what we can't have, we'll do without.'

The others came from down the pond and heard the news; but the great noonday meal cheered them. The one room was crowded, the table too small to accommodate them all; but the children sat contentedly on the floor, Susie and Philip tending them. They all ate till they were gorged, Mrs. Robbins moving busily to and fro, her urgings equally divided between insisting that they have some more and that they clean their plate. 'We've a whole ox to eat,' she reminded them, 'and the sooner the quicker. It might come off warm so the meat won't keep. Dave, it's your ox, but I guess we'll all have to share together now.'

Rich said: 'I'll butcher mine as soon as we can use the meat.'

But Philip spoke strongly. 'No, Rich,' he said. 'I dunno how we'll do it, but we'll feed them through.'

After dinner, when things were cleared away, Mrs. Robbins produced her Bible. 'Now Pa,' she said gently, 'you play minister.'

'Dunno as I can,' he demurred.

'You'll be a sight better at it than some I've heard,' she assured him.

He took the Bible, opening it, turning the leaves slowly. 'Ought to be something here to fit us,' he said, half to himself. 'In the Old Testament, I guess. I always did think there was more insides to the Old Testament. You can get your teeth into it.' He grinned. 'It's got more hell fire and brimstone to it,' he declared. 'To read it, you'd think that if a man didn't behave, he was going to get his come uppance and no mistake about it. My experience is, he does, too. This here business of having your good time first and then repenting yourself out of trouble afterward always looked to me like a pup that wets the floor and knows he's going to get a licking for it and lays on the floor with his belly up, repenting no end. But after the licking, he goes and piddles on the floor again.' He looked at Mrs. Robbins. 'I've done some repenting in my time, Ma,' he said. 'Most generally you saw to it that I did. Usually it'd be after I'd had too much rum the night before.'

His eyes were on the leaves he turned, and he said in a different tone: 'But there's other things besides death and damnation in the Old Testament. There's a pile of sweetness and comfort. Listen here.'

He read slowly: ' "The Lord is my shepherd, I shall not want." ' His eyes went from one to the other, quizzically. 'I dunno as that's so,' he said. 'Maybe we'll have thin pickings later, want more'n we've got; but I guess we've had all we want today.' He read on, in a voice deep and sonorous as the words laid their spell upon him — and upon them all:

' "He maketh me to lie down in green pastures. He leadeth me beside the still waters." ' He looked at them as though about to speak, but then continued: ' "He restoreth my soul. He guideth me in the paths of righteousness for his name's sake. Yea, though I walk through the valley of the shadow of death, I will fear no evil; for Thou art with me. Thy rod and Thy staff, they comfort me. Thou preparest a table before me in the presence of mine enemies. Thou anointest my head with oil. My cup runneth over." ' He hesitated, finished then, in calm, sure tones: ' "Surely goodness and mercy shall follow me all the days of my life, and I will dwell in the house of the Lord for ever." '

He finished and closed the Book, and after a moment he said quietly: 'Well, there's a good deal there that a man can hitch to. It fits us, some ways, too. We've come up here into a green pasture. It's mostly woods, only where we've cut them off; but there's pastures, too; Round Pond meadows and places like that, enough to feed a pile of critters if we'd cut all the hay and stacked it. If we didn't, I guess it's our own fault.' His face contorted in a spasm of remembered pain. 'Only I never thought the barn might burn.'

They waited, listening quietly; and he said, after a moment: 'Green pastures and still waters. Well, there's still waters out there under the ice. I've got a good yoke of oxen drowned in them still waters; but I'd ought to have had more sense. They've got me to blame. Anyway, the still waters are there under the ice now; but the ice won't always be there. We'll see the pond sparkling and dancing in the sun again, come spring.

'And this is a good place for restoring the soul, too. It's restored mine some a'ready. The worst thing I know to upset a man's soul is worrying about somebody else's doings. Before we came here, I used to get as haired up as anybody about the King, and the soldiers, and Tories and Doc Taylor and the rest of the mean, low-down cusses in the world.

'But up here they don't bother me. I don't even think about them one Sunday to the next. I can set here with you all, with Ma and our own children, and with you, Bess, that married our Dave and made a good wife to him, and with you, Rich, that married our Bet and has took good care of her, and with your young ones, and I feel pretty good, just watching you all going about your business, and knowing you're mine.

'Or I can go off by myself with nothing but the woods for company, and the ground under me, and the river sliding sleepy by, and that's good too. A man needs to know how to be good company for himself. Then he won't ever be lonesome.

'Restoreth my soul? Well, I don't know what a soul is, but I have an idea maybe your soul's what you've learned yourself to like to do. You get to liking to do some things; and you do them, but you don't get no satisfaction, nor no peace out of it. Or you get to liking to do other things, and every time you do them it leaves you as happy and contented as a cow chewing her cud. I judge if you like to do the things that leave you feeling good, your soul's in good shape, don't need restoring.

'I've worked hard up here, and liked it. I didn't always feel that way about work. Maybe that means that being here, and the woods, and the pond, and the busy summers and the long winters and the way spring comes every year have restored my soul.' He looked at the Bible in his hand. 'This says the Lord does that job; but maybe God and the world He made are the same thing. Maybe when you clear a field and bring it to bearing you're taking care of Him, the way Bet and Bess are, when they clean up their young ones.'

He looked at Mrs. Robbins, smiling. 'There's one thing you young ones might not get straight, out of what I read. There's a lot about being led to a nice piece of country to live in, and being shown good smooth roads to travel on, and having somebody look out for you and cut a walking stick for you, and set the table for you to eat. Well, that's what Ma's done for me for a good many years. Of course she has her ornery spells, but they just make me appreciate her that much more when she gets over them. I don't mean to be irrev'rent, but I always think she comes as near being God as I'd want to live with regular. I guess He wouldn't mind my saying so. Maybe God and love are the same thing. I love Ma. There's nothing equals a good wife — or a good husband.' His eyes twinkled. 'But I guess a good husband ain't so easy come by.'

Mima saw her mother's eyes stream with happy tears. Her own were full. Philip lifted the Bible again. 'And it talks about His anointing your head with oil,' he remembered. 'B'ar's grease is the same thing, maybe. I've always found it'd serve my turn.

'But I've got one complaint to make about this. It don't say a word about giving you a job of work to do. Me, I wouldn't give a damn for a world with no chance in it to work up a good lather of sweat every day. I like work. I don't want to be tended hand and foot. I want to do for myself — to take care of myself and my people.'

His eyes swept them all. 'You're my people,' he said. 'There's some of my blood in all but two of you, and them two are mine too, because I love them like my own. A man that loves a thing, he owns it. It's his. Nobody can take it away from him — any more than anybody can ever take this piece of land here away from me. A hundred years from now, or a thousand, there'll still be our sweat in this land. It'll always be ours, because we're the first ever loved it.'

He said, after a moment, apologetically: 'Well, I didn't aim to talk you deef and blind. That's all.' He hesitated. 'Only maybe I ought to try to pray.' He said, his eyes closing: 'Lord, we've got ourselves into a mess here. We'll work out of it the best we know how. Help us all You can. I guess with Your help we'll still be here, ready to go on, come spring.'

*　*　*　*　*

They faced the winter after that day steadily enough. They back-packed hay from Round Pond to try to keep the remaining cattle alive while another pung could be built; but just before the turn of the year one of the cows died after gorging on hemlock browse, and the others were losing flesh every day. In January, Philip and David went down-river to see if it was possible to buy corn. The snow was too deep for hand sleds; so they planned to pack home what they could get.

They found there was none to be bought; but Porterfield of Thomaston gave them a bushel. They backed it to Lermond's mills at Oyster River to be ground; then carried it home. They brought news that Mason Wheaton had bought from Doctor Taylor a tract along the northern bound of Philip's land, and touching the river.

'He'll make a good neighbor,' Philip told Mrs. Robbins. 'He's as good a man as there is in Thomaston. He was the main one in getting the town incorporated, called the first town meeting, was elected selectman. Yes sir, if he moves up here — he says he will, too — it will make the town.'

Mrs. Robbins said: 'Sho, Pa! We can make this town our-selves, without no help from him nor anybody.'

'Certain,' he agreed. 'All the same, I'm glad to have him for a neighbor.' He added: 'And I'm glad we could get this corn. There's none to buy for love nor money; but Porterfield give me this to help us get along.'

The cornmeal, doled out a little at a time, was made to last through January and into February. Before it was gone, one of Rich's oxen had died, and the others were gaunt from hunger. Philip and his sons were almost equally gaunt from laboring to find forage for the beasts; but Philip would not consent that any be butchered. There was meat enough without that. Their store of powder began to run low, but it could be hus-banded. Jess and Eben snared many rabbits, and Jess even contrived to snare a moose in the cedar swamp up the brook beyond Round Pond. When he and Eben found the animal — a young cow — caught by one forefoot and lifted half off the ground by the spring of the birch to which the snare was fast, they whooped with exultation; but the moose had still one foreleg free, and to approach it was to risk a deadly stroke. Jess felled a great oak tree in such a way that its spreading branches crushed the moose and held her fast; then he came close enough to stun her with his axe and so to slit her throat. After that it was a weary business to free the carcass from the felled oak and drag it out; but he and Eben in the end came triumphant home.

But meat alone was not enough; and of other things there was too little. Their store of potatoes dwindled. Some must be saved for seed; and by mid-February they were in sight of the end of their supply. Philip went again to Warren, and to Thomaston, to try to buy grain, but the Tories and the refugees, harrying the coast, had almost cut off imports; and there were more people in the towns than the towns could feed. He came home empty-handed.

By March, counting the ox which had been burned, and the two which had drowned, they had lost ten head of cattle, and the three families were reduced to something like starvation. The March hunts failed when rain came to shrink the drifts and clear the ground of snow so that the moose escaped from the yards. David and the Comings household, since they had young children that must be fed, were given more than a proportionate share of what grain was still available; but before relief came, David and Bess and the three children lived for two weeks on a few cupfuls of rye meal cooked in maple sap, salted with brine. When the children cried with hunger, Bess gave them birch buds to chew.

The alewives ran and they went to Warren to dip them at the fall, and Philip was able late in April to buy a hogshead of corn at twenty-five dollars the bushel. What need not be saved for seed they ate, pounding it in the old stump that served as mortar, saving every crumb. When it was gone, hunger returned to oppress them. Dave was so put to it that after he had planted his potatoes he dug them up again and trimmed away all but the seed eyes to eat.

But with the first flood of spring the danger was over. The sap ran in the maples, and they were busy with the boiling; and the snow had scarce gone before buds began to swell. They felt with the first taste of green things a flood of new life in themselves.

Then, on the fifteenth of May, Joel came.

10

EBEN brought the news of Joel's imminent arrival. He had gone to dip alewives at the falls at Warren, and he returned at dusk, paddling up the pond in a driving rain. He hallooed as he approached the landing, and Jake went down to help handle the fish he brought. Rain kept the others in the house, and Mima was by the hearth mending the fire when she heard Eben's voice as he approached.

"'Bijah Hawes is back, Pa,' he told his father in the doorway there. 'I brought him as far as his place. And the three that bought from you up at Round Pond; 'Bijah's brother and Joel Adams and that other man, they've come too.'

Mima, on one knee, facing the fire, did not move. There was a stick in her hands. She laid it on the embers, and then she was still, her back turned to them all. Joel was come! A year ago, when the ice went out and spring flowed across the land, she had thought he might return; her heart had leaped every time she saw a float coming up the pond. But this year, their own anxieties had driven thoughts of him out of her mind. They were so near starvation, hungry all the time, gathering fiddle-

heads and birch buds and every green thing to eat, that she
had no thoughts left for him. Now Eben's word ran through her
like a flame.

Behind her she heard her mother say urgently: 'Get them wet
clothes off of you, Eben, before you catch your death. Come by
the fire.'

Mima stood up and moved aside as he obeyed. The leaping
flames made shadows dance around them, made their shadows
more gigantic along the walls. Rain was driving in, so Mrs.
Robbins bade Philip close the door. Mima stood with her back
against the wall, her hands behind her, watching Eben as he
stripped to the waist, pulled on a dry shirt, changed his lower
garments. His shoulders gleamed in the firelight, and he talked,
answering their questions, talking without prompting. Her
father asked where the three were, and he said:

'At McIntyre's. They came that far last night, but they're
waiting till the rain's over. I went over there, and they were
drinking rum and singing songs.' He chuckled. 'Joel Adams
knows a lot of songs, army songs I guess; and he had the girl
that works there on his knee. The one named Fanny. He'd
tickle her in the short ribs and she'd squeal and slap at him;
but I guess she liked it!'

He was grinning at his own words, and Mrs. Robbins made a
scornful sound. Mima watched him, not moving, waiting for
every word. Philip asked another question, and Eben said:

'Why, they came from the westward in Colonel Wheaton's
sloop, dodging alongshore and in behind islands all the way.
They almost got caught down Falmouth way. A shaving mill
chased them to cut them off, but they just made it past the
point of Gebeag Island and caught the wind and got away.
They were so close the Tories shot at them!' He cried hotly:
'I'd like to get a shot at an old Tory sometime.'

Mrs. Robbins told him sharply: 'Hush your talk, Eben.
You're still wet behind the ears, and talking about shooting
men!'

'I'm eighteen, Ma!'

'There! I don't care if you're eighty-eight, you're too young to talk about fighting and all.'

'Well anyway,' he said, 'they said the war's about over with.'

His father shook his head forebodingly. 'Joel Adams said the same after they took Burgoyne, and that's a year ago last fall!'

'Well, he says the English are looking for an excuse to stop fighting now,' Eben insisted. 'After Ben Franklin got France to help us, the King sent commissioners with word we could have everything we wanted except independence.' His eyes shone. 'And the Congress told them we didn't have to ask the King's leave for anything and sent them home again.'

Philip Robbins said grimly: 'That's big talk, but up here we have to ask leave to get enough to eat! We've near starved here this winter, and we're likely to again. If the refugee pirates get any thicker alongshore, we'll be thin as picked chickens, come another spring.'

'Well anyway,' Eben repeated, 'they all think the fighting's about over. Howe had to move out of Philadelphia. They've had to get out of every place only New York and Newport, and Joel Adams said we'd have taken Newport last summer only a storm damaged some of the French ships. Joel was under General John Hancock there!'

Mima, standing, listening, watching Eben's bright face, thought she loved him best among her brothers. He was young and bold and gay; yet there was in him too a thoughtful tenderness, something as gentle as a woman. When he was for a moment silent now she asked a question in her turn.

'Is Joel Adams the same? Did he take any hurt in the war?'

Her mother looked at her shrewdly, and Eben said: 'He looks fine!' Then he said quickly: 'That girl on his knee, Mima, she just — she was just sort of setting there while he talked. They were all laughing and talking and singing and drinking rum; and there were two or three girls from the kitchen came in, and they were joking with them, that's all.'

She nodded, understanding his desire to reassure her, making no attempt to conceal the fact that she had longed for Joel's coming 'Did he want to know how we'd wintered?' she asked.

Eben nodded. 'Yes, I told him about the barn and all.' He spoke to his father. 'Joel says they can let us have a barrel of meal and we can pay it back when we make our crop.'

'I'll buy it off him.'

'I said you would,' Eben agreed. 'But he laughed and said he hadn't seen any money for two years that would buy anything he had to sell. But he'll take pay next fall in kind.'

They sat long in talk that night, each feeling that the return of Joel and the others meant something new in their lives. The rain was still drumming on the roof when they went to bed, and dawn was dull and overcast; but before the sun was an hour high, it had swept the clouds from the sky and set the drenched land steaming. The day was so hot that Mima thought you could almost see the grass grow. Already the cattle that had survived the winter were able to find a little new green here and there, and crop it greedily. Presently their ribbed flanks would begin to fill.

Since the rain had stopped, Joel would surely come today. Between her morning's tasks and when she could, Mima went to the door to look down the pond for a first glimpse of the newcomers; but in the end she heard them before she saw them. She heard the sound of voices far away, and realized that they were singing, shouting words she could not distinguish in great roaring voices. The sound came to her first as an echo flung back by the eastern shore of the pond; then as the oncoming barge passed David's point she heard it more directly, and she could see them through the fringe of trees along the water. She went down to the landing to watch their approach, her arms folded tight across her bosom, and Jess and her father, and then her mother and Eben and the younger children, came to join her. The barge, deep-laden, glided toward the landing here. Joel was steering, Matt Hawes and Jason Ware pulling at the

oars. Joel cried: 'Let her sli-i-de!' The oars trailed, and the
barge nosed lightly ashore, and Joel stood up and he called:

'Howdy, neighbors! Well, friend Robbins, we were a long
time coming — but we're here to stay!'

Mima felt her heart pound at that word. To stay! The three
young men stepped ashore, shaking hands all around. Joel
turned first to Mrs. Robbins, gave her a smacking kiss.

'You! Leave go of me!' she protested.

'We'll start right,' he told her; while she smiled and bridled
happily. 'See here, I can't be calling you Dame, or Marm.
What do they call you — your first name . . .'

'Mima,' she said, laughing at his laughter. 'Same as Mima's.'

'Ho!' His eyes were twinkling. 'Well, I'll call you Aunt
Mima.' He added flatteringly: 'That's the only way a man
could tell the two of you apart, no matter how close he looked.
You're like as peas.'

He turned to Mima, shook her hand, looked at her more
gravely. 'You've thinned down,' he said. She nodded, and
Mrs. Robbins said briskly:

'I notice you don't treat us both the same, for all your soft
soap about not telling us apart!'

'I'd not want to spoil the taste I had from you by another
so soon on top of it,' he retorted; and they all laughed. He
picked up Susie, a great girl of eleven now, and tossed her high,
and caught her coming down. 'One from the kinchen!' he
cried, and kissed Susie too. 'You're as cute a sparrow as I'd
want to see!'

Susie giggled with pleasure and straightened her petticoats
demurely. Matt and Jason made their greetings, and Joel said:
'Well, I'm suited to be here, after all the time.' He filled his
lungs elaborately, breathing deep. 'A man could live on that
air if he had to.' Philip Robbins grunted; and Joel said: 'That
puts me in mind. The boy here ——' He looked at Eben, grinning in a friendly way. 'He tells me you've been living on air
this winter gone — or the next thing to it.'

'Aye, we've been a bit short since the barn burned.'

Joel scanned their faces, one by one. They were in fact gaunt and drawn fine. He nodded seriously. 'You look peaked,' he agreed, turned to the laden boat. 'We've brought more than we'll need right off,' he said. 'We can let you have some till you've made a crop.' And without asking their agreement, he plucked a barrel off the bow of the boat, rolled it on his knees, swung it expertly to his shoulder. 'Where'll I put it?' he asked. 'You can fill the same barrel and hand it back to us when your corn is ground.'

'Why, we're obliged to you,' Philip agreed. 'I'll show you.' He led the way, and Joel, balancing the barrel on his shoulder, strode after him up the knoll toward the house. The others stayed here where they were, Mrs. Robbins talking to Matt Hawes; and Mima thought proudly that among these three men Joel was the leader, the spokesman for them all. She liked Matt, too. He spoke quietly, yet she felt strength in him and a calm composure. Jason Ware on the other hand appeared almost sullen, he was so quiet. Mrs. Robbins urged them to stay to dinner. Matt said:

'Why, we're obliged to you, marm, but we'll be getting on, I'd think.' Jason stepped into the laden ferry and sat ready at the oars as though anxious to be off and resenting this delay. Joel and Philip came from the house, and Mrs. Robbins repeated her hospitable urgencies; but Joel said:

'Can't, Aunt Mima. We've got to get a roof over our heads come night, and little time enough to do it in. I think there's more rain coming.' He added: 'But we'd be obliged if maybe one of you could come along to show us the lay of the land and help us pick a good place for the house we'll have to have.'

He looked at Mima, and she wished to go; but her father said: 'I can show you the place I'd pick. Jess, come along and give them a hand.'

He and Jess took their own float. Mima and Eben watched the two craft turn up the river toward Round Pond and disappear; and Eben looked at his sister, touched her arm, laughed teasingly.

'You'll have all three of them after you this summer,' he predicted. 'Being the only girl in the place, and no men around's dull doing — but the only girl in half a day's journey of three young bucks just back from soldiering can pick and choose.'

She smiled and hugged him close to her with one arm around his shoulders.

'They'll be working too hard to think of any girl,' she said; added with warm eyes: 'But a girl can be thinking of one of them.'

*   *   *   *   *

Philip Robbins came home in time for dinner; but Jess stayed up at Round Pond to help with the immediate business of building a house. 'It looks like raining again tomorrow,' he commented, 'and they'll need to hurry to get their stuff under cover, sure.'

Mima asked: 'Where are they going to build their house?'

Her father said: 'Why, by that spring you found, the one you showed them. They're going to build on the high ground right handy. Then soon's they get a house built, they aim to fell that stand of big pines between the brook and the pond.' He told Mrs. Robbins in a slow satisfaction: 'I'm glad they've come. We need them. It's time we were getting some people in here if we're ever going to make a town.'

The rain held off a day or two; but on the third day it came again, with a thundershower in the morning, and a great wind churned Seven-Tree Pond into angry whitecaps and bowed tall pines like wands, so that again and again they heard the crashes as trees fell in the forest near. The skies were black till it was like night. Mima thought of the men at Round Pond and wondered what shelter they had. Jess was still with them, and she had wished to go and see how their work progressed; but till now she had not gone further than the nearer shore of Round Pond, where she could hear their axes.

The rain held all that day; and Jason Ware and Matt Hawes came down-river in the afternoon, and touched at Philip's landing. Jason grumbled at the rain and wind. 'Worse ever I see,' he declared. 'Do you have it like this much, up here?'

Mima stood under the shelter of a pine on the bank above them, listening. Philip shook his head. 'We'll get wind, of course, and rain too; but it blew this morning as hard as I want to see it — and the thunder and lightning was the worst I ever see anywhere. It's soaked the ground. We can't plant till it dries some. Where you bound?'

Matt Hawes answered him. 'We want some boards to roof our house,' he said. 'It's raining too hard to use an axe today, so Jason and I thought we'd go get a load. Be back tomorrow.'

'Jess and Adams still up there?'

'Yes; we got some bark slabs, made a shelter. If the rain lets up they'll finish the walls before we get back.'

They rowed away through the pitiless downpour; and it was still raining next afternoon when they returned, with boards loaded crosswise on the barge at bow and stern, and a raft of them in tow behind. They did not land, but Mima and her father spoke them from the bank. They were both wet through, and Jason was dour and silent; but Matt was cheerful enough. 'We'll do fine with these,' he said. 'And it looks like clearing. We'll be wishing we had this rain, by August.'

That night the rain stopped, and next afternoon Jess came home. 'They're fixed for a while,' he said. 'Just a slant roof, and no chimney; but they'll manage for the summer, get a chance to finish it before fall.' He said they were expecting another man. 'Woodward, Nate Woodward, his name is. He's coming from Boston on his own feet, the way 'Bijah did. He's a soldier too; but he hasn't any money to buy land.' He spoke to his father. 'They thought he might work for you.'

'I've more hands than I've got work for them to do, with this rain,' the older man grumbled. 'Setting still and waiting for a chance to get to work always gripes me plenty.'

Jess nodded, and then he grinned. 'They call their house the Royal Mess. They're all in share and share alike, and they'll draw lots for choice of land after they've looked it over. But they aim to work together and live together.'

Mrs. Robbins sniffed scornfully. 'I guess it'll be a royal mess, all right, with three men in it, and no woman to pick up after them.'

'That was Matt's idea, calling it that,' Jess said. 'He's a mighty pleasant man.'

Mima looked at her mother. 'Maybe I could go and sort of clean up for 'em, every so often,' she suggested.

'They'll need somebody; that's certain sure,' Mrs. Robbins assented. She asked Jess: 'What did you think of them?'

'Why, Matt is the cheerfullest,' Jess decided. 'Nothing gets him down. He's the same, rain or shine. Jason's always growling about the rain, or if his axe gets a nick in it or something. Nothing suits him. But he's a worker.' He chuckled. 'Joel and me got along fine,' he said. 'He can tell more tales, men he knew in the army, and wenches and all.' Mrs. Robbins made a scornful sound. 'I guess he's a hand for them,' Jess confessed. 'And you ought to hear him sing, Mima.' He grinned. 'Only most of what he sings ain't fit to hear.'

'He'd ought to be ashamed,' Mrs. Robbins declared. 'Putting a lot of idees in your head.'

'Well, it sounds all right to hear him,' Jess assured her, a little puzzled by his own words. 'He can tell about a girl — doxy, he calls them — and you just have to laugh.' He added hurriedly: 'It ain't always himself he talks about, Mima. There was a man he knew in the army used to steal everything he laid hands on, and he was a great hand with women. Mostly Joel tells stories about him. There was one . . .'

'That's enough out of you,' said Mrs. Robbins sharply. 'Keep his nasty talk to yourself, if you have to listen to it.'

'Well, anybody'd listen,' Jess insisted. 'The way Joel tells it.' He chuckled at his memories.

*　*　*　*　*

Nate Woodward arrived next day, tramping up from Warren in the morning. He proved to be a strapping man, but morose and silent, and when Philip asked his opinion of the region, Woodward said grimly:

'It don't hit me. Too many hemlocks. I never liked 'em.'

'They ain't good for much, for a fact,' the older man agreed. 'Only to burn.'

'I wouldn't burn 'em,' Woodward declared. 'Always a-sparking and a-spitting!' He asked whether Philip needed to hire a hand.

'Can't say as I do,' Robbins admitted. 'And if I did, I'm hard put for cash money to pay with.' He said: 'I'll tell you, though. Your friends have bought up't Round Pond, a mile wide and clear through to the end of my piece at the Waldo-borough line. You clear the land south of theirs, over by the line; clear all you're a mind to, and I'll give you half of what you clear, and as much more, woodland, to boot. That'll make you a farm.'

Woodward said he might. He asked how to find his way to their cabin, and Eben volunteered to take him up in the dug-out. Mima and her father watched them start, and Philip spat and chuckled.

'Hemlocks? He'll never make a hand. Too notional!'

He and his sons were by this time breaking ground. He had bought a fresh yoke of oxen from Sam Boggs; and the rains had given way to warm winds that sucked the moisture out of the earth. Planting would not be delayed as long as Philip had feared. Now when Woodward was gone, he turned away to the waiting tasks; but Mima stayed by the river, watching Eben depart. She wondered whether Joel would send her any message by Eben, wondered whether she dwelt in his thoughts as he in hers. Since his return, since now he was so near, she seemed to herself more alive. She was intensely conscious of his nearness; thought his voice was in the very air. She turned away from the river at last, back to the house, back to the steady tasks that needed doing; but she moved in an automatic fashion, not seeing, not even thinking. She was tremendously conscious of the flood of new life in everything around her; the warm, teeming flood of spring and coming summer, seed-time for the harvest that was to come.

Eben was late returning, and when he did, he had a tale to tell. 'They've got a way of falling trees beats everything,' he said excitedly. 'They'll notch a whole line of 'em, and then touch off the driver, and down they all come. It saves a sight of chopping, too.' And he urged: 'You want to come up and see, Pa?'

'I got enough to do t'home,' his father told him. 'And so've you, Eb. Guess't I know how to fall trees by now. I'd ought to. I've done a plenty.'

'Well, I saw Jason Ware drop twenty-two trees all't once today,' Eben insisted. 'It's a sight to see. You lemme show you!' He brought a handful of chips, stood them on end in the soft ground in a line; then toppled one against the others so that they all went neatly down. 'Like that, Pa,' he urged. 'And they lay good to burn, that way. The tops of each tree help burn up the one they're laying on.'

Mima said: 'It must be a sight, Eb. It would make a man feel like he amounted to something, laying twenty-thirty big trees flat with just one axe stroke at the end.'

'They're working on that stand of big pines between the pond and the brook now,' Eben said. 'Some of 'em three or four feet through. Joel and Matt Hawes have been notching them all day. Where Jason was working, it was in the small stuff; but him and Nathan Woodward went to work with the others after, and Joel Adams told me they'll touch off the drivers tomorrow. There'll be a rucus when them big ones go down that I'd sure admire to see.'

Mrs. Robbins said stoutly: 'Well, I wouldn't! Them great fine trees that'd mast a ship or make lumber enough to build us a fitten house 'stead of this pigsty — all knocked down and burned up. It makes me kind of sick. I always liked trees.'

'Sho, Ma,' Philip urged, 'you can't raise anything without first you clear the land.'

'I know, but it's a pity all the same!'

Mima argued: 'It's kind of beautiful, though, Mother! There's hundreds and thousands of miles of land all to the westward here and nobody in it but Indians; and nothing but trees and trees. But men and women like us will be coming along and cutting off the trees and putting the land to work and making homes on it long after we're dead and gone.' She smiled. 'Maybe some day trees will be scarce and folks will want to save them; but there's more trees than there's any sense to now — and not enough men to fall them.' She said, warm at her own words: 'I aim to go Monday and watch them knock down the big pines.'

* * * * *

Sunday, soon after breakfast, Mima heard voices coming down the river. She went racing through the pines to climb the high knoll above where the river met the pond, and saw Joel and Matt and Jason passing the mouth of the cove below her, in the big barge they had used to bring up their own belongings and then the lumber for their roof. She did not show herself, standing quietly among the great trees till they had passed; but when they emerged from the river into the pond, they hailed the house. She heard Joel's call: 'Hullo-o-o! Robbins!' She stayed where she was while they shouted back and forth, but they did not land. When she returned to the house, her mother said: 'They were taking the ferry back down river, and Matt Hawes was going to hear Mr. Urquhart preach. It's safe to say Joel Adams won't waste any time in church!'

Mima thought that they would walk back that afternoon, and she expected them, but they did not appear. At dark she spoke of them, and Jess said: 'If they were walking, they'd cut across

through the woods.' This was true. Seven-Tree Pond ran
north and south; but Round Pond was directly west of its
northern end, the river between them running southeasterly.
From Rich Comings' house the shortest way was to cut across
south of the hill behind Philip's and so come to the southern
end of Round Pond and skirt its shores. Mima decided they
must have gone that way.

In the night, rain began again to fall; and it held most of
Monday, so she did not carry out her plan to go up and watch
them felling trees until the following morning. Susie wished to
go with her. The sky now was cloudless, the sun warm; and
there was new green everywhere. When Mima and Sue went
down to the landing where the dugouts were pulled up, she
could see her father and her brothers hard at work in the cleared
lands that extended southward along the shore, hurrying to
bring the fields to bearing.

To Mima the world seemed in order. The seeds they planted
now would come to life in earth's warm bosom; the first shoots
would appear; the crops would come to another harvest. She
and Susie paddled up the river, and Susie chattered happily,
but Mima said little. It was as though she saw the river for the
first time: the quicker current as she entered its mouth and
again when they passed under the pine Jess had felled for a
bridge; the two rocks facing each other above, a ledge coming
down into the water on the south bank, a cone-shaped boulder
all in the water on the north side; the suddenly opening vista
when only the swampy point lay between them and the pond.
She saw a fresh run salmon in the pool below the narrows, and
a swirl in the water as another fish changed his position as they
passed. She caught the flash and drum of wings in the thicket
as a partridge rose, and her heart leaped to the scutter of ducks
surprised in the edge of the grass. She saw the widening ripples
where a musquash swam; and a flash of red among the hardwoods where the partridge had risen might have been a fox.
She was intensely conscious of life all around her renewing

itself; and the world was fine and suitable. Even the relentless little black flies could not spoil all her pleasure in the day. Use had accustomed her to their attacks; she and the others had acquired some immunity to their poison. Certainly the occasional gesture of brushing them away was automatic, almost perfunctory.

The dugout emerged into Round Pond, and followed the low, reedy northern shore along the meadows. Mima still retained a lively fear of the water. Too often for her peace of mind they heard of this one or that one drowned in the river at Warren, or at Thomaston, or in one of the ponds. So she preferred to keep near shore. If she was with Jess, or even Eben, they might laugh at her fears and head straight to their destination, regardless of all risks; but when she was alone, she could do as she chose. She had not yet been able to teach herself to swim, but she — and sometimes Susie and young Phil — had paddled about in the shallows until she began to think she might swim if she had to do so. So within a few yards of shore she felt secure enough, confident that if any mischance did occur they could still cling to the canoe and by kicking with their feet work it to the shoal water.

Above the trees ahead, a thread of rising smoke showed her where the new house had been built; and south of it, down toward the brook, where rose the towering crests of that stand of giant pines which Joel and the others had begun to fall, she heard axes sound.

She paddled slowly. She passed the mouth of the river and saw the maple tree where she and Joel had watched for moose at the time of his first coming a year and a half before. That was long ago, and yet it was yesterday and all the long waiting for him to return was forgotten now. A salmon leaped clear of the water in the pool below the beaver dam as they crossed the mouth of the river.

The shore she followed was low and the water shallow. Nearest the shore grew a fringe of some water plant with arrow-shaped leaves, and outside this there were slender tubular reeds, just showing above the water now; and outside of them again, later in the summer, there would be pads and yellow lilies. She could see the small pads still below the surface in the clear water under her paddle. The air was full of the nearer sound of axes. The beats fell into rhythm, then broke time again, as a pair of trotting horses may fall into step and out.

They came to the angle where the shore turned southward, and put the bow of the dugout into the muddy bank, and she and Susie landed, and she dragged the bow high and dry. As she did so, she heard a long halloo of warning from the men at work, a sound like a howl of triumph. She stopped still, her heart lifting its beat, pounding in her throat. She knew that sound. Her father and her brothers shouted thus when a great tree first tottered to its fall.

She turned to look. From where they stood they could see nothing, because of the high bank above them where tall pines stood; but they heard like pistol shots the snap of breaking wood, and a susurrus filled the air, a whispering rustle as of many hushed voices murmuring in pity and in terror too. They heard crashings and splittings, and the lash of branches and the thunder and the rumble of great trunks flung prostrate to the ground. The sounds went on. It seemed to Mima minutes after she heard that first halloo before there was silence again. A fox, startled out of his wits by this collapse of his world about him, came racing past them, his feet desperately scrambling, his hackles high with fear; and the tops of the trees above where they stood were disturbed as though by a gust of wind, tossing fretfully.

Then there was a deep stillness everywhere, as though the world crouched in hidden, breathless fear. Mima felt this, and Susie too. The child held hard to Mima's hand, looking up at her, trembling; so Mima laughed and said:

'There, that's the way they do it. We'll go where we can see, the next time.'

There was a path from the landing, where the men had cleared away the underbrush. Mima and Sue took this path, and Mima listened to the axes. She could distinguish the splitting sound as keen blades bit, the solid 'chock' as the axe was driven in horizontally to free the chip started by the previous stroke. There were, she decided, four axes. Nathan Woodward must be working with them here.

The path they followed led directly inland from the pond, ascending thirty or forty feet in eight or ten rods, and it brought them to a small clearing. There on a knoll stood the house Joel and the others had built. It was, she judged, somewhat smaller than her father's; and the roof had not enough pitch to be tight against rain — or snow. In other ways, too, the house was still unfinished. There was no door fitted to it, nor had it windows. Mima in a sudden reluctance forbore to look inside; but she saw ashes where smudge fires had burned to act as a screen against the black gnats and mosquitoes. Five or six paces from the cabin, an oven had been built of stones plastered with clay; and there was a fireplace of the rudest sort, with crotched sticks and a bar across for a crane. Cooking dishes and plates and cups, all unwashed, were strewn around.

Susie was scandalized at the disorder. 'They don't clean up after themselves, do they?' she protested.

'They're too busy, Sue,' Mima reminded her. 'They have to get land cleared and things planted, first of all.'

Susie peeped in the dark door. 'There's not even a fireplace,' she said critically. 'Nor a chimney.'

But Mima hushed her. 'Come away,' she said. She was ashamed of her intrusion here, as though she had surprised a secret of Joel's which she had no right to know. 'Come along and see where they're working, Sue.'

They went toward where the axes sounded, hurrying a little as though to make up for lost time. After a long quarter of a mile, they saw ahead an opening, the sun shining down through the pines; and just beyond it, two men were at work. Mima recognized Joel and Matt Hawes.

The tree which they attacked was a fair four feet through. It was already deeply notched on the south side, through more than half its diameter; and by the pitch of the ground, or some accident of its growth, or its own great weight, it already leaned a little that way. Only the sound wood on its upper side still kept it erect; and into this, two axes were biting steadily.

Joel worked right-handed, Matt from the other side of the tree; and their axes struck in time, each one recovering as the other's blade came down. Joel had laid aside his shirt; and Mima saw the play of muscles in his shoulders and arms and along his flanks as he swung the axe and threw it home. Matt Hawes worked solidly and strongly, but Mima thought Joel was like a dancer, like a sword, like fire.

She and Sue came slowly nearer, within thirty yards; but the men were too much absorbed to see. Mima could hear the grunting breath come out of them at every stroke; the 'Huh!' that drove the keen blades home. The tree was near its fall. No more than a foot or so of sound wood still held it precariously erect. She saw that in the notch in the downhill side someone had set a slender splinter, firmly wedged. When the tree tipped even a little, the splinter would begin to bend, give warning of the slightest inclination.

Susie was quiet beside her. They went on till they were just above the stump of a tree that had been felled a while ago. From this position Mima could look down a vista, a hundred and fifty or two hundred yards long, where two or three lines of trees had toppled under the impact of drivers like this one beside whose stump she stood. On either side of this slot in the forest, the branches of trees still standing seemed to reach out to hide the wound; but looking along this vista Mima saw the pond beyond, and distant hills, and her heart lifted. It was as though by levelling the forest, men broke the bonds which hemmed them here.

She looked again at the splinter in the notch in the tree on which they worked. It was still straight. Jason Ware and Nate Woodward were chopping deeply into another great pine at one side, and she watched them for a moment, and then she heard Joel say, in a panting breath:

'She feels it, Matt!'

The splinter had begun to bend; the bend increased. Joel and Matt quickened their strokes. Jason and Nate Woodward stopped and came to watch. They were all so intent that they did not yet see Mima and Sue. Joel suddenly cried:

'Back, Matt!'

The two men jumped clear of the great butt, giving it room enough, backing up the hill toward where Mima and Sue stood. The splinter in the notch shivered into bits. High above them a bough, suddenly released, switched free of the branch that had held it with a hissing sound. Fibres in the notch cracked like shots. The tree began to fall.

Then Mima saw the working of that tremendous progression. As the tree came down, it fell against another. Their bases were not twenty feet apart. The crown of the falling tree seemed to embrace the trunk of the other, high up. At the impact, there was a louder splintering, and the second tree began to fall. Mima clapped her hands over her ears. Someone had shouted like a scream, scarce to be heard above the din of breaking branches, snapping trunks, smashing falls. She shut her eyes. Even the men drew back, as though the great trees were monsters which in their death struggles must be given room. Mima, her eyes closed, her hands across her ears, felt something touch her, and opened her eyes. Joel, instinctively recoiling from this destruction he had set afoot, had backed into her. His shoulders, streaming sweat, almost touched her breast. When her eyes opened, since the ground sloped a little downward so that he stood below her, the back of his head was just in front of her face; but he had felt her there, and turned in a startled flash till he recognized her and was quick to laugh at his own alarm.

Below them, trees were still falling; here about them the air
was choking full of dust thrown up, and of débris. But the noise
was less and less. They could be heard. He laughed and protested:

'You scared me, Mima! How long you been here watching?'

'Not long.' She saw where flies had bitten him, on his face
and on his bare chest and arms; saw drops of blood, some dry
and some fresh, and the swollen places left by old bites. She
said ruefully: 'You're awful bit up. Best put your shirt on.'

Matt Hawes came to speak to Mima, and gave Sue a toss.
Joel said cheerfully: 'Too hot to work in a shirt. Matt says he'd
rather sweat than be eat up, but I'd rather be cool as I can.'

Mima told them: 'Rubbing pine sap or spruce gum or something on yourself helps some. You get so you don't mind 'em
in a year or two.' Below her down the slope the vista was wider
now. She said: 'You knocked over a lot of trees.'

'Twelve or fifteen at a time,' Joel agreed. 'This way saves a
lot of axe work. We've been at it for five days, getting ready,
notching the trees down below. We'll have corn planted here
in no time now.'

Jason and Nate Woodward returned to their task. Matt said:
'Come on, Joel, or they'll be ahead of us.' Joel nodded.

'Better stay and eat dinner with us, Mima,' he urged. 'I
killed a salmon this morning when I went to swim, down in
that pool under the maple where we watched for the moose.
Remember?' She would not forget. 'I climbed the tree to
dive and they were lying right under me; so I got a heavy pole
and darted it at 'em and happened to get him on the head.
Stunned him and he floated up and I caught him. He'll eat
good.'

'They're better if you keep them one day anyway,' she said.
'Did you bleed him?'

Matt called: 'Hey, Joel, come on!'

'No, just hit him on the head. You stay. I'll fry you a piece
you'll like, blooded or not.'

He turned to the business in hand; and he and Matt went beyond Jason and Nate Woodward to attack another driver there. Almost at once the nearer tree on which Jason and Nate were at work let go. It fell more quickly than the others; but by some mischance it took a wrong inclination, brushed without effect through the branches of the tree it was supposed to knock over. The great butt jumped and rolled sidewise alarmingly; but the men were clear.

Woodward stared at the tree and swore. 'Acts like a damned hemlock!' he said.

Jason said to his partner: 'If we'd cut her true, she'd fall true. Come along.' They attacked the tree below. Joel and Matt, for fear of dropping their tree on the other men, presently stopped their axes, and Joel came to Mima again. She said:

'Joel — salmon's better boiled. I'll go start it if you want, have it ready time you want to eat.'

'So do, ma'am,' he agreed. 'I've ate fried stuff till I taste hog grease all day long. Seems like it's the only way to cook a thing that a man ever knows; but a woman is always smarter than a man.'

He was smiling, and she said: 'It's men that get their way, though.'

'That's just their stubbornness, even when they know they're wrong. Or sometimes it's a woman having her way and letting a man think it's his!' He stood beside her, breathing deeply from his exertions, looking down along the avenue now opened through the trees. 'I like that,' he said. 'Looking out, seeing the hills. Trees shut a man in. It's a pity we can't just start a fire running and burn them all.'

'They'd not fall till long after, if you did,' she said. 'And they'd come down at odd times, so you'd never know where you could work the land and not be mashed by one.'

'Nate says if we girdle them they'll die standing and we can plant around 'em; but I want them down and burned and gone.'

'You'll never get these big pines burned in time to plant this summer.'

He nodded. 'We're going to plant a crop along the edges of the meadows as soon as they're dry,' he said. 'Burn off the grass and plant there.'

'You'll need the meadows for hay land.'

'It's only for this year,' he said. 'To save clearing first. We'll have plenty cleared —— There it goes!'

Jason and Nate this time dropped their tree more justly; and Joel went back to join Matt, and their axes flew. Susie decided to stay and watch the trees go down; so Mima left her there, herself returned to the cabin. The breakfast embers still held heat enough to start a fire. She brought water from the spring and put it on to boil. She decided there was time to clean things up a bit before starting the salmon; so she rolled up her sleeves and went to work. Joel was yonder clearing his farm. She was here, tending his house for him. She smiled a little, felt like singing, happy in the sun.

11

May ran to June and the world was green, and the days were warm and fruitful under cloudless skies. While the earth was still too wet for planting, Philip and his sons pulled stumps, and Dave and Rich further down the pond were likewise engaged. Mima more than once went to the house on Round Pond to put all in order there; and the three young men of the Royal Mess welcomed her gratefully.

She did her best to make their quarters habitable. The house was still unfinished, lacking a chimney and a proper roof; and what furniture it contained they had made themselves. They had a table of boards on a loose trestle of poles, and they used squared logs for benches. For a bed they had built a sort of shelf some four feet above the ground, with room for storage under it; and this shelf was big enough so that they all slept together there, with a scattering of hemlock boughs laid on the split slabs to serve as mattresses. Joel and Matt and Jason were congenial; but Nathan Woodward, though he lived with them, was not of their company. He moved gloomily; his curious

obsession against hemlock trees never left him. Joel told Mima
that he spent days alone in the forest to the south of their land
toward the Waldoboro line, girdling every hemlock he found,
searching them out like enemies. He had too a lively certainty
that Indians were likely to come down on them; and he told
Mima what had happened at Wyoming and at Cherry Valley
the year before with a sour relish, predicting that the same
might happen here.

Mima stoutly assured him that hereabouts Indians and
whites had been at peace for more than twenty years; but she
had not forgotten the message brought by Dunbar of Ducktrap
the previous fall. The Indians, according to that rumor,
would come down from Canada when the leaves were as big
as thumbnails, and through May when the leaves were growing,
she had thought of that prediction more than once. She never
spoke of it, not even to her father; but she saw Philip one day
pluck an unfolding leaf off a maple and lay it across the nail on
his thumb, and she knew what he was thinking. Also he said
one day:

'I'm glad to have them up at Round Pond. Never quite
liked the idee of being the last house this side of nothing.'

But the leaves grew, and the Indians did not come, and by
the end of May Mima forgot to wonder whether Dunbar's
warning had been a just one. Not even Nate's doubts and fears
disturbed her. Trying to reassure him, she told him one day
about Jimbuck and his sons, who had lived peacefully for a
summer near her father's house; but Nate was sure those Indians had come to spy out the land and would return, leading
yelling hordes of painted devils. He was a lugubrious man,
and when his stomach began to distress him, none of them was
surprised that he decided to go back to the settlements, never
to return.

In the second week of June, Colonel Mason Wheaton came
from Thomaston to look at the land he had bought during the
winter. The river, coming south from Sunnyback Pond, when

it was within a long half mile of Seven-Tree Pond, suddenly turned northwest for a while before swinging south again into Round Pond. Colonel Wheaton's land had the river for its eastern bound; it touched the stream again half a mile north of Round Pond, just above where Bowker Brook came in from the north; and it continued west along the land Philip had sold to Joel and the others. Colonel Wheaton asked Mima's father to walk his south bound with him, and Philip agreed to do so. The Colonel proposed to set men to work clearing his land; but he had found no hands in Thomaston. The day he came up the river, three more young men from Franklin — John Fairbanks and Amos Lawrence and Moses Hawes, the latter 'Bijah's cousin — likewise made the journey. They thought of settling here; and Colonel Wheaton hired them to work for him during the summer.

Mima remembered the Colonel as a jovial man who had paid her some flattering attentions when the Sally sloop stopped at Fort Wharf on their first arrival; but there was a change in him now. He was blunt, with a loud, blustering voice, already showing traces of that sharp temper which would increase as he grew older. The war, he said — Mima listened for hours to his talk with her father that night — was all a blither'ng confusion. New England had licked the lobsterbacks, driven them out of Boston, out of everywhere along the New England coast except Newport; but the other colonies were afraid to stand up to English troops.

'Why, God's Nails and Britches, Robbins,' he said furiously, 'our sailors have chased the English off their own ocean, captured five hundred English vessels, maybe a thousand, and some of them in English harbors, under the guns of English forts! If New York and Pennsylvania and Virginia and the Carolinas would do as well, the war would be over.'

But he said people were too busy listening to the talk of Congress to do any fighting; and all Congress did except talk was print paper money. Pretty soon it wouldn't pay the cost of printing. The Colonel was buying his land on time. The longer the time, he declared, the less it would cost him to pay for it. He winked with ponderous wisdom. A man was a fool to sell in such times, but wise to buy — if he could buy on credit. As for the war, he was through with fighting unless the English landed in New England. Then he'd call out his militia and kick the bloody backs into the sea.

Philip Robbins agreed with all he said. 'Aye, so!' he assented strongly. 'They're easy licked if you've the stomach for it. I told them in Boston, the King's own captains and lieutenants, "You stick your nose into the country roundabout," I says, "and with one Yankee to every two of you, we'll paddle your backsides all the way back to Boston town." They clapped me in jail for saying it; but when they tried a march out Concord way, I was one of those had breakfast off their wagon trains in Cambridge after we'd sent the last of them skedaddling home.'

Mima lay half asleep with Susie in the trundle bed, listening to their talk. Smoke from the smudge at the door drifted under the garret floor and up to follow the ridgepole; and she saw skeins of it sucked by the draught up the chimney. She slept at last, but when Colonel Wheaton rolled in his blankets at her feet, his stumbling movements woke her; and later she smiled to hear him snore.

He and her father departed next morning to see the Colonel's land. Young Fairbanks and Lawrence and Moses Hawes had already gone up to Round Pond. Philip Robbins came back that night. He said the Colonel would stay and see the work under way. They were putting up a camp, meant to clear land along the line of the land owned by the Royal Mess.

*   *   *   *   *

By mid-June, Philip and his sons had most of their planting done. The Royal Mess had put in corn and summer rye along the edge of the meadows in land they burned there, and they were falling timber day by day, proposing to have a full twenty acres ready for seed another year. Jess killed a bear. David and Rich went down-river and succeeded in buying corn enough to tide them over till their own grain ripened. Winter's hardships were forgotten; summer was on the flood; life moved serene.

One day Philip and Eben had gone down-river to dicker with Sam Boggs for a fresh cow, leaving Mrs. Robbins at Dave's, planning to pick her up on the way home. At late dusk, Johnny Butler came paddling across from his farm at the Mill Stream. Mima heard him coming, and she and Jess went down to the landing. He did not see them in the gathering darkness till he was near the shore. When he did, he called sharply: 'That you, Jess?'

'Yes.'

'Where's Colonel Wheaton?'

'Up-river, up on his land.'

'Well listen, Jess,' Johnny directed, 'you got to go up there and g-get him. Tom Snow just got to m-my place, all played out. He c-come afoot all the way from the upper t-town, and he hurried. His tongue's hanging out. He says there's a lot of B-British ships has stood into the eastern b-bay and gone up to B-Biguyduce, and they sent for the C-Colonel.'

Jess whistled. 'Take me in with you and we'll go get him.'

'C-Can't,' Johnny confessed. 'Little Jimmie's c-cutting a tooth or something, and Lucy's worried, and T-Tom Snow's too b-beat out to go. You'll have to get word to the C-Colonel.'

Mima said: 'I'll go with you, Jess. Jake's here with the young ones.'

Jess agreed, and he and Mima pushed off while Johnny started home. They turned into the river and glided toward Round Pond, and dusk faded and dark came down; and great trees were black against the sky, the branches almost meeting above their heads. In the marsh opposite the deep cove something splashed ashore and fled noisily as they went by, and just above they saw the red eyes of some creature in the wood. Till they passed under the tree that served as bridge, Jess did not speak; but then he said in a chuckling tone: 'By gravy, Mima, some excitement! Look out for that rock ahead. Reckon the lobsterbacks will come up here?'

'If there are Indians with them, they might come,' she reflected; and she said: 'It's funny, Jess, what a difference it makes knowing things. Before Johnny told us, we weren't worried or excited or anything; and now we are. But the King's ships were there just the same before we knew, and it didn't hurt us. We can't do anything about it, anyway.'

'I guess Colonel Wheaton will do something about it, all right!' Jess told her. 'Probably Joel and the others will all go off with him to fight them.'

Mima was silent, dipping her paddle quietly. The only sound in the night was the little hiss of drops from the paddles lifted on the recover, the burble under the stern, the whisper like silk tearing at the bow. They rounded the upper bend, and the pond opened out before them, and she saw the young moon, three or four days old, in the western sky. Then another sound came — at first softly — through the night. Mima asked:

'What's that?'

Jess for a moment did not answer; but then suddenly he chuckled. 'They're singing,' he said. 'Sounds to me as if Colonel Wheaton and his men are down at the Royal Mess. Yes, and there's rum going, by the way they're hollering.'

Mima did not speak for a moment, pondering this matter that must always be a puzzle to womankind. 'Do you like rum, Jess?' she asked curiously.

'Times I do,' he admitted. 'When everybody's having some, like at the barn-raising. Or maybe when I'm cold.' They glided along the fringing reeds toward the landing ahead, and he said thoughtfully: 'Mima, you don't want to go up there to the house. They'll all be roaring. You stay in the float and I'll go tell the Colonel.'

Mima assented. The singing sounded more loudly all the

time. When the float touched, Jess stepped over Mima and ashore.

'I'll come right back. You shift to the stern,' he advised. 'I'll shove you off, and you wait till I come back. Nothing will bother you in the water.'

Mima was much more afraid of the water than of anything ashore; but she did not say so. She took the stern, and Jess thrust her free. 'I'll be back soon's I can,' he promised, and started up the path toward the house. Mima could hear whoops and yells of laughter as each song ended and before the next began. Once or twice she was sure she heard Joel's voice. There was a light southeast breeze which tended to set the dugout ashore. She backed clear of the reeds with idle strokes of the paddle, listening to the lusty sounds.

She knew by the sudden silence when Jess reached the house and began to tell them the news. But she was too far away to hear even the murmur of his voice, to hear anything at all till presently one voice rose in a shout, and then the others in a whoop together, a confusion of joined cries that went on and on and turned at last to song again.

She wondered why Jess did not return; but presently she thought she heard him coming through the woods above her. There was someone with him, for she heard two voices, heard one of the men blunder into a tree and swear mightily. She recognized Joel's voice, and chuckled at his wrath, and thought he would be here in a moment more. She thought he must be coming with Jess to say a word to her; and a deep happiness stirred in her.

Then she heard another voice and knew it was not Jess with Joel. The two men came down to the landing, and one of them — she did not know the voice — said thickly: 'Where's th' damned float, anyway? We get it and hide it and he'll have to stay!'

Joel said: 'It's bound to be here handy. You go one way, and I'll go t'other, till we find it.'

Someone came along the wooded shore toward her. The night was dark enough so that she was not easily seen. She stayed where she was, hoping it was Joel. He drew near and nearer, till suddenly he was abreast of her and saw the float. He bawled:

'Here it is, Joel! Gone adrift!' Then: 'No, by Harry, there's somebody in it!' She recognized the voice. The man was 'Bijah Hawes. He demanded: 'Who's that? Eben?'

Mima smiled in the darkness. She could see 'Bijah's great bulk only vaguely. Joel had gone out along the beaver dam, was moving back toward the shore now.

'No, it's Mima,' she said. 'Where's Jess?'

'Mima?' 'Bijah echoed, and she heard him laugh to himself. 'Why, Mima!' he said thickly. 'We don't need Jess. Say, we don't even need Joel! I'll get in with you and we'll go for a nice long ride.' He began to wade into the water toward her. He promised, chuckling: 'I'll teach you a game you're ripe to learn.'

She had dipped her paddle to back clear, her heart suddenly pounding. The dugout lay at an angle toward the shore, and when her paddle bit, the bow swung in a quarter circle. He plunged forward, trying to catch it, through water that deepened slowly. He shouted in a sudden anger: 'Hold on! Hold up! God damn it, wait a minute! Let me get hold of you . . .'

He made a diving lunge, his hands almost reaching the bow of the heavy float; but he missed, and he went face down into the water that choked his word.

Mima was shaken with something like panic. The night, the treacherous water under her, the unstable float so hard to move and to control, and the drunken eagerness of her pursuer combined to make her heart race. 'Bijah sober she could handle; but 'Bijah drunk was another matter. She back-paddled hard and drew clear. Then she heard him come to the surface and choke and strangle and begin to wade after her; and he swore zestfully:

'Why, damn your pretty hide, Mima!' he gasped, and began to swim. 'I'll paddle your backside when I catch you! No way to treat a man.'

She made sure that he could not overtake her, and then Joel called from the landing: 'What's the matter, 'Bijah?'

'Mima,' 'Bijah told him. 'Trying to get away from me! I'll show her!'

Joel laughed. 'You damned fool! Mima, come around him to me. Come ashore. I'll take care of you.'

Mima swung the float around 'Bijah toward the bank, but then she heard sounds of distress behind her. 'Bijah choked and began to cough, and he made a gurgling sound and then was quiet, and Joel called: 'Wait a minute. He's in trouble.' She heard him plunge into the water and swim toward where 'Bijah, drifting to the surface again, was splashing feebly. She swung the canoe that way, forgetting her own alarm, ready to help if she were needed; but Joel told her: 'I've got him. Keep clear. I'll drag him ashore.'

He did so. She heard them on the bank, 'Bijah gagging and retching, heard Joel's laughing voice.

'Try to drink the lake dry, did you, 'Bije? Well, this'll be a lesson to you. Puke it up and you'll feel better!' Mima heard the thump of a blow, as Joel slapped the other on the back. 'Cough it up! So!' The choking and the gasping eased and ceased; and Mima asked:

'Is he all right?'

Joel laughed. 'He's well as ever now, or will be with another suck of rum.' 'Bijah muttered something; and Joel said cheerfully: 'Here's Mima scared you're drowned, 'Bije. Tell her you're not! Then go tell Jess you frighted his sister. Bid him come take her home.'

'Bijah said contritely from the shadows: 'I'd not have hurt the wench. I'll tell Jess.' She heard him climb slowly up the bank, and she said:

'I was afraid he'd tip me over and we'd drown.'

'Can't you swim?' Joel asked.

'No.'

He laughed. 'Love us, that's a pity! I'll teach you, some fine day.' And he explained: 'We wanted Jess to stay a while, so we kept him for one drink and maybe a small song — and 'Bijah and I came to hide his boat so he'd have to stay.' He added: 'There's no harm in 'Bijah sober — and mighty little rum or anything else left in him now.'

'I want to know how to swim,' she admitted. 'I've tried to learn, but my feet pull me under . . .'

His shout of mirth rang through the night. 'So they do. So they just do!' he agreed. 'But I'll have you swimming in no time at all.' He urged: 'Will you come ashore?'

'Is he gone?'

''Bije? He'll never hurt you.'

'I was witless to be scared,' she admitted. The breeze moved her toward the shore. She neither helped it nor resisted, staring into the shadows, trying to see where Joel stood. He spoke in a low tone.

'It's a fine night for a man and a maid, Mima, and — you're the only wench in half a day's hard travel.' He chuckled. ''Bijah or any man would wade clear across this pond to come to you — if you'd wait and not run away.' She did not speak, feeling her cheeks warm at his tones. She heard Jess coming; heard his voice as he spoke to 'Bijah somewhere above them, heard 'Bijah mutter and go on. Joel was not ten feet from her on the shore.

'Now I'd not want to scare a girl,' he said softly, a chuckle in his tones, 'and maybe see her upset and drown before my eyes. But if it wasn't for scaring you, I'd be reaching for you too.' He asked, suddenly husky: 'Did ever a man sing a song to you, Mima, in the dark, so you could blush and him not see, only he could feel your cheek hot to his lips? Till he stopped singing. Did he now?' She did not speak, but she thought he must hear her heart pound. 'Or maybe teach you a new dance

with none but yourselves to call the numbers?' And when she
was still silent he laughed and said: 'Likely not, by the way you
sit there so quiet, and never a word or a laugh out of you. But
you'd learn easy. What if I was to wade out to you through the
water warm as milk and swing aboard?'

'You'd tip me over,' she said helplessly. He laughed again,
and took a step into the water. The paddle trailed idle in her
hand.

But then Jess called from the bank above them: 'Mima!
Where've you gone?'

'Here,' Mima answered; and Joel said, for her ear alone, in a
whispered challenge:

'You're scared of yourself, maybe, that you keep ten feet of
water between us, to cool the heat in a man, and him hot with
the night and the rum . . .'

Then Jess came sliding down the bank through the trees to
where they were, and Mima turned the bow of the float till it
touched the shore and he caught it and stepped in.

'The Colonel will come in the morning,' he told her, and
laughed. 'He's not fit for travel tonight; but he says he'll come
in the morning, and take them that are up here with him and
go lick the King and his whole navy with no other help at all.'
He said with a chuckle: 'You'll have to paddle me home, Mima.
The drink I had has knocked me dizzy a'ready.'

Mima turned the float and started to skirt the shore. Joel
called: 'Good night to you, Mima.'

'Good night, Joel.'

'Don't be forgetting,' he reminded her, 'you're going to learn
to swim. You've many a thing to learn.'

Then he was left behind.

* * * * *

Joel came down-river next morning with the Colonel in the
bow of his dugout. Philip had returned early from Warren —
that cow would not freshen for a few days more — so he and

Eben were there when the two men arrived. Philip had heard
the news in Warren; and Colonel Wheaton said:

'I'm on my way now to kick the rascals out, Robbins. We'll
show 'em we're not to be monkeyed with. You'll come along?'

Mima saw her mother at that challenge suddenly white and
still, while she waited for her husband's answer. Philip hesitated.

'When will you be going?' he asked. 'I'd not want to leave
the work here and go sit on my backside a month or two, waiting for the fun to start. Send me word the day you're ready.'

'Will ye come?'

'If I can.'

Colonel Wheaton roared: 'If you can! If you can! Are ye a
man, or a woman that doesn't know her mind? Can ye or
can't ye?'

'So! Then I'll come when ye're ready,' said Philip Robbins;
and his wife's hand tightened on his arm.

'Now you talk like a man!' the Colonel said approvingly.
'And I'll take a suck of grog with you. Joel here and the young
rake-hellions up-river say they've had their bellyful of fighting,
so we'll have to do it for them.' He stamped off up to the house,
Philip beside him.

But Mima stayed with Joel, and he said cheerfully: 'The
Colonel's in a fair wax this morning, with the head on him from
last night.' He sat down on the bow of the float, and Mima
stood on the bank above him. Eben and Jess were by. 'He was
bound we'd all go along with him; but I've done my stint.
We'll be put to our trumps to make a crop this summer, as it is,
enough to feed us through the winter.'

They could hear Colonel Wheaton's loud tones from the
house. Mima asked: 'Are you setting him down to Warren?'

'Just that,' Joel agreed. 'No more.'

She was glad he would not go again to risk death or hurt.
He and Jess fell to conjecture as to what the British meant to
do, what effect their presence at Biguyduce would have on con-

ditions here. She listened silently; but she saw Eben watching them both, and he was curiously white. She spoke to him. 'What's the matter, Eben?'

Instead of answering her, he challenged Joel: 'Aren't you going to help fight them?'

Joel looked at him with a lifted brow, smiling a little. 'No, Eb. I've had my bellyful of war.'

Eben turned from white to red. 'I guess one of you will have to keep working, up at your place,' he admitted. 'Are the others going, Matt and Jason, and the Colonel's men?'

Joel said quietly: 'Never a one of us, youngster!'

'I'm going,' Eben said. 'With Pa.'

Mima came near him, touching his arm; but Joel spoke easily. 'I guess you think we're a cow-hearted lot, Eb,' he said. 'You're wrong. We've all had a smell of it.' He smiled faintly. 'The worst smell about it is the foolishness of Congress, and of some of the men that try to be officers; but we've smelled powder too, and smelled dead men fly-blown in a hot sun with maggots crawling on them.' His voice was almost weary. 'I was your age when I started. Now I'm old, and I have bad dreams.' He said: 'The fighting's not so bad, Eb. You get excited, kind of like it. But you might rot in camp for a year, and run yourself to death with a bloody flux, and sleep wet and freeze your feet and never shoot a gun.' He spoke in a sudden heat. 'Man, you can go three months and never have enough powder to charge your piece, the way things are! Anybody's brave enough to fight. It's the waiting for a fight that teases you.'

'There'll be fighting enough at Biguyduce.' Eben appealed to his brother: 'Jess, you're going, ain't you?'

Jess grinned. 'Not me. I'd ruther shoot a moose. He don't shoot back!'

Joel looked at Mima. 'Likely you're thinking the same as Eb, that I ought to go?' he told her, his word a question.

She shook her head. 'You've got all you can do here. One man in an army don't help much; but one man here can do a lot in a summer, Joel.'

Eben said after a moment: 'I guess you know best, Joel. You're the one to decide, anyway. But I can go and not be missed.'

Mima put her arm around him; but before she could speak, the Colonel and her father came down the path again. Mrs. Robbins followed them. When Joel and Colonel Wheaton moved away, Mrs. Robbins came to her husband's side, watching him; and they turned back to the house arm in arm.

* * * * *

Joel did not return that day, but he stopped next morning to report the latest news. The British had seized Biguyduce and were clearing the peninsula and building a fort there.

'They'll have to be driven out,' Philip commented. 'We'll want all the men around, Joel.'

Joel said stubbornly: 'Not me. I've put in better than three years at it, and come out poorer than I went in. It's the turn of others now.'

'Aye, you've done your share, son,' Philip admitted. 'But I don't like having them so handy. The people over Broad Bay way, and some in Warren and Thomaston, half of them are ready to go for the King if they can; and with King's ships at Biguyduce, the refugees will be busy along the coast till a canoe can't slip past them.' He did not push the point of Joel's going. 'Well, we'll manage,' he said, and he added with a look at the serene and cloudless sky: 'We need rain bad. The rye's slow, and things are drying up in the ground, so hot and dry it is.'

'Aye,' Joel assented. Philip turned back to the house, but Mima stayed by the landing there to see Joel depart. He said: 'It's hot paddling.' Then, with a twinkle in his eyes: 'Good weather for swimming. You were wanting to be taught, Mima.' She nodded, and he asked: 'When will you have that lesson?'

She hesitated, and her color heightened faintly. 'How's a woman going to swim with men around?'

He laughed and said: 'Wear an old dress, and not too many petticoats, or they'll drag you down. Once you've learned, you'll be leaving off everything!'

She said, her cheeks bright: 'Then maybe I'd best not be learning!'

He chuckled. 'That would be a pity, too.' His brow lifted in that teasing way. 'There's some, the more clothes on them, the better they look; but you're not one, I'll be sure!' And he argued: 'What's to be ashamed of? Matt said I was wrong to let you see me without a shirt, the day we were falling trees. Did it hurt your eyes?'

She laughed a little. 'The flies had liked finding you so. They'd nibbled you all over.'

'Was that all you saw?' he challenged; and in a sudden confusion she turned back up the path. Then she heard him singing to himself as he paddled away, and stopped to listen. She recognized a jig tune she had heard him whistle before; but now she could hear the words.

> Oh her cheek it was bonny; her eye it was merry;
> Her ear was a shell and her lip was a cherry;
> Her smile would make any man linger a while
>   And she smiled that smile at the gentlemen!
>
> This lad he rode by and he tarried to dally
> And dandle and bundle with this pretty Sally.
> 'I'll lay me,' he told her, 'Just seeing you smile,
>   'That you've been very kind to the gentlemen!'

She began to lose some of the words as his strong strokes drove the dugout swift on its way.

> .... sweet Sally, 'There's no harm in smiling
> On any fine lad......... so very beguiling
> And as for............... being so kind,
>   '.... kind to myself as the gentlemen!'
>
> .... clipped and he tossed her,
> Till she fled.................. lost her
> And.............. she was easy to find —
>   .... of the gentlemen!

He sang another verse; but Mima could no longer hear any words at all. He disappeared around the point toward the river mouth.

* * * * *

June ended and July began and no summons came from Colonel Wheaton. Mima saw that her mother never liked tc let Philip out of her sight. There was a gentle tenderness in the older woman in these days, and many small solicitudes. She seemed unconscious of the presence of her sons and daughters, as though she and Philip were alone in the small house where they all lived so compactly. Mima perceived, in this, a similarity between herself and her mother. Her world too had contracted. Until Joel came, she had been a part of a community which included David's family, and Rich and Bet and their children, and sometimes Lucy and Johnny Butler; but now this was changed. Even here in the house she felt herself apart from her family. Her thoughts were more on Joel than on them. As for the others, she had not gone down the pond since Joel's return. Her orbit was changed. Where before she might in a free hour wish to see Bess or Bet, now she was more likely to go up to Round Pond. Sometimes she only went as far as the nearer shore, looking across to the neck of land between brook and pond where they were falling trees; sometimes she went to the cabin, to see Joel, to put the house in order for them. She was forever conscious that he was near; he was the centre of her world, just as in these days Philip was the centre of her mother's.

She might go a week without seeing Joel. She needed not to see him; but she often went to the nearer border of Round Pond, to look across toward where he was. In the second week of July, she set out one hot afternoon and walked up the river to the pine Jess had felled. The water was low, and she could see the clean bottom. It occurred to her that she might wade the stream if she chose. She tried it, lifted skirts and petti-

coats and — going on tiptoe in the deepest parts, her garments raised breast-high — she crossed. She followed the path
to the old maple, and climbed it; and she was in the act when a
float appeared in the mouth of the river. Joel was paddling.
He turned up toward her, and called:

'Hullo. You, is it? Thought I'd treed a bear.' She sat down
quickly on the bough to which she had ascended, drawing her
petticoats around her legs, so startled that she could think of
nothing to say. 'Want a ride home?' he asked. 'I'm on my way
to Warren.'

She hesitated, then nodded. 'Yes.' If Joel were going downriver, there was nothing to keep her here. But she could not
climb down from the tree with him just below her. She did
not move, and he watched her, smiling, waiting.

'Come ahead,' he said, for a moment not understanding.
But then he chuckled. 'Afraid of me? I'll shut my eyes.' He
did so, and she swung to the ground in one quick motion and
stood on the bank above him. He heard the thump as her bare
feet landed, and looked up at her and put the canoe ashore;
and he said: 'But a man doesn't have to see more than the
curve of your cheek, Mima, to be glad he's got good eyes.' She
stepped into the bow of the canoe, and he backed clear and
turned along the shore. Then he chuckled, remembering.
''Bijah says you starve a man,' he told her. She guessed from
his tone that his eyebrow would be lifted teasingly. She did
not speak, and he said: 'You know, you're a queer one, Mima.
I never saw one easier to look at — and I've an eye for them —
but there's something about you keeps a man from doing more
than look.' They turned into the river, moving easily with the
faint current. 'How did you get across?' he asked.

'Waded,' she told him. 'Down by the bridge.'

'Waded? You went deep, then?'

'Pretty deep.'

'With your clothes on?'

'I pulled them up!'

'You might have gone too deep — the way 'Bijah did — and me not there to pull you out!' He chuckled. 'Did you know 'Bijah took a handling from Matt that night?' She had not known this. 'He named you when he got back to them,' he said, 'and Matt did not like the sound of what he said. Matt's a head the shorter, but when I got there, Matt had him down and pounding him, till Jason and me hauled Matt away.' He said: 'Maybe Matt couldn't if it hadn't been for the rum in 'Bijah — and the pond water — but I don't know. I've seen Matt in a fight. He's a sudden man!'

There was a still excitement in her, wondering what 'Bijah had said, why Matt came to her defense. She could not imagine Matt fighting; he seemed so mild. They passed the deep indented cove just short of the river mouth, and she wished to ask Joel to set her ashore there, but could think of no excuse. ''Bije and I are going down to Warren now,' he told her. 'I'm picking him up. He spends as many nights there as here.'

They emerged into the pond. In a moment more they would come to the landing. She wished he would take her on with him, keep her with him always; wished this moment might not end. But she knew no way to prolong it, and when he put the nose of the float ashore she stepped out. Susie appeared in the door of the house, watching them; and he asked seriously, as though puzzled by his own forbearance: 'Why didn't I kiss you on the way?' Her cheek burned and his eyes began to twinkle. 'I would have tried it, any other girl I ever saw.'

With the house near, Sue watching, she felt secure; but she found no word to say. He backed clear. 'I'm a wonder to myself,' he said, and turned the float away.

* * * * *

Next day they were all indoors at supper, with a smudge at the door to discourage the flies, when he came up from the landing with a man at his heels. 'Robbins,' he said. 'Here's a man to see you from Colonel Wheaton. John Perry. He's a North Haven man, and he's been with the soldiers at Biguyduce. The Colonel sent him to raise men to go to drive the British out.' Joel added: 'I've told him our case at the Royal Mess, that we'll not go; but he's bound to see you, and your sons, and Johnny Butler. So I've delivered him to you. He does not like me because I won't go soldiering, so I'll go my own way and leave him here.'

Mima saw her mother, white-faced, looking from Philip Robbins to this John Perry. Perry said quietly: 'I've cause enough to want a whack at the bloody backs, and so has any man.'

'I've had my whack,' Joel told him good-humoredly, and disappeared. Philip Robbins said:

'Sit down, friend Perry. Sit down and eat. Have you been at Biguyduce?'

Perry's eyes were burning like a cat's in the dark, crowded cabin. 'I have so,' he said, in a strange tone. Jess had made a seat for him on the bench. He took the heaped plate Mima brought him and began to eat while he spoke.

'I've a farm on North Haven,' he said. 'The King's ships stood in to the eastern bay and saw my house and sent a boat ashore. I stayed to meet them. My wife was near her time, and I'd not leave her. There was an officer said they must have a pilot to show them the way to Biguyduce. I said I couldn't go, with my wife as she was; but they said I'd go or they'd put a musket ball in my belly to match the babe in hers.'

Eben asked hotly: 'Did she hear them?'

Perry looked at him. 'Aye, she heard.'

Eben was on his feet, but Mima touched her brother's arm; and Mrs. Robbins said:

'Hush, Eben. Hear his tell and be still.'

So Eben was silent, and John Perry went on, in a hollow voice drained of all emotion, as though he spoke of far-off things. 'I went,' he said. 'What could I do else? I kissed my

wife, and she was fine, and down to the boat I marched.' He
nodded. 'Aye, and I brought them safe to Biguyduce, the lot
of them.'

His lip twisted as though at a sudden twinge of pain; and
Philip Robbins asked: 'How many of them?'

'Seven or eight sail. They put seven hundred men ashore.
The first day they landed just a small party, that huddled like
a flock of sheep, looking all around, expecting some of ours
would start shooting from behind the trees all around. Fair by
Joe Perkins' house they landed; but back aboard they came
again for that night. Then the next day the ships set them all
ashore and they camped in the open ground northwest of Cross
Island and started falling trees and digging ditches to make a
fort on the hill back of the camp.'

'Is the fort built?'

'It was no more than started, ten days gone,' Perry said.
'There was plans for ditches and moats and bastions; but we
can come at them before 'tis done and butcher the last lot of
them. Aye, and will, too, if I have to go alone.'

Mima spoke gently. 'Did they send you safe home?'

His eyes met hers, burning bright in the smoky cabin. 'They
said I was a rebel and they put me to work on the fort; but a
fog rolled in and I made a run for it. I got away across the
neck and came the long way around and stole a canoe on the
eastern shore and crossed to my home.' He said: 'My wife was
dead, and the baby too. Happen if I'd been there she'd have
died just the same; but it would have been easier for her to die
with me there.' His stern eyes met Philip's. 'So I came to tell
Colonel Wheaton the case they're in. The General Court is
raising an army and a fleet to go set a heel on their heads —
six hundred men from Lincoln County, and six hundred from
Cumberland, and three hundred from York. That's two of
us to one of them, and we'll have a great fleet of fine ships of
war besides.'

Mima, watching him, feeling the heat in him, saw his hand
clench tight. Philip Robbins said: 'I'll go.'

Eben cried: 'Me too! I'll go with you!'

But Mrs. Robbins said: 'You'll not, Eben. One of my men can go, but no more. Let every other woman send one man, and there'll be men enough.'

'Colonel Wheaton wants you to be commissary,' Perry told Philip. 'Any man can fight, but that job needs a man with a sober head to him, and he'd not have to be a soldier.'

Robbins nodded. 'Jess,' he told his son, 'you and Eben stay here, tend your mother and the young ones. Jacob, I'll take you along for my waiter. You've a peaceful mind.' Mima saw Jake taut with excitement, swallowing hard, his lean neck working. 'You'll do your own job and not be wanting in the fighting all the time.' He sat in silence for a moment, his heavy face set and sombre; and they watched him, none speaking. Then his head swung toward John Perry. 'When does it begin?' he asked.

'I'll stay the night.' Perry's tones were bleak. 'Is there none. of them up above with Adams that has insides to him enough to go?'

'Ye're wrong to say that, Perry,' Philip Robbins said sternly. 'No man will come up here and knock down the trees and burn them and grub out the stumps and the roots and the stones and all, if there's any backing off in him. That's all better worth doing, maybe, than this fighting business. But — knowing the King's men are so near does make my backside itch. It's a nervous feeling. I'll go with you and pitch 'em out of there.'

12

PERRY did not easily give up his hope to enlist some of the members of the Royal Mess, or Mason Wheaton's men, for this expedition. Jacob next morning took him up the river to see them, while Philip Robbins spent the forenoon preparing for an absence that might be long or short. The rye would be ready to harvest within a month. The timbers for the new barn must be sized and fitted, mortises cut and holes bored and tenons shaped and trunnels rounded, ready for a raising in the fall. Mrs. Robbins was anxious that some flax should be grown next year; and for that crop, ground must be prepared. Philip told his sons what they might do during his absence, till Jess laughed and said:

'That's enough to keep ten men busy ten years, Pa! We'll not have time to make a scratch on it before you're back.'

Robbins nodded slowly. 'Maybe not,' he agreed. 'But a man going where there's fighting looks ahead if he's anyways sensible. I've been laying out in my mind all the things I might do here in a lifetime, give me time. If I don't come back, Jess, you and the rest will do them — but not all in what's left of this summer, sure.' He chuckled. 'So don't let the thought of all there is to do be scaring you.'

Mima said surely: 'We can just do the one thing at a time. Nobody could fall all the trees in one summer; but he can do it if he takes one tree at a time, and a summer at a time.'

Jake and John Perry presently returned, and Perry reported scornfully that the men up-river still refused to go. Colonel Wheaton had sent a message to the men working on his land that their jobs were ended; but they would not be thus coerced. Amos Lawrence proposed to hunt work in Thomaston; Moses Hawes would lodge with 'Bijah down the pond and buy land before the summer was done; and John Fairbanks said he had had his bellyful of the wilderness and might try privateering.

'They talk like a lot of lousy King-lovers,' John Perry commented, with a slow burning in his tones. 'There's as many here would like to have the English stay at Biguyduce as there are that want them thrown out. All the old-country folks have a leaning so, or most of them. Only us that come down from the westward are true men.' And he said: 'It's the King-lovers fetched the redbacks to Biguyduce, Robbins. Some in the town invited them. They'll get their needs and dues, once we lay hands on them!'

When time for departure came, Mrs. Robbins bade her husband and Jacob good-bye with a kiss and a smile; and she kept a high head and a steady eye all that day. But that night she called Mima to take Philip's place in the great bed; and long after the others were asleep, Mima held her mother, shaking with fearful, soundless sobs, close in her arms.

* * * * *

The second day after her father's departure, Mima, remembering guiltily how long it was since she had done so, walked down the shore to see Richard and Bet. Bet had gone to bake bread in the oven at David's cabin, so she found Bess and Bet there. They were laughing together as she appeared; but they hushed when they saw her and Mima asked:

'What's so mighty funny?'

Bet looked to see that the children were out of hearing; and then she said: 'It was something you'll not know about till you're married, Mima.' She laughed again, and Bess smiled; and she explained: 'We were saying, why do we always have to start our babies the wrong time of year.'

Mima's eyes flashed from one to the other in a quick happiness. 'Are you that way, Bet?'

Her sister nodded. 'I'm sure, myself; and Bess thinks she is too. Mine will be in February.' She shivered. 'Br-r-r! Makes me cold to think of it. Winter's a terrible time to have babies; but it's snug and warm to be abed, at that,' she admitted. 'And no flies in winter, anyway, to pester the life out of you.'

Bess said seriously: 'We're just like the trees, and the grass, Bet. Spring of the year and the sap starts to run in us, same as in them.'

Bet laughed merrily. 'Shame on you for talking so before Mima that knows nothing of such things!' She peered into the oven to see how her baking did, and Mima said:

'I might know more than you think.' Her eyes were still as hidden pools. 'A woman's a woman, spring or fall, married or not. She can — want to feel life growing in her, married or not.' She said rebelliously: 'Yes and she can have it, too — married or not!'

Bess looked at her soberly, but Bet said: 'You were always a queer one, Mima. The rest of us, our babies are just our babies that come along and are a nuisance for a while and a worry for a while and a blessing for a while.' She laughed. 'But your babies, when you have them, you'll take it as serious as if you were having all the babies in the world.'

'It's the babies we have that will be the world when we're gone,' Mima told her. 'Having a baby's more than just loving a man and maybe a son or a daughter comes of it.'

Bet said teasingly: 'You talk big, but you're a long time doing your share, Mima. You're gone twenty-two a'ready — and still leaving Bess and me to have the babies to fill the world.' She laughed affectionately. 'I thought with Joel back, you'd be at it by now.' She began to draw the loaves out of the oven with the long wooden peel. 'If there ever was a woman wanted a man, you're the one, gulping and swallowing every time he looks at you.' There was a mirthful amusement in her eyes, derision in her tones.

But Mima said simply: 'It's true. I'd as soon folks saw it. I'd as soon he knew it.'

'You'll scare him off,' Bet warned her. 'He's too soon out of the army to settle down.'

'I can wait. If I have to. He's in share and share with Matt and Jason till they get a start. He can't work just for himself yet. He's got to work out his share with them.'

'You're as bad as Rich,' Bet declared. 'Sometimes he's so patient I could spit! When I want something, I want it, and I'll get it and get it quick, or know the reason why.'

Bess said quietly: 'You can't, always, Bet. Dave and me have wanted another baby for three years now, and got them and couldn't keep them.'

Bet drew out the last loaf, her eyes on Bess, saying softly: 'You'll have one, Bess!' Then Mima felt someone near, and turned and saw within six paces of them a man dressed in skins, white beard flowing, long locks about his shoulders, bowing profoundly. She uttered a low exclamation, and the others saw him. Bet dropped the fresh loaf to the ground; and the old man bowed again. Mima saw in puzzled wonder that he bowed to the bread and not to them. He was tremendously tall. His cap was of moose hide shaped to his head and sewed with sinews. His hunting shirt was made of moose hide, too; but on that the hair had not been scraped away, though it had been rubbed off by long use in patches here and there. This shirt descended to his knees. Below bearskin leggings frayed by brush and brambles, his feet were bare and black and horny. Mima herself wore moccasins — she usually did so when she went far from home — but Bess and Bet were barefooted. Yet his feet were not like theirs. His were more like hooves than feet, they were so calloused and so dark. His waist was girt with a twisted strip of moose hide knotted in front; and from it hung pouch, shot poke, powder horn and hatchet. His flint-lock was rusted, and in one place it was neatly bound with thongs. He carried on his shoulder a pack of furs.

Mima saw all this in the instant before Bet spoke. Bet had been frightened; she was still, a little, and it showed in the anger in her tones.

'Where'd you come from?' she demanded. 'What do you want? What you a-doing here? What are you bowing at?'

The old man looked at her as though faintly dazed by her many questions. 'I'm Davis,' he said, and his voice seemed creaky with disuse. 'I've got furs to trade for salt and powder. I'm bowing at the bread, ma'am. I always crack a knee at sight of bread. I don't see it often.'

Mima spoke quickly, liking him. 'Here's plenty. Taste it.' She picked up the loaf which Bet had dropped, flat, hard-baked, of home-ground corn; and he took it and broke it in his hands. He held his gun in the crook of his arm as he ate, and he looked at the oven.

'I build my fires on the ground,' he said in that curious dry tone. 'Once I come in from my traps and it a-raining; so I struck me up a fire and set to dry, and the fire begun to squeal at me and hump itself and heave around, and if out didn't come a-crawling the granddaddy of all turtles that had dug into the warm ashes of my old fires to sleep or something. He et good, he did.' His strong jaws clamped down on the bread; he chewed as happily as a cow.

Mima asked: 'Where do you live?' The children had come nearer, shy as wild animals at the sight of this stranger, clinging to Bess, yet curious too.

'I live wherever I be,' the old man told them. The strange sound he made was remotely like a chuckle. 'I'm here, ain't I? I'm alive, ain't I? Well, then, right now, I live here.'

Bet insisted: 'But where do you come from?'

'Why, this time I come down through the swamps on the Madomock, looking for signs on my way to town. I might set my traps that way come winter. When I go back, I'll go up-river.'

'Up this river?' Mima asked.

'Yes, ma'am.'

'How far up does it go? I want to go, some day.'

'It goes a way,' he said cautiously.

'Beyond the next pond? I mean the second one above this? Jimbuck — he was here one summer. He's an Indian — called it Sunnyback.'

'Jimbuck's a good Indian. He's my neighbor this summer. Yes, ma'am.' The old man seemed to forget caution in enthusiasm. 'Yes, ma'am, there's other ponds above. There's one might be twenty miles the way the river runs. Half the river comes out of that. That's my way home; up that pond, and up the stream that feeds it, and around the edge of a beaver meadow that's fine to see, with moose like neat cattle, and ducks breeding, and beavers plenty. There's two fine brooks flows into that meadow. They come down out of the hills. You can call it I live on one of them. Mostly I get back there as often as I can make out to — but between times I go as far as Fort Western one way and Bangor the other. I heard tell there was a town making here, and come to see.'

'There is,' said Mima. 'We're making it.'

His eyes twinkled under shabby brows. 'Don't you go crowd me!' The last crumb of the loaf had disappeared.

Bess asked about Jimbuck. 'Are the two young Indians with him?'

'Yes, ma'am.'

'Dunbar of Ducktrap said last fall the Indians might come down on us from Canada this spring.'

'Yes, ma'am, I heard that. I asked Jimbuck about it but he says no.'

'I thought they might come to Biguyduce, now't the English are there.'

The old man shook his head. 'There ain't any Indians with them there yet, that I've heard of. Jimbuck says there won't be.' A dog barked far away across the pond, and Mima heard it and she saw the old man cock an ear; but the others seemed not to hear. Bess said more hospitably:

'Well, I'm glad to hear it. I guess you'd like a collop of bear meat to wad that bread down. David killed a young one, day before yesterday.'

'Ma'am, I've et bear meat till I can climb a tree with my toenails. But I could maybe get around a mite more bread. That dog's in trouble.'

'What dog?'

'The one over across.'

Mima said: 'It sounds like Tuner, Bess. Listen.'

They all heard it, when they were quiet now. '"Tis Tuner,' Bess decided. 'He went off with Lion. Lion came down with Bet and off they put, two-three hours ago.'

Bet Comings said: 'I don't hear Lion.'

The old man repeated: 'The dog's in trouble. He's asking for help.'

'How do you know?' Mima asked.

'He ain't trailing, and he ain't chasing, but he's hurrying and he's yelling. If something was chasing him, he wouldn't be yelling. He'd save his breath. He's yelling so's somebody will hear. Where's your menfolks?'

David and Richard had worked together the year before, clearing five or six acres of land back from the pond. They had burned the fall-piece this spring, were gone today with the oxen to roll or haul the half-burned trunks of great trees into piles for another firing. 'I'll go fetch them,' Mima offered. 'Tuner's nigh down to the shore opposite. We'll have to cross over and get him, see what's the matter.'

'Hold on,' the old man suggested. 'If there's a float handy, I can go over. That dog's in a hurry.'

'The float's down at the shore,' Bess told him; so they all moved that way. Tuner showed, on the bank across the pond, his barks coming ringingly. They could see him jumping up and down in a clamoring excitement. Bet cried:

'I don't see Lion! Reckon he's hurt?'

Mima heard the sound of a paddle and looked up the shore and saw Joel coming toward them in his dugout. The old man here beside them said doubtfully: 'I dunno. That's a big dog, and he don't know me. He might not like the smell of me.' He looked at Bess and smiled. 'I took notice you keep to wind-'ard of me,' he commented. 'These here leggings is kind of fresh — but they ain't so damned fresh, at that. But your dog might think I was a b'ar. A dead one.' He looked toward Joel, near them now. 'Your dog know that man, does he?'

Mima said: 'Yes. I'll get Joel to set me over.' Joel was near, and she spoke to him. 'Tuner's in trouble,' she said. 'You want to carry me over there?'

'Sure as a gun!' he agreed. He looked at the old man. 'I'm Joel Adams,' he said. 'I'm clearing up at Round Pond.'

'I'm Davis,' the stranger told him. He nodded toward Tuner yonder. 'You'll find the other dog's hurt, likely.'

Mima stepped into Joel's float and they pushed off. The bearded hunter called after her: 'Yo're friendly, young woman. Come see my mountains, some fine day.'

'Wait,' Mima urged; but he shook his head.

'No, I'm moving on.'

She told Joel, as they moved across the pond: 'He lives 'way up-river, says he traps and hunts all over from the Kennebeck to the Penobscot. He says there's fine river above, and a pond and brooks. I'd like to go, some day; see what there is.'

'I aim to,' Joel assented. 'When I can get a spell off.'

'Time will come,' she said. 'Look at Tuner!'

'He's crazy,' Joel agreed.

When they nosed into the shore, in fact, the great dog was in a frenzy, leaping, barking deafeningly, bounding to and fro. Mima tried to call him, but he would not come. She saw bleeding gashes in his flanks, pointed them out to Joel, shouting to make herself heard over Tuner's clamor. She stepped ashore, and Tuner raced away; so Joel landed and pulled the nose of the dugout up on the bank, and Tuner came darting back and then away again.

His barks guided them; he returned now and then to make sure they were following. He led them southeastward for more than a mile, running ten yards to their one, barking steadily in a maddening clamor, till suddenly his barking fixed in one place, perhaps a quarter mile ahead of them.

They came there and found Lion. The other dog lay on his side, his tongue out, panting as rapidly as though he had run a race. Tuner still danced about them, barking till Mima thought her ears would split. 'Oh, make him stop!' she cried; and Joel caught Tuner and forced him to lie down and somehow hushed him. Mima touched Lion. He was sadly mauled; but his visible wounds were not sufficient to account for his helplessness. There were just here no signs of struggle; but Joel backtracked a few rods while Mima stayed with the hurt dog. He returned to report.

'They tackled a bear,' he said. 'A big one. Likely it hugged Lion, or caught him a cuff, and Tuner drove it off. He must have let it go and stayed with Lion here.'

'Lion's hurt bad!' Mima said. 'He can't move; and when I just tried to lift his head he yelped and snapped at me.'

'He wouldn't bite you,' Joel told her. 'You hurt him is all. We'll have to make some way to lug him.' He looked around, began to cut poles, and strip bark for withes to tie them together. He took off his hunting shirt and passed two long poles through it. He braced these poles as wide apart as the shirt would permit with cross pieces forked at one end and bound with bark. 'We can carry him on this,' he decided, and laid the rude stretcher on the ground. He took Lion's head and forequarters, holding the dog's head securely to prevent any spasmodic and instinctive attempt to bite, and Mima lifted the great beast's hindquarters, and they laid him on the stretcher.

'He might fall off,' she said. 'Wait.' She took off one of her petticoats. 'We can tie him on with this.'

So Lion was presently secured. 'There!' Joel said. 'He's as snug as a papoose. I'll rig a harness on Tuner, make him carry one end.'

But Mima said she could do it, so they set out. Tuner, whining uneasily, trotted ahead of them. Mima carried the front end of the stretcher. Lion was astonishingly heavy; and his weight tended to thrust her forward. Also, since her hands were engaged, she could not push aside the underbrush which barred their way; and she was forever ducking and bowing to escape branches that might have struck her in the face. 'You're like a man in a fight,' Joel told her, watching the play of her slim waist as her body bent this way and that. 'Want me to go ahead?'

'No, then the branches you push out of the way would slap back at me. I'm all right.'

'You are, to a shaving!' he agreed; and she felt her cheeks warm and was glad he could not see them. They began to see the pond in glimpses through the trees not far ahead. The hurt dog made no sound; but Tuner, though he was reassured since he saw Lion in their hands, nevertheless looked up at them with low whines now and then that seemed to ask for comforting; and Mima said:

'He all but talks, doesn't he? Yes, Tuner boy, he's all right. He'll be fine.'

'Unless he's hurt inside,' Joel reminded her. 'But a dog will get over anything that doesn't kill him right off. I wouldn't wonder but he'll pull through.' They came down to the water, a little south of where Joel had left the dugout; and he said: 'Lay him down. I'll fetch the float and get him.'

Mima was glad to rest a moment. She was hot and sweating, and her face was sticky with spider webs from walking through the woods. Also, the black flies had punished her severely; and when she rubbed at her cheeks and brow, dried blood showed on her palms. She took off her moccasins and stepped into the water, lifting her dress and petticoat, and waded out. The bottom was rocky, but she saw in the clear water a patch of sand two or three steps further out, and knotting her skirts high and securing them about her hips, she waded thigh-deep. The water on this midsummer day was on the surface warm as milk; but it was cold around her feet on the sand, and she thought a spring must bubble up through pin gravel there. She dipped up water and washed her face and her throat, washed her hands and arms; and then she heard the float coming, around the small point just north of where she stood. So she came ashore again, loosing her skirt as she did so; and standing on a rock beside the water, she wiped her face and hands with her skirt, then buttoned it down the front again. Her wet legs were deliciously cool under her petticoat. When Joel nosed the float ashore, he saw tiny moist curls on her brow and said with that quick lift of his brow:

'Hullo! Have a swim?'

'I just waded in. It's like milk, so warm.'

He nodded, turning to where Lion lay. 'We'll put him in, stretcher and all, I think,' he decided. 'We can handle him without hurting him, so.' They laid the stretcher lengthwise, turning the dugout broadside to the shore to make this easier. Mima took her place in the bow, and Joel made Tuner lie down under his own feet in the stern.

Then he pushed off and they angled across the lake toward David's landing, half a mile away. They said little. Mima was always apt to be silent; and Joel was well enough pleased to watch her shoulders as she paddled, and her round arm that dipped the blade so deep her fingers touched the water and came up dripping. Once he said:

'There are the young ones on shore watching us.'

She nodded, and he whistled through his teeth, a sprightly jig tune which she recognized as that which he had sung as he paddled away down the lake a few days before. She smiled secretly. He did not know that she had heard his song that day. Her ears were so much keener than those of the folk around her. Even his little whistled jig was almost soundless, as though he whistled in a whisper. The shore was near now; Bess and Bet and the children watching their approach. Bet called:

'Did you find Lion, Mima?'

'Yes. He's hurt. A bear hugged him, I guess; but he's alive.'

Tuner had roused at Bet's call, and he stood up in the unstable craft and began to bark ringingly. Mima thought it was as though he were trying to tell these on shore all about it. In a moment now they would reach the landing, and lift Lion out, and then Joel would go on down the lake and the river to Warren. She might not be with him thus again for weeks. She remembered how he had rescued 'Bijah, almost drowning, that night at Round Pond. Shore was only two or three rods away, and Tuner's gyrations shook the boat. As though to balance it, Mima leaned too far.

They were all in the water together. The dugout did not tip completely over; but Tuner and Joel and Mima were thrown out and the clumsy craft filled and floated like a log awash. One end of the stretcher slid free; but the other held, so that Lion, fast bound to it, was supported with his head out of water. Mima had thought she could hold to the dugout; but it escaped her, and her feet pulled her down, pulled her under. She held mouth and eyes tight shut, but she ceased her clumsy efforts to help herself. If she let him, Joel would take care of her. While she was still under water, his arm went around her from behind, under her arm and across her breasts, and they came to the surface together. When her mouth was clear, she told him steadily:

'I won't move, Joel. I'll be quiet.'

'If you're not, I'll clip you one,' he said cheerfully. Still sup-
porting her, he glided around in front of her, his hands under
her armpits. 'Glad I'm down to the buff!' He chuckled.
Mima heard Bet's excited voice from the shore, and the children were crying with terror. Joel said: 'Put your hands on my
shoulders. Hold tight. Keep your elbows stiff. Push yourself
away from me.'

She obeyed, her fingers digging hard into his bare shoulders;
and he began to swim, pushing her backward toward the shore.

'Is that right?' she asked.

'To a trifle,' he assured her. 'Keep your elbows stiff, and
spread your legs, let them trail either side of mine, give me
room to kick. Let your head lie back on the water.'

She felt his shoulder muscles move under her fingers, felt
through her arms the drive of his strokes. Her eyes and mouth
were still closed, and she scarce breathed; but she could breathe
if she chose. Her face was out of water. She could feel the
powerful kicks of his legs between hers. He said in low laughter:

'Open your eyes, Mima. Your phiz is screwed up like a wench
being kissed that likes it!' She obeyed him, looking down over
her own cheeks at him as he thrust her thus toward shore; till
he said: 'All right. You can stand up now. I'll go get Lion.'

She felt firm bottom under her and waded ashore to face the
excited relief of Bess and Bet and the children; and she stood
wringing out her skirts while Joel swam off and brought the
dugout in. She dried her skirt as she could, plucked her dress
free from her body to which it clung; and Bess told her to go
to the house and strip and dry her clothes before she caught her
death. Mima wished not to go; but Joel was bringing the float
toward the landing and she was suddenly reluctant to stay and
face him. Before he reached shoal water she fled away.

13

THEY would have no news from Philip for a while, but some two weeks after his departure with Jacob, Joel one Saturday afternoon brought word that the force sent by Massachusetts to drive the British out of Biguyduce had sailed up the Bay. He had gone down to Thomaston on some errand or other, and returning hailed them from the water and they all went down to the landing to hear what he might have to say.

'Thought you'd want to know,' he told them. 'They've started for Biguyduce. The ships that came from Boston were becalmed off St. George's Islands yesterday, but they got a wind this morning and now they've gone up the Bay. There's a monster great fleet, and the Warren frigate at the head of it, and twenty more besides, and guns enough aboard them to knock down a mountain if they had a mind to, and a thousand men and better to do the shore fighting. If they'll fight, the thing will be soon done.'

Young Eben asked hotly: 'Why wouldn't they fight? It's what they went for — and one of us is worth two lobsterbacks.'

Joel chuckled. 'So we say,' he agreed. 'But there's no being sure. When it comes to fighting, militia's like a woman about loving. When they will, there's no stopping them; and when they won't, you can't bring 'em to it.'

Mrs. Robbins made a scornful sound. 'From all I hear, you're one to know about women anyway!' she said.

He grinned. 'Why wouldn't I?' he agreed. 'If I don't, it won't be for lack of trying.' He added: 'But if you want to know, they say there's twenty-four bottoms full of men, besides the fighting ships, and there's only three-four war sloops of the King's at Biguyduce and a few hundred men. We ought to do the job in one mouthful.'

He had not stepped ashore; sat in the laden dugout at the landing to talk to them on the bank. Mrs. Robbins asked: 'Had ye any news of my menfolks; my man and my boy?'

Joel shook his head. 'No more than that they went aboard a sloop with Colonel Wheaton and the Thomaston men, to meet up with the fleet off the mouth of the river. They're gone up the Bay. Might be it's all over before now, if the wind served.' He spoke to Mima, smiling. 'Want another swimming lesson some day?'

Mrs. Robbins said: 'She told me you brought her safe ashore that time down at Dave's. I'm obliged to you, Joel. I'm ever afraid of the water, and the crank boats here.'

'It's easy enough to learn swimming,' he assured her.

'There's none of mine know how.'

'I'll teach them, the lot of them.'

Mrs. Robbins said doubtfully: 'I dunno. Getting into the cold water is a sure way to get sick and laid up with aches and pains and all.'

Mima urged: 'It was fair warm that day we fell in, Mother, and it is now.' Eben and Jess supported her, and so did the younger children, except Sue; and they argued the point till Joel laughed and said:

'Well, I'll come down, maybe tomorrow afternoon, and we'll let those that want it have a try.'

He pushed off, lifted his paddle in salute, turned up the shore and into the river and disappeared. Something drew Mima after him. She walked toward Round Pond through the silent pines. She heard Joel singing, somewhere ahead of her; but she made no attempt to overtake him. She came down to the river and sat a while on the ledge that projected into the water. The sun was low before she turned back, but Jess and Eben were still at work where the new barn would stand, and a flight of pigeons went over to settle on the rye, and Susie and Philip ran to drive them out. The birds took the air with a silken rustle of many wings, and there were thrushes singing in the dusky woods. Her mother had supper cooking, and the sun's last light lay across the pond. She thought they could be happy here. She said to her mother:

'What's the use in fighting, anyway, Mother? Why can't we just go on, doing the best we know, carrying our dish right side up, tending our own business?'

Mrs. Robbins shook her head. 'Don't ask me. It's idees, Mima. Men get idees. If they'd stick to their jobs, the way women do, cooking and cleaning and having children, they wouldn't have so much time to set and think. It's thinking so much that raddles a man.' She made an angry sound. 'Call the young ones,' she said. 'Tell Jess to start a smudge to keep the mosquitoes out. We can eat any time.'

* * * * *

In the morning, breakfast done, Mrs. Robbins watched Mima and Susie clear away, and she said: 'I declare, I'm a mind to go to church today! Jess, would you want to carry me down-river?'

'Matt Hawes might be going,' Jess evaded. 'He went two weeks ago. He goes a lot.'

'Matt may, but the others don't,' she assured him. 'Joel and Jason and 'Bijah Hawes, they go rooting around after every little no-petticoats down there. But I'm a mind for church today — with my man gone and all.'

Mima said: 'We can have church here, Mother. We do everything else for ourselves. I guess we can do that.'

'Your pa could if he was here,' Mrs. Robbins agreed. 'He can find ways to say a thing.' Her eyes filled with bitter tears. 'Dod rot him, what did he have to go off and let on he's a soldier for, the plaguy old fool!'

Mima laughed softly and came beside her. 'He's all right,' she said. 'Like as not he's having himself a time, telling everybody how he always did say one of us could whip two of them.'

'Don't you go making fun of your pa!'

'I'm not, Mother. Just trying to make you laugh. He'll be back with a big story to tell.'

'Well, I wish't he'd come.' Mrs. Robbins added gratefully: 'It's some comfort having you sleep with me, Mima; but I ain't only half here with him gone.' She said: 'I ain't a-going to no church though, to hear that Mr. Urquhart spitting brimstone. So don't try to talk me into it!'

In the end, with breakfast out of the way, her children around her, she walked down to the pond and they sat in the shade there and talked quietly together. Mrs. Robbins did most of the talking. 'I just feel like it,' she said. 'You might as well set and listen to me.' She harked back to the days before her marriage. She talked of Philip, and of how the children began to come. 'Robbins may not be so much,' she confessed. 'I guess't he wouldn't be, to anyone else, and he's made me mad enough to spit, more'n once. That man will get a hold of a thing and he'll tell it over and over till I want to screech and kick my heels. He don't have but one thing in his head at a time, and he's stubborn and set as a pig. But he's took care of us better than I looked for.' She laughed a little breathlessly. 'It looked bad for a while this winter, I'll admit. I didn't know as we'd make it. Winter's like waking up in the night and you get started worrying about something till you think the world never will be the right color again. I wish't there was some way you could realize, in the night, that things'll look better in the morning. They always do. Winter's the same. Seemed like to me some days last winter, I couldn't stand it, but we was all right, come spring.'

Mima said: 'I guess things always do straighten out some way, if you just keep going along.'

Her mother nodded. 'There was once I didn't think they ever would,' she admitted. 'When Joe died. That was ten years ago last January. He was just short of four years old. I dunno but he was the best of the lot of you, or would have been. When he died, I didn't know as I could stand it, but I did.'

'I don't think any one of us, any one person, amounts to much,' Mima confessed. 'It's all of us that counts. Most of the trouble comes from thinking so much about ourselves that we get so we think if anything does happen to us, the whole world's wrong.'

Her mother laughed. 'Minds me of a halfwit boy used to be at home. He didn't have brains enough to keep himself cleaned up, and you had to keep off from him or hold on to your nose. He got the idea into his head that the whole world stunk, used to go around telling folks so, real serious about it. You couldn't persuade him that if he cleaned himself up, the world would smell a sight better to him and to everybody else.' She added briskly: 'I wouldn't wonder if that wasn't the answer to a lot of things. I mean if we all just took care of ourselves, did the best we knew how. There's too many fuss-budgets around, always trying to tell other people how to behave. I've took notice more than once that these women that are always ready to tell you how to bring up your own children, they most generally have a passel of worthless brats to home.' She looked at Mima. 'Like you said, Mima, if we'd all just carry our own dish upright, there wouldn't be so much slop spilled all the time.'

Jess sprawled on his back, half asleep; but Eben sat with them. Susie and Phil paddled in the shallow water. Mima said: 'I've noticed one thing, Mother.'

'You always were a noticing young one,' Mrs. Robbins agreed, in good-humored affection. 'What is it you've noticed now?'

'Why, it's about being scared,' Mima said. 'I've noticed that the things we're scared of never happen. It's what you don't ever think about that makes the trouble. So there's no use in being scared.'

Her mother laughed. 'If being scared keeps things from happening,' she declared, 'I'm for it.' She added in a shaken tone: 'I hope you're right. I'm scared to death Pa and Jake won't come safe home. Maybe that'll fetch 'em.'

Eben said slowly: 'I'm more scared they won't do what they set out to do, lick the British.' He moved uneasily. 'There's better things than being safe,' he said.

'Not for a woman,' his mother assured him. 'Not where her menfolks are concerned.'

The morning droned away, the light breeze died and the sun hung hot and high so that Jess thought a thundershower was making up. Mima said at last: 'This has been as good as church, Mother, all here together. I wish Dave and Rich and theirs had come.'

'I'd ruther have it the way it's be'n,' Mrs. Robbins confessed. 'Let a young one get married and it's different, some way. They ain't yours any more.' She added: 'Not but Rich is all right. I didn't used to think so, but I've changed my mind. He's a real steady, good man, and he's been good to Bet. But you're all just Pa's and mine. You don't belong to anyone else at all.' She rose. 'Well, time to get started on something to eat.' She chuckled. 'I've got to keep you young ones fed, long as Pa's away.'

* * * * *

Joel came down that afternoon to propose that those who were so minded try to learn to swim. The afternoon was hot and still, the water warm, and even Mrs. Robbins could make no strong objection. The shore below the house shoaled off gradually, small gravel on the sandy bottom, and Joel chose that spot. Mima wore a calico dress with no petticoats; the others stripped to small clothes; and when Mrs. Robbins protested, Joel laughed at her.

'They've got too much on them as it is,' he protested. 'Mima, you'll never hate clothes so much as when you're in the water in them. So! Now we'll start learning the big thing. The big thing is, you can't sink if you want to.'

Jess laughed at that. 'Man, my feet are lead! They pull me down,' he vowed.

'We'll try that,' Joel told him. 'Shut your mouth, hold your breath, let me see you lie down on the bottom and stay there, here in three feet of water. Try it.'

Jess obeyed him. He went under easily enough; but standing around him in the clear water they could see his body rising toward the surface, see him scrabbling at the bottom in a vain attempt to hold himself down. He stood up at last, gasping and laughing and mightily pleased with himself.

'Say, it's so!' he cried. 'Try it, Mima!'

Mima tried it, forcing herself to lie face downward in the water. She felt the air balloon under her skirts, felt her shoulders and the back of her head out of the water. She made crawling motions with her hands and feet, and heard voices far away, and Joel caught her arm and pulled her to her feet again. Eben cried:

'You were swimming, Mima!'

She laughed happily, wiping the water from her streaming face, clearing her eyes. 'Was I, Joel?'

'You'd have swum right out into the pond if I hadn't stopped you,' he assured her. Eben was already trying the same procedure, and Jess too. 'That's all there is to swimming,' Joel said, watching them.

'But I couldn't have breathed!'

'You could if you lifted your head. Try it. I'll hold you up a little at first.'

This time he walked beside her, holding to her dress, sup-
porting her just enough so that she gained confidence. She
managed to breathe several times without choking; while Joel,
standing still, led her around him in a circular course. When
she stood up, Jess was choking with water he had swallowed;
and Mima laughed at him; and he said hotly:

'Well, you'd sink, too, if your skirt didn't hold you up! You
ought to see what you look like, with a backside on you like a
horse!'

Mrs. Robbins called sternly: 'Jess Robbins, you shut your
dirty mouth or I'll tan your hide, big as you are! I've done it
before and I can again.'

But Jess was already past his temper. 'They got me mad,
laughing, that's all,' he said.

'The thing to do,' Joel advised, when they were all tired and
ready to quit, 'take a couple bladders and blow them up and
fasten them to your belt; or find a tree that has a good limb
hanging out over the water, and hang a rope on it with a loop
in the end, long enough so it reaches into the water. Then you
can pass your shoulders through the loop, and paddle around
and get the feel of the water, and any time you're tired just
hang on to the rope and rest. You'll learn in no time, Mima.
You're not afraid. That's the most of it.'

She was filled all that day with a deep excitement, like that
of one who enters a new world; and when they were done and
he was gone away up the river, she went back down to the pond
to sit alone there with her thoughts. The sun was still high, the
day was breathless.

She became conscious at last of a trembling in her ears; some
sound too faint to be heard, not audible, yet sensible in silent
ways. It was as though the pressure of the air on her eardrums
came in beats and heavy waves. She had thus felt the beat of
air when a night hawk, swooping, caught himself on stiff pinions
near at hand. She strained to hear, her mouth open; she stood
up, all intent. And suddenly her brow was moist with a cold
sweat; for she knew what the sound must be.

It was the sound of guns, great guns. She bit her lip, nodding. They were shooting cannons at each other at Biguyduce — and her father was there.

She told no one what she had heard; but that night the heat ended in a thunderstorm which came cannonading around the house. Mima slept with her mother, and Mrs. Robbins whispered fearfully: 'Is it the guns, Mima? Could we hear from here?'

Mima laughed at her tenderly. 'Not likely, Mother. They're miles away. I'd not know how far; but too far to hear, certain. This is thunder like we get all the time.'

'Will they be hurt?' her mother whispered. 'Will they be killed?'

Mima comforted her; but she thought rebelliously that there was nothing but folly in all this. If John Perry had not come to tell them, they would never have known the British were at Biguyduce. Her father and Jacob would never have gone. Why should they have gone? Whether the British stayed at Biguyduce or were driven out could not matter to them here in Sterlingtown. 'If we didn't know, it wouldn't worry us,' she told herself. 'I wish we didn't know.'

She woke at dawn to lie thinking where such a rope as Joel had suggested, to help them learn to swim, could be hung. She rose and went out-of-doors into a still, foggy morning, no wind stirring, light faintly showing through the fog; and she turned toward the river. The water was shallow in the narrows above where the river met the pond; and it was so warm it seemed to steam. For a while no one would be abroad. She slipped out of her garments and waded into the water, wading out from shore, finding it no more than breast-deep till it began to shoal again toward the river's further bank. She turned and waded back again; and when the water was only a little deeper than her waist, she threw herself forward on her face, her face under water, and worked arms and legs in a crawling motion till her hands struck bottom painfully. She stood up in water barely above her knees. She had made progress, two or three yards, toward the shore.

She forgot time in repeating this experiment, till she heard her mother calling her. She answered, and dressed and went home and found a towel to scrub her streaming hair; and she told her brothers:

'I went swimming. I really did swim a little. I mean I took a breath once while I was swimming.'

Jess grinned. 'Anybody could with a skirt full of air to hold you up.'

'I didn't have a skirt on!' she told him hotly. 'I didn't have anything on.'

Mrs. Robbins whirled on her. 'Well, I'd be ashamed to admit it!' she cried. 'I declare, Mima, times I don't know what to make of you. You ought to be smacked, out nekkid in the light of day!'

But Eben said loyally: 'I bet you did swim, Mima. I'll bet you learn to swim good, before summer's gone.'

'I'm going to,' she agreed, and she asked: 'Eb, where would be a good place for a rope, the way Joel said?'

'There's a big birch leans out over the cove,' he remembered. 'The bank goes off steep, and the water's deep there, but we could hang a rope from the tree and it would be out over the water.'

Mrs. Robbins demanded to know where they thought a rope was coming from for that foolishness; but Jess said they could take the towropes off the hand sleds. 'We don't use them in summer anyway,' he pointed out. 'And we wouldn't have to cut them.'

They overruled their mother, in the end; and they hung the rope that day. Jess was the first to try it, while they watched from the bank. It was a success; and thereafter Mima came often through the woods to hook the dangling rope with a forked stick, and tie it around her body, and with its reassuring support she made progress day by day.

*   *   *   *   *

The night Philip Robbins and Jacob came home, they were all abed; Jess and Eben and Phil in the garret, Mima and Sue in the trundle bed, Mrs. Robbins in the big bed alone. But Mrs. Robbins was awake, and it was she who heard the grate of the float on the gravel at the landing. She called softly:

'Mima, someone's landed!'

Mima, instantly awake, heard steps; but a moment later she heard a voice too, and recognized it and sprang out of bed. 'It's them!' she cried. She swung wide the door. 'Father?' she called; and his great answer came.

He and Jacob were safe and sound. A glance was enough to show that; but Mrs. Robbins had tearfully to hug them both, and to feel them all over as though they might be concealing from her some dreadful wound. Jess built up the fire for light to see by; and the two were bombarded with many questions. What was in the bundles they bore? Were the King's men all killed? Were they themselves surely unhurt? Was there a big battle? Had they killed any Englishmen? The rain of queries came from Jess and Philip and Eben. Mima stood quietly waiting to hear; Susie sat up in the bed on the floor, her eyes wide in the firelight; Mrs. Robbins clung to her husband's side.

Philip when he could speak said the whole enterprise was still unfinished, but that it would surely end in failure and catastrophe. 'We could have had them three days ago,' he declared. 'But the Commodore was a New Haven man, name of Saltonstall, and stubborn as a mule.' And he cried, in an agony of bafflement: 'There was enough of us to eat them before breakfast! Yes, without salt, too! General Lovell would have done it. Him and General Wadsworth, there's two men that are worth two hundred; but the Commodore kept us popping our guns at them from too far away to do a mite of damage.'

He banged his knee in a deep rage. 'Three days of that we had!' he exclaimed. 'Just their three little war sloops to stop us, and nineteen great ships of ours, and any one of ours with guns enough to blow the three of theirs out of water. But we laid there and popped at them and nothing done.'

Mima said: 'I heard the guns, Father.'

'Aye, ye've good ears,' he agreed, and he explained: 'The war sloops was anchored broadside on to us; and the Commodore's notion was to try to cut their springs and their cables with our shot, so they'd swing around where they couldn't bring their guns bearing. But Goddlemighty, all we had to do was go at 'em, blow 'em sky high.'

Mrs. Robbins spoke reproachfully. 'Mima, you didn't tell me about hearing guns!'

The girl said strongly: 'No, I didn't! You didn't have to know! We'd all be happier and better off if we never knew anything that happened a day's walk away. Knowing just keeps us stewing about things that can't be helped.'

Her father chuckled; he said keenly: 'Mima, ye've changed, these two weeks.'

'She's learning to swim,' Eben told him. 'Joel's teaching us. We're all learning. Go on, Pa.'

The older man nodded. 'Three days ago,' he repeated. 'Before daylight. That was when we tried 'em. Two hundred marines and two hundred militia we set ashore — and it might full as well have been three times that many; but the Commodore was all for cautious ways. If it was a bear he was trying to kill, he'd have put his gun down and throwed rocks at it first. But at that, the four hundred of them took a battery. They landed on the west side, where there's a bluff to climb. There was a young one named Trask played his fife on the beach all through it, and we could hear him from the ships. They took this battery, and killed a lot of English and drove them back.' His hand clenched on his knee. 'With as many more men, they'd have walked right into the fort. It's no fort at all, rightly speaking; just a ditch and a bank a man can jump over flat-footed.'

'Why didn't they?' Eben demanded.

''Account of the yellow-livered, rat-hearted Commodore,' the older man said. 'And may mice gnaw his eyes out and eels eat his guts — if he's got any insides to him. Why, look here, that day when all he needed was to give them another good lick, the Warren frigate, with him on it — and she was the best ship we had — never got into it at all till along about ten o'clock. Then she run in and popped off her guns two-three times; and a few of them little six-pounders hit her and messed her up some, and she hauled off again, had her fill of it. The Commodore had his fill, too, I sh'd judge. One more push would have done it, but what did he do? Called them all aboard the frigate for a council. Time to fight is no time to talk! General Lovell, and Peleg Wadsworth — a fine handsome beautiful man he is, too, Ma — said they could demand a surrender and get it; but this fish-bellied Commodore wouldn't do it. So they said they'd storm the fort without asking for any surrender; but: "No," he says. "Some of my marines got killed this morning, and I'll not let them fight any more." And: "No," says he, "I'll send to Boston for help. It's more men we need. Man a couple whaleboats," says he, "and tell the men to go to Boston and say we need help." ' He spat with disgust. 'I judge he thought they'd enjoy the row!'

Jess exclaimed: 'Whaleboats, Pa? To go to Boston? Guess't he was crazy, wasn't he?'

'He's a chicken-gutted, cow-hearted coward! He knew if they fetched help, he'd have to fight some more; and he didn't want that. So whaleboats it was!' He glared into the coals. 'So I told Colonel Wheaton I had better business at home than waiting for the Commodore to grow a backbone; and Jake and me came along. We stopped by my brother Eben's, Ma, on the Fox Islands. I told him like as not he'd have British neighbors from now on, the way things was going. He says it's been bad anyway, with the refugees in sloops and shaving mills and whaleboats and barges coming by all the time. I told him he'd better move up here with us, away from all the rucus. Dunno but he will.' And he went on: 'Then they set us ashore at daylight this morning at Uncle Will's house. We tramped from there today.' He said gloomily: 'They'll stay there and flip pebbles at the fort till their grub gives out, then home they'll go. Not me! I've work to do.'

Mrs. Robbins said: 'I'm thankful they'd let you come away.'

'We was volunteers,' he explained. 'Us that went with Colonel Wheaton. Most of the others from hereabouts were in Captain Olson's company in Colonel McCobb's regiment. They had the heft of the fighting, day before yesterday, and a fine job they done of it, too.'

Jess asked: 'What did you fetch?' Philip and Jacob had each borne a heavy sack slung across their shoulders.

'I took my pay in goods,' his father explained. 'Ma, the things they had you'd never believe. We could live on it, rest of our lives. Salt beef and flour and rice and bread by the ton, and better'n a thousand gallons of rum, and muskets and cartridges and balls and gunpowder by the barrel, and digging tools and axes.' He nodded toward the sacks by the door. 'I fetched you some wheaten flour, Ma, and rice; and the rest is mostly powder and ball.'

Eben asked: 'Were you in the fighting any?'

'We were aboard the sloop we went on, all the time,' his father told him. 'It's a sightly place, Biguyduce, Ma. Town's on a neck of land shaped kind of like a tomahawk, with the blade facing southwest. There's two-three islands off southeast; and the harbor runs in kind of northeasterly between the islands and the main.' He grimaced bitterly. 'Them three English war sloops, they anchored right across the harbor mouth between the mainland and what they call Cross Island; and they fit back at us like good ones. We hit 'em some; but the Commodore kept our ships so far off, nobody done much harm to anybody. If he'd sailed right in, first day we got there, he'd have just run 'em under. They pulled back up into the harbor after that.'

Jacob, his Adam's apple pumping, said eagerly: 'Pa, it was one of ours made 'em pull back. The sloops were anchored broadside on to us; but the Hazard went around back of the island and shot at 'em across the island so's to hit 'em endways, and they couldn't stand it. That's why they pulled up the harbor.'

The older man nodded. 'Likely so,' he agreed. 'I didn't see it.' Then rage at his own memories exploded in him. 'Why, Goddlemighty!' he cried. 'Their war sloops didn't have only six-pounders on them; and us with everything up to eighteens, and more for all I know. If they keep on doing the way that lousy Commodore says, them three little sloops will come out some day and sink the lot of them.' He added dourly: 'That's why I come home. If that's going to happen, I'm no mind to be there to see.'

Mrs. Robbins clipped his head against her side, standing beside him as he sat before the fire. 'You're home, Pa! And Jacob too. You'll not go again. Come along to bed with me.'

But it was a long time before any of them slept that night. Mima could hear Jake in the garret whispering his story of his adventures to his brothers there; and her father's voice was a low murmur in the big bed beside her own. The night was hot, and she was stifled and breathless. The door was closed against mosquitoes. The black flies disappeared at sunset, and they were in any case almost gone at this season of the year; but the mosquitoes kept Mrs. Robbins awake; so even in summer the door was shut fast at night. The only air came through the small window, or through the cracks between the logs, or down the chimney. Usually Mima was conscious of no need for air, but tonight she felt oppressed, crowded into the small house with all these others.

Toward morning she took her blanket and went out-of-doors and slept upon the ground. She had slept out before, on that hunting trip with Jess that seemed now so long ago; but always in the winter. Night air, her mother thought and said, would poison a body, and it was worst in summer. Mima herself half shared this belief; but for this particular night the cabin was somehow intolerable. She lay under pines north of the house toward the river, watching the stars through the boughs overhead; but then mosquitoes drove her to cover her head till no more than her nose was exposed, and suddenly she was asleep and woke to full day and her mother by her saying:

'Skies above, Mima, what's got into you? You'll take your death!'

Mima smiled up at her, warm and rested and strong. Lying on her back, still half asleep, she clasped her arms across her breasts. 'No, Mother,' she said, 'I'll not. There's too much life in me.'

Mrs. Robbins made a scornful sound. 'Too much stuff and nonsense!' she retorted. 'Mima, something happened to you the day Joel fetched you ashore when the boat tipped over. You ain't the same.'

'I was changed before,' Mima told her. 'It's just — I know it, now.'

The older woman nodded slowly; and on a sudden impulse she sat down beside where Mima lay. 'It was that way with me, Mima,' she assented. 'First time I saw your father it was so, something starting in me, like a kettle getting ready to boil.' She smiled at her own memories. 'That was when he first came to work in the neighborhood. I was nineteen. You're older, Mima. It was a year before we married; but the minute I laid eyes on him, something happened to me. Then one night there was a hay ride, and when we come home he swung me down. Feeling him hold me hard, his hands on my waist, pressing hard — I knew it then.'

'My hands on his shoulders,' Mima said softly. 'Him swimming, kicking, driving me along ahead of him.'

The older woman said slowly: 'It won't make any difference to you, my telling you this — it wouldn't have to me, with Philip — but Joel's a regular he-goat, Mima. I've heard talk. There's a wench at McIntyre's he goes to see every time he goes down-river; and he's not the only man that does. He's been a soldier; and a man that never knows the minute he'll be killed will spill his seed every chance he gets. It's a habit easy learned. Joel's got it. But I guess that won't make a difference to you.'

'No,' Mima assented. 'He'll be different by and by.'

'The rum he drinks, I say nothing about,' Mrs. Robbins said. 'And wenching is maybe natural enough to a young man alone. But he'll want you, Mima.'

'I want him,' she said. The early morning was very still, no others stirring.

The older woman did not speak at once. Then she smiled a little, chuckling happily. 'I'm forty-eight years old, Mima, forty-nine in November; but I was happy holding Philip in my arms last night, all the same, and knowing him safe and all.' She said in a low tone: 'He says Chris Newbit got his arm took off by a solid shot, in the fighting that morning at Biguyduce; but my Philip came home whole.' She spoke softly, as much to herself as to Mima. 'You and all the others like you, going into the woods with your husbands, working with them and fighting with them and all — this country we're making is going to have a new kind of women in it, Mima. They'll be good for something besides having children plowed into them by some man, like they was a field he had to seed.'

'I know it,' Mima agreed.

'But a man don't know it,' her mother told her. 'You take Joel. He's a man, to begin with; and he's a man, if I'm any judge, all he's ever had to do was lift that eyebrow of his at a woman and she'd roll over and play dead like a little dog. A man like that, Mima, ain't going to have any notion of getting married.' Mima did not speak, and the older woman went on: 'Another thing, he's been a soldier. Take it a man that goes off fighting, killing, risking being killed, he gets excitement in his blood. It'll be a long time before he's ready to marry and settle down.' She spoke very gently. 'I don't want you hurt and unhappy, Mima. If he's the one you want — why, he's the one. I know you well enough to know that. But you'll have a job to gentle him. Women mean just one thing to him. You'll have to teach him there's more to a woman than he looks for.'

Mima nodded, her eyes suddenly twinkling. 'Give me time, Mother. I'll bring him up with his toes a-digging.'

Mrs. Robbins chuckled. 'I guess likely,' she agreed. 'I don't give Joel the chance of a hen in the rooster pen, with you after him, Mima! And you'll make a good man out of him, too. Now come on and help get up some breakfast for your pa and the boys.'

14

THAT was a dry summer in Sterlingtown and all along the coast; and crops were laggard. Nevertheless the rye ripened early in August; and Philip and his sons were busy with the harvest. During the days after his return, they had only fragmentary news from the force at Biguyduce, but the knowledge of that British army so near was heavy on their minds. The old-country Loyalists toward Broad Bay were saying the fort must by this time have been strengthened beyond any chance of capture; and among those who before now had been wary of committing themselves either as patriots or as King's men there began to be talk that whatever might happen to the westward, this coast would always be the King's. Even Philip thought this might happen.

'If we've many more like that pismire of a Commodore to give orders, we couldn't beat our weight in pillows!' he declared. 'Like as not the British have sent word to the eastward and the King's ships will come and sink the lot of ours; and we'll never have as good a chance to drive them out again.'

But since her father's return, what might happen at Biguyduce seemed to Mima remote from all their lives. She was more interested in the least event at Round Pond.

One thing that happened there was that Matt and Jason and Joel partitioned between them the land they had bought from Philip Robbins. Mima had a part in that transaction. Jason Ware had bought from John Snow in Thomaston a yapping little white dog named Sambo which was reported to be a champion bear dog; and Sambo proved his worth by treeing two bears in the first week after his arrival at Round Pond. He appeared one day at the house on Seven-Tree Pond, and Mima thought him lost and took him home, paddling up the river, Sambo excited in the bow. The men were busy extending the clearing. She landed and went to the house and found it in a clutter of masculine disorder. She built up the fire, heated water, and worked till even the sooted cooking dishes were clean and shining, everything stowed in some order, the whole more seemly to her feminine eye.

Sambo stayed with her while she worked; and when she was done and would have started home, he wished to follow her. He jumped into the float when she pushed off, and when she threw him out and paddled away, he barked so ringingly that she paddled down the shore toward where the men were working, hoping his barks would attract Jason's attention. The dog bounded along the shore, still barking; and at some distance below the landing, Joel came to the top of the bank above her and saw her and called a greeting.

'I brought back Jason's dog,' she told him. 'Now he wants to follow me.'

Joel laughed. 'Don't blame him,' he said. 'Wait a minute.' He called to the others, and Matt and Jason joined him on top of the bank. They talked together there, and looked at Mima, and she wondered what they discussed so seriously. Sambo found them, and she would have started home; but when she dipped her paddle, Joel called again to her to wait.

So she waited; and Matt cut a small twig off a bush near

where they stood, and another, and another. The three men came down to the shore where a rocky ledge slanted into the water; and Matt chose a little muddy spot on the margin of the water and thrust into it three bits of twig. She saw that the men were all surprisingly serious. Matt told her:

'We've got something to settle, Mima; want you to help us. Come pull up one of these sticks.'

She felt a still excitement in her, caught from them. She put the float ashore and stepped out to where the twigs were. 'Which one?' she asked, looking up at the men.

'Any one,' Matt told her.

She drew out, at random, the middle twig. It had two notches cut in what had been the buried end. Matt took it from her hand and looked at it. 'Yours, Jason,' he said, and gave the twig to Jason Ware. Jason grinned and wiped his mouth with his hand. Matt spoke to Mima.

'Now another,' he directed.

She obeyed him. This had a single notch. 'Mine,' said Matt.

Joel spoke for the first time. 'So I'm the Judas,' he said cheerfully. 'All right, boys, help yourself.'

Jason said: 'I'll take the house lot.'

Mima half guessed, then, what they were about. Matt said at once: 'I'll take the north lot.'

Joel laughed. 'Well, if that's the way it lays — that's the way it lays,' he said.

Mima asked them: 'What is it? Tell me what you mean?'

So Matt explained to her. 'Why ma'am, we're partners here, bought all together, built the house together, and we're clearing this land together. But we can't go on share and share the rest of our lives, so we've split it into three pieces. The best land's here along the pond and the meadows; but some places it's a wide strip and some it's not. So we cut it up into three lots, one big one down here, because there's less good land here; and one with the house on, and one above. And you drew lots for us to see who'd have first pick.'

Mima nodded, shaken with disappointment because she had failed to draw for Joel the first choice. 'Jason gets the house, then,' she said. She had so often imagined herself and Joel living there.

'Yes,' Matt agreed. 'But the big job is getting the land cleared. Joel gets this we're working on, and we'll all work together till we get some cleared for Jason and for me.'

'I guess you'll build different houses after a while,' she suggested. 'So you won't have to go on living together.'

'Don't know as we will,' Joel told her. 'Long as we get along.' He spat on his hands. 'Well,' he said, 'this ain't falling any trees.'

They went back to their work again, and she turned homeward, skirting the reedy northern shore of the pond, wishing Joel had drawn the house lot, feeling that if he had done so it would have freed him so much the more quickly from his bondage to his friends. But she was not impatient. Time was long; and when a thing is sure to happen, it need not be hurried.

That evening at dusk, Joel came down-river with a haunch of meat. 'Sambo treed this bear yesterday,' he told Mrs. Robbins. 'And it eats good.' He looked at Mima. 'Somebody gave our place a cleaning up today — and this will help pay for it.'

Mima laughed a little. 'It was a real royal mess!' she said. 'Made my fingers itch. I had to give it a lick and a promise.'

'You need a woman to do for you, Joel,' Mrs. Robbins told him stoutly. 'I'd as soon clean up after pigs as men! I never saw menfolks yet that'd take the trouble to do a thing right. It takes one woman all her time to red up after one man; and as for three men! Skies above, I hate to tell you!'

Joel grinned. 'I expect we're pretty bad. But we wash our dishes when they need it, anyway.'

'Yes, with cold water! I know the way!'

He laughed, and he asked Philip: 'Mima tell you we drew lots for our land today? Or she did?'

'She was telling me,' Philip agreed. 'I sh'd judge Matt got the best piece. The meadows will be mostly his.'

'No, we aim to share the hay off of them,' Joel explained. 'There's plenty for the lot of us. I figure I got four hundred acres, more or less. There's not so much good farming land, but there's good timber. That'll be worth something, time I'm ready to sell it off. I don't know as I'll ever make a farmer; but the brook's all on my land and a good chance to get logs down to the pond. If I ever want to sell out, I've got a good proposition.'

'There won't be any call for lumber for a spell.'

'It might not be as long as you think,' Joel argued. 'If I get my bellyful of farming.'

Mima said: 'I guess you'll never sell.' Her own voice sounded strange to her, shaken by fear.

'Well, I might,' he insisted.

Her mother asked Joel: 'You going down to Warren again tonight? It's late, but I've heard you go past after dark before now.'

'Thought I might,' he admitted. 'I aim to see if there's any news from Biguyduce.'

'I know all about the news you want to hear!' she told him angrily. 'And for that matter, so do half the men in town. They've heard it too!'

He chuckled, and Mima went out-of-doors to hang the meat on the shady side of the cabin. Dark had fallen. She plucked ferns to wrap the haunch against flies and to keep it cool; and having done so, she moved aside toward the pines north of the house, out of sight but not out of hearing. The thought that Joel might sell his land was shaking her. She wanted to be alone. He and her mother stayed by the cabin door, and Philip joined them.

'Well,' he said, 'if it's news from Biguyduce you're after, Dave was down't Warren this morning. All the word is that they're still shooting off their guns and doing nothing.'

'Why then,' Joel decided, 'this is once I won't have to go to Warren for what I want. I'll sit a while with you.'

Mrs. Robbins made a contented sound. 'It won't hurt you,' she declared. 'Setting decent is a sight better than going out every night on a tom cat prowl!'

He laughed challengingly. 'How would you be knowing what's better and what's worse?' Mima, standing among the pines, could hear every word. The children were down by the shore, wading in the shallow water. Philip and Mrs. Robbins and Joel were alone. 'I could tell you some tales to take your breath out of you,' Joel assured them. 'A man never knows what he'll run into in the dark.' He laughed. 'I knew a man name of Tufts,' he said. 'In the army. He put up one night at a house where there was a pretty wench and another as ugly as a hedge fence. He found the pretty one's bed in the dark, or thought he did, and a fine night they made of it. But come daylight, he saw it was hedge fence there beside him, and he swore at her for a cheating trollop, and she told him it would be a lesson to him that all women are pretty in the dark.'

Philip guffawed, and Mrs. Robbins said hotly: 'Philip, you hush! Joel, shame on your dirty mouth for talking so!'

'I notice you didn't stop me till I finished,' Joel reminded her, chuckling. He said in politely conversational tones: 'Mosquitoes not so bad as they was, seems to me.'

'The flies is worse,' Mrs. Robbins retorted. 'The little ones have growed up to be big ones now. I'll be glad when frost comes, for one.' She said: 'Robbins, you better get a smudge going.'

Philip obeyed her, and he suddenly laughed at some thought of his own. 'Speaking of women in the dark,' he said. 'Ma, you mind old Dan Wingo, down home?'

She said hotly: 'Yes, I do! Don't you go telling that story, Pa!'

'Why, 'twa'n't nothing only a joke,' he assured her. 'Old Dan...' She rose vehemently and turned indoors, and she called back over her shoulder: 'Mima! Mima, you come on inside and let the menfolks play in the dirt!'

But Mima did not answer, and Philip went on. 'Dan had been meeting one of the neighbor's wives down by the haystack of a warm night,' he explained, 'and Mis' Wingo got onto it. She might have combed his hair with a broomstick, but she was smart. She knowed it's a sight better to laugh at a man than to cuss him out; so she went to the woman and give her a piece of her mind, and when Dan got to the haystack that night, Mis' Wingo was there to meet him. It was dark as the insides of a black cat, and it was so near the house they had to whisper, and Mis' Wingo played up to Dan so's he didn't know the difference.

'He'd fetched along a ham for his mopsy, and he give it to her, and next day for dinner Mis' Wingo gave him the ham, all baked, with hay around the edge of the platter!'

He laughed with them, and Mrs. Robbins said from the doorway: 'She'd have done better to take the carving knife to him!'

'I dunno,' Philip protested. 'The story got out on him. They say he never went near a hay pile again.'

The others came up from the shore. 'You come along in, Robbins,' she said. 'Jake, you and the young ones get to bed.'

Mima had remained a little withdrawn, near enough to hear, far enough away so that they could forget she was there. Jess and Eben and Joel stayed near the little fire on which as soon as flames began to show one or the other dropped a handful of grass and weeds so that new clouds of smoke arose. The night was overcast and warm, the mosquitoes savage; but Mima preferred to stay apart and listen to Joel's talk. He told tales of his service in the army. He had arrived too late to harry the troops home from Concord; and he was sick with a bloody flux the day of the fight at Bunker Hill. But in New York and in New Jersey he had seen fighting enough; and he was at Trenton and at Princeton. Mima, listening from two or three rods away, watching the small flames that now and then lifted

their heads, thought gratefully that he had come through un-
harmed. She saw her brothers intent on every word. Joel's
voice fell low and lower as the hush of night settled all around;
and Mima heard a night bird croak high above the river, and
an owl hooted somewhere, and down the pond, loons broke
suddenly into an insane chorus of hoots and shrieking cries.
Jess laughed at that.

'It was the loons that scared the Dutchmen over at Broad Bay
most of all when first they came,' he said. 'Dave says they used
to pray to be saved from witches and warlocks, and from the
things that scream on the lakes and say hoo-hoo in the meadows!'

'Did they so?'

'They were scared plenty,' Jess declared.

'I was only scared once,' Joel told them; and a little flame
lifted for a moment and Mima from where she stood saw the
whites of Eben's eyes gleam. 'I mean to say, what you'd call
scared,' Joel corrected.

'When was that?' Eben asked.

'Why, it was a time when I went with my father,' Joel said.
'I was a younker, and we were going somewhere I've forgot. I
might have been your age, Eben. We came to an inn for the
night, and there was a dead man in the place, and people
sitting up with him. Only mostly they were full of rum in the
taproom below.

'So my father and I went off to bed. I slept with him, and
glad I was to do it. But sometime in the night I woke up in the
wrong place.' He laughed briefly. 'Did you ever know a man
that walked in his sleep?' he asked.

'There was a woman in Walpole used to,' Jess told him.
'She got up out of her own bed one morning with clay mud
between her toes — and there was no clay mud in two miles of
the house.'

'So?' Joel exclaimed. 'Well, it was the same with me. I
woke up that night in the stable yard, and them that were

sitting up with the dead were still shouting and singing in the tap, so I was glad to dodge back up the stairs and never be seen; and into bed I dived, and glad I was to be there.' He added fresh grass to the smudge. 'But you know,' he said, 'it wasn't long before I began to be cold, and I didn't know why. I was cold all through — so I edged over to snuggle up against my father. He was always a big, warm, comforting man, and I was cold enough to want to get close to something warm.

'But the trouble was — he was cold!' His voice suddenly acquired tension, it was strict and whispering and still. 'He was cold,' he said. 'And the closer I snuggled, the colder he was. And then I tried to sneak in under his arm — and his arm was stiff so I couldn't make it bend. It was like trying to bend a stick of cordwood. Only it was cold, like ice, like wood out-of-doors in the winter, frozen stiff and hard.' He said reasonably: 'Mind you, that was my father's arm, cold and stiff. So I spoke to him. And he didn't answer. And I knew he was dead.'

Eben asked in a stammering gasp: 'Was he?' Mima smiled, coming nearer through the darkness; and Joel said:

'Why, no. The man in bed with me was dead, sure enough; but my father was in the other room. I'd got into the wrong room, when I came back from my sleepwalking.' He saw Mima draw near, watching them; and he asked:

'Did ever Dave tell you about the wreck of the Grand Design? I heard that tale in Warren one night a month ago.' They had not heard; and he said slowly: 'Why, it happened maybe forty years gone. Some Indians came to Warren, that was the upper town then, with letters from people off her. She'd been wrecked on Mount Desert Island. That's off to the eastward, a hundred miles or so around by land. She was a big ship, two or three hundred tons. They were north-of-Ireland folks mostly, going to Philadelphia to settle, and most of them had servants with them. They got what food and stores they could off the ship, but it wasn't much; and the young men — almost a hundred of them — started off, got across to the mainland on rafts, and set out to try to find help somewhere.

'They never were heard of after, not one of the lot, a hundred of them just walked off into the woods and nobody knows where they went or what happened to them.'

'Indians?' Eben suggested.

'Not likely,' Joel said. 'If Indians had taken that many scalps they'd brag about it enough so't someone would have heard by now.' The fire burned up and Jess dropped some sticks on it, kept the flames alive. Mima watched Joel's face in the firelight. He stared at the flames while he spoke. 'They might have starved, or froze, or scattered or anything. They might have gone east instead of making this way. But anyway they never came back.

'The rest was women and children and the married men. They were months there, starving and dying.'

Jess demanded: 'Why didn't they kill a bear?'

'Likely they did,' Joel assented. 'But not enough to live on. There was a Mrs. Galloway, and she had a baby and her husband. Her husband died and she buried him. They were 'most all dead before help got to them from here. The folks here brought them back to Pleasant Point, down the river, where Henderson's store that used to be a blockhouse is now. They were so near starved that they wouldn't wait for potatoes to roast, dragged them out of the ashes and ate them raw. Mrs. Galloway married Archie Gamble after they came here; and McCarter married another woman that her husband had died the same way.'

He added: 'But it's the young men that stick in my mind, a hundred of them going off into the woods, and never a hide nor hair of them seen since. Wonder what got them?' His voice was low. 'There's only a dozen of us here now. Whatever got them might be still around.'

Mima had drawn nearer as he talked, and at this word, Eben shivered and Jess laughed at him, and Mima said:

'They didn't have any women with them, or maybe they'd have got through. It takes a man and a woman together, Joel She'll fight as hard, and work as hard, as he will; and he'll fight twice as hard and work twice as hard if he's doing it for her. It takes two of them.'

His eyes met hers, but it was a moment before he spoke. He said then, nodding a little: 'Yes, 'tis so. A man alone's only half a man.' He rose, stretching himself. 'We've sat here half the night,' he said. 'I'll be going.' He spoke to Mima. 'And much obliged to you for cleaning up today,' he said. 'Might be you'd come do it again.'

'I will if I'm up by that way,' she assented, not moving, feeling her heart pound.

Jess went with him down to the landing, and Eben to his bed; but Mima, before Jess returned, slipped around the cabin and along the border of the wood and then down through the pines till she came to the river by the cove. She stayed there as Joel in the float went by. When he passed, he began to sing, under his breath:

> Oh her cheek it was bonny, her eye it was merry;
> Her ear was a shell and her lip was a cherry;
> Her smile would make any man linger a while
> And she smiled that smile for the gentlemen!
>
> Till a lad he rode by and he tarried to dally
> And dandle and bundle with this pretty Sally.
> 'I'll lay me,' he told her, 'Just seeing you smile,
> 'That you've been very kind to the gentlemen!'

He broke off as he passed under the tree bridge; but he whistled the same tune as he went on. He rounded the next point and began to sing again, yet so softly that she could not hear the words. She heard for a while the occasional thump of his paddle against the side of the dugout, till that too was lost, and the hush of night once more settled down. She turned back, glad that tonight at least he had not gone down-river, to hear the news from Biguyduce or on any other errand. If the girl named Fanny at McIntyre's expected him, she would be disappointed.

Biguyduce was a far trouble in her mind, and so was Fanny; but they were outside the borders of her world here. If she could keep Joel here, her world was full.

Yet suppose he sold his land and went away, not to return? The thought made her cold.

At the house she found that Jess had waited for her, and he said in a teasing laughter:

'Did you go tell Joel good-bye, Mima?'

She said simply: 'No. Just to hear him pass in the night.'

'You like him, don't you?'

'Yes, Jess, I love him,' Mima said.

15

IN EVERY lull in the work that summer, Philip and his sons turned to the task of getting out timbers for a new barn. He was thus engaged one day in the second week in August, when Oliver Robbins came up from Thomaston and brought his brother Ebenezer. They were both half-brothers of Philip. Mima, when she saw Uncle Eben, half-guessed his errand. Ebenezer Robbins had settled on the Fox Islands eight or ten years before. She knew where the islands lay, halfway to Biguyduce; so she was not surprised when Uncle Eben said now:

'Well, Philip, you was right about Biguyduce. There's a monster great fleet of Englishmen come from the east'ard yestiddy. Ours up the Bay, they've done nought but pop off their guns; and by this time the English have got a real fort built, I reckon. Now the whole damned King's navy's coming, to sink the lot of 'em.'

Philip nodded grimly. 'I've been looking to hear so,' he agreed. 'I c'd see, before I come home, the Commodore would set there pecking at them till they had time to send for help, 'stead of gobbling 'em up when he could.'

'He'll get gobbled now,' Uncle Eben predicted. 'And with the British settled there, Fox Islands ain't going to be any place for a man to live from now on. I picked up Oliver to fetch me up here to see you. I'm a mind to move up here with you. Guess't their ships won't come this far.'

'We need men here,' Philip told him soberly. 'And there's room. You come along.'

Ebenezer nodded. 'I like the look of it here,' he assented. 'The land's not full of stones and all. There's solid ledge shows through all over Fox Islands. Looks like a man could raise a crop here.'

'We do,' Philip assured him. 'Mostly, anyways. We've had it pretty dry this summer, though; and I had a kind of set-back last winter. My barn burned — I'm getting out timbers for a new one now — and we had critters starving to death all winter, me and Dave and Rich Comings. He married my Bet.'

'I know, certain,' the older man agreed. Mima saw his lip tremble, and she thought he was uneasy at the necessity of giving up his farm, starting all over again. She wished to comfort him. Her Uncle Oliver said:

'Lucy tells me Bet's having a baby in February.' Mima saw that he wished to give Uncle Eben time to compose himself again.

'So I hear,' Philip agreed.

'Lucy's got a fine young one, over yon.' He pointed across the pond.

'Dave's Bess has had two, but neither one of them lasted long,' Mrs. Robbins told him. 'One was stillborn, and the other didn't live but a couple weeks.'

They talked, carefully, of children and of crops, of moose and bear, of the drouth that began to be severe. Uncle Eben sat quiet, muttering to himself, shaking his head and wagging it; and they let him have time for his decision. Mrs. Robbins asked Oliver how his family were; she asked him for the news in Thomaston. He answered her at length, filling time, now and then looking at Ebenezer with a faint frown as though wishing he might say something to help the other man to a decision. Mima thought there was in men gentleness and consideration. They allowed to each other the right to reach decisions. Women in the same circumstances would have added many urgencies and pleadings. Not till Ebenezer lifted his head did Oliver wait to see what the other now would say.

'I'll come, Phil,' he said simply, in that sudden silence. 'You pick out a likely place for me.' He added: 'I'll have to get a sloop to handle my stock and all, and I'll go back and harvest my crops when they're ripe, if the refugees don't burn them out of meanness. I'll send the young ones home to Walpole for the winter; but I'll start moving now, get a house up and ready.'

'The boys and me'll give you a hand,' Philip promised. 'You'll need help.'

'Glad to have it,' the old man agreed. He looked at the barn timbers on which Philip had been working. 'Bela can help with them there,' he said. 'He's a good carpenter; and he's as able with an axe as anyone I ever see.' He looked toward the shore where their dugout lay. 'Bela wouldn't be seen in a crank dugout like that one,' he declared. 'He'll take an axe and a log and make you as pretty a canoe as ever you see, quicker'n a cat can spit.'

He was anxious to start down-river, but Mrs. Robbins made them stay long enough to eat a bite — which proved to be a feast. Ebenezer said the British fleet was not yet in the Bay when he left home the day before. 'But the wind the way it is, they'd make in today all right,' he predicted. 'They'll be up't Biguyduce tonight or first thing in the morning.' He looked at Philip. 'You c'n be glad you're not there.'

'If the Commodore runs away from a fight as hard as he holds back from getting into one, they'll never catch him,' Philip predicted. Memory raised his voice in anger. 'If he had the grit there is in General Wadsworth's big toe we'd have driven the lobsterbacks from hell to breakfast, two weeks ago!'

The two men presently departed down-river; and Mima wondered whether she actually heard the sound of distant guns that afternoon, or whether it was her own imagination. Next morning she was sure; and during the next few days there were rumors that all the American ships had been run ashore and burned, and the militia scattered. Philip Robbins was divided between a gloomy triumph because his predictions were fulfilled, and a curdling, choking rage at the Commodore. Then Colonel Wheaton came up from Warren in a ferry with three men who would work at clearing his land up the river. He sent the men on, but he stopped to eat dinner with Philip Robbins, and while they ate and afterward, he told the bitter tale. The very moderation of his language showed how hard hit he was. He spoke simply, like a man half stunned.

'We had word the British fleet was coming,' he said. 'Heard the day before, and then we see them. They was too many for us, and there was nothing for it but to cut and run; so we got off all the men from shore, and our guns. Worked all night, and we were still at it at daylight. We could see the King's ships by then, down the Bay; but it was all a flat calm, so they hung there, looking as big as mountains.'

He hesitated, as though silenced by the memory. 'One was the Raisonnable 64, I heard; and she was a sight, big enough to carry our Warren frigate for a longboat. Come daylight, the Commodore had laid our gun ships in a line across the Bay from Biguyduce to Long Island — and the transports north of them was sweeping away as fast as they could. My sloop was loaded earlier than most. We made for Turtle Head, but it was mighty slow sweeping. Then the wind came up out of the sou'west. I hauled up for the head of Long Island; and I could see the British ships catch it and come on, with ours laying to their anchors there and waiting for them, and the transports scattering every way like a flock of chick partridges. I kept watching to see what would happen behind me.'

He choked with pity and with anger and with shame. 'Well,

I saw,' he said. 'It was Hell with no boots on. The English ships came right along up to ours, and all of a sudden they wore, handy as an ox team, and let their broadsides go. Then you could see all of ours slipping anchor and crowding on sail, and trying to run and nowhere to run to, and the Englishmen to wind'ard and right on top of them.' His hand pounded lightly on his knee. 'Two of them, two of ours, tried to make around Turtle Head; and I saw the Hunter run hard aground with all sails standing, saw the men on her jumping overboard, scrabbling ashore. By the time I started across toward the main there were ships of ours afire all up and down. I could see one up toward the river burning like a torch, and a dozen smokes beyond her and around.'

His own memories silenced him. Young Eben asked in a husky voice, 'Did they sink any ships with men aboard?'

'I guess the most of them got ashore,' Colonel Wheaton told him. 'But some of them will have a long walk home.'

Philip Robbins spoke in a curious, flat tone empty of emotion. 'We could have whopped them three weeks ago.'

'We could so,' Colonel Wheaton agreed. 'The Englishmen were ready to give in, the twenty-eighth. They say the English General had his hands on the halliards one time, ready to haul down his flag. That was just before our ships pulled off. They hadn't any fort worth mentioning, nor half enough men. Colonel Brewer of ours went close enough to see, and he tried to talk the Commodore into it, but he just got damned for a know-it-all.' He added: 'The Commodore ought to be court-martialled for a coward; aye, and shot, too, if I was on the court!' And he cried again, stirred to heat by memory of the disaster: 'The woods are full of ours, dragging their tails home the best way they can, but they'd have had Biguyduce two weeks ago if he hadn't held them back!'

For a while their talk was all ejaculation, rueful curses, dis-cussion of what might have been. Eben sat with tight lips, and even Mima felt some of the shame and the pity of that disgraceful

failure. Her father said at last in a dry rage: 'Any one of ours
could handle two of them — but the thing gripes me, one
pismire of a Commodore can keep all of ours back like their
hands were tied, and get them killed and all!' He added slowly:
'It's going to be hard for us, Colonel, with the British there.
They'll stay now, no getting rid of them; and you'll see sloops
and schooners and shaving mills in and out of every cove, stealing and burning.'

'There's plenty that are glad of it,' Colonel Wheaton told him.
'For one thing, the English will be buying meat and corn and
all, enough to feed a thousand men; and there'll be plenty
hereabouts to sell to 'em.'

'My brother Ebenezer's moving up here from the Fox Islands.
He says there'll be no living there.' And Philip asked: 'What
happened to Perry, the one his wife and baby died, that came
up here to fetch me?'

'He was with me that day. He's gone back to North Haven to
get his children and put them safe; but he's not going to be
happy till he kills two Englishmen to even up for his two they
killed.'

Robbins said gravely: 'He was a wrathful man. I'd not want
him after me, not even if I had an army round me.'

When Colonel Wheaton was ready to go on up the river,
Mima volunteered to take him, so that Jess and Eben and the
younger boys could stay at their tasks here. He took the stern
and she the bow; and he went over and over the same ground
again, repeating some things, adding others. ''At Fales, that
went with me, made fools out of a whole company of the lobsterbacks,' he said. 'Went across past where they were, in easy
musket shot, to fetch the rest of us some water. All of sixty of
'em shot at him, going and coming, and never so much as
tipped his hat. I didn't see him start or I'd not have let him.
It wasn't any way possible, what he did. One of our men that
was used to shooting for meat would have knocked him over as
easy as a treed bear.'

He harked back in bitterness to the defeat of the fleet again. Mima asked no questions. She was always more apt to listen than to speak; but more by his tone and his continued talk than by his words she began to get a picture of that noontide of confusion when the American ships scattered in blind panic flight.

'We might have licked them, but the Commodore was a coward,' Colonel Wheaton told her, 'and knowing that took the fight out of all of them.' And he cried: 'Why, their three little war sloops had stood off our nineteen great ships for nigh onto a month! Just the solid shot we popped off at them, if you loaded it aboard them, would have been enough to sink them; but they stood us off. Even when their big ships came, if we'd made a fight of it as good as the sloops did against us, we'd have beat them.' He groaned. 'It was a sin and a shameful thing to see!'

They came to Round Pond; and Mima asked: 'Will I set you up the river to your land?'

He elected to go by the cabin of the Royal Mess, so they struck across the pond; and when they landed, Mima went as far as the cabin with him. The sound of axes led him to where the men were working; but she stayed to clean the cabin, wondering which of the things she handled were Joel's belongings. Sambo came back to the cabin on some errand of his own and barked at her and then recognized her and sat with his head on one side watching her activities till he decided they held no possible interest for him and so departed again into the wood. She finished and returned to the dugout and started home. The late afternoon was warm and still, the water cool upon her fingers as her paddle dipped. When she came home, the menfolks were busy with the barn timbers, the sun low in the west, fine clouds across the sky.

John Butler paddled over from the Mill Farm that night to say that a militia company, homeward bound to Falmouth after the disaster up the Bay, had camped in Crawford's Meadows. He had gone to the Meadows to try for a moose at dusk and had seen the company of men emerge from the forest, footsore and hungry, with a man from Lincolnville guiding them. He killed no moose; but he did encounter a bear in a berry patch on the way home and killed that. Jess and Eben went back with him and stopped to butcher the bear and pack the meat on for the hungry men. They stayed all night, returned next morning. Jess was chuckling at some of the tales he had heard, incidents at once tragic and ludicrous. One man had been creased by a musket ball across his backside, and Jess said:

'They were claiming he'd have to learn how to sit down standing up, or else never sit down only in the backhouse, where he wouldn't be pressing his hurts on anything. Another man, a cannon ball brushed one of his ears off just as clean as if you'd knocked it off with a brick. He had on a coonskin cap, and it took the side out of that. I asked him did it hurt, and he said no, but he thought he'd die laughing to see the fur fly.'

Jess was amused, but Eben was not. 'It made me sick!' he said hotly. 'Talking to them, knowing how hard they'd had it.' He frowned, groping for words. 'I mean, if they had beaten the English, they'd be heroes, and everyone out to meet them. But they didn't, so everybody's laughing at them — or else cussing them. But they were just as brave losing as if they'd won, and they had a sight harder time.'

Philip Robbins said: 'You'll find it's so, Eben. It ain't what you try; it's what you do that folks go by. There's a lot of fine men never got anywhere, and no fault of theirs; and there's others done well and no credit to them. But it's the ones that do something that get the credit, all the same.'

'I was sorry for them,' Eben said, and Jess agreed:

'So was I, but I could see the funny things about it, too.'

Mima asked: 'Have they gone?'

'They were getting ready to,' Jess told her. 'It's a long walk home for them, and through woods all the way.'

Philip said: 'Aye, and there'll be more of them coming along.' They did see other stragglers, and the thought of the disaster hung like a cloud in their thoughts all summer long.

*   *   *   *   *

Before the end of August, Moses Hawes bought from Philip a tract of land between his own farm and Rich's, running back toward Round Pond, and began to clear there; and a day or two later Uncle Eben brought up the river the first cargo of his household goods, his son Bela driving their oxen through the woods up the western shore of the pond. Bela was eighteen years old, Eben's age; and although he was a light-hearted, laughing youngster, his skill with an axe made him at once the leader where work of that kind was required. When he and his father set to work to put up a log house, Jess and Eben helped them fall the trees, and the oxen dragged them to the chosen spot; but it was Bela's axe that fitted the ends. In most houses, the logs were notched together in a saddle-and-rider pattern; but Bela, as though delighting in his own manual skill, preferred to cut a semicircular notch that would fit down over the naturally rounded log. Since they had not to square the logs, this if it could be well done was the quicker procedure; and Bela was able to prepare the logs as fast as the other three could fell the trees, cut them into proper lengths, and deliver them to the cabin site. The walls went up fast; and since there would be some delay in getting boards — the extreme drouth had so lowered the streams that mill work was curtailed — Bela fitted pole rafters and covered them with slabs of birch and hemlock bark for a roof to keep out the weather till later in the fall boards could be secured.

Mima and Sue helped chink the spaces between the logs. The other cabins were chinked with moss from the forest; but Bela had a better way. 'We've hands enough to do it right,' he said, 'and clay a-plenty. I'll show you.' He cut wedges, forced them between the logs like shingles overlapping, plastered the outside and the inside with clay well pressed in and smoothed against the weather. With many hands to help, the task was soon done.

When the cabin was well under way, Ebenezer went to harvest his crops on the Fox Islands farm; to take his chance of bringing their harvest safely up the river. The chance was a risky one. With the British secure in Biguyduce, marauders thronged along the coast. Colonel Wheaton, as commander of the militia, kept twenty men commanded by Captain Ludwig under arms in Broad Bay to meet any threatened attack, and a company under Lieutenant Kelloch was on duty at Clam Cove, and Ben Burton at Camden. At Philip Robbins' request, Colonel Wheaton sent nine men under Captain Crabtree to go with Uncle Eben and protect him at his harvest. All the grain that could be saved must be, for the drouth had curtailed the yield, and the corn was particularly poor. The woods were dry as tinder, and the skies were overcast with smoke from distant forest fires. Down-river, northwest of Warren, fire got loose and ran through the forest, burning itself out along North Pond.

Ebenezer returned to report that every British sympathizer along the coast had turned privateer and pirate.

'Pomeroy of Meduncook for one,' he said. 'He's got a brig now, coming out of Biguyduce. Landed the other day on Jameson's point with twenty men and put Bob Jameson in irons aboard the brig, butchered two of his oxen and three hogs and never stopped to dress them. Loaded the lot aboard the brig, and three firkins of fresh butter besides. Jameson went to school with him, and he told Pomeroy off, said what he'd do if he ever did have the chance at him — and when Captain Pomeroy tried to shut him up, threatened to kill him, Jameson told him to kill and be damned, till Pomeroy was glad to put him on shore to be rid of him. But he kept the oxen and the pigs and butter too.' He added: 'And Waldo Dicke has gone over to them from Warren, and John Nelson, and a plenty more that's likely to, and will if they've a chance at all.' He had news too of the militia that had scattered into flight after the disaster at Biguy-duce. 'It took the first lot, that headed west, six days to get to the Kennebeck,' he said. 'They were lost two days in a cedar swamp somewhere north of here, following spotted trees that kept taking them around in a circle, till an old man that called himself "I'm Davis" met them and put them right.'

Mima said: 'He's been here, a tall old man with a long beard, bows at the sight of bread.'

'I don't know about that,' her uncle confessed. 'All I heard, he calls himself "I'm Davis".'

'He lives up-river,' Mima explained. 'He told me about it. About twenty miles up from here, the river forks, and the right-hand fork comes out of a great pond three miles long; and you go up the inlet to a beaver meadow and around the west side and there's a fine brook runs in. He lives up that brook, in the hills, and traps all up and down and over.' And she said: 'Some day I'm going up there. He says it's sightly.'

Bela had given Mima from the first a boy's devotion. He was at once younger and older than his eighteen years; and something in her voice now made him look at her understandingly.

'I guess you dream about that,' he said, and laughed and promised her: 'I'll make a little canoe big enough for the two of us and take you, Mima.'

Mima to her own surprise felt herself blush; and Jess hooted with mirth. 'See her red up!' he cried. 'It's not you she'll be going with, Bela.'

'But I'll go in the canoe you make, Bela,' Mima promised him. 'So see you don't forget your promising.'

Ebenezer said: 'The British have sent some soldiers to Belfast, too. Captain Mowatt that fought off our whole fleet with three sloops at Biguyduce, he went over; and every man, woman and young one in Belfast moved out to get clear of him. Some come to Camden, and some put into the woods back five or six miles from the Bay, to Greene plantation.'

'They're driving cattle from Broad Bay through north of

Mason Wheaton's land and on to Belfast now, to sell to Mowatt and his ships,' Philip Robbins reported. 'I was up't Round Pond yesterday and Jason Ware told me. Colonel Wheaton's got two men working up there, and they say there's a beaten road, or soon will be.' He said grimly: 'There'll be some of us short of enough to eat this winter, with everything carted off to Biguyduce.'

His brother nodded in a gloomy agreement. The prospects were hard enough, certainly; but there was no recourse except to prepare as far as possible to live the winter through. Bela helped size and fit the barn timbers; and Philip Robbins began to plan a day for raising the frame. Two or three weeks, he thought, would see them ready. This time, with more hands available, the work would not be so hardly done.

*   *   *   *   *

On a day in late August, William Boggs, son of old Sam, came up from Warren one afternoon to see Philip Robbins. They were all at the site of the new barn when he arrived, Bela doing the axe work, Jess handling the oxen that dragged the heavy oak logs from where they had been felled and left to dry weeks before, Eben and his father roughing them out square. No one saw Boggs till his boat landed and he came up past the house. He was a square-set, bearded man, ponderous and firm, steady and methodical and industrious. He was in every way different from his father, who was as apt as not to start on a hunting expedition in good working weather. Mima had seen him only once or twice; but Philip had dealt with him in the matter of the purchase of a yoke of oxen, and knew him well enough. He turned, axe in hand, to greet the man.

'Well, Will,' he said. 'Don't see you here as numerous as we might. Come up and set.'

'Why, I don't mind if I do, Robbins,' the other assented. 'Hot work paddling such a day.'

'I'll cool ye,' Philip said. 'Mima, go see what you can find.'

When Mima returned with two mugs filled with rum and water, Boggs was saying gravely: 'We had news from Young Sam, finally. He's dead.'

Mima remembered Young Sam — who was as old as her father — from that day of their first arrival, when he helped them freight their belongings. She looked toward them in quick attention, and Philip asked in a startled tone:

'Is he so? He was in Ulmer's company, wa'n't he?'

'No, he just went along for the fighting,' Will explained. He wagged his head. 'I told Pa to keep him at home, but he said if Sam wanted to go helling around, best thing was to let him. They found him here a week ago, up east of Belfast in the woods. Hadn't anybody seen him since they all got ashore after they burned their schooner. Somebody'd shot him. Like as not he'd hid behind a rock along the river to pop at the Englishmen if they came near enough; but he got popped himself, in the leg.'

'Sho!' Philip protested. 'In the leg? That kill him, did it?'

'It did in the end,' William Boggs assured them. 'Looked like he tried to get home, and come down with lockjaw. The ground all around where they found him was tore up scandalous, like he'd kicked and scratched to beat time.' He wagged his head. 'I judge he'd suffered awful,' he said. 'Worse'n if the Indians had got him in the old days.'

'So! Well, I take that hard,' Mima's father said soberly. Mima watched them both, her hand pressed to her mouth; and she felt herself trembling as her imagination filled in the details of the scene William Boggs by his words suggested. She hated him for the calm complacency of his announcement of his brother's death. It was almost as though he relished the taste of his own words; as though he felt this death were a judgment on the other's brave folly — against which he had advised. Mima wanted to rage at him; and when she heard a step behind her and swung and saw Joel coming up the path from the landing, she turned to him eagerly, took two or three steps to meet him, wishing to tell him this terrible brief tale and see his sorrow and his pity go hand in hand with hers.

But before she could speak, she saw the black anger in Joel's
eye. He no more than glanced at her. He spoke to Boggs.

'You're here, are you?' he said harshly. 'Robbins, has he
told you what he's come for?'

Mima's father, when he was surprised, was always a little
slow of speech. He said, after a moment: 'All he's told me is
Young Sam is dead.'

Joel cried wrathfully: 'I just came from Warren. They're
aiming to collect taxes from us here in Sterlingtown!'

There was a moment's silence then, Philip Robbins looking
steadily at Boggs. That heavy man did not flinch under the
other's dark stare; but after a moment he said: 'Guess 't you
know I'm assessor, Robbins.'

'In Warren town you are,' Philip Robbins reminded him
quietly. 'Not here.'

'Why now, the state tax was on Warren and Sterlingtown
too, man.'

'The state tax, maybe. But what's this tax now?'

'Why, the town tax! 'Course, this ain't Warren town . . .'

'Nor it ain't likely to be.'

'But you'uns up here, Warren's your town. You can't go
nowhere without you go through Warren. You use our river
and our roads and our paths. It's no more'n right and just
you should help pay for 'em.'

'By whose lights?' Philip spoke so quietly Mima knew how
angry he was.

'By any just and right lights.'

Philip said slowly: 'Will Boggs, you're nine kinds of a damned
fool! You ain't got enough roads in the whole town of Warren
to run a wheelbarrow on; and as far as our having the use of
'em — any time you'll lay out a road to the town line, you can
start talking about taxes, not before.'

Boggs shook his head. 'You're taxed, all the same. Talk
don't mend any bridges.'

Robbins suddenly laughed. 'It gits to be funny,' he decided.

'First I come here, and there ain't a thing here only woods. Taylor agrees to sell me all the land I want. We agree on so much. Time I come to pay him he claims money ain't worth what it was and I can't have only half the land I want. Well, I trade, just the same. Then when I pay him, he wants specie; and he sues me in the courts and I have to pay. Up here, we live in a log cabin eighteen-twenty feet square, eight of us. Thirteen there was at first. We work and build us a barn and raise us some crops, and get the barn full of hay and feed for us and the critters, and it burns up!' His tone rose as memory of his wrongs returned. 'Our critters starve to death, and we come next thing to it ourselves; but we eat seed potatoes, and weeds and what all, like we was cows. Then this year we plant another crop and it don't rain!' He looked up at the cloudless skies and shook his fists in the air. 'It don't rain no more than a fly can spit, the whole summer!' he roared; and his fists came banging down on his knees for emphasis. 'Our crop don't make! We'll be eating shavings by spring, and now by Goddlemighty, you, you block-faced, horse-rumped, pot-bellied, nit-eyed, fly-blown pismire, you come to collect some taxes out of us!'

He stopped, and his jaw worked with words he could not say, and slaver showed in a small fleck of white at the corner of his mouth. He brushed his lips with his knuckles, shaking his head. 'No, Will,' he said. 'No taxes. That's flat!'

Mima saw Bela grinning happily; but when she looked at Joel, his eyes were blazing, and his lips were white, and she saw the man's anger in him, and the strength to back it. Then Boggs said mildly:

'There's no call for hard words, Robbins. I'm elected assessor. It's my job to assess taxes on your farm. I aim to do my bounden duty. You'll pay. If you don't, why then the farm will be sold at tax sale, and we'll take the tax money and give you what's left, and whoever buys it will have your farm.'

The other shook his head. 'The King of England's finding out he couldn't talk that way to Americans,' he said. 'Nor

you can't talk so to me. Massachusetts can tax me, certain; but
Warren town can't tax me no more than if I lived in Boston.'

'You'll find your farm sold, just the same.'

'The man buys it might full as well throw his money in the
fire. Farm's mine, and mine I aim to keep it.' He was mild
enough now, and by that mildness the more convincing. 'But
Will,' he said, 'don't come again on any such like of an errand.
You nor nobody else. I'm mostly a peaceful man, but not all.'

'It ain't only you, Robbins,' Boggs urged. 'It's every man up
here that's rateable.'

'Them can pay that wants to. I'm one that won't.'

Joel said quietly: 'I'm another, Boggs; and I can answer for
two more.'

Boggs nodded. 'Suit yourself,' he said. 'I'll have the sale
notice posted up this time tomorrow. You can't go against the
law, none of you, and I'm the law.'

He turned majestically and went heavily down the path.
Bela called derisively after him: 'You may be the law, but you
look more like the stern of a pig to me!' Jess chuckled; but the
others did not smile. Mima touched her father's arm.

'Can they take the farm?' she asked in a low tone.

He looked at her wonderingly. 'Take my farm? Why, Mima,
there's my sweat, and my boys' sweat on every foot of it! We
made it. It's ours. There can't nothing nor nobody take it
away from me!'

He turned strongly to where the great timbers lay, returning
to the work in hand; and the young men turned with him.
Joel looked at Mima, and suddenly he smiled. 'He's a man,'
he said.

'Yes.'

They went toward the landing; walked that way together.
'I heard about it in Warren,' he said. 'I wondered what we'd
do! Your father didn't wonder, did he? He knew.'

William Boggs was paddling down the lake, keeping close to
the bank in the shade, already past the island. Mima said, half

to herself: 'They've worked together, Father and Mother, here. She works as hard as a man, sometimes. I guess a man might give up something he'd worked for alone; but if his woman worked beside him — he'd never let it go, any more than if it was a baby they'd made together.'

He looked at her. She was watching the float departing down the lake, her face half-turned from him. He said in a tone that surprised her: 'What do women have to do with it? Working's a man's job!'

'Women have to do with everything worth doing, Joel.'

He laughed carelessly. 'Maybe. Depends on what you call worth doing.'

'Clearing farms,' she said. 'Making homes. Raising families.'

'To hear you talk, you'd think homes and farms and families was the only thing a man ought to bother with.' There was a half-sullen impatience in his eyes.

'It's the big thing that needs doing here and now,' she said strongly. 'We've claimed this land is ours; but it's not ours till we use it. We've got to make farms and homes and towns and cities out of this country we've claimed is ours. After we do, it's going to belong to us. Not to the King.' She smiled faintly. 'And not to William Boggs.'

Joel chuckled grimly. His float was here by their feet. He said: 'I'm due back up above. You talk too big for me. There's plenty a man can do alone. We're getting along all right without a woman at the Royal Mess.'

'You need one. There ain't a clean dish in the place.'

He said in a grim amusement: 'We're suited. But a woman always wants to teach a man his manners.' He pushed off, swung the dugout toward the river, called good-bye. 'We'll get along!' he said defiantly. She turned back up toward the barn as he moved away.

16

FOR the barn-raising, Colonel Wheaton came up from Thomaston, and Nat Fales; and there were others from Thomaston or from Warren, and every man, woman and child — and dog — in Sterlingtown was there to lend a hand. Preparations began days ahead. Those who came to help — or to watch — would need to be fed at noon and again at night, and there would be monstrous appetites for food and for drink to satisfy. Philip brought a stock of rum from Warren; and Jason's Sambo dog treed a bear which Jason and Joel shot and contributed to the occasion; and Jess, three days beforehand, killed a yearling moose at the spring in the meadows north of Seven-Tree Pond; and David Robbins netted eleven dozen pigeons, fat as balls of butter, rich and delicious.

Nat Fales and Colonel Wheaton arrived the day before; and Fales and Bela Robbins inspected every timber, checking the fit of each one, checking lengths and thicknesses. Fales was a man as old as Philip Robbins or older, and he wore a shabby wig to cover his bald poll. When in the heat of his labors something arose to perplex him, so that he mopped his brow too strenuously, he was apt to knock the wig askew; but he never noticed this unless it slipped so far to one side that it was in danger of falling off, when he might hurriedly thrust it back into place again, damning it as he did so. He was a master carpenter, and Bela gave him an apprentice's devotion, listening to his every word, leaping at his least command. At first the man seemed to resent the boy's attendance; but Bela was at once so humble, so willing and so skilful with his axe or his hands that Fales insensibly melted and came to better humor as the work went on.

While these two were thus engrossed, the Colonel and Philip Robbins sampled the rum; and Philip asked what news there was of the marauders along the coast. Colonel Wheaton said: 'You remember Perry, the one the King's ships made him pilot them to Biguyduce, and his wife had the baby and died.'

'So I do,' Robbins assented. Eben heard John Perry's name and came to listen.

'Well, they're after him to hang him now, or shoot him maybe, or flog him to death with the cat,' the Colonel said; and he explained: 'Perry was hot to fight them, but he couldn't do it alone, any more than the rest of us. So after they sunk us, John got across to North Haven to try to get in his crops. A sloop came from Biguyduce foraging; and they sent a dozen or fifteen men to Perry's. He moved off into the woods by his cornfield where he'd hid his gun. He put three or four buckshot in on top of the ball, and waited till he got two of them handy and their heads almost in line and let her go.' The Colonel slapped his knee. 'Dropped the both of them, by God! The rest of them chased him to hell and gone; till finally he crawled into a hollow tree.'

Eben asked sharply: 'Did he get away?'

'Sure as a gun! But he stayed up that hollow tree two days and nights before he dast to show himself; then he found a dugout and paddled across to Owl's Head. Came to my house before day. Now he's gone to Boston, but he'll be back, come spring. The General at Biguyduce says he'll pay a thousand dollars for John; so I told him to put for Boston and stay there till they cooled off a mite.' He added: 'He was saying he might go privateering.'

'I'd go with him!' Eben cried.

'I'll keep you busy here, Eb,' Philip warned him. 'You'll have a stint to do t'home.' Fales and Bela came from their inspection of the barn timbers, and Philip asked: 'Well, Nat, think she'll do?'

'Don't see what's to hender,' Fales assured him. 'This young fellow here, he'll make a hand. Done a good job, sizing and all. We'll have her up in no time, tomorrow.'

The work would be under way at first light. Before dawn Mrs. Robbins roused Mima and the others. Eben had dug a three-foot ditch between the house and the pond, to which now he carried coals to start a fire. Mima and her mother set to work at once to feed those already here; collops of moose meat broiled over the fire in the ditch, cornbread and coffee. Before they were done eating, others began to arrive. Richard Comings and Bet came first with four-year-old David trotting at Richard's heels and two-year-old Esther in her father's arms. Bet's baby would be born in February; and she was blooming, eyes shining, cheeks glowing. David and Bess and their three were not far behind; and the others from down the pond. 'Bijah Hawes came with the Bowens. Mima had not seen 'Bijah since that night at Round Pond, and he grinned sheepishly when she caught his eye.

Ezra Bowen had a pail of honey on one arm, their baby on the other. 'Found the bee tree a month ago,' he said. 'But I left it till yesterday. Thought you could use some honey for them that likes something sweet, today.'

He was burdened with the honey and the baby; but Prance was empty-handed. Mrs. Robbins told her: 'We're putting all the babies in my big bed, Mis' Bowen. Go right in the house and if you need anything, sing out.'

Prance spoke crisply. 'You heard her, Ez. Well, go ahead and do it.'

Ezra obediently went indoors where Bess and Bet were making the other babies comfortable. Prance stayed by the fire, watching Mima and her mother; and Mrs. Robbins called Eben and told him to put more wood on the fire in the ditch. 'Keep it going good,' she said. 'We want that ditch plumb full of coals by the time we're ready to start cooking.' She explained to Prance Bowen: 'We've got eleven dozen pigeons to clean this morning. I aim to spit them and broil them over the coals, and I'll roast a saddle of moose and a haunch of bear meat. We'll bake kettle bread indoors, and there's a plenty of potatoes. I guess they'll make out.'

'They'll do more drinking than eating,' Prance predicted, with a toss of her head. She called sharply to Ezra, just emerging from the cabin: 'Did you tuck her in good?'

'Yes, Experience,' he said. Mima judged he was not allowed to use the shorter name. 'And Mis' Comings is looking out for her.'

Prance went to see for herself, and Mima thought the other was like a long-legged colt in the way she strode along. 'Head up and tail erect!' she whispered to her mother, and Mrs. Robbins chuckled. Mima went down to the landing to welcome Johnny Butler and Lucy coming across from the Mill Farm with their Jimmy in Lucy's arms. The baby was fat and amiable, chuckling at everyone he saw; and when Mima took him now, while Lucy climbed out of the float, he gurgled delightedly. She carried him up to the house to put him on the big bed with the others. When she came out again, Joel and the other two of the Royal Mess had just arrived; and Joel came to Mima and said that with all these pretty girls around there was bound to be a dance in the new barn as soon as the floor was down.

'Or we don't need to wait for that,' he assured her. 'There's the threshing floor as smooth as marble.'

'There's nothing for music, not so much as a fiddle,' she reminded him; and he laughed and told her:

'A man don't need music to dance with you! But you'll find some of us can sing — or maybe whistle — a dance tune to please you as much as any fiddle ever you heard.'

Her eyes flashing mirthfully, she said: 'I've heard some of your singing, that night I took Jess up to fetch the Colonel. I guess the tunes — and the words too, maybe — would make a girl more want to run and hide than to stay dancing.'

He chuckled, and sang:

> And he found her again — she was easy to find...

'That's one of them,' she told him. 'So don't go singing any more of it for me to hear! They'll be wanting you for the first lift in a minute, anyway.'

'I'll be wanting you for that dance later, all the same!' he retorted; and he turned away toward where already the work of framing one side of the barn was under way. The thump of mauls sounded there as treenails were driven home.

Mima joined her mother and the other women and with fingers flying they prepared the pigeons for the spits. They sat under a birch by the pond side below where the barn would be; and feathers and heads and feet and entrails of the fat birds went into the water where small fish and great ones by the scores had come to feed, and Mima saw eels gliding on the pebbled bottom. Mrs. Robbins called Sue. 'Susie, you come help pick pigeons. Mima, Ez Bowen says you squeeze some honey out of the comb and mix it with the rum and put a little water in it and it makes a real tasty drink. You go mix some up and see if the menfolks like it. Sun's getting hot, and they'll be ready for the first lift any time now.'

So Mima went back up the knoll and found the honey. She put a few flakes of the comb into a pewter pitcher and crushed it with a pestle and poured the honey through a strainer into the biggest bowl she could find. Philip had set a half-keg of rum on the north side of the house, and water in a tub beside it; and Mima drew rum from the keg and added it to the honey, and added water and stirred the mixture and found it somehow lacking. But when she carried it and two or three mugs out to where the men were at work, she had no complaints from anyone.

She saw that they were ready to raise the north side of the new barn. The sills and floor timbers, her father and brothers and Bela had long since laid and spiked together; but since work began this morning the east side had been framed, and lay now on the barn floor. Bela and Nat Fales were just wedging into place the braces which would hold in place the lower ends of the posts as the frame was raised. Mima found it hard to believe that the thing could be done with the men at hand; the timbers were so massive and so heavy; the lift itself must be so awkward. But while her bowl was being emptied, Nat fixed the brace to hold the foot of the last post; and he shouted:

'Ready, men!' He saw Mima and came toward her. 'I'll have a taste of that for luck!' he said, and drained a mugful; and Joel took the bowl from her and cried:

'I'll just empty this so you can be filling it again!' He tipped the bowl to his lips and drank the last drop and pressed it back into her hands. 'So, now stand clear!'

Mima, stepping back out of the way, called to her mother and the others by the pond: 'Here it goes up, Mother!' They came to watch as the men lined up along the posts. Nat Fales shouted two or three questions:

'Props ready? Stay-laths ready, Bela? Pike poles handy? All right, boys, take right hold. Easy does it.'

They stooped as one man. The heavy posts had been laid on bits of board so that they could slip their fingers underneath to get a grip. Nat was on the east post; he saw Mima watching; and he called to her:

'You give the word, ma'am. Count and we'll h'ist her.'

She came to stand on the ground north of the barn floor, facing them. 'I'll say one-two-three-up,' she said. 'You lift on "up." Ready now?'

'Bijah Hawes drawled: 'Hurry, ma'am. My britches are splitting a'ready, staying stooped down so long!'

Someone laughed; but Mima said quickly: 'Ready!' Then, her tones clear and ringing, her voice rising in an even crescendo, she counted:

'One — Two — Three — Up!'

The bent backs bowed in an even curve; the great frame rose smoothly and with a single motion till they held the posts at the level of their chins. Then Nat Fales at one end, Bela at the other, stepped clear and set props under the posts to hold all that had been gained. The men relaxed; and Joel demanded mock-seriously:

'Say, why didn't the rest of you lift a little with me? I need a drink, doing it all alone!'

'Another lift first,' Nat told them, mopping his brow and straightening his wig. 'We'll h'ist her halfway. After that she goes easier. Ma'am, you tell 'em!'

So with Mima calling the count, the men responding like one, the heavy frame rose easily. Nat drove them to it. 'Give us the whole of it!' he urged. 'Let's not stop while we're going good. Get your pike poles this time. Easy, though. Don't hurry it, or you'll have her over the other way.'

He would not let them rest till presently the side was perpendicular, the butts of the posts well socketed in the sills; and he and Bela, with treenails ready, spiked home the stay-laths to hold it there.

While the south side was being framed, there was for some of them nothing to be done. Mima mixed another bowl of rum and honey and water, and Joel asked the secret of it, and she gave Ezra Bowen the credit; and 'Bijah Hawes said:

'Mima, if I'd had a few drinks of this that night up't the pond...' He grinned at the memory. 'I wouldn't have cared if I had of drowned.'

She smiled. 'I'd have cared. I was scared you would, as 'twas.'

He said huskily: 'I didn't set out to scare you. I was just fooling, in a friendly kind of way.'

Her father caught her eye, and she went to him. He said warningly: 'Scant the rum for a spell, Mima. There'll be half of them too drunk to lift their own weight if you keep on.'

'They'll be calling you as mean as that man that muffled his cowbells to save wearing them out,' she warned him.

'They can have all they're a mind to when the job's done,' he assured her. 'But I want 'em kept fitten to work till then. We ain't got what you'd call a full crew, as 'tis.'

'I remember Phin Butler telling about raising Doctor Taylor's barn. There weren't but eight of you, counting him and Johnny.'

He nodded. 'I was captain of that job,' he agreed. 'But we were two days at it, and rubbed most the meat off our arms doing it, and there wa'n't one of us good for a lick of work for three or four days.' And he said: 'No, Mima, you scant the rum till the heavy lifting's done. Put in some molasses instead. It'll smell all the same.'

'Some of them are going straight to the keg.'

He winked elaborately. 'That's all right. I've a'ready thinned it down a mite. There's another keg in the house. They'll have a-plenty by and by.'

Mima obeyed him, and none complained; but when the south side was raised she saw the sweat start on them all and run streaming down throats and arms. With the two sides up, and held erect by the stay-laths, the heaviest part of the work was done — and the sun was high. Mima's mother came to call them off the job.

'Time to eat a mite,' she said. 'I don't know if what we've got is fitten, but what there is you're a-welcome to.'

Joel threw his arm around her, kissed her loudly. 'Ho, Aunt Mima, you could cook for the King!' he cried.

She pushed him clear. 'Get your paws off me,' she protested. 'You're all in a lather!'

He bowed profoundly. 'That's soon fixed, Aunt Mima. Keep the womenfolks together this side the house. I'm going swimming. And save another kiss for me when I come back.' He shouted to the others: 'Anybody for a swim?' Eight or ten of them followed him on the run, racing up the shore toward the river till they were out of sight; and Mima could hear them whooping and splashing in the water there. Mrs. Robbins began to cut the moose saddle into slices; and the swimmers came back streaming and dripping, and stopped by the rum keg on the way; and Joel remembered to claim that kiss, and then suddenly as they attacked the food all the noise ended — or almost all of it. Mrs. Robbins chuckled.

'Vittles shuts 'em up,' she told Mima. 'They can't go hooting around with their mouths full of pigeon breast and moose meat.' And she added teasingly: 'Look out for yourself, Mima. Joel's apt to try to turn your petticoats today. When the mother gets kissed, the daughter better get her mouth puckered up ready.'

Mima laughed, her cheeks bright. She went into the cabin. Lucy was nursing Jimmy, Bess and Bet tending their children too. 'Father says the hard part's over,' she said.

'I'm glad of it,' Bess declared. 'Dave dropped a stitch in his back here a month ago, heaving at a log, trying to roll it over. I didn't want him to do any today, but he was bound he would. He said it didn't hurt him.'

Mima predicted: 'They wouldn't know it now if you stuck a fork in them, the rum they've drunk; but I guess Dave's all right. He acts it, kicking his heels and a-hooting.'

Bet Comings chuckled. 'Love you, Mima, don't start looking down your nose every time a man takes a drink! They work hard all the time till they're tired as knots. A drink or a fight or something looses them up again — and they love you all the better after.' She added with a wry smile: 'Seems like a man is like a pig. He's healthier if he can wallow in the mud once in a while.'

Lucy protested: 'I think that's an awful thing to say, Bet! Johnny's not like that.'

Bet put her arm around the other girl, looking down at the lusty baby at Lucy's breast. 'I'll bet he's not,' she agreed in smiling reassurance, and poked small Jimmy's cheek and laughed. 'But here's one that's going to like his rum, the way he's swigging at his mother now!'

Mima said soberly: 'I know how it is with a man, though. Sometimes he wants to do something he knows he hadn't ought to do — and he's a lot better for doing it, getting it out of his system.' She whispered half to herself: 'They work so hard, and a man has to always be thinking: If anything happened to me, what would happen to them that I take care of? It must be hard doing, knowing all the time that your wife and your babies will die if you don't go on taking care of them.'

Bet laughed at her seriousness; but then by the rising chorus of conversation outside they knew the eating was done, the men returning to their tasks again. Mima and Bess and Bet and Prance Bowen went to help Mrs. Robbins clean up, leaving Lucy with her baby. There were platters and mugs and spoons to be washed, the litter to be cleared away and burned, the fire in the trench replenished and kept alive against time to cook again. Mima, while she helped, watched the men busy with the barn frame. The sides which had been raised during the morning and secured in place were gaunt and naked against the sky; but now with Nat Fales bossing at one end, Bela at the other, the end posts were raised and the cross beams set piece by piece; and then the bays were framed in till the whole was bound together firmly. The heavy plates were lifted into place by stages, men standing on the cross beams, tipping the long timbers up like seesaws, supplementing their own strength with ropes and poles, till the plates could be spiked home.

There was a pause then, and more calls for rum and honey; and Mima filled her bowl again and again and went from man to man. Her father, seeing the end of the work in sight, was drunk as much with satisfaction as with the rum. Colonel Wheaton's voice was as loud as a bull's roar, and growing louder with his every potation. All the men were talking all the time; and Mima heard David telling some interminable story. He appeared to be quoting someone. 'So I says to myself, God, I says, Dodapher, I says, you're going to be wolf meat before morning if you don't look out. So I says, God, I says, you better throw the dog to 'em. God, I says, maybe they'll eat dog and leave you be. So I give the dog a heave toward them, but he lit running back to me; and he looked at me as much as to say, God, he says, don't do that, Dodapher, he says. God, he says, did you see the teeth on that wolf, he says. Why God, he says, he's got the hairs on my tail in his teeth now. So I says, God, I says, what am I going to do, Pete, I says. His name was Pete. And he pressed against my shins, and he says, God, he says, take your axe to 'em, he says. God, he says, you can lick twenty wolves, Dodapher, he says. And God, he says, there ain't but a dozen here. So I says, God, I says, I never chopped down no wolf, I says, Pete. I says, God, I says, I guess we better get up a tree. And he says, God, he says, I can't climb no tree...'

The tale ran on and on, and Dave as he told it was at one moment the man and at the next the dog. The man seemed to be backed against an imaginary tree, staring in affright at wolves around him. When David became the dog, he dropped on all fours, pressing against an imaginary man. Mima had heard the story before. Dodapher Richards, who lived over Camden way, was supposed to be the narrator. He had been bayed by wolves one night when he was homeward bound, and according to Dave he would tell the story endlessly, and with a singular paucity of invention where profanity was or seemed to be required. The story was a success now, as Dave's performances were apt to be. Give him a drink of rum and an audience and he was a master clown. The tale ended in shouts of laughter, and then 'Bijah came lugubriously, tears in his

eyes and a choke in his voice, to tell Mima again that he had
not meant to scare her, that night at Round Pond. 'You're so
beautiful,' he told her. 'You can drive a man witless!'

She laughed and said: 'Now 'Bije, you read that in a book
somewhere!'

'Well,' he insisted, 'it was a good book. But I didn't go to
scare you, Mima.'

'I got over it,' she said and he was reassured. She saw Joel
and three or four others up on the cross beams, high above the
ground, laying boards which those below passed up to them; and
when Joel had a floor under him he danced a brisk jig, the loose
boards rattling, and he sang:

> Oh, her cheek it was bonny, her eye it was merry,
> Her ear was a shell and her lip was a cherry,
> Her smile would make any...

His jig and his song broke off. He had stepped incautiously
on the end of a board that projected beyond the cross beam,
and it gave way under him so that he lurched back to safety
by a hair; and a roar of laughter greeted his mishap, and
Mima felt the heart and bowels drop out of her body. He might
have fallen, hurt himself, been killed. She slipped away, into
the house, to hide the sudden terror in her.

She stayed there while Bela and Nat fitted the rafters together in pairs and spiked them with collar-beams to hold them.
Each pair was wedded while they lay flat, then raised into place
and spiked there. When the last pair went up, and the purlines
bound them together, the sun was still an hour above the trees.
From the house where Mima was, the voices of the men sounded
like the clamor of a tremendous, good-humored mob. There
were only nineteen of them, but they sounded like a hundred.
She thought they could not make any more noise if they tried,
yet they made more all the time, till by and by she heard a
great general shout; and her mother came to the corner by the
door and said:

'It's done, Mima. The last lick!' Then in a different tone, looking toward the barn, she said under her breath: 'The tipsy idiot!' She called: 'Somebody get him down!'

Mima came out to see what was happening. Joel, daring the others to follow him, was straddling the rafter at the nearer end of the barn, hitching himself up to the ridgepole; and three or four of the other young men sought to imitate him. 'Bije was trying to swing his leg over a cross beam and hoist himself up. Jason Ware was standing on the plate, high against the sky, waiting to follow Joel up the rafter as soon as it was clear. Jess was climbing the post at that corner, embracing it with arms and legs like a bear; and Johnny Butler tried to follow Jess, and Lucy pulled him down, and Mrs. Robbins called to Jess a shrill command to come down out of that and have some sense and he obeyed her as though glad of the excuse to do so.

But Mima saw only Joel. He had reached the ridgepole. He sat astride it, then managed somehow to rise on his hands and knees, then got his feet under him. When he stood up, balanced, silhouetted against the sky, a great shout of approbation greeted the feat; and Mima heard little Sue screaming with wonder and delight; and she saw young Philip try to climb one of the posts, and saw her mother pull him down and box his ears hard.

Joel waved his hand to those below; he began to walk along the ridgepole. Jason was hitching himself up the rafter to follow Joel, and 'Bijah Hawes had reached the plate. Joel stopped to admire the view; he shaded his eyes with his hands, looking all around; he clowned it for them. He was halfway along the ridgepole when Jason reached the end of it. 'Bijah started up the rafter; but suddenly his stomach failed him, and he clung to the rafter with arms and legs, and those below gave way and room. He hugged the rafter, sliding slowly down it till he sat on the plate again; and when the paroxysms of his sickness passed, he rolled off the plate and slid down the post and sat on the ground to pick the splinters out of his arms.

Jason was trying to stand up on the ridgepole; and Joel near the other end of it had turned to watch him. Jason got his feet placed; but when he tried to rise erect, his balance failed. He weaved desperately, his arms flailing, till one foot slipped and he fell and caught a rafter with both arms and hung from it. Mima heard the others scream as Jason started to fall; but he saved himself and swung his feet up around the rafter, and hanging from it by hands and feet as though he were a hammock, he slid down it to the plate. Then like a shot bear dropping out of a tree, he came from beam to beam to the ground.

Joel, the only survivor aloft, slapped his sides and crowed like a rooster, loud and long. Mima could not watch him; yet she could not look away. He walked the length of the ridgepole, poised and sure; he retraced his steps, walking this time backward, and cheers applauded him. As though inspired to more extravagant efforts by the shouts from below, he chose a spot where rafters met the ridgepole, sat down astride it, rested his hands on the rafters, put his head down and his feet along the pole under him. Mima shut her eyes in helpless dread, but then there was a great shout and she had to look and she saw him standing on his head, his feet and legs moving for balance against the sky. She clapped her hand to her mouth to hold back her cry of dismay; and he dropped down astride the ridgepole again and stood up and ran along it to the end, as though he would dive off. At the last moment he checked himself, and caught his balance, and walked down the rafter to the plate. He sauntered like a stroller on the boulevard. He stood on the plate a moment, high and fine, master of the scene; then swung down to the beam below, and hung from that and swung to clear the sill and dropped and landed on his feet, as lightly as a deer leaps a log. They shouted again, and Mrs. Robbins said:

'Joel Adams, you're a fool!'

Joel laughed and kissed her. 'If I am, it's your pretty phiz has turned my head, Aunt Mima.'

She said more gently: 'There, don't kill yourself, lad! You're

good enough, some ways, so I'd like to keep you around! Now
let me go till I feed this pack of wolves.'

They ate between sunset and dark, tearing the delicious
pigeons in their fingers, breaking chunks of cornbread to wad
them down, swilling the sweetened rum. Jess set a bonfire to
give light as daylight failed; and Colonel Wheaton started a
roaring song, and Joel joined him, and Johnny Butler caught
Mrs. Robbins and dragged her to the threshing floor of hard-
packed earth, smooth and firm. Clapping hands gave the beat
and they began to dance. Philip Robbins called the numbers.
David caught his Bess, and Richard and Bet joined the dancers.
Ezra Bowen and Prance leaped as high and stamped as hard
and swung as furiously as any. Mima watched them, wishing
Joel would come to claim her; and 'Bijah hiccoughed in her
ear and said unsteadily:

'I don't want to scare you, ma'am!'

But before 'Bijah could seize her, Joel came with a bound,
and his arm around her waist swung her clear of the ground,
her skirts and petticoats flying, and they were dancing with the
others. Philip sought to bring some order out of their headlong
whirling. 'Ladies one side, gents the other!' he bawled. 'Bijah
Hawes when he lost Mima took Lucy; and Bela, mincing like
a girl, was Jason Ware's partner; and Matt Hawes led little
Sue into the line and took his place opposite her. The others
beat the time and whistled. The tune was that infectious jig of
Joel's. Philip Robbins bawled at intervals: 'First gent swing
second lady!' Then: 'Lady second gent! Greet the lady! Greet
the gent! Swing your partner four times round! Down the
middle! Now second gent swing first lady . . .'

Dark was on them, but the fire blazed high; their shadows,
thrown tremendous against the trees, danced as they danced.
Joel whistled as he danced, and when he and Mima were for a
space inactive in the facing lines, keeping time with clapping
hands and with skipping steps, he leaped high and clapped his
heels together. The dance had no pattern. Philip called what

turn he chose. He sought to confuse them; and when he succeeded, and they collided in seeking to obey him, the watchers roared and hooted and jeered. There was no end to it. Mrs. Robbins was the first to quit, panting for breath, laughing till she cried; and Johnny turned to draw his Lucy out of it, and young Eben took her place. Bet gave up, clinging to Richard helplessly; and he kissed her roundly and stood holding her in the circle of his arm. The others dropped out two by two and then one by one till only Joel remained; he danced alone, with an imaginary partner, till for laughing they could urge him on no more, and he clapped his hands against his side and crowed again that great rooster crow of victory. 'Danced you down!' he shouted, and Philip Robbins rolled out a fresh keg of rum.

Mima, standing by Bess and David while men packed around the keg, heard Bess whisper to her husband:

'Dave, Lucy's is coming in March.'

David caught Bess close, laughing huskily, and he whispered something and Bess laughed. When after a moment Bela and Eben began to dance again, and Jess swept Mima on the floor, she looked for Bess and Dave but they were gone. No one missed them for a while, as the dance went on. The fire was dying; but the moon was half-full, giving light enough. Then Jess likewise noticed that David and Bess had disappeared, and he asked Mima where they were, and she shook her head. He yelled:

'Let's find them!'

Whoops of glee greeted the suggestion, and men scattered every way, toward the river, toward the pond. Their shouts receded till there was suddenly a zone of quiet here.

In that relative quiet, Mima heard somewhere at a distance a girl singing in a clear high soprano that jig tune which Joel so often sang. The sound came from the pond. Joel and some of the hunt for David and Bess had gone that way; and Mima heard a sudden silence along the shore and heard the song more clearly. Then there was a great shout of laughter and of cheers too, and a splashing in the pond, and more shouting and a confusion of voices there.

After a while Jason Ware came back from the pond side, laughing. He came alone, and he went to Colonel Wheaton, and Mima heard his chuckling tones. 'The ferry from Warren's out there with some girls in it,' he said. 'Joel and 'Bijah Hawes waded off to them. They've gone away down the pond.'

Mima began to tremble. Her mother said at her shoulder, gently: 'Joel's full of rum, Mima. Full of rum and hell. He'll be sorry in the morning.'

Mima said through stiff lips: 'If that's all, he could have stayed.'

The older woman spoke quietly enough. 'Hush you, Mima. That's no way to talk.'

But Mima said stubbornly: 'He didn't have to go.'

17

BEFORE the first of October, the year's crop of corn and rye was safe in bins in the new barn; the cellar under the house and the pit beside it were alike stocked with potatoes and with beets and turnips; the cattle and the pigs were housed against the winter. Philip Robbins expected this winter would be hard. The wild geese had begun to fly south even in September, and through October the skies were full of them and their lonely cries sometimes came down from the starred night skies. The partridges were heavily feathered down their legs; and even the domestic cattle seemed to be putting on a warmer coat.

He prepared for the worst. He filled the barn with hay, and boated over from the meadows north of the pond enough more to make two stacks below the barn. 'And far enough away so's if we have another fire they don't have to go,' he told Mrs. Robbins.

'We'll not,' she promised. 'We've had our bad luck, Pa. We'll be fine from now on.'

'I been thinking,' he said. 'We're outgrowing this house.

The young ones ain't babies any more. I'm thinking I'll build, next summer; and we'll move where we'll have more room.'

'We c'n do here,' she assured him. 'Our family ain't going to get any bigger at my age; and Mima'll be marrying Joel first thing we know, and moving out. Then Jess and Eben, they're likely to find them a gal down in Warren or somewheres and go building houses themselves. It won't be no time at all till there won't be only you and me left here.'

'They grow up fast,' he assented. He asked: 'What about Joel and Mima? I notice he ain't been around since he went off with that Warren bitch, night of the barn-raising. I didn't know as she'd stomach that.'

'She loves him. She'll have him. She'd have gone off with him herself that night if he'd asked her, likely.' Mrs. Robbins added: 'He come a week after, one time when you was up cutting hay; fetched a fine saddle of moose meat, but Mima'd gone down the pond to see Bet.'

'Didn't he get to see her?'

'No. He asked where she was, and I said I warn't real sure. He hung around for an hour, hoping she'd come back, but she didn't. She said she was full as glad she didn't come while he was here. Mima's smart, Philip. If they'd got to talking about it, they'd have said things they'd ruther not. Thing to do with a business like that is let a man forget it. You give him the sharp edge of your tongue and it just makes him mad.'

He nodded, chuckling. 'Well,' he said, 'Joel's young and wild and crazy-headed and a gal-chaser; but I wouldn't wonder if he made a hand — if he don't go sell his farm.'

'Mima'll see to't he don't.'

'Dunno how they can do any courting, the way things are,' he reflected. 'Just one room and the garret here, and Mima sleeps with Sue.' He said cheerfully: 'Not but what Joel could bundle in with both of them, matter of that. Sue's a sleeper!' And he said: 'But he's in no case to get married, yet a while. Him and the others up at the Royal Mess, they've got all they can handle, this next two-three years. They'll have to scratch to get by, won't have no time to go building separate houses; and she can't marry the lot of 'em.'

'She don't aim to. But her and Joel could marry, and her move in with the three of them. I wouldn't put it past her. She's set on him, Philip.'

'Well, she could do worse,' he assented. 'But I wish't we had a bigger house. Make it easier for Mima and him if she had a bed and a room of her own. If this winter's as hard as I look for it to be, they'd have time enough to talk things over.' He chucked Mrs. Robbins in the ribs. ' 'Member that winter before we married, Ma?'

'Mighty little talking we did! You was always more doer than talker.'

He drawled: 'Still am.' He put his arm around her, kissed her cheek. 'We've got along, you and me. Never see a mare yet I'd swap for the filly I got.'

'You'd have had a busted head if you'd ever tried any horse-trading!'

'Guess it's been the same with you.'

'Well, I dunno,' she said teasingly. 'Colonel Wheaton's a real handsome figger of a man!'

He kissed her again. 'You roll sheep's eyes at him and I'll make him think he's been in a war,' he assured her.

'I been wondering why he don't come around,' she confessed, no longer joking.

'Busy,' he said seriously. Colonel Wheaton was in fact active in directing the movements of the militia whose task it was to protect the coast against marauding refugees. He was busy too with other public affairs. The question of regulating prices and attempting to stabilize the currency was considered at three town meetings in Thomaston during September, and the Colonel went as a delegate to the convention at Wiscasset. Then in the meeting of the town on November 29 he was elected to represent Thomaston in the Great and General Court. The

water journey to Boston entailed too many risks of capture by
the refugees. He would go overland; but before he left, he came
to Sterlingtown to engage Jess and Eben and young Bela Robbins to work for him that winter, getting out timbers for a barn
on his land up the river.

'I'll be gone till spring,' he told Philip Robbins, over their
rum and molasses. 'There's ice making in the coves along the
coast a'ready, and the God-damned King-lovers at Biguyduce
won't be doing much on the water, so there's no need of me
here.' Jess and Eben were listening; and he said: 'You two, if
you get a chance while you're working up there, kill some of the
beef critters they're driving across my land from Broad Bay to
sell to the bloody backs. I'll stand the damage, and pay off the
blasted Dutchmen in lead if they howl! Kill anything you see.'

*   *   *   *   *

From the day of the barn-raising, Mima did not see Joel,
except for casual encounters when others were about, for a fair
three months' time. First snows came early in December, two
or three inches that did not melt; and Bela and Jess and Eben
decided it was high time they made a trip up to the Colonel's
land to pick their trees and to see what they would need for a
more extended stay. Mima went with them. There was already
ice enough in the river to make water travel impossible, so they
went afoot, crossing the river by the great pine Jess had felled
at the narrows, following up its north bank and along Round
Pond to the old maple. In the deep pool below the broken
dam, ice had formed; and they laid long poles across the ice to
distribute their weight and crossed dry-shod. They followed
the beaver dam. The path Mima had cut ran along the top of
it, screened by willows which grew on either side; and as they
approached the Royal Mess, she wondered with a quickening
of her pulses whether Joel would be there.

But they heard axes in the woods to the south, and knew the
men were at work, so they did not go up to the house, but

turned north along the edge of the meadows toward their goal. Colonel Wheaton's men had built a three-sided log shelter roofed with bark beside the river where his south line touched it; and the barn he planned would stand near-by. Bela chose a stand of oak within a quarter mile where the trees grew straight and clear of branches for forty feet. He thought they could work there, cut the trees, square the logs and rough-cut the ends, then leave the great timbers where they lay till deep snow made it easier to move them. They would live here for at least part of the time, so they added a fourth side to the camp and made it into a hovel about eight feet wide and ten feet long, with a door three or four feet high through which they could crawl. They built with flat slabs a wide fireplace and laid a hearth and slanted poles to serve as a flue that would guide the smoke toward an opening in the roof. They strengthened the roof against a possible weight of snow, and laid the bark again, and added more.

'We'll have a fire inside just enough to keep us warm,' Bela said. 'Do our cooking out-of-doors.' And he told Mima, laughing: 'You'd best come keep house for us, Mima, do the cooking and all.'

'I might so,' she agreed.

'Three men alone, we'll be a mess,' he said, and she smiled, thinking of Joel, realizing how long it was since she had put the Royal Mess in order. They had brought lunch with them, and ate it now, and Eben and Mima cleaned up while Jess and Bela worked on the hovel. When she was done she said:

'I'm going to start home, Eben. I might stop by the Royal Mess and straighten them out on the way.'

'So do,' Eben assented. 'We'll like as not stay here till dark. Be hard travelling then for you. You go along.' And he said understandingly: 'You like doing for Joel, don't you, Mima?' She looked at him in a quick happiness; and he smiled and said: 'Your cheeks are bright right now, thinking of him, and your eyes kind of shining.'

'I hate seeing things a mess and dirt all around.'

He spoke with that gentleness, that capacity for understanding which he so often revealed. 'I guess he feels bad about going away the night of the raising,' he said. 'He hasn't hardly been nigh us since.'

'Does he?' She spoke almost eagerly.

'Certain!' he assured her. 'That's the way a man acts when he knows he's played the fool and don't want to be told so.' He asked: 'You mad at him?'

She shook her head. 'I guess I'll never be real mad at Joel, Eben.'

He smiled, touched her arm affectionately. 'You go along,' he said.

Mima followed their own trail back toward Round Pond. Her footsteps muffled by the thin snow on the summer's dead leaves, she walked rapidly southward through the December woods. The snow everywhere was laced with tracks of small creatures. She noted them inattentively; but once she saw the trail of a late-wandering bear, and once she crossed moose tracks. She heard at last axes somewhere ahead of her; and she was at once sorry and relieved to know that she would find the cabin still deserted. She wanted to see Joel — yet she dreaded that encounter too.

There was a thread of smoke above the chimney when she saw the small house through the trees; but they would have left the fire banked, so she went forward, expecting to find the house empty. But when she came to the door she stopped still; for Joel faced her there. He must have heard her footfall and stopped what he was doing; for he had a broom in his hand, of birch switches bound to the end of a spruce pole. He had been sweeping the earthen floor, and he looked at her in the shamed embarrassment of a man caught at any household task. He was somehow so ludicrous that she laughed, and he grinned, and she said:

'Whatever are you up to, Joel?'.

He looked at the broom in his hand in an incredulous way as though surprised to find it there. She saw that he had heaped everything off the floor indiscriminately under the big common bunk that served them all, and hung garments on pegs stuck between the logs. She took the broom from him. 'Let me,' she said. 'You'll never do it right.' She assumed command. 'Fill the big kettle and set it to boil. Build up the fire outside. A man don't know what to do — but I'll tell you.' She asked: 'Do you three take turns, cleaning up?'

Joel said, grinning: 'They've put it on me since the barn-raising. I'm the Judas.'

'Why?'

'Well, you used to come regular before; but you don't since, and they claim you got mad at my foolishness.'

She was sweeping busily. 'I just didn't happen to come, that's all.'

He drew nearer her. 'Did you get mad at me?'

Her eyes touched his. 'It was puppy foolishness.'

'I guess a girl never knows how it is with a man,' he protested.

'I guess a man never knows how it is with a woman,' she retorted. He came a step toward her, and her cheeks flamed and she said quickly: 'Go on, get the kettle on.' She flirted the broom at him; and he laughed and dodged and went to obey.

They did what had to be done together, he working under her orders, she deriding his awkwardnesses; and they were merry, laughing at nothing, some intoxication in them both, as though they felt an equal relief because the rift between them now was healed. She made him scrub the pots and pans; and he said the water was hot enough to scald him, and she said there never was a man who wasn't a baby about hot water. They shook out blankets between them, dust and pine needles and tobacco crumbs flying in their faces as they snapped the blankets like flags in a wind. Under her eye he brushed the soot out of the oven with branches of ground pine, down on his hands and knees, peering inside to be sure he got it all. They were in a breathless haste, as though they worked against time. She had him fire the oven, and she mixed up cornbread ready for baking. She kept him occupied, and herself too, feeling instinctively that there was safety in action; that when they were done, with idle hands, nothing could keep them apart. She began to be deliciously afraid of what would happen when there was no more for them to do.

But so long as she kept him busy, she was safe. He did not speak again of that September night, nor did she; but again and again as they worked he was near her, sometimes touched her hand by apparent chance when they shared some task. Once after he had cleaned the oven, he left a smudge of soot on her dress, and she said:

'Go wash yourself. You're a sight, smutting everything.'

He laughed and obeyed her; and when he returned from the pond side she made him dig a hole and bury in it the cracked bones, the discarded skins of animals they had killed and eaten, the accumulated refuse of their cooking. Whenever he thought they were almost done, she devised some new task for him to do.

But the sun was low, would soon dip out of sight behind the trees. She wished Jason and Matt would leave their work and come back to the house, since with them here she would no longer be so dangerously alone with him. But they did not come, and the end of their work was in sight. She found at last an inspiration. The hemlock browse on the long shelf that was their bunk had been there so long that it was dead and springless. She sent him to fetch more.

'Get plenty,' she said. 'You might as well sleep soft as hard.' Near the house there were only pines. For hemlock he would have to go some distance, out of sight, and she would have a chance to get away.

'We'll do that tomorrow, the three of us,' he protested. 'We've slept on what's there all right up to now.'

'You go along,' she insisted. 'Don't you argue with me. I'm going to see things right, for once.'

He still grumbled, but he took his axe and went off up toward the high ground west of the cabin, away from the pond. As soon as he was out of sight she fled, slipping away toward the spring, racing along the beaver dam. If he returned and found her track, he might overtake her; but she would have a fair start. She caught up skirts and petticoats and ran like a doe deer, headlong, till her heart was pounding. She came to the river and picked her way across on the poles they had cut and laid that morning. The ice cracked even under her weight. She stooped with a breathless laugh and caught the poles and drew them after her. The ice would not bear Joel without the poles to help, and he would have no axe to cut fresh ones. She hauled the last poles to the bank; and then she heard him coming, racing through willows along the beaver dam. She slipped away among the trees till she was hidden, and paused there, and he came plunging down to the riverside and stepped out upon the ice and broke through into water knee-deep. He swore, and floundered back to shore.

'Damn the wench!' said Joel furiously, stamping to free his legs of the icy water. Mima crouched among the bushes, wishing she dared look, wishing to laugh, wishing to run. Then she heard Joel chuckle to himself; heard him say: 'Damned lucky for her she did run!'

He turned back. Before he was out of hearing she heard him begin to sing, midway in that song she knew:

> Till she fled and he ran and he found her and lost her
> And found her again — she was easy to find —
> Far from the sight of the gentlemen!

She knew these words rather because she had heard them before than by actually hearing them now; but as he went on he sang another verse which she could not hear, his voice receding. Turning homeward presently, she wondered what he would have said, what she would have said, if he had caught her today; and her cheeks were still warm when she came home.

18

THE long night of winter was for them all a tedious time when for days on end they might stir out-of-doors only to attend the routine chores or fetch fresh wood for the fire. This winter just beginning would be remembered for the ferocity of the cold and the great mass of snow that lay deep in the forest. At the turn of the year, there was a fair four feet everywhere, and severely low temperatures had long since sealed river and pond. The snow was so deep that even on webs travel for any great distance was arduous. Day after day, they stayed in the small cabin where snow was banked to the eaves on the weather side, as much prisoners as the cattle in the barn.

But they were warm and comfortable, and well fed. The only shortage was of meat. The crocks of pigeons, laid down layer on layer and each layer covered with tried-out fat, were a delicious delicacy; but a hungry man could eat a dozen birds. Jess had hung up three or four hindquarters of moose meat to freeze, and the saddles; but eight people can eat an astonishing amount of meat when the steady cold is waiting outside the door to drain their strength every time they emerge. Also, they were idle; and idle men may eat more than those who are all day at work.

So meat ran low; and Jess projected a trip to the moose yards in the Madomock swamps where the great beasts moved along their narrow trails. He was out every day on snowshoes, testing the travelling; and one day he went as far as the Royal Mess.

'Joel thinks we can make it,' he reported that night. 'These sunny days, the snow melts a little on top and then freezes hard at night. There'll be crust enough to carry snowshoes soon. Half the time today I didn't break clear through. It just settled all around me. We think we'll go.'

He enlisted Bela to fashion special runners for one of the hand sleds, making them a fair eight inches wide, of spruce steamed and bent, with long toes sweeping upward high enough so that they would not catch in the crust and would serve always to lift the sled on the firmest footing. Philip Robbins advised that they go north to the head of Sunnyback Pond and cross from there to the Madomock. The easiest route up-river was from Philip's across the meadows at the head of Seven-Tree Pond. So they would start from Philip's, and Joel came down the night before. The others were abed before he came, but Jess sat up for him, and so did Mima. She had not seen Joel since that day she fled and he broke through the ice in the effort to overtake her. He said when he saw her:

'You left in a hurry that day, didn't wait to be thanked proper for all the work cleaning us up.'

'You did the heft of it,' she reminded him.

'You didn't have to run away. I wouldn't have et you.'

'You stayed so long cutting browse I couldn't wait.'

'I was back in no time, but you'd gone. I thought you were handy by, thought you'd come back.'

'I guess you didn't start looking for me.'

'Why no,' he declared. 'Time I decided you weren't coming back it was dark.' He chuckled. 'If a girl wants to run away from me, I don't ever aim to chase her.'

Mima said with complete gravity: 'I didn't run. I didn't even come straight home. It stayed light quite a while, and when I got across the river there by the big maple, I stayed a spell watching the sky and the sunset color and all.' She added seriously: 'There was an otter — or something, couldn't make out just what — came down and broke through the ice right across from me. I guess it was after salmon, maybe.'

Jess said in a sharp excitement: 'Was there so? I'll set a trap for him. A good otter skin'll fetch a price.'

Joel chuckled, looking at Mima. 'Guess that otter'll be back — show him the same bait that fetched him that time,' he said. They spoke in low tones. Mr. and Mrs. Robbins were in the big bed behind them, and Philip was snoring, and Sue was asleep in the trundle bed on the floor. The younger sons had climbed to their place in the garret overhead. The fire burned low while Jess and Joel and Mima stayed in talk together; and at last Mima, in the shadows behind the men, stepped out of her dress and petticoats and in her shift slipped into bed with Sue. She lay with her head toward the fire, on her stomach, her chin on her hands; and the two young men talked a while longer. As the fire died down, cold crept into the cabin till Jess said:

'Well, time for bed. Joel, take my bed in the garret and I'll roll up on the floor in your blankets.'

'Keep your bed, Jess,' Joel told him. 'I'll do fine here on the floor.'

But Mrs. Robbins said from where she lay beside her husband: 'Floor's hard, Joel. You better roll in with Sue and Mima. That's a real comfortable feather bed I fetched from home they're sleeping on. You'll need to sleep sound.'

'Why, thank you kindly, ma'am,' Joel agreed. 'If there's room.'

Mima said: 'There's room enough other side of Sue. She always curls right down in the middle of the bed.' She turned on her side, her back toward Sue while Joel stripped off shirt and hunting socks and lay down. Jess had waited to be sure Joel was comfortable. He asked:

'Covers enough?'

'Plenty. Sue's good as a warming pan,' Joel told him.

Jess banked the fire and climbed to his place in the garret. After a moment his stirrings ceased, and there was no more movement or sound. Mima lay warm and still, Sue close along her back, pressed for warmth like a plaster there. But she could feel Joel near.

* * * * *

The two young men made an early start. When during the day the wind came out of the northwest and blew bitter cold, Mrs. Robbins was concerned; but Philip reassured her.

'They'll do fine,' he said. 'With snow as deep as this they can burrow into it and sleep as snug as bears.'

'There's people have froze to death,' she reminded him.

'Them that did were mostly scared to death,' he insisted. 'Jess is smart and steady — yes, and Joel too. Let it storm and all they have to do is camp, lie down, eat, sleep — wait for it to pass.'

'And freeze in their sleep! Or starve!'

He laughed. 'You ever been real cold, Ma? Woke you up, didn't it? Nobody ever froze to death without knowing it, not without waking up.' He added: 'And as for eating, a man don't need to eat!'

'I've took notice you make fuss enough if your meals ain't ready on time.'

He slapped her shoulder in a cheerful affection. 'I just do it to keep you on the job, Ma!' He said: 'No, the only thing in the world there is to be scared of is — being scared. If you're scared, you lose your head. Things look bigger and blacker than they are. A rabbit will throw a shadow as big as a moose if he's near enough the candle.' He spoke to Mima, with an unusual gentleness. 'Don't ever be afraid of anything, Mima. If you're not scared — there's mighty few things in this world that can hurt you.'

While the two were gone, Mima had sometimes to remind herself of this advice. She asked her father many questions, which he answered patiently. Jess and Joel wouldn't hurry. Hurry made trouble. You broke a snowshoe, or you twisted a leg, or you tired yourself out. Easy was the way to do it. He told her where they had planned to go.

'Sam Boggs says there's a brook comes down from the north-east through meadows and hits the Madomock just fair west from the head of Sunnyback Pond,' he said. 'The river comes more from the northwest there, and high land in between. There's cedar swamps along the river, and grass swamps and meadows along the brook, and it's a master place for moose to winter; but they'll have to look till they find where they're using.' He added: 'Then they'll likely kill what they can, fetch what they can, leave the rest for us to go after.'

On the eighth day, at late dusk, Joel returned alone. They were all indoors and no one heard him coming till he pulled the latchstring and pushed open the door. Then they met him with shouts and questions, and Mrs. Robbins saw that Jess was not with him, but Joel said in quick reassurance: 'He's all right, Aunt Mima.' He kicked off his snowshoes and came in, warming himself before the great fire. 'There's a sled load of meat at the landing, Eb,' he said. 'If you want to go fetch it. I've dragged it all of ten miles today. The last pitch was too much for me.'

Jake and Eben leaped for the door, and Joel told his story. 'We've got enough moose butchered to go through the winter, but it will take the lot of us to haul it home.' There was deep weariness in his voice. He told Philip: 'You never saw such a place for moose. I judge they're backing off up-river from the settlements at Broad Bay. There must have been forty acres of yard, paths beat down everywhere, and the browse eaten off as clean as sheep. We could have killed twice as many; but when we'd shot twelve, that was all we could handle.'

'Bela's been putting runners on all the sleds we've got,'

Philip told him. 'I had a notion we might need 'em if you struck meat. I've got three, and Rich and Dave and the others — they'll have one apiece, anyway. We'll put out to fetch the meat first thing in the morning.'

Joel nodded. He said: 'We sledded all the meat to our camp place and piled it up there.' He told Mrs. Robbins: 'You don't need to worry about Jess, Aunt Mima. He's setting right on top of maybe two tons of moose meat, and nothing to do but cook it and eat it all day long. He'll be fine!'

Mrs. Robbins said crisply: 'I might have knowed Jess would take care of hisself, take the easy part and let you drag the sled home alone.'

'Someone had to,' he told her good-humoredly. He said: 'I'd ought to go tell Jason and Matt we're starting early; but my legs are limber as a piece of rope, they're so tired.'

Eben volunteered to tramp up to Round Pond, and Jake would go down as far as Rich's cabin and pass the word along. Joel was so weary that he went to sleep with his supper half-eaten, his head on his arms on the table. He and Sue and Mima shared the trundle bed again.

The men made an early start next morning, and they returned on the sixth day. There were fourteen men in the train. A side of moose meat was all one man could drag, but two men could pull a sled loaded more than twice as heavily; and with relays to break out the runners in the morning, or to haul the sleds up steeper pitches and over the more difficult going, they had managed well enough. They had killed four more moose to add to those Joel and Jess had butchered; and sixteen carcasses, each one split, the head and all useless parts discarded, came back that day to Seven-Tree Pond. The frozen meat would keep till warm weather; it provided for the whole settlement a bountiful supply.

*   *   *   *   *

Winter seemed interminable, but spring was coming. In

February the sun rose earlier and stayed later every day, and by the middle of the month, the last snow had melted off the roof of the house and the drifts began perceptibly to settle. Bet's baby — a girl, named Polly — was born on a fine sunny day, unseasonably warm; and Lucy's, a month later, likewise proved to be a girl, named after Lucy herself. April brought warm rains that darkened the snow across the pond, and one night Mima heard a rumbling as the ice began to break up; and on the sixteenth Joel was able to come down the river from Round Pond in his float.

Mima was half sorry for winter's end. Life during the winter months was as comfortable as a familiar bedfellow, but now first Joel and then Philip as they went down to Warren and returned brought disturbing news of the troubled world. The long war to throw off the rule of the King translated itself along this coast into savage affrays with men once their neighbors, now refugees in Biguyduce, sallying out from there in schooners and sloops, barges and shaving mills, to pilfer and to burn. They heard, now that spring was come, ugly stories of men beset in their own dooryards, seeing the fruits of their labor stolen or spoiled. Ben Burton, a Colonel now, had made the trip across the ice-covered bay from Camden in February to ask the release of young Eliakim Libby of Warren, who had been carried off a prisoner when the sloop on which he was a hand was cut out in the Wessaweskeag by a Tory crew; and Libby was released, and Burton brought him home. General Peleg Wadsworth, who had been the ablest and most energetic of the commanders in the attack on Biguyduce, early in April arrived in Thomaston to take command of all the forces in the eastern department as far as the St. Croix. John Long and McClellan and John Snow of Thomaston were turned Tory in their sympathies and their avowals; and Long was active in privateering and in smuggling provisions to the British at Biguyduce. There were ugly rumors that Lieutenant Matthews, of the Thomaston militia, had accepted a commission from the King. Belfast was deserted.

Belfast folk had on the first occupation of Biguyduce, at the demand of Lieutenant Mowatt, taken the oath of allegiance to the King; but when the fleet sent by the General Court sailed up the Bay, they broke that oath and volunteered to serve against the British under General Lovell. So now they could expect no mercy for their persons if they were captured, and nothing but destruction for any of their property that might fall into British hands. It was said that they had left most of their goods behind in Belfast, hiding their pewter, their cooking dishes, their very furniture, in their wells and in the woods around their abandoned homes. Waldo Dicke of Warren was now a refugee, he and John Nelson; they harried every small craft that showed itself at the mouth of the river. Some families from the Penobscot had come to Warren to escape the near proximity of the British. The air was full of rumors, fact and fable, that ran from mouth to mouth; and Mima hated the bitter talk and the shabby tales she heard.

But her father tried to shut his ears to the ugly news. He was full of plans for widening his fields. When the ground was a mire with emerging frost, he and his sons worked pulling stumps, using sometimes two yokes of oxen tandem, wrenching the stumps out of their beds like great teeth. His land was almost entirely free from stones, as was the land on Round Pond where the Royal Mess had felled trees the year before. The stalled oxen during the winter had produced a mountain of manure, and whenever they were driven to the fields they dragged a sledge load of it, the heavy runners slithering in the mud, to enrich even more the rich and virgin soil. The men were at work before the snow was fully gone; they worked from first light to last day. Down the pond, and across on the Mill Farm, and up at Round Pond, every man was thus engaged. There would be a lull presently when seed time was over; but now there was no breathing space at all.

May brought warm steady winds which helped to dry the ground, and most of the days were fair; but on the nineteenth

came such a day as no one of them had seen before. It began
with a thundershower in the morning, of peculiar violence; and
after the shower passed, the skies, instead of brightening, grew
darker still.   Philip when the rain stopped tried to go back to
work in the fields; but he had to give it up, and stalled the oxen
and came indoors.

'Darkest day ever I see,' he declared. 'Can't make out a
stump in the field in front of you till you're right on top of it,
dummed near too late to swing the oxen.'

'I had to light a rush light in the house,' Mrs. Robbins agreed.
'Till I built up the fire. And Mima says the fish were jumping
in the pond, and the birds went to roost, like it was already
dark.'

Jess said: 'It's dark as any night I ever want to see.'

'Wonder what makes it, Pa?' Eben asked, standing in the
door, looking out. 'Smoke in the air or something?'

'Don't smell like it,' the older man reflected. Mrs. Robbins
was boiling moose meat spitted before the fire, baking kettle
bread; and he watched her. 'And if it is smoke, it'd take a
powerful big fire to make this much.'

Susie asked with wide eyes: 'Reckon it will be all right
tomorrow?'

Her father clapped his arm around her shoulders, drew her
closer. 'Don't fret yourself. Sun always has come out again,
sometime. Guess't always will.' He nodded at his own words.
'There's been times I've took a heap of comfort out of remembering that,' he declared. 'When things were going kind of bad,
I c'd always tell myself that the worst they went, the surer they
was to get better.'

Mrs. Robbins said: 'There, I guess't dinner's ready,' and
Philip clapped Sue cheerfully on the head.

'There, y'see? Nobody can worry very long when they've
got plenty to eat and your ma to cook it up for them.'

After they had eaten, Philip and his sons went out-of-doors to
give the womenfolks room to clear away. Philip cuffed at a

mosquito, and Eben got a smudge going, and Philip sighed a controlled, well-fed sigh. 'Jess,' he said. 'One good thing, this drove them little black midges. They thought it was night, went off to bed. Wish't it'd be as dark every day.'

'I've got so I don't mind 'em so much,' Jess admitted. 'Guess I'm so poisoned a'ready they can't poison me no more.'

It was too dark to work, all afternoon; yet there was no feeling of storm in the air. Joel and Matt came down from Round Pond to ask Philip what he made of this phenomenon, and to speculate with him as to its cause. Smoke from forest fires seemed to them all the likeliest conjecture. 'Somebody burning off a fell piece, and the fire got away from them,' Philip hazarded. He himself had been clearing land west of the house, over the rise of ground and down toward the river, at odd times these two years; so that his arable lands were widening every year, and he had some down-timber to burn off this spring. The Royal Mess had during their first summer felled the great pines over about twenty acres south of their house; and this too was ready to burn as soon as it dried out from the weight of the winter snow. The men talked of these tasks, and of all the economy of the farm, and of the ravages of the Tory marauders along the coast; they spoke of the fact that Philip's farm had been auctioned for taxes, and laughed at the thought that any man would be bold enough to think he could have it by such an empty purchase. 'But the man bought it, he's agent for Colonel Wheaton,' Philip said. 'He'll keep quiet till the Colonel can do some work in the General Court, get this whole tax business straightened out.'

Mima from where she was busy indoors could hear their voices, and it was Joel's for which she listened, caring not so much for his words as for the sound of his strong tones, in which there was so often a hint of laughter. He had the trick of laughing at things; at too many things. Mima had no illusions about Joel. She saw him whole; saw clearly enough the weaknesses in him. They did not repel her. She might be wounded, but wounds healed, give them time. There was no wild passion, no hopeless yearning in her. She was not impatient. She could be patient, being sure.

He and Matt went back up-river at last, and Philip came in and said: 'Well, Ma, no sun to tell by, but my belly says it's getting on toward supper time.' Night when it fell was only a deeper blackness; but the night was warm, and after supper, Jess said: 'Eben, you and Jake want to come see if we can spear us a salmon? There's some lying in the pool up above the gray birch.'

Eben said: 'Certain!' Philip told them: 'I'll come and watch ye.' And as the three departed toward the landing, he spoke to Mrs. Robbins inside the cabin. 'Boys are going to get a salmon, Ma. Let Mima and Sue finish cleaning up. We'll walk up through the woods and see the fun.'

'I wouldn't go out in them mosquitoes for all the salmon in the river,' she assured him. 'Mima, you and Sue go along if you're a mind.'

So Mima and Sue went up the rising ground behind the cabin and — keeping in the clearing since it was too dark to see their way among the pines — made toward the river; but Philip decided to stay behind with Mrs. Robbins. 'A night like this, warm and so still you can hear the sap running, I always kind of like to hang around my gal,' he told her affectionately when they were alone; and he came in and sat down, his elbows on his knees. 'Stillest night you ever did hear, Ma,' he told her. 'I could hear the mice squeaking, making love in the barn.'

She chuckled. 'Trust a man to git ideas in his head, spring of the year.'

'Well,' he reminded her, 'the ellwives run in the spring, and the salmon, and the foxes and all.'

'Moose don't!' she argued. 'You can hear 'em bawling like a bulling cow, along every fall. I dunno about bears.'

'They pup in their sleep. Cubs about the size of chipmunks. I've dug 'em out and found 'em.'

Mrs. Robbins chuckled. 'I can remember times I'd like to have been a bear. David weighed right on to eleven pounds, and the others warn't much smaller. Chipmunks!' They heard a shout of triumph from the river where their children were engaged, and she said gently: 'They've growed up to be a fine lot of chipmunks, Philip.'

'You know what I'd like, Ma?' he said thoughtfully. She did not answer him, finishing her tasks; and he went on: 'I'd like if you and me would live a real long time. I'd like to have us die about the same time.' He added mirthfully: 'I guess't you'd better plan to outlive me a little, so you can redd up after me; but I want us both to live long enough to see some of our great-grandchildren.'

She said briskly: 'That ain't going to be so long as you might think. Dave's Jason's eight years old — and when he was a baby I never did see such parts on a young one!'

His voice rumbled with amusement. 'So, yes, he's a lusty boy. Why Ma, in say thirty years we can look to see our first great-great-grandson. Thirty years ain't much! We've been married that long, come November, and it don't seem a minute. We'll live another thirty years before we know it.'

She had finished cleaning up, came to stand beside him. 'It's funny to think, Philip,' she said softly, 'that forty years from now — or fifty maybe — you and me'll be dead and buried, gone, all finished with.'

He dropped his arm around her waist. 'Don't you believe it. Dead yes, and buried — well, I should hope so. But not gone, Ma! Not finished with! Not with our young ones, and theirs, and theirs, coming along.' He chuckled. 'You and me, we're like a spring up in the mountains, running a good flow of water. And all along, other spring brooks run into it; Rich Comings, and Dave's Bess, and Mima's Joel when he comes to it, and the others that'll come along. It gets to be a bigger river all the time — and we'll be part of it as long as it keeps running. We'll be part of it till it goes clean dry.'

'We've give 'em a good start, Philip. Healthy bodies, decent minds.' She said: 'We're healthy ourselves, and we love each other. That's all there has to be, healthy folks in love.' She added: 'But we'll be forgot.'

'They can forget us, but they can't get rid of us,' he argued. Another shout came from the river. 'They've got another salmon,' he said. 'Likely it's splashing and raising a rucus! Every splash it makes starts a ripple out across the river; but the river keeps flowing, and it takes the ripple away, down the pond, down the river again, down into the sea. But wherever that particular water goes, it take some of the ripple that salmon started.' He chuckled. 'That's you and me, Ma. We've started these young ones living. There's a ripple from us in every one of them, and it'll go on in their children and on and on. We throw quite a splash, Ma, you and me!'

She laughed with him; she asked suddenly: 'Pa, do you believe in Hell and damnation?'

'Certain! But you don't have to die to get it. It catches up with you while you're alive.'

'Do you believe you and me'll die and go to Heaven?'

He held her hand. 'Don't have to. Living with each other is Heaven enough for you and me.'

She kissed him. 'Here they come,' she said. They stepped out-of-doors and saw above the tree-tops across the pond the risen moon, blood red through haze which still filled the sky. Jess had speared two salmon of about ten pounds each; and he bound each one in a sheath of alders to keep off the flies, to keep them cool. Eben built up the smudge by the door, and they all sat a while there, watching the red moon, talking in low tones. The night was full of small, comfortable sounds. When they went at last to bed, Mima lay awake, happily listening to the teeming silences. She felt all around this small cabin the springing flood of life, of which she was a part, that filled the world.

19

WHEN the drifts began to settle, six weeks before, Bela had gone with Jess and Eben to resume that business of felling oak trees and hewing the timbers for Colonel Wheaton's barn, which the deep snow for a while had interrupted. Late in May the Colonel came up the river, bringing men to work at clearing his land and preparing for the planting, and to see how the barn job progressed. He had been all winter in Boston as Thomaston's representative at the General Court, had come home in time to see General Wadsworth installed as commander-in-chief of the Eastern District, and to tender to the General his own good frame house in Thomaston as a home. He reached Philip's cabin in the late afternoon; but he found only Mrs. Robbins and the younger children at home. She met him at the landing.

'They've all gone up-river,' she explained. 'Joel and the others are burning off their fell-piece tonight, nigh twenty acres of big pines that they laid last summer. It's dry as gunpowder, and my menfolks have gone to give them a hand, see't it don't start running.'

He said approvingly, with a glance at the sky: 'They picked a good day. The wind's coming northeast. It'll fetch rain.' He asked the family news, heard that everyone was well, heard of the new babies born during the winter, and that David's Bess was due in June.

'How's Mima?' he asked. 'No man put his mark on her yet?' And when she shook her head, he said robustly: 'By Gora-mighty, if one of 'em doesn't do it soon I'll carry off the girl myself! She's ripe as an apple in October.'

Mrs. Robbins thought there was a change in him. He was more cheerful than he had been these two years gone. 'You look better than you did,' she said. 'Wintering in Boston suited you.'

'It's a load off my mind having General Wadsworth here,' he agreed. 'I've had all the worrying to do, trying to keep the God-damned refugees from raiding alongshore and not knowing how to do it. Now he'll handle that. He's got brains in his head.' He told her honestly: 'I can cuss and swear around, but when there's a job of thinking to do, it needs a thinking man.'

She nodded, liking him. 'You're like every other man, Colonel. You talk big to prove to yourself you are big; but you ain't fooled. Inside you're as scared and shy as a girl.'

He chuckled. 'Well, I never did claim to have any brains,' he admitted. Since Philip was not at home, he decided to go on up-river, stepped back into the barge.

Mima was at Round Pond. She and her father stood together on a naked ledge thirty feet above the water at the northeast corner of the cut-down. From where they stood, every tree to the south and west as far as the boggy meadow along the brook mouth had been felled. Since they were cut the year before, the heavy trunks had settled nearer the ground; the sap had dried out of them, they were smothered in inter-lacing boughs on which the needles had turned brown and dried till they were like tinder. The cut-down was bounded on the east and south by the pond, and on the west by the boggy land along the brook where no trees grew, so that except on the north side there was little danger that the conflagration would spread.

When Colonel Wheaton and his men landed, Philip Robbins was tending a fire from which brands would presently be carried to start the down-stuff burning; and along the line of the woods, the younger men were cutting brush and piling it ready to catch the first touch of flame and nurse it into a roaring torch. Philip turned at Colonel Wheaton's shout of greeting; and he left Mima to watch the fire and went down to the pond side to meet the other man and clasp his hand.

'You're long coming, Colonel!' he exclaimed. 'I'd thought to see you up here a month ago.'

'Too God-damned busy chasing Tories,' the Colonel told him as they climbed the bank. Mima came to greet him and he caught her shoulders and told her she was a sight for sore eyes. 'If there was a man up here with any gimp to him he'd have had you in bearing before now,' he cried.

Mima said she was glad to see him back again. 'To take care of us,' she told him smilingly. 'They're driving cattle across your land to Biguyduce, and there's talk of Tories till you look for them to jump out at you from behind every tree.'

He nodded grimly. 'That minds me, Robbins,' he said. 'You remember John Perry? He came here last year?'

They remembered. Mima said: 'Eben's forever talking about him.'

'I saw him in Boston,' the Colonel explained. 'Did you hear how the British almost had him last November?'

Philip had not heard, but before the Colonel could go on, Joel and then others come trooping back to the fire to get brands. It was dusk — though on this day the sky was overcast, and dusk came early — and the story was interrupted while he shook their hands. Bela reported that two weeks' work would have the barn timbers ready for the raising; and the

Colonel said: 'We'll put it up soon's it's ready, Bela.' The men
took burning torches from the fire and ranged away along the
line of brush piles, but Mima kept Eben here.

'He's saying something about John Perry,' she told her
brother. 'Wait and hear.' So Eben let the others do the firing;
and Colonel Wheaton said:

'Why, I had it from Perry himself. He was on the dodge,
eating where he could. This was after he'd killed two of them.
He spied a raft of ducks in the Thoroughfare and sneaked alongshore near enough and let off both guns into them. Tide was
running and it took the dead ones; but he had his float in a
good place below and started for it to pick the ducks up, not
waiting to load his guns. He came to the float and jumped in,
and then four soldiers from Biguyduce with a little pismire of a
lieutenant at the head of them came charging down to the shore
bidding him come in or they'd shoot!' The Colonel chuckled.
'So Perry said he'd come in as soon as he'd picked up his ducks,
and they thought they'd have the ducks to eat, so they watched
him do it. He got off three or four rods, picked up seven of the
ducks — and then over the side of his float he went and into
the water, and the canoe between him and them to stop the
musket balls — Oh, they peppered him, too! — and away he
swam with it, canoe, guns, ducks and all, and the tide to help
him, and got clean away.'

Philip swore approvingly. 'You said last year the British had
offered a thousand dollars for him. The one that gets it will
earn it. He's a man!'

Eben asked: 'Where is he, Colonel? What's he going to do
this summer? Privateering? Gorry, I'd like to ...'

But the Colonel cried: 'There goes the fire!' The first smoke
ribbon rose at the northwest corner of the cut-down, and before
the leaping flames followed it upward, other smokes rose,
nearer where they stood, and all along this northern side of the
fell-piece, fires like sentinels began to burn. Colonel Wheaton
watched with the eye of a good tactician. 'They're firing it all

this side,' he commented. 'What wind there is will carry it away from the woods.'

Philip nodded. 'So, yes; and they've cleared a firestop with oxen and small burnings all along here. The brook and the pond will stop it at the south end.'

Already the flames were running; the fierce hungry crackling of them began to rise into a steady roar. Jess and Joel and Bela came back to join them here; and Joel was dripping with sweat.

'There it goes,' he said. 'We'll be baked on the hoof if we stay here.' The fire was already painfully hot on their faces. They retreated a little, and Joel and the young men sprawled on the ground, watching the flames mount higher and higher. The dark smoke masses were a crimson banner against the evening sky. Mima stood with her arms folded tightly across her bosom, feeling that exultation a burning always woke in her. This was so much more than a bonfire; it was victory, victory seen in the very moment of consummation. The great trees had guarded the land, jealously defending it against men who wished to seize it and make it yield a treasure of rye and potatoes and cabbages and turnips, wheat and oats and corn. So long as the trees stood, the land lay secure in idleness; but a year ago Joel — Joel and others, to be sure; but it would always for Mima be Joel who did it — had toppled them down. Their corpses still cluttered the earth; but now fire would consume those corpses, leave the good earth clean. The earth was a woman, captive of the forest, freed now to be wedded and made fertile by the men who had fought for her liberation.

Mima stood a little apart from the men, and they all retreated further as the flames swept the length of the cut-down, and twenty acres of great pines in one tremendous bonfire sent a flaming banner streaming upward till it seemed to touch the stars.

She heard, as though from a great distance, Colonel Wheaton's voice. He was telling some story. The men while they listened all watched the great fire, their eyes glittering in its reflected light, their faces golden red from its illumination. 'Loaded with lime she was,' said Colonel Wheaton. 'I'd spent all my money in Boston, needed to make a cargo quick. I went along to see her safe; but a shaving mill came out of Harpswell Bay after us. They caught us on a lee shore, and in among the islands too — and just three men of us aboard. We tried to clear Cape Small, so's we'd have the wind free; but just at the last when another two minutes would have seen us do it, they laid us aboard. Burn their Tory hides!'

Philip Robbins asked: 'Who was it?'

'Linneken,' Colonel Wheaton told him. 'And a proud cock he was. I could have her back, he said, for two hundred dollars ransom money; and I told him he could be damned. He said I'd see Metcalf Island if I didn't, and he fetched a crew aboard, set a course for Halifax.

'Well, in no time, he saw a schooner make out from Ragged Island. She was all of ten miles away. We were on the wind, but she was making to cut us off, and Linneken saw she'd have us if she was a mind to. I knew there was a militia company on Ragged Island, and I thought there might be some good boys aboard that schooner.' The roar of the flames was like the sound of a great cataract, drumming in the air. The men were close to him, listening; but Mima from a little way off could still catch every word. 'Linneken asked me to have a look at her,' the Colonel went on. 'Gave me his glass, and I put it on her. There was no more than two men aboard that I could see; and I told him so, told him she might be a fishing smack out of New Meadows; but I could smell trouble coming for him just the same, and so could he.

'She was handy by then, and Linneken told the three of us he'd turn us loose if we'd help fight her off; but I was watching the sloop, and I saw the helm go as she rounded to, half a musket shot off our quarter. So I yelled to my two men to drop flat, and drop they did and no time to spare. Musket balls went across like sleet, right above us; killed one of Lin-neken's men and punctured a couple others, and in no time twenty or thirty of the Ragged Island militia were aboard us.' He laughed till he cried. 'They grabbed Linneken by his pig-tail and took a rope's end across his backside till his pigtail and the rope were both wore down to a whisper. We sailed into New Meadows and locked Linneken up and I bought enough rum punch for them all to swim in. I had a good swim in it myself, too, before we made on for Boston. We did some sing-ing. I taught them that song of yours, Joel.'

Joel grinned, and he came scrambling to his feet. 'I near forgot. See here, I thought we might get thirsty, want a bye-blow.' He fetched a jug from among the roots of a pine behind them, and it went the rounds.

Mima did not look that way. She was watching the great fire, loving the heat of it on her face. It seemed impossible that it could burn more fiercely, yet the roar of it was louder all the time. The rising air above the conflagration created all around a brisk breeze. It fluttered Mima's skirts and she felt it cool on her neck. Even at this distance the heat made them all per-spire. They might have drawn farther off, but there was some-thing fiercely stimulating in this actual discomfort. Above the cut-down, an ascending column of flame and smoke and spark-ing embers went rushing skyward with the speed of a cataract; yet watching the burning brands high in the air Mima could see how they seemed to hang and drift slowly off to the southward, each one now obscured by smoke, now visible again. The men drank raw rum; but for the second drink all except Colonel Wheaton preferred to modify its violence with water from the pond, and after the third drink, Joel filled the jug with water, diluting the harsh spirit; and the talk, as it was always apt to do, went back to Tory depredations. Down-river a man never knew what might happen to him. Heard's salt works had been burned for sheer malice. Captain Sam Watts had some specie hid away and they came and tried to make him tell where it

was, routed the Captain and his wife out of bed, searched everywhere, ripped up the feather beds, stole Captain Watts'
Comarny cap, finally carried the Captain away as a prisoner.
But they did not get the money; and it was thought the Captain
would be presently released. There had been raiders at Camden, threatening to burn the mills, calling the houses pigsties!
The British came to Thomaston and took two deserters; and
over on Islesborough they seized Shubael Williams and charged
him with helping a deserter, and sentenced him to sixty with
the cat; but he was an oldish man, and after forty lashes the
blood had run down and filled his shoes and overflowed, and
they saw he would die from bleeding so, and let him off
alive.

Mima hated the talk of violence and all hideous depredations. She saw Eben's face tight with rage at these wrongs he
could not right, and Jess grinning like a skull with hatred of the
Tories, and Bela's eyes were blazing. They had been happy
till tonight, hard at their tasks, building their lives and their
homes, loving and kind. Now they were full of hate, and Mima
thought hate might be a poison that blunted your wits and
sapped your clean strength. She withdrew a little from where
they sat. The faces, even Eben's, were ugly to see. She wondered whether the Tories went to and fro with hate like a dark
stain on their brows. Probably the English, and the refugees,
thought as bitterly of the patriots as the patriots thought of
them. Mima wished she did not have to know about these
shabby wrongs. Winter had been clean and sweet and fine.
They knew nothing of what went on beyond the snowy walls
that protected them from hearing these tales. She wished
winter would come soon again. They were all so much happier
not knowing. Probably all over the world there were wars and
hate and violence; but if you did not know about them, they
did not harm you. A man — or a woman — had enough to do
living his own life, loving good and hating evil in himself and
in those near him. It did no good, only great harm, to hate

Linneken, and the British, and all those others whose lives never touched your own.

They did not notice when she drew away. She went back to the landing and took a float and started home; but once out on the pond she stopped paddling to look back at the beautiful fire. At this distance the roar of it began to be softened; but those great trees — she remembered trunks so thick that even when they lay prostrate they were breast-high — would burn for hours, for days, the fire eating into their hearts, following the resinous sap veins, till the trunks were empty shells, like gutted carcasses. She stayed a while there, her float drifting idly, watching that tremendous spectacle. Between her and the fire the crests of the tall pines swayed and tossed in the strong suction of the fire, as though lamenting this destruction of their brethren, as though knowing that a like fate awaited them. The glare lighted all the shores around the pond so that she could see every tree and bush along the waterside. The pond itself was red as blood in the reflected light. The men were singing yonder. She could hear the Colonel's hoarse bellows, hear Joel's clearer, truer tones. Full dark fell, but the fire burned the brighter. Flames leaped a hundred feet in the air, like tormented things trying to escape, springing skyward and perishing in the rising columns of reddened smoke against the stars. The smoke trailed away southwestward, blotting out the skies that way.

She felt a great contentment. The fire would burn all night; but tomorrow it would be reduced to scattered, smouldering trunks of trees half-burnt; and the day after, it would cool. There would be rain to damp it out; and then Joel — and the others — would plant their corn, thrusting pointed sticks down through the ashes into the fertile earth, dropping into each hole a few grains, smoothing the earth with their feet. In a little after that the first green shoots would appear, and grow so fast you could almost see them; and as summer passed, the corn would ripen and be cut, and then they would drag the half-burnt logs together and burn them and sow winter rye. Till now this land had been useless wilderness, untamed and wild, serving no useful end. Now man had set it free to serve the ends of man. Forever it would lend him its fertility.

It was long after dark when she came slowly home; but even the clearing around her father's house was half as bright as day, lighted by that great torch which flamed against the sky a scant mile away to the westward. She could see the glare, could almost see the leaping tips of the flames, from here beside the house; and after she was in bed, she could hear the far roar of the fire.

She lay half-awake, feeling the hot passion of the fire in herself. Joel had felled the trees, he kindled the flame, and presently he would seed the land and bring it to rich bearing. It was as though he were the husband, the teeming earth his bride; and Mima longed for him, full of a warm hunger, full of the pulse and stirring of this season just waking to the flood. Sleep was slow in coming, and she rose at last and went out-of-doors to lie on the ground, her eyes among the stars, lonely and afar. She lay there awake and yearning, till she heard voices from the river and knew her father and her brothers were coming home, and opened her eyes and saw first dawn's pale cast across the eastern sky.

* * * * *

Mima had other wakeful nights, till the night she heard someone coming at a stumbling run and went to the door to meet David. He was here to fetch his mother.

'It's Bess!' he gasped, panting from his run.

When Mrs. Robbins was ready, Mima went with them down the pond. 'Bess is sure this one will be all right,' David told them, as he led the way. A roll of birch bark flared in his hand to light their steps. 'She's been mightily scared, after the last two, but she saw the new moon over her right shoulder tonight.' He tried to laugh. 'I've been telling her and telling her that she'd be fine, and the baby too; but she wouldn't believe it till now. She'd sooner believe the moon than me!'

'So would any woman,' his mother assured him. 'There's more'n one girl has refused to believe a man's promises till maybe some fine night the moon told her all he said was true. And then like as not he was lying worse than ever!' She asked: 'When did she start?'

'I came the minute she woke me up.'

'I doubt she'll be long,' Mrs. Robbins reflected. 'Bess always was a quick one. Time we get there, you build up the fire, Dave, and fill the kettle, and then get out of the way. Mima and me don't want to have you on our hands just when we're busiest.'

'I'd be all right if I had a thing to do.'

Her tone was gentle. 'A man never does get used to his wife having a baby, does he?'

'She's so big,' he confessed. 'I guess she was big the other times too — but it scares me.'

Mrs. Robbins said sharply: 'Pity you didn't see the new moon yourself, to put some backbone into you.'

The baby, a boy, born without incident, was to Bess and to Mrs. Robbins and to Mima — as all babies are to womankind — the most beautiful ever brought into the world. It cried properly, it went properly to sleep in the warm nest of arm and bosom beside Bess where she lay; and David, once it was born and Bess all right, forgot his own fears and said infuriatingly that he couldn't see that it was any different from other babies. When Jason and Chloe and Joe woke in the morning, they were permitted to see the newcomer's small wrinkled countenance with tight-shut eyes and scowling brow and twisting, working, forever hungry mouth. Jason said it was awful red, and Chloe said it was awful sweet, and five-year-old Joe for some obscure reason took one look at it and ran to Mima, clinging to her skirts, screaming with fear which for a while Mima could not soothe.

Mima stayed for that week and part of the next to take care of Bess and of the baby; and Bess watched her bathe it and fondle it and hold it close, and saw her passionate hunger and thought Mima would be mighty happy some day with a baby of her own. She sought some way to please the other woman, and when she was well enough to get up, to attend to her household and her baby and herself, she said one day:

'Mima, Dave and I were talking last night what to name him. Do you think Joel would let us name him after him?'

Mima was completely surprised, and color flooded her cheeks; and the thoughts of which she herself during these days had not been fully conscious suddenly took form and substance. She had been thinking: How if he were mine, Joel's and mine? A sudden jealous anger filled her, and despair too, because Bess and not she herself had borne this baby that would wear Joel's name. Her cheeks burned, and she thought for a moment that Bess made this suggestion out of malice; but she saw Bess smiling tenderly and knew there was no malice in the other girl, and she tried to speak evenly.

'Name him "Joel"?' she repeated.

'Yes. It's a good name.'

Mima said stiffly: 'I sh'd think you'd want to name him after someone in the family.'

Bess smiled again. 'Well, I'm real fond of Joel, like he was my brother or something. 'Course he's not in the family yet; but he might be, some day. And if he'll let us name the baby after him, we'll have one Joel in the family anyway. You ask him.'

Bess was so pleased with her own suggestion that Mima could not still be angry. 'Why, all right,' she said. 'All right, I will. Next time I see him.' And she spoke more warmly. 'It'll be nice to have a Joel in the family, Bess, yes. Only I was upset for a minute, wishing it was mine.'

Bess touched her hand. 'There, Mima,' she whispered. 'The next one will be yours.'

* * * * *

Mima would speak to Joel, but not at once. She had no immediate opportunity. His own activities kept him at home, and she was reluctant to go up to Round Pond on such an errand. She told herself she would see Joel soon enough in any case, that there was time to spare. The baby was ten days old before the occasion came.

Jess went down to Warren to buy a few pounds of gunpowder and some dry groceries. He returned at supper time with a tale to tell. 'They caught John Long down there this morning,' he said. 'He'd come up last night to see a woman, and slept too late and someone saw him come out. He's about the worst old Tory around, they say, and they set out to arrest him and he pulled his knife and 'lowed he'd gut anyone that touched him; but John Spear grabbed him and rassled him down and they tied him on a horse and took him over to Broad Bay.'

Jess had other news. Paper money, he said, wasn't worth the paper it was printed on. Beef was five dollars a pound, and other things in proportion. He had taken furs trapped during the winter to trade for what he wanted. 'And they'll buy meat,' he said. 'I'm going to kill some bears and moose and freight the meat down there. It'll fetch something.' He said the town was thinking of closing the alewife fishery, another year. 'They say nobody that don't live in Warren will be let to come dip at the falls.'

The evening was warm, and Mima, hot from her work over the fire, went out-of-doors while they were still at table. The sun had set, the air scarce stirred at all, the world was very still. She heard a sound somewhere to the north, across the river; the crack of a stick, the thump of a foot. She stood listening for a moment, then spoke through the door to her brother, softly.

'If you want a moose, Jess, I think there's one coming along beside the pond up beyond the river. I can hear him.'

He caught up his gun, came to listen. 'I can't hear it,' he said. 'But you always could hear a hummingbird lay an egg a

mile away!' He told the others: 'You'd best stay here.' He
primed his pan. 'I loaded up on the way home,' he explained.
'Case I saw anything. Come on, Mima. You can listen and tell
me which way it's heading.'

They went through the pines till they reached the point
where the river emptied into the pond. The opposite bank was
heavily forested with a mixed growth, some hemlock and pine,
some hardwood; and two or three great boulders nosed out from
the bank into the water. Jess whispered: 'They come this way
sometimes to get to that swale up the river. D'ye hear him
now?' But then a stick cracked, across the river, and he touched
her hand for silence. They stayed concealed among the
bushes by the shore, the sound of footfalls now clear enough;
and Jess half-raised his gun, ready to fire at the first opportunity.
Then he saw something more, and flung the gun to his shoulder.

But he did not fire; for instead of a moose, it was a man who
stepped out on the opposite bank of the river; one man and
then another. This second man wore a red coat, sadly torn
and stained, and his leggings and trousers were ripped by brush
and briers. He was, clearly, an English soldier. Mima and
Jess were sufficiently hidden so that for a moment the men
opposite did not see them; but when the river blocked their
way, they stopped, speaking softly together, discussing what to do.

Then Jess challenged them. 'Stand still! Or I'll shoot!'

The two men stared toward the sound of his voice. He
showed himself, his gun at his shoulder, and Mima took her
place at her brother's side. Jess told her: 'Go get Pa!' Without
question, she obeyed him, running like a deer back through
the pines along the shore.

When she returned, her father was beside her, and behind
them the others came trooping. A third man had joined the
two here. Philip had his gun; and when he came where Jess
stood, he put the men to the question. 'Name yourselves,' he
said in a grave growl of a voice. 'Where do you come from?
What's your hell's business here?'

Jess felt suddenly small beside his father who seemed now to tower; and Mima thought she had never heard Philip's voice so deep and terrifying. There were no wordy threats; but there was death in his eyes and in his tones.

One of the Englishmen yonder across the stream spoke in answer. He was, Mima saw, the younger of the two, not as old as Jess; and when she saw this her fear of them began to fade. They were no more than boys, they seemed unarmed, they were certainly tired and probably hungry.

'My name's McGregor,' said the young man in a strongly accented voice, with rolling r's. There was something fearless and yet appealing in his tones. 'My friend's is Roakes,' he added. 'Mr. Miller here showed us the way across the mountains. We're from Biguyduce. We're deserters, if your worships will forgive us.' His eyes were certainly twinkling now. 'And as for our hell's business — that's to keep our backs from the cat and our necks from being stretched.'

Mima found herself smiling, felt her father's tense readiness relax before he spoke. 'Deserters?' he echoed.

'And a hard game it is to play too, sirs,' young McGregor assured him. 'As you know if you've ever tried it.'

'I've made out to stick any job I started,' said Philip Robbins scornfully; but then he confessed: 'Serving the King was never one of them.'

The young man's back stiffened and his head rose. 'The King, God bless him, sir!' he said crisply. 'I'd never quit his service!' His eyes were smiling again. 'But when his duty comes down to me through an endless line of guzzling, witless, beefy bullies who serve themselves first and give the King the scrapings — why then I'm done. We've deserted from the army, sir — not from the King!'

Philip Robbins chuckled. 'Well, young squib, I'll not argue it with you. Come to that, we hereabouts have deserted the King and all his works — if we can make him admit it.' He spoke to his son. 'Jess, set 'em across. Mima, they'll be hungry.'

So Mima turned back to the house while Jess brought the float to ferry the young Englishmen across the river. She had the fire roused and a strip of smoked moose meat broiling before they appeared at the door. Young McGregor, she saw, had stopped to wash his face at the waterside; but his companion seemed a dull young man with no spark in him. The third man was not with them, and when Mima looked for him, her father said:

'He's gone back. Miller, his name was, from Lincolnville. He agreed to see them safe away from the coast towns; but he wanted to be home before morning.' He added: 'Since the bloody backs put the cat to Shubael Williams, it's a risky business helping deserters.'

'Miller's a man,' McGregor told them. 'There was no pay in it for him.'

'It's pay enough for some of us to help men away from the service you were in. I'll give you what hand I can.'

When they sat down to eat, Philip and Mrs. Robbins sitting with them, Mima serving, the others close around, it was McGregor who answered their questions. He and Roakes had escaped from Fort George now near two weeks ago, he said; and Philip interrupted to say:

'It wasn't much of a fort when I looked at it last summer.'

''Tis now,' McGregor assured him, and he asked: 'Were you with that lot that came to try for it?' Philip nodded, and he demanded: 'Why didn't you grab it, man? If you'd pushed home one good stroke, you'd have seen the flag down. General McLean knew well we'd no chance to stand out if you were bold.'

'Some of us were bold enough,' Philip assured him. 'But there was a cow-hearted Commodore that should have led us and held us back instead.'

McGregor nodded. 'Well, it's a brave fort now, and it will need your General Washington and all his army to clear us out of there.'

'You're two — you and your friend here — that are already cleared out,' Philip drily reminded him.

'That's true.' McGregor grinned. 'We had a hard time getting clear, too. They've ditched the neck, and sentries there; but a black fog came and we made it. Since then it has been travel when we could, keep out of sight, eat when we can — and mighty little of that we've done too. Till now.' He filled his mouth again, and Mima heaped his platter and he smiled at her gratefully.

Philip said: 'We were wrong not to put our heel on that snake's nest when we could. Now your pirate rats come out of there to burn men's farms and steal their goods and scuttle home again to safety.'

'They're not always safe there,' McGregor assured him. 'Did ye hear how one of yours made right into harbor and cut out Pomeroy's brig?'

'Cut him out, you say?'

McGregor nodded. 'Pomeroy had a fourteen-gun brig, and one day he took a coaster of yours and put a crew — two or three of them — aboard her. But then fog wrapped them so they anchored to wait it out. In the night, one of your captains — I heard his name was George Little — anchored in the same harbor; and in the morning there they were, not a long musket shot apart.

'Pomeroy didn't want fighting; so he got sail on his brig and the prize and away they went, and Little after them. Pomeroy's brig had the heels, and she came into Biguyduce an hour or so before dark; but the prize was out of sight down the Bay among the islands, and Little too.' He interrupted himself long enough to swallow the last mouthful, then went on. 'But just coming dark, Pomeroy made out the prize standing in; and he hailed her and told her to come alongside. She was a handy sloop, and alongside she came; but when they rubbed, it was Little and a dozen of his men that jumped aboard the brig. They'd took the prize and hid on her.

'There was fast work for a minute; but Pomeroy had no
stomach for it. He went over the stern, him and two or three
others, into the small boat they towed there, and rowed for
shore; and Little cut the brig's cable and got sail on her, and
sloop and brig tacked out of harbor. The guns in the fort did
some practice on them, and every soldier that had his musket
in hand took some pot shots; but most were laughing at Pomeroy. He was not liked before — and since he lost his fine brig
he was laughed at afterward. I heard he shipped with another
captain to get away from that.'

Eben said: 'Captain Little must be as brave as John Perry.'
Mima saw his eyes shine at the tale.

The two young Englishmen had no plans. 'Only that we
wished to leave that place,' McGregor admitted, 'and we have
no wish to be taken back there. We were followed as far as
Belfast town, saw cutters on the shore there and soldiers searching among the cabins north of the river. So we swung north
ourselves, and we've kept well away from salt water since.' He
added in a dry tone: 'Your roads are not good, from Belfast
here. Mountains and forests and lakes and bogs.'

Philip said: 'They'll not come looking for you here. The
house is crowded, but you're welcome.'

'I'll choose the barn,' McGregor suggested. 'Then if anyone
comes asking for us at your door, we'll hear them and have still
a chance to slip away.'

Philip assured them that no one would come; and Jess promised to keep watch by the pond. 'If anybody did come, it
would have to be that way,' he explained; and he went to
show the young Englishmen where they could sleep. The night
was warm, no need for blankets. When they were gone, Mima
said:

'I like him. The other one didn't talk as much; but he was
scared.' She spoke in wonder. 'I've always thought all Englishmen must be terrible, like animals.'

Philip nodded. 'Aye, you learn to think so, in war times.

You have to think a man is an animal before you can kill him
like one and not have your stomach turned. Men are mostly
alike, I'm thinking, if you look at their insides. It's the things
he wants that makes a man what he is — and most men just
want a home and a woman and a baby now and then.'

'And a full meal,' Mrs. Robbins amended.

Mima added one word: 'And a job to do. I guess no man
was ever real happy without a job to do.'

*   *   *   *   *

The two young men departed next morning with a pack of
smoked moose meat, pork and cornmeal to feed them for two
or three days. Philip Robbins advised them to strike straight
west for the Kennebeck.

'Just keep going and keep the afternoon sun facing you and
you'll hit it,' he said. 'If you bear southwest, you'll run into a
nest of Tories in Broad Bay that might truss you up and cart
you back to Biguyduce.'

Jess volunteered to set them as far as Round Pond on their
way, and Mima, remembering that she had still to carry that
message about the baby's name from Bess to Joel, decided to
go that far with them. When they emerged into the pond at
the head of the river, they heard distant voices and Jess said:

'They're clearing up the burnt-piece, Mima. They rented a
yoke of oxen from Boggs for the summer. They got part of the
burnt-piece planted right after they burned it; but they're aiming to get the rest broken to the plow soon's they can.'

She thought she could distinguish Joel's voice, commanding
the oxen. Jess ran the float ashore at the landing, and the two
young Englishmen came with them to see the work here under
way. The fire had left the burnt-piece one great sheet of
ashes — sodden now and beaten down by rains — on which
the trunks of the great pines, some of them still smoking sullenly with inward fires, lay in a sort of order, their butt-ends all
one way as they had been felled.

The ground already planted was at the end nearest the house. Beyond, Joel and Jason Ware and Matt were at work. Joel handled the oxen; and three or four small fires were burning where half-consumed logs had been heaped around stumps and set afire again.

Young McGregor had questions; and as they moved together toward where the three were at work, Jess answered him. 'They knocked down these trees a year ago,' he explained. 'Left them lying here to dry out till they'd burn easy, and then here this spring they burned them off.'

McGregor looked at the encircling forest, which seemed already to press in upon this small clearing, as though hurrying to heal the scar man with axe and fire had made. 'Why wouldn't the fire run wild?'

'Woods are damp in the spring. Then we burn at dusk, and fires don't run much at night. They go to sleep like people. And we pick a time when it looks like a rain coming on, to damp it out before morning, or the next day anyway. And around the edges we sort of clear a fire break, burn the rubbish there first. Most generally we handle it all right. There was a bad fire down-river last year, but we've had none here.'

The ashes rose around their feet in small gray puffs; and there was wind enough to carry some of the dust away across the burnt-land. Mima saw that Joel and the others, and even the oxen, were sooted and black. When their axes struck through the charred outside of the burned logs, black dust filled the air and settled on their sweating skins. When sweat ran into their eyes they wiped their faces with black hands. Joel and Jason had laid aside their shirts and worked in smallclothes. Matt Hawes wore shirt and petticoat breeches, and they were sadly grimed. Joel saw the newcomers and shouted a word of greeting and left the oxen and came to speak to them. Matt and Jason followed him, glad of a respite from the steady toil. Jess laughed as they drew near.

'Man, Joel,' he said, 'but you're black as the inside of a bear's belly! The sweat has drawn snake-tracks down your chest.'

Joel grinned. His eye sockets and his lips were almost the only part of his face that held its natural color. The white eye sockets made him look like a man wearing a mask. 'It's dirty work,' he admitted. 'No way out of it.' He looked at Mima, his eyes twinkling. 'Time you gave another lick to our house,' he said. 'Everything in it is smeared with charcoal.' And to the two young Englishmen: 'You're a long way from Biguyduce. Quit it, did you?'

Jess answered for them. 'Aye, they deserted. We slept them in the barn last night; and Pa told them they'd best make for the Kennebeck today.'

'Say you so?' Joel exclaimed. He spoke to McGregor. 'Why then, there's a man coming along will set you on the way.' He looked at Mima. 'Calls himself "I'm Davis",' he said. 'You saw him once. He went down to Warren yesterday, said he'd come back past today; and he's going over to Fort Western.' Jason and Matt came toward them, their combs rising at the sight of English uniforms, walking stiff-legged as strange dogs. Joel said: 'Come along to the house and I'll have a mug of rum with you.'

McGregor smiled in a friendly way; and Mima thought he was amused at the patent hostility on the part of Jason and Matt. She had almost forgotten that they — and Joel too — had fought for two or three years against such uniforms as these men wore. The war was far away; it was not easy to remember that even now an English force held Biguyduce, so near that if they fired a cannon and the wind was right the gun might be heard. As they all moved toward the cabin, Joel and McGregor led the way; the other Englishman followed at their heels; Jess and Mima, Jason and Matt came on behind. Mima was glad Joel could meet these enemies so easily.

When they approached the house above the spring, I'm Davis came angling toward them through the woods. A small, nondescript dog trotted on his heels, and Jason's Sambo with ferocious yelps that at close range quickly gave way to friendly investigations raced to meet him. When Mima had first seen the old man, he was dressed in skins; but now he wore a loose white coat — or one that had once been white — over his hunting shirt, and a broad hat with a drooping brim that might protect him against a moderate squall of rain. His long white beard was tucked inside his belt in front. Mima went to meet him, a curious liking stirring in her.

'I saw you once before,' she said. "You told me where our river comes from. The pond, and the big stream that comes out of the beaver meadow, and the two brooks that run into the meadow, and the mountains where they spring. Remember?'

The old man's eyes twinkled. 'I'm Davis,' he said.

'Yes, I know. And you like bread! Joel, have you some baked?'

The others joined them and the old man looked with glancing eyes at the red coats. 'I can stir up some,' Joel promised. 'Mr. Davis, here's two want to travel with you to Fort Western. They've quit the King — the same as the rest of us.'

'Well done,' I'm Davis said approvingly. 'I'll see them clear. But there's a drive of cattle coming across north of here this day from Broad Bay, with old-country Loyalists on the heels of it. We'll best be moving before they come along.' He added with a click of his tongue: 'They've a hard way with any that harbor deserters, the King's men.'

The result of his warning was that they waited only for a mug around of rum and water before departing; but as he left, the old man spoke again to Mima. 'There's another head to your river here,' he said. 'A brook comes out of a fine pond and ker-spangling down as pretty a gorge as ever a man see. Aye, there's a main of beauty places to be looked at, up that way.'

'I'll come some day and find you out,' Mima promised. 'If I ever knew where you'd be?'

'Take the right fork when the river forks,' he directed. 'That's a dozen miles and more above here. So you'll come to a pond that's three miles long. Go up the inlet to a beaver dam, and leave the beaver meadow on your right hand till you find a brook running into it, and go up that brook that dances over gravel with great trout in every pool. You'll find it comes to meet you down rocky terraces. Go on till you find a deep basin in the rocks under a bit of a fall; a basin as deep as it is wide, and twice as long, and a rock shelf hanging over it. You'll see my hovel just below, on the west bank. If I'm gone I'll be back in a while. It's a place I go back to.'

He touched his hat brim, turned away without a word. The two Englishmen followed him; and before he was out of sight in the thickening timber, they saw the younger men half-running to keep pace with him. Joel chuckled. 'He'll walk their legs down to stumps,' he said. 'That old man can walk a horse to death, any day.'

20

WHEN the Englishmen were gone, Jess and Mima might have started home; but they lingered, standing in the sun. Jason looked toward the forest into which I'm Davis and his charges had disappeared, and said he was a mind to take his gun and go after them, but Joel laughed at him. 'Cool off, Jason,' he said. 'We're done with soldiering, and so are they.' He touched Matt's shoulder. 'You had blood in your eye yourself, Matt.'

Matt smiled. 'That red color their coats are will always make me mad as a bull,' he agreed. 'Come on, we'll go take it out on the oxen.'

He and Jason turned away, and Jess said: 'Ready to go along, Mima?'

'In a minute,' she said. 'I've got a message from Bess for Joel.' Joel looked at her in surprise, and Jess asked:

'What is it?'

She did not wish him to hear. He would be amused, would make some jesting remark. 'You go along,' she insisted. 'It's private.'

Jess laughed. 'Poor excuse is better than none!' he said derisively. 'All right, hoot and I'll hear ye.'

He turned away after the others, and Joel looked at Mima with a lifted brow, a quizzical light in his eyes that made her color. 'What's this about Bess, now?' he asked.

Mima hesitated, then blurted out the words. 'She wants to know can she call the baby after you?'

Joel's eyes widened with surprise and pleasure too, and then he grinned. 'I've not seen the young one,' he reflected. 'Is he worth the name, do you say?'

'He's beautiful,' Mima told him. 'And so strong you'd not believe it, holding on to my thumbs already till I can lift him sitting up.'

'And him no more than two weeks old?' Joel pretended to be impressed. 'Why then, he's welcome to my name and I'll have to make him proud of it. Could I maybe see him tonight, d'ye think?'

'I don't know why not.'

'I'll come down and you can show him to me,' he proposed, with that teasing lift of his brow.

'I guess you can find your way without me.'

'Dunno as I could.'

'Why — all right, if you're so helpless.' There was a happy confusion in her. She said hurriedly: 'You go along. I'll redd up the house a mite before I go.'

He laughed. 'It can stand it,' he agreed, and turned away.

Mima, when she attacked the disorder in the cabin, was fairly startled at its completeness. During the winter, when not much could be done out-of-doors, the three men made some effort to keep their few belongings in order; but now they had no time for housekeeping. Rising before dawn, attacking their tasks as soon as there was light to see, working as long as there was light enough to swing an axe, they neglected everything indoors. The cooking dishes and the eating dishes were alike smeared with food cooked on or dried on, and everything in the cabin was black with the soot and ashes from the burnt-land where they worked all day. She found bread forgotten and burned to cinders in the oven. Except for Sambo's gleanings, no one had attempted to dispose of scraps of meat and discarded bones. Flies swarmed everywhere; and the pestilential black midges, which were the curse of the region from mid-May to the first of July, seemed to have made the cabin their rendezvous.

Mima attacked the place with a woman's shuddering hatred of dirt. She brought water from the spring and set it to boil; she took blankets and skins out-of-doors and beat them with switches while the dust rose in clouds; she gathered everything that could be washed in one heap; she stripped the cabin clean. The hemlock boughs on the long bunk were matted and springless. She took all the old browse out-of-doors and brought a brand from the fire and set it burning. She carried out guns and gear; and when the cabin was empty, she made a new broom, binding birch switches to the spruce stave that had served as handle for the old one, and swept the very walls and then the dirt floor. She even laid a herringbone pattern with her broom strokes. What washing she could do, she did out-of-doors.

She put things at last back in their places, but she piled the blankets on the end of the bunk, so that no matter how tired the men might be when they came in, they must cut fresh browse tonight. Not till she was satisfied did she seek Jess and start for home.

* * * * *

At the supper table that night her father spoke again of his plan to build a bigger house. Mrs. Robbins agreed: 'It'd be a good thing, if ever you had the time.'

Philip said flatly: 'I aim to take the time, this summer. It ain't fitten to go on living here like eight foxes in one den.'

'We've got along,' she urged. 'Only Mima had ought to have a room of her own.'

Mima said: 'I'm all right as I am, Father.'

'Well, maybe so and maybe not,' he agreed. 'But Ma and

me might want a room to ourselves. I ain't too old for a little bundling on a cold winter night with a gal as pretty as Ma!'

Mrs. Robbins told him to hush up his foolishness before the children, and he said: 'Well, I mean it.' His plans had taken shape. 'I figured on one big room, with a chimney at the end of it, and two little rooms on that end. One fireplace'd heat the whole house just the same. Then make it high enough for a real shut-in garret, and beds up there for the boys. I was thinking today to build it up on the high land, against the woods. Too many rocks there to farm the land, anyway.'

'I declare,' Mrs. Robbins confessed, 'I don't know as I'd know how it would seem to have enough room to turn around without stepping on each other! But I ain't complaining. You've done as well as a body could, with the barn burning and all.'

'Well, I'm a-going to build,' he said flatly. 'We'll move out of here. I hate to live like a lot of denned bears.' He laughed suddenly and slapped his knee. 'Speaking of bears, I heard a good one. Lucy was telling me when I went over t'the Mill Farm this morning. Josh Thorndike, Thomaston man, treed a bear last week, whacking sticks at it and all; but he didn't have a gun. He figgered how to make that bear stay up in the tree while he could go get his gun, so he took off his shirt and tied it around the tree, thought that would do it. Then he put for home. Run the whole way and back again.' He laughed till he cried. 'The dratted idjit!'

'Was the bear gone?' Jacob asked.

'I hope to tell ye. Takes more than an empty shirt to keep a bear up a tree.'

'I'd like to have a piece of bear meat,' Mrs. Robbins confessed. 'I ain't put a tooth into any for a good spell.'

Someone at the door said: 'Here's your bear meat, Aunt Mima!' Joel was there, dark against the darkness outside, the hind quarter of a small bear in his hand. 'This fellow came smelling around tonight, liked the smell of our cooking, and Sambo put him up a tree for us.'

'Well, that's real neighborly of you,' Mrs. Robbins assured him. 'And I'm obliged. Jake, you take and hang it in the barn and let it mellow a day or so. Come in and set, Joel. Et, have you?'

Joel grinned at Mima. 'I've et like a man ought to, for once,' he declared. ''Mima gave us a going over today, cleaned us up proper.'

Mima laughed. 'It would have turned you inside out, Mother, to look at the place before I tackled it,' she said.

Mrs. Robbins nodded. 'I've seen men's housekeeping before now,' she agreed. 'When I was having one of you young ones, I always dreaded more than anything else the being flat on my back three-four days and letting Philip here make a mess of things. With David I stayed abed right onto two weeks; but after I see what a man can do to a house in two weeks, I always got up just the minute there was any starch in my knees.' She told Joel: 'If you had any sense, you'd get a woman to cook and tend for you.'

'Why, maybe I will,' Joel declared, something mocking in his tones. 'I know a fine wench down in Warren, works at McIntyre's, she could keep three men comfortable as mice.'

Mima shivered as though at a distant warning note; she felt a far alarm. Mrs. Robbins tossed her head. 'Guess I know the one you mean. I've heard tell that a good-looking young rip can talk her into 'most anything.'

He drawled: 'Now Aunt Mima, a girl has to please the customers.' He asked: ''Mima, you want to take me down to see Dave's baby? The moon's right on the full. We can see our way through the woods — or go down in my float.'

She hesitated, careful of her tones. 'Let's go in the float,' she said. 'Moon's pretty, shining on the water.'

'Bess was saying she might name the young one after you, Joel,' Mrs. Robbins commented. She added: 'But you two had better get a move on. Dave's working hard these days. They'll be asleep about as soon as Bess gets supper out of the way. You go with him, Mima. I can 'tend to things here.'

Mima nodded. 'I'll come in quiet,' she promised. 'Try not to wake up you all.'

Philip said mildly: 'I'll be awake, Mima, when you come.'

* * * * *

Mima always remembered that evening with Joel, paddling down the pond to David's landing, paddling back again. Yet there was little to remember except the fine moon in the eastern sky, and the softly stirring night airs, and the call of a loon down toward the foot of the pond, and the splashing of great fish feeding in the shallows along the shore. Joel behind her said little; she herself wished to say nothing; the dipping of their paddles and the soft hissing the dugout made as it sliced through the water were for long minutes on end the only sound. Mima thought that in some ways this was the first time she had really been alone with Joel. It was true that on more than one occasion they had seemed to be alone. They had been so today for a moment at the cabin of the Royal Mess. But on land, there might be someone unseen within sight or hearing. The fact that they were on land somehow made them part of the great community of land dwellers, among whom there were no solitudes. Tonight, in ways she tried to define to herself, was different. The fact that they were in this small craft, afloat upon a different element, somehow removed them from all touch with land, set them apart, protected them from any unwanted intrusion.

Yet this was not even the first time she and Joel had been in a boat alone. They had crossed to get Lion, the day the bear hugged him, the day Tuner came to summon help. But that day Bess and Bet and the children had watched them from the shore, and Tuner had met them on the other bank, and they had an errand to be done. This was certainly not like that. This was like no other time she had known before.

She sat in the bow, Joel behind her. His paddle dipped with hers; and she was conscious of this rhythm, conscious that they moved in unison. She filled her lungs deeply, her breast swelling. Joel changed his paddle to the other side and the dugout tipped, and he said:

'This float's cranky as a mean ox. I made it, but I did a poor job.'

There was something like diffidence in his tone, as though he were embarrassed by their situation, like a boy. She smiled to herself. 'Bela's good at making them,' she said. 'He's promised to make me one, so light I can carry it, and so big it will carry him and me.'

'He's handy with an axe, sure.'

'Father might get him to hew timbers for our house.'

'Robbins building, is he?'

'This summer, he says.'

'I sh'd think he would, all of you in that house no bigger than ours! There's only three of us, but we're in each other's way all the time.'

'It takes managing,' she agreed, and talk died and they paddled in silence for a while. An owl hooted in the forest beside them and there was a whistling beat of wings in the night as a pair of ducks lanced across the moonlit sky. Mima heard a splashing in the shallows half a mile away across the pond. A moose must be pulling lily roots for his supper there. She had so much to say to Joel, and he to her; but before those things could be said, many things must pass unsaid in such silences as this. There were things that passed without speech, simply from their nearness to one another, from the fact that their paddles dipped together. It was working together that bound man and woman close and closer all their lives; working and living and suffering and grieving. Even paddling the float together tonight was a part of that long binding and welding which would go on as long as she and Joel were both alive.

She knew well enough that he did not love her. It might be a long time before he did; but he would. Just now he was a young man working hard all day, drinking rum when there were other men to drink with him, turning sometimes to easy women when the day's work was done. But she could wait. She felt no press of haste upon her. Time was long, but he would come to her in time.

They turned in to David's landing. When they reached the cabin, David was already abed, Bess nursing the baby by the last light of the fire. They made Joel and Mima welcome, and Joel gravely inspected the baby. 'Now I'd call that a proper kinchen,' he decided, and Bess demanded to know what a kinchen was, and he laughed. 'That's flash talk,' he said. 'I knew a man named Tufts in the army, a thief and a liar, and a proper punk-burner. He...'

'What's a punk-burner?' Bess asked, and Joel told her gently:

'Ask Dave. Nothing you'd know about. But Tufts had a way of talking. Called the moon "Oliver". I thought of him to-night, paddling down. It's a good night to get planet-struck.' He said: 'I'm pleased you're naming the baby after me, Bess.'

'I wanted to,' she said.

'We ought to have some kind of a celebration,' he declared; and Dave agreed, but Bess hugged her baby close and said:

'It don't need that. Just us calling him Joel is enough. I won't have him bothered.' He was guzzling at her breast with an occasional loud sound, and Joel chuckled and said:

'Listen to him suck air!'

They stayed a while in quiet talk together; and David asked questions about that man named Tufts. 'He'd been a thief all his life,' Joel told them. 'Been in and out of more jails than most men have beds. Cut his way out, or burned through the walls, or something.' He laughed at a sudden memory. 'He had a dog once that he couldn't lose. It'd find him anywhere. So he used to sell it and then leave town and the dog would catch up with him and he'd sell it again. He was a great hand to steal horses. He'd paint them up so the man he stole them from wouldn't know him. He did that once and the man that owned the horse came to get Tufts to help chase the thief. So Tufts painted up the man's horse and he took it and rode it when they went hunting for it, and the man never knew the difference — or so Tufts said.'

David guffawed, and told a story of his own, about a horse trade and some devious practices, and Joel said Tufts always claimed he could tell a horse in the dark if he could hear it chew corn. 'Said he could come close to guessing how old the critter was, too,' he declared. 'Just listening to its teeth work.'

The easy talk ran on. Joel wondered who would own the first horse in Sterlingtown, and Dave said a horse was no good without a road. He chuckled and slapped his knee. 'Old Sam Boggs claims his horses is all trained to walk logs,' he said. 'Claims he can ride 'em right through a cedar swamp on the down-timber. I'd ruther have oxen for heavy work, anyway. One thing, they make ten times the dressing a horse does. I guess farming and oxen always will go together.'

Joel nodded. 'Any time I've got a horse under me, I want good footing under him,' he agreed. 'So he won't fall on me.' Mima watched him in the flickering firelight, and he yawned and she said it was time to go.

'You'll be an hour paddling home, and you'll be up before day,' she reminded him.

'I'm sleepy as a bear in the first snow,' Joel admitted. He took the baby from Bess and tossed it high, and it gurgled and a white curd formed on its loosely smiling lips and spilled on him before he could dodge. David hooted with mirth, and Bess said drily:

'That's right! Keep a-churning him!' She recaptured her small son. 'There, did Uncle Joel make him pit up his sup-sup? Well, he shall have some more.' Little Joel applied himself to bounty, and big Joel and Mima said good night and went down to the landing again. In the float, Joel said with a chuckle:

'Babies are queer. Always leaking one end or the other! I kind of like them, though.'

Mima did not say anything. There was no need of saying that babies were beautiful, or that she loved them, or that men didn't know how to handle them, or that it needed a woman. These things had been said so many times before. The water was cool on her hand as her paddle dug deep. There was the Big Dipper, there the North Star. The river came down out of the north. Some day she and Joel would go up the river, toward that star, perhaps in the canoe Bela had promised to build for her, till they came to the beaver meadow and the cascade and the rock pool where I'm Davis lived when he was at home.

Joel said: 'You know, your mother's right. We ought to get some woman to come take care of us up at the cabin. It makes me sick, living the way we do.'

'Yes, you need a woman.'

'I don't know as we can get anyone to come.'

Mima did not speak. She hardly heard him, too intensely absorbed in the hour and the night and his nearness, to care for words or even for thoughts. She felt strangeness in her. 'I feel like a bud,' she thought, amused at herself. 'Just when it begins to open in spring and let out what's inside of it. That's how I feel.'

Their paddles dipped together, and the moon was big above the trees across the pond, and it laid a shimmering path toward them along the water. Joel whistled under his breath. She wondered why he had never tried to kiss her. Except for that day when after cleaning the cabin she sent him to fetch browse and then fled and he pursued her till the thin ice stopped him at the river, he had never seemed to find her a woman and desirable. Yet he turned to other women, as casually as a man drinks water when he is thirsty. She knew that he and 'Bijah Hawes and sometimes Jason hunted together, pursuing women as dogs chase rabbits. She knew it, but for her the knowledge lacked reality. She did not blame him. It was not Joel as he was today who filled her life completely; it was Joel as he would come to be.

She had not noticed their progress till he said quietly: 'Here's your landing.' He set the float ashore. She stepped out and he pushed clear. He said good night, and she answered softly, raising her hand, standing there in the moonlight. He slapped a mosquito on his cheek and paddled away.

And that was all; yet that was everything. Mima, standing to watch him go, told herself: 'The world's different now. I'm different. I'll never be the same again. It's like we were married already.'

There was no longer that hungry yearning in her. She was serene again. The night was cool on her cheek as she turned up toward the house. Her father from his bed spoke to her softly as she came in.

21

THAT night, those brief moments alone together in the dugout on the pond, the sight of Joel as he held his namesake in his arms, had for Mima a finality she did not seek to define. Joel might not feel this, and she knew it, and did not care. It was enough for her to find in herself now this settled certainty, this sure purpose, not to be turned aside.

The longing for him which had come to full tide that night when she watched them burn off the fell-piece was by this quiet evening together somehow satisfied. She did not even see him again till toward the month's end. The surface of their lives appeared unchanged. After the hard winter, spring had come with a rush, as though to make amends, and now by mid-June, summer was in flood. Bela had the timbers for the Colonel's barn all sized and fitted; and the raising was set for the first of July. Colonel Wheaton proposed to invite a mighty host of his friends from down-river.

'We'll have enough men here to put that barn up in an hour,' he predicted. 'We'll need the rest of the day for the rum and the ladies, God bless 'em! When the floor's down we'll have a dance; and if the barn stands up under that dance, it will stand forever.' He was as pleased with his plans as though this was the first barn ever raised.

Philip went to Warren one day, and returning he saw a young moose, its horns still in the velvet, swimming the pond from east to west. David's Tuner was in the boat with him, and when Philip raced alongside the moose as it neared the shore below Richard's house, and shot it through the neck, Tuner leaped out of the float and grabbed it by the nose. He drowned the wounded moose before it could make the shore. The animal was fat as butter. Mrs. Robbins saved almost thirty pounds of tallow, and the meat was marvellously rich and tender.

At supper afterward, Philip reported that he had seen Colonel Wheaton in Warren. 'He was at McIntyre's,' he said, 'inviting folks to the raising. He asked everyone in sight and all their kin; and they're all a-coming, too. Every rag tag and bobtail of 'em!' He chuckled. 'Colonel was feeling fine. Fanny's gone to work for Boggs, but she was there, and he pulled her down on his lap and told her she was bound to come; and she said she hadn't missed a barn-raising in Sterlingtown yet, and didn't aim to. He told her if she took the men's mind off the work the way she did at mine, he'd smack her backside.'

Mima looked at her father in a slow attention, stirred as one is by the roll of distant thunder, and Mrs. Robbins cried: 'Hush you, Pa!'

But Mima said quietly: 'It's all right, Father. I knew about that.'

Philip said contritely: 'Don't fret yourself over it, Mima. She's nought to Joel — or to any man — only maybe for a roll in the bushes.'

Mima asked in a low tone: 'Coming to the barn-raising, is she?'

'So they tell!'

Mrs. Robbins said sharply: 'Colonel ought to be ashamed of himself, and I'll tell him so — fetching a parcel of hedge wenches up here!' Because she knew Mima was hurt, she was in one of her rare rages, which arose like a summer storm out of a clear sky — and might pass as quickly. 'I'll take a broomstick to him, next time he shows hisself around here. If that hussy's coming, he can get his barn raised without a decent woman to help him! He'll get no help from me or mine!'

Philip protested: 'Now Ma, I'll be there to boss the job, and I reckon the boys will go along. You can't keep young ones away from a raising, and I have to be neighborly. I'll be wanting help on my house by and by.'

Mima left them still arguing the point, and went out-of-doors. Dusk was fading into dark. She walked blindly up through the woods toward the river, not knowing where she went, wanting only to be alone. She felt as though she had suffered an actual physical wound. Joel was not responsible for the Colonel's invitation to the girl named Fanny; and yet he would be glad to see Fanny at the raising. When she sang, out on the pond the night after Philip's barn was raised, he swam off to her float and did not return; and Mima remembered now that two weeks ago, when Mrs. Robbins said the Royal Mess ought to have a woman keeping house for them, it was of this girl Joel thought first of all.

So long as Fanny stayed in Warren, Mima could forget that she existed. So long as Fanny was simply a tavern wench to whom Joel might turn in empty moments, she was nothing. But now Fanny was coming here; and in that new understanding of herself which had been born the night she took Joel to see Bess's baby, Mima knew she could not endure having Fanny near. Pacing through the darkness among the pines, she felt her fists clench till the nails bit her palms. There was in her a swelling of some deep passion which made her cross her arms and hug herself hard as she fought for self-control. She had known for months, surely and beyond disputing, that without

Joel she was nothing; and knowing that, she could wait patiently
enough for the good time to come, when in the pressing wilderness up at Round Pond he should have made himself a home
and freed himself by hard labor from that union of three to
which he was committed, so that he might — if she could so
persuade him — turn to her. Waiting thus, she could shut her
eyes to many things. What Joel might do in Warren was beyond her horizon, had nothing to do with Joel here in Sterlingtown.

But for Fanny to come here, to the barn-raising hardly half
a mile from the cabin of the Royal Mess, was a different matter.
So long as Fanny stayed in Warren, or even if she came here
secretly at night, Mima could persuade herself that Fanny did
not exist. But now she felt the winds of danger blow about her.
Suppose the three in the Royal Mess asked Fanny to stay and
cook and tend for them! Matt might protest; but Jason and
Joel would overrule him, and for Fanny to be established in
the cabin with them would be unbearable.

Mima walked stumblingly as far as the river, and there was a
fierce purpose in her, but it had yet to take shape and form.
She tried to stand still, to think; but she could not be still. Till
now her love for Joel had been passive, but it was so no longer.
Now for the first time she confronted an emergency which must
be met. Waiting would not serve.

When she turned back toward the house she did not know
what she meant to do, thought of appealing to her mother; but
at the cabin everyone was asleep or seemed to be, and she could
not bear to go in and lie tamely down and let night end another
day that could not be recaptured. The days in a lifetime were
so few. This one was almost gone.

In a blind longing to be near Joel, she pushed off the float
and got in, turning toward the river, toward Round Pond.
Night was a curtain all around her. She paddled up the river,
neither slow nor fast, not hurrying and yet with a steady stroke
that never slackened. The moon was dark, but stars gave some

light, and they shone in the calm water under the bow of the canoe like beacons summoning her on, making clear the way, giving light enough so that she could avoid the occasional rocks in midstream. The great trees on the points where the river narrowed were black against the sky, blotting out the stars. The night was deeply still, yet with a humming stillness. Mima thought it was as though she could hear the milliards of tiny streams of life running in trees and underbrush; as though she could hear the warm stirrings of the small creatures of the wood, alarmed in their dreams. She was intensely conscious of life all around her; of life within her too.

She emerged into Round Pond and the trees fell back and the sky came near her, full of stars. She struck directly across the pond to the landing, and without decision stepped ashore, and came quietly up the path through the pines to the house on the knoll. Mosquitoes, that had attacked her in the river, came to cloud again around her now; and something that must have been a moose plunged away through the meadow and went off at a trot to the westward. She could hear the diminishing beat of its hooves for a long time; and she heard far away the quacking of ducks startled from their feeding-place in some boggy spot in the great beast's path. The whistle of their wings diminished across the pond toward the fly way of the river.

The cabin when she approached it was dark and still, the night heavy with the smoke smell from the evening smudge at the door. She meant only to come near it, near Joel sleeping there; but Sambo came bounding out to meet her, barking a furious alarm, till he smelled her and knew her and leaped delightedly to lick her hand. But he had waked them, and Jason called from inside the cabin:

'You, Sambo, come back here!' He came to the door and saw Mima dimly in the night. 'Who's that?' he challenged, and she heard him catch at his gun. 'Who's there?'

She had to speak. 'It's me, Jason. Mima Robbins!'

Jason uttered a startled sound. 'Mima!' She heard the others stir, and then they all came out-of-doors, Joel still struggling into his shirt. Even in the starlight she saw his bare legs as though he had slept with no clothing at all. He asked quickly:

'What's wrong, Mima? Refugees? Indians? Somebody sick?'

'Nothing's wrong,' she told him. 'Nobody's sick.'

'What's the matter?' he insisted.

She could not think what to say, but they pressed around her, waiting. She said hastily: 'I came to talk to you.'

Joel protested: 'Talk? This is a fine time for talking; wake us up, scare the lights out of us — to talk. You could talk in daylight!'

'You're all working daytimes,' Mima told him. She knew, suddenly, what she wanted, said hurriedly: 'I had to talk to all of you. You're in everything together, working and all.' She hesitated. 'I mean, you ought to have someone cook for you, and keep things cleaned up. That way, you'd get more work done every day, not having to bother yourself — and you'd eat better and live better too.'

For a moment no one spoke. They were all silent with astonishment. Then Joel said, half amused: 'We've got along so far!'

'You've got along because every time you're just about buried under your own dirt, I come and fix things up for you. If I hadn't, I dunno where you'd be by now.'

No one spoke for a moment, and Mima began to tremble; but she stood her ground. If she were here established, Fanny could not come! She spoke in a voice she did not recognize. 'I want the job regular,' she said thickly. 'It'll be a sight easier for me keeping things clean than cleaning up all at once ever' so often, the way I've been doing.'

Matt reminded her: 'We've got no place to sleep you.'

'You don't have to. I could go home nights.'

'If you did, we'd have to get our own breakfasts! We're up before daylight most times.'

'I'd get here in time,' she insisted. 'I get up early, anyway. You could pay me something between you.' She argued recklessly: 'Father might lose his farm if he can't pay his taxes. I'd want the money for him.'

Joel laughed grimly. 'Philip Robbins won't lose his farm,' he said. 'It'd need General Howe and his whole army to get it!'

'Well, I want the job, anyway,' she insisted, trembling yet insistent too.

Matt Hawes asked quietly: 'How much would you have to have for pay, Mima?'

'I don't know. Paper money ain't worth hardly anything — and I've not been anywhere to spend a cent if I had it, in four years. Whatever's right.'

He reflected: 'I'm tired of eating my own cooking, and Jason and Joel are worse cooks than me.'

But Joel cried: 'We don't want any woman all the time around, Matt!' And Jason supported him, while Mima in the darkness listened to the debate between them. Matt argued:

'We've all been well pleased when she's come and cleaned us up. We'd have been buried in our own dirt by now, if she hadn't.'

'I can get along without a woman always nagging at me,' Jason declared. 'Have her here, and a man'd have to watch hisself all the time.' They ignored Mima's presence. 'A woman like Mima, specially. She don't know the way men are.'

'I've got a father, and I've got brothers,' she reminded him. 'I guess I know enough about men.'

Joel laughed shortly. 'You'll find it some different with us three. We're used to being alone.'

'We can get over being used to it,' Matt argued. 'We'll be a lot better off, living decent, and eating decent; and it won't do us any harm to have to be some careful about loose talk and all.'

Joel said flatly: 'When I want to get drunk and play the fool — I want to get drunk and play the fool.'

Mima said: 'You can, for all of me!'

Matt drew Joel aside; he spoke in a low tone apart, but Mima caught a word or two, enough to know that Matt was reminding Joel of some past conversation. Joel answered him wrathfully:

'I know I did, but Fanny's different! You know where you are, with her.'

Matt said stubbornly: 'Well, it's the wrong place to be!' Their voices had risen, they turned back to where Mima stood. 'I'm for it,' Matt said. 'Let's try it a while, anyway; see how it goes.' He spoke to Jason. 'What say, Jason? You've got an upset stomach, half the time, the way we cook.' His tone was chuckling, persuasive. 'You'll be a lot easier to live with if everything you eat don't set on you.'

They were silent a moment. Then Jason said grudgingly: 'Well, all right! But Gor-ram it, Mima, if this ain't a funny time of night to come hire out for a job!'

Mima said: 'I just made up my mind to it.'

'How about your ma?' Jason urged. 'Don't she need you to help her t'home?'

'Susie's growing up,' Mima said. 'She's going on twelve, old enough to help Ma. They'll manage!'

'Well, I'm willing to give it a try,' Jason decided.

Matt appealed to Joel: 'What say?'

Joel laughed mirthlessly. 'Guess't I'm out-voted,' he reminded them. 'Two out of three always has decided, for us. Nothing I can do.' He spoke to Mima, more gently. 'I'm thinking of you as much as anything,' he said. 'I've always shied off from women as a steady fare. They get to bossing a man; and the first thing he knows he's tied and bound. I'm thinking you won't like all you hear and see.'

'I'll learn when not to hear and see,' she told him, knowing she had won. Listening to her own words as though she were a spectator, she knew suddenly that this was the end of her life at home. She thought of her father and mother and her brothers and sisters as though they were strangers with whom she had tarried for a while, but to whom she would never return. She might still see them, sleep in the same house with them; but she would always hereafter be as completely a stranger in her own home as though this were her wedding night. It was like her wedding night. She was coming to spend long hours every day under Joel's roof, mending his garments, making his bed, cooking his food, cleaning up after him. She would belong to him hereafter; this house and not her father's was from now on her home. She was quick to seize her victory. 'I'll come in the morning,' she said, almost without a pause; and before they could change their minds, she turned away.

Joel said hurriedly, as though to make amends: 'Hold on, I'll light you home!'

'No, my float's down at the landing,' she told him. 'I can find the way. I'll be going back and forth all hours from now on. I might as well get used to it. You stay here.'

They let her go, but when they thought her out of hearing she heard Jason say in heart-felt tones: 'Well, I'll be God-damned!'

Joel said grimly: 'We'll all be God-damned! We'll be fighting over her before we're done!' Then he laughed in a way that made her cheeks burn.

Yet despite that laughter, something was singing in her as she went her way. She was uplifted, her head high. Waiting had been long, but waiting was done. She need no longer stand aside and let Joel go his way; need no longer keep demurely silent till he chose to turn to her. Let Fanny come! She could fight Fanny for him now! She stepped into the dugout and stood erect and triumphant in the unstable craft as she paddled out across the lake. If Joel ever looked at Fanny again, Mima would know what to do with Fanny — and with Joel too!

When she came home, slipping silently into the house, only her mother was awake. Mima heard her whisper: 'Where've you been to, Mima?'

Mima said in a low tone: 'I've got a job keeping house for the Royal Mess.' She slipped free of her outer garments and into the trundle bed with Sue; and Mrs. Robbins asked in the faintest murmur:

'Joel down here t'see you, was he?'

'No, I went up there! I wasn't going to let them get that Fanny in there! I got 'em out of bed. They gave me the job to get rid of me!'

She heard her mother chuckle, and then the older woman said approvingly: 'Go it, Mima! He ain't much yet, but there's stuff in him. Don't you let him get away.'

22

THE day of the barn-raising, Mima went early up the river and across Round Pond to reach the Royal Mess half an hour before sunrise. Mists were heavy in the river and on the pond; but even before sunrise it was warm, so that as she walked up to the house she began to perspire. The mosquitoes were a cloud around her, and the black flies came with daylight, hungrily persisted in settling on face or hands, arms or legs. There was a heavy dew, wet on her bare feet, wet on the hem of her skirt and petticoats. She slipped into the cabin to fetch embers from the hearth to light the fire outside. The three were still asleep. Joel was like a baby, lying on his back, with his right hand, palm upward, beside his head, and his mouth a little open. Jason snored roundly. Matt opened his eyes as Mima came in and she smiled at him without speaking. She took coals to the outside fireplace where in fair weather cooking was easier, and built up her fire and filled the kettle at the spring. She took the axe and split a bolt of pine into useful sizes for a quick, hot fire. This was her second day of service; and already she had the work organized. She had

even begun to form many projects; a better cellar, inside the
cabin and covered with planks; a spring house — she meant to
build this herself — to keep things cool; a wigwam for smoking
salmon or moose meat; a proper crane for this outside cooking.
Inside the cabin she meant changes too. There was not room
enough for all the gear that as often as not was heaped in a
corner somewhere. A lean-to against the small log hut they had
built as a stable for the oxen would take care of work tools that
now were as often as not littering the cabin. She thought too
that the three men ought to have separate bunks instead of
sleeping together like puppies; and there should be a garret.
The cabin had been built in a hurry; and while there were cross
beams, notched over the plates to keep the weight of the roof
from spreading the walls, these beams had not been floored
over. If that were done and the garret space used for storage,
the space in the cabin would be doubled. Mima thought it
might even be possible to have a bed in the garret; and then if
the weather were too hard for the trip home at night — in winter, for example — she might stay here.

But that lay in the future. For the present it was simple
enough for her to come and go. Her mother had approved;
her father in the end agreed, though doubtfully. 'Dunno as I
want my daughter working out by the day,' he protested; and
Mrs. Robbins laughed and said:

'It's no worse than if she'd got married. If she had, she'd be
working days and nights too.'

'I dunno about them young rips,' he admitted. 'Mima, any
of them makes you any trouble, you bring him up with his toes
a-digging.'

Mima laughed. 'Matt will look out for me,' she assured them.
'He's steady. Jason's all right, too — only he talks hard.' She
added in a different tone: 'And I wouldn't ever be afraid of
Joel.'

She had served them yesterday; and last night Joel, already
cheerfully reconciled to the new arrangement, would have

paddled home with her, but she pointed out that this was a bad habit to begin. 'There'll be times enough you won't want to,' she reminded him. 'But if you get in the way of doing it, you'd feel like you had to, all the time.' She went home alone, and came back alone this morning; and at the sound of her axe-strokes they appeared, yawning and stretching. Jason was surly as some men are on waking, with no civility in his tone till he was fed. She would find that he seldom spoke before he had eaten; and Matt was quiet too, and Mima had noticed yesterday that Joel, though he said good morning to her, said no word to them. She watched to see whether it would be the same this morning, and it was. Joel came close to her before he spoke. Even through the traces of sleep his eyes were bright. He had pulled on smallclothes and hunting shirt; carried leggings and footgear in his hands.

'I'll be back, time you're ready,' he said, and went toward the pond. Her eyes followed him and she thought it might be fine to swim in early morning under the curtain of the dawn mist. The water had been warm on her hands as she paddled across the pond this morning. Jason and Matt used the wooden basin and washed their faces with noisy gasps and blowings. The sun rose, and mist rolling up from the pond began to glow with its light and the sky was blue. They ate cornbread, and salmon which Joel and Matt had netted out of the pool under the maple the night before, broiled with pork scraps for seasoning. Moose marrow on the cornbread took the place of butter. They had neither tea nor coffee, since till their crops were made and ready for barter, dry groceries would be at a premium; but Mima planned to roast corn and pound it and try what she could do with that as a substitute for coffee. Before they finished, before the mists had lifted clear of the pond, they heard a long halloo from that direction, and another cry answered from up-river. Joel said: 'There's the first to come. Hear the Colonel hoot! Wonder who it was. Your father, Mima?'

'Not this early. He figured to get up there in time enough,

leave Jess and Eben to chore up. But he wouldn't be going now, and he wouldn't be yelling.'

'Sounded like Johnny Butler,' Matt suggested; but Jason argued that this must have been a boat from Warren. Sterling-town folk would come more soberly to the routine business of helping a neighbor raise his barn. They would not be so noisy. The people from Warren would be more bent on the festive aspects of the day.

'That's right,' Joel agreed. 'Sounded t'me they had a touch of rum in them already. Mima, you coming along with us?'

'I'll clean up first. You be back for dinner?'

Joel laughed. 'Not today, nor supper either. Colonel's laid in enough to eat and drink a hundred men. I aim to stay by it as long as it lasts.'

She thought he was like a boy starting to a party. When they presently set off together, he led the way. She stayed con-tentedly behind, with work to do; but within the hour she heard other boats arrive, heard the calls and shouts as they turned up-river from the pond. The barn was to be raised near the river where it touched Colonel Wheaton's south boundary That was a long half-mile away in a straight line, but the sound of voices carried to Mima at her work, and the clop of axes and the thump of mauls. She was soon done with routine tasks, but she found other things to engage her for a while; and she was in no hurry to join the throng yonder. She took a certain pleas-ure in letting Joel go his own gait. Whatever he did, here was his home to which he must return; here she would be when he came back to his home — and to her. When at last she did turn north along the border of the meadows, she was in no haste at all.

She had stayed at her tasks longer than she knew. When she came to the edge of the Colonel's clearing, the frame of the barn was already well done, beams and cross timbers in place, half the pairs of rafters raised, and purlines notched in. Many

hands had made light work of it. Now there was a pause for
dinner, and some were eating mightily, and around the rum
tub there was a double circle of men crowding to take their
turns. Mima did not go forward at once to join them. She
stayed in the border of the wood, content to watch the scene
without being a part of it. Colonel Wheaton was near the rum
tub, mounted on a stump there, unsteady on his feet, waving
his hands for silence. He never got it, but without waiting for
them to listen, he began to sing. Mima recognized the air.
She had heard men's voices shouting out the tune one night on
Round Pond while she waited, drifting in the float a few rods
offshore, for Jess to do his errand with Colonel Wheaton. That
night she had heard only the tune; but now she caught the
words.

> I'd been drunk for six days, also sometimes at night
> And the sloop had six masts and her sails were a sight.
> I'd a touch of the shakes as I looked o'er the bow
> And saw nine kinds of snakes squirming 'round General Howe.

The shouts and laughter combined to drown him out, and
Colonel Wheaton lost his balance and fell off the stump, and
Joel climbed up in his place, his clear voice for a moment
silencing them all.

'Hear it sung right, boys!' he shouted. 'Second verse!' And
he sang:

> So I hooked to his britches and hauled him aboard
> And scrabbled him aft where our vittles were stored.
> An ox with blue horns made a lady-like bow
> As I started to stir up some grub for old Howe!
>
> In the galley were monkeys, and devils, and rats
> And little red mice played with cream-colored cats.
> A cross-eyed old bulldog with ears like a sow
> Was dancing a horn pipe for General Howe.
>
> I saw lizards and tree-toads and fiery-eyed frogs
> Sometimes talking like persons, then barking like dogs.
> A Thing, 'twas part serpent, part tiger, part cow,
> Was among the collection saluting old Howe.

Colonel Wheaton was fighting to recapture his place on the stump, and Joel held him off and finished the song which for their shouting no one now could hear, and someone shouted: 'Sally! Sing Sally, Joel!'

Joel laughed. 'No, boys, or Fanny there'd have me by the ears. She's a jealous wench!' He jumped down into the crowd again; and a hiccoughing voice tried to sing:

> Oh, her cheek it was bonny, her eye it was merry,
> Her ear was a shell...

But the words were lost in a clamor of many voices, and Mima looked for the girl called Fanny in the crowd, and wondered whether she would know her. There were many strangers; folk from Warren and from Thomaston too, and she saw women in finery, and became conscious of the fact that she herself was in no festal garb. Her dress of tow, buttoned down the front and dyed a useful brown, was plain and unadorned; and it had been torn and mended here and there, and she was barefoot as in summer she was likely to be. But there were gay colors yonder, and kerchiefs, and caps and even one bonnet. It was so long since she had been in any company except that of those she knew well that she had no wish to go among these strangers now; and she drew back into the cover of the wood till suddenly in a sort of laughing panic, at once afraid of being seen and amused at her own fears, she turned and slipped away.

She found a faint path that led back to the cabin and followed it. The trees were not spotted to mark the way; but there was constant going to and fro between the Colonel's land and the Royal Mess, and many passing feet had left their traces on the ground in the months since he began to clear his land. Mima had seen other paths come into being around her father's house, along the lake shore or by the riverbank, skirting the cultivated fields. The first man to take a certain way might with his feet turn over a stone here and there, break a stick, crush a bit of turf; he might idly snap off a twig with his fingers as he passed, or break off a bough that swung low to brush his cheek. The next comer, a day later, or a week or a month, unconsciously followed these traces more or less completely. In the course of time, let no more than a dozen pairs of feet tread the same way, a path was born.

This that Mima followed was such a one. Probably not fifty times had anyone taken it; yet it was easily followed, leading her surely on. It pleased her to improve it. Now and then she stopped to roll some small boulder out of the way, or to kick aside the fallen pine needles across a gnarled root that might trip the unwary foot, or to move a billet of rotten wood to lie along the side of the path instead of across it. Here and there she cut across, saving a step or two. Presently the faint trail traversed a boggy spot where the footing was soft; and Mima found two or three rocks and a chunk of dead wood and laid them in the muck so that she could cross without wetting even her bare feet. Behind her the clamor of the merrymakers was loud and persistent; yet it seemed far away. These silences and solitudes protected her. She was conscious of unbroken forest stretching for long mile on mile to the north and to the west. To the south and to the east there were towns enough; but to the north there was nothing, and no dwellers except such solitary folk as old I'm Davis; and to the west nothing this side of the Kennebeck. That business at the barn back there, this small task of mending the path, were each a part in the great work upon which they were all engaged of harnessing a continent, putting their mark upon it, building homes and barns and making trails and roads.

There was so much to do. A man could do so little in any day, or in any lifetime; yet he could do something! He could do a great deal if he kept trying — and had a woman to help him. To try and try and never weary; that was what your life was for. Use your life in trying. No work was ever done; but you could try, and grow strong and fine in the trying, and breed children who would go on trying after you were done

The trail led her past a spring hole that was one source of the tiny meandering trickle which ran down through the meadows toward Round Pond. The water was cool on her feet; and she followed up the little flow of it till she came to its head. She scraped away dead leaves and found where water seeped up through pin gravel; and she went down on her knees and began to dig with her hands and with the sharp end of a broken stick. She became absorbed in the work. As she dug deeper the water came more freely. She made a bowl-shaped basin as big as the bottom of a kettle, and a thrush with a striped breast came to watch her curiously. She let the water clear, and dug some more, and let it clear again. It was cold as ice on her hands, cold when she lay to dip her lips and drink. She dug out the spring till she had a basin two feet across and a foot deep, and she walled it with small bits of flat rock collected over a twenty-yard radius. She laughed with delight to watch the water clear at last, and she found a birch tree and peeled off a strip of bark and rolled it into a flat cone and pinned it in shape with a twig thrust through and through to make a cup. She hung the cup on the end of a stick set in the ground beside the spring, and was pleased with what she had done. Thirsty men and women and children could come here to drink when they chose. A man traversing this path a hundred years from now could turn aside here to quench his thirst; or if the spring were clogged, he might kneel to dig it out, and find the stones she had set, and wonder who had cleaned the spring and walled it long ago. Mima became two people; herself, now, discovering this spring that no human being had ever seen before; and that other wayfarer a hundred years from now, or two hundred, finding the spring again and drinking from it and feeling a moment's gratefulness to its first discoverer.

She lay down on the warm earth above the spring, relaxed and all at ease. She was not tired, but she was drowsy with well-being. The noise of the crowd back at the barn came to her clearly enough, but it no more than emphasized here her solitude. She watched the clouds through the high branches, and once she saw a hawk wheel against the sky; and a squirrel scolded her for lying so still. Her eyes closed and when she opened them the sun was lower, so she knew she had slept a while. There was a fiddle going, back at the barn, and she thought she could hear the stamp of dancing feet. Joel would be dancing there, perhaps with Fanny; but Mima was not disturbed at the thought. He was a man, working hard all day and every day; and men were not like women. A man was somehow happier and gentler and more kind if sometimes he could do without reproach things that were called wrong. Mima thought: But nothing is wrong except to do nothing. Nothing is wrong except to let life spill away without trying. Nothing is wrong in the world except to live without dreams and without striving toward those dreams.

She looked proudly at her spring and lay down to drink again, and something darted under one of the stones and she laughed with a quick delight. Already a little newt had come to live in the clear water. She spoke aloud. 'I hope you like the home I made you. Wait till you see the home Joel and I will have some day.'

She left him in possession and went on her way, stopping at the cabin to make sure all was in order there. They would not be home for supper, not till late tonight; so she went down to where her float was beached beside the pond. The sun was touching the tops of the trees behind her as she paddled homeward. In the river she let the current take her. Her mother was at home before her, and the big bed was full of babies.

'There, I'm glad you've come!' Mrs. Robbins said. 'I wasn't in a mind to go, so Bess and Bet and Lucy left their young ones here, and I'm wore out trying to keep 'em pacified.'

'They must be starved.'

'I dunno as they are,' Mrs. Robbins declared. 'I guess they can get along without their mothers for once. I've give 'em milk and sugar and hot water and they've took it; but I be'n feeding one or t'other of them all day long. How was the raising?'

'I didn't go,' Mima confessed. 'I took a look at the crowd, and the womenfolks was dressed regardless, and the men all around the rum tub. I came away.'

'That hussy from Warren is up there, and I don't know who all.'

'They'll be gone tomorrow,' Mima assured her. 'And the men will be back at work again. I guess a man's better off sometimes if he's left alone.' David's young Joel woke and began to demand attention, and Mima took him up. Mrs. Robbins made a clicking sound with her tongue.

'Look out for him,' she warned Mima. 'He's worse than a young robin to make a mess.' She chuckled. 'I dunno but I'd as soon clean up after a yoke of oxen as these young ones. You tend them and I'll get supper started. Pa said he'd be home.'

*   *   *   *   *

At sunsetting, a wind began to blow, coming more and more strongly up the lake, stirring the trees around the cabin, bringing a scud of cloud to obscure the stars. Philip returned and David and Bess came with him to claim young Joel and take him off home.

'Jess is bringing the other young ones,' Dave told Mima. 'They're walking down. He'll whistle for you to fetch 'em across the river.'

He and Bess went on, Bess holding the baby, David keeping the float close to shore for easier travelling against the rising wind. Philip said half the folks left at the barn-raising were drunk or on the way to be. He laughed to himself at some memory.

'Colonel slept most of the afternoon,' he reported. 'It looked to me the rum kind of crep' up on him.'

Mrs. Robbins said harshly: 'I'd like to tell him a few things, the old Whistle Britches! Are the rest of the young ones coming along with Jess?'

'Guess so, only Eben. He struck it up with Matt Hawes today. I saw them talking about something, and they went off a while ago. Dunno where they went.'

'I ain't afraid of anything Eben'll do. He's a good boy.'

'Matt's a good man,' Philip agreed. 'He's kind of like you, some ways, Mima; always talking.' He tried to explain what he meant. 'Most men talk about weather and crops and critters and work; and most women talk about each other. But you're apt to talk about ideas, and Matt's the same.' He laughed, slapping his knee. 'Speaking of women, Ma, Lucy and Prance Bowen had some kind of a set-to today.'

'What about?'

'I didn't get the straight of it; but it was something Lucy said about the Colonel having Fanny come up here with decent folks, and Prance said it was a pity the way folks talked about Fanny just because she'd been 'prenticed out, and she said some women she could name had married 'prentices — meaning Lucy's Johnny, of course; and one thing kind of led to another, the way it will.'

Rich and Bet came up from the landing, interrupting his story, and Rich said it was blowing harder all the time. 'I'm a mind to leave my float here and us walk home,' he declared. 'But it's a long mile for the young ones in the dark. Guess't we'll make it.'

Mima heard Jess whistle from up by the river. She was astonished, when she went down to the landing, to find how hard the wind blew. She got the dugout afloat and paddled up to the river mouth, and the wind drove her against the rocks where Jess stood waiting, so hard that she lost her balance and toppled overboard to her waist in water. The youngsters with Jess screamed with delight at her mishap, and Mima splashed ashore, laughing with them, and threatened to throw Dave's young Jason into the river himself if he thought it was so funny; and he fled with shrieks and she chased him and lost him in the darkness while Jess ferried one load across the river and came back for more. Two or three other canoes and a barge came down the river, Ezra Bowen and some womenfolk, and Jess called to urge them to stay the night here.

'We can sleep you all in the barn,' he promised. 'Women in the mow and the men on the floor. Better stay.'

But they went on. Then Johnny Butler and Lucy stopped at the house where their two babies had been all day in Mrs. Robbins' care. Johnny would have taken them and gone on, but Lucy would not. 'I'm not a-going to take the two of them acrost the pond a night like this, Johnny,' she protested, 'and maybe drown the lot of us! We'll stay right here.'

'I c-can't stay, Lucy,' he pointed out, 'with the c-cows to milk and all.'

Mrs. Robbins said: 'Lucy, you stay. Johnny can go around the shore. We've room a-plenty.' And she asked: 'What's this about you and Prance Bowen?'

Johnny said: 'Whoa, Aunt Mima! Get Lucy started on that and she'll talk you deef, dumb and b-blind! I'm going along before she b-begins.'

'Well, why don't you go, instead of talking about it?' Lucy demanded irritably. He disappeared and she said: 'There's nothing to tell anyway, only I didn't like some of the Warren folks that came to the raising and Prance did, and I told her if she liked 'em so much she'd best make friends with them and not with us up here.'

From the river and the pond came recurrent voices as one after the other floats and ferries returned down the pond toward Warren town. Mima had wrung out her soaked skirt and petticoats and stood drying them before the fire while Lucy, her baby at her breast, recited to Mrs. Robbins the story of her altercation with Prance Bowen. The fire was hot, and Mima was breathless with it when her father called to her from outside the door.

'Mima,' he said. 'Come out here.' She obeyed him. He said uneasily: 'Listen and see if you hear anything. Someone was a-yelling awful, up't Round Pond.'

Mima at first heard nothing except the beating of the wind and the water on the shore. The wind blew from the southeast; Round Pond lay westerly and a little north. But after a moment she heard a hoarse sound like a shout; and then she realized that there were other voices shouting and calling in an excitement like terror. She told him:

'Something's happened. Maybe a boat's upset.' Joel was there! He might be in danger. Without a word she raced for the landing, her father on her heels.

They fought their way alongshore to the river, and the float was hard to handle; but once in the river, sheltered from the wind, they made good time. They heard voices ahead of them, the words still indistinguishable, the terror in them plain. When they rounded the point and emerged at last into the pond, someone had a birch-bark torch flaring in a float ahead of them, and there were other torches and a fire on the bank; but the shouting had ceased and a strange hush lay across the water. They paddled toward the canoe which carried the torch, and Mima saw in it Bela and his father. Philip asked a question, and Uncle Eben said hoarsely:

'Three of 'em drowned. Got to fooling, and the float spilled 'em out. Joel's be'n diving for 'em, got one — too late.'

Mima saw Bela white-faced, heard his teeth chattering. Colonel Wheaton called from the shore; and the canoes began to move that way. Mima looked back at the black water like ink into which three lives had sunk forever; she touched the water with her hand and it was warm as milk upon her fingers. Ashore as they reached the bank there were silent men and women, and Mima saw Joel standing by the fire someone had kindled. He was wet, but she did not go to him. It was enough to know he was alive, to watch the firelight touch his countenance. Mason Wheaton was telling her father what had happened.

'We heard the screeching,' he said. 'From up at my place. Most all the folks had gone. Joel and me jumped into a float and came downstream hell for leather. We could hear one of them yelling, out in the pond, and we dug for it. It was Fanny, hanging onto the float; but she let go about the time we got there and down she went a-gargling. I made a grab for her, got a hold of her too; but not good enough. Down she went, and next thing I knew, Joel was in the water. He damned near tipped over the canoe, but over he went and after her. By God, Robbins, I wouldn't have done it! Not even if I could swim I wouldn't! Go down into that black water full of drowning folks a-scrabbling and a-sclutching!'

Mima turned her head to watch Joel, seeing the weariness in him as his chest heaved to fill his lungs.

'But Joel did,' the Colonel said. 'And a minute later up he came. He had Fanny. She never made a move till she felt the air, and then she let out a whoop and grabbed him. He let her have it, a good one in the face, sounded like a poled ox; and that stiffened her and he yelled to me to hang on to her while he got the others, and down he went again.

'But it was no go,' the Colonel finished. 'It's a deep hole. He got the boy, but he was dead.'

Joel, beyond the fire, did not raise his head. Philip asked: 'Who were they, Colonel?'

'Fanny that Joel saved, and the woman that cooks for Boggs, and the German from Broad Bay that's been helping Boggs with his plowing this summer, and the boy. The German was aiming to marry the woman, they say.'

'Fanny all right, is she?' Philip asked.

'Guess so.' The Colonel looked around at the group by the fire. 'Where is she?'

Joel said: 'Jason and 'Bijah took her over to our place. She hadn't come to. I guess I broke her jaw. I hit her hard.'

Mima moved quickly. 'I'll go take care of her.' Eben was beside her and she spoke to him. 'You and Matt set me over the river, can you? I can go along the beaver dam.'

Her father said: 'Maybe I'd better get Ma. She'd know what to do.'

'I'll send word by Eben if I need her,' Mima promised. She turned toward the water, stepped into the canoe. She heard her father say he would go home and report what had happened; and Colonel Wheaton proposed that he and Joel take the body of the drowned boy down to Warren; but Joel shook his head.

'I'll stay the night here,' he said. 'I kind of hate to go off and leave them out there.' He looked toward the pond. 'That German was a good man to sing songs,' he said. 'We had many a drink together today.' He added: 'Maybe if we hadn't had quite so many drinks, he wouldn't have tipped the boat over.'

Mima could hear their voices for a while. Eben and Matt took her to the landing below the cabin. She was herself untouched by any emotion in this hour; curiously calm. She gave no thought to the three lost ones; thought only of Fanny, who was hurt and alone and needed her. The men were silent till they touched the shore. Then Matt asked in a low tone: 'See all right, can you, Mima?'

'I'm all right, yes,' she said. 'You come along. Eben, I might need you.'

So they followed her. When she came to the cabin, there was a smudge at the door, and a fire beside it for light. Jason stood near, and 'Bijah Hawes squatted on his hunkers by the fire. They looked up without speaking, and Mima asked quickly:

'How is she?'

Jason jerked his head toward the door. 'She's in there.'

Mima went quickly past him into the cabin. A few flames rose from one log burning on the hearth, giving enough light so that she could see the girl lying on bear skins spread on the floor. Fanny was breathing with long, slow, convulsive writhings, her breast rising as though it tightened into a knot at each inhalation. Stooping above her, Mima saw that her eyes were half open, the whites showing; and her lips were drawn back and her chest strained and arched with each breath she drew.

She filled her lungs, she seemed to hold them full for a minute, and then the air rushed out of her and her body seemed to deflate and to lie limp and small before the next breath began.

Mima turned to call Jason; but the men had followed her into the cabin. She asked sharply:

'Has she been doing this all the time?'

'Not the whole time,' Jason said. 'She didn't do much of anything for a while, and then she sort of come to and let out a screech, and then she started this.'

Mima bent and touched the girl's jawbone, moving it, feeling it; and Fanny's hand came up to clutch at hers with straining fingers. 'Jaw's not broken,' Mima said. 'We've got to get the wet clothes off of her, get her to bed. The lot of you get out of here, only Eben, you stay and help me.'

She made him build up the fire, and between them they undressed Fanny and rubbed her dry. Mima had thought of this girl as having golden hair and fine blue eyes; but Fanny's hair was brown and thin and ill tended. Mima thought she was not even pretty. They had no dry clothes for her, could only wrap her in a blanket and cover her warm. Her breathing had eased while they handled her. They made a bed for her on the floor, and Mima went to call Jason and Matt.

'Joel's staying out by the pond till morning,' she said. 'There's no reason you two shouldn't come in and go to bed. I'll sit up with her.'

Jason preferred to sleep out-of-doors, and Matt decided to go keep the useless vigil with Joel. He and Eben departed, and Jason took his blankets and disappeared. Mima hung Fanny's clothes to dry, and she sat down on a squared log that served as bench near the fire, leaning back against the wall. She was not sleepy, thought she did not sleep; but suddenly there was gray dawn in the doorway and the sound of voices coming up the path from the spring.

She went to the door. Joel and Matt were home. They must have swum in the pond when they landed, for their hair was wet and their faces shone. Mima wished to touch Joel, to feel his solid flesh and know it was real; but she only asked in a low tone:

'See any sign of them?'

He shook his head. His teeth were chattering. 'Colonel took the boy down to Warren,' he said. His hand tightened on Mima's arm. 'I found him on the bottom,' he told her. 'In the dark. I picked him up and he was like a baby in my arms, Mima, wrapping his arms and legs around me like he loved me for finding him. He was dead. He'd been down ten-fifteen minutes, then. But he hugged me like he was glad.'

She said gently: 'You've had a hard night. You'll feel better when you've et. I'll get breakfast started.'

Then behind Mima in the cabin someone called: 'Mom!'

'That's her!' Joel whispered; and Matt said:

'Mom's what she called the woman, the one that was drowned.'

Before Mima could move that way, Fanny came to the cabin door. She had a blanket somehow wrapped around her. Her hair was draggled and matted, her eye puffed and discolored, her cheek swollen with a great bruise where Joel had hit her. She stared at them in the gray light as though afraid to speak.

'Where's Mom?' she muttered.

The men were helpless; Mima was not much better. 'You ought to remember,' she said gently. 'The boat tipped over.'

Fanny's mouth after a moment opened, and out of it, out of that wide mouth in an expressionless face from which her eyes stared blankly, came a terrible, protracted cry. It was not human; was more like the cry of an animal than of man or woman. Then in the middle of it, she saw Joel, and seemed to recognize him, and the cry stopped, cut off short. Her mouth closed with a click of teeth, and she stared at him.

'They drowned,' she said hoarsely, as though she spoke to herself. 'All but me. You got me out!' She ran toward him, hugging the blanket around her; she dropped at his feet, holding on to his knees, hugging them. 'I'll work for you!' she cried. 'I'll work my legs off to the knees and my fingers to the bone. I'll work for you the last day I live. I'll never leave you any more than if I was bound. I'll wash and cook and mend ...'

Joel stared down at her miserably; but Mima caught her shoulders. Jason had come from among the trees where he had slept. Mima said to them all: 'Help me get her in. She's out of her head.' Fanny was down on the ground, kicking convulsively, screaming, fighting to be free. 'Help me, Joel!' Mima cried.

He caught Fanny, lifted her, carried her indoors and laid her down. She stiffened and was still. Mima said:

'Go fetch my mother, Joel. Fanny'll have to stay here a spell.' She said, as though she were listening to someone who told her what to say: 'I'll stay with her.' She looked at him. 'She's not going to work for you, Joel,' she said strongly. 'That's my job. I'll get her well and send her packing, but I'm going to stay.'

He nodded in a dull way. 'I'll fetch Aunt Mima,' he agreed. 'She'll know what to do.' He went down toward the landing.

Fanny was delirious for days, and she could not be moved for more days thereafter. The men slept out-of-doors, Mima inside. Before Fanny was well enough to go down-river to Warren, Joel had built a garret in the cabin, and a bed for Mima there. Mima slept no more in her father's house from that day on.

III

The Royal Mess

1

IN THIS campaign to make
farms and homes in the wilderness there were no final victories.
Arable lands won from the forest needed to be defended tirelessly; for the great trees left standing cast their seed abroad
upon the winds, and in that teeming soil, one season of neglect
meant that sapling skirmishers would begin to creep out to
recapture the cleared land.

The best defense was a new attack; so each man widened his
clearings year by year. When Philip Robbins brought his
family to Seven-Tree Pond, he and his sons had already cleared
about twenty acres, running from the house down along the
shore of the pond; and another clearing ran from Seven-Tree
Pond to Crawford's, north of the Mill Stream. Rich Comings
that same summer had cleared and planted about five acres,
down the pond. Except for these tracts, the rest was forest,
hardwoods predominating east of Seven-Tree Pond, and pine
and spruce and hemlock on its western shores.

Since then these clearings had been extended and new ones
had been opened. Ezra Bowen had twelve acres cleared and

under some cultivation, down along the Warren line. 'Bijah
Hawes, working spasmodically, had felled the trees and burned
them on eight or nine acres. David Robbins and Rich Comings,
sometimes pooling their efforts, had brought about thirty acres
under cultivation; and on Round Pond the Royal Mess had
during their first summer cleared about twenty acres of good
land. Across by the Mill Stream, Johnny Butler had failed to
hold all he had from Doctor Taylor, and shoots of birch and
popple stood in knee-high thickets around the border of his
clearings; but Philip Robbins, with his sons to help him, had
now brought more than forty acres to bearing. His clearing at
no point touched the river; but it ran west from his house and
also south, making an angle around that low rocky hill which
Mima liked to climb. It was at the foot of this hill, where he
could look north across his fields to the grassy bays along the
river, and east to the pond, that Philip decided to build his
house. It would be at some distance from the barn built the
year before, but this inconvenience Philip and Mrs. Robbins
were willing to accept in return for the location they preferred.
By the middle of July the work was well under way, and every
day Philip or Jess or Eben or Jake found an hour or two to turn
that way; to cut brush, to move stones ready for foundation
walls, to dig the cellar which would be big enough to store a
winter's supply of roots and grain and hog meat well laid down,
or to cut suitable trees on the hill above where the house would
stand, and with the oxen drag them down.

The building of the new house emphasized for Mima the
fact that she was no longer one of her father's family. In the
old house she might still have felt in some degree at home; but
in the new she would always be a visitor. As her home changed,
so did her world. At first when they came here, her world had
been the west shore of Seven-Tree Pond; and Rich and his
family, and Dave and his, and her father's household of which
she was a part, had been the people in that world. 'Bijah and
Ez Bowen, when they established themselves down the pond,

and Johnny Butler and Lucy, across by the Mill Stream, were her neighbors, rarely seen.

But when Joel came, her orbit changed. Dave and Rich and their families began insensibly to recede into the background of her life; Round Pond and Joel came nearer her thoughts than they. Her father's house was still the focal point; but her thoughts and she herself went more and more often toward Round Pond, and less and less often to the homes of Rich and Dave. She might go two or three weeks at a time without seeing Rich, though except for Moses Hawes who had built a hovel on his land, back from the pond, he was their nearest neighbor. Bet came often to her father's house, and Mima saw her there; Dave and Bess came and brought their children too. But Rich was a worker, and even when he came to Philip's house he was so quiet that you might not notice he was in the company.

Now with her removal to the Royal Mess, Dave and Rich and their families were far away; a mile or so in distance, much further in reality. Even her father and mother and Jess and the others became in some degree strangers, and between her and them a gulf appeared. She lived at the Royal Mess at first from necessity. So long as Fanny lay ill, delirious from shock and fright and even when she began to recover still too weak to help herself at all, Mima had no time to come down from Round Pond. Joel and the others had thrown up a lean-to shelter against the south wall of the cabin, and they slept there, leaving the cabin to the two women.

Fanny at first required constant care, and Mrs. Robbins came every fine day to give advice and aid. When she did not come, Matt was helpful. Mima thought he was like Eben, gentle and understanding. Eben had helped her undress Fanny the night of the drowning. Matt helped her sometimes in equally delicate ministrations now; and Mima felt no embarrassment on these occasions. She liked Matt. Till they were thus thrown intimately together she had only noticed that he was less apt to laugh than Joel, less apt to grumble than

Jason; and she knew that he was a sober man, knew he sometimes went to meeting in Warren. But she found in him now a
source of strength. He was always the same. She could count
on his quiet good humor, his co-operation in all she wished to
do around the house, his thoughtfulness of her.

She gave freely of her own strength and time to Fanny,
tending her like a sister. She had never felt any enmity toward
the younger girl; she did not now. Fanny was ended. The old
Fanny, gay and laughing and recklessly ardent, was dead; and
Mima knew this well enough. Joel, seeing Fanny senseless and
raving, seeing her wasted and sick, could never turn to her again.
A man could love his wife through such an ordeal, and forget it
when she returned to health and blooming tender beauty; but
this could not happen with one like Fanny who had no other
hold on a man than the passion of a moment could bestow.
Mima was sure of this long before it became apparent to Joel
and to the other two men. She thought Fanny must know it
too; for the sick girl seemed not at all surprised that as she recovered her strength Joel and Matt and Jason avoided her,
avoided coming into the cabin, tried never to meet her eyes.

When she was well enough to travel, Joel took her down the
river again. Mima went with them as far as her father's landing. Fanny was still stupid from shock, and weak and ill; and
she wept when she said good-bye to Mima. Mima kissed her,
almost loving her, wondering why she felt toward Fanny so
tenderly. 'Because I've taken care of her,' she thought. 'Maybe
taking care of people is the way to love them.' She had no
uneasiness at seeing Joel and Fanny go off down the pond together. Fanny was over and done with. That was plain.

Her mother was at the landing and she and Mima went up to
the house together. With Fanny's departure, Mima might
have resumed her place here at home, going to and fro night
and morning; but it did not occur to her to do so. She had
already moved most of her personal belongings to the Royal
Mess. The garret where she slept was her domain, much more

her own than any corner in her father's house. Mrs. Robbins had long since recognized that Mima would not return to them; and when from time to time during Fanny's illness she went up to Round Pond, she was apt to take something for her daughter. Lacking room for them in the small cabin, she still kept many of her household belongings, brought when they came four years before, in the storehouse that had been built solidly enough to serve as a possible refuge against Indians. From it she had rummaged out a feather bed for Mima, and a quilted coverlet, and today she offered some pewter and some cooking dishes which she herself never used.

Mima declined them. 'They've enough to do with, up there,' she said. 'We can get along.'

She collected today the last of her own things. Her clothes were sadly worn and depleted; and the terrible depreciation of the paper currency made it impossible to buy more. 'But I can make them do,' she told her mother, smiling as she quoted the older woman's familiar phrase. 'Make them do or do without. And Joel and the others will pay me something for the work when they can. I can buy what I need, when they make a crop.'

'Your father's planted flax this year,' Mrs. Robbins reminded her. 'Enough so's we can each have a dress out of it. I'll get out my wheel when the time comes.'

She and her mother were alone the long afternoon till Joel returned. Her father and her older brothers were working on the new house; and Susie had taken young Phil down to Dave's to play with the children there. Joel came back promptly; and when they met him at the landing, Mrs. Robbins said:

'You made real good time.'

'I didn't stop,' he said. 'I went and got Boggs' trail cart to carry her over, came right along home.'

Mima took her place in the bow, and Mrs. Robbins called good-bye and watched them move away up the shore. Joel turned the float into the river against the slight current, and he said in a sober tone: 'They've found the man, down below.'

Mima knew what he meant. They had all been oppressed, since the drowning, by the thought of those poor bodies in the deeps. Joel himself for a while patrolled Round Pond night and morning, looking for any trace of them. He found the woman on the fifth day, and he and Jess took her down to Warren; but till now the German's body had not been recovered.

'I'm glad,' Mima said.

'So am I. He's been on my mind a lot,' he admitted; and he added: 'Fanny told me today, going down, what happened. She was joking, in the boat, about wanting to sit next to him, to tease the woman; and they got to tussling and the float turned over. She calls it she killed 'em. Wishes she was dead herself.'

Mima said: 'I guess she used to be pretty.'

'Not pretty, maybe,' he admitted. 'But she was all right, lots of ways. She was friendly, and worked hard and liked people.'

'I'm glad you say good things about her, Joel.'

'Why wouldn't I?'

'Some men would let on now that they never thought much of her anyway.'

'I did,' he said without apology. 'I liked her. But that's done.'

She did not speak, watching where ahead of them the river opened out into Round Pond; but her eyes were warm with happiness. She had known that what he said was true; but she was glad to hear the word he said.

2

ONCE she was rid of Fanny, Mima cleaned the small cabin, scrubbed and swept each inch of it as though to remove every trace of an alien presence. This became her domain; the house, the small stable for the oxen, the spring down by the meadows, the oven where she baked her bread, the outdoor hearth where she preferred to cook when weather was fine.

But Mima was not satisfied with things as they were. The cabin was a little smaller than her father's, but it had to serve for storage as well as living quarters. The fireplace was built in the corner diagonally opposite the door, and the only furniture was the long shelf four feet above the floor which served as a bunk for the three men, a table hewed out of a split log with pegs for legs, and a bench by the hearth. There was no floor except the bare ground; and farm tools, barrels and chests, clothing and odds and ends were littered everywhere. Joel had floored the garret during Fanny's illness, and for that purpose he brought up the river more boards than he needed. On rainy days during the summer, Mima set the three men to dig a cellar in the corner of the cabin under the common bunk, and they built a floor over it with the extra boards. When the cellar was done, at her urgency they tore out the common bunk and each built his own. Pegs in the walls served to hang things on. The lean-to in which the three men had slept while Fanny was here they enlarged to serve as a storage place for axes and farming tools, and with this and the garret and the cellar to take the overflow, the cabin was no longer crowded. There were endless things to do. Some Mima did; some tasks she imposed upon the men. Matt was always her ally, approving every suggestion she made. Joel might laugh at her, and Jason grumble; but in the end she had her way.

They had occasional news from the outer world. Colonel Wheaton had Moses Hawes and Sam Fales working on his land, and whenever he came up the river he was sure to stop at the Royal Mess to tell them all he knew. He came one day on a more particular errand, arriving at mid-forenoon in a sweat of rage. A shower had kept them all in the house after breakfast, and the rain was just ending when he stormed up from the landing.

'Turn out!' he shouted, before he reached the house; so they met him at the door, and he said strongly: 'Get your guns and come along. We've a job to do!'

Joel asked a question; but the other needed no prompting.

'A bunch of refugees killed Levi Soule, in Waldoborough, early this morning,' he said furiously. 'They're trying to get back to Biguyduce this way, probably following the cattle trail up across my land. We're going to head them off. Come along!' And he explained: 'They thought Soule had some money in the house. They took Steve Pendleton, off the islands; made him go along and show them the way to Soule's house. They got there first light and caught Soule in the barn starting to milk.'

His own words made his cheek dark with wrath, and the three men listened gravely and Mima saw Joel's lips tighten and his eyes shadow at what he heard.

'They tied Soule's hands behind his back,' Colonel Wheaton went on, 'and said he'd have to give them his money, and he told them to go to hell for a lot of Tory bastards! So they said he'd have to come along with them back to Biguyduce. He said he'd go to hell barefooted before he'd give them anything; but his wife was sick abed and he wanted to say good-bye to her. They took him into the house and they left Steve Pendleton to guard Soule while they tried to find the money. Soon as they got out of the room, Soule backed up to the kitchen table and picked up a knife there and then he backed up to the bed so Mrs. Soule could cut the rope they'd tied him with. And Pendleton holding a gun on him all the time.'

'Did Pendleton see him take the knife?' Joel asked.

'Not first off,' the Colonel explained. 'But when Mis' Soule started to saw at the ropes he saw her, and he upped his gun and told Soule to come away from the bed, and Soule told him he could be damned and Pendleton shot him.' His own rage made his voice thick. 'Had the gun full of slugs,' he said hoarsely. 'Blew him wide open. One of them hit Mrs. Soule too.'

Jason growled: 'Him with his hands tied!'

'Yes, by God! But some folks heard the shot, and when the refugees came running out, there were men down around the water where their boat was, so they put for the woods and headed this way.' He added: 'They got word to Warren — I was there last night and a fellow came on horseback, caught me at breakfast. I sent word to General Wadsworth, and I've got men all along the river from Warren up here, and the men down at Seven-Tree Pond. I'll get Sam Fales and Mose from my place, and you three, and we'll cover the river as far as Sunnyback Pond. I figure they'll try to cross and work over behind the mountains and get back to Biguyduce, but by God, if I lay hands on them they'll not get back! I'll hang the murdering sons of bitches!'

Joel nodded, and he took his gun from the peg inside the door. 'I've shot at men myself,' he said, in a quiet voice curiously

deadly. 'And maybe hit them too; but they were shooting back
at me. They weren't tied up; and I never shot a woman sick
abed.'

Jason said: 'I'd like to kick the guts out of that Pendleton.'
He and Matt brought their guns and shot pouches and powder
horns.

'Robbins is covering everything up to the bend in the river,'
the Colonel said. 'We'll shift the boats, so they'll have to wade
the river or swim.' He spoke to Mima. 'You'd better go home
and stay till we've caught 'em. They might come through
here; and if they'd kill a man in his bed, there's no telling what
they'd do to a woman alone.'

'I'll clean up here first,' she said. 'You leave a boat here for
me.'

They trooped away down to the landing, Sambo barking
with excitement, the Colonel going over the tale again, the
others grimly silent. Mima went about her work; but when she
began to clear away the breakfast, she realized that the men
had gone without provision. They might get something at the
Colonel's place, but if they had forgotten it here, they might
forget it there. And if they stayed all night to guard the river,
they would be hungry. On the thought, she set a fire going in
the oven, mixed up bread and presently raked the fire and put
the bread to bake. She had·no meat, but her mother might
have some; and when the bread was done, Mima carried it
down to the landing and laid it — still hot — in the dugout.
She paddled down the river and found her father and mother
and the younger children at home. Dave and Rich, they told
her, had taken their families over to Johnny Butler's house,
since on the east shore they would be safe from these marauders;
and they themselves had gone up-river. 'Bijah Hawes and Ez
Bowen were guarding the river below the pond.

'I'm a-staying here,' Philip said mildly. 'If it's open season
on Tories, I'd as soon shoot one or two right at my own back
door where they'll be handy for butchering.' He added: 'They

say John Long's with this crowd. I've a hankering to see that critter, the tales they tell about him.'

Mrs. Robbins said: 'They caught him, in Warren, a while back.'

'The dummed fools let him get away again,' he retorted. 'Done it a-purpose, like as not. Well, if I ever lay hands on him, he won't get away from me!'

Mima explained her thought, that the men would need food. 'Did they take any from here?' she asked. They had not, and Mrs. Robbins said:

'Just like a pack of men, go scrabbling off and never stop to think. They'll be hungry as wolves before night.'

'I baked some bread,' Mima explained. 'If you've got some meat I could take it up to them.'

Philip agreed that this would help. 'You can pack a couple days' feed for 'em easy as not,' he said. 'Colonel Wheaton was too busy roaring about how many he was going to hang to think about grub, but I was a commissary myself last year at Biguyduce. I know a man's got to eat.'

Mrs. Robbins produced some smoked moose meat, and Philip made up a pack for Mima to carry. 'It'll be heavy,' he said. 'But you don't have far to go. I'll set you over to the carrying-place. Eben and Bela and Johnny Butler are strung along there from the pond to the river. You can give it to the first man you come to, and let him pass it on.'

'They'll have to stay where they are,' Mima reminded him. 'I'll go on till I come to two of them together.'

Her father assented. 'I'll set you over, see you started,' he said. He put Mima ashore at the northern end of the pond. 'I'd go myself,' he told her. 'But I've got to stay and look out for Ma and the young ones.' The sun was low, dusk not far away; and he hesitated, but then he clapped her shoulder. 'You'll do fine,' he said. 'You can outrun any rattlesnake of a Tory that ever lived — yes, and lick him if he catches you. If it comes on dark, you can stay with somebody. Be a fine night. Sleeping out won't hurt you.'

Mima said slowly: 'You'd shoot one if you saw him, wouldn't you?'

'Certain,' he said flatly. 'Quick as I would a snake.'

'I don't like having you want to kill somebody. It's poison in a man, hating like that. Joel's the same, and the Colonel and all. I wish't we could just live here and work hard and do the best we can and not bother about what's happening anywhere else at all.'

'Don't talk like a woman,' he said roughly. 'Go along.' He kissed her cheek. 'Look out for yourself,' he said.

When he put her ashore, the meadows were on her right, the forest on her left. She followed a faint track in the border of the wood, thinking that here too men in their casual passing began to make a path for other men to follow. A tongue of trees projected into the grassy meadow, and when she came there Bela, his gun on his arm, stepped out to meet her. 'Where you going, Mima?' he asked in astonishment.

'I thought the men might not have enough to eat, might be hungry,' she explained. 'Is this where you're staying?'

'Yes, we're watching the meadows,' he said. 'Johnny Butler's along a ways, and Eben's between him and the river.'

'You staying here all night?'

'No, we're going to get together, go back to Johnny's. The womenfolks are there. The Colonel's pretty sure this crowd will keep shy of any houses, but we're going to be on hand at the Mill Farm if they do come.'

'Then you won't need any of this I brought?'

'No.' Then he said: 'Oh say, Mima, I've got a start on your canoe. Haven't seen you to tell you. It's going to be a beauty. I got an old punkin pine, works just like cheese. Found it back of the house in the big woods. A wind had knocked it over, but the trunk's all sound only right at the bottom. I'm going to work it down to an eggshell between now and spring.'

'I'd like that mightily, having it my own.'

'It'll be the best canoe anywhere around here,' he promised.

When she went on, she looked back and saw him retreat to the shelter of the wood again; and she wondered what he would do if he saw the fugitives. He seemed like a boy to her. It was hard to think of him shooting a man, killing him. She wondered how old that Steve Pendleton was, who shot Levi Soule. The Tories had forced him to show them the way; probably they had set him to guard the prisoners under pain of his own death. Perhaps he was a boy, no older than Bela; perhaps he was younger, as young as Jacob, afraid of his own life, seeing Mr. Soule freeing himself from his bonds, pulling the trigger at last in a blind and desperate terror — to kill a bound and helpless man. A woman might do a thing like that or a boy very much afraid.

She did not see Johnny, but Eben hailed her before she reached the river. She was following the faint trail down toward the stream when he stepped out from behind a tree. He spoke at the same time, quietly so as not to startle her. 'It's Eben, Mima.' And as she stopped: 'Where did you come from? Did I scare you?'

'No. Bela told me you were here.' She explained her errand. 'Where are the rest of them?' she asked. 'Bela said you're going back to Johnny's tonight.'

'That's right. The others are strung along all the way to Sunnyback Pond. Colonel Wheaton figures the Tories will try to cross as high up as they can. He's got two men — I don't know which ones — up where they've been fording beef critters across. Jess went up-river just a while ago. He'd been moving all the boats to this side of the river so they couldn't get at 'em. He told me to fetch some meat or something in the morning. He didn't have anything; so he'll be glad to see you.'

'How far is the ford?' she asked.

'They say about a mile. Mima, don't you get into any trouble. If you see a sign of them, let out a yell and run. Somebody'll hear you.'

She nodded. 'Eben, what will you do if you see them?'

'Let off my gun. That's the signal.'

'Shoot one of them?'

He grinned sheepishly. 'I don't know as I will, Mima. I hate their guts, and I'd fight 'em; but I wouldn't want to shoot a man that didn't know I was around. Like as not I'd shoot somewhere nigh 'em to scare 'em plenty, and then kind of hang on their tail till the others could get here.'

'I guess you would,' she said. She kissed him quietly. 'You be careful.'

She went on more slowly. There was no longer any path to lead her by the easiest way, and this east bank of the river was steep, the ground rising at a sharp slope from the water. The watchers would be by the river; but there was easier going a little above the water, so she moved along the slope, sometimes descending to the stream side, sometimes thirty or forty feet above it. She found no one till she came to the ford, marked by traces where cattle had scrambled up out of the river. Jess was there with Sam Fales of Thomaston, who was working this summer on Colonel Wheaton's land; and they welcomed her heartily.

'I'm half starved a'ready,' Jess assured her. 'Just from thinking how hungry I'll be before morning.' She slipped out of her pack and he opened it to take what he and Fales would need for tonight and tomorrow morning. Mima knew Sam Fales. He had come more than once to the Royal Mess. His father, Atwood Fales, was for Thomaston folks the hero of Biguyduce because of his exploit of fetching a pail of water to his fellows across a reach of ground commanded by British fire. Sixty muskets were let off at him going and as many returning, yet he went untouched. Jess referred to this now as he opened the pack. 'Mima's bringing this is like your pa's trick at Biguyduce, Sam.'

'There's no one a-shooting guns at her,' Sam reminded Jess. 'There was at Pa!' Mima and Jess laughed together, and Jess said:

'I'll pass this on to the rest of the men, Mima. You'll have to hurry to get home before dark. Sam will stay here while I take it up-river.'

But young Fales protested. 'Hold on, Jess, I ain't staying here alone. Right here's where they're pretty sure to come, and tonight's the time they'll try it. The whole lot of us ought to spend the night here, if you ask me.'

Jess said laughingly: 'Man, your pa'd stay and lick the lot of them. It ain't any worse staying here with the woods to hide in than scuttering across with sixty men shooting at you!'

'Well, Pa was thirsty!' Fales argued; and when they shouted with laughter, he added: 'Besides, he didn't know they'd be shooting at him when he started, and when they begun, he didn't have brains enough to come back.'

Jess howled with mirth. 'Sure! I know! Like Joe Lackland back home. He was splitting wood one day and he caught his axe on a clothesline and it bounced back and hit him in the head with the flat side. Knocked him senseless, so he kept on swinging and it kept on a-hitting him till his pa had to come a-running and take the axe away from him before he beat hisself to death.'

'That's all right,' Sam stubbornly insisted, 'I ain't staying here alone!'

Mima might have returned home, if Sam had been willing to keep watch here; but at this she said: 'All right, Jess, you stay here with Sam. I'll go on up-river. I'll be fine.' She asked: 'Who's next above here?'

'It might be Joel,' Jess told her. 'But he'll be quite a ways, above the deadwater. Colonel aimed to have most of the men up handy to the pond, and just watch the likely places from here to there.'

She nodded. 'I'll find him,' she promised. If Joel was next, she was glad to go on. The sun was setting when she left the ford, and shadows were deeper in the woods, and the glory of the western sky was mirrored in the river below her. Thrushes were singing in the forest, and Mima thought their clear, liquid notes were as beautiful as the singing of a hidden brook. The sound kept her company as she went on. She had put on moose-hide moccasins, and buskins against briers, but she went softly, her footfalls making scarce a sound. The sun set and crimson glory tinted every smallest cloud across the dome of the sky and then began to fade, and dusk flowed silently through the forest, and the call of the thrushes and the murmur of the river over an occasional ripple blended into a peaceful evensong.

She kept near the water to be sure not to miss seeing any man along the stream, whether it were Joel or another; but the man she found was Joel. He stood on a flat-topped boulder close beside the water, leaning against a great pine which grew so hard along the stone it seemed to have flattened itself against the granite. He must have heard her before she saw him; for his flintlock was ready in his hand and he was peering toward her when she discovered him.

She said quickly: 'It's Mima.'

'Mima!' He leaped off the boulder, came to meet her in one bound. The sun had set long before, and in the deep woods it was already almost dark. The forest on the opposite bank, blackly reflected in the water, made the river black as ink; but along the shore on which Joel and Mima stood the water mirrored a narrow strip of reflected sky in which some afterglow still lingered. Mima was tired; she had without realizing it hurried a little, anxious not to be overtaken by darkness before she found Joel. He had heard her coming; but until she emerged from the forest close beside him he had not known who she might be; and for him the relief from taut readiness for danger, and for her the gladness at having found him, made them laugh together now. She slipped her pack, letting the boulder upon which he had been standing take its weight, and he asked:

'What have you got there?'

'You didn't bring any victuals, so I baked some bread and got some smoked moose meat from Mother, and packed them up here.'

'Say, I'm glad to see you! I was getting hungry a'ready, thinking how long it would be till morning.'

'There's plenty here for all of you till then.'

'Was it your idea, to come?'

'Yes. Jess would have fetched it on up here, but Sam Fales didn't want to stay alone — nor to come alone, either.'

She heard him chuckle. 'Didn't it scare you?'

'No.' She confessed: 'I kind of liked it, coming through the woods with the birds singing.' She looked at the river, added quietly: 'I've never been so far up-river before.'

He nodded. 'We work all the time, don't go anywhere unless we've got a reason; so there's nought to bring us so far.'

'How far is Sunnyback Pond?'

'Right close onto a mile,' he said: 'I'll pack this on to them up above. Jason's not far. We're scattered along every forty rods or so. He can pass it on to the others.'

'You'll stay out the night?'

'Colonel says so. He looks for them to cross tonight or tomorrow, somewhere between here and Sunnyback Pond.' His tone was concerned. 'I can't take you home, Mima; not without leaving my stand here. There's a place just at the next bend where they can wade over, that I have to watch.'

'I can stay, well as not. A night out won't hurt me. It's warm and all.'

'How far down is Jess?' he asked doubtfully.

'Half a mile, maybe more.'

He hesitated, then opened the pack. 'I'll take out enough for us for tonight and the morning. Then I'll carry the rest up to Jason.' He fumbled in the darkness. Mima saw the first fine star bright above the trees across the river. 'I'll be a while,' he said. 'But there's nought to hurt you.'

'I'm not afraid.'

He lifted the pack, adjusting it to fit his shoulders, and moved off. Mima could hear his movements for a while as he climbed away from the water to try for easier going. Once or

twice she heard him collide with trees in the inky darkness of
the wood, and heard him swear; and once she heard him fall
and slide almost to the water's edge while small bits of rock
cascaded down around him. Then the sounds he made were
lost in the murmur of the rips a little way upstream, and Mima
was alone. She sat down on the boulder where she had found
him standing, her shoulders against the tree. Mosquitoes
swarmed around her and she brushed at them with automatic
movements. There was a ticking silence in the wood. The
voice of the river was a murmur of many voices, as though a
company of sentries kept watch and the 'All's well' ran musi-
cally up and down the line. Mima alone in the forest was always
conscious of its intense aliveness, of the fact that creatures great
and small moved to and fro under shelter of the night upon their
own concerns; and this was true now. She imagined the crack
of twigs as soft pads passed; she heard the stir of leaves and
thought a branch which some slim body pushed aside had
rebounded to its place again. Somewhere an owl was hunting.
She heard its hoo-hoo-h-hoo that might be a few rods away or a
mile; and she heard a fox, and she thought Tuner barked, far
down on Seven-Tree Pond. She was still and warm and happy.
The night had always a mysterious charm for her, and she had
not infrequently — to her mother's fearful disapproval —
slept outside the cabin on stifling summer nights. Mrs. Robbins
was sure the mists off the pond would give her chills and fever,
but they never had; and tonight was as warm as the day had
been, though a cool little breeze came gliding up the valley
against the current of the stream.

Joel was gone an hour or more. She heard him returning,
groping and floundering; and when he was near enough she
called to him — softly so that the peace of the night might not
be disturbed — and thus brought him to her side. He was
breathing heavily with real fatigue.

'Still here, are you? I thought you might be gone.'

'I wouldn't want to travel in the dark.'

'It's hard doing,' he agreed. 'You can't see anything till it hits you, and you go thumping into trees, and branches slap you in the face. I ran a dead pine stub into my eye.' He chuckled. 'I saw glims enough for a minute then. Have you et?'

'No, I wasn't hungry.'

'I'll strike up a fire. We'll move back from the river a little so it won't show too much. There's a spring brook comes down, along this way.' He gathered up their provisions and led her toward the brook and chose his place in the angle of two boulders. He flashed a little powder in which he had laid threads of birch bark, and had small twigs ready and fed the tiny flame. The brook chuckled beside them as their meat broiled on switches propped over rocks, and he brought bark to serve as platters. He was the cook. 'It's time I cooked a meal for you,' he said smilingly. 'Just so's you'll know men aren't as helpless as you think.'

'I know you're not,' she agreed. 'But a man would rather do other work, work that shows, than just do the same job over and over every day the way a woman has to.'

'You talk like Jemima. My sister.'

Mima felt a curious surprise. 'I never thought of you having sisters and brothers, having a family.'

'Guess most folks do,' he said, amused. 'Where did you think I came from in the first place?'

'I don't know. I never thought about it. You just seemed to be — well, you didn't seem to need a family, some way.' He turned the meat, presented a new side to the hot little fire; and she rubbed her cheeks and felt them burning and he asked:

'Too hot? Plenty of room to move back.'

'No. How old is your sister?'

'Twenty. She'd like it here. She's a master hand for the woods. I told her she could come up and have a visit with me after a while.'

'She could come now and sleep in the garret with me.'

'I wouldn't risk her with so many refugee sloops alongshore stopping everything they see.' The meat was done and he laid it on the birch bark and cut it into strips with the knife that was tucked in his twisted belt, and they began to eat. Mima thought he had cooked none too much, so she ate sparingly to be sure there was plenty for him. 'I aim to wait,' he said. 'After Jason and Matt and me get things going, if I don't sell out I'll have a chance to build a cabin of my own, and then she'll come.'

She shivered faintly. He had spoken before of the chance that he might sell his land, but she had forgotten till now. She said slowly: 'Maybe Jason and Matt will marry and move out and you can have the cabin.'

'No, it's on Jason's land; but what we've cleared is mine. I'll build south of the brook, if I ever do.' He added: 'There are some sightly places on my land. I've picked out two-three that would set a house mighty fine.'

'I guess your sister will wish she could come sooner. How long will it be?'

'Depends on the crops we make and all, and how we get along. Everything takes longer than you'd think, to get it done.'

'Nothing's ever done,' she said. 'There's always more to do.'

He laughed. 'I'd hate to think that. I want to take a look around some day and say: "Well there, it's finished!" '

She looked at him in the firelight. The flames were dying down. He finished the last of the moose meat and licked his fingers and wiped them on his hunting shirt. There was a little bloody gravy on the birch bark where he had cut up the meat, and he cupped the bark and poured the gravy on a bit of bread and ate it. A two or three days' beard showed on his lean cheek, and she saw the line of his jaw, and his strong nose.

'No, you wouldn't,' she said. 'You don't ever want to finish anything. It's the doing that's the fun, working and trying and keeping at it.'

'Work? Fun?' He laughed. 'Not for me.' He lay down on his back beside her, watching the tinted smoke drift upward out of the firelight's reach. 'Not for me,' he insisted. 'I work because I have to, and I quit as soon as I can. It would suit me all right if I never did a lick again.'

Mima said almost angrily: 'That's not so, Joel. You don't know it, but you try loafing some time and you'll find out. Doing nothing's the hardest work there is.'

For a moment he did not speak. Then he said lazily, watching the smoke rising through the trees: 'That time, one little spark went clear up and up like a lightning bug. Watch!' He stirred the fire, and small sparks flew upward, glowing for a while before they died. 'Like shooting stars,' he said. 'I can see one star, up through the trees.'

She leaned back against the boulder by his side, tipped her head far backward, looking for that star. He watched her, said with a chuckle: 'What's wrong with loafing? We're loafing now — and it's easy to do.'

'Just the same, it's working and trying that's fun,' she insisted. 'Whether you do what you're trying to do or not. It's like clearing a field, Joel. You clear it, and you burn off the down-timber, and you haul out the stumps — but if you go off and leave it alone, first thing you know it's all grown up again and has to be done over.' She added before he could speak: 'And that's all right, too — and it's what happens and it's meant to happen so. Why, say we got everything done that there was to do, here in Sterlingtown, so that when the ones that are children now grew up, there wouldn't be anything left for them to do. A fine lot they'd turn out to be.'

He argued: 'They could go up-river and start over.'

'They'd come to the end of the river, sometime. There won't always be more woods to clear, Joel. I don't know how much of this country there is. Nobody does. But say it could all be cleared and stay cleared and no work left to do — I wouldn't want to live then and neither would you.'

He said, watching the stars: 'I guess't there'll always be far places — and men to go into them.' He rose on one elbow, looking at her. 'I don't mean just trees to cut, but — new things to do and new ways of doing them; roads to build, and quicker ways to get around and all.'

'A path's about the first thing a man makes in a place,' she reflected. 'Before he gets a house built, his feet have made a path to the nearest spring, or somewhere.' She added strongly: 'But I don't want roads, and comings and goings, and being all stirred up all the time about what's happening in places you've never been and that don't matter to you. I'd like to live just in walking distance, not ever go outside that. But I want to know everybody in it, and every tree and hill and river and pond; know them inside out and backward and forward, every way. I'd rather know a lot about one tree, say, than a little about a lot of trees. You love a thing so much more when you know all about it.'

'That's because you're a woman. Women always want to stay at home.' He chuckled, sitting up, hugging his knees. 'The way you tell it, you'd want to live in one clearing all your life and never go outside it. But a man keeps wanting to make the clearing bigger.' He stared at the dying fire, and she watched him and he said, half to himself: 'There's something wonderful about a clearing, Mima. I mean about making one. There you are in the woods, trees all around you, you can't see up or down or around. But you've got an axe and you go at it and pretty soon the tree lets go and comes smashing down and you can look up and see a circle of sky.

'When you do, that's your sky, by God!' His tone was hushed like a prayer. 'You've brought it down to shine on your land and make your things grow. You knock over more trees, and every one that goes, you've grabbed that much more sky and it's yours to keep. You grab sky first, and by and by you make the clearing bigger and you catch you a hill off somewhere five miles, ten, maybe a hundred. You couldn't see it before, but now you can, and that sight of it's yours, to keep. That hill's yours! It's one of the things you can look at, from your land.'

She hugged her arms tight across her breasts, watching him. The fire was almost gone. He tossed a handful of pine needles on it and the quick little crackle of flames came and passed. Something had changed, here all about them; and Joel looked up and said in surprise: 'Ho! Moonrise!' She saw above them a silvering sky; and there began to be the silhouettes of trees here in the forest. He said: 'Them that killed Soule might be travelling, now it's getting lighter. We'll move down to the river.'

The glow of the dying fire showed them the way. When they came to the waterside, the moon had caught clouds in the western sky, and in the moonlight the stars began to fade. She thought some day she and Joel would go up this river as far as they could go. He said beside her:

'I'll want to be where I can see up and down. You pick a comfortable place and sleep if you can.'

'We could have a smudge for the mosquitoes.'

He shook his head. 'Smoke smells a long ways. I want to know this crowd is coming before they know I'm here.'

She did not yet feel sleepy. 'You and Matt and Jason get along, don't you,' she said.

He assented, mirth in his tones. 'We always have,' he agreed. 'We don't ever want the same things, so we don't have anything to fight about.'

'Matt's awful comfortable to have around. You always know where to find him.'

'He'll make some girl a good man,' he agreed. 'He's the marrying kind.'

'I guess most men are.'

'Matt's fit for it, though,' he said. 'Jason and me — well, when a man like us has been soldiering for two-three years, we don't think much about marrying any woman.'

'I've got to know Matt pretty well,' she assented. She felt his eyes on her. He did not speak for a moment. Then he said almost curtly:

'You'd better settle down and get some sleep. Be warm enough, will you?'

'Plenty!'

He suggested: 'You can pull your skirt up over your head to keep the bugs off.'

'If you want to sleep, wake me up and I'll take a turn at it. I can wake you if anyone comes. Where are you going to stay?'

He chose to stand. 'If I set down I might go to sleep,' he confessed. 'I'll stand along here anywhere.'

She found a mossy bank as springy as a bed, with a hummock convenient for a pillow. The night was too warm to need any covering; but for protection against mosquitoes she unbuttoned her dress from the waist down and drew her skirt up over her head. For her legs, moccasins and leggings and petticoats were sufficient protection. Joel stood ten feet away, leaning against a tree in such a position that she could see him dark against the moonlit sky. She watched him for a while, herself wide awake, thinking long thoughts, puzzled about him as a child may be puzzled by adult ways. He was a man whom women loved easily and generously; and she could understand this. That lifted eyebrow, that gentle smile which was at once jocular and tender and understanding had a peculiar charm. And he had been recklessly eager to take the gifts such women as Fanny offered him.

Yet Mima had known him — and loved him — for months now, and he must know this; but he had never touched her, never wooed her as even 'Bijah, for instance, had sought to woo her in the past, with no word of marrying at all. She wondered wistfully what it was about her which repelled him; and she slept and waked and slept again as one does out-of-doors. Once when she waked he was not there, and she sat up and spoke his name and he answered from the riverside below her.

'Just getting a drink,' he said.

She saw that the moon was halfway done with its march

across the sky, the night more than half gone. 'Do you want to sleep a spell?'

'I'm asleep on my feet.'

'Lie down, then. I'll watch.'

'Well, if I could sleep a minute, it would wake me up,' he admitted. 'If you hear anything, just touch me. Don't speak.' He added: 'The way you can hear things, I guess they won't get by you.'

'I'll watch,' she promised. 'Rest easy, Joel.'

She heard presently his deep breathing, where he lay near her feet. She could have touched him without moving. She was alone for she did not know how long in the night that was so full of little sounds all blending. He woke at last without being roused, and spoke to her and stood up near her.

'That's as good as a night's sleep,' he said. 'Hear anything?'

She laughed at herself. 'I heard plenty. I'm just aching from listening. You can hear a long way in the night. No, I didn't hear anything the way you mean.'

They stood together for a while, not speaking. 'Mose Hawes is getting married,' he said at last. 'He's setting out to build him a cabin on his land.'

Mima was surprised. Moses Hawes, Matt's cousin, had bought land between Rich and her father; but except for putting up a hovel and clearing two or three acres and planting some corn, he had done nothing to it, hiring out his services to Colonel Wheaton instead.

'Is he up the river tonight?' she asked.

'Yes.' Joel chuckled. 'He didn't want to come along today, said he had to go to Warren; but the Colonel hollered it out of him. He's going to marry Mary Kelloch, Alex Kelloch's girl.'

She nodded, watching Joel in the darkness, wondering what had made him think of marriage, wondering whether his thoughts ran with her own. She said: 'I knew he went down to Warren sometimes.'

'He worked down there for Boggs last winter,' Joel reminded her. 'Likely it started then. You'd best sleep some more.'

'I'm not sleepy. I'm wide awake from listening. Joel, I don't think they'll come this way. They'll go up around Sunnyback Pond. They wouldn't risk getting caught — not even if it meant going clear around by the Kennebeck.'

'I don't know. Colonel's bound we'll watch tomorrow, anyhow.'

She lay down again, and thought she was wide awake, but she must have slept, for without any interval of waiting, there was dawn light across the sky; and when she looked for Joel he was gone. She waited, sure of his return. When he came back, his hair was wet. 'I had a swim,' he said. 'Even river water's warm in the morning, like milk. You were sleeping like a good one.'

'I did sleep fine,' she agreed.

'I'll strike up a fire and we'll eat.' They turned back to where they had the fire the night before, and she found a small pool in the little brook and washed her face and drank. The sun was just risen, crimson on the river mists that were rising above the level of the trees. The meat broiled in the hot small flames and they ate hungrily; and once as they ate, their eyes met and they laughed together without reason. Then Mima heard a stumbling footstep and they turned to look and listen and presently Colonel Wheaton came striding along the bank between them and the river. He hailed them and came up to where they were.

'Smelled that meat cooking for half a mile,' he said heartily, and clapped Mima on the shoulder. 'Well, girl, you had a lot of men thanking you last night up-river,' he said. 'I'm going down for more grub now. We ate all ours.' Then he seemed to realize what her presence here implied. 'Stay all night, did you?' he demanded, frowning.

'Yes.'

'You and him?' His eye was stern on Joel.

'Yes,' said Mima.

He hesitated, spoke grumblingly. 'Well, Joel, I guess with her here the King could have marched six regiments past you and you'd not have known it, man! Mima, you come along home with me and let my sentries do their job!'

Joel laughed. 'The job wasn't slighted, Colonel. There were two of us watched instead of one, that's all. Want to eat? There's a scrap left.'

'I'll wait till there's plenty,' the Colonel told him. 'Mima, you come along. I'll take you home.'

She would have liked to stay, but had no ready reason. They left Joel and tramped down-river together; but when they were clear away from Joel's hearing, the Colonel stopped and turned.

'See here,' he asked awkwardly, 'did Joel — bother you any?'

'Joel? He'll never bother me.'

He could not doubt her, and he chuckled, touched her arm. 'Well, you're the first wench could ever say that after a night with him,' he said. Then his brow clouded. 'Mima — set down,' he said. 'I aim to talk to you.'

She looked at him uncertainly, but then she obeyed, half-sitting, half-leaning on a boulder, waiting for him to speak. He watched her, expecting some question; but when she asked none, he demanded:

'You aim to go on living with the Royal Mess?'

'I work for them.'

'I know, but you live there too.' His color rose. 'What do your pa and ma think about that?'

She did not let any suggestion of her amusement show in her eyes. 'I never asked them.'

'A woman in a house with three men ain't noways decent,' he declared.

'Would it be better if there was only one of them?' she suggested, smiling a little.

He chuckled, seemed for some reason suddenly more at ease.

'You're a quiet one,' he said. 'There's some of these young ones always twisting and twitching like a fish on a griddle. They'd drive a man crazy, a man my age.' He met her eyes, humbly and yet bravely too. 'I'm forty-five years old, Mima,' he said. 'And I've lived hard — since my wife died, special. How old are you?'

'Twenty-three.'

He nodded slowly. 'Time you're my age, I'll be right on to seventy. And you're the kind that won't get old. You'll stay young, look young, feel young, act young. There's times already when I feel old, feel like an old man. There'd be many a time when you'd be of a mind to do a thing and I wouldn't.' She watched him quietly, touched and tender. 'I don't want to let on what ain't so, Mima.' He asked huskily: 'Do you know what I'm talking about? A girl like you ought to be married and having babies by now.'

Her eyes left his. The risen sun began to send lances of light down through the trees around them. The river was still in shadow below and she saw a mother duck and her brood gliding downstream under the opposite bank, oblivious of the human beings on the slope above them. The forest was full of many sounds.

'You don't give a man much help,' said Colonel Wheaton. 'Mima, I'm too old to be the kind of husband you ought to have; but — you can have me and welcome.'

She looked at him and smiled and felt her eyes sting. 'You're a real good man, Colonel,' she said. 'You amount to something.'

He shook his head. 'Don't get that notion,' he told her warningly. 'I'm a big toad in a small puddle, maybe. I talk loud, and folks kind of let me have my own way because I shout 'em down and it's easier for them to give in than to argue. I'm smart some ways; but being smart and having brains are two different things. I'm mostly talk. But I back my talk. If you'll have me, I'm your turkey! I'll do my damnedest to behave myself, and I'll aim to be good to you.'

She said gently: 'I'm not going to marry you. But I'm real happy about your asking me.'

He hesitated, and then he took off his hat and mopped his brow and grinned. 'Well, I dunno but what I'm full as well pleased,' he admitted. 'You're more woman than I'm up to, Mima. I'd have done my damnedest — but if you'd said you'd have me, I'd have been as scared as the man that throwed the bear!'

She laughed, touching his arm. 'I always have liked you — but I like you better than ever now.'

'Why the hell hasn't one of these young rake-hellions up here bedded you before now?' he demanded. 'That's what I can't understand.' He said: 'Take Matt Hawes if you can get him, Mima. He'll make a man.'

She asked, smiling, her eyes dancing: 'What about Joel?'

'That goat! You, Mima, if he ever tries his tricks on you, you tell me! I'll cut that rooster's comb!'

3

THE watchers on the river kept a fruitless vigil all that day; but they saw nothing of the murderers of Soule. General Wadsworth, as a result of the murder, issued a proclamation warning all men against giving aid or comfort to the enemy on pain of death; and the clandestine trade in provisions to Biguyduce came to an abrupt stop. Alongshore it might be profitable to slip out of some hidden cove on a foggy night and cross the bay with a barge load of provisions; but there were no more cattle driven across Colonel Wheaton's land and through the northern part of Sterlingtown.

One day late in July, Joel and the others were felling trees along the edge of their clearing, working north toward the cabin and west along the brook; and Mima was alone at her morning tasks with the sound of their axes for company. She had put in some small flower beds on either side of the front door, and she had a little garden patch down toward the spring which she herself had spaded, which she hoped to enlarge, and in which she planted radish seeds, and turnips and onions, for sauce. She was busy there when she heard her father's voice from the direction of the pond, and the sound of his paddle; and she went through the woods to the landing. There was a stranger in the bow of the float. Her father said:

'Mima, here's a new neighbor. William Jennison. He aims to buy out that damnifyed Taylor!' And he told Jennison: 'There'll be a better smell around here when Taylor's name's scrubbed off of everything.'

Mima smiled at her father's heat. His own battle with Doctor Taylor was long since ended, but not his hatred of the man. 'Maybe Mr. Jennison likes Doctor Taylor,' she suggested.

Before Jennison could speak, her father exploded: 'Like him? Who'd like that wife-killer?' He demanded of Jennison: 'Know what he did to me? Agreed to sell at one price, and then when I'd put in a summer's work, doubled the price on me so I could buy no more than half the land I wanted. And after that when we'd agreed again, he took an excuse to say I'd have to pay specie. I told him I'd not pay it, and he said he'd sue, and I said he could sue to hell and back again with the devil for his lawyer. But by Godfrey he did it — and got Continental money for his pains. But we saw to it his creditors had an attachment waiting to clap on him the minute he had the money in his hands.' He shook his head warningly. 'He'll do the same to you, Jennison, if you give him the chance.'

Jennison chuckled. 'I'll look out for him,' he promised. 'But it sounds to me he got small purchase out of you, Robbins. He never had the use of your money!'

'I say he's a wife-killing liar and thief,' Philip told him strongly. 'His first wife lasted six years; and she wasn't cold till he married again and that one lived two years. He was published again right after, but the woman changed her mind. Then the last letter I had from the westward, his last wife had died too, and them not two years married. He's a talker and a promiser and a liar, and he'll have your eye teeth if you don't

keep your mouth shut when you talk to him.' The big man
had talked himself into good humor again; he said: 'Come
along! If we're going to walk your lines we'll need to do some
travelling. I wanted to make you acquainted with these men
here. Where are they, Mima?'

'You can hear the axes,' she reminded him. 'They're over
along the brook, I'd say.'

'So! We'll go that way,' Philip agreed. He told Jennison:
'I can show you Wheaton's corner, on their north line. Come
along.'

Jennison spent a week exploring and appraising his land.
His southeast corner was at Colonel Wheaton's southwest
corner, so that they both touched the tract owned by the Royal
Mess. His purchase included some six thousand acres, and the
Madomock traversed it on a diagonal, flowing southwesterly
toward Broad Bay. Jennison had large plans to bring men to
clear farms and settle there; and Philip and all of them welcomed this prospective new strength in Sterlingtown.

Mima saw him only that first day. She was so much absorbed
in doing and in planning that she seldom went down-river,
except on Sundays. Then she liked to hear her father read from
the Bible, and perhaps talk a while as he usually did; and
sometimes they all sang together. But if she did not go down,
her mother or Jess or Eben was apt to appear at the Royal Mess
every day or two, to tell her how the new house progressed, to
tell her any news at all. It was Eben who told her about Lucy
Butler's soldiers. They were deserters from Biguyduce. 'Johnny
wasn't to home when they came,' Eben said. 'And Lucy was
so scared her teeth were chattering. They was starved, mighty
peaked-looking; and Johnny had a ham hanging in the cellar
way. They saw it and asked if they could have some, and Lucy
cooked up about half of it for them.'

'I should think she would,' Mima agreed, 'if they were
hungry.'

'They were bad off,' Eben assured her. 'Johnny came in

while they were still there. They told him that crowd that murdered Soule got back to Biguyduce all right. They went up the Madomock till they were way north of here and around back of Belfast, kept in the woods all the way. The last two-three days they didn't have a thing to eat only the bark off trees.'

Mima asked: 'Did ever you think you'd like to go up-river as far as you could, Eben, and see where it comes from and see what's there?'

Eben shook his head. 'I'd rather go down-river. I want to go help fight off men like them that killed Soule. It's about time we started fighting back.' He spoke as gently as he always did, but his words were the more emphatic for that gentleness.

'Don't you go fighting, Eben,' Mima told him, smiling affectionately. 'There's plenty to do here — and you're my best brother. I don't want you fighting.'

'I don't want to fight,' he agreed. 'But there's times a man has to, for his own sake, so he can keep his head up.' He said: 'John Long, and Dicke, and Nelson — everybody knows what those old Tories are doing, but they come to Thomaston when they're a mind, and the folks that see 'em don't dast lay hold on 'em.'

'They caught Long at Warren,' she reminded him.

'Spear did. The rest of 'em would have let him go just because he had his knife out. Spear was the only one had the backbone to grab him — and after that, them that tried to take him to jail, he scared them into letting him get away.' He smiled. 'I went to Warren with Pa three-four days ago and he was giving 'em fits for that. He 'lowed if he ever got his hands on Long, he'd hold on to him.'

'He would, too,' Mima agreed.

Eben nodded proudly. Then in sudden recollection he asked: 'Mima, you remember Phin Butler? The one that walked up the east side of the pond with you the day we came?'

'Yes.'

'He's home,' he said. 'Johnny told me. He got his discharge from the army and he's gone to work for Uncle Oliver now. Phin got some land from Taylor for being bound, on the west side of the river up above Colonel Wheaton's place; and Johnny wants him to come up there and start clearing, but Phin dunno as he will.' Mima smiled, remembering Phin's characteristic uncertainty. 'He says he likes Thomaston better.'

'I wish he would come up here,' Mima said. 'We need all the men that will come.'

*   *   *   *   *

The summer droned away. The heavy snows of the previous winter made for flood stages in the river, and the waters had been high till late June; but very little rain fell to help the crops and by mid-August the corn was suffering badly. Colonel Wheaton came up from Thomaston at intervals, fuming at the continued depredations of the refugees. Waldo Dicke had cut out the Colonel's sloop while she lay at anchor in Maple Juice Cove loaded with lime for Boston. He took it away to Biguyduce, and General Campbell, commanding there, offered its return at a moderate ransom.

'I judge he aimed to do right,' the Colonel admitted. 'The English, mostly, they're decent. It looks to me he was ashamed of the trick Dicke did on me. But I told him he could whistle for his money. Paying a ransom's too much like dealing with the enemy to suit me.'

Thomaston had decided to send no representative to the General Court this year; so the Colonel could give all his time to his affairs. He had a dozen business interests of which his land in Sterlingtown was the least. Joel thought he would build a house and come there to live, but Mima was sure he never would. 'He's too busy too many ways,' she declared. They were eating supper at a slab table she had persuaded them to build outside the cabin, under a roof of loose boards that kept off the rain.

'He'll not,' Jason Ware agreed. 'He bought the land to sell. He bought it on time, and he's waiting to pay for it till paper money gets down as far as it's going. Then he'll sell it for specie when he can.'

Joel said thoughtfully: 'That's the way to make money on land, buy and sell. Doctor Taylor bought all this from Tom Flucker for around ninepence an acre; but he got a dollar an acre from your father, Mima, and four or five times that, Continental, from Jennison.'

Mima felt a faint, deep alarm sensing the thought in Joel's mind. 'But Jennison's got his land,' she urged. 'And we've got ours. All Doctor Taylor's got is money, and not much of that; but when you've got land, you're safe.'

Joel chuckled. 'I'd take the money and risk it,' he declared. 'This clearing and getting started is fun, some ways; but I don't see myself settling down to be a farmer.'

She protested: 'I guess time you've salted the land with your own sweat you'll love it too much ever to sell it.'

'Well, I've sweated enough,' he agreed. 'And I don't aim to sell right away. We've got to get it cleared first. Then it'll fetch more. So far we've just worked this side the brook.' He added: 'We've agreed we'd work together till we've got the makings of three farms here, Mima. Most of what we've cleared so far is on my land; but we'll get twenty acres or so of Jason's cleared this year, and Matt's next year.' He said cheerfully: 'But after I'm squared up with Matt and Jason, anyone comes along and pays my price for my land can have it.'

Mima did not speak. Matt, watching her, said quietly: 'I'll never sell. I'm going to stay here and marry and farm and raise a family. It suits me here.'

Joel laughed. 'You like this part of it, where we're gaining all the time, something new every day; but you'll get tired of it when it comes down to little jobs over and over and nothing to show for them.' He brought coals and started a smudge against the mosquitoes. 'Knocking down great trees, setting a twenty-acre bonfire to send a torch up to the stars — that's big. A man don't get tired of big jobs. It's the little jobs, chopping brush instead of chopping trees, pulling weeds, and feeding pigs, and milking cows — that's what gets to be a chore.'

Matt stuck to his guns, and Mima began to wash the dishes. The men sat around the smudge, their pipes going. Matt was sure of the enduring charm and beauty of a farmer's life, and Joel was equally sure of what he meant to do. Jason said nothing. Mima listened while she worked, and sometimes when Joel insisted on his arguments she shivered a little as though she were cold. Dusk turned to darkness, and she built up the fire for light enough to see by and finished her tasks. Sambo cleaned up the scraps on the ground, and slept by Jason's knee. Mima left them talking when she went in and climbed to her bed in the half garret; but she was still wide awake when they came in, and she was awake after they all slept in their beds below her. They were so near. The cross beams which supported the garret were so low that a tall man might bump his head on them. Jason always snored, Matt sometimes, Joel seldom. She had come to know them by the sounds they made, sleeping six feet below where she lay. She lay wide-eyed, wondering what she would do if Joel sold his land and moved away.

*   *   *   *   *

That was a troubled summer. Drouth hurt the crops, filling them with concern for the winter that was coming; and as the summer ended there was a hanging in Thomaston. A man named Jeremiah Braun from Damariscotta way was tried by court-martial on a charge of guiding a foraging party of British soldiers. He was sentenced to be hung, and the word ran up and down the river. Some said Braun was a half-wit and that General Wadsworth would just scare the man and then turn him loose. Nevertheless, Braun was well and duly hanged, on the Tuesday following his sentence; and ripples of rumor about the execution spread in all directions. The ugliest report was that the hanging was an accident; and Matt Hawes heard this when he went to meeting in Warren, and came back with circumstantial detail.

'The General meant no more than to make a spectacle,' he reported. 'So a great gallows was put up on Limestone Hill, and Braun was set in an ox cart with his hands tied, and hauled up there. Outside of the soldiers, not many came to see the show. It was thought it would not be gone through with. They made Braun stand up in the cart, and tied his hands and blindfolded him, and put the rope around his neck; but some say there was no order to drive the oxen out from under him. Some say a hornet stung 'em, and some say it was a boy that threw a rock at 'em. There's no one will say he gave them the brad; but anyway, they started, and pulled the cart out from under Braun, and there was no order to cut him down, so hung he was and dead he is.'

Jason Ware exclaimed: 'Gor ram! That's bad!'

'There was a lot of talk about it,' Matt agreed. He added: 'And I heard that there's fighting against the American war in England. Some say the King has run away, and Lord North with him.'

Joel laughed. 'I'll believe none of that.'

'Colonel Wheaton told Mrs. James, and she told me.'

'It's a lie, all the same,' Joel insisted. 'Men get to be plain fools when there's a war and fighting. They'll believe anything that's told them, and pass it on for true. They'll not stop to think could a thing be so.' He said in a grim amusement: 'They told us in the army that Hessians had split hoofs, and a tail with a barb on the end of it tied up flat against their backs, and horns in their hair — and there were some believed it.'

Jason argued: 'This about the King might just be, Joel.'

Joel said in friendly derision: 'Have some sense! D'ye think the King would be so stubborn he'd give up his throne and his palaces and his horses and his jewels, just because he couldn't have the fun of sending soldiers to get their combs trimmed in colonies he never saw and never will see? Why man, the war means a lot to us, but I'll lay odds there'll be days at a time the King never gives a thought to it. You'd never see him ske-daddling out of England, with his tail between his legs, yelp-ing at every jump: "I want to be let to shoot me a Yankee!" '

He laughed, then added soberly: 'Men are all the same, wherever you find them. They mostly do what they think is right — or what they want to do — or what they have to do. They're mostly just about like you and me.'

Mima asked, smiling a little: 'Even the refugees?'

'Well,' Joel admitted with a grin, 'I'll leave out the refugees.'

Matt said, laughing: 'Trouble with you all, you stay up here in the woods all the time, never get out to hear what's going on. That's one reason I like to go to meeting. You get a chance to talk to people, and to listen to them. You ought to try it some-time.'

'I haven't been to meeting since we came up here,' Mima remembered. 'I'll go with you, some day, Matt.' She laughed at the others. 'I guess they'd never go.'

Joel said: 'I might fool you.' He said to Jason: 'It'd make their eyes stick out if you and me did go, Jason.'

They joked about the matter all that week; but Mima was more than half serious in her desire to go to Warren, and on the spur of the moment, the following Sunday, she and Joel and Jason decided to go. Matt stayed at home, declaring that he did not want to lose his reputation by appearing in such company; but the others paddled down the river and walked across the carry. Mima afterward was sorry. For one thing, she was offended by Mr. Urquhart, the minister. There was something in the man's eye which made her uneasy; and she told Joel so on the way home.

'He looked at me all over,' she said resentfully. 'And he held onto my arm. He's not a good man. I'll not have him hold forth to me again!'

They laughed at her heat; but she went no more to hear Mr.

Urquhart, whose marital confusions were sufficient evidence that her feeling had some ground.

She was sorry, too, to have heard war talk on every side, after meeting. In the remoteness of Sterlingtown it was hard to remember that the Colonies were still fighting for that independence to which they had laid claim; but the talk they heard at Warren of Cornwallis ravaging the south and Washington helpless outside New York made the winning of independence seem a doubtful and a distant thing. There was no longer need of scouting parties to watch for marauders this far up the river, but in Warren and Thomaston the militia were ready and alert. A man named Nat Palmer, leader of a refugee band which ravaged the shores of Muscongus Bay, had been captured and convicted of aiding the enemy; and he too was sentenced to be hung. But Braun's execution had been condemned by so many and commended by so few, even of the most zealous patriots, that at Warren many were sure he would never see the gallows; and a few days later they heard that he had in fact escaped from Colonel Wheaton's barn where he was confined awaiting execution.

* * * * *

In mid-October, Philip's new house approached completion, and Philip and Mima's mother invited everyone within easy distance to come for a house-warming. Jess proposed to organize a day's hunt for all comers, to divide the men into teams and make it a competition. Philip contributed a ten-gallon keg of rum for the winners; and the day was set a week ahead. On the appointed morning, Mima's axe, splitting kindling for the breakfast fire, woke the three in the first gray light of dawn; and they started down-river as soon as they had eaten, Mima staying behind to finish her work. But she hurried to be done; and she was not an hour behind them. Bela had finished her canoe late in September. It was worked so thin that she did not draw it up on shore for fear of breaking the

delicate sides. She moored it on a running line attached to a
'dead man' thirty feet from the bank. Today she drew it in and
loosed the fast and paddled across the pond. A rock in the
bow balanced her weight in the stern. The canoe was light
enough so that she could lift it herself — and Bela had showed
her the knack of swinging it to her shoulders — yet it was big
enough so that it would carry two people if they were careful.
Bela had worked it out of a great pine, and braced it with ribs
and thwarts, and laid a ceiling lengthwise to distribute the
weight when one stepped into it; and compared to the clumsier
dugouts made in haste by men less skilled than he, it was graceful as a bird.

She met Joel and Matt Hawes as they emerged from the river
into Round Pond, setting out for the day's hunt Jess had
planned; and other dugouts followed them, the men all paddling hard. Joel called, as the two canoes drew together: 'We've
got this side the river, Mima; Jess the other. He and I are
captains.' The dugouts met and passed, Mima's drifting, the
others racing for the further shore. 'Be back an hour before
sundown,' Joel shouted over his shoulder. They hurried on.

She tallied Joel's men in the floats that followed; he and
Matt, Jason and Bela, Moses Hawes and 'Bijah. Mose and
'Bijah swung to the south shore of the pond, Jason and Bela
started up the river; Joel and Matt held on to their own landing. Mima smiled to watch them race away, as eager as boys
at this game they played. She paddled easily down to Seven-
Tree Pond and called young Philip to help her lift her canoe
carefully ashore and cover it with branches to keep it from
drying out in the sun. Bela had pitched it well, but even this
October day was warm and fine, and sun would do the craft
no good.

The new house stood back from the pond almost a quarter
of a mile, at the foot of the hill where the woods began; but
they had not yet moved into it. In the old house, near the pond,
Mima found David's Bess nursing little Joel, and the other

babies were already asleep side by side in the great bed. She stayed with Bess till Joel was satisfied, watched him in a chuckling delight till his lips parted and he slept, and took hold again and tried once more to eat, till sleep and satiety overcame him.

'He's fat as a little pig, Bess,' she whispered. 'He's beautiful!'

Bess laid the baby gently down and tucked him in and led the way out-of-doors. They went past the barn and up toward the new house. Mima asked: 'Who's Jess got for a team?'

'Eben and Dave,' Bess said. 'They've gone up north of the pond. Jess and Johnny went toward Crawford's, and Rich and Jacob went down the pond on the other side.'

'Didn't Ez Bowen come?

'No.' Bess explained: 'Since that squabble Prance had with Lucy at the Colonel's barn-raising, we don't hardly see them.' She added: 'Phin Butler's here. He hurt his foot so he didn't go hunting. Cousin Mily came with him. She's up visiting Lucy. They've gone off walking in the woods, him and Mily.' She laughed. 'I noticed his foot wa'n't hurt too bad for that! She's a real pretty piece!'

'I haven't seen her since she was a young one,' Mima confessed. 'Not since the day Johnny and Lucy moved up here. Is she pretty as Lucy?'

'Prettier,' Bess declared. 'She's sixteen now, and filled out handsome.' She added with a smile: 'The men all look at her as if they'd like to bite her.'

They came to the fire. The day was for the season mild; yet it was cool enough so that the fire was an attraction. Mima stopped there for a moment with the others, then went on with her mother to inspect the new house. It was half again as big as the house by the pond, built of squared logs dovetailed together at the corners, smooth inside and out. The main part was bigger than the cabin by the pond, divided into two rooms with a great stone and clay chimney in the middle; but also there was a sort of wing, in which were two rooms, and there was a garret in the main cabin where Jess and Eben and Jacob and Philip would sleep. Susie would have one of the small rooms; Philip and Mrs. Robbins the other.

Mrs. Robbins, her eyes swimming with pride, took Mima to see the great fireplace, with an oven built in beside the hearth and an iron bar set solidly at both ends for a high crane, and a shorter crane on a pinned hinge that could be swung out over the hearth.

'Pa says the stones will burn out in a few years,' she admitted. 'But it'll do till we can get bricks enough to do it right.' She said happily: 'It'll be a comfort, Mima, having things to do with, and room for my furniture, and a good cellar and all.'

The cellar was tremendous and impressive, and in one place where the soil was sandy it had been rocked up. 'There's a rock drain to keep the water out of it,' Mrs. Robbins pointed out. 'And when we haul our boards on the ice this winter, Pa's going to build shelves and bins and all. He says he'll get glass for the windows, soon as it's safe to fetch things from the westward.' She made Mima admire the smaller rooms. 'Pa and me'll have one,' she explained. 'And long as you ain't at home, Sue'll likely sleep in the other, and the boys up-attic.' She looked at her daughter. 'Unless yo're thinking of coming home, quitting your job?'

'No,' Mima said. 'I don't look to come home. I guess I won't ever come home to live, Mother.'

'Joel — said anything, has he?'

Mima shook her head. Joel had said he meant some day to sell his land and go back to the westward; but Mima would not let herself remember that. Maybe it wouldn't happen. 'No,' she said.

'There's times I'm worried about you,' Mrs. Robbins confessed. 'Up there with three men.'

'They're real good to me,' Mima assured her. She added: 'Matt's the nicest of them, Mother. I've got to know them inside out.'

'I sh'd think you would,' her mother agreed.

'Matt's always the same,' Mima said. She smiled. 'He's even good-natured before breakfast. Joel is one way sometimes, and another way another. He's either up or down. Jason grumbles a lot, but he don't mean a thing. He just sort of seems to feel like he has to growl and complain. But Matt's easy to get along with as a dog.'

Mrs. Robbins looked at her sharply. 'Changed your mind about Joel, have you?'

Mima laughed a little. 'I guess it isn't my mind, where Joel is concerned, Mother. Maybe Matt's worth a dozen of him. I don't know — nor care.'

'Joel tried any tricks, has he?'

Mima shook her head. 'I might be a man, the way he treats me,' she said, almost ruefully.

'Well, you never was a girl had any foolishness in you,' her mother commented. 'I guess he knows it.' She added, in a dry amusement: 'And a man works as hard as Joel and the others do, he's too tired, come night, to have much foolishness in him, unless rum starts him, or unless he's like a dog running around hunting for it.' She added: 'I notice Joel don't go to Warren much since you moved up there.'

'I guess since Fanny was sick he's changed some,' Mima suggested.

'You get along all right with him?'

Mima's cheek tinted faintly. 'I don't know as I've been alone with Joel any time at all, only that night I carried the vittles up-river and stayed. We talked some, that night. Slept mostly, though.'

Mrs. Robbins made an impatient sound. 'If he wa'n't a fool, he'd have married you by now.'

'He can't, Mother! They agreed to work all together till they've made three farms. They've cleared mostly his land, but now he has to help clear theirs.'

Mrs. Robbins nodded. 'I know it. All the same, the time for folks to get married is when they want to. Some way always turns up so they get along; but if they keep waiting and waiting, either they cool off or they burn up and do some damage.'

Mima laughed. 'We ain't come yet to where we want to,' she confessed. She hugged her arms across her breast, looking down across the cleared land to the pond. 'I do,' she admitted. 'But Joel don't. Joel ain't in the notion to marry me nor anybody else, not yet anyway.' She hesitated, remembering that day when she had fled toward home and crossed the river on thin ice, removing the poles which made her crossing possible, so that Joel when he came broke through. That day, if he had overtaken her . . . Her pulse stirred at the thought. 'He hasn't said a word,' she repeated. 'It'll be time enough to start worrying about having to wait after we both know we're waiting.'

'Well, of course,' Mrs. Robbins commented, 'with all three of them there all the time, you don't have much chance alone, either one of you.' She laughed at some sudden memory. 'Mima, I'll give you my grandma's whispering rod. It's with the things in the storehouse. In Grandma's day, a boy came sparking, bundling wasn't thought of. He and the girl had to sit in with the rest of the family, so they'd talk through the whispering rod, the way you used to do when you were young ones, playing with it.' She added: 'Pa and me never used it. Times had changed in my day. Bundling was a lot more satisfaction. Joel's bunk's right under where your bed is, ain't it? You can run the rod down through the garret floor so he can reach the end of it. You might have to cut it off some.'

Mima smiled. 'I guess I'll wait till he's got something he wants to say to me,' she decided.

They came out of the house to join the others and saw two men approaching from the landing. One was Colonel Wheaton. 'There's old Whistle Britches,' Mrs. Robbins commented. 'Now we'll be deef all day, listening to his bellering!'

As she spoke, the Colonel shouted a greeting, and Philip and Ebenezer by the fire turned and saw him and answered the hail and went down to meet the newcomers by the barn. Mima asked: 'Who's that with him?'

Mrs. Robbins did not know. She and Mima joined Bess and Bet and Lucy while the children went racing to greet the newcomers. Mrs. Robbins said: 'Lucy, it's about time Mily and Phin Butler came back. They've be'n gone long enough.'

'I guess they've got a right to walk,' Lucy retorted. Mima thought Lucy began to have a sharp tongue, a scolding tone.

'As long as they keep walking!' Mrs. Robbins agreed. 'But they've be'n gone long enough to walk to Warren and back.'

The men yonder had returned to the house, and Mima saw her father bring out a jug which went around. She watched them, half-listening to the talk here by the fire. Lucy was in a spiteful mood. She had just realized that she would have another baby in the spring, and she resented it.

'Jimmy ain't two years old yet,' she said, 'and Lucy's just gone seven months. Makes me feel like a cow that comes in every year. As if I didn't have enough to do with the two I've got, and the house and all!'

Bet smiled. 'I noticed Johnny kind of had his foot in his mouth this morning, like he didn't dare call his soul his own.'

'I've give him a piece of my mind steady ever sence I was sure,' Lucy admitted. 'I've combed his beard for him. I told him this was the last, and it's a-going to be!'

Mrs. Robbins said scornfully: 'I hate a fool, Lucy! Don't talk like one.'

Mima thought enviously that Lucy, two years younger than herself, already had two babies. She spoke her thought. 'I wish I was you, Lucy. Here you've got two birds in the hand and one in the bush, and me not even married yet.'

'Well, it's high time you was!' Lucy told her. 'Living with three men! It ain't decent!'

Mrs. Robbins turned swiftly toward them; but Mima checked her. 'Hush!' she said. 'I can speak for myself.' And she told Lucy: 'I don't worry much, Lucy, about what other folks call decent or not. The only one I care about what they think is myself. I've got to live with myself the rest of my life. I aim to keep myself good company for myself, that's all.' Lucy looked at her, silenced by something in Mima's tone; and Mima said quietly: 'Worrying and fretting about what other folks think of you don't get you far, Lucy. For one thing, other folks don't all think the same, so you please one and don't suit another. Please yourself, if you're wise.' Her tone was almost stern. 'You sit still a minute and see what you think of yourself and the way you're talking.'

Lucy, after an instant, sprang to her feet, her tears a torrent of contrition, throwing herself in Mima's arms. 'I'm sorry, Mima. I'm awful sorry! I could've cut out my tongue the minute I said it.'

Mima kissed her, but Mrs. Robbins said: 'It'd be a sight more to the point if you cut it out before you said it!' She spoke in a lower tone. 'Look at them coming, Mima. Something's wrong.'

Something was wrong indeed. The stranger with Colonel Wheaton was Ben Burton, whom Mima remembered, and he brought the news of Arnold's treason, and every other matter was forgotten for a while thereafter. Colonel Wheaton was in a storming fury that did not diminish. Mima thought it wonderful that he could continue to be so blusteringly angry so long. Ben Burton had little to say. She thought there was a fund of quiet strength in him. No doubt there was strength in Mason Wheaton too; but too much of it was dissipated in wordy threats about what he would do to Arnold if he caught him, and to all traitors. Mima watched her father while the Colonel talked; and she saw his countenance settle into grave, deep lines. He spoke at last. The Colonel had begun to curse Arnold's ancestors and all his works; and Philip interrupted him.

'Hold on, Colonel,' he said. 'Don't take in too much territory. Arnold may be all you say now; but he went up the Kennebeck, and he was at Saratoga. He had good parts!' He frowned at his own thoughts. 'This that he's done didn't come from wanting money, I figger. It come from thinking too much, till he got confused in his head.'

Wheaton cried furiously: 'God's Nails and Britches, Robbins, you going to stand up for a traitor?'

'Hold on,' Robbins repeated. 'Calling names don't settle anything.' And he said, groping for words: 'The thing is, we're all Englishmen. We've been brought up to it; yes, and to be proud of it, too. And we had a right to be, only sometimes England gets her a bad king. But when you and me were boys, Colonel, nothing was thought of except that we were English and always would be. Well then, the King and us had some troubles and they got worse and we started to fight for what we 'lowed we'd ought to have, so he called the lot of us traitors and rebels! So about that time folks begun to say: "Rebels be damned. We're independent! We're not English no more!" '

'And we're not!' the Colonel cried. 'And I'll hang the man says we are!'

Mima looked around. The day was fine, the sun shone, autumn colors were at their peak across the pond and all about, fine clouds sailed the sky. They were alone here, secluded and secure, and a while ago their lives had been serene; but now this ugly tale came to sadden some of them and anger others.

Her father was speaking. '... so everywhere there were a lot of men couldn't rightly decide whether they were for the King or for the Colonies. Some were one way one day and the other the next. Some — like Flucker — plumped for the King; and we made them leave the country. But mostly we were men like me that don't know much only to work and pay their debts and try to get along. We're apt to be too tired, come night, to do much thinking.'

He shook his head. 'It's the thinkers I'm sorry for, times like these,' he said. 'I'm sorry for the men with brains enough to see that there's two sides to everything; to see that maybe it's just as wrong to burn a Tory's house as it is to burn a patriot's.

Men like that, they've had a time of it, ever since this started, trying to decide which side they really was on. Some have gone to the King, and some have come our way, and some haven't decided yet.' He seemed to have reached the point toward which he had been laboring. 'I'd say Arnold was one that hadn't decided till now,' he said. 'He's fit on our side, fit hard, and it didn't suit him; so now he's gone over to the King. I wouldn't wonder but there's a lot like him.' His eyes hardened. 'But Colonel,' he said, 'the time's come when every man has got to decide. Where there's a war, a man has to take sides, if he's a man. If a man ain't for us, he's ag'in' us; and either way, we've got to know.'

Colonel Wheaton had been impressed into silence. 'What are you getting at?' he demanded.

'Don't know as I know,' Philip confessed. 'Only — Braun got hung, but Nat Palmer got away. John Long got away. Waldo Dicke comes and goes and no one touches him. I say we ought to put a stop to that. We ought to decide, all of us, which side we're on.'

The Colonel said doubtfully: 'There was plenty, good men too, blamed the General for hanging Braun.' He added honestly: 'That's why Palmer was let get away.'

'I reckon,' Philip assented. His tone was stern. 'But from now on we've got to do different. There ain't no in-betweens in a war. A man's got to be one thing or t'other.' He shook his head almost wearily. 'A man's got to stop thinking, in war time, Colonel. Thinking's poison. You can't be thinking what you're doing when you kill a man. Arnold thought too much — and so did them that let Nat Palmer get away out of your barn.' He added: 'No offense meant, Colonel.'

'None taken, Robbins,' the other assured him. 'Palmer got hold of a nail and picked his handcuffs, that's all. Maybe he could have been stopped if he was watched close. I'm not saying. But I can see what you're getting at. We've got to do less thinking and more fighting.' He laughed and added: 'Next time we nab a Tory, Robbins, we'll turn him over to you.'

'So do!' Philip agreed. 'I mean what I'm a-saying. Give him to me and I'll see he's put where he belongs.' He seemed to relax; grinned a little. 'I've talked my throat dusty, Colonel. How about you?'

4

THEY stood around the fire in the cooking ditch near the new house; and Mima heard a shot off to the northwest toward Round Pond and thought someone of Joel's team had made a kill. The men talked themselves thirsty, and turned to their drinking. Colonel Burton drank nothing but water, and Mima remembered what Captain Watson had told her about him and about his father's death, on that day when they all came up the river on the Sally sloop, and how her own thoughts had clung to Ben Burton for a while. But that was before she saw him. He was a fine figure of a man, bold and strong, handsome, a respected leader among his fellows; yet the sight of him that first day stirred her not at all. Nor did it now. She remembered with a faint amusement at herself that she did not even now know whether he was married or not! Was it that his very virtues dulled her interest in him? After that day she had thought more of Phin Butler, the bound boy, the somewhat stupid toiler, than of Burton. She could feel some affection for most men: for 'Bijah, who had boldly sought to lead her into casual dal-

liance; for Bela who from his first coming had paid her a boy's
devotion; for Jason, always surly and grumbling; for Matt
whom she liked — loved perhaps — as she did Eben, her
brother; for Colonel Wheaton, that blunt, harsh, profane, loud-
mouthed, drunken man. And as for Joel, who drank more than
most men, who was heedless and laughing and irresponsible, a
light lover of any roadside wench, with no virtues she could
name and many easy vices, when she thought of him, her heart
stirred. There was something deeper than reason in this,
something beyond explaining. She looked at Ben Burton, that
admirable man, and almost hated him for bringing today the
news of Arnold's treason, which had turned what should have
been a merry day into a dour and sober time. Why could he
not have kept his news to himself — or stayed away?

A cool breeze from the pond chilled her, reminding her that
winter was coming and the long wait for spring. Her mother
said dinner was ready, and when they began to eat, Phin
Butler and Mily came down through the pines from the hill
behind the new house. Mima did not see them till Mrs. Robbins exclaimed:

'Well, I might know you'd be here when there was eating to
be done! Where you been all morning?'

Mima turned then as Mily answered. 'We were up on the
ledges in the sun,' she said. 'You can see all over, and it's fine
and warm.' Mima thought she had never seen anyone so
beautiful. Mily's bright hair was always escaping its bonds,
her lips were a scarlet line always a little moist, her skin was
like cream, her eyes a kitten's. She was small, inches shorter
than Mima, her figure surprisingly mature for her years.
Mima went to speak to them both, welcoming Mily, reminding
Phin that he had been her guide on her first coming here. Phin
grinned in a red embarrassment, jerking his head in that
familiar way he had, as though trying to speak. He was not a
vocal young man, but Mima remembered he had talked freely
enough when they walked up from Warren alone; and Mily

prettily demanded to know why Mima never came to Thomaston to see them. 'You just stay here all the time!' she protested. 'I don't see how you stand it.'

'Why, we keep busy,' Mima told her. 'We're too busy to think about standing it or not.'

'But you don't have any good times! It'd drive me crazy!'

'We do have good times,' Mima insisted. She smiled a little, thinking of her own happiest moments, guessing they would not appeal to Mily. 'Mostly they're just sitting and talking, but we have barn-raisings and huskings and all. We get a lot of fun out of them.'

Mily laughed, tossing her head. 'It wouldn't suit me. Sitting and talking isn't my idea of fun. Is it, Phin?'

Phin grinned again, and Colonel Burton called him. 'Phin, you got your discharge from West Point. Hear about General Arnold?' Phin went to join the men, as though relieved to escape Mily's teasing; and Mily said critically:

'Phin's awful stupid sometimes! Just sat, all morning!'

Dinner was eaten late. Afterward the men sat smoking and talking in the shade, and Mily with them. Mima thought Mily wished to be near Phin. The mothers went down to the other house to tend the babies there, and the afternoon passed sleepily. As the sun fell lower in the west everyone gathered at the landing to wait for the return of the hunters; and Philip Robbins brought from the house the keg of rum that would be the prize for the winning team. Colonel Wheaton said gustily when he saw it:

'Robbins, if I'd known the prize, I'd have been out all day, a team all by myself. I could bite a moose to death for ten gallons of rum!'

'It don't have to be a moose,' Philip told him. 'Everything counts. A moose scores a hundred, and a grown bear seventy-five. Twenty-five for cubs, and anything down to one tally for birds and critters.' He said with a chuckle: 'Ducks might win it. Dave told me he's got a place baited and a pigeon net all set. He looks to catch two-three dozen ducks.'

'I've heard guns,' Colonel Burton said.

'Each man had three charges of powder,' Philip explained. 'They was planning to set snares and all, besides.'

Phin Butler said, his neck pumping like that of a cooing pigeon: 'Johnny 'lowed he'd get him a few bears, him and Jess.'

Philip chuckled. 'They won't if they have to burn as much powder as they did that bear they treed on the island out there. Remember, Ma? I'd started for Warren, and there was so much shooting I thought the Indians had come; came back a-running.'

Mima remembered, smiling at the memory; and Phin, his tongue loosened by the rum, said: 'Johnny don't 'low he'll have to shoot 'em. He claims he can run a b'ar to death!'

'Some of these old she bears don't run so good,' Philip commented. 'Not if they've got cubs around.'

Mima said: 'There's a float coming down the river. I can hear the paddles.'

Joel and Matt were the first to return. They had killed a yearling moose up the brook west of Round Pond, and they brought back its saddle and hind quarters and the liver and some gobbets of tallow. Mily was loudest in her applause, her eyes shining, telling Joel what a wonderful hunter he must be, demanding that he recite to her every detail of the kill; and Joel did so, laughing at her eagerness, watching her lips parted in wonder and her cheeks where the color came and went. She clung to his arm till he finished, and she said then with shining eyes: 'I guess you must be awful brave to kill a great big moose!'

Joel grinned. 'Brave as all get out,' he assured her, and Bet caught his other arm and in an absurdly exact imitation of Mily's flattering tones, said:

'Now tell me too, Joel! You wonderful big man! I want you to tell me all to myself!'

Everyone laughed at that except Mily; and Mima saw that the child was hurt, and put her arm around Mily's waist and said: 'Don't you mind their teasing, Mily. You be just as excited as you want!'

'I don't care,' Mily insisted, 'I do think he's wonderful!'

Mima laughed and said, with a teasing eye on Joel: 'That's all right. So does he!' She saw his brow lift, and he chuckled; and when she turned away she caught Matt's glance upon her thoughtfully.

The other floats presently began to arrive, each with its bag of game. But after Joel's moose, the rest for a while was small fry; a pair of geese, a beaver, two porcupines, a fox, three salmon netted out of the river, a dozen or so of snared rabbits and partridges, a few squirrels on which men had used up their shot charges coming home. David arrived with two dozen wood ducks and a few over and dolefully declared that was the only game he had seen all day. Mima thought he pulled too long a face, suspected he had something in reserve. Joel's team held a substantial lead till Johnny Butler and Jess, the last to return, came across from the Mill Farm with two bear cubs. Johnny was grown almost gray. With his hat off, he looked like an old man, though his face was young. Jess reported that Tuner, David's dog, had treed three cubs for them in a pine toward Crawford's Pond. Two of the three appeared to be twins, but the other was larger, almost full grown.

'We shot him out of the tree,' Jess explained. 'He came down all spraddled out. Tuner had chased them a ways, clear out of hearing of Dave; but we heard him barking treed and got to him first. The big one we shot was about done when he hit the ground, and Tuner went for him. He tried to run, and Johnny after him, and Tuner got him by the leg and throwed him, and Johnny killed him with one whack with a club.'

He laughed and went on: 'Johnny come back bragging how he'd run a bear down, and saying he never saw the day he couldn't outrun a bear. I clumb the tree to shake out the cubs. They got out on a limb, so I took my knife and whittled at it till it broke; but before it broke, the old she bear had come around, and Tuner took after her; so he was gone when the two cubs went down. One of the cubs hit the ground, and Johnny clubbed him; but the other landed on a leaning tree and run down it just like a squirrel, head first. He lit running, and he kept on running, and Johnny put after him. I near laughed myself out of the tree.'

'It outrun me,' Johnny confessed. 'But it w-went uphill.' He spoke like a man who has been wronged. 'I'd have c-caught it on the level.'

Philip had to decide whether the moose was worth more on the score than a yearling bear and one young cub. 'It's a near thing,' he confessed. 'Johnny, if you'd outrun the cub, your side would win easy, but as it is, I'd say you lose.'

Then David said triumphantly: 'Hold on. If it's as near a thing as that, these here ought to swing it.' He produced two black ears, and he explained: 'I kept them till now, just so Joel'd think he'd won. Tuner put that she bear up a tree finally. It took us a hell of a time to get to where he was; and she was too big to lug after we killed her. I wouldn't wonder if she'd go three hundred. There's the ears off of her.'

But Joel loudly protested the claim. 'Ears ain't a bear,' he argued. 'Maybe you just outrun her, the way Johnny claims he can, and sliced 'em off as you went by. But that don't go. You had to kill her. I got to see a dead bear to count.'

'I don't go around scalping live bears,' David told him. 'Far as that goes, you didn't fetch back your moose, either!'

'That's all right,' Joel pointed out. 'A bear can travel without ears, but a moose won't go far without no back end to him! Half our moose is dead, anyway. There it lays; but I don't see your bear. No sir, I claim we win.'

Partisans supported each one in the argument; but Philip shouted them down. 'I'll do the deciding, boys,' he told them. 'Ten gallons of rum was the prize. Well, you can split it. With ten gallons for twelve of you, there ought to be enough for to-night, anyway!'

With this judgment of Solomon he satisfied them. They

stayed to start the rum, and Mrs. Robbins and the younger women began to select from the day's bag what would serve to feed them all. While they cleaned the game, young Phil went to build up the fire in the cooking trench. Time was needed for the meats to cook, and the hunters spent the interval drinking grog, straight watered rum that could be sweetened with maple syrup from the spring boiling if a man wanted it so.

And around the grog tub they digested the black news of Arnold's treason. Mima, dressing ducks by the waterside, could hear them. Joel once or twice had seen the General, and so had Ben Burton; and every man there knew Arnold's greatness. Most of them felt something like a personal shame and grief, because this man now brought by his own act so low had been a mighty figure in their eyes. But only Colonel Wheaton was loud in angry cursing. The others were more apt to follow Philip's lead.

'All is, the man thought too much, till his own thinking got him in a dither,' Philip insisted. 'War's no time for thinking. All you can do is follow the crowd, do what the crowd does. Let you change step, or fall behind, or get out of line, and they'll rip you like wolves.'

Joel suggested: 'I say a man always has a right to think for himself.'

'He can think as he likes, but he'll do as he must — and thinking different only makes him unhappy in the doing.'

The news damped the occasion. The men were grave; the rum took not so much hold on them as usual; and when food was ready, they trooped up to the new house and ate almost in silence, in groups around the fire. As darkness fell, the fire had been built up to light the scene; and Mima, sitting at one side with Bet, watched the still faces of the men, bronzed or bearded, their eyes gleaming in the firelight. Mily stood near Joel, and Mima said:

'Mily's pretty to look at, Bet.'

'Pretty as anything,' Bet agreed. 'Prettier than Lucy. That

yellow hair gets the men, too. But she's a flighty little piece making up to every man around. Ma says her mother was the same till she settled down, and Lucy's that way too!'

'Mily'll settle down soon enough,' Mima told her. 'She's still a young one.'

'She's old enough to fill out her dress,' Bet pointed out. 'And she lets the men know it, too. It's high time that dress she's got on was let out, if you ask me.' Then she said contritely: 'I hadn't ought to talk so, but I guess I'm jealous. I never was pretty the way she is. I feel like an old woman along of her.'

'She'll be a fine woman,' Mima insisted. 'Make someone a good wife, the way her mother did Uncle Oliver.'

'She'll never marry Phin,' Bet predicted. 'Not unless it's a force put.'

'She likes him.'

'He's been the only man around, anywhere near her age, all day; and he works for Uncle Oliver, so she sees him all the time. A girl like Mily, and her age, goes for any man in sight.'

'Phin will make a good man,' Mima suggested. 'After a while. He's been off soldiering, and it takes a spell to get the army out of a man.' She asked: 'Why didn't Mose Hawes come today, and bring his Mary?'

'She's three months along,' Bet explained, 'and she's taking it hard. Sometimes you do, the first one. Mose says she can't hardly keep anything down till dinner time. She's in Warren, living with her folks. He's up here most of the time, working on his house, to get it ready to fetch her up-river before winter sets in; but he's in Warren today.'

'I haven't seen her yet.'

'She's be'n up two-three times with Mose.' Bet said teasingly: 'I noticed Mily made up to Joel, Mima. Shouldn't think you'd stand for that!'

Mima laughed. 'If she didn't she'd be funny. He's the best man here.'

'He fair licked his lips, lapped it up like a cat likes cream,' Bet insisted. She said in a sudden tender passion: 'Mima, don't you let her get him away from you!'

Mima shook her head. 'Hush,' she said. 'Don't talk foolish, Bet. It's cold. Let's get up to the fire.'

The group around the fire was quiet. Usually there would have been some merrymaking; but there was no hilarity in them tonight. The news of Arnold's treason was like a shadow across the countenance of every man; the failure of the corn crop this summer with its warning that short rations might before spring be the rule was a fact no head of a family with children depending on him could forget; and winter was near, its breath on the breeze that came up from the pond. Not even the roaring fire could warm them all; and Mrs. Robbins and Bess and then Lucy moved away down to the house by the pond where the children slept. By the fire Philip and Uncle Eben, Colonel Wheaton and Ben Burton were the centre of the group, the younger men listening to them as though their utterances were gospel; and Mima and Bet stayed with them for a while. The rum went around, but soberly; they were heavy with hearty eating, and they were all used to go to bed at dark and so were sleepy now. Mima saw Jake's eyes close and his head nodded on his breast as the older men talked. Johnny Butler slipped away to find his Lucy and take her home. Rich came to speak to Mima and to sit by Bet, but presently they too departed, while the slow pendulum of talk ran down. Jason said at last:

'Joel, what say? Time to start up-river?'

But Joel shook his head. The talk had turned on hunting, and Joel started to tell one of Sambo's exploits, and Jason from simple pride in his dog stayed to listen and forgot his desire to go home and presently took his own hand in the telling.

'He's helped kill thirteen b'ars this season,' he declared. 'Treed 'em or kep' 'em treed. You holler b'ar anywhere he can hear you and he'll come a-running. He'll follow anybody that's

going hunting, and he'd sleep with a gun under his head if he
was let.'

'He came up to my place every day I was there this summer,'
Colonel Wheaton declared. 'Why, that little white dog will
chase a bear just like most dogs chase cows; keeps nipping at
their heels till they swing around after him. Then he just keeps
out of their reach.' He added with a chuckle: 'Seems like a bear
is kind of ashamed to have a little white dog put him up a tree;
so mostly he'll keep going till Sambo's got him all wore out.'

'He's the best bear dog anywhere around,' Jason averred,
and he related one of Sambo's exploits. Then David Robbins
said a bear had been stealing his corn.

'I aim to build a log trap and catch him,' he said; and they
debated the relative merits of log traps and set guns.

'Trouble with a set gun, you're apt to forget it and shoot
yourself,' Philip declared. 'Tripping over the string. Take it a
log trap and bait it with fish guts, or some rum and syrup in a
sap trough, and you'll get your bear every time.'

David was reminded of one of Tuner's performances and began to recount it, and Mima slipped away and went down to
the house where her mother and Bess were sitting by the fire,
the babies asleep on the big bed behind them.

'I'm going along home,' she said. 'They might talk half the
night now. They're telling about their dogs.'

Mrs. Robbins protested that she did not know about Mima
going off up-river to the cabin with no man to look out for her,
and Mima laughed and said there wasn't a thing to be afraid
of; but when they went down to the landing to help her put the
light canoe into the water, they found Matt Hawes there. He
rose from the bank as they came down the path, and Mrs. Robbins was startled and cried out.

'Who's that?' she demanded. He told her, and she protested:
'Well, my land, do you have to scare a body to death? I thought
you was a bear!'

Matt laughed. 'They're killing all the bears, up around the

fire,' he said. 'I've heard all the stories twenty times.' He
added, almost diffidently: 'I saw you come down this way,
Mima, thought you might be going home, thought I'd go along
with you.'

She hesitated. 'I dunno as my canoe will carry two, but you
ain't as big as some. We'll try.'

Mrs. Robbins said: 'Well, it's a relief to me you're going with
her, Matt. I don't like her traipsing around at night alone.'

'I'll take care of her,' Matt promised.

Mima yielded the stern seat to him, and Mrs. Robbins and
Bess called good night to them as they turned up toward the
river. Matt shifted his weight, and Mima said warningly: 'You
have to sit easy or it'll throw you.'

'It's nigh as light as a bark one,' he agreed.

'I never saw one of them.'

'I have, one that an Indian made. But you'd step through it
if you stepped heavy.'

Mima said nothing. There was the crispness of frost in the
air. The moon, a few days past the full, was not yet risen; but it
was brightening the eastern sky and lighting the pond till as
they turned up the river the trees wrapped shadows around
them. She was careful not to dip her fingers as she paddled. In
summer, when the water was warm, to do so was cooling and
delightful; but not tonight.

Halfway up to Round Pond, Matt said slowly from the bow:
'Mima, I came a-purpose to go home with you.'

She felt a curious whisper of surprise. She had not till then
thought much about Matt except to hope his weight would not
strain the canoe. He seemed now to wait for her to speak, but in
the end he went on without word from her.

'Since you came to work for us,' he explained, 'I've been
thinking we're a sight more comfortable.'

'I'm real glad. I've tried to keep things nice.'

He said, as though encouraged: 'I don't know as you'd ever
thought about getting married?'

'I dunno as I have, Matt,' she confessed. She was not moved
or excited. She liked Matt, liked him better than she liked
Jason. Joel did not even enter into the comparison. Trying
just now to understand herself — Matt seemed for the moment
to have no more to say — she thought that perhaps she did not
like Joel at all. That night she and Joel spent together up-river
had been friendly and fine; she liked him then. But most of the
time he made her mad; walking the ridgepole of the barn when
he might have been killed, going off to Fanny that night of the
barn-raising, talking about selling his land here as soon as it
was cleared, drinking too much with Colonel Wheaton. Sometimes she wanted to smack him!

'Well, I have,' said Matt steadily.

'You can't figure on marrying till you get a farm made and a
house of your own,' she reminded him, thinking of herself and
Joel.

'I can be thinking about it,' he insisted. 'I have been. I guess
it don't hurt to plan ahead.'

The canoe emerged from the river into Round Pond. During
their passage from one pond to the other, the moon had risen
and now illumined the pond ahead of them and the further
shore toward which they tended. Matt spoke again, and she
listened, paddling easily, a slow excitement in her.

'I'd aim to do right, Mima,' Matt said, steadily. 'I'd be good
to you, and you'd make any man a good wife and make him
proud.' He hesitated, then continued: 'I dunno as there's anything I can say to talk you into it. I guess you know me as well
as I know myself, and I know you, too.'

When she did not speak, he said: 'I used to think it was Joel
for you, the way you looked at him and all. But since you've
lived with us, you're just the same to all of us. I don't know but
you come down harder on Joel than you do on Jason or me,
when we mess up the cabin or something.' He added: 'And I
was watching you today when Mily was making up to him. She
was all over him, but it didn't bother you, and I guess if you —

if it was him — it would have.' He spoke quietly. 'So if it ain't Joel, maybe when I can get my house built you'd want to marry me.'

She was faintly irritated by his reference to Mily, and by his failure to understand her better. 'Well, I wouldn't,' she said curtly; but then when he did not speak she was sorry she had hurt him. 'Don't feel bad, Matt,' she said. 'You're a hard worker and you'll make some girl a fine husband.' Her voice rippled with something like a laugh. 'Only, don't let her boss you, Matt. You're too easy for your own good, maybe. If she wanted to, she could keep you jumping. You make her toe the mark when you do get her.'

'I kind of hoped you'd see it different,' he confessed. 'I'd just as soon toe the mark for you.'

She felt a sudden impulse to tell him the truth. 'If I had any sense, likely I'd marry you, Matt. You're — well, no girl could ask to find a better man. Joel's a lot of things he hadn't ought to be, and I know he hasn't any idea of marrying anybody. But I'm going to marry him some day, in spite of him.' She laughed in a broken way. 'In spite of everything,' she said.

For a long time after that he did not speak; but his paddle stopped, and since her strokes without his guidance made the canoe turn off its course, she held her hand. They drifted aimlessly toward the reedy shore. He said at last:

'I guess I was wrong, then. You're right to want Joel, Mima. I've been through hell on trucks with him. Take it when you're in a hobble and he'll always get you out. The trouble is, when there's nothing happening — he'll go looking for it. I don't know as he's a marrying man, Mima.'

'I don't know as he is, yet,' she agreed, amused at her own frankness, glad for the night which made it possible to say things that could not be said in daylight. 'But he's going to be.'

He dipped his paddle again. 'If you ever want me,' he told her, 'I'll be around.'

'You'll find plenty that'll have you if you want 'em.'

He said ruefully: 'Whereabouts, I'd like to know?'

'Take a trip down t'Warren sometime — with Joel. There's girls enough there.'

'Joel ain't be'n to Warren since the drowning,' he reflected. 'Not to stay the night, only to go and come the same day. He's different, since then.' He added, as though realizing this for the first time: 'There haven't any of us be'n away overnight since you came to live at the cabin.' They approached the shore and he swung the canoe to lay it along the bank while they stepped out. He secured the fast and pulled the light craft off to the mooring, and then they stood a moment together and he said, half-laughing: 'You might get him, at that. I hope you do!'

She touched his arm. 'I'm real sorry, Matt. There's plenty girls in Warren.'

He looked across the pond, nodding dubiously. 'Mebbe,' he said; and then he said: 'Here they come.' They could as yet see nothing, but she heard the paddles, and Matt said in surprise: 'Say, they're in a hurry! What d'you reckon for?'

Half guessing the reason for that haste, Mima slipped away up the path to the dark cabin and left Matt to wait for them there by the landing. She climbed to her bed in the garret, smiling to herself, hurrying. She heard Joel's angry voice at the landing, heard him come running up the path as she slipped into bed. Then he spoke to her from below.

'Mima! Mima, you all right?'

She said sleepily: 'What? I guess I was asleep.'

He came halfway up the notched log that served as ladder, till his head rose above the garret floor near her feet. 'You all right, are you?' he insisted.

She spoke wonderingly. 'Why certain, Joel. Why? What's wrong with you?'

He said almost resentfully: 'I didn't know where you'd gone to.'

'Matt fetched me home,' she explained. 'Good night.'

He descended the ladder again, but slowly, as though still

unsatisfied. The footsteps of the others were coming toward the door. She heard Jason say with a dry chuckle something about a hen that had lost its chickens. Matt did not speak. Joel roused the banked fire, to give them some light. She lay listening while the three men went to bed, happy because Joel had missed her and come jealously racing home. She thought of that day he had run as far as the river to overtake her before he broke through the ice so that his heat was cooled. She wanted, in a mischievous delight, to tell him to go cool his head in spring water tonight.

She heard him bank the fire again at last, heard him turning wakefully in his bunk below where she lay, long after the others were asleep.

5

A WEEK after the house-warming, an eclipse of the sun gave them a foretaste of the dark and gloomy days to come; and November brought first snows and began to skim the ponds. They faced the winter with uneasy minds. The summer's drouth had hurt the crops, so that to last till spring they had on hand only scant supplies; and in November, a new anxiety came to them from the outside to cause them all concern. The town of Warren, although the assessors had caused Philip's land to be put up to be sold at auction, found no profit in the transaction; and at the November town meeting a committee was appointed to try to compel him to some settlement.

Since he was the largest landholder resident in Sterlingtown, and the founder of the settlement, the other men there would stand or fall with him, but at first they did nothing. Philip went to Thomaston to ask advice from Colonel Wheaton, tramping the long miles through the few inches of snow already on the ground. When he came back, he said the Colonel advised that they write to the General Court, to present their grievances; and Joel reported this to Mima.

'Colonel's right, too,' he said. 'If we don't, they'll tax our land right away from us. Philip ought to call a meeting.'

He and she were alone in the cabin, Jason and Matt sledding home a load of firewood. Mima shook her head. 'He'll never do that,' she said. 'He'll stand alone. As long as he's the only one in it, he won't ask the rest of you to stand up for him.' She hesitated, then went on: 'Somebody's got to take the lead in a thing like this, Joel. Father's the biggest man in town, but some day he'll be old and then someone else will have to take over and be leader in things. Why don't you ——' She smiled. 'Well, why don't you sort of elect yourself captain, and tell them what to do?'

'I've no license to, no more than anybody else.'

She spoke carefully, shaping her thoughts. 'I think when everyone thinks a thing ought to be done, and someone says: "Come on, let's do it," he's the captain from then on. They think he's an able man, because he told them they ought to do what they already wanted to do. If you start out doing that, you'll be the one people will always look to, to tell them what to do.'

He chuckled at her shrewdness. 'Only thing is,' he argued in an amused tone, 'I don't know as I want to be Captain. The officer is the one gets shot. If I start any trouble, Warren will be taxing me next.'

'That's right,' she agreed. 'You wouldn't want to take any risks.'

Her tone had been without reproach, and she turned away; but she saw his cheek red, and she was not surprised when he said sharply: 'Hold on! Don't try to get me mad, Mima!' There was a sudden strength in him which made her still and happy. 'Now let's talk it over. It's all right to say we ought to do something; but what are we going to do?'

'You want to figure out ahead of time just what you want them to do; be all ready to tell them. You call a meeting, and tell them just what it is that might happen, and tell them what to do, and they'll do it; because they won't have time to think of anything better. Colonel Wheaton says a petition to the General Court. If that's right, you ought to have one all written out ready to sign. Maybe get some of them to sign it ahead of time, or to promise to. It's just like sheep going over a fence, Joel. Soon as one shows the way, the others follow him.'

Joel chuckled. 'You're a clever one, for a woman,' he admitted. 'I'll try and see what I can do.'

* * * * *

Joel found it easy enough to call a meeting of them all at Philip's house to discuss this matter of the tax. The day set proved to be stormy, half a gale blowing from the northwest, snowing a little, and sternly cold. They gathered in what Mrs. Robbins always called 't'other room'. Joel, as he had taken the lead in calling the meeting, likewise directed the proceedings; and Mima, in the background with her mother, watched him proudly. Joel asked Philip to tell them first how this matter of the taxes stood; and Philip, calmly and without heat as befitted the occasion, told the tale.

'Ain't much to tell,' he said. 'Will Boggs told me the assessors had voted to tax me, and I told him he was welcome to tax and see what he got. So I didn't pay anything. Captain McIntyre was constable; but he didn't seem to get far collecting from me; so here the end of November they voted a committee to come see me and settle it somehow. Committee was Mose Copeland and Will Lermond and Bob Montgomery. They wanted to know what I'd be willing to pay, and I 'lowed I wouldn't pay anything. I told them we'd asked them to lay out a road from Warren to the line and they hadn't done it, and I didn't see anything for us to pay taxes for.' He hesitated. 'So there she sets today,' he said and was done.

Joel spoke in turn. 'If Warren can tax him, it can tax all of us,' he pointed out. 'Colonel Wheaton thinks we ought to put it up to the General Court. He's pretty sure they'll settle it our

way. Colonel says he'll sign a petition, and I'll sign for Jason
and Matt, because our land is all in my name, so far. Phin Butler owns some land up there, that he got from Taylor, so he'll
sign; and Matt has wrote out a petition that's suitable. Matt, go
on and read it, let's hear how it sounds.'

Matt was red as an apple with embarrassment at this sudden
eminence. Nevertheless he unfolded a sheet of paper and read
his composition.

' "To the Honorable, the Senate and House of Representa-
tives of the Commonwealth of Massachusetts, Dec. 1780." '

He broke off to explain: 'Colonel told me how to say that and
the rest of it, the words and all. I didn't know.'

They nodded gravely, and he read on:

> The petition of the subscribers, inhabitants of a plantation
> called Sterlingtown, in the county of Lincoln, humbly showeth,—
> That the said Sterlingtown is an entire new settlement, consist-
> ing of nine families and a few single men.
>
> That three of the said families have been settled about four
> years, two about three years, and none of the others more than
> one year; and several of them obliged as yet to depend on their
> friends at the westward for support.
>
> That Sterlingtown, and the settlements therein, are situate at
> a great distance from any other settlement.
>
> That we have no other way of passing to said plantation from
> other settlements only through the woods, or up St. George's
> River, part of the way by water and part by land; but the pass-
> ing that way is prevented nearly six weeks every spring and fall
> by reason of the ice.
>
> That we have waited on the inhabitants of Warren (by our
> committee chosen for that purpose), requesting them to lay out
> a road through the woods from the settlements in their town to
> the line between said Warren and Sterlingtown; but they utterly
> refused to have anything to do about said road, but only would
> consent that we might clear out a road (without the same being
> laid out), the length whereof would be about six miles, as it
> must run, crossing St. George's River twice in its way, which
> would require two large bridges.
>
> That, in December, A.D. 1778, a large barn belonging to Mr.

Robbins, in which was stored almost all the grain raised that year by the (then) inhabitants of the place, was consumed by fire, with twenty tons of hay; which brought the inhabitants into great want, and occasioned the loss of ten head of cattle that winter.

That we lie exposed, as a frontier settlement, to the scouting parties of the enemy from Majorbagaduce, who, often passing this way, keep us in continued alarm; and, by order of Gen. Wadsworth, we have the summer past, and yet do keep up a watch and scouting party to discover and detect them.

And lastly, notwithstanding all these our difficult circumstances and sufferings, we were taxed by the assessors of Warren in the year 1779; and they seem further determined to assess us in all the taxes.

Wherefore your petitioners humbly pray your Excellency and Honors to take our case under your wise, just, and paternal consideration, and grant that we may be exempted from paying taxes until we are in circumstances to bear the burden thereof. And, as in duty bound, shall ever pray, &c.

He finished, and looked doubtfully around. Mima, while Matt read, had been shaking with excitement. If Joel succeeded in this first essay at leadership in plantation affairs, it would add to his stature in his own eyes and give him a sense of his own responsibilities; and if he succeeded by following her advice, he might remember that fact. She was desperately anxious that he should succeed; and watching the men while Matt was reading, she saw approval in every countenance but one. Only Ezra Bowen made no sign.

She could guess to some extent the reason. His farm ran along the Warren line; he went down-river more often than other Sterlingtown folk; and his wife since her quarrel with Lucy Butler had little contact with her neighbors here, preferred to make friends in Warren town. It was not surprising that Ezra should hesitate to commit himself to an action which Warren might resent and for which the town down the river might undertake reprisals. So while Matt was still reading, Mima left her place to move to Joel's side; and she whispered to him:

'Have them all sign that want to, Joel, before you have any talk about it. If you let Ez Bowen talk, he'll never sign.'

Joel nodded; and when Matt finished, the thing was done as Mima advised. She had quills sharpened and ready; and one by one the names were set down. Ezra when his turn came looked dubious, but he signed without a word; and when the last name was affixed, Joel sanded the petition and folded it again.

'Phin Butler's coming up next week,' he said. 'He'll take it to Colonel Wheaton, and the Colonel will see it goes where it's meant to.' He laughed. 'I forgot to ask if anybody had anything to say; but long as we've all signed, I judge we're agreed, and there's no sense talking now.' He looked at Philip Robbins. 'It's a cold day. I could handle a mug of rum.'

Mrs. Robbins said hospitably: 'A hot toddy's what you folks need.' She had made during the summer gone some elderberry wine. She put some to heat over the fire, added maple syrup, and then stiffened it with rum. The men stayed a while, drinking at first soberly; but the brew was a potent one, and their voices began to rise. Jason was sometimes made truculent by drink, and it was so with him today. Usually inclined to silence, he plunged now into one argument and then another as the strong drink went around.

It was full dark before Mrs. Robbins dismissed them. 'There, you'd better go along, the lot of you,' she said. 'Or you'll freeze to death on the way home.' Jason wanted to argue that point with her, but she laughed at him, told him to go on and sleep it off. Outside, Moses Hawes spoke to Joel.

'You all come by my house,' he proposed. 'I'd like to have you see Mary, and see how snug we're fixed.'

Joel said doubtfully: 'It's some out of our way.'

'We can go from there around behind the hill and down along the brook to Round Pond, Joel,' Mima reminded him. 'It's full as short that way.'

Jason said loudly that it was shorter. 'And we'll make Mose give us some rum,' he declared. 'I'm dry as hot ashes!'

'I'll do that,' Mose agreed. So they went with him. He had brought home his bride a month before, but Mima had not yet seen Mary Hawes. The cabin was small, no more than twelve feet by sixteen; but it was well built and well fitted.

'And I can build onto it, any time,' Mose proudly pointed out.

Mary kept them all for supper which she and Mima cooked together on the hearth; and there was rum and hot water and sugar till even Matt was in a singing mood. Outside, the wind blew cold and colder; but here they were warm, and the men sang while Mima and Mary cleaned up the supper things, and there was plenty of rum. Mima had to urge them at last to start home. She won Matt first and then Joel; but it required their united persuasions to get Jason under way.

They followed the brook bed toward Round Pond, and even in the forest the half-gale directly in their faces was bitter. Joel was in a lively humor, drunk more with his first taste of leadership than with his potations; but the cold quieted the others and him too, and they plodded at last in silence through the night, their heads bowed against the wind, Sambo silent at their heels.

At home they found the fire gone out. Joel had banked it when they started for Philip's house after dinner; but either it was then already too low to stay alive or he did a careless job. The ashes were still warm, but there was no life in them, and the cabin was cold as a tomb. The wind searched every crack between the logs, and little trickles of air like icy needles came in everywhere. Jason had frosted his nose, and his temper was surly with drink. He blamed Joel for the dead fire, and told him so, angrily; and Joel answered him in anger and their voices rose and they came near blows till Matt quieted them. They were still quarrelling when Mima climbed to her bed in the garret. The walk home had left her shift moist with perspiration; and when she had been abed a few minutes, the cold penetrated through all the covers she could heap over her, and her damp garments chilled her through. Matt and Joel were lighting the fire — Jason sullenly refusing any share in that task — and she heard the snap of the flint and presently the crackle of flames: and the light danced on the rafters close above her head. But the wide chimney, in a northwest wind like this one, drew too well. It sucked most of the heat from the fire up the chimney. Mima heard Joel say with a rueful laugh: 'I'm toasted in front, and my backside's getting frostbit.'

'You have to stand right on top of the fire to get any good out of it,' Matt agreed. 'There's cracks in the walls big enough for a squirrel to come through. We'll have to chink them some.'

Joel clapped his arms to warm himself. 'It's a hard night to sleep alone,' he said. 'Be cold as be-damned when the fire goes down. Br-r-r! Makes your teeth chatter, just standing here. Wish we had our old bunk back tonight, so we could roll in together.' He put a fresh log on the fire, and flames took eager hold.

'I'm a mind to haul in with you,' Matt declared. 'There's room for the two of us.'

'So do,' Joel agreed. 'The less room the better, a night like this.'

Jason muttered something and went to his own bunk. It was in the corner opposite the fireplace, at the foot of the log ladder which led up to the garret where Mima slept. Matt's was in the corner diagonally across the cabin; Joel's directly below Mima's bed, along the front wall, its foot against Matt's. Joel said: 'Roll in, Matt. I'll mend the fire.' He laughed. 'With you between me and the wall, and the fire on the other side, I'll sleep warm if you don't.'

He stood, by the sound of his voice, near the hearth. Mima heard Matt lie down, and for a time no one spoke, and the only sound was the crackling of the fire. Joel pushed the logs together, and Matt began quietly to snore. Joel asked in a low tone: 'Warmed up any, Jason?' Jason grumbled wordlessly; and Mima, shivering herself warm, became conscious of a tension of anger in the air. Jason was in an ugly mood; Joel humored him with the tolerant gentleness of long friendship.

After a while Joel went to bed with Matt. The fire would burn for an hour or two without replenishing; and on such a night as this they would keep it alive. She heard Joel make himself comfortable, and then there was silence on them all except that Matt seemed by the sounds he made to be sleeping peacefully enough.

But Mima did not sleep. Time passed, and as the fire burned down, the pattern of the shadows on the roof above her changed and changed. Presently she heard a sound below her and was instantly awake. The notched log that served as a ladder to reach the garret where Mima lay rested against a cross beam at her feet. She felt the beam stir a little as someone's weight came on the log; and then Joel spoke sharply below her.

'Jason! What are you up to?' His feet thumped the floor.

Jason's voice, when he spoke, was level with the garret floor, near Mima's feet. 'Two in a bed's the only way to keep warm,' he said, in a growling tone. 'I don't aim to sleep alone.'

Joel spoke cheerfully enough. 'Still cold? Why, you can sleep with Matt. Come down.' Mima, lying still, listening, heard him move nearer the foot of the log ladder.

Jason came no higher, but he held his place. 'Who says so?' he challenged.

Joel drawled: 'Why, what difference does it make who says so? You come down, Jason.' Then, as Jason did not obey, he spoke again, this time more sharply. 'Before I pull you down!'

The log ladder shifted, and Mima heard the soft thud of Jason's feet as he dropped to the floor. He said grimly: 'You'll never pull me down.'

There was a queer silence, broken only by the crackling fire. Mima knew the two men must be facing each other, ready for violence; but before the first blow was struck, Matt said, laughing as he spoke:

'You two act like a couple of strange dogs! Be sensible. You're grown men!'

Jason said in an aggrieved tone: 'Well, I'm God-damned near froze! You two are warm together. It ain't right, Matt.' He added in a ludicrous solicitude: 'I guess she's cold, too! She's bound to be!'

Mima almost laughed at the sudden change in his tone. The cold had taken the fight out of him. Joel said in a warning whisper: 'Hush up, she's asleep!'

Jason protested: 'She can be asleep and still be froze.'

Matt suggested cheerfully: 'You get in with Joel, Jason. I'll be warm enough alone.'

Mima, smiling, thought they were all still a little drunk, with rum and cold and sleep. She spoke calmly from above them. 'There's no sense any of us freezing. Joel, you can bundle in with me.'

No one spoke for a moment. Then, as though he were answering a look, if not a word, Jason said defensively: 'Well, all right, damn it! I just didn't want her froze to death before morning! She's took good care of us. We'd ought to take care of her.'

Matt said: 'This bunk's already warm, Jason. Pile in here.'

'All right,' Jason repeated. 'My backbone's an icicle a'ready.'

Mima heard the bunk creak as he joined Matt there. Joel said awkwardly: 'I'll put another log on the fire.' He did so. He said: 'If you wake, build it up, Matt.'

Matt assented, and Joel after a moment threw a blanket and a bearskin off Jason's bunk up into the garret. Mima sat up to spread them, and he climbed the notched log and helped her arrange their covering.

When they were abed, her back against his body, they lay still and felt warmth embrace them and drive out the cold. But they did not sleep for a while. She lay in his arms, his lips near her ear; and he said in a chuckling whisper: 'Jason's fighting drunk. He'll be all right in the morning.'

She nodded without speaking. Presently he said: 'Well, the tax meeting worked the way you said it would. They did what I told them to!'

She turned her head, her cheek against his, so that she might speak to him without being heard by the men below. 'And Jason did what you told him to, just now,' she whispered. 'Men get in the habit of doing what they're told.'

'How do you know so much about men?'

'How do you think wives boss their husbands? Women always knew that!'

He chuckled, and they lay comfortable and content. He said a little later: 'I never knew you were so little. My chin's on top of your head, and my knees curled up under you. Warm now?'

'Nice and warm. Is your back cold? We can turn the other way after a while, and I'll warm you.'

'Listen to that wind!' Snow like sand rasped across the boards of the roof close above their heads.

She said: 'You wake me up if you want to turn over the other way. If you get cold.'

6

SNOW lay deep that winter, and the winds blew hard. In the woods the heavy blanket settled and packed, only to be replenished by fresh falls; and on Round Pond and Seven-Tree the scouring winds rolled great billowing drifts back and forth across the ice with every change of wind. The ice cracked with cold, and reefs formed where one sheet of ice thrust up above another, and a January thaw flowed all the ice with water that turned the roots of the snow to mush which froze again. The snow was so deep that to fell a tree without leaving too tall a stump involved digging away around its foot. After the January thaw, Jess and the three of the Royal Mess went away to the Madomock after moose; and Mima went home to stay till their return.

But she felt like a strange visitor in the new house. She had never lived there; it had never been her home. Yet she thought she might have felt equally an alien in the house by the shore. All that part of her life was done, as completely behind her as her girlhood in Walpole. When they came to Sterlingtown, Walpole was forgotten; and so now her first years here were sunk in the past, not to be recaptured.

She had never felt this separation so completely as when she came now to sleep for half a dozen nights under her father's roof. She missed her own familiar bed in the garret at the Royal Mess, and it already seemed strange to her on cold nights to sleep alone. Since that first occasion when Jason's drunken advances had led Joel to climb up and share her bed, he did so more and more often. Sometimes he came because the nights were cold; sometimes simply because he wished to talk to her. Then they might lie whispering a while till sleep overtook them. Inevitably they drew together, knew each other better, talked more freely. Joel might say things in darkness, in a whisper, which he would not say by daylight and in a normal tone of voice. She discovered a shy boyishness in him she had not suspected; a diffidence hard to credit.

During this week at home she missed him. Her mother for the first day or two asked no questions; but the third morning, so casually that Mima was amused, she inquired:

'How are you and Joel getting along?'

'Just the same,' Mima said.

'I judge you feel the same about him?'

'I judge I do,' Mima assented smilingly.

Her mother sniffed. 'Well, you beat me,' she said. 'When I made up my mind about Robbins, I saw to it that he knowed it, quick! Joel said anything to you, has he?'

'No.' Mima added suddenly: 'But Matt asked me to marry him, Mother. That night of the house warming. He was awful nice about it. Matt's fine. He's like Eben.'

Mrs. Robbins was full of a lively interest. 'Did he so? I like Matt myself; but he's slow as a snake with frostbite. What'd you tell him?'

'Told him that some day I wanted to marry Joel.'

'Humph! What'd he say to that?'

'He said he had thought that was it, until he saw Mily making up to Joel that day and saw I wasn't jealous!'

'It'd be a waste of time to be jealous of that hot little piece!

She licks her lips every time she sees a pair of britches.' She said shrewdly: 'Joel came that night asking where you'd gone. I told him; said you and Matt went off together. It upset him, I could see that. He yelled for Jason and left in a hurry.'

Mima nodded. 'He was worried, all right,' she agreed. 'But it didn't come to anything.' She added: 'But Joel's different this winter. Maybe Matt told him. He's been bundling up with me, cold nights.'

'Well, that's the first sensible thing I've heard out of either of you. But don't you let him make a fool out of you, Mima!'

Mima laughed, almost ruefully. 'Don't fret yourself. He acts as if . . .' She hesitated, trying to define to herself how Joel did act. 'Well, as if he was scared I'd bite him, or something. We talk a while, and then go to sleep, that's all.'

Her mother chuckled. 'Well, it's a real cold winter,' she commented. 'He may get over being scared, come spring.'

* * * * *

Mima, during these days at home, found her father changed. Philip Robbins had always been a patriot, and he had begun to feel that the eventual independence of the United States was assured; but Arnold's treason for the first time made him doubt it, and this winter he was not content to be shut off from any contact or correspondence with the world. Twice in January he departed down-river to be gone three or four days at a time; and he was troubled when he came home. General Wadsworth when winter set in had discharged the soldiers called to serve the year before.

'He's living there in Colonel Wheaton's house,' Philip reported, 'with no more than three or four men at a time for a bodyguard. I offered to take my turn at it, and Will Boggs went down with me.' And he said: 'With nobody to stop 'em, the English can come at him any time. Colonel Wheaton tried to tell the General to keep a company or two handy; but he couldn't argue with him. Ben Burton says the same. There's got to be soldiers here next summer, or there'll be hell on trucks alongshore.'

Mrs. Robbins said confidently: 'Well, we'll not be bothered up here, whether or no. It's too far for the British to come, and nothing for them to come for.'

'We'll be bothered plenty if the English decide to move over to Thomaston instead of staying at Biguyduce — and they might — and there's none to stop them.'

Mima was troubled by this concern in her father, and she was glad when the hunters returned. They came back by easy stages, with the meat of six moose on their sleds. She went gladly back to the familiar cabin, and she told Joel and the others her father's fears.

'He's going to Thomaston for a week's turn standing guard,' she said. 'And he's talking so much he's got Eben wanting to go, too.'

Joel thought Philip's anxieties groundless, but Jason took them more seriously; and when Philip returned early in February from his guard duty at Thomaston, Jason tramped down to Seven-Tree Pond to hear what news he brought. He came back to report that this winter there were many minor forays upon farms along the shore. 'And there'll be worse before we're done,' he said.

Philip was eventually proved a good prophet, when a party from Biguyduce crept into Thomaston one night and captured General Wadsworth and carried him off. The tale came to the Royal Mess third or fourth hand. Philip heard it in Warren, and Eben came to pass the news along.

'They took him away to Biguyduce,' he said. 'And Pa's gone down-river to see if Colonel Wheaton's going to try anything to get him back again.'

They wanted details, and he said Waldo Dicke had bragged to some in Thomaston that he guided the British force which made the capture. 'They came into the Wessaweskeag River in a schooner,' Eben explained. 'There was a lieutenant and twenty or thirty men. They stayed at Snows' till the middle of the night and then they marched up to town. Hezekiah Bachelder was on his way home from the mill with a bag of meal and they grabbed him. When they came to Wheaton's house, Will Boggs was the sentry; but all he did was whoop and holler.'

Joel said grimly: 'Certain! All Will's good for is selling farms for taxes.'

Eben nodded, and his eyes were hard with rage. 'I wish't Pa'd been there. He'd have shot a couple of 'em, I bet you! They come at the house all sides. The General and his wife were asleep in the front room, and a woman from Boston, and two children; and the guards were in the kitchen.'

'Drunk, likely,' Jason suggested. 'Or asleep.'

'Might be,' Eben agreed. 'Anyway, one of them opened the door, and the Englishmen shot into the kitchen at them, and set the house on fire, and shot General Wadsworth in the shoulder and grabbed him and put him on a horse. They stopped at Doctor Fales' house. 'At Fales was there, and he run off and hid in the woods, he was so scared. They left a soldier there that had a bullet in him. I guess General Wadsworth peppered them good, before they got him. Anyway, they got back to the schooner and turned Hez Bachelder loose and got away.'

Joel asked: 'What happened to Boggs and the rest?'

Eben made a scornful gesture. 'The English turned them loose. Nat Copeland was one of them.'

Joel said respectfully: 'All the same, that took some doing, to come right into town and get safe away. Colonel's house — there's others handy, the way I remember it. I was there two years ago.'

'Were the children hurt?' Mima asked.

'No. The oldest one slept right through it. There wasn't any-body killed, but some say the General is hurt bad; and the soldier they left at Fales' is bad off.' Eben said hotly: 'With the General gone, it's going to be hard next summer; nothing to stop them from coming and robbing and burning any time they've got a mind — unless some of us take a hand.'

Mima heard him in a deep terror. She thought she could not bear it if anything happened to Eben. Matt said:

'We'll keep out of it, Eben. We're safe here.'

Eben said, his eyes on the floor: 'I don't know as I want to set here safe. Hez Bachelder, that bag of meal was about all he had. He'd worked two weeks to earn the corn, and he's got a wife and children. They took his meal.' He spoke with a calm that was more dangerous than any violence of words. 'They were clever to steal the General maybe, and he's a soldier. You can't blame them for that. He could look for it to happen. But they didn't have to steal cornmeal from babies.'

Mima crossed to stand beside him, her hand on his shoulder; and he lifted his hand to press hers. 'They say he kept fighting till they shot him,' he said. 'Then he gave up, and one of the soldiers that was hurt called him a rebel bastard and started to shoot him, but the others grabbed him. Mrs. Wadsworth said they wouldn't let her tie up his arm where he was shot. All she could do was tie a handkerchief around it to stop it bleeding. They made him walk the first part of the way, till they left the hurt man at Doc Fales'. Hez Bachelder says when they got back to the schooner, the Captain tried to make General Wadsworth help launch it, and the General told him to be damned, and the Tory threatened to stick a knife in him, and the General told him go ahead if he had a mind to.' Eben beat his knee with his fist. 'He stood up to 'em! If Pa'd been there, they'd not have got him. Him and Pa'd have licked the whole of them.'

'Well, I'm full as well pleased Philip was home,' Joel declared. 'He'd have fought 'em, Eb; but there ain't any two Yankees can lick twenty or thirty English. Them bayonets go through you like butter. When you see them come at you, the thing to do is keep shooting as long as you can — but then it's time to cut and run.'

'You talk like you were afraid of them!'

Joel chuckled. 'I'm afraid of a bayonet when all I've got's an empty gun, Eb. That's just sense. Being afraid at the right time is the best way I know to keep from getting killed.' He added: 'You know, Eb, it's damned seldom a soldier does any good getting himself killed. The ones that do the most good are the ones that stay longest alive.'

General Wadsworth's capture was a heavy blow, coming as it did just when a strong hand was most surely to be needed; and Philip went to Thomaston to discuss with Colonel Wheaton the chance of freeing the captive.

'But he's against trying anything now,' he reported on his return. 'He figures the English will be looking for something right off, but if we wait a while there might be a better chance.' He added: 'Ben Burton's trying to get a pass to take Mrs. Wadsworth and that friend of hers to see the General, and he'll tip him the wink then that we'll try something first chance we can.'

But it was toward the end of March before Colonel Burton was able to get permission to take Mrs. Wadsworth and Miss Fenno to Biguyduce. Fresh snow had buried Sterlingtown under a three-foot blanket; and Jess and the three of the Royal Mess were off for another foray against the moose. Mima again went home to stay with her mother, and Eben went down the river with his father, to hear the news Burton might bring home.

They came back before the hunters returned, and Eben's eyes were shining. 'I saw John Perry,' he told Mima. 'You remember him?' She did, well enough. 'He's back from Boston, and he's going to fight the refugees this summer. He wants to get hold of a boat and get a commission for her. He told me I could go with him.'

Mrs. Robbins said stoutly: 'You'll do no such of a thing! Pa, tell Eben to talk sensible!'

Mima watched her father; but Philip shook his head. 'Eb's

twenty years old,' he said. 'He's a man grown. We may all be in it before we're done. Ben Burton took the women to Biguyduce, and he's taking them to Falmouth now; but he says the British are going to send the General to Halifax, and maybe England. They won't give him parole or let him outside the fort. The refugees hate him for hanging Braun, and for the scare we give 'em when they murdered Soule.' He added bitterly: 'If they do ship him off to England, we'll be hard put to get anyone to handle things here. We haven't got any generals to spare, and the ones we have don't get anything done. Cornwallis licked the lights out of Gates at some place they call the Cow Pens, here a while back, and Washington can't do anything except watch outside New York, like a mouse watching a cat hole, ready to run if the cat comes out.' He said: 'If the plagued snow would go off, so's we could get around to Biguyduce by land, we might do something this winter. Not much chance in summer, with the Bay full of refugees and privateers and shaving mills. You can't go by water without they see you. When Burton comes back, he'll tell us where they've got the General shut up and all, and then maybe we can figure something.'

But Ben Burton did not come back; and they heard that he too had been captured, on his return trip from Falmouth, and carried off to Biguyduce. By that time, first signs of spring were showing. Their provisions had held out better than they feared; and General Wadsworth's capture and the discussions that followed it kept them from worrying too much about their own straits. Toward the middle of April the ice had gone out of the river, and Colonel Wheaton came up by boat to bring Philip Robbins the news of Burton's capture, and Jess brought the word to the Royal Mess.

'Pa's gone to Biguyduce,' he reported. 'The Colonel says if anything's going to be done for the General, they'll have to know where he's locked up; and he couldn't go himself, because he's an officer, and they'd just lock him up too. Eben offered

to go; but Ma put a stop to that, and the Colonel said it had to
be a man that would keep his head, anyway. He's giving Pa
some business to do with the General for an excuse; and Ma
went down-river with them, to stay at Uncle Oliver's till Pa
comes back.'

Mima watched Joel and the others to see whether they
thought her father's risk as great as it seemed to her to be;
and Joel seemed to feel her eyes upon him, and spoke to her.
'He'll be all right, Mima,' he assured her. 'They'll do no harm
to him.' He smiled in a steady reassurance. He said quietly:
'I wouldn't say so if I didn't mean it, Mima.   He'll be back.'

She passed her hand across her eyes, nodding gratefully.
'Yes, he will,' she agreed. 'He has to come back.' She smiled.
'He has to come back and get his planting done,' she said. She
was grateful to Joel for his reassurance. Last summer he
would not have understood her need of it, would not have read
the message in her eyes. She thought he was coming to be in
many ways like Eben; and she could mark the milestones
which set off the change in him. The drowning had been the
beginning; the drowning, and Fanny's long illness here. He
had not since then gone down-river on one of those forays in
which he and Jason, or he and 'Bijah once were partners. If
he went at all, he had an errand, and he returned — sometimes
after dark — in time to sleep in the cabin. That night she came
home with Matt was another marker; and his assumption of
leadership in the matter of the tax petition had made a difference too. Since he began to share her bed on cold nights,
they drew always closer, so that sometimes he seemed to read
her thoughts as he did now. She thought contentedly that this
was the essence of marriage, this capacity to enter into the
heart and mind of another person, to converse without words.
To that extent she and Joel already began to be married now.

When the talk of General Wadsworth was done, Jess had a
message for Mima too. 'Mary Hawes wanted to know could
you come down and be with her for her baby?' he explained.

'Ma was going to be; but now she's gone. Mary'd rather have you than Bet or Bess, she says.'

'I guess I can,' Mima agreed. She looked at Joel. 'If you can manage here. I can come any time Mose comes to fetch me.'

'You go,' Matt told her. 'We can bach it for a while.' And Jess said:

'She wanted you'd come and kind of stay. The wind the way it is, Mose looks for it to snow some more.'

So Mima went down the river with Jess. She asked when they were alone: 'Jess, is Eben at home?'

'He went with Pa and Ma.'

'I was afraid he did. I wish't he hadn't!'

'He'll be company for Ma.'

She said breathlessly: 'Jess, don't you go?'

'I'm not,' he promised. 'I've tried to talk Eben out of his idea, Mima. Told him we had all the job we could do here. Pa has told me I can have the land over there.' He pointed toward the south shore of Round Pond. 'Between Joel and Mose. I'm going to start clearing it this summer, soon's planting's done. Maybe I'll build a house on it too.'

Mima smiled. 'You picked out a girl down in Warren, have you, Jess?'

'I've looked around some,' he assented. 'But they don't come to suit me, not down there.' He asked with a gentleness like Eben's: 'How're you and Joel coming along?'

'It ain't time yet,' she told him. 'I mean, not for love talk, and love-making. That's a thing, once you start it, it either has to burn up hot or fizzle out like wet tow. Joel can't marry yet. He's got to help clear land for Jason and Matt.' She said surely: 'But he knows, the same as I do, Jess. We're just waiting till it's time.'

Jess chuckled. 'Look out you don't forget to wait, Sis. You know what Ma's always saying about the spring of the year. Sometimes you think a kettle isn't ever going to boil, and then it boils over before you can stop it.'

She said surely: 'I've been living in the same house with Joel
nigh on a year, Jess. Mostly, the others are there too; but cold
nights he tucks in with me, and we can talk and they not hear;
and we know each other pretty well, Jess, know what the other
one is thinking. I don't mind waiting.'

'I don't want to do any waiting, when it comes my time,' Jess
commented. They glided down the river, high with the spring
flood. The dugout picked up speed as the current caught it;
and he drove it with strong strokes. 'Being in love takes everyone his own way, I guess,' he said. A few flakes of fine snow
came lazy down; and he said: 'Guess Mose was right about it
snowing again. Look up, Mima.'

She looked and saw the solid snow masses descending toward
them like a cloud; and the flakes struck her upturned face.
Before they landed, it was smothering all around them, white
underfoot; and by the time she reached the cabin where Mary
Hawes greeted her with a passionate relief, there was already
an inch or more upon the ground. In the morning it was
packed two or three feet deep against the cabin door. Mary's
baby — a girl named Hannah — was born into a white world,
and Mima tended the baby and the mother.

* * * * *

Mrs. Robbins came home without her husband. Philip,
returning from Biguyduce, landed at Camden to hear that
Captain John Long, the Tory, had been captured there.
Colonel Wheaton appealed to him to deliver Captain Long to
the authorities in Boston, and Philip agreed to do so. Eben
went on that journey with his father, and Phin Butler brought
Mrs. Robbins up the river and home.

The day she returned, Mary Hawes was stronger, already
able to sit up in bed, soon to be about again. Her baby was
four days old, and Joel had come down to see how she was and
to find how soon Mima would come back to the Royal Mess;
and Mary told Mima to go along.

'I'll do fine now,' she said surely, 'with Mose to help me. You've given us a good start, Mima.'

Joel and Mima stopped at the new house to see Mrs. Robbins and to hear her report of Philip's trip to Biguyduce. 'He saw the General,' Mrs. Robbins told them. 'But he says there's nothing anybody can do for them without an army to help. The General and Ben Burton, they keep 'em locked up in a barred room in the officers' quarters. That's inside the fort; and the fort walls is twenty feet high, and frazed on top, and there's sentries on the walls, and outside the quarters, and right outside their door too. Then the upper half of their door, it's all open so the guards can look in any time.' She added soberly: 'And pickets outside the fort toward the neck to catch deserters.'

'Nobody could get in at 'em, then,' Joel agreed.

'That's what Philip said. They've got to get theirselves out, if they can.' She added: 'They didn't have anything to work with only a little knife to sharpen pens, and Philip didn't have any chance to carry anything in to them. But he found out the man that shaves them — his name's Barnabas Cunningham — and gave him a gimlet to take to them, first chance he gets. If they could cut a hole in the ceiling of their room they might manage some way, and a gimlet's better than a belt knife for that.'

Mima asked: 'Did Eb have to go with Father?'

'He went to help guard John Long,' Mrs. Robbins explained. 'Philip didn't want to go, but he'd made some talk about it, and Colonel Wheaton put it up to him, said it would give him a chance to see the General Court about the tax business, too; so Philip decided to go, and Eben with him.' She added: 'Eben's bound he'll stay down-river this summer.' Mima saw her mother's eyes sharply fill with tears. 'There's some excitement down there. They look for a hard time from the Tories, and no one to take the General's place. Some of the young ones that can be spared off the farms are going to go with Thompson or Perry, get boats and kind of guard the shore and maybe do some privateering their own selves.' She added: 'Eben wanted to go try to help the General, land up there some foggy morning; but Thompson warn't for it, said it wouldn't do a mite of good, so they've give up on that, and Eb went to Boston with your pa.'

Mima, watching her mother, said: 'They'll be all right, Mother. They'll be home.'

* * * * *

Joel and Mima went up the river together in his float; and the river was still high, so that Joel took his setting pole to stem the current, and kept close to the bank. The day was fine and warm; and the deep snow that had fallen late in April was melting fast. The river ran black between banks of a dazzling whiteness. The buds were swollen and bursting; and any day now the alewives would run. Mima thought contentedly that the fears of famine with which they had begun the winter had proved empty ones.

'Snow's going off fast,' she said.

'Sun's licking it up the way a cat licks cream,' Joel assented. 'But it's late. That holds us up on burning our fell-piece, keeps the frost in the ground, makes it later to get our planting done.'

'I always think a late spring's better. It makes things come fast when they do come, like they were tired of waiting and in a hurry.' He did not speak, and she added: 'And if things are later getting a start, it's not so apt to come an early frost and kill them or set them back.'

He did not speak, but as they emerged into the pond he began to sing under his breath:

> Oh, her cheek it was bonny, her eye it was merry,
> Her ear was a shell and her lip was a cherry,
> Her smile would make any man linger a while
> And she smiled that smile for the gentlemen!

Till a lad came along and he tarried to dally
And dandle and bundle with this pretty Sally.
'I'll lay me,' he told her, 'Just seeing you smile
    'That you've been very kind to the gentlemen!'

'Oh sir,' said sweet Sally, 'There's no harm in smiling
'On any fine lad that's so very beguiling...'

He broke off, and Mima said: 'I haven't heard you sing that since last summer.'

Joel chuckled. 'I always feel more like singing in the spring.'

'I guess everybody does,' Mima agreed. She hugged her arms across her bosom in that unconscious gesture. 'You feel sort of full of things that you're wanting to be doing.'

'Certain!' he assented. 'Take it in winter the bears den up, and the moose don't move out of their yard unless they're driv' to it.' He was amused at his own words. 'In winter the whole world's kind of like a dog sleeping in the snow, in a tight ball with his tail keeping his nose warm. But let the sun begin to warm up, and things straighten out, and the first thing you know, Whoosh! Everything's busting loose at once!'

She laughed without surely knowing why, catching the infection of some welling mirth in him. 'I'll be glad to get home,' she said. 'I feel like I was visiting now, when I'm anywhere except up here.'

'We've kep' it as clean as men can,' he told her. 'But I wouldn't say any of us liked it. We've got used to having you do for us.' He added: 'Matt was saying last night, when he comes to build a cabin, he's going to marry someone. He's been down to see Mose a lot this winter, seeing how snug him and Mary are. And Jason said the same; said he'd ruther spend a winter with one woman than with any two men.'

'I guess that's the way it's meant to be,' Mima assented quietly. She added, on some impulse: 'Matt was thinking, one time, he'd like me to marry him. He asked me.'

Joel said after a moment: 'I know. He told me about that.'

She wondered what else Matt had told him, but she was reassured when he asked: 'You going to?'

'I told him to get over the idea. I guess he has.'

He did not speak for a while. Then he said, a little amused at himself: 'I've thought some this winter . . .' Her heart lifted its beat, but he broke off; said instead: 'You like it here, don't you?'

'Yes.'

'Want to stay on here, probably?'

'Yes,' Mima repeated. 'I like here; and — all of us have started a job of work here that'll keep our children busy, and our grandchildren, and their grandchildren.' She said quietly: 'There'll always be some of me living here. I think if you love a place, the trees and the ponds and the river, it's like you put your mark on it. It never gets rid of you after that.'

He said stubbornly: 'I aim to sell out, when I can get my price. I'd rather live Boston way.'

'So?' she murmured.

'Yes,' he insisted almost angrily. Mima smiled to herself, in a deep sure confidence; but her back was toward him so that he could not see. He said stubbornly: 'It's all right up here when you're young, and want excitement and hard work and all; but I want to do something besides farm all my life.'

'A man's that way,' Mima assented. 'Mostly a woman's happiest taking care of a house and a man and some children — if they're hers.'

He was paddling slowly, in no hurry. The dugout moved lazily across the pond. 'You act as if you liked taking care of us, and our house.'

'I've got so it kind of seems like mine.'

Joel chuckled. 'You act it,' he repeated. 'The way you boss us around sometimes anyone would think we were your young ones.'

'I guess a woman always feels that way, some, about men she sees a lot of. They do so many tricks a young one would do.'

He said, suddenly rebellious, his tone sullen: 'I don't know as I ever will get married.' She did not answer, and he challenged: 'What's the use in it? If a man gets married, it just means he takes on a life job of working and worrying, taking care of his wife and his children, scared to death every time there's a baby coming or a baby sick, or anything. If he don't get married, as long as he don't, he don't have to work only enough to keep from starving, and no one to worry about but himself. There ain't any sense to marrying!'

Mima laughed a little. 'Maybe not, but there's a lot of company — especially when you get old. Just taking care of yourself might get so it wasn't much fun after a while. It don't get you anywhere. I mean, what's the sense of taking care of yourself just so you can go on taking care of yourself? Water in an eddy never gets anywhere till it gets out of the eddy.'

He thrust the nose of the canoe ashore and she stepped out, and turned to help him haul the float up till it lay secure. They faced each other, the dugout between them. His brow was furrowed. He said in a still tone: 'I've thought some that you and me might get married, if you wanted to, when I've got a place to live.'

She said simply: 'I've thought so too, Joel.'

'I guess you would.'

'I guess I would,' she assented.

He stepped around the bow of the canoe to grasp her shoulders with both hands. 'But I don't figure to go on living here,' he told her hoarsely.

'I guess you will, Joel, when the time comes.'

He stared into her eyes, then released her so abruptly it was like a blow. He turned away up the path. After a little she followed him toward the cabin; but he had waited for her, and when she came to him, he said in a challenging anger:

'You're so sure, you make me mad!'

She said: 'I'm sure what I want for you and me, Joel. I've be'n sure ever since the first time you came up here, that time you bought the land. You remember the day we watched for the moose, from the old maple tree?'

He nodded, watching her. 'I've always got on with women,' he said after a minute, half to himself; and he chuckled at his own thoughts. 'You know there's different kinds of women. There's some you get away from soon as you can. There's some you make love to, quick and hot; and they laugh and like it, and that's all you want of them. There's some, you like to talk to them, and to be with them, without ever thinking much about whether they're women or not. And there's some — you want to have a baby with them.' He said: 'You're both the last two kinds, Mima.'

She nodded simply enough. 'That's the kind of woman a smart man gets married to, if she'll have him.'

'I've never made love to you.' He smiled. 'There was once I would have, if I'd caught you, the day I broke through the ice.'

'I know it. That's why I moved the poles, so you couldn't cross the river.'

'Didn't you want to be caught?'

'Not that day.'

He said slowly: 'You're a new kind to me. I've spent nights with women — but that night you and I were together up-river watching for them that murdered Soule — I liked that night better than any night I ever spent with any woman.' He said: 'I've slept with you in my arms and never wanted anything only to take care of you and keep you from being cold.'

Her eyes twinkled. 'Didn't you like sleeping warm yourself?'

'Certain.' He asked wonderingly: 'Why don't I kiss you now? You wouldn't hinder?'

She said quietly: 'I might. You'll have to make up your mind to some things before you ever do kiss me, Joel.'

He laughed. 'I'm about ready to say I'm a damned fool!'

She moved past him, toward the cabin. 'You'll get over that,' she said, mirth in her tones, and went up the path toward the cabin in the pines.

7

THE last snow went off with a
rush. Under the warm May sun, the drifts shrank so fast it
almost seemed possible to watch them settle. The clots of snow
on the branches of the pines let fall for a while a cascade of
bright drops, and presently broke apart and fell away. The
trunks were black with water running down, shining in the
sun. By the third or fourth of May the bare ground began
here and there to appear; and after a few hours of sunshine the
young grass showed faint green. The nights were steaming wet.
A moist fog hung in the air, and the roar of the risen river
tumbling down the rips filled the silent hours of night. A
warm rain helped, and suddenly the snow was gone and spring
came rushing like the river, sweeping north to embrace the
land and woo it back to bearing. Maples were crimson in the
swamp lands, and shad bush was lacy white along the river and
the pond shore, and Joel saw a salmon jump in the pool by the
old maple. Where the sun struck warm on ledgy sheltered
ground, mayflowers came into fragrant bloom; and there were
early blossoms everywhere. Brazenly cheerful robins had been

here for a month, but now the woods suddenly were full of birds, flowing northward like a tide with the coming spring. Hardwoods that had been gaunt and bare the night before spread against the morning sky a delicate tracery of living green.

Philip Robbins came home, proud of having delivered his Tory prisoner safely to the authorities in Boston. His charge for expenses on the five-day trip to the westward and the return journey, in the depreciated state of the currency, amounted to £128, 2 shillings. Eben returned with him; but not to stay. He went down-river almost at once to offer his services to John Perry; and Mima saw him go with a strange deep sense of loss, as though he were gone forever, leaving a place that must be filled. Bela Robbins departed too, enlisting secretly under the name of William Robbins to avoid interference by his father who was bitter against his going. He had told Mima what he meant to do.

'So if word comes that anything has happened to William Robbins of Sterlingtown,' he said, 'you'll know it's me.'

She thought war took men so easily, enticing them away like the strange woman in the Bible, and killed them and maimed them; and a woman could do nothing but bear more sons to fill their empty places. In this spring season, all the world was busy with the business of reproduction. Wherever trees had been cut and bushes cleared away, new growth began to show itself. Lucy Butler's baby was born on the eighteenth, and it was a boy; but that was only one boy, and Eben and Bela were two who had gone, two young men, and Mary Hawes' baby had been a girl, and there were two men gone to war, who might not return, whose empty places must be filled.

Philip when he came home said the General Court would settle the tax question in their favor. 'I talked to them,' he said. 'I had promises enough. They say Warren will have to pay back all the taxes they've collected, and they'll not be let try to tax us again.'

The word came presently that on the eleventh of May a resolution had been passed in these terms. William Jennison brought the news of that vote. He had bought from Doctor Taylor, the year before, the land northwest of the holdings of the Royal Mess; and he arrived to lodge the night with Philip, came up to Round Pond next morning with four men whom he meant to put to work clearing some of his land, and with Ephraim Tucker to whom he hoped to sell a part of it.

Jess and Philip came with them this far. Mima and Joel and the others met them at the shore; and Philip made the introductions. 'Jennison's having as much trouble with Taylor as I did,' he told them; and Jennison explained:

'He heard I wanted to sell some land to Mr. Tucker here, and he told Tucker my land was no good; said it would take a thousand acres of it to keep a red squirrel alive. I told Tucker that Doctor Taylor was a thief and a liar. I had to sue him in March to get my deed, and he's suing me now for calling him a thief.'

Philip said heartily: 'I told you what to look for, man! Best settle up here with us and be rid of him.' He added with a proud chuckle: 'You'd get no purchase doctoring here, to be sure. Nobody's ever sick in Sterlingtown. But the land will take care of you.' And he explained to them all: 'Mr. Jennison's been educated for a doctor.'

Jennison smiled. 'You have babies up here, don't you? Doctors do other things besides doctor sick people. Some day doctors will help women have their babies.'

Philip shook his head. 'Womenfolks will always 'tend to that, I guess, Jennison. That's one time a woman don't want a strange man around. And our women here drop their babies with no more trouble than a mare.' He said: 'You'd best be moving along if you want to get up to your place and back today.'

'I think we'll stay over the night,' Jennison explained.

Philip nodded. 'So do, then. I'm going down-river now, but

Jess'll show you anything you're a mind to see. He knows every tree in the woods.'

Joel elected to go with them, and they set out. Jason and Matt were digging stumps in the cleared land. When they came in for the dinner Mima had cooked, they said the ground was already so dry that it would soon be ready for planting. During the afternoon, Mima was alone and she went to her own small garden patch to try the ground. Its surface when she turned it with her hand was warm from the sun, but underneath, it was cold and wet with the last emerging frost. There would be time enough to plant a week from now, or two weeks. When the soil was ready, the seed sprouted quickly and grew strong.

Joel and Jess returned in the late afternoon, and they were agreed that Doctor Jennison would have trouble selling land to Ephraim Tucker. 'Tucker thinks it's too far to get to,' Jess explained. 'Jennison picked out where he wants to start clearing, and he aims to spot a trail down to where Matt's clearing will be, and make some kind of a road. He told Tucker he would, but Tucker wants to be on the water.' Jess looked at Mima. 'He wanted to buy on Seven-Tree Pond,' he said. 'But I told him that was all took up, except on the neck. He asked about here on this pond, but Pa's already said I could have the land right up to Joel's. I dunno but Tucker might try to dicker for the neck. It's a good piece, but it's mostly hardwood, and he wants pine. He figures if he can get pine handy to water, he can raft it down-river and sell it for enough to pay for the land.' And Jess added: 'I told him yours was mostly pine, Joel.'

Joel nodded. 'Yes, he was talking to me. He's coming down to look at it on his way out.' As though uneasy under Mima's quiet eye, he said: 'It's sightly, up there, Mima. We climbed a hill and I got up in the top of a tree and I could see all over. Kind of a haze today, but I could see smoke off t'the westward thirty-forty miles. They're burning off a big cut-piece over on the Kennebeck, maybe. A clear day, you could see plenty. We'll go some fine day, and I'll show you.'

' I'd like to go,' she agreed. 'I like hills. Here it's all shut in, with the woods and all. We can't see far.' Jess went on his homeward way and she got supper started, and Joel watched her move to and fro. She asked: 'Are they staying up there?'

'They packed in enough to start with, and Jennison set them to building a house. He's going to send what they'll need up-river when him and Tucker come down. They'll be working there all summer, anyway.'

She said: 'I've kind of liked thinking we were the furthest ones, thinking there wasn't anyone west of us.'

'I think Tucker's right,' Joel said. 'Jennison's too far from water. It's all of three miles, and hard going, up the brook to a muddy little pond and then up a steep hill. I'll hit a straight line when I take you over there. It might be shorter, and it will be easier walking. We can spot out a trail.' He added: 'It's real pretty, up on that hill. Some big old oak trees, and ledges, and moss.'

'I'd like to go,' she said again. 'Maybe Sunday, if it's fine.'

'We'd want a clear day,' he agreed. 'Before the leaves are full out. When they get thick, you couldn't see anything.'

She asked, looking at him suddenly: 'Joel, are you going to sell Mr. Tucker your land?'

'I might,' he admitted, not meeting her eyes. 'If he wants to buy.'

* * * * *

Tucker and Doctor Jennison returned on the second day. Joel had gone to work with the others; but Mima was at the cabin. Tucker inquired for Joel; and Mima hesitated for a moment before answering.

'Did you buy some land?' she asked at last.

'Not yet,' he said, and Doctor Jennison explained:

'He's not satisfied to be so far from the water. I told him there might be some he could buy down here.'

Mima pointed to a path through the pines. 'You go along that path,' she said. 'You'll come to where they're working. They're getting ready to burn a cut-piece tonight.' She watched them stride away along the trail. She was cold; yet the sun was warm, the day was fine. There was no reason, no outward reason, why she should be cold, but she was. She went in and fetched a shawl. She felt a deep tremor shaking her, and her teeth wanted to chatter. She thought: I guess I'm going to be sick. Then she told herself honestly: If Joel was to sell out and go away, I guess I'd die. I'd want to die.

Joel did not come back with the others at dinner time. Matt said he had gone to show Tucker his land south of the brook, steep rocky hillsides heavily grown with pines. When Joel did return in the late afternoon, she saw excitement in him, in his voice and in his eyes; and she had no need to ask questions. He told her, without inquiry, what had happened.

'Tucker liked my land,' he said. 'He wanted to see if your father had any he'd sell, so I took him down there and we went over on the neck, but that was too much hardwood and he wants pine. He'd rather have mine. Amory that owns the neck is asking two dollars. Tucker said that was too much for hardwood.'

She asked: 'Did you put a price on yours?'

'I told him to make me an offer.'

'Did he?'

'He wants to talk to Lermond, to see what pine will fetch at the mill; and he wants to find out about spars and masts, see what they'll bring. He's going to let me know.'

Mima's voice was strange in her own ears. 'What would you have to get?'

Joel said after a moment: 'If he was to offer me a thousand hard dollars for the lot, I dunno but I'd be satisfied.'

'Would you sell for that?' she insisted, and he told her in a half-defiance:

'I've been planning all along to sell if the price was right —

and that price is right.' He turned abruptly away, and brought coals and started a smudge fire by the cabin door to keep away the flies.

The others came back for early supper, to be through in time to start burning the fell-piece before it was full dark; and Mima hurried her work afterward and went to watch them. The tract they meant to burn was something over a dozen acres in extent. It was bounded on the south by the clearing they had made the year before, and by the brook which flowed into the pond. It ran west from the pond a quarter of a mile and extended somewhat north of the cabin. In a triangle of which cabin, spring and landing were the corners, the trees had been left standing; but tonight this tract would be an oasis surrounded on three sides by fire. Breaks had been cleared to protect it, and there was no wind worth mentioning, so the three — and Mima if she was needed — would handle the burning alone. She helped fire some of the brush piles prepared along the east side of the tract. A heavy dew was falling as the fire took hold, creeping slowly across the fell-piece, the flames illumining a pillar of smoke that rose straight upward toward the stars. The fire made no trouble, and they had nothing to do except watch warily for any change of the wind. They were all together near the cabin when Jess and Jacob came up from the landing to find them.

'Got word from Tucker for you, Joel,' Jess said. 'He talked to Johnny Butler about Lermond's paying. He's gone down-river now, to see Fales about titles; but he said to tell you if the title was good and you'd take two fifty an acre, hard money, he'd buy.'

Joel nodded, his eyes on the fire; and Mima watched him. 'I've got right around four hundred acres, or some over,' he reflected. 'That'd be a thousand dollars. Thanks, Jess.'

Jess looked at Mima while he spoke to Joel. 'He said you could let him know any time till Tuesday. He'll be at Uncle Oliver's.' He added then: 'I'd hate to have you sell, Joel. We'd miss you here.'

Mima stood a little at one side, and the fire's roar and crackle was in her ears. She felt Joel look at her. Then he spoke to Jason and Matt.

'If I sold, I'd keep out my piece that we've cleared, make it over to you,' he said. 'That'd square it up for my leaving you to clear the rest.' They did not speak, and he asked: 'How do you feel?'

Jason said wrathfully: 'You know damned well!' And Matt added his word. 'Don't you sell, Joel. You'd miss it here, and we want you.'

Joel said doubtfully: 'Well, I don't know. It's a good price.'

No one spoke for a moment. Then Jess remarked: 'Going to be fine tomorrow.'

Joel nodded. 'So 'tis.'

Mima moved a little nearer him. The heat of the fire pressed them back, and she felt it scorching her. She looked up and the stars were fine. The smoke pillar, full of sparks like jewels, mushroomed high above them in a crimson glare. The fire seemed to be within her own body, consuming her. She wondered to hear her own voice seem now so serene and calm.

'If it's real fine tomorrow, Joel,' she said, 'it'll be Sunday. We could go climb that hill.'

*   *   *   *   *

An hour after full dark, Mima left the men together, to watch the fire till it burned down to harmlessness; and alone in the cabin she bathed herself, and thought she would be glad when — soon now — the water in the pond was warm enough for swimming. She had learned to swim well enough, even in hampering garments; and sometimes when she was alone and secure against disturbance, she stripped naked and revelled in the greater freedom thus achieved. The long winters imposed this hardship, that she could not swim; and in the narrow quarters of the cabin she had to pick her times for bathing when the men would be away, drawing the latchstring against their chance return.

She was asleep when they came stumbling home, and thought the night far gone, and slept again and woke before day; and she woke knowing that she had dreamed happily of Eben. Yet the Eben in her dream seemed not to have been her familiar brother, but another, younger and more fair and finely beautiful. She lay half awake a while, trying to recapture that dream; and it was bliss to try, even without succeeding.

In their bunks below her the men were asleep. She waited till full sun before descending from the garret. Out-of-doors she found wood ready for the fire so that she need not use the axe. The morning was warm and misty, but she knew it would clear, and when the men woke and came sleepily out of the cabin, the sun was fine and the sky a cloudless blue.

Joel was the first to appear. He said to Mima: 'Never a better day, by the way it begins. We'll eat and go.' Sunday was a day when only necessary work was done.

'I'll take some bread,' she said. 'And some moose meat. We might stay the day before we're done.' And she asked, watching her fire: 'Will Matt come with us, and Jason?'

'Somebody'll have to keep an eye on the burnt-piece, see it don't start up again; but it don't need all of us.'

So after breakfast, Mima and Joel set out. She had a pouch of bread and meat ready. Joel fetched his gun and horn, and he carried his axe. 'We'll spot a trail,' he said. 'I want to see how nigh I can come to running straight to where we're going.'

'You'll need both hands, with the axe,' Mima reminded him. 'I'll carry the gun.' Sambo watched their preparations with an interested eye; and when they presently set out, he went racing ahead of them and back again, and then settled into a brisk and businesslike investigation of every inch of ground within twenty rods of the course they took. He was a busy little dog, with a passion for bears; and he ignored chipmunks, red and gray squirrels, and every other creature except the one that was his chief concern.

From the cabin Joel set his course at first parallel with the brook, ascending at an easy grade through pines. He had slung the lunch pack on his shoulder, leaving both hands free; and he began at once, although the pine woods were open and clear of underbrush, to spot trees. He sliced away bark on both sides of each tree, so that the blazes could be seen by anyone who followed this trail in either direction. Mima said behind him: 'You don't hardly need to do that through here, Joel. Just scuffing our feet a little in the pine needles on the ground leaves marks enough. If we come this way a few times there'll be a regular path.'

'I know it,' he agreed. 'It's queer how quick you begin to notice paths around, even up this way where nobody hardly goes. When we went with Jennison, we went the same way your father took him, first time he came, last year; and we saw their tracks, or places where they'd walked, all the way to where they hit the line. But I want to spot this trail for winter. That's why I'm doing it high, above where the snow will come to.' He lopped off an occasional branch that hung low across their path, struck off a chip through bark and into white wood every rod or two. She liked to watch the smooth power flow into even these light strokes, from his thighs up his flanks and into his shoulders and arms.

'I guess anywhere men ever have lived, you'll find the paths and the roads they've made,' Mima suggested. 'Maybe the houses they build burn down or blow away or something and never leave a sign, but the paths they made without thinking, just wherever they happened to go, will be there after the men are dead and gone.'

'That's because the animals use them too,' he assured her. 'A bear or a moose don't like busting through the brush any better than a man does. They make their own paths, or they use them that men make.' They reached a low crest from which the ground descended in all directions; and Joel said: 'We don't want to go down grade any more than we have to. When you're trying to climb, every time you take a step down, it makes it that much harder.'

'That's the way with everything, isn't it,' she reflected. 'You've got to decide where you're trying to get to — and keep heading that way all you can.'

He assented, moving on. 'That's right,' he agreed. 'Pick out what you want to do and keep at it.'

'Maybe that's why paths last so long,' Mima suggested. 'I mean, the men that made them weren't thinking so much about the way they went as about where they wanted to get; so they took what looked like the best way, and the next man in the same place, wanting to go to the same place, took the same way, and pretty soon there was a path.'

'I wouldn't wonder but there'd be a road through here some day,' Joel agreed. 'It's a good way to go.' Their course was level for a while, along a slight slope that ran down to the brook on their left, that rose a little on their right. The pines gave way in some degree to hardwoods as the ground ahead of them began to rise; and Joel said exultantly: 'Here's where we start to climb.' They ascended a hardwood ridge where ledges broke the ground, and it pitched upward steeply for a while, so that before they came to easier going they were both breathing more quickly, and dripping with perspiration. The day was very still, the sun warm. At the top of the sharp ascent they paused to rest a moment, and in the sudden silence Mima heard voices somewhere below them toward the brook, she could not be sure how far away. She bade Joel listen, and they stood quietly together, and Joel said in a low tone: 'Jennison's men, likely, taking the Sunday off, going down to our place to visit.'

They stayed where they were till not even Mima could hear the receding voices. For this part of the ascent, Joel had chosen to follow a narrow ravine cut by a spring brook which ran tributary to the brook below; and at its head, he dug out a little basin from which when the water cleared they drank. They had come, he judged, about a mile from the cabin; they presently went on, ascending the rounded shoulder of a rising height, shaping their course by the conformation of the ground, pausing every few paces while Joel spotted a tree. Hardwoods here predominated, although a few young hemlocks and spruce and pine were growing among them. The leaves on the hardwoods were well started now.

'You can almost see them getting bigger, a day like this,' Mima said. 'So warm and all.'

'They'll be full out in another two weeks,' Joel agreed. 'There was a blossom this morning on one of the little apple trees Matt set out when we first came. It's the first time they've bloomed; but most years, they say down at Warren, you won't see blossoms on an apple tree till later than this. About the twenty-fifth of May is as early as they come, and some years it will be into June.' He stopped to knock chips out of a spreading beech beside their path; and when he moved on, he whistled under his breath a lively jig tune which Mima remembered, and he sang the line which finished the verse:

And she smiled that smile for the gentlemen!

But he sang no more of the song just then, falling into an abstraction which engaged him so deeply that she thought he had forgotten she was here. Sambo came back, panting apologetically, to report that try as he might he could not find a single bear; and since Mima had the gun, it was to her he reported. She stooped to scratch his ears, and he licked her hand and swallowed hard and raced away again to try to turn this splendid opportunity to good account. Joel, pausing to mark a tree, said with a grin: 'He's having a real good time.' Mima smiled and they went on. They came to a growth of young spruces packed close together, so that Joel had to use his axe freely to clear a way through them. He attacked them with a sort of passion. They were no more than an inch or two in diameter at the foot, and a single axe stroke for each one was enough. As he cut them, he pushed them aside against their fellows, cutting a sort of trough with slanting sides straight through the thicket. Mima suggested:

'We could go around, easier.'

He said, amused at his own stubbornness: 'I want to lay this trail as straight as I can. Then if anyone comes after us, they'll see I did a good job.'

Mima, happy at some thought of her own, made no further protest. The spruce thicket seemed for a while interminable, and they saw charred trunks of what had been tall trees, some prone across their path, some erect yet lifeless. 'It's an old burnt-piece,' Joel panted; and she asked:

'What would set it afire?'

'Indians maybe, or maybe lightning. Must have burned ten or fifteen years ago.' Their progress was slow, and the black flies clouded around Mima's head, and the sun came baking down. Behind them the trail Joel had cut was as straight as a string, and ahead they began to see the crowns of tall oaks which came nearer till they emerged from the spruce thicket into hardwoods again.

They welcomed the cooler shades and stopped to rest, Joel mopping his brow; and Mima heard a sound strange to her, in the forest to the north of them. It was a rumbling, thunderous roar, but there were no clouds in the sky. She spoke to Joel, but it was minutes before he could hear it.

'It sounds like thunder, sort of,' she said. 'Or like a lot of horses tramping, with sleigh bells on them. Listen.'

He caught it then, as it drew steadily nearer. There was something curiously exciting in the sound, yet it was not alarming; and suddenly Joel recognized it.

'It's pigeons,' he said. 'Coming along the ridge below us.' He caught her hand. 'Come down that way. It's a thing to see.'

She followed him; but they had not far to go before they saw in the hardwoods below them the first comers, and a moment later they were in the fringes of the flock. The pigeons were here by thousands. It was impossible to guess at their numbers. They flowed through the forest like a wave rolling up on a beach and about to break, pouring through the upper branches or just above the tree-tops, dropping down to alight on the untouched ground in front of the advancing horde. They were like a cascade of birds, their plumage gleaming in the sun-flecked forest in every shade of blue and gold, crimson and green, set off against the slaty background of their body hue. Mima was at first too confused by their numbers to see individual birds at all; but as she and Joel stood quietly, there began to be pigeons all about them, and she saw that they were in ardent pairs, perching on every inch of the limbs of the trees, their wings half-extended and quivering with the rapture of the nuptial flight. It was their coo-coo-cooing which suggested the sound of bells. Joel held out his arm, and a pair of birds alighted on it unafraid; and Mima's breath caught and her breast filled with the pounding of her heart. This mating of millions all about them seemed to fill the air with a warm passion, forever rising and as quickly appeased. She tried to speak to Joel, saw his lips move, heard no word he said for the steady throb and pulse of the love note of the birds, the roar of many wings. In the beech woods below them she heard, even above the tumult, branches break under the weight upon them; and Joel caught her arm and drew her away back toward their path again. Behind them the steady roar of wings like thunder, and the undertone of bells, receded till they could speak once more; but they had even then for a while to raise their voices, almost shouting.

'They'll nest along there,' Joel predicted. 'In those beeches. We'll be able to get young ones by the hogshead this summer; more than we can use. They eat better than the old birds, so fat they're like chunks of butter just before they fly. You can push them out of the nests with poles, get all you want.'

'They were mating,' she said. 'All of them. That was a sight to see.' There was a deep tumult in her. The air was still full of the roll and rumble of the wings, the bell-like whisper of that wooing.

'I've heard they'll nest two or three times every year,' he told her. 'The young ones will be ready to fly in five or six weeks. The old birds won't feed around here while they're setting. They'll go off, miles at a time; leave the feed handy here for the young ones that can't hardly fly. You'll see them roll through the woods just like water, churning up everything on the ground and on the trees.' They walked on, Mima silent, still too deeply moved to speak, feeling as though she had witnessed some hidden mystery not meant for human eyes. He was talking, but she scarce heard him, still listening to the tumult now far behind. The wind was against them, and the sound receded, as though the birds were quieter. They came to a knoll from which in all directions the ground seemed to descend, and she thought this might be the summit to which Joel led the way; but he said:

'No, this isn't it. Where we're going is higher, with a big old oak right on top, and it's steeper on the southwest side. We're heading right, as near as I can judge.'

They proceeded straight ahead until the ground began to descend more sharply. 'We don't want to go downhill at all,' he reminded her. 'I'll keep along the edge of this.' He bore a little more northerly, following a course approximately level, and Mima came silently behind him, thinking of the pigeons, of the nests they would build, the young they would rear. The pulse in her ears was like the pulsing of their mating call. Joel was tireless at the business of lopping off small bushes in the way, or low boughs that crossed their path. The ground fell away on their left, and at the end of a half-mile that pitch below them grew steeper while at the same time they saw a steep slope ascending to the right.

Joel called back exultantly: 'This is it, I think!' He turned up the slope. They climbed two or three hundred feet in half a mile more, and suddenly he bounded ahead and struck his axe into the bole of a huge oak which reared its head above those of its neighbors. 'Here it is!' he cried. 'Here's the one I climbed!'

She came there to his side. They were both hot and breathless, and the sun was drenching through the thin leaves. Sambo at their heels now panted hard and looked at them inquiringly. By the foot of the oak there was a sunned ledge warm and smooth, and Mima sat down on it to rest a moment, and lay at length, looking deep into the sky above her, feeling the sun's caress like hot hands along her body. Joel turned aside, and she heard his axe going. He came back with a notched log to brace against the foot of the oak.

'You can step up on this and reach the first branch,' he said. 'After that it's as easy to climb as a ladder. We can see all over to the south and west from the top. Can't see much the other directions. Too many trees in the way; but it's worth it if you want to climb.'

'I'm going anywhere you go,' she said, and stood up again; and he laughed and bade her come along. He swung up on the great bough, and he said:

'Hand me my axe. I'll maybe want to cut off some branches up above.' She passed the axe up to him and he hung it in the band of moose hide knotted around his waist. Then he gave her a hand up; and when she stood beside him, he climbed higher and she followed. Sambo barked at them two or three times, inquiringly; and Joel laughed and called down to the dog:

'No place for you up here, Sam! Go find a bear!'

Sambo sniffed at the packet of bread and meat which Joel had left on the ledge, and Joel warned him off, and the little dog departed on business of his own. They climbed till they came into the topmost branches where the oak's crown spread out in all directions. Joel decided to lop off two or three boughs that obscured their view; and Mima, with one arm around the trunk, held to his belt to steady him while he used the axe till he was satisfied. He had opened a sort of window through the half-grown foliage, and they could look off toward far horizons that were knife-sharp against the blue of the sky. Mima saw, infinitely far away, what she thought were white clouds just peering above the nearer hills. She watched them in breathless silence, and Joel too was hushed now. They sat with the trunk of the oak between them, each with an arm around the tree; and she remembered that they had watched thus from the old maple by the river, the first time Joel came.

Those white clouds so far away did not move nor change their shape. She said at last in a hushed wonder: 'Why, they're mountains!'

'They're the White Hills,' Joel told her. 'I saw them once from off Falmouth when I came up here. There's snow on them now, but they're always white. The Captain said there's some kind of white moss grows on them, makes them that way; but I never saw white moss. Likely it's snow, stays there all the time because they're so high.' He pointed down into the valley below them. 'See that pale green? That's the grass bog beyond the Madomock. You can't see where the river runs, from here. And you can just see a pond off northwest, and another one that way, and some more mountains off there, not so far away. They may be over by the Kennebeck.'

Her eyes were deep. 'Nobody lives between here and the Kennebeck,' she said. 'It's all just woods. And beyond, there's nobody much from there to those white hills; and on beyond the white hills, there's nobody. There are mighty few of us, yet, Joel, to clear up all that country and raise children to live on it.'

He laughed grimly. 'We don't amount to much yet,' he agreed. 'We're nothing but the first maggots on a dead moose. But there'll be more of us.'

'It's a fine country.'

He said: 'Jennison's started his men clearing down right below us here, not more than a mile. There's a sort of level place there, half a mile one way and a mile the other, fine land.'

After a little she asked quietly: 'Joel, do you aim to sell your land?'

He did not answer at once, said at last: 'I've always figured I would, when the price was right. Tucker's price is right. I might go down the river tomorrow and see him.'

'I don't want you to sell,' she told him.

It was a moment before he spoke. 'I don't know as I want to,' he confessed.

'Then what makes you do it, Joel?'

He laughed suddenly, so that she leaned forward to look around at him and see why he was laughing. 'I was thinking of a man in my company under Captain Folsom,' he said. 'We were at Winter Hill, building forts at Lechmere's point, dodging cannon balls while we worked. His name was Hal Tufts. I guess I've told you about him. He was the slickest thief in the army. We were on short rations, and he tricked the commissary out of a side of pork. He and Jim Hall got the pork, and then got a gallon of rum from the sutler and gave him an old summons for debt instead of money. Told him it was a four-dollar bill and the sutler had never heard of such a thing so he took it. Tufts used to brag and blow about how slick he was. He used to say he could steal anything he wanted, whether it was a horse, a full meal, a gold piece or a woman.' She was puzzled, trying to understand; and Joel explained: 'I was just thinking what Tufts would say about a man that set to work to cut down a lot of trees just so he could spend the rest of his life plowing and planting the ground, sweating himself dry all the time.'

Mima said, after a moment: 'Remember you wanted to leave a straight path through those little spruces, so that any man who came after you would know you'd set your course and kept it?'

'I know.'

'That's the reason, isn't it, Joel? A man is proud of doing the best way he knows. He's happy, knowing he's tried. He's happy setting a straight path for his sons to — judge him by.'

Joel protested stubbornly: 'That's only if he's going somewhere. Making a farm isn't going anywhere! It's staying in one place!'

'It's the start of going some place,' she insisted. 'You come this far and keep the road open and your sons will go on — over beyond those white hills and on and on, making other farms the way you showed them, always trying to do a job the straight, true way.'

'Farming's a job you never get done,' he argued. 'The minute you stop cutting brush, your farm goes back to woods again.'

'You don't want to stop cutting brush! You don't want a job you can finish. There wouldn't be any fun in the world with no more jobs to do. Finishing anything just means you have to hunt up something else to do to keep you happy. It's not finishing a thing that gives you the satisfaction. It's tackling it and trying to do it right.' She said quietly: 'I guess the real happy people are the ones that tackle something too big for them, so they never quite finish it; so they always have the fun of trying.'

'Maybe,' he said, and chuckled. 'But Mima, I haven't got any sons to go making farms beyond those white hills.'

'You can have sons,' she said quietly. 'Any time you want.'

He looked at her and then away again; and for long minutes no other word passed. Some vagary of the wind brought to Mima's ears again from far away the soft, pulsing, bell-like murmur of the pigeons in the beech wood. The world lay spread below them, mile on mile of forest, roll on roll of hills shining green in the sun; and the surge of spring beat in them both. His shoulder was against her arm that circled the trunk of the tree between them; his arm was between her waist and the rough bark.   A little gusty breeze made the new leaves whisper as a whisper runs through a crowd of listeners waiting for some word. It was he who spoke at last.

'If I don't sell, if I stay here, we'll get married, Mima.'

'Yes. I've known that since the first day you came.'

He said honestly: 'I've known it too, I guess. Knowing it has made me shy off. I don't know as I want to marry anyone. It ties a man down.'

'You have to plant a tree to let its roots take hold.'

'I don't know as I want to root in one place.'

'A man, no more than a tree, can't grow without roots.'

'You figure we'd get along?' he asked doubtfully.

She said slowly: 'I don't know what you mean by getting along. I'd love you, Joel, and you'd love me; but likely we'd have fights enough. If that's what you mean. If you mean would we make money and save it, I don't know — nor care much. But we'd try. Anything there was to do, we'd tackle it together; and the more we worked together, the closer bound we'd get to be.'

'You figure you're in love with me?'

'As much as a woman can be with a man she's not married to. Women love a man more, the more they give him, Joel.'

He laughed in a sudden tenderness. 'There never was a woman like you,' he said. 'Brave enough to ask a man.'

'I guess most women do, one way or another,' she declared, but her cheeks were bright, and he saw them; and he sang teasingly:

> Oh, her cheek it was bonny; her eye it was merry;

She smiled and he sang on:

> Her ear was a shell and her lip was a cherry.
> Her smile would make any man linger a while
> And she smiled that smile at the gentlemen!

He broke off, told her in laughing accusation, his eyebrow lifting: 'You're smiling that smile, Mima.'

She said, her own eyes dancing with a sudden happiness. 'I want you to linger a while, Joel.'

'I'm going to!' he cried, in a sudden sure decision. 'We'll do it, Mima. To hell with Tucker! I'll not sell my land. My sons will want it.'

Her eyes filled with sudden blissful tears. 'I've been so scared you wouldn't,' she confessed.

He leaned toward her, and she toward him, and he tasted tears on her warm cheek. 'But we'll have some waiting, Mima,' he said. 'Till I can work out my stint with Matt and Jason. Till I can build a house.'

'I can wait, long as I'm sure of you.'

'I don't want to wait,' he told her strongly. A hawk soared by below them and their eyes followed it. He said: 'Spring is no time for waiting.'

She smiled, thinking of her mother; and he saw her smile, and sang again, laughingly:

> Her smile would make any man linger a while
> And she smiled that smile at the gentlemen!

She said: 'Mr. Jennison's gentlemen have all gone down to Round Pond long ago. You're the only one around.'

He laughed aloud, and turned to straddle the branch on which he sat, his arms around her but with the trunk of the tree still between them. He kissed her again, a fine intoxication in him, and holding her thus awkwardly, he sang:

> So this lad came along and he tarried to dally
> And dandle and bundle with this pretty Sally.
> 'Now I'll lay me,' he told her, 'Just seeing you smile
> 'That you've been very kind to the gentlemen!'

He laughed, releasing her. 'You've been very kind to Matt and Jason and me, that's certain sure!'

'Sing,' she said, her cheek against the rough bark, watching him; and he sang:

'Oh, sir,' said sweet Sally, 'There's no harm in smiling
'On any fine lad that's so very beguiling,
'And as for this matter of being so kind,
    'I'm as kind to myself as the gentlemen!'

Mima sang the last line with him, laughing with him; and she watched him while he sang:

So he caught and he bussed her, he clipped and he tossed her,
Till she fled and he ran and he found her and lost her
And found her again — she was easy to find —
    Far from the sight of the gentlemen!

She repeated after him, looking out across the forest below them: 'Far from the sight of the gentlemen.' She asked: 'Isn't there another verse?'

'The best of all,' he promised her.

For a moment she did not speak. Then she said, suddenly grave: 'Sing it to me, Joel.'

8

SUMMER came that year with a sweep and a rush, like a fine ecstasy. Mima thought the new green had never been so beautiful, and there had never before been so many birds singing at dawn around the cabin, and the skies were never so fine before and the days so rich and full. She herself wore a radiance like the earth on a sunned June morning after a night of rain. She did not know this; but Matt saw the change in her and spoke of it to Joel. Joel reported the conversation to Mima.

'But I didn't let on to him,' he said. 'We'll keep it to ourselves a while.'

They stole moments together when they could. He might rise when she did in the morning, or come back to the cabin a little before the others at noon; or they might sit outside the cabin by the smudge fire after Jason and Matt had gone to bed. Sometimes they paddled down the river at dusk to see her mother and father, and they might be late coming home; and on the full moon early in June, thus returning, they stopped at the pool under the maple and swam together, sleek as seals and as silent, speaking in whispers in the secret night, laughing in soft breathless ways. She pretended to drown and he to rescue her, and she was the sleek salmon and he the otter pursuing her in the pool's depths and grappling with her there and bearing her to the surface and ashore. They thought they played their parts well enough to deceive every one; but Matt one day, with a twinkle in his eyes, called her Mrs. Adams. Mima's heart leaped in such rich happiness that she knew Matt was no longer deceived; but Jason had not heard him, and Jason did not know.

June was speeding. Colonel Wheaton came up the river to put men to work on his land, and he gave good reports of the war. General Gates had lost all his battles in the Carolinas, but he had somehow won his campaign. 'All the same,' the General admitted, 'that doesn't help us here. The Tories are thick as seals alongshore, and with the General locked up in Biguyduce there's no one to fight them off.'

Joel said soberly: 'It needs General Wadsworth to keep 'em down.'

The Colonel agreed. 'I do the best I know how,' he said. 'But he had the trick of making folks do what he told them to.' He grinned ruefully. 'I cuss and yell and carry on; but they don't pay any heed to me. The British are sending the General off to Halifax any time, I hear. We'll have to stiver along the best we can without him.' He said Eben was with Thompson on a little sloop, privateering to the eastward, harassing the traffic from Halifax to Biguyduce. 'But most of the time they're between here and Falmouth, picking off the shaving mills and anything they can handle.' He added: 'John Long, that your pa took to Boston, Mima; he got away. He's back here now.'

He went on up to his land, and he was still there on the twenty-first of June when word came that General Wadsworth and Ben Burton had escaped. Mima's first hint that anything had happened came in early afternoon when she heard a long halloo from the direction of the river and a shouted answer, and then voices to and fro. Joel and the others had gone to begin a

The Royal Mess

517

new clearing on Matt Hawes' land, next to Colonel Wheaton's line, on the headwaters of the little brook that came down through the meadows near the spring; and she heard them shouting too. She went out to listen. There was something in these distant voices which made her pulse quicken, but she could not hear any words. She started that way, but before she had gone far she heard the pound of running feet, and then Joel, with Jason and Matt following a little behind him, burst from the woods beyond the clearing and came racing toward her, his feet kicking up puffs of black ashes from the burnt-land. She waited for him, and he come to her and gasped out the news.

'Mima, the General's come! He and Ben Burton broke out of Biguyduce. He's over beyond Crawford's Pond, played out. Ben Burton came to get help from Johnny Butler; and Jake came up to tell the Colonel. We're going over.'

The others were on his heels. They raced on toward the landing, and Mima followed them. Jason and Matt took the big float. Joel and Mima pulled in her light canoe that Bela had made for her, and stepped into that. Colonel Wheaton, with Jacob, emerged from the river into Round Pond ahead of them and they raced to overtake him. When they came out into Seven-Tree Pond, other canoes were crossing toward the Mill Farm from down the pond, and from Philip's own landing; and Joel and Mima overtook Philip and Jess in one, and Joel called:

'Is it the truth, Robbins?'

'True as gold,' Philip told him jubilantly. 'Burton came to Johnny's. He says the General is plum tuckered, with that arm of his still bad. Johnny yelled across the lake to us, but the wind was so we couldn't hear; so I sent Jess over, and he came back and told us. I knew the Colonel would want to know. I sent Jake up river. I'd have started before now, but nothing would do but Ma'd cook up some hot kettle bread for me to take him, so I had to wait.' And he said with a proud chuckle: 'I'm thinking he'll want to give me back that gimlet I give Cunningham to give him. I'd have got a compass saw too, if there was one to be had in Biguyduce, or a screw auger; but watching me the way they did, a gimlet was all I could do.' He cried in a hilarious satisfaction: 'Ben said they ate their way out with it like a mouse in a cheese box!'

The canoe grounded. Colonel Wheaton had landed a minute before, and he was already on his way across to Crawford's Pond, a file of men on his heels. With Jess to lead the way, they set out at a fast pace, so that Mima had to hurry to keep up with them. It did not occur to her to stay behind. Their excitement infected her; their high voices ringing with an almost personal triumph whipped her to an equal zeal. When they reached Crawford's Pond and left the cleared land behind and began to round the head of the pond, the forest shut them in; and Mima saw that the feet of the men ahead of her had already marked something like a path, on which she trod. Wherever man went he left his imprint. Probably everything a man did left its imprint, no matter how casual the moment, how light the action. Perhaps great men — like General Wadsworth — were great because they left on the minds of men their mark, deeper and more permanently than lesser folks. But any man, no matter how humble his own life, had put a foot on the ascent to the heights if he had sired a son; for the son might be great. The woman who bore that son to him helped him, and herself too, to immortality, whether for good or ill. You had to try your best to make it be for good rather than for ill.

Their pace had slowed a little, and she came easily behind them through the wood, stepping where they stepped, catching the small branches that switched back from Joel's passing, glad they were preceding her so that the spider webs everywhere were broken by them and did not touch her cheeks and cling and need to be rubbed away. They left Crawford's Pond behind and began to ascend the rising ground to the eastward. The forest was for the most part hardwood, with more undergrowth than among the pines west of Seven-Tree Pond; and they picked their way, dodging thickets, skirting rocky knolls, sometimes turning aside to pass a great tree that had fallen to bar their path. A mile or two beyond Crawford's they came to a meandering brook that wound through a ravine whose sides were deeply corroded. Beyond, the ground rose steeply; but Jess turned up the brook, and Mima presently heard voices ahead of them, and spoke to Joel, and he called the word along. The others stopped to listen, and Colonel Wheaton shouted in a great voice, and someone answered him, and then they were all running toward the sound.

Mima came last of all, and more slowly. She smelled the smoke of the fire Johnny Butler had started, and the fine fragrance of meat boiling; and as she came near she recognized Ben Burton, taller even than Joel. General Wadsworth was sitting on the ground, the others around him; but Burton saw her over their heads, and grinned a welcome as she came near. She passed around the group to his side.

'Is he all right?' she asked quietly. Colonel Wheaton was talking in such a loud excitement that only Colonel Burton could hear her.

'Will be as soon as he's et,' Burton promised. 'We've had a hard three days of it, and his arm bothers him.'

Her father heard that word and turned in astonishment. 'Three days?' he exclaimed. 'Did you make it from Biguyduce in three days? Who set you across the Bay?'

Colonel Wheaton and the others, turning with him, opened out the circle to include Burton. Burton looked at the General, but Wadsworth smiled and said: 'You tell them, Ben. I'll watch that meat cook. Never saw anything handsomer!'

Johnny Butler grinned at him from the fire, and propped the broiling strips nearer the coals, and Ben Burton chuckled and said: 'Well, I could eat a fair-sized bear myself, right now.' And he told Philip: 'Why, no one set us over. We found a dugout, about first light, and crossed for ourselves, up where it narrows, seven or eight miles above the fort. It was after sunup before we landed on the point there. We saw a barge full of soldiers coming up the Bay toward us, but they didn't make us out, or if they did, they were too far away for us to tell it. Time we got ashore we didn't wait to watch them. We put through the woods kershackling, the way old I'm Davis said the scared moose went; and we haven't hardly stopped since. Had a time finding the neck, getting off the point we were on and onto the mainland.'

'Come all the way by land?' Philip asked incredulously. 'Man, you've walked some. Have anything to eat on the way?'

'Some,' Burton admitted, and he grinned at his own word. 'But mostly we were in too much of a hurry to eat. We made it to Belfast about noon the first day, to Tolford Durham's house. Mistress Durham wanted us to set and eat; but we could see three-four boats full of soldiers coming across the Bay. Durham said he'd set us across the river; but when we got down to the shore one of the boats was too handy to suit him.'

Colonel Wheaton roared indignantly: 'God's Nails and Britches! I'll go up and hang the Tory bastard myself.'

'Easy, Colonel,' Ben told him. 'Don't blame Durham. He had to stay there and meet them when they came. He was afraid what they'd do to him for helping us, and I'd been afraid myself in his place.' He went on: 'So we took his canoe and crossed ourselves.'

The meat was cooked; Johnny said: 'Eat it while it's hot, C-Colonel.' Burton took a piece of the cornbread, laid a slice of meat on it, borrowed Joel's belt knife to cut it, and talked while he ate. General Wadsworth ate without talking, listening to Burton, watching them all; and Mima saw that he was like a man drugged with hunger and fatigue.

'Time we got across, the Englishmen were handy,' Burton said. 'But Jim Miller's boys, Jim and Bob, took us into the woods by a brook about a mile from their house, and we laid up there the rest of the day. They fetched us food and blankets and made up a hemlock camp for us in case it rained. Then yesterday we come along down through the woods along the shore, to Nash Miller's at Lincolnville; but we could see barges in the Bay, so we slept out, and we got an early start from there today. It looked to us the Tories or someone would be watching in Camden, so we came around behind the mountains.' He glanced at Philip and laughed. 'Thought we might get a chance to give you back your gimlet,' he explained, and squatted on his hunkers to take another strip of meat.

Philip hooted mirthfully. 'I had a notion you'd find some way to use that,' he declared. 'Cunningham give it to you all right, did he?'

General Wadsworth answered him while Burton ate. 'That's what got us out,' he assented. 'Here it is.' He fumbled in his pocket. 'I'm afraid we dulled it,' he said with a chuckle. His strength was returning; there was color in his cheeks and a twinkle in his eyes. Philip took the gimlet, turning it wonderingly in his hands. 'We cut a hole in the boards in the ceiling of our room,' the General told them. 'We bored holes in a row with the gimlet and then filled them with bread so they wouldn't show. We were three weeks doing that.' His face twisted at the memory. 'We had to be careful all the time, so that if the sentries looked in, we could stop what we were doing and look innocent. We saved some food every day toward the last, stowed it in our pockets; and then when a good dark, rainy night came, we had a try for it.' He looked toward Burton gratefully. 'Ben here insisted on going first. I think he thought that if there was any shooting, he would be the one to suffer. We went to bed as usual, blew out our candle; and then Ben climbed up through the hole — it only took us a minute to cut through the last few slivers of wood at the corners — and up he went!'

They were watching him, and Mima saw Joel tense and eager, his lips a little parted, his eyes shining. She thought smilingly how young he was, listening like a child to a fairy tale. But even Colonel Wheaton was quiet for once and willing to listen.

'Ben did most of the work cutting the hole,' General Wadsworth said. 'I couldn't reach the ceiling without standing on a
chair, and the sentries were always looking in; and a chair under
the hole would have looked suspicious; but he was tall enough
to reach it from the floor.' He smiled. 'My job was to chew
bread and have it ready to fill the holes he made.' And he went
on: 'So Ben climbed up and out. He had to crawl along over
the rooms next to ours. The officers slept there. I waited till
he'd had time to get to the entry, and then I started after him.

'But this arm bothered me. I had trouble swinging up
through that hole. It wasn't much bigger than I am through
the middle.'

He smiled at the memory, and Colonel Wheaton muttered:
'By Balls and Belches, that was a thing to do! Did you make it,
General?'

General Wadsworth chuckled. 'Well, I'm here,' he pointed
out. 'I made it, yes; and I crawled along on the cross beams,
listening to the snores under me. I slid down into the entry
and got out-of-doors.'

Burton spoke a word. 'It was raining like a pond falling out
of the sky,' he said. 'I never saw it rain harder. We couldn't
find each other in the night at all.'

Philip demanded: 'But how'd you get out of the fort, with a
twenty-foot drop outside the walls, and them frazed on top
and all?'

'Climbed the bank on the inside and lowered ourselves down
with blankets,' Burton said. 'Tied the end of the blanket strips
to the pickets.' And he added: 'The relief came along while the
General was there on top. They as near as anything stepped on
him, but it was raining so they couldn't see him.'

General Wadsworth took up the tale. 'I got as wet in that
rain as I did when I waded the cove afterward — and I went in
to my chin in the cove. I had to wade to get past the sentry
line.' He shook his head. 'It was all a blind business in the
dark, dodging past the sentry boxes. I kept hoping to find Ben,

but I didn't. Not then. After I got clear of their lines, I headed north, kept going till daylight. Part of the way I followed the road I had cut to move guns on, two years ago.

'I'd given Ben up; but when it was light enough to see, I stopped to rest — and he came along, and here we are.' He ate a last scrap of meat. 'Almost as good as ever!' he declared, and he asked Philip: 'How far would you guess it is to Boice Cooper's?'

'Five miles, say.'

The General rose. 'We'll have to move to make it tonight,' he decided. 'I travel slowly. I'm soft, shut up in one room so long.'

'We'll carry you if you say so,' Philip offered. 'There's enough of us here to do it, easy as scat. Or you could come along back to our place, only it's about as far.'

General Wadsworth thought not. 'I can make it, all right,' he said. 'If we find the way.' He saw them disappointed not to be of more service, and he said: 'But I'd appreciate it if some of you would come along, in case I do play out. I'm sorry to be a bother to you.'

In the end, Colonel Wheaton, with Johnny Butler and Jason, Jess and Matt Hawes as escort and guard, went off with them down brook toward Warren; and Mima with her father and Joel and the others turned homeward. It was dusk before they reached the cleared land, and Mima saw the thin crescent of the new moon above the trees ahead. Philip led the way, David and Rich followed him, and she and Joel, a little behind, heard Jacob's voice still keen with excitement as he asked his father a thousand questions, demanding to hear again and again the stirring tale. Joel walked by Mima's side, his arm around her waist, secret in the darkness; and the night was warm and still, the mosquitoes for once not savage. She said in a quiet happiness:

'I like nights, Joel. You can hear so many things when it's still, like whispering.'

'You always did hear like an owl,' he agreed.

'No, I mean, things you can't really hear,' she explained. 'Like his voice. The General's. I can still hear it. Did you notice how it kind of sings, like music? I guess he's a great man, isn't he?'

Joel chuckled. 'A General looks great to me. A General's God in the army.'

'I don't mean that! Only — he's good stock. You know, like a fine tree. He'll have fine sons and grandsons.' She looked up at him in the darkness. 'I want to have fine sons for you, Joel.' He kissed her warm mouth, almost without breaking the rhythm of their steps as they walked together arm in arm like one.

* * * * *

They heard when Jason and Matt returned next day how the General came safe to Warren, and how Boice Cooper hailed Captain McIntyre across the river at the ferry, announcing the General's return in such a roaring voice that any lurking Tory parties within a mile must have heard.

'The General's gone on to Falmouth now,' Matt said. 'With a guard to see him safe. Ben Burton went down-river to Cushing to see his wife, but he won't dare to stay only overnight. He aims to go to Boston then, maybe try privateering. If he stayed here they'd nab him again sure.'

The excitement lingered for a while, and the tale of that escape would be told over and over; and Philip hoped that the General would curb the Tories now. But they were reported to be as active as ever, and early in July, Eben came up the river to find his father. Captain Long, the refugee whom Philip had once before conveyed a prisoner to Boston, was again at his old trade. John Snow had received a letter from him like an impudent challenge, in which Captain Long said he would have business in Thomaston presently and would call to settle an old score. Eben proposed to his father that they make it their business to recapture the Tory; and Philip swore he would.

'Aye, and take him to Boston again, alone if I have to,' he declared. 'If he makes good his brag, does come to John Snow's, we'll be waiting for him there. I'll lay him by the heels!'

He went down-river with Eben, and it would be late July before they saw him again. He came home then triumphantly. He had made good his boast, seen Captain Long safe to Boston for a second time. 'And if he gets loose again, I'll nab him again,' he declared, proud of his success.

But there were not many like Mima's father, bold to strike back at the refugees who harried the shore towns and farms; and the militia was disorganized. Colonel Ulmer at Camden, Colonel Wheaton at Thomaston, and others like them did their best; but reports came up the river every day of new harassments. There was no trade to the westward, no fishing beyond the confines of the river, no sale for casks or spars or lumber even in Thomaston, no source of income for any man except farming or salt making. Some Wessaweskeag men bought a schooner and sent her to Boston loaded with salt to trade for supplies; but on her return she was taken. About the same time a party of Tories invaded the east part of the town and made their way to the house John Perry had built, almost two miles from the water. Perry was off with Thompson in that small sloop on which at the time Eben was serving; but Mrs. Perry and the children were at home. The Tories ordered them out of the house and set it afire; and when Perry's two-year-old son screamed with fright, one of the marauders cuffed him, knocked him head over heels, called him a damned little rebel. Mrs. Perry was allowed to save nothing; the house and all it held was burned to ashes while she watched helplessly.

The tales came up the river day by day. Captain Long escaped again, and he sent word that he meant to come with a regiment of British soldiers and burn out the whole nest of rebels in Sterlingtown; and a watch was kept for a while thereafter, and flintlocks were loaded and ready for any alarm.

But Mima this summer heard the rumors with a sense of unreality. They did not trouble her as they had in the past. Her horizons were narrowing more and more; her life began to distil out of the diffuse the concentrate; her world included only Joel and herself, although others sometimes shared with them a moment or an hour.

She and Joel were more often alone together. After the planting was done, the work was not so steady and demanding; and on days when rain made outdoor work impossible, and on Sundays when only necessary tasks were done, they were apt to leave the cabin after dinner at noon and go for a long tramp up the river, or up the brook. They followed more than once that trail Joel had blazed, to the hilltop to the westward; and they climbed again the oak from which such a wide prospect could be seen. They were happy, and Matt Hawes said one day to Mima: 'It's good watching you both. It's like you wore bright garments. You seem to shine!'

'I think it's so, Matt,' she agreed. 'I feel all bright and gleaming like polished pewter, yes or silver. There's so much happiness inside me, it's bound to shine through.'

He said understandingly: 'Joel's a grand man in the making, Mima; and you can hold him and help him as he needs.' Often when he and Joel and Mima were together he called her Mistress Adams, and Mima always felt her pulse pound at the word; and once Joel laughed and said:

'You're a year ahead of time with that, Matt. I'll have to have a house, before I can marry a wife to put in it.'

But Matt reminded them: 'There's more to marrying than parsons.' He was more understanding than Jason. They both talked with him more freely than with the other man. Among these three it came to be accepted — and freely spoken — that Mima and Joel would be married next summer when Joel could get his cabin built.

Yet though Joel seemed ready enough to speak of this with Matt and Mima together, he was not so ready to talk about it with Mima alone. 'Time enough for talking when the time for doing comes,' he said. So she, to please him, never spoke of next year. They lived in the present rapture.

The work at the cabin took not all her time, and in the long afternoons she liked to walk through the forest alone. Sometimes she went as far as her father's house, but when she did so, instead of taking her float, she might go the long way, around the south shore of Round Pond; or she went along the old beaver dam where there was by this time a well-trodden path. Joel made a raft of logs to let her cross the pool below the old maple, and that tree Jess had felled across the river still served as a bridge below.

She seldom stayed long at home. Her mother, seeing her wear happiness like a garment, was apt to ask questions which Mima was not yet ready to answer. One day, returning from her father's house, she made a discovery. East of the river, between where it flowed into Round Pond and out again, there was a reedy cove, with banks grown to low bushes. As she approached the dam, she heard the faintest stir in the underbrush at the water's edge, just below her, and she looked through the bushes and saw ripples widening. She thought a musquash had dived there, but after a moment a loon came to the surface just outside the cove.

In a sharp excitement Mima parted the bushes and stepped down into the water and waded along the shore, looking closely for what she knew must be there. She found the nest, a wide platform at the water's edge and so low that even a small wave must have wetted the single big egg. Mima saw loons every day through the summer, and often at close range; but she had never seen a nest, nor had she ever seen one of the birds on shore. She wished to spy on this nest and the birds themselves, and sought a vantage point. Fifteen or twenty feet from the nest there was a low, thick-growing spruce. Mima broke off some branches and set them in the ground like a screen. She lay down under the spruce on a warm carpet of fallen needles, and peered through the screen; and she cleared away brush and weeds between her and the nest till she could see the egg from her hiding place.

Then she went home; but next afternoon she returned, and made a cautious circle through the tall grass in the meadow and crept up to the spruce, and slid under it like a snake. She peered through the screen. The loon was there, her slim black head turning uneasily as though she were alarmed; but Mima lay so still the bird's fears subsided. Mima watched her for an hour, lying on her stomach, her chin resting on her clasped hands, heedless of the mosquitoes which came to feast upon her arms and throat and cheeks, her bare feet and legs. Not till the loon slid clumsily off the lip of the nest into the water and departed to feed did Mima stir.

The next day was Sunday, and she brought Joel, making a mystery, refusing to tell him what to expect. She led him through the meadow grass, making him crawl behind her on hands and knees. As they approached the nest, he caught her ankle and held her and crawled up beside her, laughing at her silent protests, forcing her down, clipping her tight. The sun was bright, the strong sweet smell of the grass in their nostrils, and she clung for a moment as close as he; but she whispered insistently:

'No, Joel. Wait! I want you to see something!'

'I see all I want to see,' he told her huskily. The sun was in her eyes, and his lips were on her throat, but she hushed him, made him follow her, till they came to the spruce and crawled beneath it. Mima, leading the way, looked through the screen, but the loon was gone.

'There!' she said, disappointed. 'You've frightened her away with your foolishness.'

'What is it?' he asked, sliding up beside her.

'A loon's nest! See the egg!' She pointed it out to him. 'She was sitting on it yesterday. She's so beautiful close to, I want you to see her. Let's wait. She'll be back if we keep quiet.'

He laughed lazily. 'What do we want to see her for?'

'We might as well wait,' she argued, eyes dancing. 'It's too hot to do anything else!'

He laughed and drew her near him. A cool current of air came gliding from the pond so near, and the spruce under which they lay kept off the sun, and the mat of needles on the ground was comfortable under them. 'It's like a roof over us,' Mima said happily. 'Like a house just big enough for us. What an ugly great egg, Joel. Do you suppose she loves it?'

'I've seen women love some mighty ugly babies.'

'There never was an ugly baby,' she protested. 'Joel, how long does it take a loon baby to grow up to be a big loon?'

'I don't know. All summer, maybe.'

'I'd rather have a baby,' Mima declared. 'They take so much longer growing up. You have so much more fun.'

'I never saw the fun in babies — after they're born,' Joel argued, his eyebrow lifted teasingly. 'They're always having to be cleaned up after.'

She smiled wisely. 'You'll feel different with one of your own.' They talked lazily, and now and then Mima peered through the screen. She could see out into the cove, catch glimpses of the pond beyond. Joel lay beside her, on his back, watching her while they talked, and when he stirred she cautioned him to lie still. 'She might be coming and you'd scare her away,' she told him; and Joel was obedient enough. The sun moved to shine in his eyes, and she broke off a small branch and held it to shade him, looking down at him, her eyes ranging across his countenance, watching the way his lips moved when he talked, the muscles in his throat. 'Your nose twitches just like a rabbit's when you laugh, sometimes,' she said.

'It likes the smell of you,' he said.

She nodded. 'I've always liked the way you smell,' she agreed. 'As if you'd just come out of the pond. You sort of smell of fresh water, like grass after rain.'

'You smell like pine needles,' he said. 'Pine needles and sunshine and hay.' He laughed. 'I'd rather smell you than a drink of rum.'

'You wouldn't stop to smell the rum!'

He drew her down to him. 'You and your loons!' he whispered; but she said:

'Sh! Be still! She might come.'

The loon did return at last. Mima saw her in the cove, already near the nest, and warned him with a touch. He moved as secretly as an owl on a dark night, turning, lifting his head till he could peep through the screen. The loon came nearer the nest almost imperceptibly, head turning warily this way and that. While they watched breathlessly, it reached the shore and after a moment shoved itself clumsily up out of the water, till it was on the nest. It turned then to face the water, settled itself with comfortable small motions till it was satisfied.

After that, only the black head moved. Mima felt Joel beside her as intent as she; but nothing else happened. The loon seemed to have settled to stay indefinitely. Mima watched it still, but after a while Joel turned to look at her close beside him here. A lock of hair lay on her cheek. He blew it aside, and her eyes turned to his and she smiled. He drew her near.

When they looked toward the nest again the loon was gone.

*   *   *   *   *

At supper Matt asked where they had been, and Mima told him about the loon's nest. 'I'll take you to see it tomorrow,' she promised. 'Or Joel can. It's funny to see her, how clumsy she is when she's on land.'

'I saw a loon come ashore once,' Jason said. 'On a pond down home. Two of them were fighting, and one got the worst of it. The other one kept driving him, under water and on top of it, till he drove him right onto the beach and I went and picked him up. Kept him two-three days in a pen. They can't fly off the ground. I had to carry him back to the pond finally.'

'I'd like to see this one,' Matt declared, and Mima took him to the nest next day; but thereafter, for fear her attentions might disturb the old birds, she stayed away; and the next Sunday afternoon when Joel proposed that they go to the nest again, she would not. They walked, instead, up across Colonel Wheaton's land. The Colonel since planting time had had no men at work; and he himself seldom came up the river. As they crossed his clearing now, a flock of pigeons that seemed endless streamed across above them; swinging in a great arc from the direction of Crawford's Pond toward the nesting which Joel and Mima had seen in its inception; and Joel said:

'They're the old birds coming back to the nests. They take turns at it. One stays on the nest till the other comes and all but pushes him off.' He added: 'We were figuring to go get what we need, right off. The young ones will be just fat and right now. Jess was up to see, two-three days ago.'

'I kind of hate to bother them,' she confessed. 'When we saw them mating and all.' She watched the flight passing high above them, and a hawk struck down. Directly under his stoop the pigeons dove straight downward in a solid waterfall of birds, their colors glancing and changing in the sun; and the air thundered with their wings. Past the danger spot they arched upward again, and as though these birds had marked a trail through the sky, those which followed them dove at the same spot, arched up again and so went on.

'There's plenty of them,' Joel reminded her. 'We'll kill maybe three-four hundred; but that won't be a shaving to what there is up there.'

'I wonder if a pair feels bad when you kill the young one they've loved and fed and raised.' She watched the last of the flight pass. 'Where there's so many. They like company, don't they?'

'Same as everything else,' Joel agreed. 'The ellwives in the river and the moose in their winter yards.'

'I wonder if moose stay together for company, or just because the best feed's where they yard. They don't herd up in breeding time, the way the pigeons do.'

'An old bull will get all the cows he can,' he argued. 'I killed

one last fall had three cows with him.' He added: 'But I didn't
have him dressed out before one of the cows was calling and
another bull answering.'

'Served him right,' she said laughingly. They were walking
slowly on. 'He didn't need to have three cows!'

'That's the bull way,' he assured her. 'He'll take all he can
serve. A man's the same, till a woman makes him stay at home!'

She knew he meant to torment her, and she said, as though the
idea offered interesting possibilities: 'So the cow, as soon as the
old bull was dead, started calling for another bull right away.'

He laughed and caught her, kissing her breathless. 'Try it
on me and I'll teach the other bull something — and you too!'

'If you ever went away, I might.'

'It's for you to make me stay home.'

'Only if you want to, Joel. I'll never keep you unless you
want more than anything to stay.'

'I'll never go,' he said. They walked on in silence for a while,
and the day was warm, the air still and fragrant with the
baked scent of the pines. After a mile or so they came down to
the river, deep black water above a rocky ledge like a dam,
below which ran the ripples; and Mima's ivory body glided
into the water while Joel was still stripping off his smallclothes.
She laughed up at him over her shoulder, swimming strongly
upstream; and he dove from a rock and came racing after her
and caught her. On their backs they floated side by side, motionless as frogs, watching the high white clouds in the blue
ribbon of the sky between the trees, drifting down with the current till it shoaled and quickened, standing up to wade into
deeper water and swim upstream again. He distanced her, and
without his knowledge she slipped ashore and ran up the bank
till she was well above him, keeping out of his sight among the
trees; till he missed her and called, and then he called again
with a sudden panic in his tones; and before she could answer
he began to race downstream again in a desperate haste to find
her. She called him, but he swam so hard he did not hear her

till he paused, looking right and left. Then she called again and he saw her standing in the shallows upstream above him, her hair streaming, plastered wetly to her body. He was rods away; but he shouted wrathfully:

'Damn your tricks! I'll smack you!' He plunged ashore and raced toward her, and she ran, and he came plunging through the woods where sun dappled the ground till he caught her and held her. His face was stern. 'Don't ever scare me like that,' he said furiously. 'I thought you'd drowned or something.'

She had been laughing, but she laughed no more. 'I'm not drowned, Joel,' she said warmly. 'I'm all alive.' A fleck of sun was golden on her shoulder and her side.

When they floated down the river again, contented and at peace, Mima said, as much to herself as to him: 'I never knew a woman could be so happy, Joel.'

'I never knew a man could be so scared as I was a while ago!'

'I think,' she decided with a quick laugh, 'I like you scared!'

The sun struck the east bank and warmed the ledges there. They lay till the sun dried them, and dressed and presently walked slowly homeward. Where a flat rock lay in their path a line of ants was crossing, keeping to a course a few inches wide. Mima saw them and made Joel look, and they knelt down to see more closely. These were small red ants, and some of them were burdened with white eggs bigger than themselves, and some straddled black ants, likewise larger than they were, moving purposefully along, dragging the black ants between their legs. 'Look,' Mima whispered, as though the ants might hear her and take alarm. 'There are some going in each direction.'

'Going back for another load,' Joel told her. He lay at length, resting on one elbow, lazily at peace with the world.

'Are the black ones dead?' she asked. 'Have the red ones killed them for food? Why don't they all carry something?'

He took a pine needle and brushed one of the carrier ants over on its back. It held fast to its burden, but when he had turned the ant over two or three times, it released the black ant, which promptly scuttled away.

'Now watch, see what it will do!' she cried; so they watched the black one till a red ant caught it and in a businesslike fashion turned it on its back again, straddled it, and proceeded on its way.

'Was it the same red one?' she asked, and he said:

'We'll try it again and see. When the red one lets go, I'll watch the black one and you watch the red.' He brushed another carrier over on its back.

But this time two red ants seized the pine needle with their nippers; and when he lifted it, they clung to it. He and Mima forgot the carrier, watching these two. They hung on like bulldogs till he lowered the pine needle to touch the rock again. Then they let go their holds and joined the hurrying stream.

'They must be the fighters,' Mima said delightedly, 'guarding the others. How did they know she needed help? Do you suppose she called for help, Joel, when you pestered her?'

'How do you know it's a she?'

'She's doing the work, isn't she? And he's doing the fighting. Try it again, Joel. I want to see if the same red one catches the same black one.' They tried, and Mima exclaimed delightedly: 'She did, Joel! Have they eyes? Can they see?'

'Must have.'

Mima said: 'I wonder where they're coming from, where they're going to? Let's follow them and see.'

He said lazily: 'You do it. I'm too comfortable. I think I'll take a nap.'

She laughed, looking down at him. 'Poor man! Are you all worn out, Joel?'

He grinned at her. 'Greedy! Go watch your ants!' She stooped to kiss him, laughing at him, brushing his arm away when he would have held her. She followed the moving line of ants up the slope away from the river for a surprising distance, sometimes almost losing them in the scattered underbrush, to a great ant hill into whose many entrances they plunged. She watched them there a while, and then returned, counting her steps, to where Joel lay apparently asleep; but as she passed him he caught her ankle. She protested:

'Don't! I'm counting. Sixty-four! Sixty-five!'

He released her, and she went on down toward the river. The course the ants took was almost straight, turning aside only to avoid hard travelling. They were emerging, she found, from another, smaller hill; and as many seemed to be going into it as were coming out. She returned and told Joel: 'It's a hundred and forty-one of my steps from one hill to the other. I wonder how long it takes them to walk so far?'

'Sit down,' he said comfortably. 'Make a pillow for me.' She obeyed, taking his head on her lap, leaning over to kiss him upside down.

'Do you suppose the red ones are robbing the black ones, Joel?' she asked. 'Or maybe they're just moving into a nicer hill!' He grunted sleepily, and she said: 'Your hair's wet.' She unwound the eelskin and loosed his hair and rubbed it between two folds of her petticoat till it was dry enough and clubbed it again. He seemed asleep, lying now on his side, his cheek pillowed on her leg; and she tickled his ear with a pine needle till he brushed it aside and said:

'Stop that or I'll paddle you!'

'It's what you did to the poor little ant!'

'I'm no ant! You said yourself it was a she!' She tickled him again and he swore. 'Damn the woman!'

'Are you as mad at me as you were when you thought I was drowned? You don't act the same!'

He looked up at her, smiling lazily. 'You're mine, Mima,' he said. She nodded in vigorous assent. He said: 'I never thought anyone could be as sweet as you.'

'Am I sweet?'

'Sweet as rum and honey.'

She was still smiling. 'Are you glad you love me?'

'Sure.'

'Will we move into a new house, pretty soon, like the ants, Joel?'

He saw that, though she smiled, her eyes were steady and serene. 'Why?' he asked sharply, half alarmed.

'Because,' she said, with a happy break in her tones. 'Because and because we're going to have our baby in February.'

He sat up, the movement of his body like a steel spring, his hand gripping her arm.

9

THEY came home at dusk; and crossing the burnt-land, ashes black under their feet, they did not speak at all. But when they came among the pines by the spring and turned up toward the cabin, Joel said in a low, tight tone:

'I feel like a rabbit in a trap!'

Mima smiled, but it was for him to see. She kept her tears to shed after she was abed in the garret above where he slept with Jason and Matt below. Her tears even then were few and controlled. If she cried as much as she wanted to, he or Jason or Matt might hear her. They were her tears, not to be shared.

Joel had not blamed her. 'I suppose it was bound to happen,' he admitted. 'But — I never thought about it.'

'I wanted it to happen, Joel.'

'So did I,' he assured her. 'But not yet. Not the way things are. You say February?'

'Yes.'

'Why didn't you tell me before?' he demanded, almost angrily.

'I guess I was afraid to, Joel.'

'Afraid I'd — act the way I am acting?' He laughed mirth-lessly. 'I don't mean to, Mima. I'm all right. I want to marry you. I do love you, you know.'

'I do know.'

He tried to explain. 'It's just that — well, a man not married doesn't have to worry about anyone but himself. He can do what he wants, and if it goes wrong — he's the only one hurt. Now every time I plan anything, or do anything, I'll have to think about us.'

Mima said quietly: 'I know. I guess most good men are scared at the idea of getting married. They're afraid they won't turn out to be good husbands and fathers. But I'm not afraid of that with you, Joel.' She added: 'That's the way a man's life grows, facing his job and doing it. It's what makes him fine, the way he does or doesn't.'

He shook his head. 'You're talking about ideas, Mima; but my job isn't ideas. My job's building a house for you, and keep-ing you and the baby fed and warm and clothes to wear.'

'You don't have to marry me till you want to. You don't ever have to, unless you want to.'

'I have to, the way things are.'

'No.'

He made a harsh sound. 'Your father and mother would say different.'

Mima said: 'They don't count. This is you and me, Joel. It's our lives, and our baby; and you're the one decides what we'll do. Not Father, or Mother, or anybody.'

'You don't know.'

'I'm a grown woman. I know enough.'

'I know what they'll say.'

She said quietly: 'Believe what I say. If you don't want to marry me this summer, don't. If you don't ever want to marry me, don't. I'm not ashamed. I've been happier, since that first day, than I ever looked to be, and I'm happy having the baby coming and knowing it's yours.' She shook her head, as much to steady her voice as for any other reason. 'If you never do marry me, Joel, I'll always have the baby, have that much of you.'

He held her close and gently. 'We'll be married the day you say, Mima. You know that. I can't help talking so. I'm never going to talk anything but straight to you, even to make you happy. Anything I do say, it will be true. It's true now that I wish this hadn't come the way it has. I'd rather it was next year, maybe after the war's over, so's I can take better care of you.' He kissed her eyelids and then her lips. 'But we're getting married soon now.'

'You're the one to decide, Joel.'

'We'll go down to Mr. Urquhart.'

She cried: 'No, not him! He'd look at me as if he knew, as if — as if 'twas his! I'll not let him marry me.'

There was a shaken passion in her which startled him. 'Why, we'll go to someone else, then?'

She held his hand. 'Don't let's hurry, Joel. There's time enough till February.' She smiled up at him. 'I want you should get used to the idea, not take it too hard. We'll wait a while.'

So they came back to the cabin, and Joel said he felt like something in a trap, and Mima cried softly that night till she slept and woke to a shining day. She climbed down from the garret quietly in order not to wake these others till she could make their breakfast ready; but Joel's bunk was empty and she had a moment's dreadful fear that he was gone, was gone forever.

He was in fact just coming up the path from the pond when she stepped out-of-doors; and he strode toward her tall and shining, his face still wet, his lips sweet with the cold water on them when he kissed her. Seeing his eyes was enough so that she needed no words; but when he said she was brave and beautiful and altogether fine, a rich flood of strength and pride and sureness welled up in her again.

Matt presently heard the axe going and at the first crackle of
young flames he appeared; and he smiled when he saw Mima,
and called her Mistress Adams, teasingly, and said he hoped he
would find a woman who would seem as beautiful in the morning. 'There's something new about you this summer, Mima,'
he said. 'You were always as smooth as cream, but there's more
now; something in the way you look and smile and all, as if
everything was right, inside you.'

She laughed at him, happy at his word, and said — with a
sidewise glance at Joel — that everything was right, inside her,
and always would be; and Joel's eyes promised her that this was
true.

When the men had eaten, and went off to their work, Mima
sang a little at her own tasks; and with them done, she went
out-of-doors. She turned toward the higher ground west of
the cabin, emerging from the trees which had been left standing
all around it into the land they had burned this spring. She
walked at an angle down toward the brook and found a place
where she could wade across. South of the brook, no trees had
been felled at all. As the stream approached Round Pond, it
found its way blocked by a tongue of high land which rose
fifty feet or so above the pond level. The brook there turned
north for ten or fifteen rods, then east past the end of this higher
ground, and south again through a boggy little meadow to the
pond. When now she crossed the brook, she climbed steeply
till she stood on a ledge fifty or sixty feet above the water. The
ledge was hidden among pines that rose high over her head;
but through the trunks of the trees, she could glimpse the pond
below her, bright in the sun. The pines here were tall, but they
were not as big as those which the men had had to fell to clear
the land across the brook. They were not too big to be used to
make the walls of a house; and Mima thought their house might
stand here, one day. Water could be brought from brook or
pond. This would mean carrying it up the steep pitch; but Joel
would make her a bucket yoke, to simplify the task.

She went down the west side of the tongue of high land and came into a fairly level sweep, free from stones so that when it was cleared it would be easily brought under cultivation. She crossed a trickle of water which ran down to the brook, and followed it up and found that it came from a spring at the foot of a rocky hillside. The spring was no more than a boggy patch at the base of the hill, but she saw that it could be dug out and give a good flow of water. She decided to come some day with a shovel and dig out this spring, and make a basin, and rock it up with the stones that were plentiful enough on the high ground just above where she stood.

She climbed back up to the ledge. It was surprisingly near. From a house here on the ledge it would be easier to go to the spring for water than to the pond. She stayed a while, standing, leaning against one of the pines, imagining where their house would be, and what it would be like; and she thought she would bring Joel, at the next occasion, and choose the very spot. She wondered whether he would build their house this summer, to bring her home when they were married presently. She wanted a house that would be their own, wanted it terribly; but if it could not be built in time, why then she could wait — as she had waited so long.

She heard, without for a while being conscious that she heard it, an axe at work off on the south side of the pond. Joel and the others were almost a mile away to the north, so this could not be they. This was toward Seven-Tree Pond. The strokes came in a steady rhythm, with occasional pauses when she waited for the crash of some great tree falling; but none fell, and she remembered how Joel and Matt and Jason had notched many trees in a row and then dropped one as a driver in such a way as to topple them all. She went slowly toward the sound, not so much curious to see who was at work there as because it was pleasant to move idly through the forest, smiling at her own thoughts, smelling the woods smells, hearing every faintest sound. Once she caught the muffled padding of great feet on the hillside above her and saw a bear go cantering off up the slope, startled by her approach; and she thought he was clumsy as a porcupine, soft and lumbering despite the speed with which he covered ground.

The axeman was nearer, on the lower ground ahead of her. She slanted down to the lake again and followed the shore till she saw a deep white notch in a pine beside the water, and in another beyond it, and another. She followed the line of notched trees, eight or ten of them, and saw Jess at work. He had not seen her. He was alone, his axe swinging steadily, and the clean chips flew. She stood a while unseen, watching him, thinking of him and of their childhood and of the years since. Jess was two years younger than she; and although he had a rough tongue and a joking humor that sometimes hurt, sharply contrasting with Eben's gentle ways, there had always been a bond between them. She smiled now at some of the things she remembered; and when he stepped back and wiped his streaming brow, she spoke to him. He turned sharply at her word, saw her.

'Ho, Mima!' he cried. 'Been there long?'

'Just a minute, waiting till you stopped. I heard your axe and came to see who was working on your land.'

'It's all mine from the brook to Joel's line,' he said proudly. 'I aim to clear this along the lake, knock over the trees now, maybe burn them off this fall if the weather holds, burn it clean next spring.' He came to sit beside her, glad of a respite, looking at her approvingly. 'You look good,' he said.

'I'm fine.'

He touched her cheek lightly with his finger-tip. 'Red enough so you'd think it'd be hot to touch,' he declared, smiling. 'And dew on your eyelashes, to look at them. All crinkly.' He seemed suddenly to realize what he was saying. 'Say, I never noticed you were so pretty before. I mean something in your eyes, and the way your cheeks are, like an apple before it's handled, before the bloom is off.'

'I feel fine,' she repeated, but she colored happily, and he said in a lively amusement:

'You're as red as if it was Joel had told you you was handsome, instead of just me.' He asked curiously: 'You and Joel any nearer getting together, Mima? The way you look now, I don't see how he can keep his hands off you.'

'We've talked some,' she admitted guardedly; but then in a rush of happiness she told him: 'Yes, Jess. We're going to be married, any time.'

'Good for you!' he said approvingly; and he laughed. 'I'm going to kiss you for that, Mima. I never saw a girl looked like she needed kissing worse!' He did, and she said:

'I guess it's because I'm pretty happy, Jess. I mean, if I do look different.'

'Well, you certainly look it,' he agreed. 'When you going to do it? Can't, till Joel builds a house, can you?'

'We can marry and stay on where we are. I can't leave Jason and Matt to do for themselves.'

Jess laughed. 'Won't be much fun being married, with two other men under your feet all the time. Time I come to get married, I don't want anyone around till I get my wife broke to bridle, anyway.'

'Joel's more sensible,' she declared. 'We'll manage.'

He seemed belatedly to realize fully what she had said. 'Well, so you're getting married, are you. Told Ma?'

'You're the first one I've told.'

'We've been looking for you and Joel to fix it up any time, ever since we could see the way you felt.'

Her cheeks burned. 'Did I show it so plain?'

'Well, you never fooled anyone,' he assured her. 'But I don't know as you ever tried. If Joel didn't know, I guess't he was the only one. When did all this happen?'

'We've been talking it over, lately. We just decided yesterday.'

'Who'll you get to do it? Urquhart? I wouldn't let him marry me.'

'Me either,' she agreed. 'I don't like to have him near me.'

'I didn't like the way he got married himself,' Jess declared. 'Claiming his wife died and all. I don't believe she's dead. Never did.' He added: 'They hire him regular now. Part of the taxes they tried to make us pay was for him. They voted that the paper about his wife being dead was satisfactory for the present, but I hear folks are staying away from meeting and claiming he wrote it himself.'

'Well, he's not going to marry me,' Mima insisted. She added: 'We probably won't marry right off, anyway. There's time enough.'

Jess chuckled. 'You'd better do it before winter,' he advised. 'Fix it so you can sleep warm when cold weather comes along.' He stood up, lifted his axe. 'Well, better stand clear. I'm going to knock over the driver, lay this line right down to the lake. Branches might break off and fly and hit you if you stay here.'

Mima moved around behind him, watching till the tree toppled with a splitting crash. One by one the other trees let go under the impact. Jess had notched them truly; each in turn fell where it was meant to go; and when the last was down, Mima could see along this slot cut through the forest the shining waters of the pond. They walked down to the waterside together so Jess might start to notch another line; and Mima said:

'I'll go along back and get dinner started. I saw a bear on the way over, Jess.'

'An old she and two cubs was at our corn last night,' he agreed. 'I'm going to rig a set gun, surprise her tonight if she comes again.'

Mima said: 'Jess, don't tell Mother yet. I just felt like telling someone, so I told you. Being happy's more fun when you can tell someone, but I kind of want to keep it for a while.'

'I won't spill it,' he promised. 'You tell Joel I said he's won the turkey!'

She laughed happily and turned away toward home. Behind her she heard his axe begin again. The sun was almost overhead. She hurried to be ready for the hungry men.

* * * * *

They would be married, but summer sped and Joel said no definite word. Their days were busy ones. The rye came to harvest and the corn was ripening and would need to be ground. The mill Doctor Taylor had built on the stream that came down from Crawford's Pond, and which Johnny Butler now operated, was never reliable. The stones were small and poor, with no burr; there were only two runs; and the water was apt to fall so low it would not turn them. The nearest mills except this one were at Oyster River, or Molineux's in Camden; and to carry corn so far was a business of two or three days; a day to go and a day to return and a day in between.

Mima thought they could mill their corn themselves. She set Joel to make a sort of mortar like her father's. He cut a billet of oak two feet through and three feet long, and with a tapping iron dug out one end to a depth of a foot and a half, and a foot or so across. He flattened the bottom except where it met the sides, and burned and scraped it and burned it again till it was smooth; then scoured it hard with sand. He made a pestle out of a hardwood maul, and Mima found that she could break the hard kernels into a coarse meal. She shaped a sheet of birch bark into a trough and punched many holes in it with the tines of a fork well heated in the coals, and with this contrived to sift out a finer meal that was as good for bread as the samp was for porridge. The process was laborious; but to take a grist to mill was more so. 'This way,' she proudly pointed out, 'we can get along and never go to mill at all.'

Joel was not so enthusiastic as she. 'Going to mill makes a good excuse,' he said. 'A man might want to go down-river and see people and hear the news once in a while.'

She saw now and then this restlessness in him, and it could frighten her. They were happy enough, and he was tender and ardent too; but the careless rapture of their first weeks of mutual possession was tempered now, and there might be a shadow in Joel's eyes which Mima tried not to see. She could understand that he felt himself beginning to be enmeshed in frail bonds, each one in itself as easily broken as a spider web across your face in the forest at dawn, but all of them together strong enough to hinder him and hamper him and bind him in the end.

'You don't have to have an excuse, Joel,' she said. 'Any time you want to go down-river, you just go.'

'Oh, I don't want to go just to be going,' he protested. 'But I liked setting around the mill waiting for my turn, seeing them that came, hearing what they had to say, maybe stopping for a bowl of grog or a glass of flip at the tavern.' He said: 'A man likes getting away from his womenfolks once in a while.'

She said understandingly: 'You're thinking you'll be tied hard and tight when we're married. You will, too. I'll never let you go. But Joel, I wouldn't marry you if I didn't know for sure that I can make you happier married to me than you ever would be any other way.'

He said slowly: 'I don't want any wife but you, Mima. I don't want any woman but you.'

'But you're not real sure you want any wife,' she suggested, and she promised him: 'You'll be sure by and by! You're going to be a great man, Joel; but a tree can't grow right unless it's got its roots planted in good earth, and it's the same with a man. He has to have his roots planted in some woman, to be the best kind of man it's in him to be. I'm going to be the earth, and you the tree.'

He laughed uncertainly. 'Maybe. But I'm not so much, Mima.'

'You're fine, and you're going to be finer. We're going to have such a good life, Joel, you and me. We're going to be good people.'

He took her in his arms. 'I'll be top man if I can keep dead up to you.'

She could always for the time dispel his doubts; but they returned. Mima would not hurry him; yet she began to be afraid someone would guess the truth. She had no mirror, could see herself only in the mirror of the spring or of the pond or of some secret pool in the brook; but sometimes she thought her eyes must be shadowed betrayingly, and she wondered if her dresses were not a little harder to button than they had been. If there was any change in her appearance, the men did not appear to notice it; and she avoided the eyes of her mother, of Bet, or Bess, or any of the other women. She was not afraid, not in the least ashamed; she had no sense of guilt or wrong. She had been so sure, so long, of what Joel would one day mean to her that to be bearing his baby in her body now was natural and beautiful and as right as the rising of the sun. Yet if it were known before they were married, Joel might be blamed; and she did not want that to happen. More for his sake than for her own she hoped no one would see. She could not altogether avoid an occasional trip down to Seven-Tree Pond; but she contrived to go at dusk, or after dark, seeking thus to be screened from her mother's eyes. She was herself so intensely conscious of the new life that shared hers that it seemed impossible that others could fail to realize that she was no longer one person but two; but if her mother knew — or suspected — the truth, she made for a while no sign.

* * * * *

One evening in mid-September Joel and Mima came down from Round Pond after supper, dipping their paddles lazily. When they walked up from the landing toward the house, Colonel Wheaton and Philip and Mrs. Robbins and the children were sitting or standing by the fore door. Mosquitoes were by this time almost gone, giving place to swarms of greedy flies that buzzed fatly everywhere; but Jess had a smudge going, and he was squatting beside it, feeding it with chips, adding handfuls of grass to smother every little flame. Mima heard the Colonel's

booming voice before they left the landing, and her steps lagged
doubtfully. When they were halfway to the house she began to
distinguish words, and she stopped in a strange dismay.

'Let's not go up, Joel,' she said, 'with him there.'

'What's wrong with the Colonel?' he protested. 'He'll have
news from down-river. I want to hear what he has to say.'

'I hate seeing folks.'

He said in a tender amusement: 'You're all right, Mima.
You don't show. He'd never notice, anyway.' And he exclaimed: 'Say, maybe he'll marry us, Mima! We want to do
something about that pretty soon. If the Captain of a ship can
marry folks, I should think a Colonel could.'

She clung to him, suddenly trembling. 'Could he, Joel?'

'We'll soon find out! Come on.'

But she held him back. 'Not now. Don't ask him before all
of them. He'll be going up-river. We can ask him there.'

He chuckled at her reluctance. 'Nothing to be ashamed of,
wanting to get married.'

'I know, but I don't want to talk about it before them all.'

He promised silence, and they went on together. Colonel
Wheaton as they drew near was speaking of Eben. 'Thompson's
going to stay ashore this winter,' he said. 'So Eben'll be home.
He might come along any time.' Mima and Joel drew near, and
Jess saw them and spoke to them; and Mima came to kiss her
mother and her father, and the others.

Mrs. Robbins said: 'Throw some chips on, Jess, and let it
burn up. I like light enough to see by. I'll be glad to have
Eben home, Colonel.' The chips caught and blazed up, and
Mima sat down hurriedly beside her mother, her arms around
her knees, watching the fire, trying not to feel her mother's eyes
upon her. The Colonel talked on and on. The Tories had been
active all summer, the worst since the war began; but cold
weather would drive them back to Biguyduce. Jonathan
Nutting was back visiting in Cushing with the damnedest tale
to tell. 'He was up to Thomaston yesterday,' the Colonel said,

'and he was telling me the whole of it, and six-eight of us listening.'

Mima had to say something to her mother. The fire was brighter and Jess kept a small flame dancing. Joel stood there with the Colonel and Philip. Mima, under cover of the Colonel's steady declamation, asked:

'How's Bess, Mother?'

'Good,' Mrs. Robbins told her. 'She was up to see me day before yesterday.'

There was no suggestion of reproach in her tones — but it was week before last, instead of day before yesterday, that Mima had last come to see her mother. She heard the Colonel's words.

'... for Martinique; but a frigate laid her aboard and took 'em off and carried 'em into St. Lucie's in Barbadoes. Put 'em on the prison ship, with more'n five hundred others, French and Yankees...'

Mima asked in a low tone: 'When's her baby coming?'

'Not till October. She's still real spry.' It was now Mrs. Robbins who looked at the fire, Mima who watched her mother's calm countenance.

'... four months,' the Colonel was saying. 'And hot as the ungreased hinges of hell, and they was locked up below most of the time, and not enough to eat. Jonathan said there was ten of them begun to figure...'

'I haven't seen Bess for a long time,' Mima murmured.

'You don't get down here much,' Mrs. Robbins agreed. 'And she can't make out to go so far.' Jess came and sat by Mima's other side, and Mima was glad to have him there, as though he gave her some security. She did not want to be with her mother alone.

'... and they thought if they could get to the privateer, they might take her. The ones in the scheme could all swim...'

Mima looked at Joel, thinking how straight and lean he was, and how the muscles rippled along his flanks and shoulders when they swam together. He had been a soft, helpless little baby once, in someone's arms. Colonel Wheaton's tale ran on.

'... so for the rum, the sentries, long as it was a hot night, let 'em come on deck to get a breath of air; and they'd come up five or six at a time, only one would hide behind the water casks or something when the others went back down. That Barbadoes rum is hot stuff, and the sentries warn't in no shape to count. So when they were all on deck, hid forrad, they slid down a rope onto the main chains and stripped nekkid and set out and swum to where the privateer...'

'How's Bet?' Mima asked in a low tone, under cover of his words. 'And Lucy? Lucy still say she's never going to have another one?'

Mrs. Robbins laughed. 'The women say, but the men do,' she commented. 'Bet's expecting. She always tells me, soon's she knows.'

'... and climbed up her cable,' said the Colonel. 'Nought but a couple of sentries on her deck, and they grabbed the one on the windlass before he woke up. Then quicker'n scat they grabbed pikes from the racks, and guns and all; and they clamped down the hatches and the companion scuttle before anyone could roust out the men below.' His roaring tones went on and on. '... and they sailed her right out of harbor,' he declared. 'They had to go close by the fort, but the soldiers didn't even hail them. They sailed her to Martinique and sold her for four thousand crowns to divide up among the ten of them.' And he cried: 'And by Balls and Belches, I say that's better than dying of the pox in a hulk! Jonathan's a man!'

Philip said that this was certainly true, and he hospitably proposed that they bend their elbows once for Jonathan. The rum was ready, and after Jonathan there had to be another drink for the men with him. Young Jake threw more chips and scraps on the fire; and Mrs. Robbins slapped a mosquito and said: 'They're at me again! Minute the smudge stops, every mosquito on the lake comes gnawing at me. Come in and set a while, Mima. Be neighborly.'

Mima, at thought of going indoors where there would be more light, felt a sudden panic in her. She wished for rescue, and looked at Joel; but it was the Colonel who saved her. 'I want to get along up-river,' he said. 'I footed it from Dave's, Joel. Can you carry me as far as your place?'

'Certain,' Joel agreed, and caught Mima's eye. Mrs. Robbins said the Colonel might full as well stay the night here; but he would not.

'I didn't figure to come, anyway,' he explained. 'Not till I see Dave in Warren and he said he'd fetch me up. I'll take a look around, tomorrow early, and start back. There's a lot to tend to at home, these days.'

Philip and Jess moving with them, he and Joel started toward the landing. Mima turned hurriedly to kiss her mother good night before she followed them, but Mrs. Robbins held her for a moment.

'There, baby, we miss you,' she said. 'Don't ever forget home folks, Mima.'

'I'll come again soon,' Mima promised.

The older woman chuckled. 'If you don't, I'll be up to find out what's keeping you,' she declared. 'Now go along with your Joel!' She added amiably: 'But Mima — don't try to teach your grandmother to suck eggs!'

Mima wished to run, to dart away; but she could not move. She stood still, trembling with a deep alarm; and after a moment her mother kissed her again. 'There, it's all right, baby,' she said reassuringly. 'I don't blame you a mite.'

Mima whispered: 'Does Father know?'

'Him? A man never knows till it's shoved in his face,' Mrs. Robbins confessed. She added: 'But Mima, he'll be bound to notice pretty soon. You and Joel better go see the parson before that, or Robbins will be raising a rucus.'

'We're going to!'

'Well, see't you do. Now go along with you. If your pa starts getting his dander up, I'll cool him down.'

Mima clung gratefully to her mother for a moment, then went swiftly after the others toward the shore.

On the trip up-river, the Colonel and Joel paddled, and Mima sat between them. The moon was dark, the night still with stars; but the light breeze from the northeast promised bad weather to come. The Colonel talked, of Tories and of the war; and Mima waited for Joel to speak, and they reached Round Pond.

'I'll go on to your landing,' the Colonel suggested. 'Walk it from there.'

But Joel said: 'We'll carry you up the river.' He turned the canoe into the stream. 'Colonel,' he said. 'Something I want to ask you.' He coughed in embarrassment, and Mima smiled at the sound, trembling where she sat between them. 'Did you ever marry anybody?'

Colonel Wheaton exclaimed in surprise: 'God's Nails and Britches, no!' Then he added, chuckling at his own word: 'Only Mrs. Wheaton, if that's what you mean. Who wants to get married?'

'Me for one,' said Joel, more strongly. 'And Mima for another!'

The Colonel made a startled sound. 'Well! Do you so?' He hesitated, was silent for a long minute. 'Damn it!' he protested then. 'What do you want to get married for? You're still scratching gravel, Joel, trying to get along.'

'Well,' Joel told him in a dry amusement, 'we thought some of raising a family.'

'My God, ain't there enough paupers in Sterlingtown a'ready!'

Mima laughed, full of a delicious excitement. 'Our babies won't be paupers, Colonel,' she protested. 'Joel's got four hundred acres, and he's a worker. That's all any man needs. And all any baby needs is its father.'

He said over his shoulder: 'I hate to see you go spoiling your shape having babies for a no-good soldier! I told you not to marry this tom cat! Why don't you wait for a better man to come along?'

'There isn't any finer man than Joel,' Mima said, so simply that the Colonel was silenced, while they threaded the meandering stream through the meadow, but he said at last:

'Well, I'd admire to marry you two, but I don't know as I've got a right to. I never heard of a Colonel doing any marrying. Why don't you go to Mr. Urquhart?'

Joel said: 'Mima don't like him.'

'He's an old goat,' the Colonel agreed. 'And I guess he's fetched a bleat out of half the nannies in town in his time; but he could marry you. I'll tell you.' They reached his landing and he stepped ashore and stood on the bank and they sat in the canoe at his feet. 'I'll get a J.P.'s commission, then I can tie you up tight as a drum. When did you want to be married?'

'Well, before cold weather,' Joel said; and the Colonel chucklingly agreed that a wife was a comfort in the winter.

'I'll 'tend to it,' he promised. 'I'm coming up the last of this month to fetch someone to dig my potatoes. I'll get my commission, and hitch you when I come.' He laughed and said: 'Go along home. It's a fine soft night. If it was me, Joel, I'd call myself as good as married a'ready. If you two should happen to feel the same, go ahead! It'll be all right. I'll be up in two-three weeks, marry you tunc pro nunc, as the lawyers say.' He laughed with a great guffaw. 'Good night.'

He turned up the shore, and they moved away down the river again. Mima crawled forward on hands and knees to take the bow paddle. Joel did not speak, nor did she. She waited for his word; but when it came, it contented her.

'Well, that's settled, Mima! I'm real glad, now't it's done. I'm going to be almighty proud of you.'

10

JOEL, once committed, wished the world to know. Matt and Jason were asleep when he and Mima came home; and there was a rule of old standing among the three men that they did not speak to one another before breakfast, when tempers might be short, and small differences too often flamed at a touch into open quarrels. So the announcement was delayed next morning till they had finished eating. Then Joel said proudly:

'Well, we're going to have a wedding in the Royal Mess. Colonel's going to marry Mima and me, next time he comes up-river.'

Jason said whole-heartedly: 'Well, that's good! It was about time!' Then at Joel's sudden, half-angry turn, he realized that he had said the wrong thing and added quietly: 'That's fine. You're all right, Mima. And so's he!'

Joel grinned, and Matt said affectionately: 'Far as that goes, you've been as good as married all summer. Words said over two people by some outsider don't make them married. It's the way they feel about each other. They're married from the time they both know they're always going to be the same. I've called you as good as married ever since May.'

Mima colored richly. They had thought their secret so well concealed, but these two, like her mother, had guessed the truth. Joel told Matt agreeably: 'I knew that, when you started calling Mima "Mistress Adams" — for a joke.' He told Mima, his arm around her waist: 'Matt's a hard one to fool!'

'It wasn't for a joke,' Matt said, and Jason assured them:

'You didn't fool anybody.' He grinned, clapped Joel on the shoulder. 'You been like a b'ar that's been at the sap troughs, licking your chops all summer, Joel.' He told Mima: 'And you've had a look in your eye, your own self!'

'I've been real happy,' she said honestly. 'I guess I couldn't be as happy as I have been and you two not know, us living here together the way we do.'

'When's it going to be?' Matt asked. 'Told your folks yet, Mima?'

Joel explained that the Colonel would have to get a commission as Justice of the Peace, that they would be married before the end of the month; and Mima said: 'We'll go down tonight and tell them, Matt, if Joel wants to.'

They were to find that even at Seven-Tree Pond no one was surprised by their news except the younger children. Her father nodded when they told him.

'I judged we'd hear the like before frost,' he assented, and he said dryly: 'Drawed it kind of fine, didn't you, Joel?'

Mima asked: 'Did you know too, Father?'

He touched her shoulder clumsily. 'I never know anything till I'm supposed to,' he said. He chuckled. 'That's the best way to get along with young ones, Mima. If they start to acting up so they need a whopping, you have to either pretend you don't notice, or else whop them. I never laid a hand on you. Any time you needed it, I'd always let on not to notice.'

She clung to him, thinking how often she had found in him wisdom thus commingled with forbearance. Her mother was equally prepared for the news they had to tell, but she thought badly of their choice of Colonel Wheaton.

'I wouldn't let that old Whistle Britches marry my hens and roosters!' she declared. 'Always a sky-hooting around, and talking till he'll deefen you if you'll listen to him, and drinking hisself stiff, and slapping backsides, and laughing at his own jokes till his puckering string lets go. I'd have Urquhart if it was me.' And to Mima's protest that Mr. Urquhart was a carnal-minded man, she said: 'Well, the Colonel's as bad, if it comes to that; and a parson's a parson, no matter what he does.'

Mima insisted: 'I think different, Mother. The way I see it, there's two parts to getting married. One's the law, so it'll be all legal; and the other's the sort of holy part.' She spoke in a quiet certainty. 'Joel and me can 'tend to the holy part ourselves. We have, long ago. The law part, anyone can do. I don't mind Colonel Wheaton being the way he is. He's just doing the law part. But Mr. Urquhart would let on to be doing something holy — and he's not a holy man, and him pretending to be one would physic me!'

Yet because her mother was persistent, she agreed to go to meeting and hear Mr. Urquhart again and see if that did not change her mind. She and Joel went down the river in mid-September, and they sat through the sermon in a meeting house not one-third full; and Mima hated every minute of it. She made Joel hurry her away afterward before Mr. Urquhart could speak to her. Joel laughed at her panic, told her there was nothing to be afraid of; but she insisted:

'I hate him, and I'm afraid of him. I don't want him near me at all.'

So they held to their intention that Colonel Wheaton should marry them. He sent word ahead of time that he would come up-river on the last day of September, duly armed with his commission; and Mima watched the days drift by and thought each day was fine. But the delay troubled Joel. He had been ready to go forward. To be compelled to wait was hard for him now. She saw that he was restless as the day drew nearer; and she was careful not to oppress him with tendernesses, nor harry him with questions, leaving him to work out the matter in his mind.

He turned more to Matt than to her for companionship in this last fortnight, and she made no effort to recall him; but one day Matt made occasion to speak to her.

'Don't worry about Joel, Mima,' he said. 'He'll be all right.'

'I guess men are always scared of marrying,' she assented. 'I'm leaving him be. I don't want to scare him more.'

'There's not many women got as much sense about men as you.'

She smiled. 'A woman can't live in the same house with three men as long as I have, without finding out a few things about them.' And she added warmly: 'I've found out one thing, Matt; you're a real sweet man.'

Matt laughed. 'I don't know as that's a compliment.'

'Well, it's meant to be,' she assured him. 'I've wondered sometimes why I don't feel this way about you, instead of Joel. I've always liked you, but I never thought much whether I liked Joel or not. Only, from the first time I saw him, I knew how it was bound to be with him and me.'

'Same as drinking rum,' he reflected, amused at his own thought. 'You don't drink it because you like it, so much. You drink it because of the way it does to you, makes you warm and happy and wanting to sing.'

'Joel said something to me once,' she remembered. 'He said there were some women you liked, the same as you would a man; and he said there were some you wanted to make love to; and he said there was another kind, the minute you saw them you wanted to have a baby by them.' Her eyes were for a moment dim with happiness. 'I want to have Joel's babies,' she said, and smiled at herself. 'Even if I hated him, or if he hated me, I'd want that just the same.'

He said: 'I hope I'll find a woman like you.'

'You will, sure, Matt.'

Matt colored suddenly. 'Matter of fact,' he said, 'I don't know but Sally Payson's the one. Know her, do you? Down in Warren?'

'I saw her at meeting. She's real nice, Matt.' And she said warmly: 'If it turns out so, I'll be mighty glad for you.' Yet she admitted to herself, before she slept that night, that she had been startled and even a little resentful at Matt's word. Once he had asked her to marry him; unconsciously she had come to think of him as loving her still, as one of her possessions. She was amused that she should begrudge him to Sally Payson now.

Mrs. Robbins wished Mima and Joel to be married in the house on Seven-Tree Pond. Joel was reluctant to agree to that. 'I don't see the sense of making a big to-do about it,' he protested. 'It's just you and me and Colonel Wheaton, Mima.' But she pointed out that there would have to be witnesses, and that her mother wanted everyone to come.

'She's already figured what she'll cook for them,' she said. 'She's got a lot of pigeons from the nesting, and she's got them put down in fat. She's going to make a pigeon pie, and they raised some onions this year. She aims to bake the pie in the ground, in the big kettle, and then put a crust on it and build a fire on the kettle lid to brown the crust. It's going to be about the biggest pigeon pie ever was baked, Joel.' And she urged: 'You let Mother have her good time.'

Joel chuckled and agreed. 'All right, then. You might say there were pigeons at our real wedding, Mima, that day last spring under the big oak on the hill, after we saw them nesting.'

'That was our real wedding, wasn't it.' She looked at him with twinkling eyes. 'You didn't know it was going to happen, Joel; but I did. I wasn't going to let you sell your land and go away, if I could make you stay.'

He drawled dolefully: 'Mean to say you dragged me away off up there a-purpose to get me in trouble?'

She tossed her head. 'I did that. I didn't want anybody coming.' And she said in a sudden urgent pleading: 'Don't ever be sorry, Joel! I couldn't let you go.'

He laughed reassuringly. 'I never will,' he promised. 'I guess I did know it was coming, too.' And he said quietly: 'But that day was a lot more than just a roll in the hay for me, Mima. Remember how fine the sun shone, and the clouds?'

She nodded, smiling. 'And the red squirrel scolding at us from the branch over our heads, and Sambo barking on the bear track way down at the bottom of the hill and wondering why we didn't come, and that bee buzzing around.'

'You could see Sambo was just plumb disgusted,' he agreed, 'when he caught up with us on the way home. He thought we'd plumb wasted the whole day. A lot he knew!' They laughed together at the memory; and Joel made no more objection to Mrs. Robbins' plans.

* * * * *

Theirs would be the first wedding in Sterlingtown, and Mrs. Robbins was bound to make it an occasion. She invited everyone, and everyone came. There had been no recent word from the Colonel, and Mima and Joel thought he might arrive the night before, and they were at her father's house to receive him. But he did not come. 'Probably came as far as Warren,' her father guessed, 'and he'll be up in the morning.' Mrs Robbins insisted that Mima stay here at home this last night before her wedding, so Joel went back to Round Pond alone. The older woman had a new dress of tow she herself had spun and woven, for Mima to wear; but it needed some fitting and they worked on it together, and talked late before they slept.

Joel and Matt and Jason came down from Round Pond soon after breakfast, and in mid-morning the others began to arrive, old and young. Babies could not be left at home alone, and the older children amused themselves. Mima was sorry Eben would not be here. Mrs. Robbins was early at her cooking.

The Colonel would surely come in time to marry them before dinner. Bet and Bess and Lucy brought in pine and spruce boughs to adorn t'other room where they would be married, and they admired Mima's dress; and out by the cooking fire the men drank rum, moderately and gravely, holding in check their jollity till the wedding should be done.

After a while they began to wonder why the Colonel did not arrive, and there was talk of going to fetch him; but Philip was sure he would be here in good time. When the pigeon pie was well and duly baked, and all was ready, he had not yet arrived. Bet went out now and then to ask for news of him, but there was none. Mima herself finally joined the others out-of-doors. They waited, and they watched down the pond, and Jess at last took his float and went as far as the outlet to see if by any chance the Colonel's float had overturned.

When he came back, with nothing to report, Mrs. Robbins said stoutly that her pie had to be eaten while it was hot, wedding or no wedding. The pie proved to be a work of art, with a crisp crust like bannock, of well-bolted meal; and the fat pigeons were rich and delicious in their own gravy; and there was rum enough, and mirth enough. But the afternoon waned. The sun dipped toward the tree-tops, and everyone said the Colonel would surely be here any time now; but he did not come, and Joel was black with rage at this humiliation.

The Bowens were the first to depart. Prance Bowen told Mima maliciously: 'I liked your wedding, Mima. I hope you have lots of them. A little later won't matter, anyway.'

Mima had kept a steady heart through the day's weary waiting; but she wanted to slap Prance Bowen. She wished to go to Joel; but others were beginning to leave, each saying a joking word to him. From where she stood she could hear them. 'Bijah Hawes drawled: 'I call it durned hard, Joel, just when you're primed to make a night of it!' Johnny Butler said, grinning: 'Well, this way you'll g-get some s-sleep, anyhow!' Even Uncle Ebenezer cackled mirthfully: 'Hold your fire, Joel, till you git the word!' She saw Joel grinning stiffly at their jests, clamping his temper under bonds. Her mother came to where she stood.

'Wait till I see old Whistle Britches!' she said furiously. 'I'll give him a piece of my mind!'

'Well, anyway, Mother,' Mima said bravely, 'it was a mighty fine pigeon pie!'

When the last guests were gone, Joel went down the river to find the Colonel, to find out what had happened. Mima wished him not to go, afraid — without admitting it even to herself — that if he went he might not return; but he may have guessed her fears, for he said:

'I'm going, Mima, but I'll be back. I'll bring him back, too. Tomorrow. Don't fret yourself. I'll be back tomorrow, sure.'

He went alone, and she returned to Round Pond with Matt and Jason. She was empty of all feeling, lost for once in something like despair. This day just gone had been planned so long; now it was come and gone and — nothing done. And Joel was gone, perhaps not to return. She slept to hopeless dreams, and woke and saw frost across the ground, and realized that October was here, and winter on its heels. She thought Joel was surely gone; and when he came back in mid-afternoon next day, she could not at first believe her eyes.

Matt and Jason had planned work near the cabin so that they might know when he came; and Joel hallooed from the pond, and Mima ran to meet him at the landing, and they came after her. Mima clung to him as though to make sure he were real; and Jason asked:

'Where's the Colonel, Joel? Didn't you fetch him?'

Joel shook his head. 'He forgot it!' he said furiously. 'Just plain damned forgot all about it! He hasn't got his commission yet, won't have it for a week.' He explained in a more tolerant tone: 'But they've had news down there that drove us right out of his head. That God-damned Benedict Arnold captured Fort Griswold and killed every man in it!'

Matt Hawes said quickly: 'Griswold? We went past there, marching to New York, Joel.'

'It's right across from New London,' Joel agreed. 'They say Arnold came up from New York and went through the town, stealing everything first and burning the rest.' Mima felt the anger shaking them all as they listened, pressing a little closer to Joel somehow ominously. 'Then he tried for the fort, and they wouldn't give in without a fight. He knew the militia were getting together, so he stormed the fort. Colonel Ledyard commanded, and they killed three-four hundred of the bloody backs, just like Bunker Hill; but they couldn't kill 'em all!' He added in a rasping tone: 'And after they'd surrendered, Arnold lined 'em up and shot 'em. Shot over sixty, wounded and all. If they were hurt too bad to stand up to be shot, they stuck 'em with bayonets!'

His teeth seemed to grate, as though they were on edge with rage. Jason said slowly: 'Why, the bastard!' His face was purple with congested blood. He stared at Joel unbelievingly. 'Did he, for a fact?'

'They say so,' Joel repeated. 'Guess't it's true. Down-river, everyone's standing around damning him and wishing there was some way to get hold of him.'

'I'd like to pick his hide off of him with skewers,' Jason said in a cold deliberate tone. 'I hope he cooks over a slow fire in hell for a million years.'

Mima had not spoken, content to be in Joel's arms, her cheek against his breast, holding him tight; but she felt the passionate anger in him that seconded Jason's words. Then Matt said quietly:

'Well, that's done and no help for it. When's the Colonel coming, Joel?'

'As soon as he gets his commission,' Joel said. 'He'll come right along up.' He added: 'I saw Eben in Thomaston, Mima. He's coming home for the winter, but he's going to stick with the Colonel and fetch him up here.'

She looked up at him through happy tears. 'I don't care if he ever comes,' she whispered. 'Long as I've got you home again. It's you I want, more than colonels or preachers.'

Joel laughed warmly. 'You've got me,' he told her tenderly. 'Hand and foot and — heart, Mima. But he'll come. I told him if he didn't I'd nail his hide to his own barn!'

* * * * *

Joel had said it would be a week before they could expect the Colonel, and when toward the end of that week a northeast storm set in and rain came lashing on the wind, penning them all indoors, Mima thought he would not make the trip up-river till the weather changed. But on the third day of the storm they were all in the cabin, the door closed, when Mima heard voices outside; and Joel went to see and cried in a great voice:

'Here's the Colonel, Mima! And your folks with him.'

A moment later the newcomers were in the cabin, shaking the water off their garments while Matt built up the fire. Philip and Mrs. Robbins and Jess and Eben had come with Colonel Wheaton; and Mima kissed Eben, and she told the Colonel and them all:

'I never thought you'd come a day like this. It's a wonder you ain't drowned!'

Mrs. Robbins said crisply: 'Well, it ain't my idea of a good day for a wedding, that's certain. When I think what a nice day it was the other time, and my pigeon pie and all, I could cry.' She said decisively: 'Colonel, get on with your rat killing!'

Colonel Wheaton said in defensive tones: 'Well, that's what I came for, ain't it?' Mima judged that her mother had already laid her tongue heavy on the man. He looked at Joel. 'Ready, are you?'

Joel said with a chuckle: 'Been ready ever since the first day I saw Mima, but it took me till now to talk her into it.' He put his arm through Mima's. 'Come on,' he said. 'Don't try to hang back now.'

Mima for an instant hesitated, feeling something inadequate and unsatisfying in this abrupt realization of all her dreams. Five minutes ago she and the three had been here alone, the rain beating on the board roof, the door closed, the only light coming from the fire and from the small west window on the side away from the storm. Now the cabin was full of people; now Colonel Wheaton was going to marry her to Joel. She moved her hands in a helpless gesture.

'I'd ought to change my dress, or something,' she protested.

Jess laughed; but Joel linked his arm in hers and said understandingly: 'All right. I know how you feel. You go change, and I'll slick up some. We want to do this right.' He led her toward the notched log ladder to the garret overhead, and because he had understood, she loved him so that she seemed bursting. She kissed him happily before them all, and climbed to the garret, and called to her mother, and Mrs. Robbins climbed the ladder to help her. Close above their heads the rain lashed the roof. A fresh log on the fire, wet when Jason brought it in, hissed and steamed and burst into leaping flames that threw a black shadow where they were. Below, Mima heard Joel moving to and fro. She could see Colonel Wheaton and her father, facing the fire, bulky silhouettes there. Eben stood near them. Eben was changed, she thought, with a quiet strength of manhood in him, and some sadness too. Matt and Jess and Jason were helping Joel, just as her mother was helping Mima.

Mima stepped out of her garments. 'I couldn't get married the way I was,' she told her mother. 'I couldn't get married barefooted.' She put on a fresh shift, petticoats, stockings and shoes she had scarce worn at all these five years since she came to Sterlingtown. Her mother, with strong hands that were healing and reassuring, loosed her heavy hair and brushed it long and braided it and did it up again. Mima buttoned her new dress with steady fingers, and when she was done she faced her mother, smiling appealingly. Mrs. Robbins took Mima in her arms.

'There, you're pretty as an apple,' she said. 'Want to go down now?'

When she saw Joel, he was changed; he seemed tall and straight and shining. She saw only his eyes. They were enough. They were all of him she wished to see. The cabin was full of shadows from the leaping flames. Outside the window, the day was gray and dark. Each person here seemed only half here. The bright light from the fire illumined one half, left the other half in shadow. Joel met Mima at the ladder foot and drew her arm through his.

'Here we are, Colonel,' he said quietly.

The Colonel had turned as Mima descended. He stood by the fire, his back to it. The chimney was built in the corner of the cabin, the slab table at one side under the window in the east wall that was closed now against the storm. A bench seat projected from the end wall on the other side of the chimney. The Colonel stood between the bench and the table. Philip was by the table and Mrs. Robbins crossed to him. Eben and Jess, Jason and Matt, grouped together with the bench between them and the fire; and Joel and Mima stood in the middle of the cabin, so that Philip and Mrs. Robbins were on their left, the others on their right.

The Colonel doubtfully confessed: 'First time ever I did this. Don't know just how it goes, only what I can remember, but I'll do the best I can.'

They were all silent for a moment, watching him. He said, frowning with the effort to recall the proper words: 'Well — uh — we're all here to see these two people, Joel Adams and Jemima Robbins, get married in the sight of God and man. Anybody knows any reason why they shouldn't, speak up or keep quiet from now on.' He looked around. In the hot cabin their wet clothes were steaming. After a moment he said: 'Well, that's all right, then. Now Joel, you take this woman for your wife, and you'll look out for her, and love her, and everything you've got you'll share and share alike with her, and you'll never have any other wife but her as long as you both live. Do you?'

'Yes, sir.'

The Colonel mopped his brow. 'Mima, you say the same, do you? Only you'll do everything he tells you, besides all the other things he said he'd do?'

'Yes, Colonel,' she promised.

Colonel Wheaton hesitated, gropingly. 'Well, let's see,' he said, 'I guess the next thing is to pray. I never tried that much, but here goes.' He shut his eyes, lifted his head. 'God,' he said. 'Please be good to them. They're good people. Amen.'

He opened his eyes. 'There,' he said uncertainly. 'I guess that's all. Damned glad it's over.' He laughed with a great relief. 'Now it's time to kiss the bride. I'm some better at that.' And he caught Mima and kissed her rousingly, and the others crowded toward her; but Mrs. Robbins said in sharp tones:

'Hold on, Colonel! Leave her go! You ain't finished! You have to pronounce them man and wife.'

'Goddlemighty, I forgot!' he confessed. 'That's so! How does it go?' He hesitated for a moment, said then carefully: 'By virtue of I'm a Justice of the Peace, and that gives me the right to, I do pronounce you man and wife.' He looked at Mrs. Robbins. 'You reckon that did it?' he asked hopefully.

'I reckon,' she assented. 'I sh'd judge they're married now.'

11

FOR Mima to be married to Joel made surprisingly little difference in the Royal Mess. Joel made his bed beside hers, in the garret, and the removal of his bunk gave more room in the crowded cabin; but that was the only surface change. The business of preparing for winter engaged them all. The crops were harvested, the roots dug, the cellar below the cabin was well filled; and the bins in the corn house were overflowing. They had bought a yoke of oxen from Boggs this summer, and there was hummocky hay cut and stacked in the meadows to feed them through the winter. For man and beast, provision in plenty had been made.

The war had come to be accepted as the background of their lives, something that would go on and on interminably. From Biguyduce west to Boston and beyond, Massachusetts had cleared herself of every major British force; but Washington still lay helpless outside New York, and Cornwallis was operating in Virginia, and there seemed no end in sight. Mima sometimes thought that this baby of Joel's which she bore so happily might be born and grow up to find the war still going on.

'But our children will go farther up the river,' she told Joel, and clear new farms; and theirs will go on, west, beyond those white hills, Joel. Remember? It isn't the King in London owns this land he never saw. It's people like us, that cut down the trees, and do our planting, and bring it all to bearing. We're the ones who will own it — even if the war never ends.'

Philip Robbins had raised a fine crop of corn this year; and Dave and Rich Comings, too. They still stored most of their crop in Philip's barn; and when the corn was cut, the ears were hauled up to the barn behind the swaying oxen, the sledges lightly loaded so that they would slide easily across the bare ground. Mrs. Robbins, disappointed in her plans for Mima's wedding feast, wished to make the husking a merry-making; and the Sunday after Mima and Joel were married, when they went down to have dinner at the house on Seven-Tree Pond, she spoke of this.

Philip readily agreed. 'We'd ought to do something to celebrate,' he said. 'We've had good crops, all of us. No fear but there'll be plenty to eat this winter. We've got a right to feel pretty good.'

Joel said: 'The Colonel's boated his corn all down to Lermond's. He don't aim to come back up here this fall.'

'We can get along without that old shitpoke,' Mrs. Robbins declared. She had become increasingly violent in her dislike for the Colonel. 'There's enough of us here in Sterlingtown to have ourselves a time.'

Jess reported: 'Johnny Butler says Phin's coming up this week sometime to have a look at his land up-river. He aims to build a hovel up there before snow flies, or this winter anyways. So maybe Phin'll be here.'

Mrs. Robbins predicted that Prance Bowen would not let Ez come, and her prediction was proved correct; but when the day arrived everyone else in Sterlingtown was there, and Phin, and Mily too. Joel and Mima were the last to arrive; and they found these two the centre of interest, Phin grinning in a happy embarrassment, Mily vocal with excitement. Mrs. Robbins came to meet Joel and Mima at the landing, and Joel looked at the group around Mily and asked what the to-do was all about, and she said sharply:

'It's Mily! They're getting married, her and Phin, day after tomorrow. They came up yesterday, visiting Lucy and Johnny across the pond, so Johnny fetched them over.'

Mima smiled at her mother's tone. 'Phin's lucky, I say. Mily's awful pretty.'

'They'll make a pair!' Mrs. Robbins declared. 'He's as dumb and gawkish as a turkey, always bobbing his head that way, and she's a flighty little flibbertigibbet! She'll keep him in hot water, and every other man around, too.'

'She'll settle down,' Mima said surely. They walked up past the old house, used for storage now, and went on toward the barn where the others were gathered, and Joel told Mrs. Robbins with a chuckle:

'Nothing against a girl, being pretty. I married one that's hard to beat that way.'

Mrs. Robbins sniffed scornfully. 'No credit to you! I'll bet a pretty Mima had to drag you to it.'

Mima smiled, undisturbed; but Joel said: 'Wrong, Aunt Mima. I've been after her for two-three years. She led me a chase, but I wore her down.'

When they joined the group by the barn, Mily came running to meet them, kissed Mima, told Joel: 'I'm a mind to kiss you, too, but I guess Mima would scratch my eyes out!'

He laughed. 'That's right. We'll have to watch ourselves,' he said. 'What's this about you and Phin?' he demanded. 'You ain't old enough to talk about getting married. You're still wet behind the ears.'

'No I'm not either!' she cried. 'See?' She drew aside her hair, turned her ear forward. 'Look!'

He chuckled and touched his finger to her smooth throat there and said: 'Well, kind of dampish anyway. Going to marry him, are you?'

'Day after tomorrow,' she declared. 'We came up to see where he's going to build a house for us. I've always said I'd never live away off up here away from everything, but Pa said if I was going to marry Phin, I'd have to; and I guess it's worth it, to marry Phin.' She whirled away to where Phin stood, and drew him toward her. 'Isn't he sweet?' she demanded, and Phin burned red so that they all laughed at him. Joel, to rescue Phin from his embarrassment, asked what the news was down-river, and Phin said that a French army and a great fleet had come to help Washington; that Clinton might at last be driven out of New York. 'I dunno, but they say that's why Arnold came up to New London,' he told them. 'So's Washington and De Grasse would chase him up there; but Colonel Wheaton 'lows they're all going to get together and lick Cornwallis instead. I dunno how it'll come out, but the Colonel says they'll do it.' His head jerked out the words.

Mrs. Robbins was scornful of the Colonel and of his predictions, and said so; but Phin's news, since it gave them something for which to hope, put them all in a more festive humor. The great pile of ears at the end of the barn floor was a mountain when they attacked it; but it began to shrink as snowdrifts shrink in spring. Even Mrs. Robbins took a hand for a while in mid-afternoon, before it was time to get the cooking started. Eben got the first red ear, and he chased Mily, screaming, thrice around the barn before he caught her. Because she was so soon to be a bride, she was fair game; but Joel when he found a red ear leaped toward Mrs. Robbins and caught her and kissed her, and had his ears boxed, and kissed her again for that, laughing and holding her so tight she could not fight him. Under cover of the laughter of them all, she whispered:

'Be good to Mima, Joel. She always was bound she'd have you.'

'I aim to,' he told her. 'The best I know. But I ain't much, some ways, Aunt Mima.'

She said in an affectionate ferocity: 'You behave yourself or

I'll bring you up short mighty quick!' She pushed him away. 'And for the matter of that, so will she!'

When it was time to begin cooking supper, she called Susie to help her. For this occasion, since the husking was in the barn and the new house was some forty rods away, the old house by the landing would do service; so Sue need not have gone far. But she did not want to go at all. She was thirteen years old, no longer a child and not yet a woman; and she had watched Eben chase Mily around the barn, her own cheeks as bright as Mily's, her eyes wide and wondering. She said: 'Can't I stay and help here, Ma?'

Mrs. Robbins' eyes twinkled. 'All right,' she agreed. 'But as soon as young Jason finds a red ear, you come along, you hear me! I judge that's all you're waiting for.'

Everyone heard her, and laughed; and Sue was furious because Jason — Dave's oldest — was only nine years old. She flounced her skirts indignantly at the suggestion, and she and Jason were both as red as apples. But while they were still laughing, big 'Bijah Hawes let out a whoop and held up a red ear and caught Susie and swung her high above his head, so that she squealed with delighted terror. He tossed her till her skirts flew embarrassingly high, and she commanded him to let her down. He kissed her, in his great arms like a baby; and she fought to get down, but he would not let her go till she kissed him, hugging him tight. When he put her down she fled toward the house in silent shame.

Mrs. Robbins started to follow her, but then young Philip — he was a year older than Jason — found a red ear and pounced on Mily and kissed her so hotly and so long that Mrs. Robbins took him by the ear and marched him away, and Mily was left all tumbled and disordered and crimson. Matt ran after Mrs. Robbins to claim his kiss, and then Mily was racing around the barn again with Johnny Butler leaping like a panther on her heels, till she darted into Phin's arms and from that sanctuary paid the forfeit.

After a while Philip called a halt for refreshments. There was
a great wooden bowl of rum mixed with molasses and water,
and the men drank and returned to the work. The sun was low
and the shadows crept toward them down the slope from where
the new house stood against the wood. For a while no red ears
appeared; and Philip halted the proceedings and set them to
toss all the corn that was still to be husked into a pile outside
of the barn.

'Be dark soon,' he told them, 'and I don't aim to have a light
in the barn.'

'Bijah roared: 'Don't need light for the kissing, Robbins.'

'Can't see if an ear's red or not without a light,' Philip insisted. 'Out here we can see by the light from the fire.'

When that task was done the men turned to the rum again,
and voices were louder, and red ears were so hard to find that
men began to base their claims on a few scattering red grains
in an ear otherwise of normal color. There were laughing arguments with Philip as judge and jury, till he ruled elaborately
that one red grain was worth a kiss on the forehead; that a
scattering of red kernels might lead a man as far as the cheek;
that a whole red ear was good currency for a smack fair on the
mouth if you could get it.

Joel found a prize and clipped Mima; but she did not resist
him, and Jess protested that she had cheated. 'No fun for the
man unless you run,' he claimed; but Joel said he was satisfied.
The bowl of grog was handy, and this was thirsty work. Mily
was fair game; and as dusk came down she was panting and
flushed from many races around the barn. Once Jason Ware
caught her midway of her first circuit, behind the barn, out of
their sight; and they heard her squeal as he kissed her, and Joel
sang:

> So he caught and he bussed her, he clipped and he tossed her,
> Till she fled and he ran and he found her and lost her
> And found her again — she was easy to find —
>   Far from the sight of the gentlemen!

Everyone shouted with approval, but Mima saw Phin scowling, his hands clenched, watching the corner of the barn for Mily's return. She came back with her hair disordered, her cheeks flaming, Jason chuckling on her heels; and Philip bellowed for silence.

'No more running around the barn,' he ordained. 'All of us want to see the fun.' After that, when she was pursued, Mily scampered like a squirrel, darting into the barn, scrambling over the grain bins, running up the ladder into the haymow and pushing the ladder away behind her and dodging to and fro on the hay till she saw her stronghold about to be entered, then sliding down to the barn floor again. Mima wished Phin would find a red ear; but he was for a long time luckless, and his frowning humor deepened till at last Mima herself started to pull back the husks from an ear, and saw its color. She tossed it to Phin, and he ripped it open and scrambled to his feet and bounded toward Mily. She escaped his first leap and was halfway up the ladder to the mow in a flash. He was at her heels instantly. She disappeared on top of the hay, and so did he; and they did not at once come into sight again, and Jess shouted:

'Whoa back there, Phin! This ain't day after tomorrow!'

'Fetch 'em down,' Philip ordered. Jess and Joel jumped for the ladder together, and 'Bijah bawled derisively:

'Hold her, Phin, her tail's afire!' Phin and Mily appeared at the ladder top as Joel began to climb, and they tried to push it clear so that Joel could not ascend; but Eben swarmed up a post at the other end of the barn, and David followed him and came on them from behind, and the two of them grappled Phin and pinned him; and Joel swung Mily up in his arms and, holding her so, slid down off the hay to the barn floor again. He landed on his feet, but he lost his balance and fell and they rolled over and over on the floor, and Philip cried:

'Bring 'em up before the magistrate! We'll put 'em on trial. I won't have nobody dancing Sallinger's round on my good hay!' Dave and Eben held Phin, and Joel marched Mily forward, and the culprits were set side by side; and Philip said:

'All right, now, order in the court!' Phin was grinning redly, and Mily pretended to be excessively demure. 'What's the charge against these two, and who brings it?'

Joel said: 'I do. I'll whisper to the judge.' He did so, elaborately; and Philip held up his hands in shocked disapproval.

'So be it,' he told them. 'I won't state the charges, but they're bad enough. Who's witnesses?'

Dave held up his hand. 'I was, for one. I saw . . .'

'Never mind what you saw, young man,' Philip warned him. 'What say these here hellions? Phin, you guilty or not guilty?'

Phin grinned and answered nothing, confused by this foolery, not knowing whether to laugh or to be angry; and Philip said: 'Well, I find you guilty, and I'll sentence you to a double drink of water with no rum in it, Phin; and you've got to save up five red ears before you take another try at her. You, Mily . . .'

But Johnny protested: 'Hold on there, Judge! What if Phin don't find that many before they're married day after tomorrow? You better let him off!'

'Well, mebbe,' Philip agreed. 'Long as he behaves.' And Mily said eagerly:

'Oh, he behaves real good!'

They roared with delight at that, and Sue came running to say it was time to eat, and they trooped away to the bounty Mrs. Robbins had provided. Jess built up the cooking fire for light, and they sat around it on bear skins or piles of hay. The starlit night was mild enough, the fire made a circle of heat, the smoke rose straight upward. Mima was a little uneasy. Phin, she thought, had been angry before and might be again, and with some justice. Mily was pretty and little and gay, and quick as a cat; and her eye was a challenge to any man. Half the men here had towsled her already, and Mima saw 'Bijah watching her now with a speculative eye. If the rum held out, there might be trouble before this husking was done. Mily had

been the prize they all sought to seize. Mima herself had been
kissed only by Joel. Bet was heavy with the baby that was
coming soon; and Bess was quiet too, and Lucy Butler had been
ignored so that Mima once or twice saw a malicious anger in
her eyes as she watched Mily's flights.

She saw her father, moving from one to the other of the men,
speaking to them quietly, and guessed what he was saying; and
when he spoke to Joel and moved on, she whispered: 'I can guess
what Father said, Joel. Something about not making Phin mad,
starting a fight or anything.'

He nodded. 'He's right, too. Fun's fun, and she's a hot little
piece; but Phin don't like it. He's apt to climb somebody before
we're done.'

Whether or not it was because of Philip's warning, or because
red ears were rare, the husking after supper was almost decorous.
Mily was kissed, but so were others; and Mily did not run beyond
the firelight to escape any pursuer. As the end of the pile
approached, Mima went to stand with her mother for a while;
and she said: 'They're near done.'

'And no bones broke,' Mrs. Robbins agreed with relief. 'Take
a pack of men and a flighty girl and anything can happen. If
she comes to live up-river here the way Phin figures to, there'll
be doings around here, I tell you!'

'Mily's all right,' Mima insisted. She said: 'I'm going up to
the house to see the babies, Mother.' Bess and Bet and Lucy
and Mary Hawes had as usual bestowed their youngest indoors,
leaving the husking at intervals to go up to nurse or tend them.
Mrs. Robbins went with Mima, and Bet called Rich and followed them.

'I guess we'll start home,' she explained. 'The young ones
had ought to be abed.' At the house, she picked up their Polly,
just coming twenty months old; and Rich carried Esther, and
when they set out through the darkness, six-year-old David
trotted between them. Mima looked after them thoughtfully,
and when an hour later she and Joel in the float started for
home, Mima said:

'Bet's Polly looks kind of pindling to me, Joel. Don't she to you?'

'She looks like all the rest of 'em, to me. I can't tell one baby from t'other.'

'You'll find out they're different,' she promised him. 'But Polly's always been kind of croupy. She's a sickly child. I c'd see Bet and Rich are worried about her. Bet kept going up to see how she was, all afternoon.' She said, half to herself: 'It must tear a woman all to pieces to have a sickly young one. I hope ours never are.' And she asked: 'What do you want, Joel, a boy or a girl?'

He said teasingly: 'Well, I c'd get more work out of a boy.'

Mima laughed. 'All the same, I'll bet you'd be a perfect fool about her if you had a daughter.'

'I'll be that way about any baby you have for me, Mima.'

'I hope I have lots of them,' she said. 'Oh, Joel, I hope we live to have grandchildren and great-grandchildren and everything! Do you think we will?'

He said affectionately: 'What's to hinder? We've got a head start a'ready.'

'I'm real glad we didn't waste any time.'

When they landed, he turned to her, not touching her. 'Mima,' he said soberly, 'I want you should know one thing. This business of having babies is a woman's job; but there may be ways a man can help. I want you to tell me what to do.' He colored a little, awkwardly, at his own words. 'I want to be good to you, Mima; but I don't always know how, the best thing to do. You tell me, and I'll do the best I can.'

Her eyes were bright with tears. 'Just be like you are, Joel,' she told him. 'That's all I ever want in the world, to just have you.' Her hand touched his arm; they went up the path together silent side by side.

12

BET'S baby came a week later, and the baby and Bet were fine. The baby was a girl, named Betsey. Mima saw it when it was a week old; and she held it close in her arms, sitting on the side of the bed, rocking it with movements of her body, crooning over it happily. Bet watched her with smiling eyes; and she asked at last:

'When's yours coming, Mima?'

'In March,' Mima said. 'I thought first off it would be the middle of February, but Mother thinks about the tenth of March.' She asked: 'Did she tell you about it?'

'Nobody'd have to tell me, watching you look at mine.'

'Do I show much?'

'Not to mention. It's more the way your eyes look, as though you were thinking about something wonderful; and your skin's so clear, like it was transparent. You look fine. It agrees with you. I get all blotchy.'

'I've felt fine, right along.'

'Didn't it bother you at first, mornings?'

'No.' Mima laughed a little. 'The only thing, I want queer

things to eat. I keep thinking of things I wish't I had. One day it was raw onions. I must have ate five or six. They tasted so good. Joel said you couldn't come in ten feet of me for the smell of them.'

'I ate a whole dish of pickles once,' Bet agreed. 'But I'm always sick every morning for the first two-three months. Fetch up my breakfast half the time, before I've had any use of it at all.'

'I guess I was too happy to be sick.'

'Didn't it fret you, not being married?'

'I knew we would be. I didn't tell Joel till along in the summer.'

Bet looked at her curiously. 'Did he jib at it any?'

Mima shook her head. 'He wanted to go right off down-river and get married then, but I made him wait. There wasn't any hurry as long as I didn't show, and we had a lot to do this summer.'

'I'm surprised Joel didn't carry on about it. I didn't know as he was the marrying kind.'

'Nobody could make Joel and me any more married than we were, just by saying so.' The baby began to fret, and Mima said: 'There, she's hungry! I wish I could feed you, baby.' She watched Bet give the breast, watched her sister's countenance. 'That makes you happy, doesn't it?' she said.

Bet laughed. 'Yes, but she's awful rough a'ready, hurts me sometimes, nuzzling like a colt, as if it didn't come fast enough to suit her.'

Mima stayed a while, talking happily with Bet, playing with little Polly. Polly's nose forever needed wiping; and Bet said: 'She's had the snuffles ever since the baby came.' She laughed. 'I guess her nose is out of joint!' Mima tried to teach Polly to blow when a kerchief was held to her nose; but Polly resented this procedure, shaking her head to escape the kerchief. She seemed fretful. 'She coughs some, nights,' Bet confessed. 'I guess she's kind of croupy.' Mima felt the sharp edge of fear in her sister's tones.

She left them presently and started home, paddling slowly up the shore toward her father's landing. November was upon them. The leaves were gone from all the hardwoods except the oaks, which still wore tattered garments of rusty brown. A scud of ducks went over her head with a quick whisper of wings. The day was sunless, with a penetrating cold. It might snow any time. Before spring came, her baby would be born; but she felt no fear. Blrth was life. It happened all the time, to every living thing. Unless you gave life, you were not yourself alive; but to give a part of your life to another was to start a stream flowing that would go on and on. Life was a chain, and you a link in that chain; it was your task to be sure the chain was never broken. She heard a shout far down the pond behind her; but she paid at first no heed. She paddled slowly, her own thoughts engaging her, till she heard a shout again, and an answer from the shore. Someone was coming up the pond, perhaps with news which he cried to Ez Bowen, or 'Bijah Hawes, or to David as he passed. Mima let her canoe drift to see whether he would hail Richard's cabin too; and she heard him do so, and then the float appeared around the point, angling across the lake toward Johnny Butler's, and the man in the canoe saw her, and waved his paddle, and — still well over half a mile away — bawled something at her. She could hear his voice, but not what he said; yet clearly this was news worth the hearing. She paddled out to cross his path, or to come near enough to hear him. He was racing, as though speed were vitally important; and her heart began to beat harder in a shared excitement. When the man saw that she was moving toward him, he did not shout again. The canoes drew together, his making for the point opposite the island, which he must round to go in to Johnny's landing, Mima moving across from the island to approach his course. She came near enough to recognize Phin Butler; and she hailed him at last.

'What did you say, Phin? I couldn't hear.'

He bawled: 'Cornwallis surrendered. His whole army.

They cotched him, Mima! He give up. He surrendered.' He did not slacken his speed. 'Tell your folks,' he shouted. 'Fetch Joel and them down. We'll have a rankiboo tonight to celebrate!'

He was passing not thirty yards away; and she said, smiling at his haste: 'It's a wonder you didn't stay down-river.'

'Mily's up here with Lucy. I just only went to Warren this morning. Besides, I wanted to fetch the news. You tell 'em.'

He passed her, and she turned back across the pond, herself in some haste now, her heart pounding strongly. Maybe if Cornwallis and his army were captured, the King would not send any more armies. Maybe the war was over. Maybe the King would keep New York and let the rest of the country go. He might keep Biguyduce, too; or maybe there would be another expedition to drive the redcoats out of Biguyduce and end the Tory raids along the coast. Eben had come home for the winter, had come in time to see Mima and Joel married; but he talked of going with John Perry next year. Perry hoped to get a commission, to command a privateer; but perhaps now that Cornwallis was captured, there would be no more fighting to do. Maybe Eben would stay home.

She angled toward the mouth of the river, and saw Jess and her father at the landing and swung in to speak to them. She called, before they asked the question: 'Cornwallis has surrendered, Father!' Jess uttered a cry and turned to run toward the house to tell them there, but her father waited where he was, not moving, asking no questions, standing heavily as though digesting this word. She drifted near the bank. 'They caught him and all his army,' she said, watching her father's grave countenance. Phin had been like a man half-drunk, his tones shrill, his eyes shining; but her father seemed almost to be saddened by this news which she had thought would make him glad. 'It might mean the fighting's over, Father,' she said. 'Aren't you pleased at that?'

He looked at her as though in surprise, as though he had forgotten she was there. 'So, yes!' he assented. 'But the hard part's coming, Mima. If we've thrown the King out — who'll govern us now?'

'Why, we will, ourselves.'

He nodded. 'So we will,' he agreed. 'But that's a trick will take some learning — with no two men of us thinking the same about what has to be done.' He said half to himself: 'A king's not so bad. There's this to be said for him: you don't have to fret yourself about doing this and not doing that. He says what you're to do, and you can just do it. It's a sight easier to take orders than to give them, Mima. The soldier may get killed day times, but he can sleep good nights — while the general is figuring how to keep the soldier from getting killed the day after.'

'We don't have to worry about that,' she protested, puzzled by his concern. 'There'll always be someone to tell us what to do.'

'Trouble is, we won't have to do it,' he reminded her. 'It's having to do a thing that makes it easy. Soon as you start wondering whether you will or not, you go and get idees, same as Arnold did. Idees has been the ruin of many a man. Most of us ain't fitten to handle 'em.'

'There'll be big men,' she insisted, 'great men, like George Washington, to figure out the best thing to do. We don't have to fret ourselves.'

'You're wrong there, Mima,' he said. ''Course there'll be some like him, and there'll be others that think they're like him. But they ain't the ones will make this country, Mima. General Washington didn't capture Cornwallis by hisself. He had a good many men — men like me and Ez Bowen and Joel and Phin Butler — to help him. He couldn't have done it without them. We're the ones that have to make this country now, not the Congress or the generals or any two-three dozen big wigs off somewhere that nobody ever saw. It's the ones like us, making farms and towns, that will make the country when you put them all together. Don't ever think different.' And he said strongly: 'You get to letting someone way off in Philadelphia run your business for you and you might full as well have a king.'

Her canoe drifted toward the shore and touched at his feet and for a little she did not push it off. 'I guess I know some what you mean,' she agreed. 'But I've always figured it was the great men that did the great things.'

He said strongly: 'It is, certain. But it isn't doing the great things that amounts to so much, Mima. It's the little ones. If somebody keeps doing the little jobs all the time, the big jobs will get theirselves done, one way and another.'

'They always tell you about kings doing things,' she urged doubtfully.

He chuckled. 'That's just because kings are more int'resting to talk about than ordinary folks,' he told her. He looked up and down the clearing. 'Take it this here, I've done it, me and them that came out of me and Ma. We've done it with our hands, mostly, and our heads some. Done it by working and saving and sticking to it.' He chuckled. 'Clean your plate. Wear it out. Make it do. Do without. Give me enough men that will go along on that pattern and I'll match any king.' She saw a strong serenity settle on his countenance. 'I'll take folks like us,' he said. 'And you can keep your kings.'

* * * * *

Mima, when she came back to the Royal Mess and told them Phin's news, was still thinking of what her father said; and while they were all at supper she repeated it. The three looked at each other thoughtfully; and Joel said: 'Well, there's something in that. We'll have to run the country.' He chuckled. 'But I guess I'll let others 'tend to it. I don't like having to decide things. It's a strain on a man.'

Matt said in an amused tone: 'You always were a long time making up your mind, Joel.' His eyes caught Mima's. 'I'm some different. I like to figure what's best to do — and try to see it done.'

Jason said: 'Well, Phin had one good idee, anyway. We'll all go down to Robbins' house and celebrate tonight. I'm for a celebration any time you've got the excuse for it, and the rum.'

Mima decided not to go. She was beginning to feel heavy and awkward; and sometimes she was conscious of the fact that she had nerves, feeling an impulse to tears at the least mishap, wishing to cry out in storming protest at scant excuse. When she said she would stay at home, Joel protested in something like irritation:

'Come along, Mima! I don't want to miss this.'

'You go, Joel,' she urged. 'The men will all be there, and you can have a better time without us women around.'

'I'll not go and leave you,' he told her sullenly.

She did not want to go, and she knew he would go without her. She at once wished him to go and resented his going. 'There, I'll be all right,' she declared. 'Nothing will happen to me here. You go have a good time, Joel. Don't think about me at all.'

In the end, he did go; but she saw that he hated to go almost as much as he would have hated to stay. When she was alone, she cleaned up the supper things, and cried a little because she was so sorry for herself, left drudging here while everyone else had a good time. She climbed to the garret with some difficulty, thinking what would happen if she fell and started things with no one here to help her; and in her bed she lay with her hands on her abdomen, feeling her baby stir, trying to guess whether it was a heel or an elbow or a small head that thumped under her palms. Feeling the baby move she could not be lonely, and she fell asleep and lay smiling in her sleep.

She waked when they came home. Jason Ware's hoarse voice roused her; and then she heard Joel singing:

> Tippies! To your lovely lasses
> Kindly pledge the brimming bowl.
> Nought pure love and rum surpasses,
> Or so sings the jocund soul.
> Should tomorrow...

The song ended in a three-cornered argument, Matt urging the others to keep quiet; and Mima heard her name, and then Matt somehow hushed them and they came into the cabin with elaborate precautions, hushing each other hissingly. Joel started to climb to the garret, and lost his footing on one of the notches in the log and slipped and swore; and then Matt and Jason together seemed to be steadying him and helping him and he crawled up beside her. She said softly:

'Hello, darling.'

Joel hissed loudly. 'H-s-s! Don't wake up!' he urged. 'Ev'rything's al-l-l right. Don't wake up!' So she was quiet, and she heard him ridding himself of moccasins and bear-skin stockings and he rolled in his bed beside her own. After he began to snore she heard a whisper of sleet on the roof, and then it ceased and there came a hush that filled the night with whispering; and she knew it had begun to snow. A few flakes sifted through. The roof was leaking here and there. It would need to be mended and strengthened before winter settled down.

In the morning, Joel was the first to wake. When Mima roused, he had built up the fire. She lay still, indolent for once, and not till the three of them were gone out-of-doors did she descend, careful as nowadays she always was against any mischance, conscious every waking hour of the burden which she bore. Joel had filled the kettle and put it to boil. The light fall of snow was already melting; but it made bad footing, so she would cook indoors. Till spring came they would be denned here, with no escape from one another. The men returned, and Joel gave Mima a hug and a clip on the shoulder and asked whether he had waked her last night; and she said: 'Just barely. I was asleep again before you were.' She asked about the celebration, and they told her; but she saw that Joel was thoughtful and quiet, and wondered why. When the others went out again, he stayed behind and spoke his mind.

'I've been thinking, Mima — I haven't been out of here, only down to Warren or Thomaston, since I came; and that's right on to three years. Or it will be, come spring. I'm thinking we might go home for a visit.'

'This is home,' she reminded him. 'It's all the home I've got. All my kin are here or down-river.'

'I want to show you off,' he said cajolingly.

She tried to laugh. 'I'm not much to show, the way I am, Joel.' She was ice-cold with fear. If he went to Boston without her, he might never return; and yet to go with him would be fearful.

'Might be we can fetch Jemima back with us,' he suggested. 'My sister. I've told you about her. She's going to like you — and you her.'

'Don't ever tell two women that,' she protested, smiling. 'Or they'll never do it. Joel, it'd be an awful trip, looks to me, so cold and all. How could we go?'

'Phin says Colonel Wheaton's sending a sloop load of lime. He'd carry us down, and we could come back the same way.' He added: 'The Tories have mostly pulled in for the winter by now.'

'It'd be so cold.'

'Thing is,' he confessed, 'there'll be a celebration, Mima! I want to see it! Capturing Cornwallis just about means the war's over. Probably the Congress will set a day for thanksgiving and all.' He urged like a small boy: 'I'll buy you a lot of pretties, too; and there's things we need.'

'I declare, Joel, I don't know how I ever could! Besides: Jason and Matt would have the place a mess before I got back. How long would we be gone, Joel?'

'Middle of December, maybe.'

'The pond will be froze up, and the river. We'd have to walk it, coming home.'

He laughed at her fears. 'I never saw the day you couldn't walk me into the ground.'

'I'm some heavy and clumsy now, Joel.'

'Well, that young one you're carrying might as well start walking now, Mima. He'll never learn any younger.'

She held back until she saw him begin to grow sullen and angry at her reluctance. She said then that he could go alone and leave her here; and he retorted: 'No, if you won't go, I'll stay here!' She wished they might wait for summer and fine days; but he reminded her that summer was a busy time. The question was still unsettled when he left her and went to work with the others, and Mima was wretched between her reluctance to go and her dread of letting him go alone, perhaps never to return.

It was Matt in the end who decided her. He came back to the cabin before the others, and he said at once: 'Joel's talking about you and him taking a trip to Boston, Mima.'

'Yes, he was telling me. I don't know as I want to go.'

'Well,' he said, 'it's a sight easier to gentle a colt than to force break him. The thing to do is get him used to the bit before he rightly knows it's in his mouth. You haul him up short the first time, and he'll be bit-shy the rest of his life.'

She trusted Matt, and she valued his judgment. 'I told Joel to go without me,' she said in a low tone.

Matt shook his head. 'You go to Boston with him, Mima,' he said surely. 'You fix and go.'

* * * * *

They were six weeks away. The trip down along the wintry coast was a bitter ordeal of aching cold in the sloop's small cabin with no fire worth the name; and the return was worse. Ice made on the rigging and the rail. Mima did not come on deck at all till they made into the river.

Yet she was glad she had gone. She did like Joel's sister; and Jemima promised to come, as soon as Joel and Mima had a house of their own, and spend a summer with them. Jemima was twenty years old, two years younger than Jess; and Mima judged they would take to each other. But she made no such suggestion to Jemima.

Mima had been happy and proud to be with Joel too, and to

see his pride in her, and to hear him boast about what a fine farm he had, and how witless others were not to come to Sterlingtown and buy land as he had done. She did not remind him that he had planned once to sell that land.

They made many purchases, buying small presents for everyone, and also acquiring some of the things they would need when their own house was built. They bought a chair, and a cord bed, and a small wheel for spinning tow, and a loom, and pewter porringers and platters, and a new baking kettle with a tight top and a rim around it to hold the coals, and a tinder pistol and a dozen odds and ends. There was room and to spare in the sloop's hold, once her cargo of lime had been discharged, and they brought back a surprising bulk of goods. But when they came to the Fort Wharf at Thomaston, it had all to be left there, since ice had clogged the river from the narrows up, so that the sloop could go no further. Uncle Oliver would store their things for them till Joel could come and fetch them, packing everything home a load at a time through the winter.

They walked the long miles home. The snow was not yet deep, and the trail was well packed by the feet of other passers as far as Warren. Beyond, the walking was harder. They followed the river and then the pond; and in some places the ice was scoured bare by the wind. Ezra Bowen waved to them from his cabin as they went by along the shore, and Mima felt a quick happiness.

'We're home, Joel,' she said.

'Not yet,' he reminded her. 'Three-four miles still to go. Tired, Mima?'

'I'm taking it easy,' she assured him. Joel was packing as much as he could carry, the metump line cutting hard across his forehead, pushing his eyebrows down so that he seemed to frown. She had the new gun he had bought, slung over her shoulder; and a bag of odds and ends meant to delight the babies hung from its barrel. They stopped at David's house on the way up the pond, and David and Bess were there with the

children to give them welcome. Mima opened her bag and dis-
tributed to each his allotted treasure; a belt knife for Jason, a
bag of buttons for Chloe, a jew's-harp for Joe, a knitted hood for
baby Joel. But she saw that David and Bess were troubled, and
she asked, suddenly afraid without knowing why:

'Is everyone all right?'

She saw Bess's eyes fill; and David said: 'Little Polly's awful
sick, Mima. Got the croup terrible. Ma and Bess have been
taking turns with her at night, so Bet could get some sleep; but
I guess she's going to die.'

Mima looked at Joel, and he came and took her in his arms.
She said, against his breast: 'I'll help, Joel. Let's go on now.'
She told Bess: 'I'll stay there tonight, Bess. You're wore out.
You stay home or you'll be sick your own self.'

Bess said in a helpless relief: 'I'm real glad you're home,
Mima. Seems like things straighten out when you take hold of
them.'

Mima remembered a night four years ago when she was with
Bess here, and the baby came; and she remembered the sudden
terror in Bess's tones when she asked: 'Why doesn't she cry?'
She caught Bess and kissed her. 'You're the bravest one there is
anywhere, Bess.'

Bess said wretchedly: 'Seems like I can stand it better when
it's my own. That hurts so bad you don't feel it. But Mima, it
just tears me to pieces to see little Polly gasping and choking,
that awful moaning hollow way. I help all I can, but it's been
three nights of it now.'

Mima said: 'Dave, you put her to bed. I'll stay with Bet
tonight.'

'Ma's there now,' Bess told her. 'She'll tell you all there is to
do.'

There was a trail broken through the thin snow from David's
to the other cabin, a scant half-mile away. When they set out,
Joel said: 'Mima, you hadn't ought to, the way you are, and all
tired out from tramping through the snow and all.'

'I ain't a mite tired,' she insisted, smiling up at him. 'There's two of me now, Joel, and I'm strong as both of us put together. Bess and Ma have been at it till they're wore out.'

'Mary Hawes could come.'

'Bet's my sister. Don't you fret yourself, Joel. I'm up to doing anything I have to do.' She said: 'But I'd like it if you'd stay too. Rich'll need company; or if he wants to sleep, you can maybe help me.'

'I aim to stay,' he assured her. 'I aim to keep an eye on you.' His tone was at once jocular and deeply tender. 'You've got something of mine and I don't aim to let you out of my sight till you give it to me.'

'I'm taking good care of it, Joel,' she promised him. 'And I'll give it to you, safe and sound, some fine March day.'

They found Mrs. Robbins and Eben at Richard's. The older children were all at Philip's house. Only Richard and Bet and the sick baby and small Betsey, not yet two months old and wholly dependent on her mother, were here. Polly was asleep when they arrived. Eben opened the door for them, and they entered quietly. Bet, without a word, came into Mima's arms; and Mima held her close, patting her shoulder, whispering things. She felt her own baby stir as though resenting the pressure of Bet's body against her own. Richard and Joel and Eben went out-of-doors where they could talk without waking Polly; and Mima bent to look at her, and at what she saw her heart stood still. She thought Polly was already dead, she lay so quietly; and her face was shrunken and dark-shadowed and small. But Polly stirred restlessly, moving one hand, and Mima drew back, turning to her mother and Bet again.

'I'll stay tonight, Mother,' she whispered. 'What do I do when she coughs?'

Mrs. Robbins pointed toward the hearth; and Mima saw a birch-bark tube, rolled small, three or four feet long. 'Steam is all there is to do,' the older woman said. 'Make a kind of tent with a blanket, and put one end of that birch-bark pipe over

the kettle spout and the other under the blanket, and let her
breathe it — only don't scald her. Breathing the steam helps
some.'

'Does she get any better?'

'She'll have spells, choking and straining to get her breath.'
Mrs. Robbins sat down weakly, staring straight ahead, dry-
eyed. She shook her head from side to side. 'I declare, it takes
the tuck all out of me to have a young one sick,' she said whisperingly.

Bet took Betsey and began to nurse her, sitting on the bed
across from where Polly lay. Mima went to her. 'I guess you
wouldn't go home with Mother, and let me and Joel 'tend to
Polly?' she said gently.

Bet looked up at her, and she smiled, her lips tight across her
teeth. 'Not tonight, Mima,' she said. 'Not tonight. I'll sleep
tomorrow night, I guess. We'll both sleep tomorrow night.
Polly'll sleep then.'

Mima felt, rather than heard, a thudding vibration in the air,
as though a night hawk had swooped and checked itself on still
wings somewhere just out of hearing. She stared at Bet, her
eyes widening at what she saw. She whispered: 'Ain't there
anything to do?' Bet shook her head; and Mima said almost
pleadingly: 'Then — do you have to be here?'

'She'll want her mommy with her,' Bet said surely, and
smiled again, this time beautifully, looking down at the baby
at her breast. Mima moved toward her mother again, touching
the older woman's weary head. Someone opened the door,
and she saw that dusk was falling. Mima said: 'Mother, you
and Eben go along home. There's nought to do.'

'I've done all I know,' Mrs. Robbins said in a dull tone, and
wrung her hands. She rose and came to Bet and touched her
shoulder. She said: 'Mima's more good to you than I'll be,
Bet. I'll come first thing in the morning.' She went out of the
door.

Polly began to cough, coughing till she choked, straining for

breath with a protracted, hollow, moaning sound. Mima took
her up, holding her erect; she gave Joel instructions and he and
Richard together arranged the blanket, swung the kettle over
the fire, fitted the bark tube to convey the steam. Bet said
gently: 'She's better lying down, Mima. Rich makes a bed up
for her on the floor. I want to hold her myself, but she's better
lying down.'

Rich was arranging the bear skins, thick and warm, a blanket
over them. He fixed another like a tent to hold the steam.
Mima laid Polly down under the tent, sitting beside her. It was
a long time before Polly was any easier. Her wheezing and
coughing were terrible to listen to, they were so strained and
weak. The strength was gone out of her. It seemed impossible
that she could endure so long. Mima saw Richard's hand,
hanging at his side, tight clenched so that the knuckles were
white. She could not remember that he had spoken at all since
they arrived; but he was always a silent, steady man. Betsey
was still nursing sleepily. Polly's coughing eased and stopped;
and Mima lifted the blanket away.

'Can you feed her anything?' she asked.

'It makes her cough,' Bet said.

Polly seemed to be asleep again, her small chest heaving as
though to catch her last breath. The fire gave the only light
in the cabin. Cold air flowed from under the door along the
floor toward the hearth, crossing where Polly lay; and Mima
told Joel to contrive a screen to keep it off the sick child. He
did so. After a while Polly began to cough again.

The night was long as long. Whenever Polly coughed, Mima
trembled terribly, as though she were cold, with chattering
teeth. Once she saw Bet watching her with a still sympathy;
and Mima saw with wonder that Bet seemed calm enough.
What was it Bess had said? 'It hurts so much you can't feel it!'
Bet seemed to feel nothing. She watched, and when there was
anything to be done, she was quick to do it, supplementing
Mima's activities. Rich did not sit down all night long, but

Joel came to sit on the floor behind Mima, offering his shoulders as a support for her back. When there was nothing that needed doing, she leaned against him, grateful for his strength. Once she drew his arm around her and pressed his hand against her body to feel their baby stir.

Polly died toward dawn. She had been coughing. Her wheezing inhalations were no longer so protracted, nor so loud; and presently one of them began and stopped midway, and the stillness was like an alarm bell. Bet was on her knees in an instant, snatching aside the blanket tent, catching up the little body, cradling it in her arms.

'There, baby!' she said, in a clear tone like a silver wire, smooth and bright and thin. 'There, Polly. It won't hurt any more.' Mima saw Bet smile, transfigured in the firelight, triumphant because her baby's torment now was done. The grave was hard to dig, for frost was like granite, deep in the ground.

13

SNOW held off, and in early January, Joel made several trips down-river to bring up their purchases. Phin Butler finished building his cabin up the river above Colonel Wheaton's land; and on the seventeenth, he brought Mily there to live. During the winter when the river was frozen, their cabin was most easily reached by following the carrying-place from the head of Seven-Tree Pond, along the west side of the meadows there, so that they did not cross Round Pond on their way; but Jess brought the news of their arrival 'I didn't see them myself,' he said. 'But Johnny helped sled their alls up from Warren. He told me Mily's going to have a baby before spring, by the looks of her.'

Mima was curiously touched by this, feeling between herself and Mily a common bond. She wished to go and see Mily and welcome her. Once during the early fall she and Joel had walked up the river to where Phin was building. The small cabin stood on the west side of the stream, almost opposite where they had spent the night together watching for the Tory band who had murdered Captain Soule. She proposed now

that they go see the newcomers; but Joel would not let her walk
so far.

Nevertheless Mima thought often of Mily, and she wondered
whether the girl — Mily was only seventeen — would fret at
the loneliness there. She remembered how Mily had run in
pretty terror around the barn when at the husking any man
pursued her; and she suspected Mily had enjoyed those hot
pursuits and tumbling captures, despite the fact that she was to
have a baby now so soon.

Her own days passed in a calm serenity. Joel was everything; and Jason and Matt conspired in kindliness. It was
Matt's proposal and insistence that Mima should no longer
climb every night into the garret. The ascent had become
laborious for her; so he and Jason gave up their beds and took
to the garret, Joel and Mima sleeping thereafter in the bunks
below. Mima was often all day alone in the cabin. They had
made rapid strides, in the last year, in widening their clearings.
Immediately around the cabin, along the shore of the pond and
the margin of the meadows, forty or fifty acres was more or less
ready for planting, the trees cut and burned; and another ten
acres had been cleared on Matt's land to the northward. This
open winter permitted them to work almost every day, and
they began to clear a tract south of the brook and to the west of
that projecting ridge which rose fifty or sixty feet above the
level of the pond and around which the brook drew three parts
of a circle. Since to tramp the half-mile back to the cabin for
their midday meal would have consumed time, they sometimes
took along bread and meat to eat on the spot; but Joel always
came home to see how Mima fared. He was wholly tender and
protective during these last weeks before the baby's coming;
and sometimes, almost deliberately, she fretted and complained
in order to taste the happiness she found in his solicitudes.
But more often, seeing the haunting terror in his eyes, it was
she who was the comforter, laughing, bidding him not to be
afraid.

'Women have babies all the time, Joel,' she reminded him, 'and so do bears and squirrels and cows and dogs and everything. I guess if a cow can, so can I.'

He always protested that he was not afraid at all; but she was not deceived.

*   *   *   *   *

Early in February, Mr. Urquhart came to preach a sermon at Philip's house. He came at his own suggestion. His troubles in Warren were persisting. He had sued the town for unpaid salary and won a verdict, but the vote to continue him as minister 'for the present' was not reassuring, and the party which despite his marriage to Miss McIntyre still refused to believe that his wife in Scotland was dead gained strength all the time. He may have sought to win supporters in the plantation up-river; or he may have thought Sterlingtown might some day offer him a place when Warren refused to keep him longer. For whatever reason, he proposed to come; and though Philip might have refused, Mrs. Robbins thought it high time a proper sermon was preached in Sterlingtown.

Mima and Joel went to the service because her mother wished it. When they arrived at the house, Mr. Urquhart was already there, and he remembered her. He surveyed her without pretence and came to grasp her hand. 'So, Mistress Adams,' he said. 'Now you are at God's holy business.' His tone was so unctuous that Mima wanted to laugh — or to slap him.

'I'm going to have a baby,' she said. 'If that's what you mean.'

He smiled, and when he began to speak he took for his text the verse: ' "And the man called his wife's name Eve, because she was the mother of all living." ' As he proceeded, Mrs. Robbins stared in a stony rage, and Joel was red with anger, and Mima saw her father's fists knotted as though he would have liked to strike the man. Mr. Urquhart's sing-song voice

went on and on interminably. He beamed approvingly on
Bet and Bess, and on Lucy Butler and Mary Hawes, sitting with
their children around them, their babies in their arms. Adam
and Eve peopled the world, he said, even without benefit of
clergy. Let those who were without sin cast the first stone.
Was not marriage still sacred even though it were solemnized
with only God and the forest for witnesses? They were to go
forth without fear; to increase and multiply, to people the
wilderness.

'As if we was so many heifers!' Mrs. Robbins said afterward
indignantly. When he was done, Joel and Mima went directly
toward the door, and out into the clean whiteness of the snow.

They walked quickly at first, to be rid of him; and presently
Mima laughed a little, and said: 'Joel, I'm thankful, more than
ever, that he didn't marry us. I never was ashamed till he said
we hadn't ought to be. Just his way of talking was shameful.'
Her head rose. 'But I'm not ashamed now, and I don't aim to
be, ever. Having a carnal man like him say we were married
wouldn't have made us any more married than we were. He
thinks marrying is just — babies. Joel, he's a bad man.'

Joel's hot wrath had given way to sober judgment. 'I've
known some fine men were preachers,' he said, 'and some
preachers that were fine men. There was one with our regiment, and there was one at home when I was a boy. There's
a lot of strength and — beauty in a good preacher, Mima; but
there's nothing but a rotten stink to a man like Mr. Urquhart.'

She said: 'Father reads the Bible aloud sometimes Sundays,
and talks about what he reads. I like to hear him. We talk
over what he says, but we think more than we talk. I guess
thinking about things, all by yourself, is as good as going to any
church.' She slipped her arm through his. 'Thinking is good
for people, Joel. Just going off by yourself and sitting down and
thinking about yourself and the things you've done — or
mean to do.'

Joel nodded his agreement. 'I know one thing,' he added.

'If you've been doing something you hadn't ought to, you don't like to be alone where you've got nothing to keep you from thinking about it. You go hunting company, so you won't have to think. I've always had a notion it was the things a man thinks about when he's alone that makes him the kind of man he is.' He looked at her bravely. 'I'm a sight different since I think so much about you than I was when I was always thinking about Fanny and them like her.'

'I know, Joel. But — I can see how a man might like Fanny. Taking care of her that time, I got so I kind of liked her myself. She was a real friendly thing.'

'She was fun to fool with.'

Mima looked at him in a shy way. 'It hasn't been much fun for you lately, Joel, with a wife like me; but I'll be different pretty soon now. I'll make it up to you.'

He held her and kissed her gently. 'You're always everything to me,' he said. 'This now is sweeter, some ways, than having you all slim and laughing and loving. It makes me feel big and proud, makes me want to be fine, having you so.' And as they went on he said: 'I never was calm and happy till lately, Mima. It used to be I was always wondering what I'd do next, whether I'd sell my land, all things like that. Now I know what I'm going to try to do all the rest of my life. It's like being in the army, where you didn't have to worry about what to do as long as you obeyed orders, only I've given myself my orders now, and all I have to worry about is doing them.'

'I hope we live a long time, have a lot of fine children, make a good farm. I hope we're always good people, Joel, doing the best we know. We'll get a lot done in our time.'

'There's not an awful lot one man can do.'

She smiled. 'There's not an awful lot one ant can do, either. Do you remember the ants we saw moving their nests? One of them couldn't carry but one egg; but a million of 'em could carry a million eggs.'

He laughed. 'And a million eggs is a lot of eggs,' he agreed.

'We're just like them,' she insisted. 'All up and down this country there's a million of us doing the same thing. Every time you cut a tree, Joel, a million other trees come down; and every time you make a farm, it's a million farms; and every time we have a baby it's a million babies.'

He linked his arm around her waist. They were crossing Round Pond in the blinding blaze of the winter sun. 'And two million if it's twins!' he said, and chuckled, looking down at her. 'I wouldn't wonder if it was, Mima. You're big as all outdoors.'

'Mother says it's a boy, the way I carry it. Do you want a boy, Joel?'

'I just want you and a baby.'

'You've already got them, Joel.'

'I'd rather have 'em in separate bundles.'

She laughed. 'Wonder if he can hear us talking about him? Wonder if he's as anxious to be here as we are to have him?'

'I guess he figures to wait till spring. This cold weather, he's a sight more comfortable where he is.'

'I'll keep him warm and snug after he comes,' she said, suddenly a little husky. 'I'll never let him freeze his little nose.' She began, absurdly, to cry, laughing through her tears. 'Ain't I the fool, Joel? But it makes me so happy, talking about him.'

*   *   *   *   *

The days passed gently. For one or two nights each week they were apt to be alone in the cabin. Jason and Matt this winter made regular trips down the river. Jason might go as far as Thomaston; but Matt usually lodged with Captain Payson in Warren, bundling with Sally Payson. He told Mima late in February that he and Sally had about decided to marry as soon as the mutual obligations which bound the Royal Mess together should be satisfied. 'Jason's thinking of it too,' he said. 'If he can find a wife to suit.' He promised to bring Sally up-river when the ice went out in the spring. He and Jason stayed sometimes two nights away, leaving Round Pond Saturday, returning Monday morning; and when they were gone, Joel never went far from the cabin and Mima.

Mrs. Robbins thought the baby would arrive about the tenth of March and she proposed that Mima come down a few days before — to be safe — and stay with her. There was room for Joel too; and Mima reluctantly agreed. 'But I'd rather it was just you and me, Joel,' she said.

'You'll need your mother,' he insisted. 'I wouldn't know what to do.'

'I could tell you,' she promised him. 'I've done it. And it's going to be hard for Mother. Mothers take it hard when their own little girls have babies. They get mad at the husbands sometimes.' She laughed and said: 'When Bet had her first, Mother chased Rich right out of the house with a broom, like she was crazy. Don't you worry if she does get mad at you.'

Joel grinned. 'Guess I can outrun her. What did she do that for?'

'It's the way mothers are, sometimes.' She told him wisely: 'There's a lot of things about having babies that no one can really understand. We just know how to do it when the time comes, that's all. But she was all right with Bess, and with Bet after the first. She won't bother you.'

He asked: 'Do they always come on time? I mean, will ours come right on the tenth?'

'The first one is a little late sometimes,' she said. 'Or it might be a little early. You can't tell for sure.'

Her mother and Eben came up to see her on the last Sunday in February; and Mrs. Robbins confirmed her former prediction. 'It will be around the tenth,' she was sure. 'It's settled some already. You'd better come down next Sunday to be in plenty of time. I've got his clothes all ready, enough for a dozen babies. Bess's is coming in April, and she can have what you don't need.' She chuckled comfortably. 'With her and

Bet and you all at it, you keep me as busy as a sheep farmer in
lambing time.' Mima herself had brought some things from
Boston, and Mrs. Robbins approved them. She stayed for
dinner, and spent the time taking in some of Mima's own
garments, so they would be ready to be worn after the baby
came; and at dusk she and Eben started for home again.

Wednesday of that week Jason and Matt went down-river to
Warren, expecting to return that afternoon. During the night
before, the weather had changed. The February thaw set
water dripping off the eaves; and an hour after they departed,
it began to rain; a warm, slashing rain with a southerly wind
behind it, so that except when Joel fetched wood from the great
pile by the door, or brought water from the spring, neither he
nor Mima went out-of-doors at all. The fire was warm and the
great chimney sucked so much air out of the cabin, drawing
fresh air in through every crack and cranny, that the smell of
the rain was in their nostrils. Joel thought that with this rain
the others would stay the night in Warren. He and Mima had
much quiet, happy talk together all that day, and they sat
late by the fire till Mima went to bed to be more comfortable,
and Joel lay beside her in the narrow bunk a while. He did not
bank the fire. Mima slept fitfully nowadays, waking often,
and she could rise and add a log now and then to keep it burning. He went to his own bunk by and by, and she slept and
woke and replenished the fire and slept again.

The first pain woke her sharply, and she lay quiet, feeling her
heart pound, wondering whether this was in fact the beginning
of it. She knew that sometimes pains started and stopped again;
but the next one was stronger. Joel lay so still she knew he was
asleep. The rain was beating hard. For him to go down to
fetch her mother would be to leave her here alone an hour or
more, while her mother dressed and collected her needs and
came the wretched journey through the rain. Mima did not
want to be left alone. The pain came again, but that meant
nothing. It might still be hours, might be daylight, or noon
tomorrow, before the baby came.

The pains were bad. There was no denying that. They seemed to crack her very joints, as though her bones were breaking. She lay tight-lipped while they lasted; and in the blissful relief between them she remembered that she had thought it would be beautiful and splendid to feel them racking her. But there was nothing splendid about them. They were terrible, a flaming torture which seemed unbearable and which each time was worse. She wished Joel would wake, and once she whimpered a little, lying there alone, whispering his name.

'Please, Joel. Please, Joel. Please, Joel.'

But he did not wake, and when the pain passed she did not want to wake him.

After a while, she did not know how long, she thought the pains would be easier if she were on her feet. She got out of bed and drew a blanket around her shoulders over the soft wool shift she slept in. She put on moccasins over her heavy stockings; and she added a log to the fire. Joel stirred but he did not wake. She stood near the fire to be warm, walking two or three paces from side to side; and when the pains came again she tried to stand still, tried walking, tried sitting down to ease them.

But they would not be eased; and she remembered that she did not want these pains to cease till they should have come to their fruition.

She began at last instinctively to help them. This intensified the agony, yet also it produced a numbness too. When she held her breath and bore down, the pain became a living flame that consumed without destroying her. Mima worked hard. If this was her baby, trying to be born, she must help him all she could.

Joel woke and saw her crouching, bent double, her face congested with her effort. He said sharply: 'Mima!' His feet struck the floor; he was beside her in one long stride. 'What's the matter?'

The pain passed and she stood up, smiling at him. 'I think the baby's coming, Joel.'

He tried to speak, tried again. 'I'll bring your mother.'

'Don't go away, Joel. I don't think there's time.' She saw sweat start on his brow. She said: 'We can do it.'

'I can get her quick.'

'It would take an hour. The baby might come before she got here. I don't want to be alone then.'

'I don't know what to do.'

'Put some clothes on you. You'll catch cold. I'll tell you what to do.'

He turned to obey, and that great fist in her body contracted in a hard knot that swelled irresistibly, breaking her apart, breaking her open. Joel saw her crouch again, and sprang to catch her; and when she could she straightened up.

'Joel, you dress,' she said insistently. 'You'll catch your death of cold!'

He was white as stone, but he steadied himself; he put his arm around her shoulders. 'You're my wife,' he said. 'I love you, Mima.'

'Put some clothes on,' she repeated. She was sweating. The cabin was hot, but that was fine. The baby would need to be warm. She put more wood on the fire while Joel dressed.

She lay down on the bunk again. There could be no question now that the time was near. She held her voice steady, telling Joel what to do, telling him what he would need. She made him find blankets and linen, brought from Boston this winter, now stored in the garret. She herself was able to make the bed up fresh, crouching when she had to, working when she could. He put water to heat, set basins ready, laid clean clothes and towels where they could be had. At her direction he hung before the fire, where they would warm through and through, a soft blanket and a heavy one; and she told him where to find scissors and thread. She no longer tried to rise, lay watching him move to and fro, smiling at him, but once he saw her lips strain back over her teeth; and he knelt beside her, holding her, whispering endearments.

'I'm all right,' she said when the pain was gone. 'But that was a pretty big one, Joel.'

He tried to laugh. 'I'll take care of you, Mima. I've helped heifers and sheep and mares, many's the time.'

'I love you, Joel.'

'I love you.'

She could not speak for a while. When she could, she said: 'I can brace my feet against the foot of the bunk. Fix something for me to pull on, Joel.'

And after a little: 'Joel, after he's born, you tie the cord in two places, not too near his little stomach. Then you cut it between where you've tied it. Don't tie it too tight, or the threads will cut it.'

She spoke faster and faster, to finish her instructions in time, because a pain was coming. He said something, but his voice receded and was lost in a swimming blaze of flame. The pains came almost without an interval between them now. She heard herself saying over and over in a silly, babbling, toneless voice: 'I love you, Joel. I love you. I love you. I love you. I love you.' He kissed her streaming brow. She braced her feet and held to the twisted blanket he had fixed and pulled hard, the sinews cracking in her wrists. He was talking, but she could not hear him. She heard her own voice. 'I love you. I love you.' She heard her tones rise to a louder pitch. She told herself, speaking very fast: 'Quiet, Mima. Be quiet. Be quiet.' She cried: 'I'll be quiet! I'm quiet!' She tried to whisper: 'I love you. I love you.' She tried to look at him, and saw him far away, but she must make him hear her, so she called, louder and louder: 'I love you, Joel! I love you! I love you!' He was black against the firelight, tremendous and so far away. She whispered: 'Sh-h-h! Mima, be quiet.' She said: 'Yes, yes, I'll be quiet. I'm quiet!' She cried in ringing tones: 'I'm quiet! I'm quiet!' She heard her own voice like a trumpet blast: 'I'M QUIET!' Her mouth opened till her dry lips cracked, and she heard herself utter a terrible, hoarse, inhuman, long-protracted scream.

Then there was relief from unendurable agony, and sudden peace. Joel was holding her, his arm under her shoulders. She said in weak urgency: 'He's come, Joel. Help him. I'm all right. Help him.'

Joel obeyed her. She heard a clacking, spitting, ridiculous, small, fussy, resentful sound, and her heart swelled in a dreamy ecstasy; for it was not Joel making that small sound. Then Joel was saying, in a breathless tone:

'Try again, Mima. He's almost here! I'll help!'

She obeyed him. This was not so bad, not so blinding, not so all-consuming. She felt herself emptied. She tried to raise her head; and, looking down her length, thinking how thin she was, she saw him busy at something. Then he said: 'It's a girl, Mima.'

There was a sound like someone trying to cry, and hiccoughing between cries; a little 'Hah-up-hah!' And then, very small, but lusty all the same, complaining at recent discomforts, complaining at being ejected from warm quarters into this cold world, there came the first cry: 'Yah-h-h! Uh-yah-h-h!' It went on and on, small but mighty. Mima thought how Bess had asked: 'Why doesn't she cry?' She whispered happily: 'Someone's awful mad! Wrap her in the blankets, Joel, the soft one first. Nice and warm.'

He obeyed her, and she said: 'I'll hold her, Joel. Here beside me.' The great roll of blankets was big within the circle of her arm. She lifted a fold aside to see the small wrinkled countenance from which these 'Yah-h-hs' of rage and complaint emerged.

'There!' she whispered. 'You're all right now, baby. It won't hurt you any more.' She thought of Bet when Polly died. 'Joel, may I name her Polly?' she asked. 'It would tickle Bet.'

He agreed, busy tending her. But the rest was nothing. When it was done, she drifted into blissful sleep, her husband beside her, her baby in her arms.

14

THE baby was lusty, with a jocund eye and an infectious, bubbling smile; and she was forever brimming with Mima's bountiful milk, her smiles as often as not flecked with small white curds. Joel was sufficiently fatuous about her to satisfy even Mima. They had her to themselves till toward noon of the day she was born, when Jason and Matt returned. Matt, having properly admired the newcomer in the cabin, went to summon Mrs. Robbins to welcome her new grandchild; but not before the three men had drunk a noggin of rum to Polly's health. Joel had to drink more than once that day. He was congratulated not only as the father, but also on his part in delivering the child; and Mima, content to lie quietly with her baby in the curve of her arm, watched him happily and proudly, her world completed. Even Mrs. Robbins told him she could have done no better job herself. Eben came up with her, and Philip came later, bringing Susie, now almost fourteen and tall for her age. She was allowed to hold the baby, and Eben held her too. He told Mima: 'A baby's wonderful, I think. I want to have one of my own pretty soon, after the war's over.'

Mima, at his mention of the war, felt a cold wind of fear across her heart. March was here, and spring would come, and Eben would go away again to join John Perry in that petty warfare between small boats along the coast. When Cornwallis surrendered last fall, she had hoped that meant the end of the long struggle; but through the winter they had heard no peace talk. There was even a report that another British army would presently be landed in the colonies. And unless peace came, if Perry again went privateering, Eben would surely go. Mima knew that. So his word now filled her with a still terror. But she did not let him see this. He was a man, must do what he thought best to do. He had praised her baby; and she said, smiling:

'Everybody acts as if it was the first baby ever born. I guess it's no different from the others.' Then her arm tightened around the bundle beside her. 'But it seems a sight different to me.'

She had thought her mother would bathe the baby; but Mrs. Robbins said stoutly: 'She's full as well off the way she is, for a few days. There's too much bathing babies, I always say. Keep them warm and keep them fed and let them sleep; that's all they need. Wait till it comes a warm day.'

She asked what the baby's name would be, but Mima evaded answering. She and Joel thought that decision must wait till they had talked to Bet. Rich and Bet came up to Round Pond on Sunday; and when the baby had been sufficiently admired, Mima said:

'We were wondering, Bet. Would you let us call her Polly?'

Bet's eyes filled, but she was smiling. 'I'll be real glad if you do,' she said. 'I always did think Polly was a pretty name.'

So Polly the baby became; and through March she throve mightily. Mima at Joel's insistence stayed abed a full week, though she felt able to be up and doing before that term of quiet passed. Before she was on her feet, Jason and Matt went with Jess and Johnny to hunt moose on the Madomock, and

Joel and Mima and the baby had the cabin to themselves while the men were gone. The hunters came back with sleds heavily laden. Down-river in Warren supplies were low; and Matt took a haunch of moose meat to Captain Payson.

'They needed it,' he told Mima when he returned. 'They're all out of meat, and corn too. Sally says there've been times when she was so hungry she'd just have to put her head down and cry a spell before she could go on with what she was doing.' He added: 'She's weaving a piece of cloth for a coat for me, with some wool I got her from Lermond.'

'I guess it's harder for them to get meat down there. The bears and all don't go near the town.'

'Cap'n Payson don't manage good. He's witless, some ways,' Matt explained. 'Here last summer he shot at what he thought was a bear, along in the evening in the green corn, and killed their cow.' He added: 'But Sally's sensible, and she's a worker. She'll be a good wife for me.'

Mima asked in a curious tone: 'You love her a lot, don't you, Matt?'

He looked at her for a moment uncertainly. 'Why — I guess so, Mima.' Yet his eyes were eloquent, saying what he did not say in words; and she was troubled.

'You'll get so you love her more and more after you're married to her.'

'I guess I will,' he agreed.

* * * * *

Mima's was not the only baby born that winter. Mily Butler's came in April, just before the river cleared of ice. It was a boy, and they named it Will. Bess ten days later presented David with a girl, and Philip jocularly told Dave and Joel:

'Well, Phin's a jump ahead of you two. Womenfolks are all right, as long as there ain't too many of them around; but it takes men to clear the land and make a farm. Boy babies is what we need in Sterlingtown.'

Joel said he was satisfied. 'Polly's the spit and image of Mima,' he declared. 'That suits me to a shaving, boy or girl!'

Spring was on them. The ice was gone out of the pond; and the river was high, flooding the backwaters. Mima was hungry for the first green things. She told Joel: 'I'll be glad to taste a mess of fiddle-heads.'

'I'll get you some, as soon as they start sprouting,' he promised, and when he brought her the first that appeared, she set them to boil with a chunk of salt pork for seasoning, and ate them greedily, the men insisting that she eat them all, and laughing at her happy gluttony.

The babies were not the only newcomers to Sterlingtown. There had been these two years and more no new settlers, but this year Colonel Wheaton, abandoning once for all any thought of settling here himself, put a tenant on his land. He had cleared some twenty acres, had built a good barn; and there was a hovel which Bela and Jess had made habitable the winter they cut the barn timbers, and which would with some repairs serve till a better house could be managed. Mima and Joel heard that the newcomer's name was Elisha Partridge, and that he had a wife and baby; and Joel said: 'I've a notion I know him. If he comes from Franklin, í do. We'll go see them.'

So at the first opportunity they took the path around the head of the meadows, past the spring which Mima had dug out and walled up the day the Colonel's barn was raised, to bid their neighbors welcome.

Partridge proved to be a man as old as Philip Robbins, or even — Mima thought — a little older; a full-blooded, fat man with purple cheeks and a way of laughing soundlessly till his face became congested with blood. Mrs. Partridge was a buxom young woman as merry as he. They welcomed Joel and Mima robustly, and Mrs. Partridge said:

'I hear you two are just married yourselves. 'Lish and me got together three years ago.' She chuckled merrily. 'The old goat was bound he'd have me, one way or another; and I decided I might as well marry him as have to sue him for the baby's keep. I didn't waste a minute. Lucky, too. Baby came on the dot of nine months. Alibeus, his name is. Ain't he a chubby young one?' Alibeus was chewing contentedly on a crust of corn-bread, sitting on the floor; and Mrs. Partridge shook all over with mirth to watch him and added: 'And now the old roncher there has got me charged again. I'm due to let go in September.'

Her husband roared with appreciative laughter and slapped her backside soundingly. 'Hurry it up, Sal,' he said. 'Make room for another passenger. A man my age can't waste time!'

'Well, I've seen you waste a-plenty of it,' she told him briskly. 'For all your sweating and trying!' And they laughed again, in a hilarious mutual appreciation, and Joel and Mima laughed with them. Their mirth had an infectious quality hard to resist. Partridge produced rum, and Mrs. Partridge tossed off a lusty jorum with the men. Mima declined, and the other woman said: 'I s'pose you can't, long as you're nursing the baby.' She added flatteringly: 'It ain't hurt your shape any. Alibeus ruined me. I'm spread out all directions since. 'Lish says it's all the better; says I'm so fat I won't show this one at all, says if I ain't careful I'll have it and never miss it. I tell him if he was having it everyone in ten miles would know it, to hear him bawl.' She asked abruptly: 'Anyone up-river from us be-sides this Butler? Ever Indians bother you around here?'

Her husband said: 'Don't be a God-damned fool, Sal! These folks have still got their hair, ain't they?'

'Well, I guess an Indian buck might do something to a woman besides scalp her,' she retorted.

'Not by a jugful,' he told her. 'Indians don't like white meat. A hatchet in your head is all you'd ever get.'

Joel said suddenly: 'You're Sally Fales!' He clapped his knee and laughed. 'I thought you had a familiar look about you. Sally Fales from Franklin. You remember me! Joel Adams?'

'I'd say I do,' she assured him stoutly. 'But I wasn't going to be the first to say it!' She looked at Mima, in faint doubt. Mima, a little to her own surprise, found herself liking Sally Partridge. She thought the other woman was full of fears of this new life and now laughed to hide them. She said reassuringly:

'I wish I'd known Joel before, too.'

The other chuckled. 'He was a hellion,' she said. 'You did well ever to get a yoke on him! He's hopped many a hedge with the young gipsies back home. I always did say he'd tickle the wrong set of ribs some day and get his finger caught and there he'd be! But you look to me you could handle him! Keep his toes a-digging and you'll do it.'

They stayed a while, and drank again, and these two were forever shouting out some broad jest at which they roared with laughter; but Mima was surprised to find herself free of all resentment. She told Joel on the way home:

'I didn't mind her talk. She's scared, Joel, and whistling not to show it. That's the bravest kind.'

Joel chuckled. 'She was always the same,' he said. 'As loose-mouthed as they come. She talks like a trollop, but she'd talk more and do less than any girl around. I've had her box my ears many's the time. Partridge got a good one when he got her. His first wife was alive last time I knew. I heard she died four years back, and he was after Sally Fales before his first was cold. He's an able man at that, they say.'

'Did he have other children?'

'Five or six. I judge he left them t'home. Likely he'll send for them if he makes a go of it here.'

*   *   *   *   *

The alewives ran that year on April 27. Matt, coming home next day from Warren, reported their arrival. 'So the Warren folks will have enough to eat from now on,' he said. May came in with a fine sun to clear away the last snow lingering in the forest, and a wind to dry the ground. Joel and the others

burned the trees felled during the winter, and hauled the half-
burned logs into piles to dry a while before they were burned
again, and they sowed summer rye and stuck in corn on the
burnt-land. They worked from dawn till dark. By the first of
June, green things were showing everywhere. On the seventh a
light frost fell, just heavy enough to kill the sauce in Mima's veg-
etable garden.

Two days later Eben went away to Boston with John Perry
to get Perry's commission as a privateer. He came to say good-
bye to Mima and the baby. Mima held him and kissed him,
and she was cold when he was gone. He departed down-river,
and they had no word from him for a while.

When their planting was done, the three men plunged into
the business of widening their clearings. There was a common
mind in them all. They had at first united in every enterprise;
but now Joel and Mima began to plan to build a house of their
own, and Matt Hawes talked of marrying before another winter. He too would need to build a cabin. The house where
they lived was on Jason's land, would be Jason's when their
three-cornered partnership dissolved.

But they still worked together. The point south of the cabin,
between the brook and the pond, was Joel's. They had begun
their clearings there, and some twenty acres of that first land
cleared was his. That around the cabin and to the north and
west was Jason's, to the extent of approximately thirty acres.
South of the brook and west of the low ridge around which the
brook curved, a few more acres of Joel's land had been cleared
and the trees burned; but this summer they concentrated on
Matt's land, north of Jason's, till he had as much acreage as
they. They were working a full half-mile north of the cabin;
and Mima liked to carry their midday meal to them. Since she
could not leave Polly behind, she and Joel contrived a sort of
basket of birch and alder shoots, soaked in the brook and then
split and woven into shape while they were wet and pliable. She
could carry this like a pack, with shoulder straps and a metump

line to use if need be; and in it Polly rode, wrapped like a cocoon, her head bobbing on Mima's shoulder. The black flies and mosquitoes bit her sorely; but there was no escape from them except to stay indoors and keep a smudge going; and Mima was so full of the pulse of life that to sit indoors was intolerable.

This summer, Jess was again at work on his land south of the pond, his axe ringing all day long, and sometimes Mima went to see him at his tasks. He told her one day that they had word from Eben.

'The Council commissioned Perry,' he said, 'and Governor Hancock signed it. He's got the Fly for a boat. Eben says she's seven tons burden, and fourteen men aboard. Perry 'lowed to cruise t'the eastward and then make back this way. Eben wrote us a letter before they started.'

She asked in troubled tones: 'Is there any talk of peace?'

'There's talk, yes,' he said. 'But that's all it's come to yet. They're talking peace in Paris; but they say the King won't give in till he has to.'

'I'll be glad when Eben's home.'

'Me too.' Jess said in a lower tone: 'Ma don't think he'll ever come home, Mima. She looks for him to be killed. She's got herself all ready to hear he's dead.' He chuckled and said: 'That baby's blowing milk bubbles all over your shoulder.'

Mima laughed and took Polly out of the basket and tended her, Jess watching in the baffled way men do watch this operation, as though unable to understand how anyone can do it. He even said so; and Mima said:

'Why, it's sweet. I love doing it. I'd like to know where any of us would be if our mothers didn't love us when we were little!' Jess chuckled and spat on his hands, turning back to the tall pine he had been notching when Mima arrived. She said: 'You've done a lot here, Jess. It's a pity you haven't got anyone to help you. It'd go faster.'

He looked up at the tree, and down along the land already

cleared to the pond. 'I dunno as I want help,' he confessed. 'There's a heap of satisfaction in doing it alone. When I get a farm here, it'll be mine, that I made.' He said: 'We're going to make a new kind of country here, Mima, where a man can keep what's his, and where he knows that if he does work and save and get something together, no king's going to come along and tax it away from him. We're starting even, the whole of us. The best of us will maybe go farther and faster than some of the rest of us — but we'll all get along better than men ever did anywhere else in the world — as long as we're let to work and save and keep what we earn.' He struck his axe into the tree and freed it again and said strongly: 'I don't want help. I ain't a baby, like Polly there, that still has to have someone clean up my messes. I want to do my own job — and if I get into a mess, I want to get myself out of it.'

He struck again and a great chip flew. Mima said quietly: 'Guess you want a wife, though, Jess, to rest you when you're tired.'

'Certain,' he agreed. 'But she'll work with me, her at her job and me at mine. She won't have to help me, nor me her.' He laughed at his own high pride. 'I'll get her,' he said, 'and we'll make a farm here, and it's going to be ours.'

Mima thought, walking back along the hillside above the pond, that Jess was right. The war would not make people free. They must make themselves a free people, and keep themselves so, or see their liberties drop off one by one like beech leaves in the fall. The freedom to work and save, to do the best you knew how, to try; and the freedom to keep and have what you had earned: these were the things to be treasured and defended, with an earned security for high prize in the end. She came home along that tongue of higher land on which Joel planned to build the cabin that would be their home, and went down to the shore and sat a while with Polly chuckling and squirming in her arms, looking out across the pond, enriched by all she saw. 'I own it all,' she told herself. 'It's all ours, Polly — by working

for it and loving it. Something no one can ever take away.'
The axes were ringing in the forest to the north, and she heard
presently the long crash and thunder of a line of trees falling as
the driver thrust them down. As soon as Matt's land was
cleared, Joel meant to make a start on their cabin; and in these
days of early summer he and Mima thought of little else, spoke
more of that than of any other matter when they were together.

Mima sat a while happily, with Polly kicking on the ground
beside her; till it was time to put the baby back in the basket
and go home to start supper for the men. She found them at the
house ahead of her, because Matt and Jason had decided to go
down to Warren. They were both more and more often away
overnight, and Mima sometimes suspected that this was because they were a little uncomfortable in the cabin, felt like in-
truders there when she and Joel and Polly were so sufficient to
themselves. Matt went to Warren to see his Sally. She said to
Jason while she served them now:

'It's about time you got yourself a wife to suit you. With
Matt and Sally planning on marrying this winter, and me and
Joel moving out, you'll be lonesome.'

Jason grinned. 'Well, matter of fact, I have found one,' he
said. Joel exclaimed in surprise, but she saw by Matt's smile
that he already knew. She asked the questions and Jason answered them. 'Her name's Polly Peabody,' he said. 'They used
to live in Saccarappa, but her pa moved to Warren this summer.'

'Are you going to be married?'

'Yes, ma'am,' Jason said.

'When?'

'Soon's there's room here,' he told her. 'In September,
maybe, when I see how the corn does, see how we're going to
winter. I wouldn't want to bring her here if I couldn't feed her
through to spring.'

Mima was happy for him, as young wives are at such news as
this; and when they were gone Joel said: 'We've got to start
building, Mima; make room for Jason here.'

'I hope we like her,' Mima said. 'They'll be our nighest neighbors. But her name's Polly. She's bound to be as nice as her name!'

* * * * *

Bela returned from the war before the rye was ready to harvest; and on the Sunday after his return he paddled up the river to see Mima and the baby and Joel and the others. He said there was talk of peace.

'I signed up for three years or the duration of the war,' he explained, 'and they've sent me home and a lot more, so I guess the fighting's done.' He had spent most of his service at West Point, seen no action worth the name. 'All the same, I'm glad to be out of it,' he confessed. 'Too much drill and marching without going nowhere. It feels good to get an axe in my hand and go to making something again.'

Joel laughed and said: 'I can give you plenty of that, if it's axe work you want, Bela. I'm building a house this summer.'

Bela promised to lend a hand when he could. He asked for news of Eben. 'If I'd went with Perry, I'd have had something to show for it, anyway,' he said. The coaster on which he came home had been chased, off the mouth of Muscongus Bay, by a shaving mill. 'But we got a breeze and ran away from her. I'd have stayed and fit 'em if it was me.'

The first Sunday in August, Joel and Mima took Polly down to see — or to be seen by — Philip and Mrs. Robbins and the others on Seven-Tree Pond. Jason and Matt went on to Warren; but David and Bess with their five — their Nancy was two months younger than Mima's Polly — and Rich and Bet with their three came for dinner, so that except for Eben, the whole family to the third generation was there. In the afternoon, a southeast wind blew up the pond, so they all went down to the landing where the breeze would drive the flies away; and they were together there when Mima heard a paddle clack against wood far down the lake.

'Someone's coming,' she told her mother, herself half-asleep in the sun.

'It's Phin and Mily likely,' Mrs. Robbins said. 'They went down this morning. Mily ain't satisfied without she goes down-river every Sunday, to Warren or somewheres. Phin better give her another baby. Be the only way he can settle her down.' She added: 'That's the only reason she ever married him. He give her a baby, and Oliver said she had to get married before she started to show it!'

Mima smiled. 'Guess she's no worse than me, if it comes to that, Mother.'

Mrs. Robbins tossed her head indignantly. 'She is so!' she cried. 'You was as good as married to Joel the first day you saw him, and you never looked at another man; but nobody can say the same for Mily. Mind how she cut up at the husking, and her three months along already? She ought to be smacked, if you ask me.'

Mima said: 'There's the float just coming around the point. It ain't Phin and Mily. It's a man by himself.'

'Might be Phin! Maybe she's carried on once too often and he drowned her,' Mrs. Robbins suggested with a chuckle. She called to Philip, a little way off: 'Who's that coming, Robbins? Can you make out?'

They could not yet be sure, but Susie cried: 'Maybe it's Eben, Ma!' Mrs. Robbins at that came strongly to her feet, looking toward the canoe now not a quarter-mile away.

''Tain't Eben,' she said in a low tone. Mima moved near her mother. Susie insisted that it looked like Eben; but Bet hushed her, and after that no one of them spoke. The dugout came nearer; and Joel came to Mima's side and she looked up at him, needing him.

He said in a low tone: 'It's John Perry, Mima.'

Mima looked again, and she saw that he was right. Her mother had gone down nearer the water, stood there now with her hand over her mouth. Mima's breasts ached with fulness.

It was time to nurse Polly; but Polly was asleep up at the house and Mima must stay here now. The canoe turned in toward the shore. It grounded at their very feet, and Perry looked up at them with still eyes. It was a moment before he spoke.

'I had to come myself,' he said.

*   *   *   *   *

So Eben was dead. The afternoon was very still, the breeze dying, the deep blue of the sky broken by cloud masses. They stood along the bank, looking down at John Perry in the canoe; and after a while Philip asked in level tones:

'What happened to him, Perry?'

'It was off t'the east'ard,' Captain Perry said, still sitting in the float as though uncertain of his welcome here. 'We'd landed to cook our dinner, and they snuck up on us through the bushes and let off their pieces before we knowed they was there. Eben got a ball in the calf of his leg. We chased them out of there; but they got away from us in the woods. The hurt he had wa'n't nothing to fret about at first. He helped us run 'em. But it mortified. I done all I knowed for him, Robbins. He was the best man I had aboard. The others was in it for what they could get; but he was the same as me, in it because he wanted to lick the God-damned Tories to hell and gone.'

Mima remembered how Sam Boggs had died of a like wound, how the ground was torn up where he had thrashed in torment when they found him; and her heart was sick. Mrs. Robbins asked: 'Where is he?'

'We buried him on Cranberry Island, marm.'

She said: 'I want to go there some day, just so's I can set with him a spell.'

'I'll take you, marm, any time.'

Her husband spoke strongly. 'Perry, you light and stay the night and tell us about the boy.' He added: 'You tell us all you can, so his mother will have more to hang on to.'

Perry stepped ashore, and Joel helped him beach his boat and the others turned toward the house together. They stayed a while in quiet talk before the fire, and Philip led John Perry to tell them more about Eben; not about his death, but how he had lived. David said a word now and then, but except for these three the others did not speak at all. Susie's eyes were big as she listened, and young Phil, almost eleven years old, stood by his mother's side, his arm around her neck, hers around his waist. Mima wished her mother would cry, wished grief might break its bonds and so be eased; but Mrs. Robbins sat with dry eyes through Perry's long recital.

Only when he paused she began to speak, half to herself. 'Eben was a good boy,' she said. 'Always good to me from the first.' She made a sound like a dry chuckle. 'From the first pains it wasn't over an hour till he was born. He never even made me feel bad when I was carrying him. You remember, Robbins?' Her husband nodded, and she went on, in a low tone, dreaming: 'He never cried when he was a young one. He'd fall down smack on his nose and make it bleed and come to have his face washed and that was all. Remember the time he fell out of the apple tree, Robbins; hit his head on a limb coming down and like to tore his ear off and never a whimper out of him.

'And when he come to be bigger, he was always thinking of things to do for me, catching fish for me, or picking berries, or lugging stove wood. He never had to be driv' to it, the way the rest of you young ones did. Seemed like he wanted to do what a body wanted him to.

'He'd never carry on if you took a thing away from him. Jess, you and Jake was always plaguing him, taking his things. Remember how he'd kind of watch you and smile as if he was glad to have you have a thing if you wanted it?'

Jess said huskily: 'Never was any fun quarrelling with Eben. He wouldn't fight back.'

'He'd always fight quick enough if he thought he'd ought to,' Mrs. Robbins insisted. 'He wouldn't fight for himself, but he'd fight for other children. Jake, you remember the time the Hodgkins young one was bullying little Willie Day, pulling his hair and making him cry, and you let him, and Eben come along and he sailed into Joe Hodgkins, big as he was. Joe bloodied his nose and cut his lip and pounded him scandalous; but it didn't stop Eben. He kept fighting till Joe got scared and put out down the road like hell on trucks was after him. Eben didn't chase him. He went back and gentled Willie Day and stopped his crying. The only fights I ever knew he had was when he fit for somebody else.'

Jacob said: 'He'd mix into a fight every time if it was one-sided. He'd always be for the one that was down.'

'He was a real good boy,' Mrs. Robbins agreed. 'I'm going to miss him.' She rose. 'I'll get supper started,' she said. 'No use crying over spilt milk. I'd like to have kept him; but long as I can't have him back again, I'll just have to do without.'

Mima's own eyes at that for the first time filled. 'To do without.' It was a part of her mother's philosophy, which Mima had heard so many times. 'Clean your plate.' That meant so much more than just eating the last scrap that was set before you. It meant living to the full reach of your capacities; it meant converting everything you possessed to its proper use. 'Wear it out.' Nothing was ever thrown away till the last ounce of good had been drawn from it. 'Make it do.' Some people might complain of scant means, of small opportunity; but wise men made the most of what they had, did the best they knew, tried as hard as they had strength for trying. 'Do without.' If you can't have a thing — why then you can't, and to spend your days in empty wishing is futility. Mima thought her father had never had very much, except honesty and strength and industry and thrift; yet their lives were rich and full.

She and Joel did not stay for supper. On the way up the river to Round Pond, Mima sat in the bow, Polly at her breast; and she and Joel talked quietly together, and not unhappiiy.

'Eben wouldn't complain,' Joel reminded her. 'He risked it, knowed what he was risking, thought he ought to.'

'He was sweet, like a woman,' she said. 'It's queer to think of him fighting and getting killed. Do you reckon he ever killed anyone, Joel?'

'Might have.'

'I hope he didn't,' she said. 'He wouldn't have liked that part of it.'

When they came into Round Pond, the western sky was a blaze of glory, cloud masses crimson and gold in the sun's last light. She said: 'There's a lot of beautiful things in the world, Joel.'

'There's nothing any finer to watch than you, with our baby having her supper. Just looking at the back of your head I know how your eyes must be watching her. You're the finest thing I ever saw — or hope to see.'

'I'm happy, nursing her,' she said. 'Nobody can make me as happy as she does, Joel, only you.'

He said in a low tone to match the hush of evening: 'Eben's being dead makes me want to have another one, Mima.'

'I know. I guess women always feel that, too. One to take his place.' She said: 'But the way I want it, I'd like to have them two years apart, Joel, so each one will have a good start before I have to begin taking care of the new one. I'll be nursing Polly into next winter, likely.'

He nodded; and he took Polly from her as they started up the path. In the forest beyond the clearings, thrushes sang their silvery, lovely evening song. A bear snuffling around the half-burned scraps in the dead fire outside the cabin scurried away at his rolling gallop as they came in sight, and the baby stared with wide eyes, and Joel shouted and the beast made greater speed and disappeared.

15

On THE second Sunday morning in August, Joel and Mima took Polly across the brook to help them decide where to build their house. The brook was just now low enough so that they could step across, but it ran high in the spring. 'I'll drop a couple trees, later on,' Joel decided, 'peg them together for a bridge.'

They climbed to the ledge among the pines, well above the lake; and Mima thought they might set the cabin there, but Joel said: 'No, Mima, it's too far to carry water. And another thing, I want a good cellar. We couldn't dig in that ledge.'

Mima remembered the spring she had found, on the west side of the high land, and took him to see it; and he agreed that it would when it was dug out give them a plentiful supply. 'It might go dry when the trees are cut off,' he admitted. 'But if it does, I can dig a well. But we don't want the house down here, Mima. We want to be up as high as we can and still be handy. Let's look around.'

He started back up through the pines toward the ledge, and a moment later he called to her. She heard the satisfaction in his tones, and climbed up to join him. He had found, four or five rods from the spring and just below the saddle of the ridge, a sort of shelf in the hillside, almost level, and big enough to set a cabin on.

'This is it!' he said exultantly. 'This is the place! We'll be high enough to see over the top, and low enough to be out of the wind.' He scratched at the soil with a stick. 'It's easy digging,' he said. 'We'll have to build a foundation wall on the lower side, maybe; and bank up all around to keep the weather out, and dig away a little on the uphill, but it'll do fine.'

Mima agreed with him. Even in that first moment she imagined the house already here. She freed herself of the basket in which Polly rode; and the baby, beaming and chuckling, approved their selection of a site. She rolled and tumbled on the ground smoothly carpeted with the fallen needles of the pines, and tried to eat a pine cone. Joel would have taken it away from her; but Mima said: 'No, she's cutting her teeth on it, Joel.' Two teeth showed white through the gums. Polly got sticky pitch on her fingers to which some needles clung, and for minutes on end gravely tried to pull these needles free and throw them away, while as fast as they were freed from one hand they clung to the other. Joel and Mima rocked with laughter watching her, as though no baby had ever done anything so amusing before; and she laughed with them, shaking her hands to shake the needles off, finally holding up fat palms, the fingers spread, for Mima to clean them; and Mima swept her up and hugged her hard and kissed the place under her ear; and that tickled so that Polly squirmed and wriggled in a helpless ecstasy.

Joel left Mima and Polly there and returned to the Royal Mess for a shovel and began to dig out the spring; and Mima went to the near-by hillside to find stones and carry them to him. They made a basin two feet deep and three feet across and dug down to pin gravel and walled up the sides and watched the water clear and flow out across the stones. They worked all afternoon, and when they went home at dusk, Mima felt that their home was already begun.

Joel felled the first trees next day, on the house site and above where it would stand, and Mima said:

'I want us always to cut toward the pond, Joel, when we need logs or firewood or anything, till we have it so we can see the water and see out from the ledge up there.'

'We'll cut toward the west, too,' he reminded her. 'That will let the breeze in on hot days. Wind's always west — if there is any — when it's hot. It helps blow the mosquitoes away.'

'The wind will be cold in winter,' she reminded him, but he said proudly:

'Don't worry. I'll build tight. I'll keep you warm.'

The pines here were of a size suitable for the cabin he planned. They had grown in a close thicket, thinning themselves out by sheer pressure of tree population, the trunks more slender as they reached up toward the sun; and he was to find that from some trees he could get two twenty-four-foot logs clear of branches and with no great difference in diameter from the butt upward.

After the early rye was harvested, Joel worked every day on the cabin. 'We're going to have the stylishest house anywhere around, before I get done,' he promised Mima. 'There's clay down by the brook will make bricks. Next summer I'll make some and build us a real chimney. I'm going to shingle the roof, too.' He had Matt bring back from Warren a rifting iron, and a maul was easily made. He sawed out shingle blocks four feet long, and when summer rains kept him indoors he worked making shingles, splitting them out, smoothing them with an axe till they would serve. Most of the houses in Sterlingtown were roofed with boards brought from the mills down at Oyster River, although that of Phin Butler, and 'Lish Partridge's hovel, were covered with hemlock or elm bark laid on poles and held in place with withes. Theirs would be the first long-shingled house in Sterlingtown. Even Johnny Butler's, built by Doctor Taylor, though it was framed and sheathed, had a boarded roof.

The day Joel laid his sills, Mima and Polly were there to watch him; and Mima helped roll the heavy logs into place. Joel used the saddle-and-rider to notch the logs together at the corners. The notch in the under side of each log, cut to an accurate right angle, fitted over the end of the log below which had been planed by careful axe strokes into a corresponding angle so that the fit was snug enough to leave no play at all. Joel levelled the sills, bedding those on the east side half their diameter in the earth, so that the lower sides of the end logs, resting on top of the others, almost touched the ground. He notched the side sills in two places, and saddled two cross sills into place; and Mima, watching happily this birth of the house that would be her home, always with many questions, asked:

'Are those for the floor, Joel? Are we really going to have a floor?'

He told her proudly: 'Yes. I aim to split out some basswood planks and hew them smooth. I've got the trees all spotted.' He started to say something else, then seemed to change his mind. 'I'll only fetch the floor out to here, first,' he said, indicating the cross beam nearest the north end. 'Then we'll build the fire on the ground. It will be down some from the floor level, but it will be good enough so, till I can get a brick chimney built.'

'We could do the chimney cat-and-clay,' she said. 'I could help with that, and not bother making bricks.' And she asked: 'What did you start to say a minute ago?'

But he would not tell her then, bade her wait and see. Not till the second course of logs went on did the wonderful truth appear. The cabin was to contain three rooms!

'Bedroom and buttery and kitchen,' Joel told her, happy in seeing her happiness. 'I've lived in one room as long as I aim to. It ain't decent, and I don't ever want to have to do it again.'

There were tears in her smiling eyes. 'You're awful good to me, Joel.'

He came and kissed her, holding her tight, laughing down at

her. 'I aim to be,' he said. 'I aim to spend the rest of my life being awful good to you.'

For the dividing walls inside the cabin, he used the slender tops of the trees he felled. The outside walls were some eighteen inches thick, a little less or a little more, and they were squared inside and out; but the partition across one end, and the shorter wall which divided that end into two rooms of which one was somewhat smaller than the other, were no more than eight or nine inches through. As the partitions rose course by course, Mima thought the two inner rooms seemed very small, hardly big enough to turn around in; but she would not say so, to spoil Joel's happiness by any criticism. He himself spoke of this one day when the walls were high enough so that standing on the ground he could no more than look over them.

'Rooms look to be kind of pindling,' he confessed. 'Wish't I'd made the whole thing bigger.'

'Well, I don't,' Mima told him loyally. 'They'll be bigger when we're living in them. It suits me to a trifle, Joel.'

'Guess anything I'd ever do would suit you, Mima,' he said, smiling; but she shook her head, her eyes twinkling.

'You're wrong about that, Joel. You ever try some things I could mention, and I'll bring you up so short your back hair will grow upwards instead of down.' She added: 'But I guess I'll always like anything you do to try to please me.'

Polly was with them there day by day as the new house took form. When logs were to be rolled up to their places on the rising walls, Mima could help, and her strength added to Joel's, with the purchases he contrived, did whatever was needed. Polly might lie happily on a bear skin, or on the sunned ground, wondering at her own toes, soberly plucking those sticky pine needles from one finger to another. So long as Polly was content, Mima helped Joel; or she stood near him, watching his axe bite with a clean accuracy into the clear pine. When it was time, she fed the baby, sitting comfortably against one of the trees, Polly in her arms, her husband there, her home taking form and substance every day.

She was happiest when they were thus alone; but they were not always so. Almost every day someone came to help. It might be Jason, saying jocosely that Joel was a long time about this business, saying he had come to finish the job in a hurry so that Joel and Mima could move out of the cabin. 'Me and Polly are getting tired of waiting,' he told them one day. 'The day you move out, we move in.'

'All the same,' Joel declared, 'I'm going to do this right if it takes till snow.'

Jason nodded. 'I don't aim to hurry you. I just like to come over and give a hand.' He colored in some embarrassment. 'I like being with you two and the young one,' he admitted. 'Makes me feel kind of warm and comfortable, watching you together.' And he said: 'I hope my Polly turns out as good as you have, Mima.'

Mima was deeply pleased. There had always seemed to be a roughness about Jason, a harsh way of talking. Matt was the gentle one. She thought now that perhaps Jason was shy, like a boy; that he hid his softer aspects behind that rough exterior.

'Don't ever say that to her,' she warned him smilingly. 'Or she'll hate me.'

Matt too came often; and one Sunday Matt and Jason brought Matt's Sally and Jason's Polly up from Warren to have a picnic dinner at the new house. Mima had been building — while Joel worked on the larger task — an oven near where the door would be, of wattles well plastered with clay; and they fired it for the first time that day. Mima had seen Sally Payson before but never Polly. There was a physical frailness about Sally; she was small and slender and her skin seemed almost transparent; and she was quiet as though always a little afraid. Mima remembered Matt's saying how near Captain Payson's family had sometimes come to the starving-point; and she saw that Sally ate with a furtive, ravenous haste as though afraid the food would be snatched away from her. But she saw too a living flame of courage in the girl, courage that would not down, that would always rise after each defeat to valorous life again.

Polly Peabody was as old as Jason, a year older than Mima; and Mima thought Jason had chosen well, had done well to win her. She was not pretty, unless health is beauty. There was a lumpiness about her, and her cheekbones were high and broad. She was almost as big as Jason, bigger than Mima; and her hands were as strong as a man's. But her ways were gentle, and she pleased Mima by approving little Polly, her namesake; and the baby liked her at sight, crowed and chuckled and went into her arms and stayed there. Sambo, Jason's little white dog, liked her too. Mima, herself rather quiet all that day, watching the other two women, thought: 'They'll be my neighbors all my life. Polly across the brook, and Sally up beyond. And of course whoever Jess marries, down the other way.'

She watched the young men too, each of them responding in small ways to the intoxication of feminine presences. She had lived with them so long and so intimately that she knew Jason and Matt almost as well as she knew Joel; and she was tenderly amused to see how different they were today, with Sally and Polly watching them. Even Jason displayed a prankishness curious to see. She thought they were like turkey cocks strutting before their hens. Once Jason and Joel became involved in a wrestling match, rolling over and over like grappling bears; and Jason had the better of it, and Mima was astonished by that, because she had seen them tussle together many a time before, and Joel always pinned Jason to the ground. She wondered whether Jason was stronger now with Polly watching him; and then she decided that Joel had been willing for the other man to best him with Polly looking proudly on, and Mima loved Joel so much for that consideration that she wanted to cry.

They were merry that day, with sweetened rum and water before dinner for the men; and they sang odds and ends of songs. Jason's voice was a deep bass; Matt had no ear and was as often off key as not; and Joel sang with a pleasing liveliness that made up for any deficiency of tone. He sang:

Oh, her cheek it was bonny; her eye it was merry;
Her ear was a shell and her lip was a cherry.
Her smile would make any man linger a while
     And she smiled that smile at the gentlemen!

Till a lad came along and he tarried to dally
And dandle and bundle with this pretty Sally.
'Now I'll lay me,' he told her, 'Just seeing you smile,
     'That you've been very kind to the gentlemen!'

'Oh, sir,' said sweet Sally, 'There's no harm in smiling
'On any fine lad that's so very beguiling,
'And as for this matter of being so kind,
     'I'm as kind to myself as the gentlemen!'

So he caught and he bussed her, he clipped and he tossed her,
Till she fled and he ran and he found her and lost her
And found her again — she was easy to find —
     Far from the sight of the gentlemen!

But he stopped there. Jason shouted for him to go on and
sing the last verse, and Sally blushed, and Polly Peabody without knowing why still looked uneasy, but Joel refused to continue.

'You can each one sing it to your own,' he said, laughing; and
he caught Mima close against his side. 'Mima likes it best!'

Jason roared and Matt smiled; and it was Mima's turn to
blush and tell them dinner was ready. Joel kissed her, amused
by her confusion, and told her she was red as a bride. 'Blushing
like Mily Butler at a husking,' he declared. She looked at him
in a quiet surprise, wondering why he thought of Mily now; but
then she remembered the rum.

At mid-afternoon, the others started down-river; and Joel
and Mima and the baby went back to the cabin together at
last, walking slowly through the fragrant forest with sunned
spots like gold under their feet, and up across the cleared land.
'But I'm already beginning to think it's home over there,' Mima
confessed, 'and to be homesick every time I leave it. I'll be glad
when we don't have to leave it any more.'

*   *   *   *   *

Whenever he could, Joel worked on the house, and Jess might come to help him; and one day Philip and Mrs. Robbins and all of them came for the day, and that day the last logs went on the walls. Bela had come often, and much of the more careful work he had done. He came, too, to help Joel cut and set the rafters and purlines, till it was time to put the shingles on. Joel had board nails for them, paid for with bear skins and with some furs he had taken in squat traps, up the river toward Sunnyback Pond the winter before. He had rifted out enough shingles; but they needed some smoothing still, so that they went into place slowly. Bela laid the shingles while Joel squared off the inner surfaces of the logs, hewing them smooth so that the clear pine, free from all but the smallest knots, gleamed like white gold.

Joel and Mima resented every interruption; but she and Joel and little Polly went down to Warren to Jason's wedding in mid-September; and that was a merry time. Everyone was there. Joel drank more rum than was good for him; but so did all the other men, and even Mily Butler was more flushed than she should have been during the dancing. She and Joel, dancing together, danced the others down; they danced till they were both red and dripping and too exhausted to laugh, till Mily pretended to collapse, and Joel caught her up and carried her across to give her back to Phin.

'There she is, Phin,' he said. 'What's left of her!'

Everyone laughed except Mima, who only smiled, and Phin who did not laugh at all.

Mima had no taste for merrymaking just now. She was anxious for the new house to be done. Winter was not far away. September was warm and hazy and beautiful, but the fine days were deceptive, and in the morning and at night it was apt to be crisp and cool. Three or four days before Jason's wedding, there had been heavy frost; and when they came back up the river afterward, Mima saw that some leaves had begun to turn.

Through September and October, there were the crops to be harvested, hogs to be killed, provisions to be stored away against the winter. Also, Matt was anxious to plant some winter rye; and late in September they burned off the trees they had felled on his land in June and July. The down-timber, not yet thoroughly dry, burned in a half-hearted fashion; but the small stuff was all consumed; and they brought the oxen and worked in the burnt-land, dragging the half-burned trunks together into piles and firing them again. Mima helped, fiercely resenting this interruption of the work on the house, swinging an axe as tirelessly as a man if not as skilfully, driven now by a feverish impatience to hurry, hurry, hurry. The first great fire had burned two days in the green wood before it died down sufficiently so that they could attack the débris; and after that they kept smaller fires burning till, except for the biggest trunks, the débris was all consumed. Matt sowed his rye on the burnt-land, and harrowed it in; and Joel and Jason worked with him to harvest their common crops of rye and corn and to dig the potatoes. But it was not till well into October that Joel could pick up his work on the house again.

He felled the basswood trees he had chosen for his floor planking, and sawed them into proper lengths and with the oxen dragged them home. He had dug the cellar at odd times. It was seven or eight feet wide and fifteen feet long, running under where the buttery would be, and extending to the great cross beam which would mark for the present the limit of the cabin floor. The dirt from the cellar, used to bank outside the foundation walls, or thrown under where the bedroom would be and under the floor of the kitchen, had been smoothed down so that the floor timbers touched it in many places. Joel squared his basswood logs and began to rift out his flooring; he sent for a single wide pine board from the mill down-river to make a door, and hung it on wooden hinges in which treenails served for pivots. The narrower door into the buttery he made of basswood, and he laid his floor as fast as the boards were ready, smoothing them on one side with the axe, nailing them down with board nails left over from shingling the roof. When the supply of nails was exhausted, he laid the rest of the boards loosely in place, to be nailed when nails could be found.

The whole cabin was by inside measurement a little more than twenty-one feet long, about twenty feet wide. The door was on the uphill side toward the pond. The bedroom was in the southeast corner, about seven feet one way and eleven the other; the buttery in the southwest corner nearest the spring was a little more than eight by seven. All the rooms were floored over except for a space six feet wide in front of the fireplace. The floor was about eighteen inches above the ground level. The buttery had two small windows, each one made by notching a log; and these openings, only big enough to admit a little air, were barred with treenails to exclude small pilfering animals. A sliding shutter closed the bedroom window, about a foot wide and half as high as a log was thick. There was a window somewhat wider in the big room, likewise with a shutter which would be closed all winter; but Mima planned to put up a sheet of paper smeared with goose grease to admit some light during the summer. She was full of designs for small improvements to be made as time went on; and she herself had chinked the walls with moss, jammed firmly in between the logs which had been squared top and bottom to fit as snugly as possible. She plastered clay into the cracks to complete the job.

They had brought a bedstead with cords from Boston, and Joel had a straw tick to lay on the cords, under the feather bed. Joel built a small bed beside their own for Polly.

'And on cold nights we'll bring her in with us,' Mima said.

'Not between us,' Joel insisted.

Mima laughed and said: 'No, nothing's ever coming between us, Joel. We'll sleep with Polly in my arms, and both of us in yours.' And she said: 'I'll like that. I hope it's an awfully cold winter!'

The fireplace was the last thing Joel built. He set slabs of stone against the north wall of the cabin, to protect the logs against the heat, and packed clay into the cracks between them.

Other slabs made a hearth. He had left a hole in the roof for a chimney; and he thought of putting up a temporary chimney of catted clay to carry them through the winter. But on the last day of October the first snow fell; and Jason was as impatient to bring home his bride as Mima was to move into her new house. Matt Hawes was building on his land; and he and Sally Payson planned to be married as soon as his house was ready to receive them. Mima and the three sat late together the night of the snow, discussing what to do.

'We can get along without a chimney,' Mima said. 'The smoke will go out through the hole in the roof. We're not going to use the garret yet, Joel. It isn't even floored. So it won't matter if there's smoke up there.'

'I can fix something,' Joel decided. 'I'll split out some boards long enough to reach from the floor up through the roof; put the bottoms of them ten or twelve feet apart so they won't catch fire, and hang some moose skins across the front of them. They'll take care of the smoke as it rises.' He asked: 'When do you want to fetch your Polly, Jason?'

'Soon as there's room,' Jason told him. 'Whenever you and Mima and the baby can move over there and be comfortable.'

'I'll get some boards split tomorrow,' Joel promised. 'Build a fire over there and see how the smoke works.' He said thoughtfully: 'It won't seem the same, not living together the way we have. We've got along, got a lot done.'

Mima saw them all silent, agreeing with him, each wondering how it would seem to be separated. Jason said uneasily: 'Wonder how Polly and me will get along? We've had some rows a'ready.'

'You'll have plenty,' Joel assured him. 'But you'll get over them.'

Matt said: 'I'm hoping it won't be too hard on Sally; but she's a good worker, little as she is. I aim to see she gets enough to eat, anyway.'

Mima thought in a tender amusement that they were all

whistling for courage. 'You won't really be separated,' she reminded them. 'We're all going to be neighbors, helping each
other.' And she said thoughtfully, with a smile at her own
words: 'We'll grow old together, till I'm gray, and Joel walks
with a cane, and we lose our teeth and get rheumatism and
everything. We'll be funny, hobbling around, with about ten
children apiece.' They laughed dutifully with her; but they
were all a little subdued and thoughtful in the face of this imminent change.

On the fourth of November, Joel and Mima and Polly moved
into their own home.

IV

Home

1

WHEN Mima prepared to leave the Royal Mess, she was surprised to find her heart a little sore. It was no more than half a mile from one house to the other, and she could walk the distance in ten minutes. She would be returning often, to fetch things forgotten, or to grind corn in the mortar Joel had built; and Joel and Matt and Jason would still in many ways be a partnership. Nevertheless there was a finality about this removal now. Something would end, today, for good and all, and as truly as on the day when she came from her father's house to the Royal Mess to live.

She wondered faintly how it would seem to be alone with Joel and Polly and no one else. Mima knew quite well that marriage was not all one rapture. There would be moments when Joel was in ill humor, or when she herself was angry. There had been such moments already; but the presence of Matt or of Jason had always been enough to put at least a momentary curb on them both, so that the bitter words that might have been said were not said, and silence left no wounds. But now she and Joel would be alone, and a momentary anger might give fire like flint on steel, and Mima was at once uneasy at the prospect, and amused at her own concern.

The process of removal was not lengthy or involved. For household utensils and furniture, they had the bed they had brought from Boston and the chair, an iron pot, an iron kettle with a snug top for baking, a spider, a long-handled skillet, and two wooden trenchers which in addition to regular scouring had to be boiled in lye from time to time to keep them clean. Joel had two blankets, and Mima had two quilted coverlets and her feather bed. Joel had a sea chest to keep his few garments and small personal possessions; and Mrs. Robbins by way of wedding present and dowry gave Mima three white chairs, three knives, three forks, three flowered china cups and saucers with plates to match, two pewter porringers and three pewter plates. She gave her also a sort of dressing table with one drawer set on slender legs and with a mirror eight inches one way and ten the other, bordered with flowers, to stand upon it. Mima had bought in Boston a wheel for spinning tow, and a loom. The cord bedstead and other furniture, their own cooking dishes, the small wheel and the loom and the gifts from Mrs. Robbins were all put in place in the new house before the actual removal; and Joel's axe and hatchet, his saw, his knife and his flintlock with a small store of powder and ball were likewise carried over the afternoon before, together with some small supply of provisions from the common store.

Mima went to bed that last night in the Royal Mess too much excited to sleep, and she lay a while, and slept at last and woke early to prepare breakfast for the three men for the last time. They were all at that meal silent, the men feeling as Mima did the finality of this that was upon them; and baby Polly became conscious of some restraint in her elders and watched them with puzzled, uneasy eyes.

As soon as breakfast was done, Joel packed up their bedding in a great bale and slung it on his shoulder, and Jason gave him a hand with his sea chest; and the two men, well burdened, set out for the new house. Joel would have waited for Mima, but she told him to go along. 'I'll stay and redd up,'s he said. 'I want to leave things nice.'

So they departed, but Matt stayed with her, and he said understandingly: 'You're feeling bad about moving.'

'I guess I am,' she confessed. 'Only don't tell Joel. You've all been real good to me here.' She asked wistfully: 'You think you'll get along?'

'Not as well as when you were here,' he told her with a smile. 'But we'll manage. Jason's Polly will be here tomorrow. And I'll be moving, soon as I can build my house.'

She laughed at herself. 'I'm going to be real jealous of his Polly in here. I've lived here so long it seems like mine.' She finished the dishes. 'Well then,' she said, 'I might as well go.' She picked up baby Polly, wrapped her warm, looked at Matt again. 'Well, I'm ready,' she repeated, her voice husky.

They set out in silence, Polly in Mima's arms; but once the door was closed behind her, Mima's spirits rose and her thoughts leaped ahead. When they came to the new house, her doubts were soon crowded out. They found Bela there. He had made a table for them by splitting off a slab, hewing it smooth, and setting four stout legs in it; and he had brought it up in his float this morning before Mima arrived, so that she had it to admire. Then there was other largess presently. David and Bess brought two great crocks full of pigeons put down in their own fat. 'And you can keep the crocks,' Bess said, 'after you've et the pigeons.' David had also a jug of rum. 'In case anybody did get thirsty,' he explained, with a jocular wink. 'I never touch a drop myself!' So he and Joel and the others had a drink to start the day. Then Rich and Bet arrived with a two-bushel bag of real cornmeal, mill-ground; and Rich, who had as a boy learned the tanner's trade, brought Mima a bed covering made of three or four bear skins beautifully cured and stitched together. 'I guess you'll find it comfortable, come a cold night,' Rich said, that little scar on his cheek making his eyes seem to smile; and Mima, full of welling affection for everyone today, kissed him for thanks.

'You're a real comfortable man, Rich,' she said gratefully. 'You always were.'

Johnny Butler and Lucy contributed a peck of seed corn which Johnny said was of particular excellence. 'You d-don't have to p-plant m-more than one grain to a hill,' he declared. 'It's the b-b-best c-corn to grow I ever see.' He was even more excited than usual today, his tongue tripping him on almost every word.

All that day their friends brought tribute. Elisha Partridge, paddling up the river one moonlit night not long before, had seen a bear feeding on acorns on the east bank. He whistled for Sambo, and treed the beast, and shot it next morning; and he brought the saddle to add to their larder. Jess produced a dozen salmon which he had speared in June and smoked and put away; and Phin and Mily arrived in the afternoon, and Phin presented to Joel an iron bar to make a crane to set over the fire, while Mily inspected the new house, peering into every corner, even going down cellar, telling Mima it was wonderful, telling Joel flatteringly that he was the kind of husband to have. 'Phin's got me living in a hut no better than a pig sty,' she declared. 'I tell him I'll stand it about so long.' Phin's head jerked nervously as though he wished to speak, but she gave him no chance. 'If he don't build a proper house next summer,' she declared, 'I'll move out on him.' She told Mima: 'You be careful or I'll move right in here with you. I guess Joel could take care of both of us better than Phin.' Mima thought Mily was not so pretty as she had been. Phin wore always now a puzzled frown, as though Mily were an enigma he could not solve.

Mose Hawes brought them six partridges which he had snared, and Mary fetched Mima a bleach of linen, enough to make a dress. Mima was so happy that she cried, and Polly stared wonderingly at her tears, and waved her hands up and down and crowed reassurances, and Joel and the others laughed at Mima for crying; and she laughed at herself.

'But I have to,' she confessed. 'I can't help it, when you're all so good to us!'

Philip and Mrs. Robbins and all the children came just after dinner. 'I guessed you wouldn't be fixed to feed a crowd the first day,' Mrs. Robbins declared. 'And I see floats turning up-river all morning, so I judged you had enough company around.' She inspected the cabin and declared that everything looked real nice, and Joel had a noggin of rum with Philip. He had drunk with everyone today, yet it seemed to have no effect upon him, and Mima judged that the excitement in him was stronger than the rum. Soon after Philip, 'Bijah Hawes arrived, as tall and lank as ever, with that wide grin of his that showed all his teeth like those of a snarling animal. He was just up the river from Warren, and he brought for a gift the news that the war was over; that a provisional peace had been agreed upon!

The news scarce touched Mima. This fall, the activity of the Tories alongshore had fallen off, and some of them were even returning to their farms to take up life among their old neigh-bors who had such good cause to hate them. There would be word now and then for a long time to come of the reappear-ance of men who during the war had preyed upon the pa-triots, of affrays and violences; but for Mima, the war was over when Eben died.

The men discussed the news endlessly. Philip thought the British might stay on at Biguyduce. 'They'll likely try to claim it's theirs and keep it,' he predicted. 'But by God if they do, we'll drive them out even if it means another war!'

Joel laughed. 'Not for me,' he declared. 'My fighting days are over. Mima'll give me all the war I can handle from now on!'

They were still talking about 'Bijah's news when Ez Bowen and Prance arrived. Ez brought a forty-pound pig which he had butchered, and a live goose.

'Figured it'd keep better alive,' he said. 'Till you're ready to eat it. I like a good goose as well as anything.' And he told Mima: 'When Prance goes to cook one, she hangs it up by the legs in front of the fire, not too near. You put a spider under it to catch the dripping, and give it a spin every oncet in so often, and let it cook till it's a good brown all over, and you'll have to go a ways to beat it for eating.'

Prance when she came in had picked up little Polly, and the baby crowed happily. Mima heard a hint of tears in Prance's laughing voice, and she said:

'She likes you, Prance.'

Prance, on her knees on the floor, looked up at her with brimming eyes. 'I had a Polly once, myself, you know,' she said. 'Six years ago, before we came up here. She was about as old as your Polly is now, when she died.'

Mima felt a sudden tenderness for Prance. She touched the other woman's shoulder. 'I'm glad she takes to you,' she said.

Philip and Mrs. Robbins were the last ones to leave. When they departed, it was dusk outside the cabin, but a fine fire burned on the hearth. Mima and Joel stood in the door to watch them go up over the saddle of the ridge and down to the landing. Then they were at last alone. When the door was closed, firelight filled the cabin. They stood a moment, watching Polly happy on the floor; and then Joel laughed and drew Mima close to his side.

'Well,' he said, 'Here we are, the three of us.'

Mima clung to him. 'Glad you're married, Joel? Glad you married me?' She had her answer in his arms.

2

It was a day or two before Mima saw Jason's Polly. She told herself she was much too busy putting her new home in order to go over, denying that she still felt a faint resentment because Polly had so quickly taken her own place in the Royal Mess. She wondered whether Jason and Matt would miss her, and how long it would be before Polly learned that Jason liked bread baked a little too long, almost black on the outside, dry and crumbling inside; and that Matt preferred his hardly browned at all. She herself had always taken out the first loaves for Matt, left some a little longer for Joel who liked his baked just right, left Jason's till last of all. She had always catered to the individual tastes of the men; but probably Polly would cook to suit Jason now. Mima thought Matt would be the third that made a crowd in the small cabin. Three men and a woman had lived more harmoniously than two men and a woman ever could.

When she and Joel did go over, Mima carrying baby Polly in that basket on her back, Mima was prepared to be critical; but Jason's Polly was so glad to see her, so eager for advice and for encouragement, that Mima warmed to her at once. Polly made them stay for dinner, and afterward she and Jason kept the baby while Mima and Joel went on to where Matt was building his house, half a mile to the north. The snowfall of a few days before had disappeared; but the hardwoods were bare of leaves, and winter's stripped and naked aspect, without any white graces, lay across the land.

Matt had not appeared for dinner, and he was glad to see them. 'I fetch my lunch to save going home,' he explained. 'It's no place for me back there, with Jason and Polly setting and looking at each other like a couple of planet-struck sheep.' They laughed with him; and he said: 'I'm fixing to move soon as I can. Sally and me are marrying the first of January; but I'll likely move and settle before. If we get a snow to haul some boards on, I can finish real soon.'

Joel helped him for a while, and they discussed the weather with a heavy gravity, so that Mima guessed there were in each man many things he wished to say, without knowing how to say them. On the way home, Mima told Joel: 'He'll feel better, time he gets his Sally up here.'

'He's the odd one now,' Joel agreed. 'But it won't take him long, come a snow.'

The snow Matt waited for began to fall on the seventeenth; and early in the morning Mima, still abed, heard him coming with the oxen. He crossed the brook and climbed the knoll past their door, and Joel went out to speak with him.

'He figures he'll get back tomorrow night,' he told Mima when he returned. 'But he's got a long trip of it. He'll have to pick his going through the woods, thinks he can cross the bog, thinks it's froze enough. I told him he'd do full as well to wait till there was ice enough to go by the pond, but he's bound to go now.' He chuckled. 'Says being over there with Jason and Polly is more than his stomach can stand. Says they act as if he wasn't there at all, they're so haired up about each other. Kissing and a-mauling, and Jason slapping her backside, and her a-poking Jason in the ribs and then squealing when he grabs her like she was a studding mare. Matt says he's about got his fill of married life a'ready!'

'We never acted like that,' Mima protested.

'Not for folks to see, anyway,' Joel agreed. 'But they'll settle down.' He added honestly: 'I'd have been as bad as Jason, only I always had an idee it would bother Matt, him feeling about you the way he did.'

'Matt's mighty gentle and fine, Joel,' she assented. 'I'll always like him.'

'You'd have done well to marry him. Matt's worth two of me.'

She smiled at him. 'I don't want two of you, Joel. Loving one of you as much as I do is almost more than one woman can handle. Two would be more than I could stand!'

'Ever been sorry you didn't marry Matt?'

'No.' Her one word was complete; but he persisted teasingly:

'Not even the day of Jason's wedding, when I played the fool with Mily?'

'Not even then,' she assured him. 'Mily's a pretty little thing.'

He nodded. 'She's the sort any man that sees her wants to give her a clipping,' he said.

'I can see they might. She's pretty enough to eat. But I've always had a notion Mily'd be all right, give her time.'

'Maybe,' he agreed. 'But if she makes an eye at the wrong man some day, he'll roll her quick as a cat grabs a mouse. I guess she'd let him, too.'

She said thoughtfully: 'I remember you said once there were three kinds of women; some you like the way you would a man, and some you — really love, and some you just want to get your hands on.'

He laughed a little. 'I thought I was being pretty wise, when I said that,' he remembered. 'But I didn't know a thing, Mima. I know, now, from you, that one woman can be all three kinds,

one time or another. There's times I'm plumb satisfied just
sitting and talking to you, just comfortable being with you;
and there's other times when I'm out working maybe, and I
think of you at home here with our baby, and know you're
going to have more babies for me, and it makes me feel clean
and brave and strong as any two men.' He went on, his voice
thickening: 'And there's other times when the sight of you, or
the way your hair looks on the back of your neck, or the look in
your eyes, or the smell of you can just drive me crazy. You're
all kinds, Mima, different times.'

'Which kind am I now?' she challenged; and he chuckled and
said:

'The kind I like best.'

'Which one is that?'

'It's whichever way you are, any time. There's nothing about
you, ever, that I'd want to change!'

She said in happy scolding: 'Get on with you, sitting here
saying pretties to your wife, and the breakfast dishes not done
and us old married folks! Go on and make some shelves for my
buttery, Joel, so I won't have to put everything on the floor.'
He laughed and came to kiss her before he began.

*　*　*　*　*

Next day after dinner it came on to snow and rain, and the
wind to blow, and Joel thought Matt would stay the night in
Warren, or perhaps at one of the houses of Seven-Tree Pond.

'He said 'Bijah was going down with him,' he told Mima.
'They might put up at Captain Payson's.'

They themselves were secure and comfortable; the long-
shingled roof was tight, the cracks were well chinked; the door
and the window shutter fitted snugly; and except when some
vagary of the wind drove the smoke back down the chimney
and for a moment set them coughing, the storm outside did not
touch them at all. Once during the night Mima woke to hear
rain slatting against the roof, and the wind was harder. She

turned, pressing close to Joel, happy and warm; and in his sleep his arm came around her and he patted her shoulder as though in reassurance, and she smiled and slept again.

They did not see Matt next day; and Mima was uneasy about him. Joel thought he must have returned up the east side of Seven-Tree Pond. 'It's a sight better going there,' he reminded her; but that afternoon he went over to the Royal Mess to see whether Matt was safe home.

'He's there, but he had a time of it,' he told Mima when he returned. ''Bijah stayed in Warren. 'Bije says he's going to be married before Matt, if he can find a girl to go it with him; and he figured a night like last night was a good one to go snugging up somewhere. But Matt was in a hurry; so he started home, and it came dark early, and he got mixed up somehow, over around the head of that little brook opposite Dave's place, along where we found Lion the time the bear hugged him. Remember?'

Mima smiled. ''Course I remember. And I tipped the canoe over on the way home so you'd have to save me.'

'Did you so, you scalawag?'

'I wanted to see what you'd do.'

'You're lucky I didn't leave you to drown.'

'Well, I guess you're lucky you didn't, too!'

'I kind of had a notion at the time that you got clumsy awful sudden.'

'I was doing every way I knew to make you pay some attention to me.'

'Well, I never saw a woman yet that didn't wag her tail when I came along,' he said in pretended complacency; and she said crisply:

'Well, if you ever take notice of one of 'em doing it again, I'll take a broomstick to you. What did Matt do?'

'Oh, he chained the oxen to a tree and stayed the night in the woods, walking around to keep warm.' She shivered, thinking of the wind and the driving rain; and Joel went on: 'The rain spoilt the hauling snow, too. He got his load as far as Mill River this morning; but he had to leave it there till it snows again.'

The delay was not a long one. Four or five days later another snowfall let Matt finish hauling his boards. December was cold, but it was clear and fine; and the snow was not deep. Mima, with baby Polly in the basket on her shoulder, two or three times went across the brook and stayed with Jason's Polly while the men were working. The big, awkward, somewhat homely woman was blissfully happy in her new estate as Jason's wife, and she talked with a frankness that Mima found curiously touching.

'Jason's so clever you'd never think it to look at him,' she told Mima happily. 'Being married to him before we came up here wasn't much fun, but now sometimes Matt's away overnight and we're alone, and that's fun.' She asked, suddenly grave: 'Does Joel ever act like he missed Jason and Matt around?'

Mima smiled reassuringly. 'Men act all kinds of ways,' she said. 'The thing is, you don't want to notice. Half the time the reason they get mad, or go around with their lower lip stuck out a foot like a sulking baby, or go off by themselves, is something you'd never think of at all. You ask them why they're acting so and they'll claim they're not acting any different from usual — and be mad at you for asking.' She laughed softly. 'And most of the time the reason is they're studying about some job of work and don't want to be bothered. Men don't like to take it out in talk, the way a woman does, Polly. Or maybe they haven't had their morning office and their head aches or something; and they're always cranky if they're hungry.'

Polly said gratefully: 'I guess you know a lot about men, don't you?'

'Well, I lived with three of them till here about a month ago. I'd ought to know something about them. Polly, there'd be times they'd all eat their breakfast and go off to work and not say a word to me or to each other. Not a civil word, anyway '

She added: 'And if they drink too much rum, or cut up scandalous the night before, they'll be grumpy, barking at you if you open your mouth, like a mean dog. But that's because they're ashamed of themselves and they're afraid you'll tell them they ought to be.'

'Well, they had ought to be,' Polly declared.

'They know it,' Mima assured her. 'Men don't fool themselves about things the way a woman does. If a woman wants to do something, she'll most generally figure out some way to pretend it's the right thing for her to do — no matter how wrong it is. But a man will know it's wrong, and do it anyway for the fun of it, and then be mad at himself for doing it and go around with a chip on his shoulder daring anybody to tell him he's made a fool of himself.'

'I guess they're different from us, all right.' Polly smiled suddenly. 'Mima, Jason don't like to have me see him with no clothes on.'

Mima chuckled. 'He'll get over that. But a man's different that way, too. Women get so used to tending babies, and nursing them and all, that seeing people naked, or maybe showing themselves doesn't bother them. If men had to nurse babies, they'd go into a dark closet somewhere to do it. When I used to change little Polly in the cabin, Jason would always blush and get all red and go out-of-doors so he wouldn't see.'

Polly asked in a low tone: 'Did he like her? Did he like babies?'

'He did when she had her clothes on.' Mima suddenly understood. 'Are you going to have one, Polly?'

'I think so.'

Polly sounded so forlorn that Mima laughed and came to her and kissed her. 'Told Jason yet, have you?'

'I didn't dast, yet, for fear he'd be mad.'

'He'll be the proudest you ever did see,' Mima promised her. 'As if he was doing it all himself. You watch him. I know how he'll act.'

'I hope he is. I want it, Mima.'

'It won't be the first baby a woman ever had, or the last,' Mima reminded her. 'Bet's expecting in April or May; and there'll be more coming right along, maybe before yours. There've been a lot of babies born in the world, Polly; and every daddy always was proud of 'em.' She comforted Polly and had her laughing presently. They had more than one of these days together, while the men rushed Matt's house to completion.

* * * * *

Matt moved into his new house on the twenty-fifth of December. David had seen some celebration of the Saint Nicholas legend among the German settlers in Broad Bay; and Joel and the others who had been soldiers knew that the Christmas feast among the Hessians had made Washington's surprise crossing of the Delaware possible. But the Puritan distaste for Christmas merrymaking had still some influence upon New England thought and practice; and in Sterlingtown they had observed the day, if they marked it at all, as though it were Sunday, by abstaining from work, by gathering at Philip's house to hear him read from the Bible and perhaps talk a while. Today as many of them as could do so came to see Matt settled; and 'Bijah Hawes was there, boasting that he had beaten his brother to wedlock, as he had said he would.

'I married Maggie Hawes,' he told Mima. 'She's my second cousin, and she claimed it wouldn't seem like being married when it don't even change her name, but I've taught her now that there's more than names to marrying. She's giving my hovel a going-over today till it won't know itself; told me to git out and stay out till she had it put to rights. I ain't hardly had my nose inside sence we came up-river, only to sleep with her.' He added with a chuckle: 'She lets me in for that, all right.'

Mima thought it curious that 'Bijah should be so different

from Matt, who was gentleness and strength commingled. She remembered the first day 'Bijah came to Sterlingtown, appearing so startlingly while she and Bess were working on the oven; and she remembered that night of the dancing on the threshing floor, and the day he found her in the maple tree by the river, and other days. 'Bijah had always been bold to lay his hands on her; and she thought now that he had not grown and matured as had the other young men through their labors in the wilderness. Their fibre had toughened, like that of a slow-growing tree; but 'Bijah was still as soft and heedless as a boy. Anyone knew it was wrong to marry your second cousin. 'Bijah had probably married her just to make good his boast that he would beat Matt.

When she and Joel started home, Joel said with a grin: 'Funny to think of 'Bijah marrying. He's made his bed behind every bush and haystack in Warren before now.'

'He'd have made it up here, and me in it, if I'd let him, more than once.'

Joel chuckled. 'Certain! 'Bijah'll dance Sallinger's round with any woman he can find. We used to run together.'

'You never chased after me, Joel. He did, but you never did. Why didn't you?'

He looked at her in amused understanding. 'You act like I'd hurt your feelings by not!'

'You did, some. I knew you went to Warren, right along. I thought there must be something wrong with me.'

He said gently: 'I had a feeling for you from the first day, Mima; but the trouble was, I was in love with you. Wanting a woman that other way, not loving her, is a fierce kind of feeling. You want to handle her hard, to hurt her till she likes it. I always wanted to be — gentle and fine to you.'

She laughed. 'Only that day you chased me to the river and broke through the ice!'

'That day was different,' he agreed. 'If I'd caught you that day, cold as it was, I'd have made you think it was hay time.'

'I'd have let you,' she admitted. 'That's why I ran away. And that night Father raised his barn and you went off with Fanny in the float — I told Mother if that's what you wanted, you didn't have to go.'

He grinned, his hand touching her arm. 'Looks to me I wasted a lot of time. But I'm glad I did, Mima. I came a little nearer being fit for you, when the time did come, the way it was.'

They walked in silence for a while. Matt had asked them that day to come down to Warren for his wedding a week later; but it would be too far to take Polly through the winter woods, so they could not go. Joel spoke of this now.

'Well, with Matt marrying, that's the end of the Royal Mess, Mima.' He smiled almost sadly. 'Men are never the same to each other after they get a woman.'

She knew this was true; had seen the difference in the relationship between Joel and the others after he was married. 'I guess you always have to give up something to get something,' she said. 'I'll see to it you'll never think you made a bad trade, Joel.' They crossed the brook, and Polly in the basket on Mima's shoulders shouted with glee as they came home.

* * * * *

Through that first winter in their own home, there was no single snowfall of more than a few inches; but a singing cold lay strictly on the land, so that the scant snow squeaked underfoot, and they heard the rumbling of ice heaving under pressure in the pond, and the cracking of trees when the deep cold froze them to the heart and rived them as though with wedges.

Joel worked at odd times on planks for the garret floor; and he made molds in which in the spring he meant to pattern the bricks for the chimney. For lack of nails, he dovetailed all the corners, and with no other tools than axe and saw and old belt knife, this was a laborious procedure. But there was no hurry on them. Winter was long, and except for keeping up the wood supply and cooking their meals and carrying a pail of milk every day from Mima's father's house to supplement baby Polly's ration of corn mush and meat broth as she began now to be weaned, there was nothing that had to be done. Joel ran a line of squat traps and caught a few mink and marten and skinned them out and stretched the skins; and he found a house of beavers on the muddy little pond where the brook rose and trapped them out. Sometimes he cut brush and piled it around stumps in his cleared land and struck up a fire; and once when the day had been so warm that it seemed like spring by comparison with the pitiless cold that had gone before, Mima put Polly in the basket and went at dusk to watch him; and stars were yellow in the winter sky, and many fires lifted yellow flames the length of the clearing.

That was the day Joel said he was afraid their rye might winter-kill, with so little snow and such extreme cold; and although Mima did not know it at the time, he went next day to fetch Matt to the Royal Mess, and the three men tallied the stores still on hand to see whether they might be on short rations before the alewives ran. They were a little disturbed to find how much of their common stock had already been consumed. What had in the past been enough to feed four of them might not be enough for six, and Joel came home in some concern of mind.

But there was nothing to be done except make what they had serve; and Joel did not at once suggest to Mima any curtailment. Something would happen before the pinch became too hard. He set snares and caught rabbits and partridges, and Mima began to make a rabbit-skin robe for baby Polly to sleep in, curing the skins with smoke and leechings, cutting them into strips, then plaiting these strips into strands and weaving the strands into a loose warp and woof. But rabbits were scarce that winter and the enterprise was a long time in the doing.

One night she woke without knowing why, to a sense that something was happening; and she got out of bed and opened the window a crack to listen. She thought she might have heard a wolf pack hunting over toward the Madomock, but if she had heard anything, the sound was not repeated. Then she realized that there was some strange light, brightening the darkness; and she went to the door and looked out and saw through the tall crests of the pines towering high above the cabin northern lights that played across the sky. She pulled on her moccasins and buskins and drew a bear skin tight around her and went out-of-doors and up to the ledge three or four rods from the cabin door. The sky was all one play of color that came up out of the north in waves and streamers; and she thought she could almost hear the rustle and crackle of those ribbons slowly undulating in the sky. They came from the north; and Mima thought that except for the two or three cabins beyond their own — Jason's, and Matt's, and Elisha Partridge's hovel — there was no living soul in all the wilderness this side of Canada. She crept back into Joel's arms, glad for the security and warmth she found there, glad their baby slept beside them, glad this was their home.

Joel found a coon's track in a light fall of fresh snow and traced it into a huge hollow tree; an old hemlock, four or five feet through, the heart all gone. He thought to smoke out the coon; but the tree proved to be the winter lodgment of a bear. He went to fetch Jason and Matt and they felled the tree and routed an old she and two cubs a year old out of their retreat. Jason shot the she bear, and Matt and Joel killed the cubs with their axes. The fresh meat was welcome in their cabins and on Seven-Tree Pond, shared out among them all.

That happened late in February; and the meat reminded Jess that it was time to go after moose, over in the Madomock swamps. March was the best hunting; because by that time the accumulation of winter snows would normally have penned the great beasts in their yards and made them easy victims. This year the snow was not deep enough to serve that purpose; but Jess thought they could strike game all the same. Steady hunting by the settlers from Broad Bay had driven the moose to the northward; and it became necessary to go further and further to find them in numbers. Nevertheless Jess was eager to go, and Joel and Jason elected to go along. Polly came to stay with Mima while the men were gone. Bela and Jacob made up the party; and five of them set out, each dragging a hand sled, planning to go up the river past Phin's, and up Sunnyback Pond to its head, before crossing the ridge to the westward to the swamps where moose had in the past been plentiful.

Sambo went with them, bounding and barking with delight. It was six days before the hunters returned; and Mima found herself happy to have Polly Ware for company. The big homely woman was in the fourth month of her pregnancy, and she was radiantly happy, wearing for this while a sort of beauty. Jason knew the baby was coming, and he was as proud as Mima had said he would be.

'He treats me like I'd break if the wind blew on me,' Polly said, between laughter and tears. 'He acts as if no woman had ever had a baby before.'

Mima remembered something Joel had said once, when she laughed at him in these same terms, and she told Polly: 'He just means no woman has ever had one of his babies before.'

Polly's face darkened. 'If ever one had,' she said, 'and I knew it, I'd find her and twist her head off her shoulders, slow, turning it around till the bones cracked.' Suddenly she clung to Mima. 'It scares me, Mima, loving him so. What if something happened to him while he's away?'

'Never was a wife yet didn't wonder that.'

Polly half smiled. 'You're always saying things like that; but I don't care about other women. I don't care if they loved their husbands, or had babies, or anything. All I care is me and Jason.'

'I know,' Mima assented. 'But there's a heap of comfort sometimes in thinking that we're all just little parts of the world and not the whole of it. I like to think of women in England

and France and China and all over, loving their husbands and
having their babies, and worrying when their husbands are
away. Thinking of them is company for me.' Her eyes clouded
with thought. 'When I was having Polly, it seemed to me like
I couldn't have done it if no woman had ever done it before.'

'Is it awful bad?'

Mima said gently: 'I guess so, Polly, but it's soon over. I'm
going to do it again, and keep on doing it. It's worth it and
more.'

'I'm going to love having mine.'

Mima laughed. 'I wouldn't put it past you, Polly. I loveu it
when it was done.'

*   *   *   *   *

The day the men came home, there had been a sudden snow
flurry during the night; and a few inches of fresh fall lay atop
the half-crusted carpet already on the ground. So the runners
of the sleds made no sound, and Mima and Polly had no warning till Joel and Jason were almost at the cabin door. Then
Mima heard the thump of their feet and sped to the door and
threw it wide and saw them coming up the slope from the
brook, hauling the sled behind them. The third man at first
she hardly saw at all, running to meet Joel, throwing herself in
his arms, kissing him hard, laughing at the week's beard on
cheek and chin, crying out a hundred questions. Polly and
Jason were as rapt as they; and Polly was crying with happiness
to have Jason safely home. The sled, neglected, began to slide
backward down the slope, and the third man checked it; and
Mima, her eye drawn by his quick movement, recognized him.

'Oh, you're Mr. Davis?' she cried.

'I'm Davis,' he assented, his eyes twinkling under bushy
white brows. His white beard was longer; but in no other way
was he changed. She bade them in, and they came, the men
stripping off their heavy garb, sitting down on the edge of the
floor in front of the fire, their feet hanging down; and Joel gave

them rum, and Polly asked questions faster than they could be answered, till she realized that there was trouble in Jason's eyes.

'What's the matter, Jason?' she asked in a hushed tone. 'Are you all right? Are the others all right?' Then suddenly she looked all around, seeking something. 'Where's Sambo?'

Jason said reluctantly: 'Sambo's dead, Polly. Bear killed him.'

She would not at first believe it. 'A bear couldn't catch that little dog!'

'He found its den, coming back over the ridge,' Jason said. 'He roused it out, Sambo did; and he was sure pleased with hisself. We heard him barking, and chocked the sleds and went on over. Bear was more'n half asleep, but when he see us he tried to move. So I said we'd drive him up the top of the ridge before we killed him, so's we wouldn't have to haul his carcass. We driv' him, too, quite a ways, right on to a quarter of a mile, with Sambo yapping at his heels all the time. The bear would whirl around, the way they do, and Sambo would jump back; but before we got to the top of the ridge, Sambo kind of slipped in the fresh snow and bounced ag'in' a tree, and the bear clipped him. Knocked him up in the air and give him another when he come down.'

'Kilt him?' Polly whispered wretchedly.

'Dead as a smelt. Caved his ribs all in. Never a yip out of him.' He added, nodding toward the old man: 'Davis heard us shoot the bear. He was coming down the ridge.'

Mima wished to ease his grief. 'I guess you're starved,' she said. 'I'll cook up something for you.'

But Jason shook his head. He had struck up a fire in their house as he came by, had left his sled load of meat there. 'We'll be getting back,' he said. He looked at Polly apologetically. 'I fetched Sambo home,' he said. 'I figured to fire the ground till I can dig a hole and bury him handy.'

Polly caught Mima's eye in one of those looks of understanding which women exchange; and she collected her belongings, and she and Jason departed. But I'm Davis stayed, and Mima remembered that he liked bread above every delicacy, and fetched cornmeal and mixed up some fresh, mixing it thin, brushing back the hot ashes to bake it on the smooth stones of the hearth. The old man watched her while he and Joel talked; but he did most of the talking, as though he were a vessel filled with conversation which, now tipped on its side, spilled its contents in a steady flow.

He was on his way down-river with a pack of furs. 'Got twenty-one beavers out of one house at the dam that flows the meadows below my place,' he said. 'And some besides. Come down to trade for what I'll need. That bread's coming fine, ma'am.' He bowed his head in the curious way she remembered. 'I've et moose and bear till I don't know whether to growl or bellow. Bread or gruel or some pudding now — they'd go good with me.' He rambled on without prompting. 'Been all over since I come this way the last time. Mostly on the Kennebeck. Had a sick time last November, five-six weeks. I couldn't git off my back at all, and nothing but smoked moose meat to chaw. Some men found my traps that hadn't been tended and carried them off. Belfasters, they were. Time I got so's I could travel, I put after them; but I had a time to make 'em give 'em back.' He spat into the fire. 'Can't never do no dicker with the Belfasters. They pulled their foot out of there when the British come to Biguyduce, but they're going back some now. I tried to sell some prime moose meat in the settlement in January, but all they'd pay was paper. Guess mostly they live on herring out of the Bay. Too mean to pay for meat and too lazy to kill it.'

The bread was done and he wolfed it, hot from the hearth. Mima asked sympathetically: 'Were you awful sick? And no one to take care of you?'

'Cured myself finally,' the old man told her. 'A cat-fawn came nosing around my hovel and I shot him. Used to be a quack name of Taggart over on the Kennebeck, if a man was real sick he'd skin a black cat and wrap the skin around him and guarantee he'd get well. This warn't a cat, but it was as nigh as I could come to it. I'd had belly pains and broke out in a sore that kept pussing, but I wrapped the raw skin over it and it healed up instanter, in time for me to get after them Belfasters that stole my traps.'

'But you got the traps?'

'Yes, ma'am. And I've had a good purchase this winter, too; enough to lay me in powder and lead and all.' He cackled in a sudden mirth. 'If I don't git my powder wet like Jem Dunlop. He lives over on the Kennebeck, fetched some home one day and it got rained on, so he raked out some coals and put a pail full of powder on top of 'em to dry. It went off ker-whoop! Singed all the beard off of his face and his eyebrows till he looked halfway between an egg and a baked potato. Jem always claimed if he hadn't dodged it would have killed him!' He laughed and slapped his knee resoundingly. 'A queer one he was. He was nigh as queer as Jemmy Davis, the one they called Born-Drunk. Jemmy Davis was always drunk, always had been; but he claimed the trouble was there was two of him. He said Born-Drunk Davis was the one that drunk the rum. He claimed Jemmy wouldn't touch it. "Jemmy's sober as a church," he'd say. But Born-Drunk, he'll want a drink, and Jemmy'll say no, and they'll go at it, arguing like the Devil and the parson. But Born-Drunk always gets the drink into the both of them in the end.'

They sat late before the fire, and the old man talked as a stream flows. Joel said the hunt had not been overly successful. Moose were scarce and hard to come by, and the old man told him:

'They're thick as flies up my way, no more trouble to kill them than butchering neat cattle. Next time you want you a few, just keep going up the river till you come to where it splits. The main river comes in from the westward; but the branch from the north is the one for you. Go up there half a mile above the forks and you'll find moose signs everywhere, and moose to match.'

'They've been hunted hard, over west of here,' Joel said. 'We went up to the head of Sunnyback Pond and crossed the ridge there. There's a meadow and a cedar swamp, a good place for them, right where a brook runs into the Madomock, and last time we went, there were plenty moose. But this time we had to work for what we got. Couldn't find a yard anywhere; and there was enough wind to make trailing hard.'

'You have to have the know-how,' I'm Davis explained. 'Take a moose moving, not scared, and he'll always be watching the wind. Mostly he'll feed up-wind; but if he wants to bed down, he'll kind of circle back so he can keep an eye on his own trail. If I'm working a moose up-wind, I don't follow his trail at all. I keep going off one side or t'other, and cutting back. That way oftentimes you'll jump him out of his lie.

'But if he's working down-wind, then it's blowing from you to him; and if he gets a noseful of man smell, he'll go clear out of the country. So I keep off to one side of his trail, eight-ten rods, maybe more, and then I head in to cut his trail once in so often and maybe jump him that way. But it'll be a long job, like as not, to come up with him.'

'We found it so,' Joel agreed. 'Jess is pretty good at it.'

'I know that swamp you mean,' the old man said. 'It runs up the other side of the ridge. The ridge is about ten miles long from here north; and the river makes a circle most of the way around the north end of it — just the same as the brook does around your house here.' He leaned down from where he sat on the end of the floor near the fire, and with a horny finger tip scratched a rough map on the ground. 'Where the river hits the side of the ridge and turns north to run around it, it's all cedar swamp,' he said. 'You can follow the river right through the swamp; get good going that way. River comes down out of a mighty sightly pond, up in the hills. I call it George's Pond, myself.'

'And the brook where you live is up beyond?' Mima asked; but he explained to her again about the fork in the river.

'You follow the north fork, ma'am. It comes out of a pond all of three miles long; and a good-sized brook comes in at the head of the pond. You go up that about a mile to a beaver dam — an old roncher of a dam, but it's broken down now. Keep around the north side of the meadow till you hit my brook. It's the second one you come to that's too big to jump across. You follow it up into the hills.' He said quietly: 'They're good hills, good to climb, and ledges to set on and look around with no trees in the way.'

Mima caught Joel's eyes. 'I like hills,' she said, smiling a little. 'Even when you have to climb a tree to get the view. I'd like to go there.'

Joel slapped his knee. 'Mima, let's us go, after planting. There'll be a week then with nothing that has to be done. I can look out some moose country, and we'll see the river, and climb them hills!'

'We couldn't take Polly.'

'Your mother'd be tickled to keep her.' He appealed to the old man: 'Can a canoe make it up the river?'

'Well, you'll have some dragging and some carrying,' I'm Davis told him. 'But a canoe'll take you to the beaver dam on the north fork. Or on the west fork it'll take you right to the foot of the steep pitch below the pond that lays off t'the west'ard. You'll have to h'ist it over quick waters some, and there'll be rocky places where you'll have to drag it, but there's dead waters, too. I'd say it'd be a sight easier than walking.'

When they were abed that night, the old man snoring soundly on the floor near the fire, Mima held tight to Joel. 'I'd like that, Joel, you and me,' she said. 'Can we go?'

'I wouldn't wonder a mite,' he promised. 'After planting. Be kind of fun, Mima, you and me off all alone.'

She laughed softly in his arms. 'Climbing hills, and climbing trees and everything!' And she said, 'I'm sorry about Sambo, Joel!'

'He was a useful little dog.'

'You might say he was the only one there at our wedding. I'll always remember him.'

3

THE ice went out early that year. On the second of April it was possible to go down the river in a float; but the ponds were open only around the edges. Toward the middle of the month, though Round Pond was still clogged with ice, Joel thought it was ready to crumble, and he was impatient to see it gone; so he and Jason launched the big dugout, and with Jason paddling and Joel in the bow breaking away the rotten ice in front of them with blows of a heavy pole, they tried to open a channel along the shore. The ice was thick; but it was honeycombed. Under Joel's blows it collapsed in a meek fashion, and dissolved into many slender pencils a few inches long, half an inch thick, round and true. The water around the float was full of them, tinkling against each other and against the canoe. They worked along the north side of the pond and reached the open water of the river; but before they could return, a light south wind moved the floe ice against the shore they had followed and closed their way behind them; so they had to complete the circuit of the pond to reach home again.

But there was now open water along the south shore, and that night the south wind strengthened, and all night Mima could hear the ice crunching soggily against the shore. In the morning the pond was clear, the water seeming strangely dark after the white of snow and the gray of ice to which the winter had accustomed their eyes.

Seven-Tree Pond went out that same night; and a few days later two new settlers arrived. Josiah Robbins, Mima's uncle, came from Franklin. The other man was Samuel Hills who had worked for Oliver Robbins in Thomaston. They had bought land before they arrived, and Hills began at once to clear on the point opposite Richard's farm. Uncle Josiah had acquired the whole of the neck of land north of Philip's house and bounded by the river, the ponds, and the old possession fence which followed the line of the carry from the head of Seven-Tree Pond across to the river. He would live with Philip while he cleared and planted a part of his land. He planned to bring his family next year, when he should have made ready to receive them. He was younger than Philip, not yet fifty years old. Sam Hills, a man in his early twenties, had been apprenticed to the blacksmith's trade; and his coming filled one of the needs of the settlement. With Richard for tanner and Sam Hills for blacksmith and every man able to use an axe, Sterlingtown could be self-sufficient. Hills was very deaf, but he laughed at his own misfortune; said he was glad of it. 'Keeps me from hearing the Gor rammed noise when I'm pounding out a shoe,' he said.

Uncle Josiah arrived just before Bet's baby came; and Joel and Mima did not see him till after that event. The new baby was a girl, and Bet named it Susanna — to the delight and pride of her sister Sue, who was helping tend the house and the baby and the older children till Bet should be on her feet again. Joel and Mima walked down to see and to admire the new arrival, leaving baby Polly with Mrs. Robbins on the way, and when they came back and remarked what a fine baby Bet's had turned out to be, Mrs. Robbins said:

'Well, that's the first this year, but it won't be the last. Lucy Butler and Polly Ware have begun to show theirs, and Bess says Dave's got her primed.' She said, with a curious break in her voice: 'I'm hoping hers is a boy.'

Mima knew her mother must be thinking of Eben, in a lonely grave far away on Cranberry Island, and wishing there might be a new Eben Robbins to take the place he had left empty. 'Mary Hawes is four months along, too,' she reported.

'I know. I forgot her,' Mrs. Robbins agreed. 'And I saw Mag Hawes the other day. She had the look.' She chuckled comfortably. 'There'll be babies dropping around here like apples off a tree, by and by.' She looked at Mima keenly. 'You and Joel, it's about time you filled your house. You've got room enough.'

'We're planning to,' Mima told her. 'Next winter, may-be.'

'How about Matt and Sally? Is she expecting? They keep to theirselves, don't they. We ain't seen them all winter.'

'They haven't come to our house,' Mima admitted, but she explained: 'Sally had a hard time at home, didn't have enough to eat most winters; and we've all had to cut it fine this winter. We went to see them two-three times, but she didn't ask us to stay; and Matt told Joel she was scared they wouldn't have enough, kind of wanted to hold on to every bite.'

Mrs. Robbins protested: 'We wouldn't let her starve, long as we had anything ourselves!'

'She'll be all right when she's better acquainted,' Mima predicted. 'I guess folks wasn't as neighborly down't Warren as we are up here.'

'It's a bigger place,' the older woman agreed. 'You don't get to know people so well when there's too many folks around. Where there's so few of us, we pull together better.'

Joel had left Mima at the house and crossed the river to where Josiah was at work, starting his clearing. She and Polly stayed with her mother till he returned, and Mrs. Robbins told her what news Josiah had brought. 'They're trying to agree on what the peace will be,' she said. 'And the Congress is trying to get money from the States, and the States won't give it, and money isn't worth the paper it's printed on, anyway. Some of the States are fighting over western lands; and the Congress aims to put a duty on everything if the States will agree to it; and the States say if Congress would quit spending so much there wouldn't need to be any taxes, and so it goes, squabbling and a-quarrelling.'

'Men are queer,' Mima said. 'Getting so excited about what's happening way off somewheres. Our job is making our farms, and having our babies, and doing the best we know how. Fretting and talking about the rest doesn't do any good. It just uses up our strength that we could use better tending to our own business at home.'

Mrs. Robbins chuckled. 'You'll find there's a lot of things a man does that a woman can't understand,' she admitted. 'Men and women are different as cats and dogs, Mima. You can sleep with a man every night for thirty years, and then not know ahead of time what he's likely to do any minute. They're as supprising as lightning — and I guess we supprise them full as much as they do us. The plain fact is, there's an ocean between men and women, some ways, and no way to cross it. A woman knows more about some things than a man will ever even suspect; but she knows less about some other things than a boy baby a month old. You might as well make up your mind to it.' She added comfortably: 'That's what makes men so much fun to have around, nuisances if they be.'

Mima smiled assentingly. Joel and the others returned, and she and Joel stayed for early supper, and Uncle Josiah told her she was a handsome woman and Joel a fine young man. At supper she listened to the talk among the men, her father and Josiah and Joel; and on the way home afterward, Polly in her arms, Joel paddling easily, she spoke her thought, told him that their own lives were their only true concern.

'All that other business can't ever really matter to us,' she urged.

But he said it might. 'For one thing,' he argued, 'the Loyalists will be wanting to come back, some of them, and claiming they still own their lands here. Warren's electing a committee of safety. They aim to vote not to let the refugees come back; but it may take more than voting to stop them.'

He added: 'Then there might be land trouble. I bought from your father, and he bought from Doc Taylor. Taylor bought from Flucker, and Flucker claimed to represent the Waldos, but he was drove out for a Tory. He agreed to protect Taylor when he sold to him; but I don't know as he agreed to protect anyone Taylor might sell to; and Taylor's been fighting with Jennison, so he's deeded what all land he still owned here to a man named Reed. Reed's his son-in-law. S'pose the Waldos claim Flucker hadn't any right to sell to Taylor? Taylor won't stand up for us. I don't know what it will come to.'

Mima smiled, shaking her head. 'You can't scare me, Joel. This is our land. It's not ours because we bought it. It's ours because we've worked on it, and loved it, and we're going to keep it. You can't scare me.' And she said quietly: 'Nothing outside of you and Polly can ever scare me, Joel. Nothing outside of what might happen to you and Polly.'

He laughed happily. 'You're the kind of a wife a man wants, Mima; never worrying and fretting.'

She said in a low tone: 'I want us always to be good, Joel. I mean, to try to work hard and live right and like people and make ourselves as nice as we can, every way.' She spoke thoughtfully, fumbling for words. 'I don't mean going around doing good works for people all the time. I guess them that are always helping folks and telling them how to do are kind of a nuisance. It looks to me doing good to folks can make 'em mad, do 'em a heap of harm. I guess the best way for anyone to do to help others is to be as strong and fine and decent as he can his own self. That's what I want us to do.' She looked at him apologetically. 'Maybe that sounds kind of selfish; but it's really the generous way in the end. If you've got a lot to give — you don't have to give it. People are better just from knowing you.'

Joel smiled at her earnestness. 'What's that about: "By their works ye shall know them"?'

'I don't care,' she insisted, 'I guess it's a heap better for me to keep my own house clean, and my own husband happy and my own baby healthy than if I was always worrying about what Polly Ware does to Jason, or Mily to Phin, or anybody else at all.'

'Jake was saying he saw Mily at Johnny's, day before yesterday,' he told her. 'Says she's pretty as ever.'

'She's a real pretty thing,' Mima agreed, looking straight ahead, and then she smiled and asked: 'Remember how she made up to Jake when they were both young ones, and how it bothered him? I guess that was before you came here to live. She came the time Johnny and Lucy moved up here, and she couldn't keep her hands off Jake at all. She was about thirteen years old, I guess.'

He chuckled. 'She'll always be making up to someone,' he agreed. 'It's in her.'

Mima said: 'I guess it's hard for her, up-river all winter, not seeing anybody.'

'We saw her when we came back with our moose meat,' he remembered. 'We stopped to leave her and Phin a haunch, and she was chirping like a cricket. Guess the sight of so many men all at once kind of went to her head. Maybe Phin's smart to keep her up there, much as he can, keep her out of trouble.'

Mima did not speak. She herself had not seen Mily since the day they moved into the new house; but there had been times when she remembered how at Jason's wedding, both of them flushed with rum, Mily and Joel had danced till Mily collapsed in helpless laughter, and Joel carried her and set her on Phin's knee, Mily hanging with eyes closed in his arms. Mima was glad now when the canoe touched and they were home.

*   *   *   *   *

Light snow and heavy cold had left deep frost, but as soon as clay could be worked, Joel began making bricks for his chimney. He had built his molds in such a way that the sides could be freed a little to release the bricks as they hardened; and the ledge above the cabin offered a place where they could dry in the sun till they were ready to be fired. The work took time. His bricks were about nine inches long and half as wide, and less than two inches thick. He dug the clay out of the bank near the brook, wetted it as much as was necessary, molded the bricks and sun-dried them till they were hard enough to handle. Lacking any proper kiln, he baked them on the ledge where they lay, building a fire on top of them, a few at a time. Mima helped fill the molds, and Polly chuckled with delight over the fire; and April was warm and fine. Joel was in high spirits as the air began to sing with spring; and Mima laughed at his ardors even while she shared them. She told him her mother had always said a man in the spring of the year was not to be trusted; but she was as lavish as he was eager, denying him nothing.

When they had bricks enough, and when the fire in the house could be let die down, Joel began to build the chimney. Mima was to have an oven at one side of the hearth. The fireplace would have for the present no jamb on the other side, so that long logs could be more easily thrust in on top of the fire, and the maximum amount of heat would be thrown out into the room. A column that measured two bricks on a side supported this outer corner of the chimney; and squared oak logs would carry the weight. For a while as the work progressed, they left in place those long boards which guided the smoke to the opening beside the ridgepole in the roof; but when the end of the job was in sight, they let the fire go out altogether, and Joel carried the chimney up through the roof and put birch-bark flashing all around it, so that Mima said the chimney looked like a woman with a shamefully scanty skirt tied around her waist.

He fitted new shingles over the flashing, and another strip

of birch bark over the shingles, till the roof was tight against any weather. The bricks were set in clay that would bake as hard as the bricks themselves; the chimney drew to perfection; and Joel and Mima were mighty proud when it was done. Her first baking in the new oven, they agreed, was the best she had ever managed. There was a drunkenness of happiness in them both in these weeks; and Polly, without knowing why, felt this in them and was forever laughing. She was almost fifteen months old, and her babblings began to be now and then intelligible. A rabbit which lived near the cabin had somehow tamed itself and they often saw it cropping the first green down by the spring. Mima tried to teach Polly to call it a bunny; but Polly's best effort was 'bittum'. If when they went to look for it she saw it first, she squealed with delight. 'Ditty Bittum', Mima assured Joel, meant 'See the bunny.' He claimed that Polly was trying to say 'Little Bunny'. She had been saying 'Dah-dah' since February. She had seven actual and demonstrable teeth, and Mima claimed for her others which Joel would not allow. Early in May she took four real steps, and her new ability to move from place to place led her to many tumbles; but she had never been a crying baby, and she was not now. She was as ready to laugh at her own mishaps as at her successes. Mrs. Robbins declared she was the spit of Mima, and so did Joel; and Mima said Polly was so like Joel it was just funny. So everyone was satisfied.

The sun was already high and warm; and the black flies began to appear and to harass them. Joel, in haste to make a crop, nevertheless forced himself to delay till the time was right; and in the meantime he could burn stumps and brush on his cleared land.

He used some of the stumps to serve as the backbone of a fence along the little brook below the spring. Mima and Polly watched him one day, and when he took a breathing spell he said: 'Stumps make a good enough fence to hold a cow, if you lay some poles along them. We'll get a heifer from Boggs,

Mima, and have our own milk; and we'll need a pasture walled in. I'll build a stable for the critter, too.'

'We can raise our own pigs, when we have milk,' Mima agreed, and she said happily: 'It's going to be fun, Joel; saving up and getting this and that, right along, till we've got a farm all stocked and all.'

Joel laughed and took Polly and tossed her till she screamed with delight. 'Can't raise pigs with this wench to guzzle all the milk she sees!' he protested.

Mima said in pretended wrath: 'Don't you go calling her a wench, Joel!'

'She is!' he declared. 'See her roll her eyes at me, making love to me like a good one. She takes after her ma!'

'Well, I hope she learns sense enough not to go falling in love with a rip like you before she's old enough to be sorry for it.'

'You been sorry, have you, Mima?'

'Oh, I knew how to handle you!' He laughed and caught her; and she cried: 'Stop it, Joel, with Polly watching you!'

But she kissed him, just the same; and Polly said: 'Dah, dah, dah,' approvingly, and the sun shone and new leaves everywhere were unfolding so fast and growing so fast that Mima thought she could almost see them do it. These warm spring days were like the lifting of a weight off the land. Everything expanded in a surging riot of growth, as though there was not time for all the growing that must be done.

*   *   *   *   *

They made many plans for that trip up the river to which they both looked forward. The light canoe which Bela had made for Mima would carry them both, with what gear they would need. It had begun the year before to crack a little with alternate wettings and dryings, and early in June Mima ground up some flax-seed and boiled it till the boiling oil would scorch a feather and with this rubbed the wood till it was well primed. To make assurance more sure, Joel payed the widest cracks with pitch boiled down and laid in hot till the float was as dry as an eggshell.

They discussed what they would need to take. 'We'll have some carrying to do,' Joel reminded her, 'so we'll get along with mighty little.' They settled at last on a blanket apiece, a fish spear, Joel's axe and gun, powder and shot, a sack of meal and some smoked moose meat. These with the clothes they wore would supply all their needs; but Joel thought of something else. 'You'll have to do some wading,' he told Mima. ' I'm Davis says there'll be places we'll have to drag the canoe. You don't want to be getting your clothes wet all the time.' He suggested, laughingly, that she wear some of his garments, cutting them to fit; but she would not agree.

'I'll fix it so I can tuck up my petticoats easy,' she told him. 'I'll get along.'

Mrs. Robbins was delighted at the prospect of keeping Polly with her for the week or so they would be gone; and they waited only for Joel to finish the planting. The season served him well; and June was not ten days old when he decided he was ready to set out. He proposed that, in order to make an early start, they leave Polly at Seven-Tree Pond the night before; but Mima would not be separated from the baby one night more than was needful.

So on the chosen morning she paddled down-river with Polly, while Joel made the last preparations. The sun was just above the trees across Seven-Tree Pond when she left the baby happy in Mrs. Robbins' arms; and the dawn mist was rising off the water. She turned back up the river in the dewy coolness of early morning; and now she was in haste. The water in the river was high enough so that there was some current from one pond to the other; but when she came into Round Pond again, the canoe glided effortlessly. Joel was at the landing to meet her with everything ready; but despite his laughing protests, Mima insisted on going up to the house to make sure that he had left things in order there. He packed their gear into the canoe while she climbed the hill; and she came racing down to join him again, her eyes shining, laughing like a girl.

'Now!' she cried. She stepped into the bow, and he the stern; and a moment later the canoe swung and headed for the mouth of the river where it entered Round Pond.

4

MIMA, as she and Joel pad-
dled toward the mouth of the river to begin this adventure
of which she had so often dreamed, was like a wild thing, intensely alive, intensely alert to every sight and sound. Her
nostrils caught every drift of fragrance on the faintly stirring
morning airs. The last skeins of mist were still rising from the
water. A loon hooted at them from over near the island where
she had dried her garments in the sun that day she fell, wading
out from shore. A pair of black ducks rose from the reeds as
they approached the river mouth; a bobolink was singing in the
meadow opposite the old maple, beginning so sedately with two
long, sweet, pure notes, then pouring forth a jumble of liquid
melody without pattern or design, as though the bird's sheer
joy at being alive in mating time threw it into an incoherent
rapture; and blackbirds with red epaulets upon their shoulder
were teetering among the cat-tails, with creaking, raspy song.
Things long familiar were new, now, and beautiful. Merely to
look at the arrow-shaped leaves on some of the water plants,
at the tubular stems of others, at the small lily pads below the

surface and the massed ferns along the banks and the bright blue of flags growing here and there by the waterside produced in Mima a delicious, sensuous joy.

They entered the river; and in the pool just below the wreck of the old beaver dam, where the maple hung out over the water, they saw salmon lying, the great fish swirling lazily away from beneath the canoe. Alders and moose bush fringed the stream on the western bank; the forest touched it on the east. A musquash swam down-river to meet them, its head sending ripples in a widening arrow behind it; and it saw them and dived with an effortless ease as they drew near. A mother sheldrake with a flock half grown scuttered away upstream ahead of them, the young splashing along the surface, the mother clumsily pretending to have a broken wing, seeking to entice Mima and Joel to follow her while her brood dived and hid among the bushes that overhung the water along the bank. Mima saw one and then another of them, still covered with down, a pale stripe along their heads, watching her with bright eyes as the float passed where they lay. This first flock was hardly left behind before the canoe disturbed another. The river was like a nursery in which the birds bred by thousands. Mima watched the mother's pretended distress and smiled at that transparent deception, and Joel behind her chuckled and said:

'They make as much fuss as if we wanted to kill them.'

'Jess killed some once,' Mima remembered. 'But they're not good to eat. Tough and fishy.'

'I've et them,' he assured her. 'Take one that's about ready to fly and bake him in the ground and he's pretty good — if you can't get anything better.'

After they passed the old beaver dam, the river might for a while have been merely a continuation of the pond, the flow was so slight. They crossed the shallow bar where Mima one day had bathed, and paddled easily against the faint current till they reached the mouth of Bowker's brook and saw 'Lish

Partridge's dugout lying in the water there; but the banks of
the brook and of the river were high enough so that they passed
unseen and unseeing. Then the river turned and led them easterly and a little south, and there began to be more current
against them. After they had gone twenty or thirty rods along
this easterly reach of the river, they could look back and see
smoke rising from Sally Partridge's breakfast fire; but no one
came out of the hovel till the river's course changed again, leading them northward, and the smoke was lost to view. The current stiffened, but their paddles drove them on. Mima said, her
voice a little hushed as voices are in solitudes:

'I've never been even this far up-river in a float before.'

'Neither have I,' Joel agreed. 'But I've been as far as the
head of Sunnyback Pond in the winter on the ice.'

'And we've walked up,' she reminded him.

'I'm going to have to walk it in a minute now,' he said.
'There's a ripple ahead.' He took his setting pole and stood up,
and she held her paddle across her knees while he drove the
float against the current, holding, thrusting, catching another
purchase on the bottom to hold and thrust again; till at last he
had to step out into the shallows and wade, pushing the canoe
ahead of him. Mima offered to help, but he told her to wait.

'No sense getting your petticoats wet,' he said. 'Long as I
can manage.'

'I'll tuck them up. Or I'll take them off.'

He laughed. 'No and you won't! Not yet, anyway. Like
as not I'll have you naked on my hands before we're through;
but I'll keep you decent till we pass Phin's, if I can! I don't
want to start Mily's tongue clacking.'

He was able to push the float for a while, but then the channel
was broken by rocks, and he saw a stiffer fall above, so Mima
had to step out. They were both barefoot. She tucked up
skirt and petticoats and secured them, and with him now at the
bow, Mima at the stern, they worked the float up through the
quickening water and lifted it over two or three small cascades,

and pushed it through the ripples above. They labored thus till they came to easier water above the rips, and Joel showed her where a float had been drawn up on the east bank. 'That's Phin's lower landing,' he said. 'He packs across from Seven-Tree Pond, paddles on up from here.'

She asked where it was he and she had watched together that night for the murderers of Soule, and he told her: 'Up about opposite Phin's. I'll show you.'

Mima hoped they might pass Phin's house unseen, and when they approached his landing and she saw his heavy float hauled half out of water there, she suggested: 'Keep in close to the bank, Joel.'

He obeyed her; but Mily came down to the river for a pail of water just before they reached the landing, and saw them, and called to Phin, at the house some distance away:

'Oh, Phin! Here's Joel and Mima!' Phin appeared on the bank as they reached her, and she said welcomingly: 'We're real glad to see you. Light.'

'We can't, Mily,' Mima said. 'We've a long ways to go today. Hello, Phin.'

Phin's head jerked. 'Morning,' he said, and Mily demanded: 'Where you going?'

Joel said: 'Up-river. We don't know just where, yet. Going to call on I'm Davis if we can find him, Phin; and I aim to look out some moose country. Old Davis says it's sightly up there; lakes, and hills to climb.'

Phin's neck pumped. 'I hear so,' he agreed; and Mily cried: 'Oh, Phin, let's us go with them! I'm awful tired of staying here!' Her tone was fretful and querulous, and her bright hair was matted and her cap soiled; but she was as pretty as ever, soft and fair and young. Mima thought her full mouth was made for kissing — or for sullen complaining.

'Can't, Mily,' Phin reminded her. 'Can't leave the young one.' His eyelid twitched nervously.

'We can leave him with Lucy,' Mily urged. 'Let's, Phin!'

'I've got too much to do to be going away,' he insisted.

'There'll be time enough to work after we get back.' She laughed bitterly. 'There's all our lives to work in!'

Phin shook his head, looking at Joel appealingly. 'Anyway, they don't want us traipsing along,' he protested.

Mily said recklessly: 'Oh, they don't care! They can go off in the woods or somewhere, if they want to get away from us. Please, Phin, can't we?'

Mima felt a slow anger burn in her. She took a strong paddle stroke, and Joel followed her lead. They passed the landing. 'See you in a week or so,' he called back to them. 'We'll stop on the way down.'

They moved on upstream, but behind them for a long time Mima could hear Mily scolding. 'She ought to be smacked,' she said. 'Even if she is my cousin.'

'Phin better get her in the way of another baby,' Joel declared. 'That'll take her mind off things.'

They had for a while easy travelling; but then the dead water began to break up into a series of little pools with gravel bars between, or rocky runs. Sometimes Joel poled up over these obstacles, sometimes he stepped out to push, sometimes they both waded. Ahead, louder and louder, they heard the song of stronger water. They came into a deep pool, almost circular, three or four rods across, and with rocky shores; and they passed from that into another, larger, where the water was so deep and dark that even with his setting pole Joel could not touch the bottom. On the left bank a huge rounded ledge projected into the river, rising ten or fifteen feet above the water, and against it the current swirled and eddied before dropping into the smaller pool below.

Mima said: 'Let's swim, Joel. It's a fine place for it.'

'Not yet,' he said. 'By the noise up ahead, we're going to have to carry pretty soon. We'll be hot enough to want to swim after that.'

'We don't have to hurry.' She laughed softly. 'We've left

everyone behind, Joel. There's just the two of us now, going on where we want to. We could swim first. It's an awful nice place to.'

He laughed at her. 'We'll never get anywhere if we stop all the time. The morning's half gone now.' He took his pole to negotiate the rip above the pool. 'Wait till we get to Sunny-back Pond,' he said. 'We can swim there.'

So she helped him, but the difficulties in their way increased. The river came toward them in a series of low falls, with no respite between; and they labored till Joel said at last:

'Well, I guess the easiest way to pass this is to carry a piece. I can swing the canoe on my shoulders if I get a fair purchase; but I'll pick out the best way to go, first.' He put the float ashore and lifted out his axe and gun and their gear; and they drew the canoe high and dry. 'Come along,' he said. 'We'll have a look at it.'

Mima thought the canoe too heavy for him to carry alone, and said so; but she went with him to prospect the easiest path past the quick water. He had chosen the west bank; and they climbed steeply till they were twenty feet above the water and found themselves in a stand of fine pines, with no underbrush to make travel difficult. Below them the river sang, dancing in the sun; and they walked along above it side by side, even Joel in no hurry now. 'We've nothing to hurry for,' he reminded her; and she nodded and said:

'That's what I told you. We don't know where we're going, nor how long it will take; but we know we're going there. It's just like living, isn't it? We just want to be sure to keep going in the right direction — and to have some fun along the way.'

She looked at him smilingly, caught his hand as she walked beside him through the pines; they came to the head of the rapids, and saw that though there was a strong current even above them, the water spilling down from the pond, the canoe could make way against it. With his axe he clipped away a few alders by the water to make room to launch the canoe;

and they laid the gear they had brought in a small heap near-by and turned back along the bank again to fetch the float.

But where a boulder half as big as a house jutted out into the water, he turned aside and clambered up on it to look up the stream and down; and she came and sat beside him in the sun, their feet dangling. The sun was not too warm for comfort, and the river sang below them, and Mima lay back on the flat top of the rock, her feet hanging over its edge, one arm extended, the other shading her eyes, smiling up at him. He leaned on one hand, looking down at her; and he chuckled and said:

'Hot, laying here in the sun?'

'Like a cat by the fire.'

'We won't get anywhere, this gait.'

She smiled lazily. 'We're here, anyway.'

'Aren't you too hot? Want to go back in the shade?'

'I can't decide what I do want to do,' she confessed, shading her eyes with her arm, smiling up at him. 'I like the smell of the pine needles under me, and it's cool in the shade; but I like being hot in the sun too.'

He watched the river, and he watched her, and after a moment he laughed. She asked what he was laughing at and he said: 'I was thinking of Jemmy Born-Drunk Davis. Remember, I'm Davis told us about him? He said Jemmy and Born-Drunk were two men in one. They never did agree about what they wanted. You're the same. You want to be in the sun and the shade too. Make up your mind!'

She smiled assentingly. 'I guess there are two of us in each of us, aren't there, Joel? Maybe Jemmy's the inside one, our heart, or our brain or something; and Born-Drunk is the body part. Jemmy always has reasons for what he wants to do; but Born-Drunk just wants to do things because he wants to.'

Joel nodded, playing the game with her. 'Right now my Jemmy wants to go get the canoe and bring it up and go on. He's saying: "You've got to hurry! You can't stay here for a week sprawling in the sun." '

'What does your Born-Drunk say?' she challenged smilingly.

'He says he doesn't want to carry canoes! He says canoes are heavy, and he says it will be a job getting ours up the bank, and a harder job swinging it on my head and packing it up here.' Joel chuckled. 'And he says this is a handsome piece of river, and you're a mighty handsome woman, and any man would be a fool that wasn't satisfied right here.'

'My Jemmy is scolding me too, about lying here so lazy and happy,' she agreed. 'He keeps reminding me about the mountains and the ponds we're going to see, reminding me we could lie in the sun at home, claiming we ought to go on and keep going on and getting ourselves all tired out.'

He chuckled. 'But your Born-Drunk just wants to lie there in the sun looking beautifully at her husband?'

'Or even in the shade,' she amended, turning her head sidewise on the hot rock, her cheek against the lichen which covered it. 'Where I can smell the pine needles on the ground.'

'We're wasting time,' he reminded her.

'You sound just like Jemmy. I don't think it's wasting time. I want to waste time.'

'You sound like Born-Drunk!'

'I guess I feel like him. He wants to do things because he wants to do things. He keeps telling Jemmy to stop being so energetic.'

'Jemmy keeps thinking about that canoe he's going to have to carry.'

'He'll probably make Born-Drunk carry it in the end — to punish him.'

'Punish him for what? Born-Drunk hasn't done anything!'

'I think he's going to,' she predicted. 'Sometimes I think Born-Drunk has more sense about things than Jemmy, too. If Jemmy was always boss, Born-Drunk would never have any fun, and neither would Jemmy. When Born-Drunk has his way, Jemmy really enjoys it — even if he won't admit it beforehand.'

'Jemmy says I ought to go get that canoe first.'

'Born-Drunk says Jemmy ought to forget the canoe. It will be there, afterward, but this minute won't be here except for just this minute.'

'What does Born-Drunk want?'

'Wants to be kissed some,' she murmured; and then: 'Wants to be carried into the shade, where she can smell the pine needles under her cheek.'

He laughed deeply; and he came to his feet and lifted her, warm from the sun, and held her across his body as he stepped sure-footed back along the great boulder. He bore her up the bank among the pines and laid her down again.

'Anything else your Born-Drunk wants?' he asked, on his knee beside her.

She shook her head, her arm across her eyes. 'I guess it's your turn to think of something.'

When the time came to carry the canoe past the rips, Mima gave a hand with the task of getting it up the steep bank to the level. After that Joel was able to poise it on his shoulders, and Mima walked behind him, watching the muscles in his legs work, tensing and relaxing with each step, his toes gripping the ground. She was full of a delicious peace and happiness and fine content; and the crests of the tall pines whispered high above them, and the river sang, dancing in the sun. She did not speak, nor did Joel, as they came up to the quieter water above the ripple. They floated the canoe and loaded it again and started on; and Joel sang behind her:

> Oh, her cheek it was bonny; her eye it was merry;
> Her ear was a shell and her lip was a cherry.
> Her smile would make any man linger a while
> And she smiled that smile at the gentlemen!

Mima said over her shoulder: 'Born-Drunk likes to hear you sing.'

'What does Jemmy think of it?'

'He's one of these prim and proper people, thinks it's a wicked little song, but he really likes it, Joel.' She said serenely: 'Every bit of me likes every bit of you.'

He poled up over the lip of gravel and out into Sunnyback Pond. Mima had never seen the pond before; and she exclaimed with pleasure as Joel set the float ashore on a sandy beach on the west side, just above the outlet. 'Time for that swim,' he said. 'And we'll eat a bite before we go on.' So they swam in the clear water, and dried themselves in the sun, and ate bread without troubling to strike up a fire. Then they went on, and Joel guided the canoe out into the middle of the pond, the shores falling back on either side. To the west the forested slopes rose to a bold ridge, dark with pines, that ran parallel with the pond two or three miles away and extended far ahead of them. On the east side the immediate slopes were easier; but at some distance the ground pitched sharply upward in a cluster of wooded summits. In the middle of the pond lay two or three islands, dense with cedars, so little out of water that they might be overflowed if the pond was high. These two landed to explore them, wading from one to the other when the water was no more than knee-deep, and Joel said: 'I like islands. I'd like to live on one, just big enough for a farm, with no way for anyone to get at us unless we wanted them to.'

'People have to keep part of theirselves, of their lives, where no one can get at it,' she agreed. 'Even married people. I have part of my life where you can't come, and you have part away from me. That's the way it ought to be. Anybody needs to be alone, some. The rest of the world can bother you awful if it gets too much into your mind. Like worrying about Warren taxing us, or the British at Biguyduce, or the way Mily treats Phin, or anything.'

'All a woman wants is the inside of a house, and her husband and her children.'

'That's all there is,' she said. 'That's her job to do.'

They left the islands and went on at last toward the head of the pond. She said: 'It's beautiful, isn't it, Joel? But it's not as big as Seven-Tree Pond.'

'It's wider,' he said. 'But not as long. That ridge to the west, when we go after moose we cross that, from the head of the pond. It's about three miles across to the Madomock; an easy climb on this side for maybe two miles, and then steep down the other side.' He swung the canoe in toward the western shore again; and they paddled briskly on. He said once:

'We don't have to hurry. You're working too hard.'

'I want to get out of the pond into the river again,' she confessed. 'It's more secret in the river. This is fine, but — I feel as if people could see us.'

He chuckled. 'No reason they shouldn't.'

She asked: 'How far will we go today? We'll stop early, where it's a good place to sleep, won't we?'

'Sleepy?'

'Born-Drunk is.'

He laughed. 'Born-Drunk's had his way once today,' he reminded her. 'Let's give Jemmy his turn. I've seen all this before, as far as the head of the pond. I want to get into new places as soon as we can.'

They settled to their paddles, keeping close to shore to be free of the light westerly wind. Half a dozen times they started flocks of ducks out of the reeds along the shore; and as the pond narrowed at the upper end, the banks became sedgy, and black ducks and teal rose from the marsh by hundreds; and Mima heard a crashing in the tall grass and brush and caught a glimpse of tossing horns as a great moose fled at their approach. Joel cried:

'See that old boy! We'll want to get a shot at one, tonight, maybe; need fresh meat. Not much chance to get a bear without a dog, unless we run right onto one.'

'I brought enough smoked meat to last us, but we can spear a salmon, Joel; or shoot some ducks. Let's not kill anything that's too big to eat.'

'I fetched small shot for ducks,' he agreed. They entered the mouth of the river which here meandered aimlessly, with a wide marsh meadow on either side; and he said: 'I'll load up for ducks; see if we can't get up close to a bunch of them before they hear us.'

He nosed the canoe into the grass; and Mima stepped out and steadied the canoe while he pulled the slugs out of his gun and poured in small shot from his cupped hand. He primed the piece and was ready. 'You paddle stern,' he said. 'Go along easy and keep on the inside of the bends. River's full of ducks. I can peek through the grass and see them before they jump.'

He might have had a chance almost at once; for the marsh was alive with birds, feeding along the edges of the grass. But he waited to be sure of a sufficient kill. They approached a bend that turned sharply to the left, and heard a splashing of many ducks in the straight reach ahead. Joel signalled with his hand for silence, and Mima eased the canoe along close to the grass, her paddle never lifting from the water to betray them by the drip. They approached the angle where the stream turned; and Joel crouched low, peering to the left, till presently he raised his head high enough to see over the grass and threw up his gun and fired.

The air instantly was full of ducks, and Mima heard a crashing toward the forest to the west of them where a moose took flight. She drove the canoe around the bend and saw the water well littered with dark bodies. Some floated motionless, breast down, perhaps with a broken wing thrown up at an awkward angle; some had turned over on their backs and their feet paddled furiously in the air; some, crippled, swam toward the banks and crawled ashore and vanished in the grass. Joel had got a fair shot into the thick of the flock, and they picked up a dozen dead, and caught two or three wounded that had hidden in the grass and betrayed themselves as the canoe came near.

'They breed all through here,' Joel said. 'Must be hundreds of nests in this bog, by the birds in the air.' Above them the ducks were wheeling in great circles; and Mima wondered how many nests would be abandoned now, and spoke her thought.

'Not many,' he guessed. 'If there was an old bird in the river to get shot, the other one was likely on the nest. Anyway, we've ducks to eat.'

He told her to put the nose of the canoe ashore, and plucked grass and covered the ducks to keep off blowflies, and they changed ends in the float again and so went on.

They left the marsh meadow behind, and as they ascended, the current began to come to meet them. The river was full of sheldrake, startled mothers monotonously counterfeiting a broken wing, young chicks peering at them from cover along the bank. Dense forest pressed close on either hand, and at the foot of the next quick water they saw a bear fishing in the shallows. They were close before he discovered them and splashed ashore and away. The stronger current drove Joel to the pole again, and presently to wade; and sometimes Mima too had to step out of the canoe. Once a cow moose and her calf waded across a few rods above them. The hard going continued, and the sun was descending in the west so that they were in the shadow of the trees. Mima said at last: 'Born-Drunk's getting awful hungry, Joel. Have we come far enough today?'

'Let's clear this quickwater,' he proposed. 'Get to the next deadwater and sleep at the foot of it.'

So they went on. The way became rougher, the banks steep now on either side of the river, and there were cascades a foot or two in height with deep water between. They were hot from their own exertions, so they stripped and waded sometimes waist-deep; and with Joel at the head, Mima at the foot, they worked the canoe up through the steep run. Once a salmon jumped so near Mima she cried out in startled surprise and then in delight at his beauty shining in the sun. The east bank rose fifty or a hundred feet above them; but the slope on the west began to ease. They toiled and rested and toiled again, sometimes sitting neck deep in the pleasant water and holding the canoe while they rested before pushing on. Joel said: 'Born-Drunk likes the resting better than the hauling.' And Mima laughed and said:

'Well, Jemmy's boss now. Let's go on. He says Born-Drunk can rest and eat and sleep later on.'

The high ground on the west bank broke back at last and they passed the head of the rips and reached easier water. Joel said: 'All right. This is far enough. If we go on, we might find another ripple and Jemmy would want us to pass that too before we stopped.'

Mima pointed upstream. 'Look at that tree, Joel.'

A willow near the bank had, years before, toppled over till it lay horizontally, and the branches thus brought uppermost had grown and thrived, reaching for the sun. They were six or seven inches through where they left the trunk, thirty or forty feet tall. 'It's all sideways,' she said. 'Lying on its side, growing up that way.'

'There's a leaning tree opposite,' he said. An oak inclined out over the stream at an angle of forty-five degrees. 'We'll sleep there. It's a chance to dive if we want to.'

He put the canoe ashore, and they swam before they dressed, with the leaning oak as a diving stand. Then among the pines Joel levelled a place for their bed and laid hemlock boughs in a shingled couch. It was still full sun when Mima plucked three of the ducks, one for herself and two for Joel, and drew them. He struck up a fire with a spare flint and a pinch of powder, and they spitted the ducks on upright sticks leaning toward the fire, with birch bark below to catch their drippings, and broiled them slowly, turning them on the spits when it was time to do so. Salt rubbed on, and wild onions wrapped around them, gave them seasoning; and while the birds were cooking, Mima stirred up meal and water, the meal a mixture of rye and corn, and made a batch of kettle bread, baking it among the coals.

They ate while the sun was still high enough to brush the treetops above them all with gold, and Mima cooked another

duck to make a cold bite for their lunch next day. Then dark
came down, and before the fire paled to glowing embers they
were asleep on the couch he had prepared. They were warm
enough so that Mima in her sleep thrust the blankets down; and
once or twice she woke and the night was unutterably still
and at the same time full of sounds. The murmur of the
quickwater downstream below their camp was a steady undertone of which the ear ceased to take notice; but there were many
small sounds of living things, and Mima, always preternaturally
keen of hearing, was intensely conscious of the stir of life about
them everywhere; and conscious too, as she so often was, of the
tremendous reach of wilderness that lay on every hand, in
which they were no more than the smallest and least considerable spot. Once when she woke in the night so did Joel, and
they talked a little, quietly, before they slept again; and that
was the sweetest waking of them all.

*   *   *   *   *

The world was all blanketed with pale mist when Joel
stirred. He went down to the water, but she pretended still to
sleep till he returned and roused her and said she must swim
in the river to wake properly; and she cried out that it was too
cold, that she would not, and he insisted that she would. They
tussled together like puppies, he trying to unbutton her dress
and she to prevent it, till a button was torn off and she surrendered; and a moment later they plunged into the water
together. It was warm and caressing, so warm that she dreaded
coming out and would not do so till he had struck up a fire.
Then he threatened to wet her clothes and tie them in many
little knots unless she came and put them on. Once out of the
water she made haste to dress; for the flies were savage in the
humid, windless dawn.

So presently they breakfasted and then went on. The river
seemed to welcome them and ease their way; and for a mile
or two their paddles served sufficiently. The ground on either

hand rose only a little above the water, and sometimes grassy coves broke back from the river into the forest and ended in pleasant meadows. Several times they startled moose, and there were young sheldrakes in constant panic flight before them, and every muddy path along the bank was marked with the long-fingered tracks of raccoons. Trails came down to the river where the splayed hooves of moose had cut the mud, and they saw an otter slide, and mink peered boldly at them from the bank. They came to a bend where the river widened in a deep pool with a spring brook flowing in, and the water was so clear that they could see the salmon lying packed in the cold deeps below. They paddled slowly, talking quietly, savoring everything. The morning mists disappeared, and the sun was fine. They passed through a grassy bog; and beyond, tremendous elms arched above their heads, so that they traversed a shaded grotto; and then they began to meet murmuring waters and harder going. This continued, no better and no worse, with an occasional cascade where they had to step out and haul the canoe up through the sluicing water. They came at last to where the river ran in easy curves, deep pools between gravel bars, so that now and then Joel had to take his pole, and almost imperceptibly their way became more difficult. They swam once, where a fine pool invited them under a leaning gray birch, and they ate cold duck and bread, and passed the mouth of a considerable brook that came in from the east, with a few rods of deadwater above. Then they came to rapids again, where bold water was broken by boulders and diverted by shingled bars, and the banks on either side were steep and rocky so that even a short carry would be difficult. Joel left Mima and scouted ahead upstream to see if this rip were a short one. Mima rested on a gravel bar in midstream where a few flags were in bloom, and a tuft of ferns, and a clump of reedy grass rising two or three feet high with a yellow-green tassel pendant from the tip of each stem. She saw on a rock just above the level of the water many little oval black water

bugs, and she pushed at one of them with a stick and found it
was an empty shell. She turned it over and discovered that it
sheltered a small, grub-like thing no bigger than a grain of
coarse meal, yet which seen closely, had members already
forming. Exposed to the sun, the small white thing put out
legs like hairs and crept into new shelter between two grains of
sand. She guessed that these were young water bugs in process
of development, and the tassels on the grass would go to seed,
and the fern roots would unroll new sprouts in the spring, and
the river was full of young ducks, and in every bit of shallow
water there were tiny fish almost too small to be recognized as
fish at all. Water bugs and grass and ducks and fish were all
alike engaged in the proper business of the flooding season; and
the young would mature, and prepare themselves to endure
the winter, to be ready to pass on the stream of life, come spring.

She was half-asleep, her arm across her eyes, her thoughts
far away, when Joel returned. He had found no end to the
hard going ahead of them, so they stripped and began to wade,
hand-hauling the canoe upstream.

For the first few rods it was good fun enough. The water was
warm and friendly, wrestling with them amiably. But the
bottom was rocky and began to be painful footing, and the
steady pulling and hauling became laborious. Half a mile of
it — a long hour in the doing — left Mima trembling with
fatigue; and Joel saw this and pulled the canoe ashore.

'Tired?' he asked. 'Want to leave it and go on afoot?'

'No. I'm Davis said we'd need the float in the pond, up
above,' she reminded him. 'But I am tired. Let's rest a while.'
She sat down limply, leaning back, then lying prone; and he
said quickly:

'Hold on! The flies will eat you. Put your clothes on. You
can walk up the bank and I'll take it on alone.'

'You need me,' she protested.

'I'll always need you,' he reminded her. 'So don't wear
yourself out! Put on your clothes.'

She obeyed him; and when she was ready they went on again, she following the bank, he in the water. But as though relenting before their persistence, the going presently improved. After a while she was able to get into the canoe. Joel pulled on only his shirt, not yet sure he could trust this easier current to continue, and took his pole again; but within another half-mile their paddles alone would drive them.

Mima had not thought how time had sped; but Joel asked now whether she were hungry. 'Starved!' she admitted.

'We'll eat,' he decided. 'I don't want to stop for the night yet, but it can't be much further to the fork old Davis talks about. I want to make it to the pond tonight, but I'm hungry myself. Being wet and working too . . .' He saw a little trickle of a spring brook coming in from the west bank, making a small sandy estuary where it met the river; and he landed and felt the water and found it icy cold, and followed it a rod or two till he came to where it bubbled up through pin gravel at the foot of rising ground. Mima came with him and they began to dig a basin in the clay and shale through which the gravel ran in slender veins, scooping with their hands, and Mima remembered a day that seemed long ago and told him how she had dug out that spring beside the path from Colonel Wheaton's barn to the Royal Mess and walled it with small flat stones.

'And I thought the spring would always be there,' she said, 'and the little rocks I put for a wall. Springs and brooks and rivers are the life in the world, aren't they, Joel? They're as much alive as people and birds and animals; only they stay in the same place and keep on living. When you think of life going on, you always think of a river.' He was lying flat, relaxed and resting while the water cleared in the basin they had made. 'Like this river today. Maybe we're about the first people that ever came this way, except Indians; but the river has always lived here and always will, and this little spring will keep bubbling up through the gravel.'

'You're always thinking about things going on and on,' he

said gently. 'It never seems to matter to you what happens in just one day. You like to think of things that keep on happening.'

'I hate to think of anything ending, ever.'

'Like dying?'

'Dying isn't ending. If you've had children, of course it isn't; but even if you haven't, you've put some of you into every person you've ever fought or hated or loved or known or even talked to. Just the way sunlight goes into trees and makes them live.'

He chuckled, and she asked why, and he said: 'Laughing at the notion of me shining on people like the sun!' He sat up suddenly, looking at her. 'But Mima, you never care about what's happening in the rest of the world right now! You like to think about what you will be doing later on, or what other people will be doing in the place where you are.' He nodded toward the spring. 'It makes you happy thinking that maybe a hundred years from now a man and a woman like you and me, or maybe a man and his daughter like me and Polly, or someone, will come down and dig out this spring the way we did just now. But you don't care a hoot if all over the world right now today other people are digging out other springs.'

'I know it,' she admitted. 'Where I am, and the people I love, is all the world I want.' She said almost fiercely: 'It's the only world anyone can live in, Joel; his own world. If he tries to live a lot of other lives in a lot of other worlds, he doesn't really live anywhere. Like I'm Davis. We're going where he lives; and even if he's not there, he'll be alive there. Just our looking at places he has looked at will bring him close to us. But when he comes to the settlements, he just comes out of nothing and goes back to nothing afterward. He's not real alive to us at all.'

Joel laughed, lying on his belly to drink, then getting to his knees. 'Well, if you don't feed me, I'll not be alive either!' he warned her. 'I'll strike up the fire.'

When they had eaten, they went on. They came in a scant mile to the fork where two brooks met to make the river. The west fork was a brawling stream, but they held north against an easier current, never too severe for strong paddling, and presently the trees fell back on either side as a marsh meadow opened out before them.

Here was the moose bog I'm Davis had promised they would find, and they had evidence enough before long that he had told them true. They were hidden between grassy banks; but the wind was westerly so that their scent alarmed the moose in the bog to the east of them, and Mima heard the plop of great hooves pulling out of mud, the swish of bushes flying back into position after some huge body passed. Joel stood up once to look ahead, and then sat down again and drove the canoe on with faster strokes; and so it was at some speed that they came darting out through the suddenly widening river into the sedgy foot of the pond.

A cloud of ducks rose as they appeared; and then to right and left there was a confusion of splashing as moose feeding at greater or less depths in the shallows plunged at a trot — even through water belly-deep — toward the shore. Mima saw to their left a tremendous bull, a smaller one beyond him; and there were cows and lanky calves and yearlings to the number of twenty or more, all in flight to the shelter of the forest on either hand. In a matter of seconds the nearer scene was deserted; but Mima saw other dark forms, at a distance looking almost black, take the spreading alarm and turn to disappear into the cover of the pines that lined the banks of the pond.

She and Joel watched in silence except when they cried: 'There's another! There's another!' As they paddled slowly up the pond, Joel chose to keep near the middle, so that they could see a range of fine hills ahead, five or six miles away; and when Mima looked back she saw another hill southeastward, dark with spruce against the sky.

'But those ahead,' she said, 'must be the ones I'm Davis told about. Will we climb them, Joel?'

He chuckled and said: 'Not tonight, we won't. I've had all the climbing — or the work — I want for a while. We'll pick a good spot for the night here, Mima; go on tomorrow.'

So they proceeded up the pond; and a deep indented cove on the left ended in sedgy bog where Joel saw a moose feeding undisturbed, ignoring their approach. 'I could get him,' he said; but Mima reminded him they had meat enough. They swung out from the cove around a rocky peninsula that was almost an island; and Joel thought the northern end of this island would be free from mosquitoes if any night breeze rose. But they went on, skirting the shore, swinging into the deep bay west of the camp site already half determined, and saw fine sand bottom there; and they proceeded to the head of the pond and found a moose feeding in water almost deep enough to cover his back, and by approaching when his head was under water they came so near him before he saw them that he fled with a snort of panic, and Mima saw his small eyes blaze red with mingled rage and fear.

The head of the pond was all ringed with boggy shores; and Joel thought there would be no difficulty here in killing as many moose as a man might want. 'And easy hauling home down-river on the ice,' he said. 'If it was froze hard. I'll say we come here next year.' Mima said she would like to come, and he laughed and said: 'Jemmy might like it — the head part of you. But Born-Drunk wouldn't. Hard work, Mima.' He swung the float back across the pond to the point which he thought would catch a breeze; and they landed there and made their beds and ate again, broiling split ducks propped upright before a blazing fire, and Mima made corn pudding, and the drippings from the ducks were its seasoning. The moon, two or three days short of the full, rose before they were tired of slow quiet talk together; and a pair of loons screamed mockery and protest at the fire they kept blazing till the moon left them with no further need of light. Joel smothered the fire with grass and green stuff, and the rolling smudge just above them where they lay kept the mosquitoes clear till they slept. Mima woke not that night at all.

*   *   *   *   *

They left the canoe next day, a mile or so up the inlet brook, where ripples and shoaling water seemed to make further progress difficult; and they packed their gear and divided it and pushed on up the stream. Half a mile brought them to the beaver dam of which I'm Davis had spoken. Beyond there lay a level meadow grown to reeds and rushes and alder and willow scrub and moose bush, that seemed to extend a mile or two, widening till it reached the foot of the hills. They thought to follow the brook's course upward; but bog ground made going hard and harder; so they drew off till they found good footing, and pushed on along the rising slopes north of the meadow. Once and then again Joel tried experimentally to descend to the brook again; but each time bog turned him back, till at last they came suddenly upon a lively brook slipping secret through great pines.

'This is the first brook,' Joel remembered. 'It's the second we follow up to his place.' They crossed that brook and pressed on, and now and then they crossed a strip of sedgy meadow and looked down its length toward where they had seen the beaver dam.

The two brooks proved to be not half a mile apart; but where the first had been dark hued, with deep pools like ink, the second was a sunny, laughing stream, wide and shallow, with many gravel bars and deep pools in the bends so clear that every pebble on the bottom could be seen; and trout lay in them, and where in one angle of the current the spring floods had scooped out a four-foot basin, they found two salmon lying waiting for a spate of water to help them higher still. Joel managed to get his spear into one of them; and they went on with a change of diet assured, Joel carrying the salmon, his gun and axe and the heavier pack, Mima with the blankets on

her shoulders, and their remaining ducks, tied together by their
necks, dangling from her hand.

They followed the brook till its character began to change.
The sandy pools and gravel bars gave way to rocky pools and
ledges; and cascades sang to them as they drew near. 'We're
climbing all the time,' Joel pointed out. 'And it's steeper all
the time, and the banks go up steep both sides.' They pushed
on a mile and more, sometimes in the brook, sometimes following the banks, till Mima said suddenly, half-startled at what
she saw:

'Joel! Here's a path!'

She was on the bank, he on the ledges beside the water. He
came to join her and saw what she had seen; a padded foot
trail, a little continuing depression in the needles which
covered the ground, the scrape here and there where a foot
had brushed them roughly.

'Must be nigh where his house is,' he decided.

'Do you guess he made the path here?'

'Bound to. Nobody else lives anywhere in here, and mighty
few come through. The Belfasters come as far as the bogs
east of the pond, sometimes; but not this far.' He led the way,
watching the faint track that picked the best going along the
brookside; and Mima said:

'It's queer how quick even one man will make a path, Joel.
Just camping in a place two or three days, and he'll have
paths all around; and if enough men come along, pretty soon
there's a road.' And she said: 'I wonder how long before
there'll be a road from Sterlingtown to Warren?'

'Not likely to be one till we get incorporated as a town,' he
reminded her. 'I've been thinking we'd ought to, if we get a
few more families started, and people coming in to live.'

'You talk to the men about it,' she agreed. 'See what they
think. I don't care so much about a road to Warren; but it'd
be better to have a town with a school for the young ones and
all.' She added, remembering something long forgotten: 'Your

sister Jemima was saying one time that she might come up here and start a school and teach. Is she coming this summer, Joel, the way she said?'

'She said she'd come when we had a house, and we've got one. I haven't heard from her; but I might not.' He stopped, and Mima came beside him; and he pointed ahead. 'There's his hovel,' he said in a low tone. 'Through there!'

Mima could not at first see what he meant, the old man's habitation lost itself so completely in the shadows by the brook-side; but as they went on a few paces, she saw it, and a moment later they came to where it stood. I'm Davis had built his hovel in an angle between two ledges, and against the flat side of one of them. The door, the only door, faced into the angle, so that to reach it they passed between the other ledge and the hovel's wall. The corner where the two ledges met had been blocked with stones and made into a hearth and fireplace; and for his house the old man had simply wedged into the ground four crotched stakes, laid poles across them, and made walls and roof with elm bark slabs laid on and bound with withes.

Mima and Joel hailed as they approached, and had no answer; so they knew the old man was away. They dropped their burdens, and Joel went through the crevice to the door; and he called to her: 'The ashes are cold. He's been gone since yesterday, anyway.' She came to join him. The hut beside them was so low that Mima on tiptoe could almost look over it. Its bark roof pitched away from the fireplace; but even at the front it was not much higher than her head. She thought of the old man huddling in his den like a hibernating bear, thought how snow must heap and pile down here among the litter of great rocks above the stream; and her eyes for a moment filled with tears. Where they stood in the three-cornered nook between the front of the hovel and the boulders, there was no more than room for both of them. Joel turned to lift aside a door made of bark on a frame of poles, which closed the entrance to the little hut; but Mima said quickly:

'Don't, Joel. We wouldn't want him going into our house and us away — not unless he needed shelter; and we don't.' And she said ruefully: 'The poor old man! Think, Joel, when it's cold!'

He nodded, his voice hushed like hers. 'You can see where he's piled firewood on the flat tops of the rocks,' he said. 'To keep the wind off, and the snow from drifting in.' They moved here and there, surveying the surroundings; and Joel by certain poles and frames and slabs of bark of birch and elm guessed that in winter I'm Davis might roof over his house and hearth and make them doubly secure. 'He could keep the snow off,' he said, 'keep warm enough in there.' He pointed out frames for stretching skins, and an elevated rack on which meat and skins too could be stored against wild marauders; and they admired the completeness of the old man's household economy.

'But I keep thinking of him lying there sick so long that time,' said Mima, 'not knowing if he'd get well or die and things would eat him.'

Joel tried to cheer her. 'He doesn't have to live here,' he pointed out. 'He could take a farm in the settlements if he wanted.'

'I don't know whether to be glad he's not here, or sorry,' she confessed. 'Will we stay here tonight — so if he does come home?'

They decided to do so. They ascended the brook a little further. Just above the hut there was a deep basin in solid rock, ten or twelve feet long, half as wide, and deeper than it was wide. A cascade, falling eight or ten feet in two or three steps, poured in at the head of the pool. The basin was deep and cool, the water clear as sunshine; and it was flecked just now with slanting sunrays which pierced its depths, leaving black shadows under the ledges at the sides. Mima's fingers flew down her buttons; and she stepped out of her petticoats. The water, faintly amber, tinted her body a pale and lovely golden hue, and Joel watched her sink down to the little pool's deeps and send the great trout flying to hide among the rocks that walled the sides. Below the surface Mima turned on her back and came drifting to the surface, the current moving her a little. Water got in her nose, and she choked and coughed and laughed; and he laughed at her, and she said:

'I always get water in my nose. Makes me so mad! Joel, I could see you, from the bottom, all big and white and shimmery. No wonder fishes are scared!' She stepped up out of the water. 'It's cold,' she warned him as he took his turn, and watched him slide in like an otter and come up gasping. Through the trees above them the sun penetrated only in slender shafts; but the air was warm, and a warm little breeze flowed up the stream bed. When they lay on a ledge half-awash over which some water grass grew in long streamers, this breeze kept most of the mosquitoes away; but not all. She said:

'Look, Joel.'

A mosquito had lighted on her breast, and Joel leaned nearer and they watched together while it filled itself with her rich blood, and Joel said: 'You'll have a welt!'

'Not if we don't scare him,' she insisted. 'Mosquitoes are just like us. If they're scared, they try to hurt people; but they're all right, left alone.'

The insect turned red and swelled tremendously; and Mima lay very still, and Joel, watching her, laughed and said: 'You act as though you liked feeding him.'

She nodded. 'I think I do. It doesn't hurt, and he's having such a meal of it. I like feeling that I have lots to give, and giving it.'

'He's had enough,' Joel jealously protested, and leaned nearer, blowing on the mosquito gently till it flew away; and a moment later, looking down at his dark head, she laughed deliciously and said:

'Mosquito!'

When they had gone into the cold water again, they rubbed dry and dressed; and Joel made their bed and their fire while

Mima cleaned the salmon he had speared. There were no wild onions here for seasoning; but she laid it flat between two tough green switches and tied their ends together and hung the split fish from forked sticks to cook before the fire, and Joel ripped a trencher of birch bark off a great white tree to receive it when it should be done. Then I'm Davis came home, descending the steep bank to the brook, with the hind quarters and saddle of a moose, snug bound with withes, on his shoulders. They did not see him till he was upon them; but he heard their low laughing voices even before he smelled the smoke and the cooking salmon. He came to them and greeted them with a grave courtesy; and at Mima's urgency he shared the salmon with them; but he asked for bread, and Mima made small cakes of meal and water and cooked them on hot rocks hauled out from the fire, and he ate them ravenously.

'I been to the Kennebeck,' he said. 'Two weeks gone. Come back through the bog three-four miles south of here, where I had a snare on a moose run there. He'd been in it long enough, choked hisself to death; but he was still warm when I got to him.'

Jess had once snared a moose, and Mima said so, and I'm Davis said: 'Yes, ma'am, I snare what I want to eat. It saves powder and ball and fuss and trouble too. I take a twisty rope made out of bark and fetch a good birch down, as big as I can bear down climbing it. I spread the noose so he'll get his head through it if his horns ain't too big; and that pulls it off the trigger and it hauls him up enough so he can't get a purchase to fight it. Mostly they choke, but I have caught 'em by the leg and had to shoot 'em. Lost one that way last summer. Shot and cut the rope instead of killing him; and he went off ker-snorting and ker-shackelling through the woods.'

They sat late that night by the fire, and Mima, lying on her back, listening to the old man's tireless talk, watched the tree-tops dark against the moonlit sky, and followed the small sparks ascending when one man or the other chunked the fire;

and the brook song **was** sleepy in her ears. I'm Davis told a dozen tales, and to some of them she did not listen. There was one about a denned bear which he tried to kill with an axe. 'I hit him,' he said, 'and he hit me. Knocked me and the axe ker-slishing and ker-sliding. But he was more'n half-asleep, and he thought he'd settled me, so I got the axe and chopped a chip out of the top of his head.' He cackled, a strange laugh. 'And he turned out to be a she, with two cubs in the hole with him — her.'

'Him and her,' Joel echoed. 'Like Jemmy and Born-Drunk that you told us about before.'

'The same,' the old man assented, and Mima, lying half-awake, saw Joel watching her and smiled at him in the fire-light. Davis said: 'And speaking of names, what would you say to three Dutchmen named Midstaff, and Pancake, and Christian?'

Joel said the last was a good name, anyway; and the old man cried: 'That just goes to show you! Let me tell you what them three done to a man and a woman and five young ones!' There was a sudden heat in his tones. 'I only just heard about it,' he said. 'And my bile riz and it's stayed riz!'

He went on without prompting. 'This man, his name was Forbes,' he said. 'He'd gone to live in Canada, but he didn't like it and decided to come back. He had a boy, John, that was fourteen years old, and four other young ones down to a baby just over a year. They was up in a place on the Chaudière, named Nouvelle Bois, means new woods or something.

'Some God knows reason, he decided to travel in the winter. These three Dutchmen was aiming to come through, and they 'greed to help him. Anyways, they started, on snowshoes, with the three youngest ones on hand sleds. Forbes hauled one, and Mrs. Forbes hauled one, and Johnny hauled the other. The other young one walked. She was a girl.'

Mima watched the stars through the pines above her. Joel laid a fresh stick on the fire, and the old man's voice droned on.

'They come along all right the first eight days,' he said. 'This was back in March. But then they left the river, aiming to strike across t'the Kennebeck, and they got theirselves lost. So Forbes and the three Dutchmen left the woman and the young ones, and they went back to try to find out where they'd got off the right way. They come to a lake and made camp and stayed the night; but they was still lost, and in the morning the Dutchmen told Forbes they'd had enough of travelling with a woman and children. They wouldn't go back to where they'd left the woman. They took all their stuff and put out on their own.'

Joel asked: 'What happened to them?' Mima heard the quiet anger in his tones.

'Nobody knows,' I'm Davis admitted. 'I'd like to run into them sometime. But they'd better not let Forbes, or any decent man, run into them again.'

Joel nodded. Mima saw his jaw clench as the old man went on.

'Well,' he said, 'all Forbes had left was an axe and a gun and a couple loaves of bread. He made it back to where his wife was, somehow; but the river they'd come by was breaking up, so they couldn't go back to where they'd started from, and they couldn't stay where they was. So they decided to make it to the Kennebeck settlements, if they could. They hadn't any way of knowing how far it was.'

Mima found herself listening to the dark tale as one listens in a dream; the old man's voice was now toneless and unvaried, with no expression in it at all. 'So they started,' he explained, 'dragging three sleds the best they could, him and his wife and the oldest boy, letting the children ride. Only the oldest girl, she walked. She was eleven years old.

'Well, naturally, they run into rain and snow and all; and about the time they'd et up most of what they had, they met up with an Indian that had just killed a moose. The Indian wasn't no Dutchman. He done the best he could for them.

He give them all the moose meat they could drag or carry, and he went along with them two-three days, till he fetched them to the Kennebeck. He had to go back home from there because his wife was sick, but he drawed a map for Forbes, showing him where he could save a few miles cutting across the bends different places; and he gave them what meat he'd packed that far.

'After that they come on alone. They travelled on the river all they could, when the ice looked safe; but it was coming into April and getting more open water all the time. They kept on a week or so. The moose meat begun to give out. Then finally the woman had to quit. She couldn't drag the sled no further.'

Mima covered her eyes with the back of her hand as though to shut out the picture his words evoked. She knew enough about the woods in spring, when even moose could not travel through deep snow, to know the woman's dreadful fatigue; and she wondered about the little girl, not as old as Susie, who walked so long and so far. The old man's monotonous recital, more terrible because he spoke so calmly, went droning on.

'They had three pounds of meat left,' he explained, 'and about the same of suet. They decided Forbes and the boy would leave the others and come on and get help.' Mima's lip was caught between her teeth; she lay still and tense. 'So Forbes built a shelter for them, and he struck up a fire, and dragged some wood handy so they could keep the fire going. He didn't know how far it was to the settlements, or whether he'd make it, or whether he'd ever get back to them. They give the woman and the children most all the meat and suet, and him and Johnny come on.

'They done the best they could. Mostly they followed the river, but then they come to falls, and below that it was all open water, so they had to take to the woods. That was a week or so after they'd left the woman. It was hard going through the woods, so Forbes made a raft and they tried to ride it; but it broke up. They held on to the logs till they floated into an eddy and got ashore.

'They hadn't et only the first day after they left the woman, so they et their leggings, and then their moccasins, boiling them and drinking the water and chewing up what was left. They come on barefoot. There was still some snow on the ground; but it was mostly froze and rocks. Their feet cut up some and froze some.'

Mima only half-heard him. She was thinking of the woman and the children left behind. She wished to ask about them and dared not, fearful what the answer might be.

'Well,' he said. 'They come nigh the settlements at Seven-Mile Brook and met some men hunting, and the men fetched them in. Their feet was in bad shape. Forbes wanted to start back with help, but he couldn't travel. So he told where he'd left his wife, best he could. It'd been ten days a'ready. Three men started right off, and Forbes took sick and stayed sick.

'Well, the three that went after them was gone thirteen days and come back and hadn't found 'em.'

Mima was watching the old man's beard move as he talked, and the fire shadows play across his face. Her teeth were locked, holding back the pitying words. Joel said in a low tone: 'They'd be dead by then. Over three weeks.'

'A man'd think so,' I'm Davis agreed. 'A man'd pray to God they was dead, if they was his. Everybody told Forbes they was bound to be; but he wa'n't satisfied. It was all he could do to walk, but nothing would do him but he'd go find them. He got two men that 'greed to go with him if he'd show the way. Johnny couldn't go. His feet had froze in the snow after he et his moccasins, so he still couldn't stand on 'em. The man's feet was in bad shape too, and he couldn't make out to travel till toward the end of May. But then he finally tried it.

'Well, he played out, the first day; but he talked the other men into going on.' He was silent for a moment, said then slowly: 'They found her. They fetched her down-river, here last week, her and one of the young ones.'

Joel cried: 'Alive?'

'Just barely,' the old man assented. 'The men had built a canoe to fetch her home in, and they carried her when they had to.' He said in mild tones: 'She'd had a time. It was just fifty days from the time Forbes had to leave her till the men got to her. The second day after he left her, it rained and put out her fire. That was the middle of April. They hadn't any way to light it again. The woman kep' count of the days, scratching on a stick with a knife. They et the meat, and then they et the inside bark off fir trees. They had water enough.

'The baby finally died on the thirty-eighth day, and the next one the day after, and the oldest girl four days after that. The woman couldn't bury 'em, hadn't the strength to dig. All she could do was lay 'em out, and crawl for water, and scrape the trees for bark to gnaw at. The men 'lowed she didn't weigh over seventy pounds when they found her, and the young one that was still alive looked like a picked bone.'

His droning voice died and was still, and the brook chuckled in its run below them. Joel sat staring at the fire, and Mima lay with her arms tight across her breast, her eyes streaming. Death was so near them here. The quiet wilderness was so impersonal and pitiless, in no hurry, willing to dawdle forty days over the business of killing a little child. Forty days to kill a baby! Probably his mother fed him while she could, giving him meat and tallow, giving him her dry breasts with a prayer that they might be fountains again, even if her own life flowed out of her with the milk they gave.

Mima wanted to come home to Polly! She wanted to be sure that Polly had enough to eat, had the right things. She wished Joel would tell the old man good night and come to her. The bed he had made for them was close by. She moved to lie there, as a sort of signal to him to join her. But he and I'm Davis were talking again, and Joel did not heed her movement, and her own healthy weariness made her at last fall asleep. She only half roused when at last Joel came to lie beside her, his arm across her shoulders, holding her protectingly.

5

THEY stayed one day there. When Mima woke, the sky was gray and the crests of the trees were black; but light crept through the dewy wood and there was a clamor of bird voices in the morning song. Mima still wanted to return to Polly; but daylight dulled her haste, and I'm Davis had plans for them. He proudly showed them his hovel, and Mima found it surprisingly comfortable. It was lined with birch bark; a hut within a hut.

'And rushes packed in between the walls,' he told them proudly. 'Makes it warm any time. Too hot, sometimes. I sleep out, only in winter or a bad rain.' His bed was soft with bear skins, his few belongings were neatly stowed. She admired the compact completeness of his arrangements; and he said:

'Yes, ma'am, even in the coldest weather I'm warm as mice. I put an extra roof up, so my hovel sets in a kind of cave. I do good.'

He wished to show them, and Joel to see, one of the mountains of which he had spoken; and she would not dissent. He led them some three or four miles, striking off at right angles to the brook up a steep grade, and then along more level ground and down again, and then at an increasing pitch up and up till they came out upon a ledgy summit that ran from southwest to northeast. At one place they could look off to the eastward across the tops of the trees on the steep slope they had climbed; and they saw the tumbled mountains toward where Camden lay, and traced the nearer length of that lower ridge, ten miles long, which ran down to Sterlingtown; and north of the mountains, across the lower land, they could see the upper Bay and beyond it the peninsula leading down to Biguyduce where the British were, and beyond that again, forty or fifty miles away, another higher rounded mountain mass. But neither the old man nor Joel knew what that mountain was.

'It's off t'the east'ard,' I'm Davis said. 'That's all I know.'

Mima thought of Eben, buried on a lonely island somewhere off that way. Perhaps those mountains looked toward where he lay.

They slept that night as they had before, by the brook below the old man's lodge; and he kept Joel late in hungry talk. In the morning they told him good-bye, and promised to come again another year; and he to come by their house on his next trip to Warren. Mima was glad to be away from him; and following Joel down the brook-side trail she wondered why. It might be just because she was happiest alone with Joel; but she did not think so. It might be that the old man's endless talk tired her, and the tales he told were terrible, making her anxious to come home to Polly. They had been four nights away, and it seemed as many years. In four nights, anything might have happened. So long as she and Joel were travelling further and further from home, she liked it, was eager to go on; but now, when they had at last turned homeward, she was full of a driving desire to hurry, hurry. Four days? Four days was forever. Polly might be sick! Polly might in four days have died and been buried, never to be seen again. It took forty days to starve a baby in the cold and wintry wilderness; but death had quicker ways ...

She and Joel had planned to explore the west branch of the river too; to ascend it as far as that other pond of which I'm Davis had told them. She wondered whether Joel still meant to do this; but she would not ask him. With him leading, she close on his heels, they followed down the brook till they reached the great meadow, and they retraced their former course to the beaver dam and so down to where their dugout lay.

They talked not much on that tramp back to the canoe; and when they were afloat again, they still said little. The canoe glided down the inlet and they emerged into the pond; and Joel set their course straight across to the point where they had slept the second night. They passed it and pushed on. Their coming scattered the feeding moose out of the bog at the foot of the pond, and they entered the outlet stream; and the current helped them.

So at last they reached the mouth of that other brook which flowed in from the westward; and Joel checked the canoe, holding to a hazel branch that overhung the water.

'What do you say, Mima?' he asked. 'Will we go up this one too, see that other pond?'

'Do you want to?' In the bow her back was toward him, so that he could not see her eyes.

'I'm Davis said it's hard getting a canoe up very far,' he confessed.

She laughed a little breathlessly. 'I guess I want to go home, Joel.'

He laughed too, with a great relief. 'Say, I'm glad to hear it! I was afraid you'd want to tackle it.'

'I was afraid you would!' she admitted.

He released his hold on the hazel branch and their paddles dipped. She asked: 'Can we get home tonight?'

'Not tonight,' he told her. 'There's a lot of river ahead of us, and some carrying and hard going, and it's noon now. Time to eat. We'll go as far as we can.'

They ate by the spring they had found on the way up; and

that afternoon they pushed on as far as the sideways tree where they had slept the first night. The quickwater had given them scant trouble today. Running with the current, they had only to be careful that no rock broke the bottom of the float. Mima before they slept asked:

'When will we get home, Joel?'

'Dinner time or a little after.'

She said after a moment, happy in his arms: 'Joel, I missed, last time.'

For a moment he did not speak. Then he cried in a clear delight: 'That's fine! Why didn't you tell me, Mima?'

She confessed: 'I was afraid you wouldn't let me come. I didn't want to give up this trip. So there'll be four of us, next summer, Joel.'

He laughed triumphantly. 'We've room for a dozen, Mima, and we'll have 'em, give us time.'

She whispered: 'But — I keep thinking about that poor woman watching her babies die! Take care of us, Joel.'

He said strongly: 'I'm going to.'

* * * * *

They were early awake, and swam, and ate, and pushed on down the long quick water and so presently emerged into Sunnyback Pond. They worked hard, both of them now in haste. The wind was southeast, so they kept toward the east side of the pond, to catch the lee. As they approached the outlet, Mima heard something coming down the steep bank through the oak wood ahead of them; and she turned in the bow to sign to Joel to listen. They both heard a splashing sound as some large animal descended into the water, and then the hissing suck of a moose drinking.

The wind was toward them. Joel without a sound swung the canoe toward the shore and stepped out in shallow water; and Mima with her paddle on the bottom held the float while he primed his gun. When he was ready, he went silently forward,

wading along the bank, crouching, peering ahead. He passed
out of her sight, and almost at once she heard the crashing report of the gun, and then a great splashing in the river, and then
Joel's triumphant cry.

She beached the canoe and ran to see. The moose was dead.
Joel had been able to come close to it unseen, to take the neck
shot at such short range he could not miss. The moose was a
year-old cow; and the carcass lay now in shallow water near the
shore, half-awash. Joel already had his knife in its throat; and
a red ribbon tinted the water and flowed away downstream.

'I was right on top of it, Mima,' he said, delighted with this
easy luck. 'Not twenty feet away! Broke its neck. I'll dress it
out where it lays.'

She was as pleased as he. She went back to bring the canoe,
then returned to watch him at his work. Below the carcass she
saw trout gather, attracted by the blood taint in the water.
They came up nearer Joel, darting aside as he moved, fighting
over the small bits of meat and tallow that floated free when he
opened the belly. He passed the liver and the heart to her, and
she plucked ferns and wrapped them well.

'This critter's fat as butter,' Joel said exultantly. 'She'll eat
good, Mima. I'll have to come tomorrow with the big float to
fetch the meat home. Your canoe won't carry all of it.'

She nodded, watching him contentedly. The meat would be
welcome, shared among their neighbors. Joel asked for the axe
and she brought it; and he cleared the head and split the carcass
with skilful strokes. He dragged the two sides ashore, the hide
still on, and looked for a chance to hang them. There were no
birches near, to spring them into the air; so he climbed an oak
and chose a horizontal branch ten or twelve feet above the
ground and cut off two boughs that projected upward, leaving
stubs a few inches tall, sharpened at the top. He descended and
cut a pole with a crotched stub like a hook at one end, long
enough to reach up to the branch he had chosen, and slipped
it through the leg tendon. Then he climbed the tree again, and

she passed the end of the pole up to him and he pulled and she lifted. He hooked each side of meat over the stubs he had sharpened for the purpose, so that they hung well clear of the ground, and he stuck skewers into the flesh to scare away carrion-eating crows.

'There, it will do till tomorrow,' he said. 'Till I can come fetch it.'

'The flies will get to it.'

'Not enough to hurt. We'll hang some ferns over the meat.' They did, till she was satisfied.

He washed himself in the river and they went on. They glided down the quickwater, easing the canoe over the cascades. 'I'll just bring the big float to the foot of these rips here tomorrow,' Joel decided. 'Easier to pack the meat down than to drag the float up.' They passed Phin Butler's landing this time unseen, slipping quietly along under the bank. Phin's axe was going on the slopes toward the house, and they heard its chick and chock and presently the splitting crash and then the ground-shaking rumble as the great tree fell. They fairly raced down the last stretch of rapids, resenting the delay when they had to step out and lower the canoe through the worst places, then hurried on. They saw no sign of anyone at the Partridge clearing, and so they came down through the meadows to Round Pond.

As they emerged into the open water, Mima heard an axe on the south shore of the pond. 'That's Jess, I guess, working on his land,' she said. 'He's burned his fell-piece while we were gone, Joel,' she pointed out. 'I feel as if we'd been gone forever. I don't know as I ever want to go away again.'

'I had a good time,' Joel protested cheerfully.

'So did I. But I feel as if we ought to stay here and work hard every summer, so we'll never be hungry and starving the way Mrs. Forbes and those babies were.'

'That was hard doing,' he agreed. 'But we'll be staying home, not traipsing through the woods. Don't you fret. I'll take care of you.'

They continued down the river toward Seven-Tree Pond, for Polly was there; but Mima could not wait to come to the landing on the pond side, and at her insistence Joel turned into the backwater below that leaning tree where she had learned to swim. When the canoe touched, she leaped out and ran along the edge of the clearing toward her father's house, racing up the rising ground. Joel drew the canoe ashore and overtook her, but he did not try to outpace her, and they ran like children side by side and came panting and breathless to the door. Polly, sitting on the floor just inside the door, looked up and saw them and her eyes opened wide and she cried: 'Dah-dah!' and came to her feet, saying things meaningless to any ears but Mima's. Mima swept the baby in her arms, hugging and kissing her, rapturous with tears. Polly crowed and gurgled and chattered many words all her own; and Joel watched them happily, and took them both in his arms, and Mrs. Robbins turned from the hearth at their coming, and Sue, fifteen years old now, tall, and lumpy in new places, came from somewhere, and suddenly everyone was here, all talking at once, welcoming them home. They had to tell all their adventures, and Joel described the new hunting grounds they had found, and they both talked together like excited children till the tale was told.

'Well, it's been good for the both of you,' Mrs. Robbins declared at last. 'Mima, you look fresh as cream; and I guess you'll do, Joel, time you're shaved.' She added: 'Joel, your sister's here.'

'Jemima?' Joel exclaimed. 'Good! Where is she?'

'Up with Jess, watching him work,' Mrs. Robbins said. 'She come day before yesterday.'

'How'd she get up-river?'

'Colonel Wheaton sent her as far as Warren, and Boggs fetched her the rest of the way. She's a friendly nice young woman.'

'She is that,' Joel agreed. 'Mima, ready to go along? We can stop on the way and pick her up.'

Mima assented. 'I want to be in my own house,' she said happily. 'Polly, want to go home with Mother and Daddy?'

Polly made assenting sounds; she cried: 'Mudda Dah Dah. Mudda Dah Dah.' But when they departed, she looked doubtfully at Mrs. Robbins and said hopefully: 'Gaga!' And when it was clear to her that her grandmother would stay behind, she wailed despairingly, and Mima comforted her; but in the canoe she said jealously:

'I wish we hadn't gone, Joel. Polly's forgotten us already.'

He laughed and said Polly would remember them quickly enough. 'But it tickled your mother,' he pointed out, 'to have her want to stay.'

'Of course it did,' she agreed. 'And Mother says she's cut a back tooth, and sometimes she tries to run.' She said to Polly: 'Show Mother the great big new tooth, Polly!' But Polly with twinkling eyes, now content enough in Mima's arms, refused to put her tooth on display. Mima hugged her and kissed her, and demanded that Polly give her a kiss and Polly lavishly did so, and Mima cried delightedly: 'Oh, what a wet one! She's learned to kiss, Joel. Who do you suppose has been teaching her?'

'Comes natural to her.' He chuckled. 'Gets it from her mother.'

'Well, her father's pretty good at it too,' Mima declared.

They landed at the foot of Jess's clearing. There was no sound of an axe to guide them; but Mima heard voices and called, and Jess answered; and a moment later Jess and Jemima came down through the pines. Jemima ran to meet Joel, into his arms; and she kissed Mima, and baby Polly welcomed her, and Joel said with a chuckle:

'Didn't hear your axe going, Jess. Showing Sis the woods, were you? Sis, look out for him! He's a bad man in the bushes!'

'I was showing her where I'm going to build my house this summer,' Jess said; and at his tone Mima was suddenly alert,

and she spoke quickly before Joel could say anything more.
Mima knew Jess well. There was already something between
him and Jemima that easy talk might spoil. She asked:

'How did you come, Jemima? We'd have been down-river to
meet you if we'd known.'

'I came in Captain Watson's sloop,' the other girl said. 'And
I had another friend of yours for company. Colonel Burton.'

Joel exclaimed: 'Ben Burton? Is he back? The English took
him, right after he and General Wadsworth got away from them
at Biguyduce.'

His sister nodded. 'Yes, he told me. He didn't dare stay
home in Cushing then, so he went to Boston and went off with
Captain Dennison privateering. They got caught in a gale of
wind off Newfoundland, and captured; and they were locked
up at Cape Clear, and then sent to England. He was in a prison
ship there, the old Dunkirk; and he had a bad time till the first
peace was agreed to. He was turned loose then, and he's been all
over since, trying to get home; France and all. He got back to
Connecticut with eight shillings money; and now he's home.'

'We came with Captain Watson in the Sally sloop,' Mima said.
'He told me a lot about Ben Burton, and then I met him when I
got to the pond.' She looked at Joel, smilingly. 'I thought
maybe I'd marry him, but I never had a fair chance, never saw
him only a few times afterward.'

Joel laughed. 'You never got him up a tree where he couldn't
get away, the way you did me,' he said; and she reminded him:

'You didn't try very hard to get away!'

'I was satisfied to be caught,' he agreed, his arm around her,
facing Jess and his sister who watched them smilingly. 'Sis,
what do you think of Mima here? Turned out all right, ain't
she?' And he asked: 'You ready to come along home with us
now?'

'My things are down at Robbins's.'

Jess said: 'I'll fetch her up tonight, Joel. Her and her alls.'
He added wisely: 'Mima'll want to get the house spick and
span before she comes.'

'Land, yes!' Mima agreed. 'Probably the squirrels have got in and made a mess of it. Come on, Joel.' She picked up Polly and turned back toward the canoe. 'You come any time, Sis,' she said. 'I'll always be glad to see you. Don't mind what Jess says.'

Joel told them about the moose he had shot. 'I hung it,' he said. 'I'll go fetch it home tomorrow.' Jess offered to go with him; but Joel said there was no need. They left the two together; and in the canoe Mima said softly:

'Joel, your sister and Jess have took to each other right from the go off!'

'Looks so,' he assented with a chuckle. 'Him talking about a house a'ready!'

'You'll have to fix a bed in the garret for her,' Mima reflected, beginning already to plan the new household. 'We've got covers enough, and we'll give her the feather bed, and we can get some more blankets before winter.'

He looked at her in surprise. 'She'll be going back before that.'

Mima smiled. 'If Jess will let her, maybe.' Her thoughts cast ahead in a flash, and backward too. If Jess and Jemima decided to get married, who would marry them? She thought of her own wedding, and she said: 'Colonel Wheaton sent her up as far as Warren, Joel. We don't see him much since he married us.'

'They say he's got to be cranky,' he said. 'Yelling at people worse than ever. He's fixing to build mills down in Thomaston, and start a store. Got a woman keeps house for him — and like as not sleeps with him, too.' He turned the canoe into the mouth of the brook. There was water enough so that they could go well up the little stream, where the light craft lay sheltered from the choppy seas that sometimes drove across the pond. 'Well, Mima,' he said. 'We're home.'

She and Polly went ahead, and Joel came burdened after them. Mima found instantly so much to do. They thought

Jess might bring Jemima to supper, and waited till dusk. 'Guess they're not coming,' Joel said at last, and she assented.

'There's a moon,' she reminded him understandingly. 'Jess might rather bring her up-river by moonlight.'

Her guess proved a good one. It was in fact so late before the two arrived that Joel twice had threatened to go to bed, and Polly was long since asleep. They walked down to the shore of the pond and sat there, and Joel brought coals to build a small smudge against mosquitoes, feeding it twigs and grass, and the moon was fine, and they talked about how pleasant it would be if Jess and Jemima did in fact agree and live so near; and Mima said: 'We're not too old to like sitting in the moon together, are we, Joel?'

'Never will be!'

'I like to kind of pretend sometimes we're not married, just awful in love and wishing we could be. Then it's more fun to remember all of a sudden that we are married, and — act it!' And she said in laughing wonder: 'We acted like heathens up-river, Joel, no clothes on half the time, and making love and all.' He made a comfortable sound, lying well fed and contented beside her; and she said: 'I guess some would call it wicked; but it wasn't, was it?'

'It didn't feel wicked to me.'

'People don't get older inside, do they? We go on feeling just as young as we ever did, inside. I think loving is meant to be happy, and fun, like playing together. I mean, like children, playing games.'

'It's funny, but I used to think that game wouldn't be much fun if you were married.'

'Still think so?'

'I've found out different.' He reached to put his arm around her shoulders, to draw her down to him; but she said quickly:

'No, Joel! No! Here they come.' The canoe was out in the middle of the pond, drifting slowly nearer them. She said warningly: 'It's going to be — we're going to have to behave ourselves, Joel, with Sis living with us, in the garret right over our heads.'

He laughed, and Jess heard him and called; and across the pond a loon shrieked at them, and the canoe came gently in to the shore below where they sat. Jess said, elaborately casual:

'Looks like weather, Joel. Ring around the moon.'

'You and Sis been studying about the weather, have you?' Joel asked. Mima held out her hand to steady Sis as the other stepped ashore.

'Well, we've noticed there was a moon,' Jess said, half defiantly; and Mima said:

'Come along, Sis. Let them fetch your things.'

In the cabin she lighted a rush light at both ends, touching it to the smoldering fire. 'You'll be sleeping up here,' she told Joel's sister, and climbed with her to the garret. Below them Jess and Joel came in with their burdens. The fire and the rush light made the cabin unusually bright. 'Mostly you'll have to go to bed by firelight,' Mima confessed, and Sis said everything was fine. They descended again, and they all went down to the landing to see Jess depart; and Joel called after him: 'Come often, Jess, now you know the way!'

Jess said he aimed to; but Mima warned Joel in a whisper before they slept: 'Don't you go teasing them, Joel. You can spoil it, easy as can be. Just let them alone to work it out theirselves.'

In the morning he was up before her; and she slept till after sun. He came at last to wake her, leaning down to kiss her in her sleep. He had shaved since he rose, and he rubbed his cheek against hers, and she laughed and drew him down and kissed him in turn.

'I like it when you've just shaved,' she told him. 'Your cheek's smooth as Polly's bottom.'

Jemima called down from the garret overhead: 'Is that any way for old married folks to talk?' They had both forgotten she was there, and looked at each other in startled amusement.

'It's the only way for a wife to talk, Sis,' Joel called to her. 'Keeps husbands good-humored. You can take lessons from Mima.' He whispered to Mima: 'Lucky she spoke when she did!' And she laughed, and Polly awoke in the small bed by their own and beamed at them, climbing out of bed, demanding that the day begin.

Joel started up-river, immediately after breakfast, to get the moose meat; and Mima and Sis and Polly, with the house to themselves, had time to get acquainted. Sis said Jess had promised to take her to spear salmon by torchlight; he had undertaken to catch a bear cub for a pet for her later on; he was going to show her how to trap pigeons. His name came often off her tongue; and Mima listened and smiled and said nothing she should not have said.

The morning had been cloudy, and toward noon a heavy thunderstorm swept down the river. It lasted an hour or more, then cleared to sun and piling clouds in the west that promised more disturbance later on. She wondered why Joel did not come home. She had thought he might be back for dinner; but she presently decided to wait no longer, so she and Sis and Polly ate.

It was mid-afternoon before he appeared. She had begun by that time to watch for him, a little uneasily, going up to the ledge from which she could see, across the intervening point, the river mouth and the north shore of the pond. At last she saw him going toward Jason's landing, and guessed that he was taking a cut of the moose meat to Jason. She went down to the shore to wait for him, and when he presently came around the point and angled toward where she stood, she hallooed and waved to him. He paddled toward her, and the canoe touched and he jumped out and kissed her, rubbing his cheek against hers, saying some laughing word. She saw that one of the sides of moose meat was gone, and she knew he must have divided it among the cabins coming down the river; given some to Phin and to Elisha Partridge, to Matt and Jason. His garments were dry. He had taken shelter somewhere from the shower.

'I'm glad you got in out of the rain,' she said.

'I'd just put in to Phin's to leave them a piece of meat, the time it started,' he explained. 'I hadn't hardly got to the door before it came down a-b'iling; so I stayed till it stopped.' He looked at the meat in the canoe. 'I'll cut off as much as we can use and take the rest down-river. It won't keep, this weather. We'll get some more to smoke, later on.'

She agreed in an absent way, wondering how long he had stayed with Phin and Mily. The rain had lasted all of an hour. 'But you don't have to take it down right now,' she suggested, faintly unwilling to have him so soon depart again. She laughed a little at her own fears, confessing them. 'I worried about you when it rained so hard, and then when you didn't come and didn't come, I thought something or other might have happened to you.'

'What would happen to me?' he protested, almost impatiently, not smiling. His tone surprised her.

'Oh, I don't know, struck by lightning or something?'

He took his knife and began to cut the haunch off the side of moose meat still in the canoe, dissecting out the joint. 'I stopped at 'Lish Partridge's, too,' he said. 'His daughter Dorcas has come to live with them. She's a sightly young one, fifteen-sixteen years old, pretty yaller hair. And young Alibeus is getting to be quite a boy.' He chuckled. 'I walked up to the hovel with a piece of meat for them. 'Lish wa'n't there, but I met his Sally coming up from the spring with a bucket of water and Alibeus tagging along and her laughing fit to split herself. I asked her what the matter was and she said she went down to get some drinking water — spring's all of forty rod from the house and mostly downhill — and time she got back pretty near up to the house, Alibeus he was bent and determined he'd piddle in the water. She told me, laughing fit to kill: "And you know, he was so cute about it I let him." ' He freed the haunch, tossed it up to where she stood. 'And I give Jason some for them, and some for Matt too,' he reported. 'You want to take this up to the house? I'll go along down and get rid of this and be back.'

'You didn't go up to Matt's, then?'

'No. Jason's Polly said she'd see to't Matt got the meat. I'll take this on down.'

'You could eat first,' she urged.

'I want to get rid of it, clean up the float.' He pushed off and moved away as though anxious to escape her. She watched him, wondering at the storm of doubts in herself. Perhaps it was because there was still the feel of thunder in the air that she felt as she did; or perhaps it was just one of the fancies that went with pregnancy.

She remembered that he had had nothing to eat since break-fast; and when he came home an hour later she offered to hurry supper, said he must be hungry. But he said: 'No, I et at Phin's while I was waiting for the rain to get done with.' He added, after a moment: 'Phin wa'n't there. Mily said he was working on his back piece, too far from the house to get home quick; so he'd squat under a tree or something. I left as soon as it quit raining, so I didn't get to see him.'

The rain had lasted an hour. She nodded. 'Then I don't need to hurry,' she said. 'If Mily fed you all you want, I guess you'll do till supper time.' There was a curious humming in her ears. He had been an hour alone with Mily, the house cur-tained by the rain. Mima felt suddenly tired.

6

SUMMER swept on them in a flood, and Mima's uneasy doubts were crowded out of her mind by the full passing days. Joel was busy from first light till dark, and Mima and Sis had long hours alone. Sis was small, almost frail; but there was a tireless energy in her, more nervous and mental than physical. She had a way with children. Mima's Polly loved her from the first; and older children turned to her readily. She had taught school the winter before in Franklin.

'I might stay on here and start a school,' she told Mima one day. 'You need one bad enough.'

Mima said: 'I guess we do. Of course most of the children are too young for it. But my brother Phil will be twelve, in August, and he hasn't had a day's schooling since we came here, and that's seven years; but Mother's taught him to read and write and figure. Susie's almost fifteen, but she could stand some schooling. Then David's got Jason and Chloe and Joe, not counting the babies. Jason's eleven, and even Joe's eight this month. That's four. And Bet and Rich have Dave — he's eight, and Esther's six; and there's 'Lish Partridge's Dorcas — but Joel says she's around sixteen.'

'Well, that's seven,' Sis pointed out. 'That's a start, and there'll be others coming along.'

Mima laughed. 'Plenty of others,' she agreed. 'There's ten or fifteen babies under five years old, and about everyone has either just had one or else she's going to; Polly Ware and Lucy Butler next month, and Mary Hawes in September, and Bess the month after, and then Prance Bowen.' She hesitated, her cheeks mantling richly. 'And Joel and me are going to have our second in January. I haven't told anyone only Joel.'

Sis smiled. 'You don't have to, Mima. You look so happy all the time I thought it might be so.'

'Goodness, I hope I don't look all drawn and peaked the way some do!'

'You look like an apple just starting to turn red,' Sis told her. 'I get a lot of fun out of watching you and Joel. You've been real good for him, Mima. He always was a rake-hellion when he was a boy. He used to worry Pa and Ma.'

'He's never worried me.' Mima did not think of Mily. 'Maybe I wouldn't worry, anyway. I love Joel, whatever way he is.' She said: 'Oh, and Uncle Josiah is bringing his family next year! He's got two that are old enough for school, and a baby, and two girls that are already married. So if you did start a school there'd be enough to keep you busy, with all of us having new ones for you all the time. And Mother told me Mag Hawes is having hers in January.'

'I'd have to have a schoolhouse or something,' Sis reflected. 'I couldn't have the house full of children here.'

'We'd ought to have a school,' Mima agreed, 'and preaching, too. There's never been but one preacher come up here, and he's worse than none; Mr. Urquhart down't Warren. He married a girl there, but some claim he's still got a wife in Scotland. The only church we have, Father mostly reads the Bible Sundays when we go down there, and sometimes he talks a kind of a sermon.' She smiled a little. 'But he doesn't have to talk a sermon. He lives one, working hard and taking care of all of us.'

'Joel says he's a fine man.'

Mima nodded. 'I guess the menfolks could put up a school-house for you any time.' She added, smilingly: 'But Sis, Jess has got a good start on his house already.'

Sis looked at her, and she asked suddenly: 'Do you think Jess likes me, Mima?'

'Guess he does,' Mima assured her. 'Looks to me you both like each other.'

'I like him awful,' Sis confessed, her cheeks crimson. She rubbed them with her hands, laughing at her own confusion. 'I can just sit and watch him cut a tree down and want to cry, the way he does it; and the way he talks to me, always kind of joking.'

'Jess always was a hand to joke about things,' Mima agreed. 'But he's a good boy, Sis.'

Sis said honestly: 'He hasn't said anything; but it scares me to think of going back to Franklin and leaving him here.' She confessed: 'That's why I got to thinking about a school, so I'd have some excuse to stay.'

Mima laughed and took Sis in her arms. 'Jess will think of some excuse for you to stay,' she promised. 'If I have to put a bug in his ear myself.'

'Please don't, Mima.'

'I won't,' Mima agreed. 'But he won't need it. Wait and see.'

* * * * *

Mima saw Jess more frequently that summer than at any time since she had moved from her father's house to the Royal Mess. He was working on his land, widening his clearing, burning off the felled trees and then burning the fragments that remained, preparing to sow winter rye for next year. Also, he had put in some corn in the fresh-burned land, and it promised to do well. He worked on his cabin when he could, and Bela, who would always rather use an axe than a farming tool, often came to help him. This activity on Jess's land, bordering theirs, meant that he was near-by; and more often than not he came to have dinner with them, and Sis might go back with him, perhaps take little Polly with her, to sit and watch him at his work for a part of the afternoon. He usually came up from Seven-Tree Pond by water, and if the evening promised to be fine, or if there were a moon, he might stay to supper and take Sis out on the water afterward. Mima saw that they drew together day by day; but she said nothing, warned Joel to discretion. 'More young folks have fell out of love from people egging them on than have ever fell in,' she declared.

Joel laughed. 'Let 'em go their own gait,' he said. 'I've got other things on my mind.' This was true enough. With the war surely ended, waiting only the agreement on a formal treaty, the question of national finances demanded some attempt at a solution; and the General Court had laid a levy on Sterling-town. The tax was twenty-five pounds on each man in the set-tlement; and to pay it was beyond their power. Hard money had disappeared with the continued depreciation of the paper currency. The only commodity that could be spared, and could at the same time command a market, was furs; but fur-bearers were already becoming so scarce that even the most diligent trappers reaped a scant harvest. What furs Joel had trapped the winter before no more than paid for the few necessities — pow-der and shot, farming tools, coffee and tea — which they must have. There was talk of petitioning the General Court to abate the tax for one year, or until the settlers could establish them-selves more securely; and Mima urged Joel to take the lead in calling a meeting for the purpose.

'You remember the way it was before, Joel,' she reminded him. 'Everybody was saying somebody ought to do something; and when you decided what to do, they were all for doing it. The man that says: "Let's do a thing" just when everybody else is making up their minds to do it, they'll get so they look to him to tell them what to do.'

He nodded. 'We plain can't pay the taxes,' he pointed out. 'We've nothing to pay with. But we're lucky, one way. It's worse t'the westward, where the collector can get an execution and take a man's farm. Phin Butler was saying the other day that his folks are likely to lose their farm in Framingham.' Mima wondered where he had seen Phin, but she would not ask him. Joel went on: 'Phin says they might come to Thomaston to live. What this will all come to, we'll have to incorporate a town here, to handle things. The General Court might abate the tax for this year, but they won't go on doing it.'

He decided at Mima's urgings to call a meeting of all the men in the settlement. Philip Robbins' house on Seven-Tree Pond was a natural centre at which to gather; and Sunday they all went down to spend the afternoon, and Joel and Mima's father consulted in the matter.

Philip had been in Thomaston the week before, had talked with Colonel Wheaton there. 'I told him we hadn't no way to collect taxes — nor no money to pay them,' he reported. 'He says Lithgow, the county treasurer, don't aim to press us; but he's got to collect 'em, get an execution maybe, if we don't get 'em abated or do something.' He added: 'Colonel Wheaton said the best thing was to call all the men together and act just the same as if it was a town meeting, pick out a moderator and a clerk, and assessors and collectors and all. Have 'em hold office for a year, just like a town; and send a petition to the General Court for an abatement.'

Joel considered that. He and Philip were standing at the corner of the house; and below them the ground fell away toward the pond. Cleared land lay between, where already the corn was well started. Jess and Sis and the womenfolks were all down at the landing; and by the cries and laughter there, Joel guessed that Mima had the children swimming or paddling in the shallow water near shore on this hot summer afternoon. Beyond, a float was coming across from Johnny Butler's; and Joel recognized Phin and Mily and saw them draw in toward the landing.

'We'll come to incorporating a town, sooner or later,' he

said. 'I'd like to see it done, but it's too soon yet. I'd say send a petition.' He spoke with a sudden heat. 'Man, we're right on the edge of starving to death every spring as it is, living on birch leaves and fiddle-heads and alewives when they run! We can't pay taxes.'

Philip said: 'We don't get anything for any taxes we might go and pay. Warren won't build a road. We can't get in or out only by water. If we was to starve to death some winter, the lot of us, nobody'd know it till they found our bones, come spring. We're up here at the back end of nowhere, holding on by our teeth.' He looked across his cleared lands with a twinkling eye. 'But we're doing better right along, getting our teeth into it. I'd like to see any tax collector try to take my land away from me!'

They walked down toward the water while they talked, drawn by the happy voices and the laughter there. Phin and Mily had landed, and Phin and Jess came to meet them; and the four men sat together under the pines a little above the water. Susie was swimming, out beyond the shallow water, her bright hair streaming across her shoulders. She had taken off dress and petticoats and was in her smock, the long single garment not much hindering her movements. Mima, with skirts and petticoats tucked up around her thighs and pinned there, had waded knee-deep, carrying Polly; and she was holding the little girl while Polly paddled and splashed and screamed with delight. Young Philip wished to take Polly into deeper water, but Mima would not let him.

'You'll let her choke and scare her,' she said. 'I don't ever want her to be scared of water. Besides, she's been in long enough. She'll get cold and have an upset.' She swung the plump, wet, wriggling, naked little body to her shoulder, and waded ashore and loosed her skirts, letting them down, rolling Polly in a petticoat, rubbing her till she was pink as dawn. Everyone laughed at Polly's protests at coming ashore; and Mily jealously decided that her baby should have a taste of the water. He was two months younger than Polly; a quiet, lumpy boy. Mily undressed him, and Phin called, his head jerking:

'What you going to do, Mily?'

'Let Willie play in the water the way Polly did.'

Phin looked doubtful, spoke under his breath. 'He'll catch his death.' But he did not protest to Mily herself. It was as though he were unwilling to invite an argument. 'I been over talking to Johnny about fixing up the mill,' he told Joel and the others. 'Millstones he's got are too little, and too smooth to do a good job. I told him if he'd put in a good run of stones, and maybe build a higher dam so's he'd always have water, he'd do a good business; but he says he dunno.'

They discussed the matter, only half attentive, watching the swimmers. Sue, ready to come out of the water and unwilling to face masculine eyes in her single wet garment, swam away up the shore around a bushy point to where she had left her outer clothes. Mily gathered up her skirts and carried her baby into the water. He screamed with panic and she tried to soothe him and Phin watched restlessly. Mily dabbled the baby in the water, and his howls of terror filled the quiet Sunday afternoon, and Mily grew red and redder with embarrassed anger. Mrs. Robbins said to Mima:

'If she'd pay more heed to him and less to hitching up her skirts as high as the law allows, she'd do better. She acts as if she was the only woman around had a pair of legs to show off.'

Mima said: 'Mily's all right, Mother. She's still pretty young, that's all. She's only nineteen.'

'She's a hussy,' Mrs. Robbins firmly retorted. 'I've always said so and I always will.'

Mima did not speak. On the bank above them where the men sat, she heard Joel say: 'We need a mill. Jason and Matt and me between us keep our pounder going pretty steady. It's slow work, beating up samp and sifting meal and all.' He added: 'Another thing, Sis is saying we need a school. There's six-seven young ones old enough for it a'ready, and more coming along. I wouldn't mind paying taxes if I could work 'em out building a school.'

Mily lost patience with the baby and spanked his bare bottom till he howled for better reason than before; and Phin watched with a strained face, flinching as though he felt the blows. She waded ashore and plumped young Will down on the ground; and Sue came — now fully dressed, her wet hair knotted up — to comfort him back to silence again, and dry him and dress him. Mily surrendered him to Sue and sat down with Mima and Mrs. Robbins. She seemed to feel the older woman's disapprobation; for she said:

'I hadn't ought to have spanked him, but I'm just about crazy. I guess I'm going to have another. I'm right onto a month overdue.'

Mrs. Robbins said with a ready sympathy: 'It always upsets a woman till she's sure. Once you make up your mind to it, you'll be all right.' She added: 'Guess it's in the air this year. You and Sally Hawes were the only ones left, that weren't that way.'

Mily looked sharply at Mima. 'You?' she asked; and Mima nodded. Mily said grimly: 'Well, it takes more than something in the air.'

Mrs. Robbins chuckled. 'I don't know as it takes much more than that. Some women, you shake a pair of britches at them and they're charged.' She told Mily: 'You'll be fine, soon's you make up your mind to it. You've probably give Phin fits, wondering whether 'twas or 'tweren't!'

Mily said sharply: 'Guess I have. He makes me so mad, never saying anything. All he wants to do is work and eat and sleep.'

'There's worse things,' Mrs. Robbins assured her.

'Times I think if he don't laugh or sing or something I could kill him!' Mily declared. She rose sharply. 'Come on, Phin. If we're going to get home, we'd best start.'

They departed, but Joel and Mima and Polly stayed to supper and started home at dusk. Joel had decided to call the men-folks together and have Matt Hawes write another petition to the General Court; and Mima was glad and proud.

'They'll get so they look to you to tell 'em what to do,' she said. 'Men are easy led, Joel, if you lead them where they already want to go.' She spoke happily. 'We'll have a town here some day, and you're going to be the big man in it.'

'Your father always will be the big man around here.'

'You and him. You after him,' she insisted. 'You're a good man, Joel. Men listen to you.'

He said laughingly: 'You keep on telling me how smart I am and you'll have me believing it.' Then he added more seri-ously: 'I wasn't much, you know, till you got hold of me. But you're so sure I'm going to — work hard and do right — that I have to do it to keep you from being disappointed.'

'I guess that's the way with men,' she agreed. 'A woman's the root and a man's the tree. She's the ground he grows out of. That's a wife's job; to be good growing ground, so her man will be fine.'

'What if she isn't? Say she's sour land, or sandy, or dry?'

'Then he'll be a stunted sort of a man, or else he'll find an-other woman, that's all. A man don't get far without some woman loving him and always telling him he's wonderful.'

He said, half to himself: 'If I was a tree, I needed pruning pretty bad when you took hold of me, Mima.' After a moment he added: 'I still do, for the matter of that. I ain't all you keep telling me I am; but I mean to be. If you keep telling me, I'll get to be.' There was a deep tenderness in his tones. 'You're good growing ground, Mima.'

She asked smiling: 'Which one of me? Jemmy, or Born-Drunk?'

'All three of you. All three of you suit me.'

'You keep saying there's three of me.'

'That's right. Jemmy's the one I like to talk to, the one I like being with; and Born-Drunk's the wild one. There's part wild in every man, Mima. He likes a wild streak in a woman.'

'One of me's Jemmy, and one of me's Born-Drunk. But we ought to have a name for the third one.'

'That's the one with a baby in her arms and another coming,' Joel said gently. 'Mima will do for a name for her.'

They came slowly across the pond, and it was dark when they turned into the brook. A whippoorwill was calling on a rock by the landing place as they approached; and they heard his wings flutter as he moved a few rods along the brook and began again his whip-poor-will.

*   *   *   *   *

Summer was a time of long toil from dawn till dusk, with Sundays for the only respite. Joel and Matt and Jason traded work, day by day; and sometimes when they did this, the three wives also spent the day together. If the other men were to work with Joel, Mima asked Sally and Polly to come over; and so did Polly in her turn. But Sally did not always accept these invitations, and she never suggested that the two come to her house for the day. She and Matt lived to themselves; and once or twice Mima suspected that Sally knew or guessed Matt's old fondness for her, and resented it. Even Matt began to draw apart and go his own way. The three men owned a yoke of oxen jointly, but this summer Matt bought a half-grown steer from William Boggs and trained it to work. It was a lean animal, and its pace was faster than the lumbering gait of the heavier, more powerful beasts. Matt taught it to travel at a trot. The steer wore a bell, and on still days Mima could sometimes hear that bell even when Matt was working on his own land, a mile to the northward. She thought it had a lonely sound.

Joel bought from Will Boggs — old Sam was dead — four ewes with their lambs. Boggs brought them up-river in a ferry, tied hand and foot, and he stayed to dinner. He was not so dour and sober as Mima remembered him to be; and he told them how old Sam brought the first flock of thirty sheep from Pemaquid.

'They was loose on the deck,' he said, 'and Pa setting on the windlass watching them and almighty proud of them; but he got sleepy and kind of leaned forward, his head down on his arms. The old ram took one look and give him a butt, knocked him tail over tea kettle. Pa was so mad he throwed the ram overboard, and I be damn if the rest of them didn't jump over after him. Lucky it was ca'm, and no land near enough for them to get to, so all they could do was swim around till he picked 'em up again. But was he mad! Said he'd butcher the lot when he got 'em home, but he didn't. These here come from them.'

Joel had made a deal to pay a part of the purchase price with furs trapped next winter, and Boggs was to have one ewe lamb a year for six years, besides.

'But you'll need to house 'em in the winter,' Boggs warned them. 'A hard winter, wolves come around; and a bear will kill 'em if he can.' So Joel built a low log house with a pole and bark roof, in the nearest corner of the pen; and later with juniper posts and split boards he made a smaller pen for winter. Boggs's ram would serve the ewes at the proper time. 'You'll want it so they drop their lambs in May,' he said. 'Even so, the sheep storm might catch them; but mostly that comes in April, so you'll generally be safe enough if they come in May.'

Joel put his mark on the ewes, a crop and a notch on the right ear. They were forever working through the fence; but he scattered salt in the clay pit where he had made the bricks for his chimney, and that attracted the runaways and let him recapture them. That summer, too, he made a paper window, shaping a frame with corners mortised and pegged and covering it with a sheet of white paper well-oiled with moose tallow so that it allowed some light to penetrate.

'And next summer I'll send to Boston for a piece of glass,' he promised Mima. 'With a glass window we'll have a real fine house.'

She told him it was already the finest house in town. Its only drawback was that the chimney sooted up and began to smoke. Joel borrowed a goose from Ezra Bowen, and tied its feet and lowered it down the chimney where its beating wings scoured the worst of the soot away. Then he raised the chimney two feet higher, making more bricks for the purpose, and laid up a course or two around the hearth so that the fire, resting on its own accumulating ashes, was a foot above the floor, and the draft improved.

They had except on Sundays hardly an idle moment all summer long. Jess, in order to get help handling the logs for his house, traded work with Joel; and Sis was apt to be much with Jess at his work there. She helped build the catted clay chimney and to chink the cabin walls. Josiah Robbins was building a house across the river north of Philip, and getting out timbers for a barn, and Sam Hills had erected a hovel on his point across Seven-Tree Pond from Rich and Dave. The whole settlement was a hive of industry. Even Johnny Butler had about decided to improve his dam and get new stones for the mill; but Joel predicted that he would never do it.

'There's a shiftless streak in Johnny,' he told Mima one day. He had come in from his work for dinner, and he stayed a while afterward. Sis took Polly away to be with Jess; and Mima for once resented her going. The day was sullen and hot, with no air stirring; and it was uncomfortable carrying a baby in hot weather. She had cooked dinner; it seemed to her that Sis might have stayed to clean up afterward. She even resented the way Joel sat at ease, talking idly while she moved to and fro about her tasks.

'Yes, sir,' he said, 'Johnny's plain lazy. Phin too. They work, but they go at things thumb-handed, and they're easy discouraged. If Johnny had any git up and git to him he'd have had his mill in shape before now.' He warmed to his theme, expansive after his hearty meal. 'Here Johnny is, he's got the only frame house in town, and a good piece of land that was already cleared before he came to live there. He had a couple years' head start on the rest of us; but his place is all gone to pot, brush in his fields and all. It takes work to make a farm up here, Mima; and it takes a sight more work to keep it.' He added: 'Phin says his father and mother did lose their farm in Framingham. They're coming to Thomaston, figuring to live on Phin and Johnny. I guess shif'lessness runs in the blood!'

Mima made a resentful sound. 'I'll thank you to remember that they both married cousins of mine,' she said.

He failed to catch the warning in her tones. 'Well, Lucy and Mily could have done a sight better than marrying a couple of bound boys,' he said. 'Lucy's easy to look at, and Mily when she gets prettied up is as fancy as they come.'

She felt a sharp anger rise in her. 'What's the harm in being bound out?' she demanded. 'Phin and Johnny worked hard — and got paid for it.'

'Well, working for pay's one thing and working for yourself is another,' Joel argued philosophically. 'Anyone can do a job if someone tells him what to do; but being your own boss is different.'

'Being your own boss doesn't get you anywhere unless you keep yourself working.' He could sit there, well fed and half-asleep, while she scoured a dirty, sooty kettle.

'Well, all I'm saying is — they don't even do that,' Joel insisted. 'Here's Johnny letting the mill run down, and his fields going back to woods! That's just the way his father lost his farm.' He added: 'I wouldn't wonder if Thomaston warned the old folks out, if they do come. Can't let them come in if they're going to be on the town.'

There was an anger in her she would not understand — nor could she silence it. 'Phin and Johnny will take care of them!'

'Not if Mily has anything to say about it, they won't,' Joel reminded her. 'Phin told me he wanted to have them come up here to live, and she put her foot down.' He said flatteringly: 'Trouble is, Mima, Lucy and Mily aren't like you, even if they

are your cousins! Like as not if you'd married Phin or Johnny, you'd have made something out of them.'

He was trying to get around her with a lot of soft soap. She said sharply: 'Well, maybe Lucy and Mily had too much spunk to let their husbands' relatives move in on them.'

For a moment he did not catch the implication in her words. When he did, his face reddened and he looked at her sharply. 'Meaning Sis?' he demanded.

She wondered at herself, wondered why she wanted to anger him and hurt him. 'Well, if the shoe fits, I guess you'll know which foot to put it on,' she told him.

'It was your idea her coming, as much as mine!'

'You didn't ask me before you invited her. After you'd gone and asked her, I couldn't tell her she couldn't come.'

He said, hurt and bewildered, striking back: 'I guess a man's got a right to ask his own sister to visit him in his own house!'

'I suppose you'll be saying next that I'm living in your — own — house!' She spaced the words for emphasis. Her tone was bitter with sardonic rage, and she wanted to cry, and she wanted to slap him and she wanted him to slap her.

'I meant to say our house, Mima,' he told her placatingly.

'Oh, it's yours, all right!' she insisted. 'You built it, didn't you! I just live in it and you wait on me hand and foot. I never do a lick of work, I suppose!'

'Doggone it, Mima, you're talking foolish!'

'I know, I'm a fool!'

'I didn't say you were a fool; but you talk like one. You're talking foolishness.'

'Well, take it from whence it comes! What sort of talk do you expect from a fool? I know I don't amount to anything in your — own — house!'

He protested incredulously: 'You want I should put Sis out, tell her she can't stay?'

She began to find a certain satisfaction in being as infuriating as possible. 'I've got nothing to say about it!' she assured him loftily. 'It's your — own — house. You said so yourself! Maybe you'd rather keep her and tell me I can't stay.'

He rose and came toward her appeasingly. 'There, I didn't mean to make you mad, Mima.'

'You never mean anything!'

'You don't mean half you're saying.' He tried to take her in his arms. 'You're three-four months along. I guess you're entitled to be as cranky as you want.'

She pushed him away. 'It's not the baby!' she told him fiercely. 'If there's anything makes me mad it's to be treated like a spoiled young one that has to be let have its tantrums. I mean every word I say, and just because I'm carrying a baby doesn't have a thing to do with it!' Yet she knew she was wrong. She was hot and wretched.

'You're talking crazy as a loon!'

'I know! You told me! I'm a crazy fool. Well, you've been a long time finding it out. If you thought that, what did you marry me for?'

The words escaped him. 'Had to, didn't I?'

'Not on my account you didn't! Who made you?'

'I'd got you in trouble . . .'

'I wasn't in half the trouble I've been in since I married you!' She laughed bitterly. 'And anyway, what you mean is I got you into trouble. Ever since Adam and Eve, whenever a man got into a mess he's been saying a woman got him into it. Men have made women an excuse for everything they did — including the way they treat their wives. All right, say it then! I made you marry me and I guess you've always wished I hadn't!' Her own voice was a stranger's, and Joel was a stranger looking at her, pain fighting with anger in his glance. If he were Joel she could not hate him so; if she were Mima she could not hate him so. She could not face him, see the hurt in his eyes, without crying. Her kettle was empty and she started for the door, to go to the spring to fill it. Joel tried to take it from her hand.

'I'll fetch the water, Mima.'

She had to escape. 'Get away from me!'

'I didn't mean that. You know I didn't. There's never been a day or a minute I wasn't thankful we're married.'

'Get away from me!' She was almost screaming. She wrenched the kettle free and stumbled down to the spring, gulping with dry sobs. She was hating herself now. She filled the kettle and turned at a stumbling run back up the knoll to throw herself into his arms and beg him to forgive her.

But when she came to the house, Joel was gone; gone without a word. So, she thought, to him this quarrel was nothing but an incident, to be forgotten! He would come back at supper time, hungry, demanding food, forgetting this violence of word and thought which had shaken her like an earthquake. Probably he was still telling himself it was because she was going to have a baby, assuring himself that she would be her usual serene self when he came home. Well, he would find out his mistake, find out that she meant every word she said!

Every word? She tried to remember what it was she had said which she meant so positively. She could remember words enough, but they were meaningless. Certainly he was right about Phin and Johnny Butler. They were a shiftless pair. And certainly she had no real fondness for Mily or for Lucy. Lucy had a mischievous tongue, and Mily ... Mima's throat constricted when she thought of Mily, and a dark terror filled her. Perhaps Joel had gone to Mily now!

Or perhaps he had gone down-river, never to return. The thought sent her running to the landing, but the floats were still there; hers that Bela had made for her, pulled up in the shade, turned upside down, and the big one Joel had taken that day he went up-river to get the moose meat. That was the day the thundershower caught him and he took shelter at Phin's, and Mily gave him dinner, and the rain lasted for an hour, and Phin was not there! The floats were here, so he had not gone by water; but he might have walked. He might walk all the way to Boston. 'Bijah Hawes had walked all the way from Boston when he first came; and Mima remembered the day he came and found her with Bess, and she remembered the night 'Bijah kissed her while they danced ... He was so strong, strong enough to walk from Boston, strong enough to pick her up and hold her crushed against his breast.

But Joel was strong too; strong enough to carry her from the sunned boulder back into the shade, so that she smelled the warm pine needles under her cheek on the ground ... She wept with the sweetness of that memory.

If Joel had gone, he might have stopped to say good-bye to Jess and Sis, or perhaps to take Sis with him. Mima began to run through the woods toward where Jess was working. She did not hear his axe ahead of her. Joel might be there with them.

She slowed her run to a walk, watching through the pines ahead for any sight of them, listening for any sound. She heard low warm laughter presently, and was guided by it till she could see Sis and Jess. Sis was lying on the ground under the pines by the water. Her head was turned away, her cheek resting on the pine needles fragrant from the sun. Jess half-sat, half-reclined beside her, leaning on his elbow, facing toward Mima but not seeing her. He was looking down at Sis, murmuring something at which they laughed together; and his hand was on her hair, stroking it, stroking her cheek, touching her throat. He leaned above her and her arm went up to draw him down and hold him tight to her breast; and then Polly crowed delightedly, and Mima saw the little girl half-hidden behind the trunk of a pine just beyond them. Sis without sitting up turned her head that way, and Jess too, and Mima went forward, smiling to hide her own unhappiness.

'Well,' she said, 'I sh'd judge you two have come to it! You've been long enough.'

Jess swung toward her, and he sprang to his feet, startled and laughing. 'Right!' he said proudly. 'We're going to be married soon as the house is done.'

Sis sat up in a bright dismay, and she got to her feet and began to order her hair, and Mima laughed and said: 'Don't bother, Sis. He'll just muss it up again.'

Jess promptly did so, catching Sis's head in both hands, shaking it to and fro, kissing her roundly. Sis cried: 'Stop it, Jess!' And Jess demanded: 'Ain't she sweet as honey, Mima?'

Mima wanted to cry with loneliness for Joel. 'She is so!'

Sis was hot with delicious embarrassment. 'I guess you think we're awful,' she declared.

'You're awful nice and young and in love,' Mima told them. 'I'm not going to stay. I just came to fetch Polly home, case she was getting tired.'

'She's been asleep,' Sis said; and Mima laughed.

'So there was no one to keep an eye on you! Jess, you'd better spend more time building the house and less making love. Be time enough for that after the house is done and you in it!'

She went home, Polly in her arms. Joel was not there, but she had no longer any fears. He would come presently. She told herself that he was right in thinking that this storm which had so shaken them both was no more than a ripple on the deep river of their lives, to be forgotten.

Sis was at home before he came. Mima saw him doubtful and uncertain of his welcome; but when he had watched her for a while, his doubts were wiped away. At supper she told him that Jess and Sis had decided to be married, and Sis blushed and smiled, and Joel said he had known that was coming for two months past.

Not till they were in bed together did Mima speak of what had happened. Then in his arms she said: 'I'm all right now, Joel. I didn't mean any of it. I was a crazy fool, just the way you said I was, saying things a-purpose to hurt you. I'm sorry as can be; but I'll make it up to you.'

It was a moment before he spoke. 'I didn't mean to make you mad, Mima.'

'You didn't. It was me. I was so hot and all.'

'It scared me awful.'

'Poor Joel!'

'You've got so you're so much of me.'

'I want to be all of you. I want you to be all of me.' She was close, pressing in his arms. She tried to laugh. 'I'm so happy I think I want to cry,' she said, half-sobbing; and he laughed, and his lips lay long on hers wet with her tears.

7

THAT quarrel between them, which while it was in progress had been so terrible, became in retrospect ridiculous; but it might have been repeated. For it had begun because Joel said something critical about Johnny and Phin Butler; and he found other occasions to criticize them during the weeks that followed. He spoke to Johnny one day, tentatively, about sending a petition to the General Court asking that their taxes be abated; and he reported to Mima afterward, half angry, half amused:

'Johnny don't see the sense to it! His idee is that as long as we're let alone, there's nothing to worry about. He says he don't see any sense in fretting till they try to sell our farms out from under us. He don't want to have anything to do with it.'

'I guess you wouldn't want to send a petition unless everyone would sign it. Maybe you can talk him around. Have you said anything to Phin?'

'Not yet, but I know what he'll sav! He'll say: "Well, I dunno!"' Joel jerked his head backward and forward, pumping out the words as Phin did. '"Well, I dunno! We always have got along so far, never had to pay a tax yet. I dunno!"' And he said in a wrathful scorn: 'They're the same about this as they are about everything. They never plan ahead, never want to do anything till they're pushed to it. It's a wonder they don't wait to plant their corn till they're hungry for some bread to eat! Johnny keeps saying he'll think it over. If he could think, there'd be some sense to that, but he hasn't the head to do it with!'

Mima smiled at his heat, feeling today no slightest disposition to defend Phin and Johnny, wondering why she had been so easily roused when Joel criticized them before. This was a Sunday afternoon, and she proposed:

'We might go up and see Phin, anyway, Joel, and maybe stop and see Matt and Sally.'

He agreed. 'We don't hardly see Matt at all, nowadays,' he reflected. 'They kept to theirselves all winter.'

'I think Sally's scared of everything,' Mima confessed. 'I know she was scared they wouldn't have enough to eat.' She laughed at a sudden memory. 'When Jess was a young one, he was that way. He'd take more of everything than he wanted, more than he could eat, for fear someone else would eat it before he could have another chance. Mother started making him eat all he'd taken before he left the table, and that finally cured him.' And she said understandingly: 'Sally's gone hungry at home sometimes. She can't forget it, that's all.'

'Plenty to eat this summer,' he reminded her, and she nodded; but it was true that Matt and Sally did keep much to themselves. She saw that Joel felt this, was hurt by it; and to make him forget it she spoke again of Phin.

They set out presently, leaving Polly with Sis, and stopped at the Royal Mess to say a word to Jason and his Polly there, and stopped at Matt's a while. Matt and Sally seemed glad enough to see them, and Joel told Matt his errand, and Matt agreed that a petition should be sent. Mima thought Sally looked even more frail than usual, pale and weak and shaken, with

harried eyes. She asked the other woman a kindly question, but
Sally said quickly:

'Oh, I feel fine!'

'Don't you go working too hard,' Mima warned her. 'Things
always get done, give 'em time.'

Sally insisted that there was nothing wrong with her; but
when Mima and Joel presently started on, Mima said: 'I think
Sally's going to have a baby. She acts to me like she was
scared.'

He chuckled. 'So? You're always saying that the things
we're afraid of never happen, but if that's what she's afraid of – –
it'll happen all the same.'

'She's not really scared,' she argued. 'She'll be all right when
she knows for sure.'

They followed the path toward 'Lish Partridge's hovel, and
they discussed what Joel would say to Phin. 'You don't want to
argue with him,' Mima suggested. 'Take a man that knows
he's wrong, if you tell him so, he'll deny it and get stubborner
and stubborner. But if you start saying maybe he's right —
specially if he's not sure whether he is or not — he'll start
arguing with you that maybe he's wrong after all.' She said
almost gently: 'Men like Phin and Johnny, they're never sure
of theirselves. They really know that everybody else is smarter
or stronger or better some way than they are; and they try not
to let anyone find it out, and stiffen their necks and r'ar back
in the breeching. You can't ever push them, Joel, or pull them
either. You have to agree with them about nine things so they'll
agree with you about the tenth.'

'Is that the way a woman works it?' he asked, his eyebrow
lifting teasingly. 'Give in to a man — so she can get around
him?'

'It's the way she does if she's smart,' Mima assured him.
'A man's like a cat when you've got hold of its tail. You pull
one way and the cat will pull the other, every time.'

Mily and Phin were glad to see them, Mily volubly so. 'Away

off up here we don't ever see anyone,' she declared. 'You two
are the only ones ever do come up-river this far. Come up and
set.'

Phin said not so much; but Mima thought he too was pleased
at their coming. She tried to shut her eyes to the disorder in
the small log house and the litter all around; but the contrast
to her own home, where everything after it had been used was
returned to its appointed place, was too marked to be over-
looked. The mess here was, she admitted to herself, Mily's
fault. It was a woman's job to keep a place picked up. Mily
was certainly pretty, with her golden hair of which she was so
proud that it was nearly always well brushed and neat under her
mob cap, and her skin like cream, and her kitten's eyes, and her
lips so startlingly red, the lower lip protruding almost as though
she were pouting, always moist and warm and inviting a kiss.
Mily was pretty, certainly, but she was no housekeeper. Probably she was more interested in kisses than in housework.
Probably a man felt that in her and responded to it. Just now
she was laughing up at Joel, saying something to him, smiling
with a sidewise turn of her head. Mima wondered whether she
ever smiled at Phin so; she wondered whether Mily stirred that
phlegmatic, slow young man. Joel was not phlegmatic. Mima
could see the responding excitement in him now.

He and Phin walked away — Joel made some excuse about
seeing Phin's corn, which Phin said was doing well — and
Mima and Mily and little Will were left alone. Mima could
not remember that she had ever been alone with her cousin
before; and Mily now seemed conscious of this too. She was
almost embarrassingly affectionate and friendly, chattering so
steadily that it was as though she were afraid she would not
have time to say all she had to say. The late August afternoon
was as cold as a day in October, with a blustering northwest
wind; so they stayed indoors and Mily built up the fire, and
Mima thought the hot little house smelt of clothes that needed
washing.

She was glad when Phin and Joel returned. Mily urged them to stay for supper, but Mima said they would have to go back. 'I left Polly with Sis,' she explained. 'She's got to have her supper.'

Mily insisted, appealing to Joel: 'You want to, don't you, Joel? Stay, do! We never have any company. Sis can feed the baby, Mima. Oh, stay, Joel!'

'Got any of that corn pudding you gave me before?' Joel challenged good-humoredly. 'Best thing I ever tasted. I'd stay for that.'

'I'll make you up some!' Mily promised.

Phin asked, looking at Joel: 'When was that?'

Mily answered quickly: 'The day he brought the moose meat, when it came on to rain. I told you he stayed for dinner.'

Phin said: 'You never told me.' And Mily cried in exasperated tones:

'I did too! Why wouldn't I tell you, I'd like to know? You never listen to me, that's all!'

Her voice rose in shrill complaint and anger, and Joel said hurriedly that he guessed he and Mima had better start home. 'It's blowing up cold,' he declared. 'Wouldn't wonder if we had a frost tonight, if the wind stopped.' And without prompting from Mima he held to that decision. They started home through the woods, leaving Mily protesting sullenly.

When they were away, Mima asked: 'What did Phin say about the petition, Joel?'

He laughed shortly. 'Said he dunno,' he confessed, mimicking the other's tones. 'But I tried agreeing with him and he might come around.' He reflected, faintly disturbed: 'You know, Mily ought to have told him about me being there that day. Phin gets mad any time a man looks at her.' He chuckled. 'Can't blame him much. Remember the husking bee when she carried on so before they got married?'

'It takes two for that kind of carrying on,' Mima reminded him. 'I was glad you didn't find any red ears after she started cutting up that day.' She added: 'Not that I'd blame you. I can see a man might like kissing Mily.' Watching his back as he strode on ahead of her, she asked: 'Can't you?'

He said after a moment: 'Yes. There's no Jemmy in her. She's all Born-Drunk, Mima. She's the kind I've told you about. You see her — the way she laughs, or that wet mouth of hers, or the way she switches her backside when she walks, and you get idees. Any man does.'

'I guess every woman's partly that way — or that way to some man.'

'Mily's more that way than most,' he told her. 'But Mima, a girl like her, a man might want to borrow her long enough for a quick coupling, but he wouldn't want to marry her and keep her and take care of her and all.'

She said, half to herself: 'You never do take as good care of borrowed things as if they were your own. And you feel guilty every time you look at them, and you're always glad to return them, get rid of them. Maybe it's the same with a borrowed woman.'

He chuckled at the justice of that, and they walked on in silence, and a question took shape in Mima's mind, a question she wanted to ask him. But it must be asked in just the right words, in just the right tone, so that it might not seem too important. She chose the words. She would ask him: 'Did you find a red ear, that day you ate Mily's corn pudding while it rained?'

But the tone was important, too. She was trying to decide just how to ask the question, when he spoke, in a sober fashion, of the matter of land titles. News had come late in July that the General Court confirmed to the Waldo heirs title to all this territory, only providing that the heirs must satisfy settlers who had been in possession before April 19, 1775; and he referred to this. 'But the trouble is, we all came in here since then,' he pointed out. 'Even your father. So that don't do us any good. We might have to buy our land all over again.'

She was already glad she had not asked that question about Mily, ashamed that she had doubted him. 'It takes care of Taylor,' she argued. 'It makes his title good, and Father bought from him.'

'He might not bother to protect our titles.' Joel added: 'But Matt says we're all right. They won't put us off. He says the Waldo heirs will make the land over to us with turf and twig.'

'What's that?'

'Why, just hand us a piece of sod and a piece off a tree, like they were handing us the land and everything on it. Matt says they call it livery of seizin. I'll be glad when it's all straight.'

Mima refused to be concerned. The land was theirs, would always be; and no one could ever take it from them now.

＊　＊　＊　＊　＊

What happened that night drove other problems for a while out of their minds. Crossing the pond to their own landing, they were chilled by the northwest wind, now biting cold; and Joel hoped it would keep on blowing. 'Or there'll be a killing frost, sure,' he predicted. Before they slept they heard the wind begin to die; and during the night it was so cold that Mima put more covers over Polly. Joel was up before her, and even before he roused the fire, he went out-of-doors. It was not yet full day, and Mima fell asleep again and woke when he returned. He came to the bedroom door and she saw by the way he stood that evil had befallen them. She spoke to him, and he said:

'Been a bad frost, Mima. That patch of spring wheat I sowed is killed, and so's the heft of the corn and the rye. We won't have a crop at all to speak of.'

She was quick on her feet. 'I went back to sleep,' she said contritely. 'I'll get breakfast started.' A man in trouble needed food. She kissed him, said assuringly: 'It'll be better than it looks, Joel. We'll get along.'

But a closer examination only confirmed the extent of the disaster. Except on hillsides, the frost had been deadly. Philip

Robbins estimated that at least half the expected crop would be lost; and Joel told Mima:

'It'll be tight nipping to get through the winter. We'll be gnawing birch bark before we're through.' He added half-heartedly: 'But we'll get along.'

'We'll get ourselves along, Joel,' Mima said strongly. 'We can live on meat mostly. That means killing all the pigeons we can and putting them down, putting away all the smoked moose meat we can get, and salmon, and bear meat too. We'll eat sauce and fresh meat, long as we can get it, and we'll have a crop of potatoes.' She smiled at him. 'You'll have to turn hunter, Joel. You can go up-river to that place we found, and kill all the moose you can smoke, and freight it home. And you can hunt all winter too.'

They planned a dozen measures to meet this emergency, and in the sudden new activity they had no time for fears. Joel organized a party to go after moose up the river. He was able from his knowledge of the obstacles in the way to plan how they might be surmounted. Canoes would serve for the trip up-river; a flexible raft of logs, long and narrow, which they could control with snubbed ropes in the quicker reaches of the stream, would bring the meat home. Jess would go, and Johnny Butler. Lucy and Polly Ware had had their babies on the same day; but though Jason was staying home, Johnny said Lucy was as well off without him as with him. 'Bijah Hawes from the foot of the pond, and young Jake and David, with Joel, made up the party.

'We'll be gone a week or ten days,' Joel told Mima. 'Depends on how soon we kill our meat. Takes a while to smoke it right.' He proposed to bone the meat and hang it in bark lodges with a smouldering fire to fill the lodge with smoke. 'Hal Tufts lived two-three years with the Indians,' he explained, 'and he said they'd build a green fire under it first and let the flames char it some, and then smother out the fire and build the lodge around it. He said it would keep a year, smoked so; but it takes time, so don't look for us till we come. We'll stay till we get a-plenty.'

'I'm going to miss you.'

He said, laughing huskily: 'There's only half of me going. You'll have the other half of me here.' Polly came to kiss him a second good-bye; and he tossed her high and added: 'More than half, when it comes to that, with you and Polly and January staying here.' January was Mima's month, and they had begun to use the name when they spoke of the new baby.

Jess was indoors, saying good-bye to Sis, and Joel, with Polly on his shoulder and his arm around Mima, called:

'Ho along, Jess! Sooner go, sooner come.'

Jess joined him and they all went down to the landing and watched the two men paddle away around the point, then climbed to the ledge to see them reach the river mouth. Jake and Dave were waiting there in another float. Johnny Butler and 'Bijah Hawes had already started up-river. Not till they passed out of sight did Mima and Sis turn back to the house.

While the men were absent, they went to see the new babies in the settlement. At the Royal Mess Jason's Polly beamed with happy pride, and Mima told her the baby was uniquely beautiful, and Polly laughed and said:

'I know you're just telling me that to make me feel good — but it does make me feel good, Mima.' She was not yet able to be about, but she had urged Jason to go with the others. 'I told him to,' she declared. 'But he wouldn't. He let on he was afraid some man would come along and run away with me. As if I would!'

Johnny Butler had left his Lucy; but this was Lucy's fourth in the six years since she and Johnny were married, and when Mima and Sis crossed the pond they found her already moving about the house. Jimmy, now almost five years old, was helping her manfully, amusing the younger children and keeping them content.

'Jimmy's more help with them than Johnny would be,' Lucy

declared. 'And as for me, having a baby don't bother me at all, any more than a new calf does an old cow.' There was some bitterness in her tones. 'I'm getting so I feel like a cow! I got Johnny's breakfast for him the third day.' She added: 'Mily's upset about hers; raising Cain, giving Phin a time. She said you and Joel was up there to see her, Mima.' Mima assented; and Lucy said: 'Mily thinks a heap of Joel. She's always throwing him up to Phin.'

Mima smiled. 'I think a heap of him myself,' she said; and Lucy laughed and warned her:

'Then you'd better keep him away from Mily.' She asked Sis: 'You and Jess set the day yet, have you?'

'Just about,' Sis admitted. 'The house is all done only finishing the cellar and chinking the rest of the walls. We'll get married soon as we can move right in.'

Later, when she and Mima were on the way home, she said resentfully: 'I was a mind to slap her face, talking that way about Joel, Mima.'

'Lucy always did like to say things to bother people,' Mima told her. 'You have to pay no attention, that's all.'

She and Sis finished chinking the new cabin and daubing the cracks with mud, and they worked some on the cellar; and when a week had passed, Mima began to look for Joel to come home. Johnny Butler and 'Bijah Hawes returned on the eighth day, with a long slender raft well loaded, floating it down the river, towing it when the current slackened. Mima, apt to watch the mouth of the river every afternoon, saw them and paddled across to hear what news there might be of the others; and Johnny said in a lively enthusiasm:

'They've got more m-meat to smoke, b-be two-three days yet. It was like b-butchering c-cattle, Mima; more m-moose than ever I see. We killed five at the head of Sunnyback P-Pond on the way up, left Jake and D-Dave there to smoke the m-meat; and we went on up-river, and 'Bijah and me started home with this load yesterday m-morning. Dave's b-been killing right along. He's got enough smoked to f-feed an army; but he'll be ready to come along with Jess and Joel. They'd k-killed three the night before we left, b-besides what we had a'ready.'

Mima nodded, content to know the hunt had gone so well. 'Did you go up the west fork at all?' she asked.

'Jess and m-me did, one day. It c-comes out of a big cedar swamp that's f-full of m-moose, b-but they're hard to get at with no snow to d-drive 'em into yards. I fuf-figure we can get all we w-want there any time.' He laughed. 'I guess we w-won't starve as long as we c-can chaw!'

'Uncle Josiah's corn is doing real good,' she said. 'It's mostly on the high ground where the frost wasn't so bad. And Matt and Jason have been netting out salmon and smoking them to trade for moose meat.' She had been paddling beside them as they towed the sluggish raft toward the mouth of the river that ran down to Seven-Tree Pond; but now the faint current began to take it and she turned homeward again.

She thought that meat alone would not carry them through the winter. While there were still garden things, no one was eating any grain at all. There was none to be had in Warren, for there too the frost had hurt the crops; and if there had been, no one had money to buy, and little with which to barter. The day was fine and warm; but there was a smoky autumn haze in the air, and soon it would be cold. Cold and hunger went to-gether. She remembered the tale I'm Davis had told, about the woman and the children alone in the wilderness, with no fire and no food. It had needed thirty-eight days to kill the little baby, to starve it slowly, freeze it slowly, till it was frozen bones. She wondered how Mrs. Forbes kept it warm so long. . . . The pond today was clear and beautiful, the forest all about mur-mured gently in the light breeze, the sky smiled with clouds. There was no hint of danger anywhere. But the corn house, almost empty and with no corn in the fields to fill it, was a con-stant warning; a reminder of slow, patient death that might wait till spring to clinch its hold upon them.

Mima stepped out of the float and walked up to the house with strong steps and lifted head. Whatever happened, they could meet it and beat it when it came. They could manage all right till April or May; till April at least. And April was far away, September hardly begun.

* * * * *

September sped on wings. The gentle days passed so quickly they left no mark at all. Joel returned, and he built a shed of stout poles against the side of the house and racked their meat there where cold would help keep it in condition. Jess worked on his cabin, now almost ready for him and Sis to move in; and Mima and Sis — and every other woman in the settlement — helped with the harvest. Mima found herself picking up single kernels of grain which fell on the ground; and she smiled and told herself that one grain of rye or of wheat could not greatly matter. But she began to drop into a pocket of her dress the grains she thus picked up at random; and at the end of the second day she had a fair handful, enough at a pinch to feed Polly for a day, or even two! She no longer laughed at her own folly in thus gleaning every kernel.

Jess and Sis were ready to be married; and Jess thought they might go to Mr. Urquhart in Warren. Mima's old dislike for the preacher persisted. Jess was inclined to laugh at her prejudice, and the matter was still in debate when Mrs. James, the midwife, came to stay a few days at Moses Hawes' house, where Mary's baby was expected. Mrs. James had been the minister's stoutest partisan; but she was now as violently his enemy, and full of talk about the blackness of his shame.

'I always said it,' she assured every listener. Mima and Sis had gone down to see Mary and were there the afternoon she arrived. 'I said from the first he was a liar when he swore his wife at home was dead.' Mima smiled, remembering otherwise. 'Now there's a letter from that same wife,' the old woman told them. 'It come unsealed, so the men read it that fetched it up the river; and you can be sure it was passed around for some to see before ever it got to Mr. Urquhart, the black-hearted lying devil. I read it myself, and a poor sweet letter it was from the wife and babies he deserted.'

She recited parts of it, talking on and on; and when Mima and Sis started home — they had chosen to walk, coming from Round Pond across through the sunned September woods and thus returning now — Sis laughed and said: 'She's a rattle tongue, Mima. But it must be true.'

'It's bound to be,' Mima agreed. 'Mrs. James was always one that stood up for him. When he wanted to marry down there, he had already told people about his wife at home; so he showed them a letter that said she was dead. But no one knew where he'd got the letter, or how it came to him; and some said he was lying.' She smiled. 'I remember Mrs. James saying Mr. Urquhart would no more tell a lie than George Washington. She's changed her tune now.'

'Well, I certainly don't want him marrying Jess and me,' Sis decided; and the event was that she and Jess went to Thomaston to be married, and Mima left Polly with her mother so that she and Joel could go with them.

They descended the river in two canoes, walking across the carrying-place to the ferry in Warren town; and Phin and Johnny Butler overtook them and made one with them for the rest of the journey, by boat and then on foot again. They had made an early start and they hurried on the way, proposing to come home that night. Phin and Johnny had been summoned by Colonel Wheaton, who sent word that their father and mother had come from the westward, proposing to settle in the town.

'Colonel says the town will warn them out,' Phin ruefully explained. 'On account they haven't got anything to eat, or anything to do with.' His brow was furrowed. 'I dunno as we can do anything about it. Mily and me'd take them in, or Johnny would either; but we haven't got more than enough put away to feed us through the winter. Pa's an eater, too,' he added hopelessly.

Mima wished to urge Phin to make the old people welcome; but if these two who must be fed devoured Phin's substance, then the others in Sterlingtown would have to share with Phin their own scant supplies, and Phin's father and mother would eat food little Polly might have eaten! So Mima said nothing. Her own baby was her first concern.

Phin and Johnny meant to see Mason Wheaton, and Jess and Sis planned to ask the Colonel to marry them; so they went all together to find him. He had this year built a mill on Mill River; and he lived in a small log house halfway up the hill west of the bridge, and kept a store near-by. They found him at the store; and Mima was startled to see the change in him since the day he married her and Joel. It was a change not easy to define, comprised of many small changes; a sort of weariness in his eyes, a hoarseness in his voice. He greeted them heartily, catching Mima by both hands, then kissing her roundly.

'I missed my chance to kiss the bride when I married you!' he exclaimed. 'And I've been thinking about it ever since, Mima. No man ever did kiss you — or didn't when he might have — without remembering it.' And he looked at her full figure and said: 'Ho! Another coming? How many at home?'

'One,' Mima told him.

'A bird in the hand and a bird in the bush? That's not much to show for — how long is it? Two years? And you had a head start, too. Joel, man, you better stay home nights and 'tend to your business. And who's this?' he demanded, looking at Sis, very small and a little startled by this big man who shouted so.

Jess told him. 'Jemima Adams, Joel's sister.'

Colonel Wheaton looked at Jess. 'I know what you two came for! I can tell it by the eye on you. God's Nails and Britches, Jess, ain't there enough paupers in Sterlingtown a'ready, and the women dropping babies back of every bush like a flock of yoes, but you have to go get married too?'

Sis turned pale; but Mima laughed at him. 'You said the same to us, Colonel; but we've got along.'

'Ha! Got along, have you? Got enough to last you through the winter?' he demanded. 'If you have, you're lucky. We'll be starving here. Frost did us bad, and there's no money in town to buy cargoes from Boston.' He burst into a roaring rage at the times. 'Every coaster brings folks from the westward that think they'll settle here; and half of them with nothing in hand. Town's warning them out unless they've fetched enough to live on till they can make a crop next year.' Phin and Johnny till now had not spoken, and he demanded: 'You two — what about your folks? They got taxed out of their farm in Framingham, and they tried to get along in Needham, and now they've come here with nothing to eat, nothing but their clothes and an axe and a gun. Town says they can't stay. They'll be a public charge if they do; and we've got all we can do taking care of ourselves.'

Phin said: 'I dunno. I aimed to talk to 'em, see what was best to do.'

'They're down at Oliver Robbins's. He lets them sleep in his barn on account of Mily and Lucy; but he can't feed them all winter.'

'I ain't got room for them,' Johnny admitted. 'M-me and Lucy and four young ones is all the house will hold.'

Colonel Wheaton snorted. 'Got four, have you? You better start sleeping in the barn yourself, Johnny.' He said violently: 'Go on and talk to your folks and let me know. I can get 'em passage to Boston. They better go.'

The brothers turned away; and he mopped his brow. 'Makes me mad enough to bust a gut,' he confessed. 'And — sorry too. Them are good boys, started from nothing, getting somewhere now. Too bad to have this come on them where they have to send their folks away or run the risk of starving themselves.' He looked after the two young men departing. 'How's Mily?' he asked. 'Pretty as ever?'

'Just the same,' Joel told him.

The Colonel chuckled. 'Phin better keep her covered. She's a ball of fire.' He turned to Sis. 'Well, Miss Adams, aim to marry this young fellow, do you?'

'Yes.'

'Love him and honor him and do what he tells you?'

She nodded, smiling. 'Yes, of course.'

'You feel the same way about it, Jess? Aim to love her and cherish her and all?'

'Certain! That's what we came for, to get you to marry us.'

'Well, all right. I pronounce you man and wife.' He laughed at Mima. 'Didn't forget it, this time, did I?' He clapped Joel on the shoulder. 'Words damned near choked me, when I hitched you two. Been good to you, has he, Mima?' Mima smiled; and he said: 'He better be! If ever he ain't, let me know. I'll handle him.'

Jess said: 'Look here, Colonel, how about marrying us?'

'Why, I already done it, man. Didn't you hear me a minute ago?' The Colonel roared with laughter. 'That's all there is to it, Jess. All of my part, anyway. You'll have to do the rest yourself, work it out between you.'

Sis looked as though she wanted to cry. 'It's not very — sacred,' she protested.

The Colonel touched her arm, his tones suddenly gentle. 'I meant it so, sister,' he said. 'I'm not a sacred sort of man, on the outside. You promise to take care of Jess and him to take care of you. That's the sacred part. There's nothing finer than a good man and woman married. God bless you and help you through the winter. It's going to be a tough one for all of us. I didn't go to hurt your feelings, sister; but nobody can make a marriage the way it ought to be except the man and the woman themselves. That's your job.'

Sis smiled suddenly. 'You fooled me, the way you talked before,' she said. 'You're a good man.' She came and kissed him. 'I'm glad it was you married us, and we'll try to make it the way it ought to be.'

8

PHIN and Johnny walked
back up-river to Warren with them, and Phin said he had arranged with Oliver Robbins to let his father and mother live in
the barn for the present. 'I dunno how we'll manage,' he admitted, his head pumping out the words. 'But I aim to take
care of them somehow.'

Mima thought well of Phin. A man might be measured by
the extent to which he accepted his responsibilities, or by his
evasion of them.

'Don't c-count on me to help,' Johnny said stubbornly.
'If you ask m-me, Phin, we don't owe them anything, anyway.
They n-never d-did for us, only to have us and b-bind us out to
Doc Taylor. We've scratched for ourselves ever since.'

'I'll do the best I know how,' Phin insisted. 'It's going to keep
me humping; but I always have worked. I ain't afraid to.' He
said to Joel: 'But I guess if we can do anything about the taxes,
we'd better. If I had to pay taxes too, I couldn't do it nohow.'

'I talked to Colonel Wheaton,' Joel agreed. 'He says a petition
is the thing. We'll have a meeting right away.'

'Johnny'll sign,' Phin promised, 'and so will I.'

It was already dusk when the three canoes started from the carry up the river. Phin and Johnny, in haste to get home, drew away; and Jess and Sis dropped back, in no haste at all. Mima could hear their voices murmuring in the night, long after she and Joel left them behind. They stopped at her father's house to get Polly and to tell what news they had heard in Thomaston; and Polly slept in Mima's arms on the way up the river and across the pond. Once Mima said:

'I'm going to kind of miss Sis. But at that it will be fun having our house to ourselves again, Joel.'

'Is she coming tonight to get her clothes?'

'No, we took the most of them over yesterday. They'll go right to their own house.' She smiled. 'If they ever get that far. Jess was paddling mighty slow.' And after a moment she said, like one who has won an argument: 'Joel, Phin's going to take care of his folks.'

'I give Phin more credit than I did,' he assented. 'You know, dumb people do the right thing more than you'd think. A smart man might know he couldn't do it and just not try; but Phin's just dumb enough to try — and maybe do it, too.'

'You get a lot done sometimes just by trying,' she agreed. 'If you're satisfied to try, and to keep on trying, and not worry too much about how it's going to come out, you have the fun of trying, anyway. And sometimes you get a thing done where you never expected it.'

'With him and Johnny willing to sign the petition, we can go along and do something about taxes now,' he reflected. 'I'll get Matt to write it out, and we can have a meeting maybe Sunday.'

She said happily: 'We ought to go places more than we do, Joel. It's so much fun to come home.' The canoe left the pond, glided up the brook to the landing, touched the familiar shore.

*   *   *   *   *

It proved unnecessary in the end to call any actual meeting of the men in Sterlingtown to discuss the tax petition. Matt drafted it and brought it to Joel; and Joel went down to discuss it with Philip Robbins and to consider any amendment to its terms. Ebenezer, Philip's brother, was there; and Joel read the petition aloud to them:

> To the Honorable the Senate and House of Representatives of the Commonwealth of Massachusetts, Sept. 1783.
>
> The petition of the inhabitants of the plantation called Sterlingtown, in the county of Lincoln, showeth, — That your petitioners feel themselves insupportably burdened by being heavily taxed, and exposed to execution, considering the smallness of our number now, being only seventeen ratable polls, though we have had twenty-seven; the newness of our settlements, and being in the wilderness at a great distance from other inhabitants (though bordering on other incorporated towns, through the uninhabited parts whereof we have not as yet been able to procure any roads), our sufferings by fire and from the war, and our having been taxed as adjacent inhabitants to another town; all which we have largely set forth in former petitions to the Honorable Court. Add to these, that we have no power or authority amongst ourselves to assess and collect a tax, though it has been requested of the Court of General Sessions of the Peace in this county.
>
> Wherefore your petitioners humbly pray that our taxes may be abated until we are in circumstances of ability equal to our other brethren in the commonwealth, and then we will gladly pay our proportion; and that we then may be invested with proper authority to assess and collect the same. And your petitioners, as in duty bound, shall ever pray, &c.

Philip said when Joel finished: 'Good. That's all there is to say.' He reflected: 'Matt's smart, putting in that about our sufferings by fire. It sounds good, and if anybody says where's the fire, we can tell 'em about my barn burning.' He added grimly: 'We suffered enough, certain. He'd ought to have put in about this frost, too. Looks to me this coming winter's apt to be full as bad as that one was. Fire or frost, we starve either way.'

'I figured we could have a meeting Sunday,' Joel said.

Philip advised against it. 'You call a meeting and you'll get them started arguing, and everybody'll have his own idees. Best way is just take the petition and an ink horn and a pen and go around and tell 'em to sign it. Take 'em one at a time and you can handle them, Joel. They've kind of got in the habit of doing the way you say. I'll sign first, and Eben here; and that'll give you a start. Then you can go over and get Josiah. The others won't hold back, after we've signed.'

Joel accepted the advice. When the two older men had set down their names, he went across the river to where Josiah Robbins had Bela and Ezra Bowen at work on the frame of the barn he meant to raise before he went home for the winter. Joel was surprised to see how well Josiah's corn looked, and he spoke of it, and Josiah agreed.

'It's mostly on high ground,' he said. 'The freeze didn't hurt it much.' And he added: 'I be'n thinking, Joel. I can bring some up with me when I fetch my family in the spring; so I aim to donate this to you folks that need it here. Philip can pass it out.'

'It'll help mightily,' Joel agreed.

'We'll get it cut and shocked and ready,' the older man said. 'Have the barn-raising and then the husking after. I'll get some rum from Philip and we'll make a time of it.'

Joel showed him the petition; and Josiah approved it. 'But you don't want me signing it yet,' he objected. 'I ain't a ratable poll here, won't be till next year. You just want the men with families already living here. Ez Bowen's here. He'll sign it.'

Ezra and Bela were at work on the long oak timbers, squaring out a sill; and he called them over. Ezra signed, the quill awkward in his heavy hands. 'I don't see no justify to pay taxes till we get something for them,' he declared. 'I took up the land nearest Warren, figgering on a road; but there's no road yet. Let 'em build a road to my place and I'll pay taxes — if I can raise 'em.'

Bela, at Josiah's advice, did not sign. 'You're not married yet,' the older man pointed out. His eyes twinkled faintly. 'From what I hear about you and Maggie Meservey, you're likely to be; but right now you're living with your pa — and he's a'ready signed.'

So it was with three names that Joel went to Johnny Butler. Johnny scrawled his name and reminded Joel to sign on his own account. Then Joel crossed the pond to Richard's landing and got Moses Hawes and Rich and David Robbins. He stopped for Jess's signature on the way home and found Sis blooming with happiness in their snug small house still shining new; and laughed and said:

'New married ones have a look to 'em every time, Sis. Jess treating you all right, is he?'

'Best I know,' Jess declared; and Sis said: 'Oh, he's wonderful!' Jess and Joel both laughed at that, till she was crimson and told them to stop it; and Joel cried:

'You're red as Mily was the night of the husking.'

That reminded him of Josiah's generosity, and he told them about it. 'We'll make his husking a wedding party for you, Sis! Only if you cut up the way Mily did, Jess'll paddle your behind — or I will if he don't.'

Jess with his arm around Sis said that any time she needed a paddling he'd tend to it himself; and Sis said: 'You try it and I'll make you rue the day!'

Joel went home for dinner. David had told him that 'Bijah Hawes was at Matt's, helping Matt build a stable for his trotting steer.

'So I'll go over after dinner and get them to sign,' Joel explained to Mima. 'And then I'll get Phin Butler and that's all. We won't need to have a meeting.'

He told her too about the corn husking Uncle Josiah planned. 'We'll raise his barn in the daytime and have the husking at night, after. I'm about ready for a high time, Mima. Take our minds off our troubles.'

She nodded. 'I guess a man always feels better if he can cut loose about once in so often,' she agreed. 'He behaves a sight better after he's got some of the cussedness out of him.' Then, remembering: 'But Joel, don't you go walking any ridgepoles, the way you did the time you raised Pa's barn. I was so scared you'd fall and kill yourself I could have killed you.'

He laughed teasingly. 'Why didn't you say so? I was just showing off for you.'

'Were you, honest, Joel? You hadn't hardly looked at me then.'

'I knew you had your eye on me. I was kind of halfway between holding back and grabbing you.'

'You might a sight better have grabbed me than walked that ridgepole. Why didn't you?'

'I was more scared of you.'

'You don't ever have to be scared of me, Joel, no matter what you do.' And she said: 'Dinner's ready.' Polly was by the spinning wheel, turning it, watching the spokes, slapping at them with her hands, and Mima said: 'Num-num, Polly. Get your chair.'

Polly protested: 'No. No. Wheel!' She did not move to obey, and Joel, while Mima was busy by the hearth, said:

'Come along, Polly.'

She looked at him appraisingly, then came running toward him, making kissing sounds. He picked her up and she kissed him and then wriggled out of his arms again and ran back to her play; and Mima laughed, watching them together.

'She knows how to get around you, all right. Just a kiss does it.'

'I know where she learned that trick,' he retorted. Mima set the heaped trenchers on the table; she swept Polly up in her arms and brought her to her chair. Joel said:

'I'll walk over to see Matt and Jason — and Phin. It's easier than taking the canoe up-river.' Mima was putting corn pudding and some bits of salmon in Polly's porringer, and Polly, forgetting her play now in her desire for food, cried insistently: 'Me! Me!'

'In a minute,' Mima told her. 'There!' Polly gripped her spoon firmly and attacked her victuals. Mima said: 'I'll go with you. I haven't seen Jason's Polly, or Sally either, for a week.'

They set out together presently, and little Polly walked sturdily beside them for a few paces; but then she demanded to go pick-a-back on Joel's shoulders, her arms tight around his neck, demanding that he run. He trotted down the knoll, Mima coming more slowly behind them, laughing at them both; and when Joel leaped the brook, Polly screamed with delight, and kissed the back of his neck for thanks. They waited beyond the bridge till Mima caught up with them and she said: 'She's an awful little kisser.' And she added, unconscious of the sequence of her own thoughts: 'I'll leave her with Polly and go up to Phin's with you.'

Joel laughed teasingly. 'Scared Mily'll make up to me if I go alone, Mima?'

'Well,' she admitted smilingly, 'Phin might not be at home! I guess I'd better keep an eye on you. I'm not very much fun for you, the way I am.'

He was moving at a walk despite Polly's urgencies. 'You suit me,' he said, and they came to the Royal Mess.

Jason's Polly was alone there with her baby. She said Jason had gone to help Matt, so they would find him there. Small Polly was delighted with the baby, crowing over it, bidding them: 'See babee! See babee!' They left her and went on to Matt's; and Matt and 'Bijah and Jason signed the petition Matt had drawn. Mima went in the house to see Sally, and the other woman clung to Mima for a moment almost desperately.

'I'm awful scared about next winter, Mima,' she confessed. 'Do you think we'll have enough to eat till my baby comes? I've seen times at home I was so hungry I just cried. I'll have to eat enough for two all winter — and we haven't got much put away, only meat and potatoes.'

Mima smiled, thinking that her guess about Sally had been correct. 'You'll be fine,' she said. 'When's it coming, Sally?'

'April,' Sally sobbed. 'And — I feel awful, Mima. Do you?'

'You'll be all over feeling bad in another month,' Mima promised her. 'Till you get heavy toward the last of it.' She said: 'I'll come over, often as I can. If you set here alone and think of things to be scared of, it's bad for you.'

She brought Sally to some serenity at last, and when Joel was ready, they went on around the border of Matt's cleared land, where the stunted corn, despite the heavy frost, still bravely bore a few small ears; and they passed Elisha Partridge's hovel. It was empty now. 'Lish, when he saw the certain failure of his crops, had decided to go back and spend the winter with his married children in Medfield; and he had departed a fortnight ago. Joel said:

'I guess there's others would go if they had anyone to go to. He'd have had a hard time, wintering here; but he'll be back next year if he can buy the land from Colonel Wheaton. He told me so.' He slipped his arm through Mima's. 'Remember once I thought I'd sell my land and go? But I'll not be scared away.'

'I'm scared sometimes,' she confessed. 'Remember that woman I'm Davis told us about? Will we have enough to eat, Joel? Polly eats so awful much. And there'll be four of us before spring.'

He clipped her close, laughing reassuringly. 'You'll feed one of the four, Mima. No worry about that.'

'I'll have to eat a lot myself. I was hungry all the time nursing Polly.'

He said, suddenly grave: 'There'll be enough. Don't be scared, Mima. I'll take care of all of you.'

'I'm not — really. Only when I wake up at night sometimes and get to worrying.'

They came up the river path to Phin's landing, and Phin and Mily and the baby were by the water there, Phin pulling a salmon net through the pool. The net drew blank. Mily greeted them sullenly, and Joel explained: 'I brought the tax petition for you to sign, Phin. The rest of us have all signed it. Come up to the house and put your name on it, and I'll send it down-river first chance I get.'

'I'm going down tomorrow,' Phin said. 'To see Ma and Pa. I can take it.'

'Yes, and you're a-taking me with you, this time!' Mily warned him sharply. 'I've got something to say to your folks, coming up here and taking the bread out of our mouths and us already starving.'

Phin said mildly: 'You hush, Mily.'

'I won't either hush! I guess I can talk, anyway.'

'Come on, Joel,' Phin muttered. 'I'll sign it.'

He and Joel went up toward the house, and the baby trotted after them, but Mily stayed behind and aired her wrongs.

'Phin said you was down there with him and Johnny, so you know about it,' she told Mima. 'His folks come up here paupers, so the town warned them out; and they moved in on Pa and Ma, and now Phin says he's going to take care of them!' Her voice rose in a shrill querulous anger. 'He don't even take care of me and little Will, and we're his own. I don't know how he thinks he can take care of them! I notice he don't make them live in a hovel, way up here a hundred miles from nowhere. It's good enough for his wife and his baby and another one coming, but it ain't good enough for them! He makes me mad enough to spit!'

Mima said: 'You'd ought to be proud of Phin, Mily. There's some things a man has to do; and if he does 'em he's a man, and if he don't — he isn't. Taking care of his old folks when they need it is one of them.'

'I guess taking care of his wife and babies is a sight more important!'

'He's took care of you the best he knows. The best he can. That's all you can look for a man to do.'

Mily laughed, with a toss of her head. 'Well, I want my

husband to do a sight more than keep me fed and housed.
There's plenty of things I want to do besides eat and sleep —
and living up here in this God-forsaken hole ain't one of 'em.'

'Phin'll have a good farm here, give him time.'

'Him?' Her tone was sour with scorn. 'He'll never have anything if he keeps taking care of every pauper that comes to town.'

'His father and mother are his job, Mily!'

'Well, so am I his job.' Mily added sharply: 'And he'd better
pay more attention to it, too, or I'll find someone that will.'

Mima was slow to criticize anyone, but she thought Phin had
chosen bravely; and she had old cause to disapprove of Mily.
'That's no way to talk,' she said, almost sternly. 'You'd do a
sight better to start worrying about whether you do your own
job as well as he does his.'

Mily's eyes narrowed, her resentment taking a new turn.
'Who made you so high and mighty, telling me what to do?'

'Well, it's time someone told you, Mily.'

'You're a fine one to talk!'

'I don't claim to be anyone special,' Mima said quietly.
'But anyone knows you've never tried very hard to be a good
wife to Phin.'

There was a calculating anger in Mily's eyes. 'Who set you
up to be a judge?'

'Nobody. But I'm entitled to my judgments.'

'I suppose you think I'd ought to be satisfied to be stuck away
up here slaving all the time, and never seeing a living soul from
one week's end to the next!'

'You married Phin,' Mima reminded her. 'This is his farm
and his house, and you're his wife.' She spoke more gently.
'Mily, you're a real sweet girl when you want to be. You'd be
a sight happier your own self if you didn't all the time do things
you know you hadn't ought to do. Let alone how much happier Phin'd be.'

Mily laughed harshly. 'I didn't marry Phin from choice,'
she declared. 'And well you know it! It was a force put, same

as your marrying Joel.' Her eyes were inflamed with anger.
'You talk mighty high and mighty for one that had a baby
pretty near as soon as she got her lines!' Her own words
whetted her wrath; her face was contorted in a dreadful fury.
'You make me so God-damned mad I'd like to kill you! Letting
on to be so good and noble! You're as bad as I am, any day.'

Mima asked, as though in an impersonal interest: 'Are you
ashamed, Mily, because it was that way with you? I'm not
ashamed. It didn't matter to me when Colonel Wheaton married Joel and me. I'd married Joel long before that, and him
me; and I was proud of it then and I am now. Maybe it's being
ashamed of it that makes you so unhappy now. You hadn't
ought to be ashamed of loving Phin, Mily.'

'Loving him?' Mily was almost screaming. 'Loving him?
I hate his insides! He was just hired help around the house;
but I thought anything on two legs was a man!' She pounded
her clenched fists against her thighs. 'Hired help! That's all
he is and all he'll ever be. He was a bound boy to begin with,
and hired help after; and now he's gone and bound himself
again to take care of his folks that are no better than paupers on
the town! He'll be all his life working for somebody else.'

Mima said almost pleadingly, smiling at the angry girl:
'You can't fool me, Mily. You're too mad to talk sense now, but
you was in love with Phin. I saw the way you were with him
before you were married. You were crazy about him, Mily.
Don't you ever remember nowadays how you felt about him before you were married? Phin's just the same as he was then.'

'The same my foot! I'll have you know there's some difference between rolling in the haymow on a hot summer day
and sleeping in the same bed with a man every night of your
life, listening to him snore and hating the way he smells and
every damned thing about him. The same? You make me
sick!'

'There's a lot more than that to being married to a man.'

'I'd like to know what!'

'You try to find out some of the other ways you can be a good wife to Phin and you'll be a sight happier.' Looking past Mily, Mima saw Joel and Phin come out of the house a hundred yards away and start toward them. 'Hush,' she said quietly 'They're a-coming.'

'It's all right for you to talk!' Mily said hotly. She saw Mima watching Joel, saw the sudden light in her eyes; and a heedless rage in her burst all bonds. 'You and your Joel!' she exclaimed.

'Yes, me and my Joel,' Mima said contentedly.

Mily spoke in a low hot tone. 'I married Phin because I had to, or Pa'd have skinned me alive.' She laughed harshly. 'But I can't marry every man I'm going to have a baby by. I'm already married, and so's Joel; so I can't marry him, nor him me!'

Mima looked at her in a slow, deep astonishment, unable to speak; and Mily clutched her arm, her eyes red with rage. 'I've got as good reason to marry Joel as you had,' she whispered. The men approaching were not twenty yards away. She said in a low, triumphant tone: 'I guess you remember that day last June he stopped here when it rained!'

Mima said through dry lips, almost soundlessly: 'You're a little liar, Mily.'

'Ask him!' Mily challenged. 'Ask him! He'll lie about it, but you can see by the way he looks that it's so. Ask him! I dare you to!'

Then Joel and Phin were near; and through a storm of great winds that blew her world to shreds Mima heard Joel saying: 'All right, Phin. Much obliged. You give the petition to Colonel Wheaton, and he'll see it gets to the General Court this winter. Good-bye, Mily. We've got to go along.'

Mily was sweet as cream. 'Good-bye, Joel,' she said meltingly. 'You're real good to come. We don't see many here, but I specially like seeing you.'

Joel grinned, Mima watching him. 'The way you say that gives a man some big ideas, Mily,' he told her, laughing. Mima had turned helplessly away along the path, and he followed her, and Mily called after them:

'I mean it, Joel! You come again — if Mima'll let you. With Phin going down to see his folks so much, I'll be a heap alone.' She called sweetly: 'Good-bye, Mima! We had a real nice talk, didn't we?'

Mima said: 'We did so. Good-bye!'

She and Joel moved away together; and when they entered the forest, hidden from view, he asked:

'What did you two talk about?'

Mima hesitated. 'I was telling her she ought to be proud of Phin for taking care of his folks the way he's going to.' She confessed strongly: 'I was trying to talk some sense into her.'

Joel said scornfully: 'It's no good to talk to her. She's a slut, Mima. The house is a mess inside, and the baby is just about as dirty as a pig. All Mily's good for is making eyes at men. With only Phin around to do for, she don't even keep herself cleaned up. I wouldn't wonder but she'd be better down in Thomaston where she'd have to keep slicked up, seeing folks all the time.' He said proudly: 'It takes a woman like you to live up here and keep things the way they ought to be.' He chuckled, tucked her arm in his. 'But if you didn't, I'd take a birch shoot to you!'

'If you ever did, I'd comb your hair with a broad axe,' she assured him, smiling too, matching her steps to his, hiding the storm which shook her. She knew already that she would never question him.

'I'd want you should,' he agreed.

They were silent then a while, coming back toward 'Lish Partridge's hovel, striking there the path that led to the Royal Mess. They were silent so long she thought he might wonder why, and she said at random: 'We haven't been very neighborly to Phin and Mily, Joel. We'd ought to go see them more than we do. Mily'd be happier, having more company.'

'We ought, at that,' he agreed. 'But when I'm not working,

we most generally go down to Seven-Tree Pond to see your folks.'

'I'm getting big enough so it's kind of hard for me to tramp through the woods; but you can go up and see Phin and Mily sometimes. They'd like it if you did.'

'I'd as soon not go without you,' Joel admitted. 'Even if I was sure Phin was going to be there. Mily always acts as if I'd sneaked up secret to see her. She goes twittering and whispering around. That day last June, she was as excited as if Phin was after us with a gun. Remember she didn't tell him about it till it came out accidental.'

'She has to get some excitement out of life,' Mima agreed. 'I guess she does it pretending to herself that men are in love with her.'

Joel laughed. 'She'll pretend it to the wrong man, some day. But she'll waste her time on me.'

They came to the spring beside the path, which Mima had dug out and walled up on a day which seemed so long ago, when Major Wheaton raised his barn; and they stopped to drink there and to rest a while, for Mima, heavy with her baby, was a little breathless. October was almost on them and the hardwoods had begun to turn, the birches showing yellow as gold, the beeches bronze, the oaks deep red and rich brown. This day had been warm, but now as the sun descended a chill began to touch them in the shadows. Mima said slowly: 'You talk as if it would always be Mily's fault, like Adam saying it was Eve started it.'

He sprawled at ease, looking up at her with twinkling eyes. 'Well, ain't it always the woman starts it?' He drawled teasingly: 'Like that day we'd clumb the tree, I was satisfied to set there and look at the view. I hadn't even thought of anything else; but you was bound I'd sing you a song. Putting notions into a man's head.'

'I noticed it didn't take much arguing.'

'Well, I always was quick on the uptake.'

She nodded, and then she said: 'I've always had a notion men blamed Eve, just so they'd have an excuse to treat women the way they do.'

'I always thought we treated you pretty good,' he said lazily.

'You know what I mean. Men have treated women, ever since, like they was kind of dangerous pets, somewhere between a tame wild cat and a slave.' She spoke slowly, working out her own thoughts. 'I guess here in this country is about the first time men and women have ever worked together, the way two men might, the women working just as hard their own way. We're going to have a different kind of country here, Joel. Specially where the women are concerned. Women are going to be more the same as men.'

'They're not the same,' Joel argued. 'Women are more grown up than men, for one thing. Girls fifteen-sixteen years old are grown women, a lot of ways; but men go on being boys, doing fool things just because it's fun, or because they've had a drink, or because they've seen a pretty woman.' He laughed. 'Old I'm Davis was right, Mima. There's a Born-Drunk in every man; and there's not always a Jemmy to keep him calmed down. Be better if there was, maybe. A man wouldn't be so many kinds of a damned fool.'

She rose suddenly. 'We've got to get Polly home before dark,' she said. 'It gets cold.' They went on together and she said in a sterner tone: 'Maybe men are right. Maybe the women do start it. Animals are different. The only she-thing that wants a he out of season is a woman.' She spoke slowly. 'Maybe a man never would get ideas unless a woman put them into his head.'

He looked at her understandingly. 'Mily's got you upset, hasn't she?'

'Birds and animals are both more decent than women,' she reflected. 'Some of them stick to one mate as long as they live. That same pair of geese used to come back every year to the island in Seven-Tree Pond. I got so I knew them, could tell them.' Suddenly she smiled. 'Maybe birds and animals are smarter than humans, Joel. Maybe mating in season, the way they do, it's as if they had a honeymoon every year, like you and me the trip we took last June. We want to do that again, or something like it, every chance we can. There's no reason why married folks shouldn't keep right on being excited about each other.'

He said, his arm around her waist: 'There's nothing but honeymoons for me, married to you, Mima.'

'I'm not in any shape for honeymooning now.'

'You suit me,' he said.

They came to the Royal Mess, walking side by side; and small Polly greeted them with that: 'Hulloa,' protracted so caressingly, which Joel loved. She climbed into his arms, kissing him under the ear; and he kissed her in the same spot and she squealed with ecstatic laughter, pushing him away when his rough chin tickled her. He told her laughingly:

'You're as bad as Mily, wanting to be kissed and then squealing when you get it! Come along, young lady. You're going home!'

Mima said: 'You go along, Joel. You and Polly. You can chunk up the fire. I'll visit a while.' She stayed with Jason's Polly, approving the new baby, till Joel and small Polly were well away; and when she followed them she walked slowly, wishing to be alone, wishing time to think calmly and quietly, free from Joel's presence which could always color her every thought with her love for him.

Before she came home, she knew her heart and mind and was serene again, but when they were abed that night and he had gone quickly to sleep she woke him, asking somehow desperately:

'Joel — glad you married me?'

Sleepily he drew her close and held her so and slept again, while she lay, still awake, but happy in his arms.

9

THAT scene with Mily, as it receded into the past, lost reality. Its outlines blurred, and even Mily's words became in Mima's memory so altered and modified that she was no longer sure of their meaning. She had decided to forget, and she sought with a steady determination to do so. Mily was a liar; Mily had lied. But even if Mily told the truth, truth can be forgotten. It may be the part of wisdom to believe the false and refuse to believe the true. Life must be built sound and strong, just as a house is built; but for some part of the structure a crooked log may be more useful than a straight one, a broken brick than one that is whole. If out of a handful of sand a few grains escaped, that was no reason for throwing all the sand away. Mima did not know whether she believed Mily or not. She commanded herself to forget what Mily had said, and tried to learn to do so.

Around her, life went on unchanged. Bess had her baby early in October. Hers was the fifth baby born in Sterlingtown since the first of the year; and there were as many more to come. The baby was a boy, and Bess named it Ebenezer; and Mrs. Robbins wept with quiet happiness because in this baby her Eben had come back to her from that unmarked grave to the eastward. The river was full of wood ducks that fall, and David caught sometimes a whole flock in his pigeon net. They had a feast of them to celebrate the new baby's arrival, all the Robbins clan gathering at Philip's house as soon as Bess was able to be about again. The hardwoods on the east side of Seven-Tree Pond were a blaze of color; but already in the quiet forest leaves began to fall, and there was at night and morning the feel of winter in the air and the fear of winter lay in the back of every mind. Except for the corn, everything had been harvested; so the full effect of that August freeze could now be measured, and the truth was only a little better than their first fears. They begrudged the winter rye that had to be sowed to make next year's crop; but from this necessity there was no escape.

'It'll bring us through, too,' Philip Robbins told them. 'I made up my mind when I decided to come up here that rye was the crop to bank on. They said I was crazy to think of coming up here to get a living off a farm. Anderson down in Warren was one that said so. "What'll you raise?" he says, and "Rye," I told him. He laughed till he durned near bust; and I says: "Anderson," I says, "I'll get a living off my farm, and I'll raise rye, and you'll be coming up to buy it off me yet." He will, too. It wa'n't two years before I was raising as much rye here as there was raised on the whole river.'

Joel asked: 'Why was Anderson so sure?' and Philip said:

'He thought the land had to be ploughed for rye, and that we couldn't clear it and plough it and still make a crop in time. But I cleared it and burnt it and sowed winter rye right on the burnt-land, and made a crop the next year. Summer rye, it's better if you plough; but winter rye don't need only a chance.' He added: 'Corn's the same. We made as good crops just pegging in the seed as we do now when we plough. And the first year I raised fifty bushels of potatoes off of one bushel of seed ends, before ever a plough touched the ground.'

They were at the house on Seven-Tree Pond for Sunday afternoon. Mrs. Robbins said: 'I made a good crop of beans this year, freeze or no freeze. I've got two-three bushels. And the roots did good, the turnips and carrots and all. We can eat them ourselves, 'stead of feeding them to the cattle. The critters can live on fodder and hay if they have to.'

The talk was all of crops, of the scant provision which must carry them through the winter. From the privation to come there was no escape except by flight — and no place to which to flee. These were their homes; here they would stay and wait the issue. Uncle Josiah said presently:

'Philip, I've been thinking. Say I move my corn over and have the husking here. I don't want to leave it in my barn when I go, or someone will get at it. Dave and Rich and Jess can fetch theirs, what they've got, and we'll husk all of it same time and throw it right into the bins.'

'When you going to be ready for the raising?'

'End of the month, it looks like now. We've got all the big stuff sized, and they're working on the mortises and tenons and the gains and splices and all; and we've got the timbers ready to work out the cross sills and braces and purlines, but there's still a pile to do. Bela don't want to give the word till everything's just so.'

'Guess't we might full as well have the husking first, any time we're ready,' Philip decided. He chuckled. 'That way, we'll have two shindigs instead of one; get twice the fun out of it.'

Jess said: 'The raising is going to be more work than fun. Them are heavier timbers than yours were, Pa. They'll be something to handle.'

'We'll h'ist 'em,' Philip promised him. 'No trouble about it.'

Sis took the opportunity offered by this gathering of the clan to speak of her plan to keep school for those children in the settlement who were old enough to need it. 'I taught school at home,' she said, 'and I like it, and the children got along. I could do it just as easy, at our house.'

Mrs. Robbins approved. 'They need it, land knows,' she declared. 'But Sis, you and Jess will be filling the house with your own young ones. You won't want other folks' brats around.'

'They're not brats!' Sis protested smilingly. 'I like them, and I like teaching them.'

'Well, a school would be a good thing,' Mrs. Robbins agreed. 'But it'd be a pile of work and worry for you. You'd ought to get pay for it.'

Sis said, coloring a little: 'Why, I want to. I could do it to sort of help Jess. This is our first winter, and we didn't make much in the way of a crop; so outside of the meat Jess can kill we'll be sort of living off all of you this winter. It'll help pay our way.'

Mima said in a quick affection: 'You don't have to work your way with us, Sis.'

'Well, I feel like I'd married Jess at a hard time, when you're all going to be short on things anyway.'

Mima laughed. 'You're worth more to us than full corn bins! Don't fret about that. But if you want to run a school, you go ahead.' She looked at them all. 'It'll kind of tie us together,' she said. 'Having children from different houses seeing each other every good day and coming home and telling what's going on.' She told Sis: 'Like as not I'll be over there every day to hear the latest talk. It'll be a sight better than all of us denning up in our own houses all winter long like a lot of bears.'

'I haven't any books,' Sis confessed. 'But I can print their letters for them to start on, and show them figuring, and I can send for some books next year.'

When they were agreed, Sis with characteristic energy began to organize her plans. 'We've room in our house,' she said. 'For this first year, anyway; and we're handy to get to.' Jess's cabin south of Round Pond was easily reached by walking through the woods from the farms along Seven-Tree Pond from which most of her pupils would come. She canvassed the list of prospects. 'There'll be your three, Dave,' she said. 'Prance

Bowen's Sally isn't six yet, but if Prance wants to bring her as
far as your place, your Jason can bring her the rest of the way,
even if he has to haul her on a sled. Then they can pick up
Rich's two on the way and all come together, up past Mose
Hawes's place and through the woods to ours. It's not far, and
nothing will bother them.' Her cheeks were bright, her eyes
shining with a fine excitement. 'Then there's Jimmy Butler.
He's a fine big boy for his age; and if they set him across the
pond, he can come with Phil and Sue.' Young Philip was twelve
years old, and he scowled dubiously at this prospect; but Sis
smiled at him so appealingly that he blushed and grinned. She
spoke to Sue. 'You're bigger than I am, Susie; so maybe you
won't want to come to school to me.'

'I would too,' Sue declared. 'Maybe I can help you with the
little ones, some.'

Mima saw that both Phil and Sue were devoted to Sis. She
thought the school would be a success. Before they separated
that day, the plan was complete; and except when the weather
was too severe for the children to tramp through the woods, Sis
kept school all winter in the house on Round Pond.

*   *   *   *   *

Mima did not see Mily again for two or three weeks after that
day she walked up the river with Joel; and the last of the harvest, bringing them face to face with the full extent of the damage the frost had done, drove all thought of the other woman
for a while out of her mind. Joel's corn was almost ruined.
What ears matured were small and scantly kernelled. He had
built a corn house large enough to hold the fine crop he expected, but the ears he had garnered, even in their husks, made
only a sorry show there. The rye was not much better, though
they wasted not a grain. Matt and Jason were as well supplied
as he, but no better. 'Lish Partridge had thought his crop not
worth harvesting; but the three of them, since 'Lish had gone
away to the westward for the winter, saved what they could from
his planting and shared it.

Joel and Mima had a good store of potatoes, and of beans, and smoked moose meat racked in the shed, and pigeons put down in their own fat; and rabbits were plenty along the brook and could be snared; and in mid-October Joel shot a bear that came nosing around the sheep pen. So they had fresh meat a-plenty for a while. Also, they ate every scrap of garden sauce as long as it lasted, and Joel and Mima ate no bread at all while there was anything to be had from the garden; but small Polly demanded her pudding and had it, and cornmeal mush and bread too.

Mima had to fight, day by day, against the faint persistent terror like a live thing in her breast. She saw Joel's anxiety, and to help him she tried to hide her own. She was frantic with wishing there was something they could do. Sometimes she tried to calculate what their need would be, and to measure it against their supply; and she tried to think of something that would supplement the corn that must be their staple fare. She thought of gathering beech nuts on the hardwood ridges, but the pigeons had fed fat on them, and on the acorns too. There was nothing. There was no corn to spare down-river, and no money to buy it with if the supply had been available. They could only wait, while as the days passed inexorable winter came nearer all the time.

She thought jealously of Uncle Josiah's fair crop that would be added to the common store. As it was harvested, it was ferried across the river and piled in her father's barn; and David and Rich and her father hauled their scant crops. Bela said the barn timbers would be ready for the raising by the first of November; and the husking bee was set for the day before. For that occasion, since this was no time to waste provisions, Mrs. Robbins at first planned to have nothing to eat at all, and she told folks to bring their own; but three days before, Johnny Butler killed a bear, and offered it for the feast, and Mima persuaded her mother to boil some beans.

'The more they eat, the less rum they'll drink,' she pointed

out. 'But if there's nothing but drinking to do, the men will all
be at it, all the time.'

Mrs. Robbins reluctantly agreed to the beans; but when Joel
and Mima came down the river soon after dinner of the day appointed, Mima found her mother in an intoxication of preparation. The beans were bubbling merrily, with a chunk of pork to
season them, and Jacob had a fire going in a deep trench to
make coals to roast the best cuts of the bear, and there was a
fire in the oven too. Mima cried in surprise:

'Mother, you're baking bread!'

'Yes I am,' Mrs. Robbins said stoutly. 'And nobody's going
to stop me!' She added in an apologetic tone: 'If folks are going
to half-starve this winter, I aim to give 'em one good feed to remember anyway. And we haven't had bread ourselves since the
freeze, nothing but pudding and sauce and meat. I'm hungry
for it myself.'

Mima said honestly: 'So am I.'

Her mother laughed a little, half-embarrassed. 'I just got to
thinking,' she confessed, 'and the more I thought, the more I
couldn't bear to do things in a meeching way. Folks that come
to eat at my house are going to have plenty, long as I've got it
to give 'em!'

She and Mima worked together on the further preparations;
and Joel and Philip hung lanthorns in the barn, high enough so
that they were not likely to be knocked over by any skylarking.
'Not unless the pack of you start chasing Mily into the haymow,
the way you did the last time,' Philip reflected, and Joel grinned
at that memory.

'That was a high time, sure,' he agreed. 'But she didn't take
to the haymow till Phin put after her. Mostly she'd run around
the barn.'

'Yup!' Philip agreed. 'And she'd always manage to git herself
caught out of sight the other side.'

They brought shingle blocks and boards and built a table at
one end of the barn floor, opposite where the corn to be husked

was piled; and then Philip mixed a rum and water grog and put the tub just outside the barn door, a little around the corner. 'I've took notice lately, Ma keeps an eye on me when I go to take a drink,' he explained. 'So I'm putting this kind of out of sight, where we can hit it when we're a mind to without our wives jumping down our necks.'

'Speaking of which?' Joel suggested, and Philip said amiably: 'Well, I don't know but I would.'

So they did; and as the others presently began to arrive, the libations were repeated. Dave and Bess, with their train of children, came first. Jess and Sis walked over, picking up Mose Hawes and Mary on the way; and as more and more children appeared, filling the afternoon with a pleasant din, Mrs. Robbins said to Mima, helping her by the oven: 'Seems like every time a fresh young one comes along there's twice as many as there was before. The new ones screech, and them that's already here yell and holler, and then a fight starts or something. They'll deefen me!'

Small Polly, excited by sight of so many other babies, just then emitted a bagpipe squeal at the top of her pitch just behind her grandmother; and Mrs. Robbins jumped like a spurred horse. 'My stars and moon!' she exploded, and then saw it was Polly who had offended, and caught up the chubby young one in a mock ferocity, shaking her to and fro. 'What are you a-doing, Polly?' she demanded. 'Scaring the juice right out of your old grandma!' She laughed and kissed Polly hard and set her down, and Polly went trundling off to join the pack of children. Sis took them in charge; and she half-lured, half-herded them away toward the house. In the barn some of the men were already at work on the corn. Ezra Bowen hallooed from the landing, and Joel and Jason went down to see what he wanted. He and Prance had brought along the carcass of a fifty-pound pig.

'Tain't as fat as it might be,' Ez confessed. 'They be'n running wild all summer, but the old sow dropped nine of them last spring and I ain't lost any, so I 'lowed I'd fetch one along.' He added: 'I'll have to kill the lot of 'em anyway, soon's snow flies so's they can't get at the acorns and such. I ain't got a thing to feed 'em.'

Jason slung the pig over his shoulder and started up toward the barn; and Joel was about to follow with Ezra when he heard another hail, from up the shore across the river. Since Uncle Josiah had begun to clear the land there, a float was kept handy for ferrying; and Joel went to see who it was who wanted a lift across the stream. He discovered Mily perched on the rock on the other side, flushed as though from running, laughing and calling to him.

'Set me over, quick, Joel,' she begged. 'So's I can beat Phin!' Something in her tone, and the brightness in her cheeks, and the eager pleading in her eyes, filled him with a quick excitement. He pushed the float clear and stepped in and poled across. Jess too had heard Mily's call and he arrived at the river bank as Joel started across. He stood there watching. Two or three thrusts of the pole drove the float to the other bank, and Mily stepped in and told them why she came alone. 'Phin was bound we'd come all the way by the river,' she explained. 'And I said it was quicker to walk across the carry place; and we argued till I told him to put me out at the big bend and I'd show him. So he did and I did. He ain't come, has he?' The canoe touched where Jess stood, and she leaped out, and Joel said:

'Not yet. Or leastways he hadn't a minute ago. Where's the baby?'

'With Phin!' She linked one hand in Joel's arm, the other in Jess's; and they went through the pines toward the barn. 'I'd be full as well suited if Phin don't get here,' she declared with a toss of her head. 'Maybe he'll get mad and not come or something!' Her smile flashed up at Joel. 'I feel full of the old Nick today, Joel. How about you?'

Joel laughed, and Jess said: 'Hold on, you two! Don't go playing games with me around. I'm an old married man!'

Mily said audaciously: 'I never saw a married man yet that didn't know some games — only Phin!' Then they came in sight of the barn and saw Mima and Mrs. Robbins and half a dozen others by the fires, and Mily uttered an exclamation and pushed Joel and Jess away from her, with an effect of freeing herself from them. She ran forward to greet Mrs. Robbins and to kiss Mima and call her darling and to fill the silence that met her arrival with a butterfly-swarm of words. Mrs. Robbins asked Mily where Phin was; and Mily said:

'Oh, I don't know as he's coming. He says I carry on so at a husking it makes him mad.' She told Mima sympathetically: 'You're awful big, aren't you! I haven't begun to show yet, but I'm four months along. I got caught in June, you know.'

There was a malicious light in her eyes, but Mima spoke quietly enough. 'You don't show it,' she said. 'You look mighty pretty, Mily.'

Mily smiled complacently and looked toward the barn. Most of the men and some of the children were already at work there; and she laughed and said: 'Golly, they're hard at it and no girl handy!' She moved that way; but before she got there, Sue, fifteen now and ripening like an apple, exploded out of the barn with 'Bijah Hawes brandishing a half-husked red ear and bounding on her heels. He caught her, and Sue writhed and twisted in his arms till he kissed her cheek and released her. Then she demurely returned with him toward the barn.

Mrs. Robbins commented with a dry amusement: 'Funny how it always looks kind of indecent to see a man catch a girl and kiss her in broad daylight! Kissing is a night-time business. The less you can see, the better you like it.'

Mima smiled. 'Susie's getting to be real handsome,' she commented.

'She's filling out,' Mrs. Robbins agreed. 'Susie's a good girl, a pile of help to me.' She said: 'We'll feed this crowd, Mima, quick's we can. Get some vittles into 'em before the rum takes hold too hearty.'

Phin duly arrived; and a little before sunset, the table in the barn was loaded down, and Philip and Joel cut the meat, and Mrs. Robbins ladled out the beans, and trenchers and slabs of bark served for plates. There was a mound of fresh-baked bread, enough so that everyone could eat his fill without exhausting the supply; and Mrs. Robbins beamed proudly as she watched them. The sun set before they were done, and dusk began to come and an evening chill to fill the air; but they were warm enough with food and drink, and those who had eaten attacked the corn while Mrs. Robbins and Mima and Bet cleared away. Mima saw the men by ones and twos at the rum; and as dusk turned to darkness, the voices rose louder, or seemed to rise louder in the quiet evening air. There were things to be carried up to the house, some distance off; and Mrs. Robbins called Jacob to help, and she and Mima and Bet, well loaded, stumbled through the darkness. When they came out of the house again, the lanthorns in the barn converted its door into a lighter rectangle across which dark figures moved; and the fire in the trench, fed with fresh logs, lifted a torch of flames. Mima heard Joel singing, and she recognized the quick jig tune, and wondered whether he had drunk enough so that he would sing the last verse, and remembered that she had never heard him sing the last four lines if there were others than herself to hear. As she and Bet came nearer — Mrs. Robbins had stayed to chore around the house, and Jacob had run ahead — she heard him break off the song, and heard them crying to him to go on. She was near enough to hear Mily teasing him.

'There's bound to be another verse, Joel!' Mily cried. 'You can't just end it there.'

Jess said: 'There is, but 'twon't do to sing, Mily.'

Mily pleaded: 'Sing it to just me, sometime, Joel?'

Before Joel could answer, while Bet and Mima came past the fire, Bela found a red ear and leaped toward where Sue sat, and caught her before she could escape; and she fought him and they rolled tussling across the heaped hay on the barn floor. Sue was a strong, wiry youngster. Bela could not use all his strength for fear of hurting her; and she fought as a boy might have fought, grappling and twisting and pounding at him while the others laughed and cheered. Mima and Bet came to the barn door as finally Bela pinned her down and kissed her; and Joel called Mima to come sit by him, and Sam Hills, who had worked all summer clearing land across the pond and who was so deaf it was almost impossible to talk with him, nodded and smiled at her welcomingly.

Everyone was talking at once, none listening. The three older men, Mima's father and Uncle Josiah and Uncle Eben, sat on the shingle blocks which had supported the table, just inside the barn door. Johnny Butler suddenly leaped toward Sis, and she dodged him so cleverly that he went headlong into the post against which she had been sitting, and cracked his poll. The thin trickle of blood made them all laugh, and Sis said:

'Oh, I'm sorry!' She tore a ruffle off her petticoat to tie around his head for a bandage; and Johnny caught her to claim the kiss and she gave it to him. 'I'm afraid if I didn't, you'd go hurt yourself worse,' she declared, laughing up at him. 'I didn't ever know you were so desperate, Johnny!'

Jason Ware found a red ear and gave his Polly a rousing smack; and Mily protested: 'No fair kissing your own wife! You can do that to home.'

Jason grinned. 'Dunno who I'd ruther kiss than Polly,' he declared. 'She keeps me on short rations all the time.'

'Go on,' Mily insisted. 'Kiss someone else! That's the rule, Jason.' So Jason good-naturedly rose and looked along the barn. They were sitting or standing in a double row, the pile of corn at one end; and at intervals one or another went to fetch an armful of ears and carry them to a convenient place. Jason scanned them all.

'Well now, let's see,' he reflected in a fine judicial tone. 'Not you, Mily. You're a squealer! Susie, you been run ragged already.' He came toward Mima, and his eyes met hers; and

she smiled, not seeking to escape him. 'You suit me, Mima,' he
said. 'I've watched you through hell and high water. You're a
fine woman.' She colored with pleasure, and he kissed her and
turned back to his place again. 'There, Mily, you satisfied, be
ye?' he demanded.

'I don't get no satisfaction out of seeing another woman get
kissed,' Mily assured him, tossing her head; and there was some
laughter. Mima reflected with a malicious triumph that she had
not seen anyone chasing Mily to claim a kiss. Susie and Sis had
had, thus far, the lion's share of attention. Probably Mily was
feeling slighted. Philip from where he sat called:

'You all are wasting too much time, with the corn all piled in
the end of the barn that way. Two of you go throw it down this
way where the rest can get at it handy.'

Jess and Bet went to obey him, and Jess made a game of it,
pretending to open each husk at the end, asserting now and then
that he had a red one, asking who wanted it while the men
shouted their demands.

Bess found a red ear and came to kiss Uncle Josiah. 'Because
you're really giving the party,' she reminded him. 'And we're
going to miss you when you're gone and be mighty glad to see
you back again, come spring.'

Everyone shouted agreement, and Uncle Josiah beamed.
'But I ain't giving this party,' he reminded them. 'Thank'e
kindly for the buss, all the same, Bess. You're all mighty welcome to the corn, and I'm glad I made a crop. But my party
comes tomorrow, with a barn to be raised and all.' And he
said: 'I be'n counting noses. There's sixteen of us here, men
folks. Sixteen men, and twelve women — not counting Susie
— and five young ones here, and Lord knows how many babies
up at the house. Philip, you reckon I better get some of the
Warren folks up to help?'

'Don't you,' Joel told him. 'Just us here can raise a bigger
barn — and drink more rum — than the whole of Warren.
We'll put her up so fast she'll bounce!'

'Bijah called: 'Who said rum? Where is it?' Half the men trooped out to drink. Mima saw Mily rise and follow Joel. He came back quickly, chuckling.

'Keep her off me, Mima,' he said, amused. 'Mily's hot as love in hay time, tonight.'

Mily came back and fell over Matt Hawes's legs, where he sat on the floor, and she screamed with laughing dismay and grappled him, crying to him to let her go, while Matt neither held her nor repulsed her. Mima thought this was a curiously different occasion from that other husking before Phin and Mily were married, when everyone wanted to kiss the prospective bride and Mily was chased around the barn and around. Mily was no longer so pretty as she had been, for one thing; and they were all older. She thought there was something hollow and sham in Mily's determined high spirits tonight. Except for her, they were all quiet, as though sobered by the thought of the winter to come; by the realization that here in the barn was a major part of all the corn in Sterlingtown. They talked in low tones, in small groups, working listlessly, till Philip said: 'How if we make a race of it? Joel, you and Jess choose up sides and see which one has the biggest pile husked when you're done.'

Mily said there would have to be a prize; and Philip agreed: 'Well — a gallon of rum to drink at the barn-raising. Go ahead. Joel, you take first pick.'

'I'll take Mima.'

Mily protested: 'No fair, husbands and wives on the same side!' and Philip seconded her.

'Any fights come out of this, we want to keep 'em in families,' he agreed. 'Take someone else, Joel.'

So Joel chose Sis, and Jess took Mima. Joel took Phin, and since by her own rule this meant that Joel could not choose her, Mily looked at him with resentful eyes; and when at last Jess called her name, she said:

'No, I'll throw down the corn.' She went to the end of the

barn where the ears still to be handled were piled, and 'Bijah went to help her there. The first ear he picked up was already partly husked. He saw the red kernels and grabbed for Mily, but she squealed and dodged him and caught at the ladder to the mow and started up it.

Philip called: 'Hold on there! Keep out of the haymow tonight, Mily. I don't want the barn catching fire!'

'Bijah had caught her as she hesitated, and now as he kissed her, she clung to him so hard that Jess shouted: 'Hey, who's kissing who?' Then the ear in his own hand showed red, and he turned to Sis; and she evaded his rush and he chased her to and fro, the others scattering out of her way. She dodged around groups and scrambled over sitters, astonishingly swift and agile, fast as a rabbit. Mima watched her smilingly. There was something about Sis so like Joel in so many ways that Mima's heart warmed to her more and more. She wondered why Mily did not protest because Jess had chosen to pursue Sis — if husbands were not to kiss wives — and she looked toward Mily and saw her turning back husks from one ear after another with flying fingers, looking for a red ear, while the others watched Jess and Sis.

But Mima watched Mily, half-guessing what she was about to do. Jess caught Sis and tossed her up in the air like a child and caught her as she came down and kissed her hotly; and then Mily called: 'Here, Joel!' He turned to look and she tossed an ear so sharply at him that he caught it in self-defence. Mily sidled past him toward the door; and 'Bijah shouted:

'Open it, Joel. Open it, man! She's getting away from you!'

Joel stripped back the husks. They were all watching him; they all saw the glowing color of the kernels as soon as he. He hesitated; but Mily leaped through the door, racing toward the fire, and everyone shouted, urging him on. So Joel bounded after her. She dodged around the corner of the old house, the one in which they had all lived together for the first winter here; and Joel was sharp on her heels. Everyone pressed out of the barn to see Mily reappear or to hear her scream when Joel caught her; and everyone was shouting, cheering, laughing.

But Mily did not reappear, nor did Joel; and after a moment the mirth here dulled and died in a curious embarrassed silence. Mima heard Prance Bowen say: 'Well!' The tone said more than the word. A minute passed and another. They drifted back to attack the corn again. Mima saw her father watching her with expressionless eyes.

She began to strip the husks off an ear of corn. Phin stayed outside, and she saw him turn to the rum. Then Joel came back, striding angrily past the fire toward the barn. Mima wondered how long he had been gone. It seemed long. She watched him coming, and Phin went to meet him and everyone looked that way. They stopped for a moment, speaking together. No one heard what passed between them, but everyone saw Phin's swinging blow start — and saw Joel grapple him and hold his arms till Phin was still.

Then Joel released the other man and came on, leaving Phin behind. Phin after a moment went on past the fire, stumbling toward the pines beyond. Joel reached the barn door and stopped there, looking at Mima, at them all.

'I chased her halfway to the river,' he said in a flat voice. 'She was dodging, hiding, whistling at me. So I came back. Phin's gone to get her.' He spoke harshly. 'Let's get this job done, quick's we can.'

There was no more laughter as they settled to the business in hand. Mily presently slipped in through the door, laughing, her hair disordered, a twinkling mirth in her eyes.

Philip Robbins said slowly: 'Phin's gone looking for you, Mily.'

'I'd ruther have him find me here,' she declared. She looked at Mima, laughing. 'Joel's fierce, ain't he!' she said, as one who speaks of a fact mutually known. 'Time he got through with me, I didn't dast come back till I'd tidied up some!' 'Bijah Hawes laughed, but no one else laughed with him. Mily sighed. 'Lah, I thought he'd be the death of me!' she declared.

Joel ripped at the ears in a savage rage, tearing the husks away. He found a red one and tossed it with the others on the pile; and no one commented on his neglect of the amenities. Phin returned. They saw him at some distance, beyond the fire. He came to the barn door. 'Mily here?' he asked. Then he saw her, and he said in a heavy tone: 'I'll get the baby, Mily. We're going home.'

He strode away toward the house. No one spoke till he returned, the baby in his arms. 'Come on,' he said.

Mily protested: 'Phin, I ain't ready to go!'

He said: 'You come along.'

She cried in a flaming rage: 'Don't try to boss me, you God-damned bound boy!'

Phin said: 'Get up, Mily.' His voice was not raised nor threatening, but she turned white as death under his steady eyes; and after a long moment she rose without a word and went with him down to the landing where his dugout lay.

When they were gone, no one said anything till suddenly Lucy Butler rose with flaming cheeks. 'I'll get the young ones, Johnny,' she said. 'We'll go home and let these folks start talking about my sister, or some of them will bust with the things they want to say!'

But when they had departed, no clamor of talk arose. That would wait, Mima thought, till wives and husbands were alone; till woman and woman got together, or man and man. She worked with a steady industry, ripping off the tough husks, tossing the ears on the growing pile; and she was glad when the last was done and they could all depart.

When she and Joel and Polly started up to Round Pond and were alone, Joel said: 'I played the fool, Mima. I'm real sorry.'

She spoke gently. 'You had to, Joel. There was no other way you could do.'

'I didn't catch her.'

She said with something between mirth and malice in her tones: 'I know it. I kind of wish you had.'

10

FOR sixteen men to raise a barn frame is a task not easily begun and finished in a day, and Joel left at first light next morning to be early on the ground. He had not spoken of Mily again, nor did Mima. When he departed, she stayed behind to finish her breakfast work, and in mid-forenoon she took Polly in her light canoe and paddled down to her mother's. Susie would stay at home and mind Polly and the other babies; and Bet and Mima and Mrs. Robbins ferried across the river and began to carry up to where the barn would stand the substantials for a noonday meal for all of the men.

Neither Bet nor Mrs. Robbins spoke of Mily, nor of Joel's brief clash with Phin; but their silence was eloquent. Mrs. Robbins had not come down to the barn after supper, staying at the house with the children; so she had not seen the incident, but Bet must have told her. Mima could imagine Bet's very words. '... threw the red ear to Joel so he had to chase her. If he hadn't it'd have been like slapping her face. And then she ran off in the woods whistling him to follow her.' And

Mima could hear her mother say: 'The little bitch! Joel'd ought to have smacked her.'

Mima was glad they did not speak of the incident to her. She did not want reassurances. Above all, she did not want Joel to guess her unhappiness. When they came to where he was working with the others, he stopped to come and kiss her, not ostentatiously but in a fashion so completely matter of course that it was more reassuring than many protestations. She asked how the work progressed, and he said:

'Good. Bela's done a master job of sizing and fitting. Everything goes together like grease. We've got the sills laid and levelled and pinned, and the cross sills and floor timbers in.' Mima saw the men hard at it, laying upon the floor timbers boards which Uncle Josiah had bought from Lermond at the mill on Oyster River. Joel stayed with her, watching while they finished. Bet and her mother had gone back for another load of eatables. The day was, for the season, fair and fine enough; but the leaves were long since gone off the hardwoods across the pond, and the sun shone thinly as though already discouraged and doubtful of its powers.

'I'd ought to be helping Mother and Bet,' Mima said doubtfully; but Joel, his arm around her waist, protested:

'No, you stay here. You're too heavy to go tramping around. They can manage; or some of us can if they can't. I'll fix the fire so she can cook over it.' There was a bonfire already burning, great logs rolled together, and chips and fragments from the long business of hewing out the barn timbers lay everywhere for fuel. Mima moved with him nearer the blaze and he fashioned a crane of forked sticks and a long pole as Mrs. Robbins and Bet returned from the river with their burdens. Mima asked in a low tone:

'Phin all right this morning, is he?'

Joel said, looking toward where Phin worked with the others: 'I dunno.' He chuckled. 'That's what Phin would say his own self. I mean, he'd say he dunno. He ain't spoke to me.' He added fairly: 'He didn't go out of his way not to — but he didn't go out of his way to, either.'

'It's too bad Mily acts so, bothering him. But he had no call to be mad at you.'

'Phin's got plenty on his mind,' Joel reminded her. 'His folks and all. He must be nigh crazy.' He said: 'They're starting to frame one side.'

They moved nearer where the work went on. Bela was everywhere, supervising the whole operation. Joel said: 'He's got every piece marked to show where it goes. See here.' He showed her where the sills had been halved together at the nearest corner, with a square mortise cut down through them both. A figure 'I' had been cut on the upper surface of the sill, beside the mortise there; and the butt of the post lying in position ready to be raised was likewise marked 'I.' 'See that tenon?' Joel said. 'When we get the post up, you'll see it'll slip down into the mortise like it had growed there.'

'Can just the men here raise it?' Mima asked.

'Long as we leave the plate to go on after, we can do it,' Joel assured her, and she said:

'I always hate to see you lift so much. You might drop a stitch in your back or something.'

He laughed reassuringly. 'I don't lift enough to hurt me,' he declared. 'If you heave and grunt enough, and the side goes up, nobody can tell whether you're lifting your weight or not.' The side that was to be raised was ready; four oak posts some eight inches square and fourteen feet long, with heavy cross timbers pinned in place, and braces mortised in, all held by treenails driven well home. 'Here we go,' he told her. 'We'll give her a h'ist and then knock off for first rum.'

He left her, and Mima shivered and wondered why. Bela called commands. 'Get your props ready,' he shouted. 'We'll put her up as far as we can and block her there till I see the butts are caught in the mortises.' Stout timbers to serve as props to hold what they might gain were at hand; and he saw that one was ready at each post. Then he placed his men. 'Jake,' he told Mima's brother, 'when we get her up, you set the brace under your post.' Jacob and David, Joel and Phin Butler worked together there. 'Matt, you set the brace on the second, and you, Ez, and Mose Hawes. Now get ready.'

The men arranged themselves. The ends of the posts had been laid on blocks before the side was framed together; so that it was easy to get a grip on them. Bela, his voice ringing, shouted: 'The short props are five feet long. Take her that high first hike. I'll count three; and we lift on three. When she's up, I'll yell "Hold." Then get the props under her, one at a time. Mose, you first, then Ez and then Matt, and Jake, you set yours last! Ready?'

Jason Ware bawled: 'Let her go!' They took their holds, four men at each post, standing two by two, facing each other with the post between them. Joel and David, taller than Phin and Jason, had the outer end of theirs. Bela counted:

'One! Two!'

No one heard him say 'three,' if he said it; for with one simultaneous grunting breath they lifted the heavy squared beams. Their backs straightened; they held the ends of the posts waist-high, pausing for a second, understanding what they were to do. Then, twisting sidewise as they lifted, getting hips and shoulders into it, they raised the end of the post high enough so that they could take its weight on their shoulders. There is a knack to such things. Each man knew it well.

Bela gasped: 'Hold!'

Joel could not look, but he heard the thump of the prop as Mose set it, felt suddenly a greater weight on his own shoulders as the men on the other post eased it down to rest on the prop. Mose shouted: 'Prop's in!' He stayed to steady his prop as one and then another was inserted; for sometimes the whole framed side might corkscrew sidewise and topple the props and come down again. Joel felt the heavy oak grind his shoulders hard before their turn came. When their prop was in, he stepped back and filled his lungs and saw Mima standing by, watching him whitely.

'You all right, Joel?' she asked.

'Fine!'

'You got all purple in the face.'

He laughed. 'I had a right to. Didn't you see me holding the whole heft of it? Dave and Phin didn't no more than half take hold!'

David cuffed him good-humoredly; but Phin scowled and turned away. Mima watched him go. 'I'm cold, Joel,' she said, and tried to smile. 'It's funny, but I feel as if I was standing in a cold, sneaking little wind.'

'You come and have a suck of rum. That'll warm you up.' Bela and Sam Hills and Philip and Josiah were making sure the props were steady; but the other men had already turned to where a keg of rum and a tub of water waited for every man to dilute his drink or not as he might choose. Mima saw Phin take his at a gulp, with no water to cool its fires. She tasted Joel's, gave the cup back to him and turned away. A thin haze had begun to obscure the sun; and though it still shone, there was scarce enough light to cast a shadow. She joined her mother and Bet by the fire where Mrs. Robbins had a kettle boiling.

'I'm making them a stew,' Mrs. Robbins said. 'Potatoes and onions and garden sass and what we had left over last night of the bear and Ez Bowen's pig. A stew goes good a day like this.'

Mima nodded. She felt tired, and this was strange to her. Usually, even heavy as she now was, she was a stranger to fatigue. The baby thumped against her diaphragm, and she clasped her arms across her breasts, trying not to let her teeth begin to chatter. Bela went for his drink and then called the men back to their task.

'She's a mite slanchwise,' he said. 'The two posts this way, the butts slid out an inch too far. Joel, take a maul, and you and David drive 'em back. The rest of us, we'll tail onto the posts and see to't they don't fall off the props.'

Mima saw Joel pick up the heavy maul, made of a section of
an oak butt eight inches in diameter and twice as long, with a
stout handle. He went toward one of the offending posts.
The squared tenons that when the posts were upright would
drop into the mortises were as yet only a little inclined downward; and Joel thought they would engage the mortises as the
posts rose. But Bela knew his business, so Joel, and David at
the next post, began to swing their heavy mauls. Joel was
careful that his blows fell fair, so that Bela's good fit should not
be marred by any splintering of the wood. Nevertheless when
they were done, Bela would not be satisfied till he had shaped
the ends with his axe again.

They got another lift, shifting their vantage as the ends of
the posts rose higher, inserting longer props to hold what they
had gained. The more nearly the posts assumed the perpendicular, the easier the lift became. When they could no longer
reach high enough with their hands, they used iron-shod poles
to push the posts higher and higher. The side which they were
raising was not rigid. There was some play to it, and the post
at which David and Joel — with Phin and Jason to help them
— were stationed was the first to reach the perpendicular.
The butt dropped six inches into place with a jarring thud, and
Joel whooped with glee. He ran around to the other side to
steady the post with his pike pole, David staying where he was;
and another post and then a third settled into place.

But the fourth caught on the edge of the mortise. While men
steadied the upright posts, Joel took the maul again and drove
the bottom of the one which was refractory a half inch inward
till it dropped heavily into place. Bela had stay-laths ready,
and the men with pike poles steadied the side, keeping it
perpendicular, while he braced and secured it to stand till
the other side should have been raised. Then cross timbers
would bind them together permanently, to endure the gales
and buffets of a hundred years.

Joel turned back to Mima by the fire, while the other men
crowded toward the rum. 'Warm now?' he asked.

She was not. She was cold in her very bones, and without reason. The fire spread a circle of heat around it so that Mrs. Robbins shielded her face as she tended the stew; and Mima stood within this circle, so near that her cheeks felt scorched. 'I don't know what's the matter with me, Joel,' she confessed, smiling ruefully. 'Something I et, maybe; but I feel all right, only I'm cold, like when you wake cold in the night and you're still half asleep and can't do anything about it.'

'Want to go home? Go ahead,' he urged. 'Aunt Mima and Bet can feed the lot of us.'

'I don't want to leave you,' she confessed. 'I don't ever want to leave you, Joel.'

He laughed warmly. 'You're never going to. We're going to be together all our lives, Mima.' He said: 'I'll fetch you some rum,' and he did, and she drank it and felt it burn pleasantly in her stomach.

'I'm all right,' she assured him. 'Don't you fret about me.'

'You could go along home as well as not.'

'I don't want to — not till you do.'

'We're going to be at it all day, right up to dark, maybe.'

'I might go after dinner,' she admitted. 'I'll wait and see how I feel. I don't want to go till the heavy lifting's done, anyways. You be careful, Joel.'

He reassured her, and went back to help with the task of framing the other side. Once that was raised, the hardest work would be done. The inside posts and the cross beams that held the whole together would go into place one by one. Under Bela's orders men carried four more posts and laid them ready on the barn floor, their inner ends propped up on blocks, their butts overhanging the mortises into which they would fit; and Bela supervised the placing of the cross timbers and braces.

'We'll get this up and then we'll eat,' he promised them. 'Aunt Mima's stew smells so good it takes my mind off the job.'

Mima, standing by the fire, watched the light mauls rise and fall as the treenails were driven home. The sun was gone now, the sky all overcast with an increasing haze that came from nowhere and grew thicker all the time. She thought it might snow tonight; might even snow today, before dark. Certainly if it were colder it would snow. She herself was cold. A damp chill pierced her through and through, but she knew that in fact the day was, for November, warm.

The side was framed, and Bela stationed the men for the first lift. Mima heard his shout as the groups took their places, and the ends of the posts rose and were propped again. The first lift was in many ways the hardest, since it involved rising from a stooping position, then changing grips and lifting again till the heavy timber came shoulder-high; so now there was a recess and a drink of rum around, while Bela made sure the posts were properly placed. This time too it was necessary to use the mauls to correct a slight misplacement, but two or three blows promised to be enough. David and Joel took their positions; the other men took their stands by the props to steady them.

Joel was at the butt of the post nearest what would be the front of the barn, his position a little cramped by a huge boulder with a sloping side just behind him. Mima, watching him, unconsciously moved a little nearer. Phin and Jacob were at the raised end of the post, Jacob holding the prop, Phin with his shoulder braced against the timber. At the next post, Jason Ware and Ez Bowen started some good-natured scuffling, their voices loud with rum. The men were inattentive, grouped along the posts, standing at ease. Joel swung the maul.

As the blow struck, and for no reason that was apparent, the prop which supported the inner end of the post tipped sidewise and let go. The whole side, thus thrown off plumb, slewed ponderously; and another prop fell. The men with shouts and warning cries tried to hold the side, and saw they could not, and jumped clear. Something knocked Jacob off the barn floor, and he fell sprawling on the ground beyond the sill.

Matt Hawes tripped and fell and his head cracked hard on the boards of the floor.

The side fell with a slight pivoting motion, and the post which Joel had been trying to drive back with the maul slid toward him two or three feet. The heavy timber framework came down with a thundering crash, men scattering every way; but Joel did not move. When he saw the first prop fall, he had tried to leap aside, but that boulder at his back, cramping his position, betrayed him. He bumped against it, and the end of the heavy timber slid out over the sill as the side pivoted, and pinned his leg against the boulder, holding it there.

Joel looked down at his leg stupidly. The maul dropped out of his hand. He tried to lift the timber, leaning down, tugging at it. His leg was firmly pinned.

Mima reached him, holding him up. All the color was gone out of his face; but he managed to smile at her.

'I'm all right,' he said thickly. 'It just pinched my leg some.' He looked down. 'It didn't come all the way,' he said. 'If it had, it'd have smashed everything.'

Mima as though from far away heard Jake screaming. 'He pushed me!' Jake cried. 'Phin kicked the prop and pushed me, God damn his soul!'

The men were here! Philip Robbins said sharply: 'Grab a hold, everybody. Pull that timber back. It's caught his leg.'

Joel said, hoarse with shock and pain: 'Somebody shut Jake up. He hadn't ought to say that. Phin never meant to.'

They ignored him. Their united strength slid the post back far enough so that he could pull his leg free. He tried to take a step and crumpled in Mima's arms.

'Hell!' he said. 'The God-damned thing's broken!'

Then he grinned feebly and closed his eyes and slumped down on the ground, too heavy for her to support. Philip knelt beside him. Mima pillowed his head on her knees. Jason Ware said: 'Give him some rum.' Mrs. Robbins somewhere cried: 'Jake, you shut your mouth!' Jacob insisted shrilly:

'I tell you, he did!' Mima heard many voices, saying many things. Her perceptions were curiously clear. The noise and confusion was composed of many elements, cries and movements; but she heard the voices as though each word was spoken in silence, and she saw everything. Her father was slitting away Joel's bear-skin leggings from foot to knee, feeling the bruised red flesh. Jason brought rum, and she poured it between Joel's lips, and he coughed and opened his eyes.

Mrs. Robbins said sharply: 'Let me tend him. Broke, is it, Philip? I've handled broken bones.' She knelt by her husband's side. 'Pull his foot, pull the leg out as hard as you can, so the broke ends won't cut him, or maybe come through.' She spoke over her shoulder to the others. 'Get some slabs. We'll stretch it and get it splinted and get him home.'

Mima heard herself ask: 'Is he hurt bad?'

Her mother said briskly: 'It might be a sight worse. He'll be as good as ever three months from now.'

Three months from now? Mima saw something white on Joel's shirt. It disappeared, but another flake fell to take its place. The baby stirred within her, kicking at Joel's head pillowed on her body. Three months from now, Joel would be as well as ever, and the baby would be here.

But another flake fell on Joel's cheek. It had begun to snow. Winter was begun. Three months of winter lay ahead before Joel would be well again.

The snow continued implacably to fall. It came one flake at a time, with no vehemence, not intrusively; and unless you looked for it, it was hardly noticeable. Mima would always remember that faint whisper of snow which fell while her mother tended Joel here.

'Do you know what to do for him?' she asked.

'Guess't I do,' Mrs. Robbins assured her. 'My father was a bone-setter, and I've seen him fix a broken leg. The main thing is to stretch it and keep it stretched, so it won't be shorter than the other one when it heals. And splint it so it won't bend where it shouldn't. If the bones come through, it's bad sometimes; but they didn't, and they won't now.' Joel found Mima's hand and held to it, grinning up at her; and Mrs. Robbins said:

'You lay still, Joel. We'll fix you up right here, before we take you home.' She called to her son: 'Jake, you run home and fetch that bleach of linen on the shelf back of our bed.'

Jacob departed on the run, and she looked up at the men standing helplessly around. Matt Hawes was there, blood on his temple where it had struck when he fell. 'You all right, Matt?' she asked.

'Yes, marm.'

'You help me here, then,' she said. 'Hold his foot. Keep a pull on it. Don't let it move, and don't pull too hard yet.' She spoke to her husband. 'You hold his knee, Robbins. Just hold it till we get some splints ready.'

She left them and took Bela and set him to making splints of the size and shape she desired. His axe clip-clopped as he worked, neat and dextrously. Joel meanwhile was sweating with pain, holding Mima's hand, grinning up at her as he lay with his head in her lap. 'Bijah brought him more rum, and he drank it gratefully; and Phin Butler came to stand beside him, looking down.

'Guess't you know I didn't go to do it, Joel,' he said in a slow tone. 'If you don't know it, it's no use my telling you.'

Joel said cordially: 'Sure I know, Phin. Don't bother about what Jake says. I know.'

'I dunno just what did happen,' Phin confessed. 'Maybe I'd drunk too much rum or something; or I might have lost my balance; but I didn't go to.'

'Sure,' Joel repeated; and Mima looked up at Phin and said quietly:

'Nobody's blaming you, Phin. Jake was excited; that's all. He didn't mean it. It's all right.'

Bela and Mrs. Robbins came with the splints prepared; and Bela heard Phin and he said in some indignation:

'Matter of fact, if we'd all be'n hanging on to the posts the way we was supposed to, we could have held 'em. There was too much skylarking going on.'

Philip Robbins commented: 'There've been times I thought rum and raisings didn't mix; but they always have gone together. Likely they always will.'

Mrs. Robbins tried the splints and told Bela to shorten them, to narrow them a little. 'And work 'em out some right here,' she said, marking a spot with her thumb. 'That's where his knee's got to come.'

Joel said cheerfully: 'You get all that timber on me and I might full as well have a peg leg.'

'Peg leg fiddlesticks!' Mrs. Robbins told him. 'You'll be as spry as ever, come spring.'

A flake of snow touched Mima's cheek. The day was darker, with a cold dampness in the air; but Mima was no longer cold. Bet fetched a mug of stew for Joel to eat; and Mrs. Robbins said: 'The rest of you might full as well be eating too. Here comes Jake. I'll call for all the help I need.'

Some of the men turned away, but Matt and Jason and Philip stayed. Bela brought the splints, and after some further fitting they were ready. Mrs. Robbins tore the linen into strips.

'Now we'll set it,' she said. 'Joel, you want some more rum. This is going to hurt the gizzard out of you.'

'I'll hold on to Mima's hand,' he told her. 'She'll do me more good than rum.'

'High time you found that out,' she agreed. 'Mima, get yourself out from under his head. I want Pa to hold him so we'll have a purchase to pull against.' She added: 'You can stay where he can hold on to you.'

Mima gave place to her father, and Philip knelt to hold Joel's thigh, and Matt put a tension on Joel's foot while Mrs. Robbins twisted the leg to suit her, making them pull and then ease. Joel's hand tightened hard on Mima's and then loosed again.

Mrs. Robbins at last was satisfied. 'There's two bones in there,' she explained. 'One of 'em's right, I sh'd judge, and we'll have to resk the other. I guess it'll do.' She looked at Joel and saw his eyes rolled up and she said: 'Skies above, he's fainted! Well, no matter! He'll come around, and what he don't feel won't hurt him.' Her hands were as busy as her tongue. Mima, watching them, felt in her own leg the agony that racked Joel; and the baby in her stirred and kicked and turned.

'Trying to get out and help his father,' she thought, and in her thoughts said soothingly: 'Don't fret, baby. He'll be fine — come spring.'

But it was snowing now, and spring was months away.

Bela, at Mrs. Robbins' instruction, had made the splints long enough to project beyond the sole of Joel's foot and to extend above his knee. Careful not to shut off the circulation, she nevertheless bound them in such a way that the leg was held at full stretch, with bands of linen passing around heel and toe and over the projecting ends of the splints. The business was a long one. Joel came back to consciousness again, and cursed them with a cheerful violence, and Mrs. Robbins, seeing her task almost completed, laughed at him.

'Takes a man to make a fuss,' she said. 'I'd like to know what they'd do if they had to have babies! There, I guess that'll do. Now we'll get you home.'

They contrived a litter, and Matt and Jason carried Joel down to the water's edge. Joel by that time was himself again. 'This is one way to get out of helping raise the barn,' he said, grinning. 'I dunno but it's worth it. You two better hurry and get back and go at it again. You'll have to hump to get it up by dark.'

Jason said in a rough tenderness: 'You hold your water, Joel. We'll take care of you first. Barns can wait.' And Matt said affectionately:

'You never dodged work yet, Joel.'

They put him in Jason's big dugout and Jason paddled him up the river and across Round Pond, while Mima and Matt and Mrs. Robbins kept pace with them in another float, and Philip and Jacob went ahead. When they came to the cabin, Jason and Matt carrying the litter, the fire had already been blown to life and a cheerful blaze was crackling. They put Joel in bed, and he lay helpless there; and Mrs. Robbins sent the men away.

'Go on back and give Josiah a hand,' she said sharply. 'We can manage here, get things straightened out.'

'I'll go by and send my Polly over,' Jason offered; but Mrs. Robbins said:

'No need. There ain't a living thing to do.'

Mima remembered that baby Polly was still at her father's house and spoke of it; and Jacob went to bring her home. Before he returned, Mrs. Robbins and Mima had made Joel comfortable. Little Polly was puzzled by the fact that her father lay so white and helpless. Joel slept a little, and Polly, warned to quiet, whispered at her play while Mrs. Robbins and Mima talked in low tones about what lay ahead.

'He'll do fine,' Mrs. Robbins assured Mima. 'But he might run a fever for two-three days. All you have to do is sponge him off with cold water and don't wipe him dry. That will cool him; and rum helps too. Rum's handy to have around. It warms you up when you're cold, and it cools you off when you're hot.' She chuckled agreeably. 'I wouldn't admit it to yore pa, and I've give him fits all his life every time he took too much; but if there's anything wrong with you, one way or another, a good drink of rum will help it.' She added briskly: 'One drink, or maybe two. Three's enough and four is nasty, as they say.'

'Same as everything else,' Mima commented. 'Too much of anything is bad. Even too much water'll drown you.'

'Trouble is with a man,' the older woman reflected, 'they're never satisfied with enough. They find something they like and they use it to death, till it turns on 'em, or they get sick of it.' Her voice was hushed, not to disturb the sleeping man. They were by the fire, Mima alert for any sound from Joel.

'Will he be three months?' she asked.

'He'll be a long time,' her mother said. 'Chances are he'll be thinking he can stand his weight on that leg in two-three weeks; but don't you let him. Bela can make him a pair of crutches, and the longer he keeps off that foot the better, till the bones are mended.'

'Will his leg be tied up that way all the time?'

'I wouldn't want to touch it for two weeks anyway,' Mrs. Robbins declared. 'Unless it starts going to sleep on him. Then I might have to ease it a little.'

Mima went to bring in a fresh log for the fire. There was a small pile of logs near the door, each one four or five feet long, some of them a foot thick. Mrs. Robbins did not move to help her; but she watched thoughtfully. Mima carried the log in her arms like a baby; she thrust one end in through the front of the fireplace and out through the open jamb, dropped the other end on the fire, took her broom made of birch shoots and brushed up the hearth. Her mother said:

'I'd have helped you, but I wanted to see how you'd manage. You'll have to do plenty of that this winter. The menfolks will help all they can, cutting firewood for you and all; but they can't be here to mend the fire for you.'

'I'll get along.'

'Don't strain yourself. You're carrying a baby, you know.'

Mima smiled. 'I ain't likely to forget. He's been scrabbling around like a salmon on a spear ever since Joel got hurt.'

'Mine were always lively as crickets,' Mrs. Robbins agreed. 'I dunno but you was the worst of the lot.' She said: 'You'll have a hard time here alone. Somebody better come stay with you.'

Mima said: 'I'll be fine. I'll get Bela to make a chair Joel can set in, out here. He won't want to lay abed all the time.

He can take care of Polly and keep her happy. I won't have to go out only to look after the sheep, and get wood, and fetch meat from the rack around the other side of the house.'

'You'd ought to have Sue, or Jake, or someone.'

Mima said: 'I want to do it myself. I want to take care of him.'

'I'll have Jake bring you up milk for Polly.'

'She don't have to have it.'

'She might as well. We don't use all we get, and the more milk she has, the less she'll need of other things. We're all going to be short before spring.'

'We've got enough to get along. We'll eat what we have and make it do, clean our plates.' Mima smiled. 'Many's the time I've heard you say that, since we were young ones.'

'I hate to see anything wasted,' the older woman agreed. Joel waked and called, and Mima went in to him, sitting on the side of the bed, leaning down to kiss him. He held her close for a moment, tenderly.

'This is going to be hard on you, Mima,' he said.

'I'll like taking care of you.' She smiled. 'It'll be the same as having two babies.' Polly heard her father's voice and came in, and Mrs. Robbins stood in the doorway, watching them all. Polly cooed over her father, crawling across the bed; and Mima caught her, warning her. 'Daddy's leg's hurt, Polly,' she said. 'Don't touch it.'

Polly shook her head vehemently, wide-eyed. 'No, no,' she promised. 'No! No!' But immediately she crawled across the splinted leg to kiss him, and Joel laughed and said: 'It's all right. I'd let her jump up and down on it for a kiss.'

Mrs. Robbins made a scornful sound. 'You always would make a fool of yourself to get a girl to kiss you. If you hadn't chased Mily off into the woods last night, you wouldn't be laid up now. I hope you're satisfied!'

Joel protested: 'Phin didn't do it on purpose!'

'Jake says so!'

'Jake's wrong! For one thing, Phin couldn't have figured out it would have happened just the way it did. And I don't believe he'd do it, anyway.'

'Well, if he did,' Mrs. Robbins said furiously, 'I don't know as I blame him! Mily's a fool. But you didn't have to let her make a fool out of you!'

Mima stroked Joel's brow. 'He's hot, Mother,' she said. 'I'm going to get some water, make him cool. You leave him be.' She spoke without heat, firmly, rising to pass her mother in the door; but Mrs. Robbins was not silenced.

'You're as bad as him,' she declared, her own words feeding her indignation. 'Letting him carry on so! You'd ought to have brought him up short, long ago. But there, you was so crazy about him from the first minute you saw him that nobody could talk a word of sense into you.'

Mima smiled at Joel. 'I still am,' she said. 'No matter how many times he chases Mily through the woods!'

'Hah!' Mrs. Robbins blew through her nose expressively. 'He'll catch her, one of these days.'

'Maybe,' Mima assented laughingly. 'If he does, she'll get a sight better than she deserves. Don't fret Joel now, Mother. I'll go get some cold water.'

She left them together, and Mrs. Robbins said triumphantly: 'Well, one thing's sure, you won't be running after Mily or anybody else for a while.' She said: 'Mima's a sight too good for you, Joel — even if she is my daughter.'

Joel told her quietly: 'I know. I've always known that. But — she's doing a job on me, Aunt Mima. I'm better than I was, and I aim to be better all the time.'

She relented, her eyes twinkling. 'You've got the makings,' she assented. 'If I was Mima's age I'd feel the same as she does about you. You suited me to a trifle, first day you came.' She touched his forehead. 'Skies above, you are hot!' she agreed. 'But we'll cool you down.'

Jason and Matt stopped on their way home soon after dark,

to see if they were needed. The barn frame was all in place, they said, except for the rafters. 'We kept things humping after we got rid of you,' Jason reported. 'Josiah figures him and Bela and two-three others can handle the rest of it.'

'Snowing, is it?' Joel asked.

'No, just about what you saw, a little white on the ground.' Jason told Mima: 'I'll get you out some firewood in the morning.' He said cheerfully: 'The Royal Mess always did stick together. Need anything tonight?'

'I'm a-staying,' Mrs. Robbins told him.

'Then you're all fixed,' Jason agreed; and he and Matt went on their way.

After supper, Mima put Polly to bed, and Mrs. Robbins made up the bed in the garret. 'I guess you'll want to sleep with him,' she said.

'Yes,' Mima agreed.

'Well, call me if you need me,' Mrs. Robbins bade her. She came to feel Joel's brow. 'He's hot, but he'll do. Don't keep him awake more than you can help.'

'I won't,' Mima promised.

When her mother was abed, she banked the fire and went into the bedroom. In bed, warm beside him, she took Joel's head on her shoulder. 'There!' she whispered. 'You're going to sleep right there, Joel.'

'You'll get cramped. I'll keep you awake.'

'I want you in my arms.'

He said: 'It's going to be bad, Mima. Everybody'll help; but you'll have a lot to do.'

'I want to do everything I can,' she told him. 'It's doing things for people makes you love them, Joel. That's why mothers love their babies. It's what you do for folks, not what they do for you.' She laughed, a little breathlessly. 'I'm going to be so good to you you'll hate me for it, but it will make me love you all the more.'

He kissed her throat. 'You've got everything that's good and fine in you.'

'Sleep!' she whispered. 'Go to sleep, Joel. I'll take care of you.' Long after he was asleep, breathing like a baby, his head heavy on her shoulder, she lay wide awake, holding him close. Polly slept in the small bed within reach of her hand. Joel slept in her arms. The new baby, big below her heart, lay quiet there. Her love embraced them all.

11

THE morning was bright with sun and the thin snow of the day before vanished in its first warm rays. There was the deceptive mildness of Indian summer in the air. Mima plunged into her daily tasks, reorganizing her household to meet the situation created by Joel's helplessness.

Mrs. Robbins stayed till the third day, when Joel's temperature returned to normal. 'All there is to do now is let that leg take its time,' she said. 'I'll come up every two-three days, Mima; and Sis and Jess are handy one direction and Jason and Polly the other, if you need anyone.'

'We're all right,' Mima insisted. 'We'll be fine.'

But she had no desire to put their friendly solicitudes aside; and at first she had company almost every day. Uncle Josiah finished his barn and came to see them before departing to the westward for the winter.

'I'll be here early in the spring,' he promised. 'Bela's going to build a house for me this winter, have it all ready; and if he can't make it, we'll live in the barn till it's done.' He told Joel:

'I'm real sorry about your leg, Joel; but I don't know how it could be helped.'

'Bound to happen,' Joel agreed. 'I don't want Phin feeling bad about it.'

'Guess't nobody blames him,' Josiah agreed, and said good-bye and went his way.

On the sixth day Bela came and built an easychair and a pair of crutches, so that Joel could come out into the big room every morning and sit with his leg stiffly extended on a rest Bela fashioned for the purpose, playing with Polly and watching Mima as she went about her tasks. Jason or Matt stopped in almost every day, and Jess and Sis came often, in the late afternoons when her pupils had gone home. Her school was well established now, and even Prance Bowen approved. She had brought her Sally the first time herself, walking the two miles from Ezra's farm and carrying Sally most of the way. Sis described to Mima and Joel her arrival. 'Her nose was in the air,' she said, 'so high and mighty. But I think really she was scared, because as soon as she saw how nice we were fixed she unbent right away; and she's going to send Sally every day she can. She'll bring her up to Dave's, or Ez will, before time for them to start to school.' And Sis told other tales, about her pupils; how Dave's Jason rebelled at learning his A-B-Abs and wanted to start reading right away; how little Jimmy Butler came swaggering through the woods alone the first day. 'He's only five,' Sis said. 'But he's the oldest at their house, and he's helped Lucy so much he already feels like a man. He has the sturdiest little back.' She said school let out the day Jess caught a bear in his trap on the hill south of the house, and they all went to see him dress the animal. Mima, watching Sis, saw her eyes glowing happily as she talked; and at some of her stories of the children Joel laughed till his sides ached.

One day in the second week in November, Colonel Wheaton unexpectedly appeared. He offered Joel rough sympathy.

'But it served you right, from all I hear,' he said, with a gust of laughter. 'There's been other men played the fool at huskings and didn't get off so easy. Some of 'em had to marry the gal!'

Before Joel could speak, Mima said strongly: 'Colonel, I'm sick and tired of that talk. It don't hurt me and Joel; but it can do a heap of hurt to Phin and Mily, and that ain't right. Mily was just carrying on the way everybody does at a husking, and Phin wouldn't hurt a fly — much less Joel. You hush up!'

Colonel Wheaton looked uncomfortable — and wrathful too. 'God's Nails and Britches, can't a man have a joke?' he protested. 'You don't have to get your dander up. I ain't blaming Joel!'

'You better not,' she assured him. 'Nor don't go blaming Phin either. If the rest of them had been holding on the way they was supposed to, it wouldn't have happened; but I'm not blaming the whole of Sterlingtown.' She added, smiling suddenly at Joel: 'Besides, I'm going to like having him in the house all winter instead of off after moose or something!'

'Sho,' the Colonel insisted, 'I didn't mean it. If I'd really thought Joel was shining up to Mily — or any other trollop — I'd have come up here and combed his hide with a birch shoot before now. I've told him long ago he'd better keep his shoes under his own bed or he'd have me on his tail.'

Joel said, grinning derisively: 'That's right! It's the only thing that's kept me toeing the mark, being so scared of you.' His arm around Mima's waist, he drew her close, his head against her side; and her hand pressed against his cheek. He asked: 'Send our tax petition along, did you, Colonel? Or do you aim to take it when you go?'

'I sent it,' Colonel Wheaton explained. 'I'm not going. Too much to do at home this winter. They're sending Oliver Robbins to get a permit to name somebody in my place. The petition'll be taken care of all right.' He added: ''Lish Partridge wants to buy some of my land up here, all of it maybe.

I come up to see how he'd made out, so far, renting. He says he'll give notes. Think he can make a go of it?'

'Certain,' Joel declared. ''Lish is a worker.'

'He didn't make a crop this year, had to pull out for the winter.'

'The frost hit him harder than most,' Joel explained. 'But he'll do all right, give him a chance.'

Mima asked: 'Are the Butlers still living in Uncle Oliver's barn?'

The Colonel nodded. 'But Phin's moving down there,' he said. They had not heard this, and he explained: 'He talked to me. There's a house empty that he can get for the winter, and he can take his folks in to live with them. Phin figures to hire out and earn enough to get along.'

Joel looked at Mima. 'We'll be sorry to lose Phin up here,' he said. 'He's a good man. Slow in his judgments, but a good man.' Colonel Wheaton nodded, and Mima said thoughtfully:

'Phin's fine to do that. He'd rather stay here. He's put a lot of work on his place up-river.'

'He can hire out, down below,' Colonel Wheaton repeated. 'He can make more hiring out than he can farming. He couldn't fetch his father and mother up here. There isn't even a garret in his house. Johnny's got room, but he won't have them — so Phin's the Judas, has to carry the whole load.'

'He'll be a better man doing it,' Mima said surely. 'A man gets strong and fine by — seeing his job and trying to do it and not dodging.'

Joel suggested: 'But Mily'll be a sight happier down there. She gets lonesome up here all alone. There's some women don't belong to be alone. They stew in their own juice. Let Mily have folks around her that she can see when she's a mind to, and she'll be fine.'

Mima moved away to some household task, her eyes shadowed as they were apt to be when she thought of Mily. The

Colonel stayed in talk with Joel a while; and when he was gone, Joel asked uncomfortably:

'Mima, do you think Phin's pulling out of here account of the talk about him and me?'

She did not believe this was the case. 'I think it's just so he can take better care of his folks,' she said. 'He's probably figured it out that way.'

Before their final departure for Thomaston, Phin and Mily came to the cabin. Joel and Mima had no warning of their coming till Mima heard Mily's voice outside. She went to open the door, and she saw a malicious triumph in Mily's eyes, and the other cried:

'We've come to say good-bye, Mima! We're moving to town.'

Mima said: 'Come in. It's real raw. Morning, Phin. Colonel Wheaton told us you were going to move. We'll miss you up here.'

Mily went past her to where Joel sat in his new chair. She was exclamatory with sympathy; and Phin grasped Mima's hand at the door.

'I hate it, pulling out,' he admitted. 'But I kind of had to. I've got a chance to work for Lermond, and it makes it so I can take care of the folks.'

'You'll come back some day.'

'I dunno. It don't seem so now.'

He came in, and Mima shut the door, and Mily drew a chair near Joel's her tongue rattling merrily. 'Phin took the baby down, day before yesterday,' she said. 'To stay with Ma. Pa's gone to Boston to see about a representative in place of Colonel Wheaton. We're going to live in a house with rooms in it, Mima, bigger than this, and people around and a chance to talk to someone! It's pretty near killed me up here never seeing anybody. Or hardly ever.' She looked at Joel, laughing for no reason. 'You've got a nice house, Mima!' she said. 'Can I look around?' She rose to inspect the buttery and then the bedroom. 'Why, it's real pretty,' she said, in surprised tones. 'That's an awful pretty mirror.' Small Polly watched her with wide eyes and came to Mima's knees and clung there; and Mima felt her trembling and swept the baby up in her arms. 'Well, you'll have a hard time this winter, I guess,' Mily decided. 'With Joel laid up and you having to do everything. Don't you work too hard, Mima. You strain yourself and you'll mark the baby. I heard about a woman once had a baby . . .' She laughed, as though at a jest she alone could appreciate. 'Nobody knew who the father was, only her, and she wouldn't tell. But a married man that lived near her broke his arm, and when the baby was born it had a broken arm too! So everybody claimed he was the one!' She warned Mima gaily: 'So you look out. They say if you even think too much about it, it will mark the baby.' She patted Joel's shoulder. 'I don't dare feel as sorry for you as I want to, Joel, for fear my baby will be born with a broken leg! Lah! If that happened, just think what folks would say about you and me!'

Joel grinned, and Mima held Polly close as though the baby warm against her breast could heal the wounds left by Mily's barbed chatter, and Phin said: 'Your leg's been on my mind, Joel. I might have been to blame some, and it bothers me.' Mima noticed that his head no longer pumped when he talked.

Mily cried: 'Maybe even your thinking about it will mark my baby, Phin! Do you reckon it could?'

Phin looked at her in a slow reprobation, and Joel said: 'Forget about it, Phin. My leg's pretty near all right already. It's been two weeks. I'll be on it again in no time.'

'I hadn't ought to have drunk so much rum that day,' Phin confessed. 'It had made me kind of shaky.'

'He was mad at me,' Mily explained with a malicious enjoyment. 'Because I throwed you that red ear, Joel. You mind he tried to fight you, and you handled him. He went and got himself drunk to get even with me. He wanted to whop me that night, but he didn't dast. But he wouldn't break your leg a-purpose.' She looked at Mima with innocent eyes. 'He wouldn't have any cause to, would he?'

Mima's lips were dry. She managed to smile, and Polly clung to her, and Joel watched them both; and Phin suddenly rose.

'We'll have to be going,' he said. 'But Joel, don't hold it against me.' There was a new strength in the man.

Joel extended his hand. 'I don't, Phin. It was an accident. You come up this winter, and we'll go kill some moose together.'

'I'll do that, if I get some time.'

Mily made more of a to-do about her good-byes. Mima thought for a moment that she would kiss Joel; but she did not. She did kiss Mima. 'And come see us,' she said. 'First time you're down. You've been real good to us. I don't know how I'd have stayed up here this long if it wasn't for seeing you — or Joel anyway — once in a while.'

She would have kissed Polly too, but Polly hid behind her father; and when the last good-byes were said and they were gone and the door closed, Polly said: 'She dawn! Aw dawn!' She nodded in vigorous assent to her own words, and sighed with a great relief.

Joel chuckled. 'Polly doesn't like Mily,' he commented. Mima put a log on the fire; and he said: 'Makes me mad to see you have to do that!'

'It doesn't hurt me.'

He said after a moment, in a puzzled tone: 'Mily talked funny, Mima. As if she was — trying to get us mad or something.'

'Did she? She didn't bother me, Joel.'

'What was she getting at?'

Mima shook her head. 'I didn't pay any attention. Phin will make a man. Joel, I'm a mind to cook some pigeons for supper. What do you think? Seems like they'd go good.'

'They would, for a fact,' he agreed, still abstracted. She saw his concern, and on her way past his chair to the trap door that led down cellar, she stopped to kiss him and to say: 'Don't worry about Mily, Joel. She doesn't bother me.'

* * * * *

For these first two weeks after Joel was hurt, the weather was treacherously warm and mild; and there was not a day without some visitor. Mrs. Robbins came up the pond to see how Joel did, and at the end of a week, with Philip and Jess to help her, she readjusted the splint more to her liking. Jason and his Polly, Matt and Sally, came often; and they planned ways to help Mima get along. The most immediate problem was firewood. Joel during the summer supplied the pile outside the door a few days at a time; but in preparation for the approach of winter he had felled trees between the house and the pond, dropping them right and left away from the path, leaving them to dry where they fell so that they were now fit to burn. They were pines, of good growth, sometimes two feet through at the butts. Hardwood would have made better fuel; but Joel wished to clear the slope between the house and the pond, and pine made a roaring hot fire, and the wood once down might as well be used. He had also, at odd times, knocked over what few oaks and maples grew near the house, and a few birches which had not yet been smothered by the pines; so that there was within two hundred yards enough wood already on the ground to carry them easily through the winter.

But the felled trees needed to be worked up into usable lengths, and to be brought conveniently near; and Jason and Matt came and spent two days at this task. Sally and Polly came with them, Polly bringing her baby, Sally now very proud of the fact that she began to show hers. The men carried Joel's chair out into the sun where he could watch them work, and the three wives visited together.

Jess and Sis came the second day to work with them; and when the men were done, there was a great pile of logs ready to burn, and Mima had only to carry wood in as she needed it.

Joel protested at her doing that. 'I'll get them to keep a pile of it inside, in the corner back of the oven,' he suggested. 'It will save you that much.'

But Mima said: 'Don't you, Joel! They've got their own work to 'tend to; and they've done a-plenty. I can always make out.'

Yet she was surprised to find out how much there was in fact to do. She had never thought of herself as working hard; but when now to her routine were added the things Joel had always done and which could not now be left undone, she had few minutes during the day when she could sit down and do just nothing without feeling a sense of guilt at thought of some neglected task. In the house there were, as always, meals to be prepared, and eaten, and cleaned up after; there was Polly to be kept clean and fed and happy; there was the floor to sweep, bedding to be aired, beds to be made; and there was always Joel for whom she delighted to do small services. His splints extended downward below his foot, and when he went on crutches this extension was treacherously likely to catch on things. She was always fearful when he moved about the house; and when it was necessary for him to go out-of-doors, she hovered beside him, her hand under his arm, to save him from the fall she dreaded.

She had to carry in the wood she needed; and the pine burned so fast that this was a task constantly recurring. Each time it taxed her strength. The logs too heavy to carry, she could roll, up-ending them through the door, then rolling them across the floor and letting them drop to the ground level and working them into the fireplace endwise through the open jamb, using a short stick like a lever to pry them in as far as they would go. They ploughed through the ashes and embers and half-burned stuff, scattering it across the hearth and out on the ground, so that each time she fed the fire, the house was filled with smoke, and she had to sweep up the ashes afterward. Also, the logs were so long that the ends projected through the open jamb. She could not pry them all the way in until after their inner ends had burned away; and the fire sometimes worked along them till it was outside the hearth as well as in, and the log

walls of the cabin, beyond the protecting backing of stones and
bricks laid up in clay, began to char, so that she lived in fear
they would catch fire. Once in the night she was wakened by a
flickering light in the other room, and sprang out of bed with
her heart pounding; but it was only that a little flame had come
up through the ashes with which she had banked the fire for
the night, and was playing there.

Out-of-doors, her chores were not many. They had acquired
a heifer, but Joel before he was hurt had driven it down to
Seven-Tree Pond to be housed in Philip's barn for the winter;
so Mima need not have it on her mind. But the sheep were in
their fold, and Jess and Bela one day tied them up and boated
them down to Warren to be served, according to the terms of
Joel's bargain with William Boggs. To feed them through
the winter, Joel had cut hay on the meadows and stacked it on
top of the shelter house he had built for them and all around
it on three sides; but when they were brought back, Mima had
to throw some hay to them every day. Their constant, flat,
inane baa-ing sounded all day long, and the fact that they
always fled in hysterical panic when she approached their pen
irritated her so intensely that she dreaded going down to them.
Once in October Joel had seen bear tracks outside the fold,
and there were times when Mima wished the bear would return
and kill them all!

She had another daily task which became more and more of
a burden. All the water they used had to be carried from the
spring. Joel had till now done this chore, except for an occasional pailful which she brought when he was not at the house;
but now she had to carry it all, and she was surprised to find
how much they used — cooking, washing, drinking — in the
course of a day. To make the task easier, Joel whittled out of a
piece of bass wood a bucket yoke, which fitted around the back
of her neck and rested on her shoulders, with thongs depending
from the projecting arms, and forked sticks on the ends to serve
as hooks in which the bails of the buckets could be hung. This

took the worst strain off her arms and hands; but two full pails still made a heavy load for her.

With all her activities, she went to bed every night desperately tired, woke in the morning not adequately rested; but Joel, though he might guess this, never knew it from her. There was a steady readiness and cheerfulness in Mima, and if she was where he could see her she met each task serenely, laughing at her own awkwardness in handling the great logs and feeding the fire, telling him her adventures with the sheep in such terms that he roared with amusement. He resented his own helplessness and sometimes fretted at it, and she sought ways to cheer him. She learned to imitate the silly sheep, her mouth and jaw protruded, baa-ing absurdly, grinding her jaw sidewise as they did in quick, nervous rumination, moving with stiff bounds as they did when they fled at sight of her. Small Polly hugely enjoyed this game, screaming with mirth, and so did Joel too.

In the house she could be cheerful; but outside, where he could not see her, sometimes she let go. Once she went to the spring and, with two pails of water hung from the neck yoke, trudging like a beast of burden, she started back up the steep path. This was late in November, and her baby — they still called it January — was heavy in her. Her foot caught in a bared root and she stumbled and fell to her knees, and the buckets struck the ground and spilled their contents. The water ran down the path in which she knelt, wetting her skirts, and she scrambled aside and in a sudden rage beat on the ground with her fists, tears in her eyes, weeping in a silent fury. But Joel, since she had left the door of the house open, heard her fall and called: 'All right, Mima?'

So she had to answer him. 'All right,' she assured him. 'Just dropped a bucket, that's all.' She hurried to fill them at the spring again and came back to the house dry-eyed and smiling.

Once at the sheep pen, throwing hay to the vapid creatures, she stuck a brier in her hand; and the sight of the swelling red drop of blood made her so sorry for herself she wanted to cry.

She went on past the fold to the brook and sat alone a while there, telling herself how lucky she was because this was November and there was nothing to do except use up their accumulated wood and their stored supplies. 'Just suppose you had to hoe corn all day in the sun,' she said in a chiding whisper. 'Or to plant it, or to sow the rye and drag it in, or to swing a scythe.' In summer everyone was busy. No one would have had time to come and help her, and there would have been so much more to do! Now, so long as their food lasted, they had no real concern.

And there was for the present food a-plenty. The pinch would not come till March and April. She prayed for an early spring. But of course by March the baby would be here, and Joel would be all right again and able to take care of them. She thought when that time came she would go to bed and just lie and rest for days. She was always tired now; so tired she thought she would never be rested again.

Wood and water and the inane sheep were her heaviest burdens. Sometimes when the fire burned low she thought she would rather freeze than move another of those great logs. Her back ached like a boil, all the time. She was too tired to think. She seldom even thought of Mily, of what Mily had said that day by the river; but sometimes when she was weary enough to feel sorry for herself she thought: 'I guess Mily wouldn't do all I'm doing. I guess Mily wouldn't work this hard for him!' The certainty that she was a better wife for Joel than Mily would have been was surprisingly comforting.

* * * * *

The burden of her days grew heavier. At first they had daily visitors; but as November drew near its end there might be four or five days in a row when they saw no one. Once Joel spoke of this, and she said: 'That's natural. When something happens, first off people are pretty sorry for you, and want to help; but after a while they get used to the idea. And they've all got their own jobs to do.'

She was at this relative neglect neither surprised nor resentful; but at last she had to use the axe. There was plenty of wood at hand; but most of it was still to be cut into short lengths suitable for the fireplace. Jason or Matt or Jess had been coming at odd times to do this, but now for three days they failed her. Joel blamed them, and urged her to go summon one of them to do it for her, but she refused.

'I can do it, well as not,' she said. 'They've a'ready done a lot, Joel; and they'll do more when they have the time. But they're busy too, and I don't want to go yelling for help all the time. I can manage.'

'Nobody's been near us,' he protested, 'since Matt was over day before yesterday. No, it was the day before that.'

'Well, Jason probably thinks Jess has been,' she suggested, 'and Jess figures Jason has come over. Don't get in a stew about things, Joel.' He was sometimes querulous; and she tried as hard to keep his mind at ease as to tend him physically, understanding and forgiving the fretting temper which his helplessness inevitably produced.

'I hate to see you do so much,' he insisted. 'Wood and water are a man's job!'

'Well, I won't have to carry water all winter,' she reminded him. 'We can melt snow, when it does snow.' Except for that thin fall which came down the day he was hurt, there had thus far been none at all. She added, laughing: 'And snow will make it easier to get the wood, too. 1 can slide it instead of carrying it.'

'I'll be glad when I get rid of these boards down my leg,' he said glumly. 'I can get around better then, help you more.' Mrs. Robbins had after the third week put on lighter splints, satisfied that the bones had begun to knit. 'How long have I got to wear it, do you know?'

'Till your leg's right again,' she told him. 'You don't have to hurry, Joel.' And she said, smiling insistently: 'I don't know but it's a good thing you did break your leg! Setting there all

day, you don't have any appetite. We're not eating up things
half as fast as I was afraid we would. If we can keep you flat
on your back all winter, Polly and I will live high!'

'You've got to eat,' he said more gently. 'With two to feed.'

She looked down at her swollen body. 'January's a whopper
already,' she assented. 'I don't know but it'd be a good thing
to starve him a while. I'd have an easier time when he comes.'
She laughed. 'If he's as big as he feels,' she declared, 'I wish
he'd hurry up and get here. He could take care of the wood
and water for me as well as not.'

He grinned. He said: 'Come here.' She went to him and he
drew her down and kissed her. 'I just want you to understand
one thing, young woman,' he said. 'You don't fool me! I
know how lucky I am, and I know what you're doing, working
all day long, doing my work and yours too, and smiling and
cheering me up all the time besides. There's never been a
hard word out of you.'

She laughed. 'A lot you know! You ought to hear me swear
at the sheep. I work off my disposition on them.'

'Give it to 'em plenty!' he applauded. 'If it makes you feel
better. As long as you don't take it out on me.'

'I'll never take anything out on you, Joel.'

He held her in the circle of his arm, while she knelt on the
floor beside his chair. 'Don't ever get over feeling that way,'
he said. 'Stay the same. You suit me to a shaving!'

She kissed him and released herself. 'You suit me too,' she
said. 'But I can't stay here dandling you. I've got too much
to do.'

'I'd rather have the dandling.'

She looked at him with warm eyes. 'Every littlest thing I
do, Joel,' she said, 'and every thought I think, and every word
I say, and every time I look at you and every breath I breathe
and — everything, is all just my way of making love to you.'

He watched her go about her tasks, and his eyes a little
clouded. 'I guess I'm not worth all you've given me, Mima,' he
said after a while.

Her heart checked with terror, thinking what he might mean by that, thinking what sense of guilt might be oppressing him; but she said steadily: 'You're worth every breath of it to me.'

* * * * *

The first snow came early in December, and there was, after weeks that had been as warm as Indian summer, a sudden grip of winter in the air. It was this snow that brought upon them a new catastrophe. Mima one day heard a note of terror in the baa-ing of the sheep; and she went out to look down toward the fold. She saw through the snow that was still falling a black shape that moved like rubber, clambering over the hay on top of the fold and down into the pen, and she ran back into the house and cried:

'Is the gun loaded, Joel?' She caught it off the pegs. 'There's a bear at the sheep!'

He sat up sharply, spilling Polly off his lap to the floor. 'No it ain't! Let him be, Mima. He'll hurt you.'

She dropped the useless gun, her eyes blazing. 'I'll drive him away, anyway!' she cried, and ran out and caught up the axe and hurried toward the fold. She heard Joel call to her to come back, yet she ran on, screaming at the bear that was now trying to squeeze through the narrow low door which Joel had made only large enough to let the sheep get in and out of the fold. The beast heard her and stood up to look at her, and she came to the fence and shouted: 'Scat! Get out of there!' She beat on the fence with the axe, and the bear flowed away from her like a black balloon, and scrambled over the fence on the further side of the pen. She peered into the fold through an opening between the poles that supported the hay piled on top of it, and saw that all the sheep were there unhurt, blatting in panic, huddling in a corner. She spoke to them soothingly, and looked for the bear; but he was surely gone, and she turned back up to the house again, shaken and panting with her own excitement.

She came around the corner of the house and saw Joel sitting on the doorstep, grinning at her foolishly, white with pain. He was covered with caked snow, so she knew that he had fallen; and one of his crutches lay ten feet from where he sat. Polly at his shoulder said in sympathetic tones:

'Da-da aw faw down!'

Mima felt her heart catch. She dropped on her knees beside Joel, holding him, crying out questions. She saw that one of the slender splints had snapped, and his leg was twisted awkwardly. He said in shamed tones:

'I guess it's broken again, Mima. I tried to call you back, tried to go along, thought you might need me. My crutch slipped in the snow. I fell, caught the leg under me.'

She would not let him see her despair. 'Maybe it's all right. I'll get Jason,' she said. 'He'll fetch Mother. But I'll help you indoors first.' He submitted meekly to her direction now. 'I scared the bear away,' she said. 'The sheep are all right.'

'Are you all right?'

'I'm fine.'

She helped him to his feet, and he balanced himself while she got the crutch that had flown out of his hand. Polly was in the way, and Mima's helpless despair seized on any outlet. She screamed at the baby: 'Polly, get away from him!' Polly at her mother's unaccustomed tone fled as much in bewilderment as in fear, and hid in the bedroom; and Mima helped Joel to his chair. She removed the splints, thought the leg was surely broken.

'I hate to leave you,' she said. 'But I've got to have someone. I can't fix it myself.'

'You go along,' he said. 'I'll be all right.'

She went into the bedroom for her shawl and saw Polly on her knees on the bed, wide-eyed and still, and Mima caught her up and kissed her. 'There, baby!' she whispered. 'Mother's sorry. Daddy's hurt himself again. You'll have to take care of him while Mother goes and gets Uncle Jason.' Polly's arms hugged tight around her neck, and Mima carried her out into the other room. 'Polly'll take care of you,' she told Joel. 'Don't move your leg.' She saw that his lips were white with pain, and fled away along the knoll through the steady snow and crossed the brook at the footbridge Joel had made, and went on across the cleared land to Jason's cabin.

The ice was not yet strong enough to let Jason cross the pond, so he came back with her and went on around the pond to fetch Mrs. Robbins. He stopped to tell Jess what had happened, and Sis sent her pupils home and she and Jess came to be with Mima. When Mrs. Robbins arrived, she scolded Joel roundly; and when they set the leg again and he sweated with pain, she said it served him right.

'Maybe next time you'll do what you're told,' she said. 'You play the fool again and I'll let it set itself!'

Jason and Matt helped her stretch the leg and splint it. Jess had gone off on the bear's trail, and since the beast must be sluggish and sleepy at this season, he was confident of coming up with it. Joel took their chiding and their tending with an equal humility, and they put him to bed, and Mrs. Robbins decided to stay a day or two, and see him on the road to mending. Jess came back at dark. He had killed the bear two miles up the brook, dressed it out and loaded it on two poles and dragged it this far.

'It's yours by rights, Mima,' he said. 'I'll dress the skin for you. I'll leave it here tonight, come 'tend to it tomorrow.'

Mima nodded, too tired for words. This month past was all wasted now, Joel's recovery all to do over again. Lying awake beside him after he fell asleep, she clenched her hands hard and bit her lips to keep from crying. But in the morning she was strong again; and she told Polly about the bear and showed her how the silly sheep acted in their terror, and Polly was delighted, and Joel and Mrs. Robbins laughed as much at her laughter as at Mima.

But though they laughed, Joel's leg was broken again; his recovery that much delayed. This was December. Three months more? It would be March before he was himself again. Mima squared her shoulders to the load.   She would not let herself think of the weeks ahead. The thing must be done one day at a time.

12

DECEMBER snows were deep, and by the middle of the month snowshoes were necessary in order to go abroad. Mima heard from Sis that Prance Bowen had a baby girl born on the eighth. Her own time was only a little more than a month away. Her days now were somewhat easier. Snow outside the door made it unnecessary to go down to the spring and sometimes to chop a hole in the ice in order to get water; and Mrs. Robbins, when she discovered that Mima had been using the axe, gave Jess strict orders to keep her supplied with firewood, fitted to a proper size and piled indoors handy to the fire.

'That's the worst thing for her,' she declared, 'using her arms, reaching up. Lifting's bad enough, but swinging an axe is awful!'

Joel, sobered by his second accident, no longer rebelled at his own helplessness; he watched Mima at her steady round, and he made small Polly his particular care, calling her to him when she needed attention of any kind, keeping her amused and happy so that Mima need not think of her at all. The days dragged by, and at intervals more snow fell to add to the deep blanket already on the ground. Jess now came every day to be sure all went well with them, and he fed the sheep, so that except to scoop up a pailful of snow and hang it over the fire, or to walk around the house to bring some of their store of smoked moose meat from the racks, Mima had no occasion to go out-of-doors at all.

Yet sometimes she was sorry Jess did so much. So long as she had been too busy to think, she had almost forgotten the danger that their provisions would run short before spring. Now she had time to think, and whenever she fetched food from their dwindling store she was reminded of that spectre of starvation which haunted them. She tried in self-defence to keep busy all day long, inventing tasks to make the days go more swiftly, anxious for her time to come so that she might be rid of the weight of the baby that more and more wearied her. If there was nothing else to do, she worked at the loom; and while she worked and Polly busied herself at many occupations on the floor, Mima and Joel talked long hour on hour of a thousand things, drawing close to one another in many new ways. Once when she was tired, and desperately tired of the weight she bore, she confessed:

'Sometimes, Joel, I think — what if I died when this baby comes?' And she added quickly: 'I'm not afraid of it. It's just that I keep thinking, what if I did? What would become of you and Polly? I guess you'd marry somebody. You'd have to.'

He did not protest that she was wrong to think so and to speak so. Instead he said simply: 'You'll never die as long as I'm alive, Mima. You've put too much of yourself into me, and into Polly.' And he said: 'Remember once we were talking about dying, and we said no one ever could die, as long as people that had known him were alive, because we all put part of ourselves into people?'

'I think the way not to die is to live the best way we know

how,' she agreed, and she said: 'Maybe God puts us to live on earth just for practice, to see if we can learn how to live right; and if we do, maybe He lets us go on living forever. If we don't do a good job of living here, He knows it would just be a waste of His time — and ours too — to let us go living on and on.'

'How is anyone going to know whether he's living right or not?'

'By whether he's happy or not,' she suggested. 'I mean, if you try to do the best you can, you're happy.' And she said: 'Oh, Joel, I want us always to try! We're bound to make mistakes, plenty of them; and we may not ever accomplish much of anything. But we can teach ourselves to have the right ideas about the way to do, and then try to live up to our ideas, and be happy so.'

He looked at her thoughtfully. 'Do you really believe we can go on living after we die?'

'The life in us goes on living,' she insisted. 'The way I see it, there's just so much life in the world, and we're let use part of it for a while, and then we have to give it back. But we've put our mark on it, just the way you mark everything you use. Like the handle of your axe. After a while it gets to have hollows where your thumbs go, and your fingers. I've noticed them when I used your axe this winter. It's the same way with your clothes. You wear them out in certain places, and Jason wears his out other places, and so does Matt. Anything a person uses gets to have his marks on it. I guess using our share of life marks it the same way. If we don't use it right, then when we pass it on to our children it's worn out in spots, and maybe dirty in spots, so they don't get such a good piece of life to use as we had to start with.' She laughed a little, trying to put her thought in words. 'I don't say it right, Joel; but ... well, of course our bodies die, but they're just something we use to keep our piece of life in. When we die, it's like breaking a jug full of rum. The jug is gone; but the rum's still there.'

He chuckled. 'It's there if you're quick enough to catch it

before it runs away!' he agreed; and he said: 'Mima, with a mother like you, our children are bound to be fine people when they grow up.'

'We'll always love them, won't we, Joel? No matter what they do.' She smiled. 'I guess that's why mothers like babies so much; because the babies are always making messes that have to be cleaned up. But the mothers know the babies will get over making messes after a while.' She added, in a different tone, suddenly turning away to the loom so that he might not see her face: 'Not that kind of messes, anyway.'

'But they make other kinds,' he said. 'Like me breaking my leg and making things so hard for you.'

'You didn't go to do it!' she cried, quick to defend him against himself. 'It wasn't your fault.'

'Maybe it was,' he said in a low tone. 'Maybe Phin did do it, Mima; and maybe he did it because I chased Mily at the husking. That was my fault.'

Busy at her work, her back to him, she said: 'You couldn't do anything else after she throwed you the red ear. If Phin was mad at you — that was his fault. But I don't believe he was.'

'I've noticed you're mighty slow to blame people for anything they do, Mima.'

'I never could see the sense of blaming anybody, once a thing's done,' she assented. 'Holding a grudge is poison. And I have enough to do 'tending to my own business, without going around blaming other people for things.' She asked: 'Hungry? I'll get supper started.'

Her movement was like flight. Their words made her think of Mily, and that could not be borne. She went to chunk up the fire and then to bring in some moose meat. Early dark had fallen, and in the still winter dusk she heard off to the westward the howl of a wolf, miles away on the Madomock, one wolf or a pack hunting there. They seldom came near the settlements, and Mima had never seen one, had rarely even heard their distant howls. In this deep snow, with no crust as yet formed, she

thought they must flounder at the chase, must sometimes go
hungry. At the thought of their hunger, she felt a deep kindliness toward them. There was nowadays never an hour when
she did not remember that she and Joel and Polly might know
hunger before spring. The piece of meat she chose today was a
little tainted. The warm weather in November might have been
responsible; but she thought it would be all right when it was
boiled. Joel smelled it while it was cooking and protested; but
she said:

'It's all right. It will taste all right. I'm glad I found it before it got any worse. We can't afford to waste anything that's
fit to eat at all.'

*   *   *   *   *

Deep snows made hard travelling; so for a while Mima did
not see her mother. Then late in December a thin rain and the
freeze that followed it made a crust strong enough to support a
person on snowshoes, and Mrs. Robbins came to see how they
did and to try to guess how soon Mima's baby would arrive.
She said cheerfully:

'Well, I guess you're going to put it off till summer, Mima, by
the looks of you! You're still carrying it high. You better
change its name to February!' She thought it would be a boy,
by Mima's shape. 'And this time I aim to be here,' she declared. 'Let Joel try to take care of you the way he did when
you had Polly, and he'd go break his leg again, like as not. I
had my mind all made up to stay now, if I had to; but you've
got two-three weeks to go by the looks of you, so I guess I'll go
along home.'

Mima was curiously depressed by her mother's prediction.
It seemed to her she could not remember when she had not been
heavy and malformed; and she told Joel so, that night when
they were alone.

'I feel as if I'd always been this way,' she declared.

'You wasn't last June,' he assured her, smiling. 'You was just right, pretty as a picture. Every once in a while I get to thinking about you, swimming and all, when we went up-river!'

She made a scornful sound. 'And me the way I am, and you with a broken leg! You better think about something else. But I won't always be this way, will I?'

'No. But you suit me the way you are. I like to watch your eyes. They're warm all the time, and kind of dreaming.'

'Kind of swearing, more like it!' she told him crisply, and laughed at herself. 'I'm getting so I sound just like Mother,' she said. 'She always kind of bridled and sniffed when Father said nice things to her.'

'You two are as like as can be, sometimes, the way you talk,' he agreed. 'I heard you telling Polly to clean her plate at dinner today.'

'Mother always made us,' she assented. 'Clean our plates, and wear out our clothes before we threw them away, and make things do, or do without. Will it bother you if I'm like her, Joel?'

'It'll suit me fine,' he assured her. 'That's why I married you, figuring you'd turn out like her.'

She looked at him in sudden understanding. 'Joel, you've been mighty cheerful since you broke your leg the second time. You've been real sweet to me, always laughing and joking.'

'Why wouldn't I be cheerful, sitting here and taking it easy while you wait on me hand and foot?'

She came and kissed him. 'You can't fool me. You're doing it a-purpose to keep me chirked up. And it helps mightily, Joel. I'm much obliged.'

* * * * *

She needed his cheerfulness as the year ended. Their supply of corn was shrinking faster than she liked. Polly was always demanding bread or pudding, and though they kept themselves on scant rations they could not stint her. Their other supplies diminished; and several times Mima found cuts of moose meat that were beyond use. Jess talked of going hunting, but the crust had softened, and fresh snow fell, and transport was difficult or impossible. He was setting snares for rabbits, and Mima put out a score or so in runways down by the brook. Sometimes she had luck, sometimes not. Joel protested at her going out in the deep snow, fearful that she might fall; but the fresh meat was welcome, and she insisted. Matt Hawes killed a denned bear and they had their share of that; but there was no longer any hope in Mima's mind that their corn and rye would last through the winter. She calculated that by the first of May, perhaps even earlier, it might be possible to get fiddle-heads, or young leaves of the birch or beech for greens. That was four months away. She divided what corn they had into four parts, and the rye too, and resolved to make each part last a month. With Joel unable to move — his crutches helped him around the house, but the snow barred him from going out-of-doors — she sometimes went over to Jason's cabin to use the apparatus she and Joel had contrived there for breaking up the corn into samp and meal. The trip was for her a long one, and Jason offered to come and get their corn and grind it for her; but she was jealous of every kernel, afraid he might spill it in the snow, hoarding it like gold; so she persisted in going herself.

As the new year began, everyone in Sterlingtown faced the same certainty of approaching famine; and on the first of January Philip Robbins apportioned out the corn from Uncle Josiah's land, and delivered to each his share.

'I don't want the responsibility of keeping it,' he said when he came to Joel's cabin. 'The barn might burn or something. It's better to have it divided up, and this way everyone will know just what they've got to do with.'

The supplement to their store seemed to Mima like bounty; and she fondled it as a miser does his hoard, letting the bright kernels trickle through her fingers. Her father had hulled the corn, to make a more accurate division. There were some red grains — off the red ear Mily had tossed to Joel, perhaps. Mima picked them out one by one, half-minded to throw them away: but she did not. They could not be spared.

She divided this addition to their store into four, and added one part to what she had measured out for their supply for January. She counted twelve quarts scant; say a pint a day for twenty-four days — and none at all for the other seven days. A pint of kernels would not make a pint of meal; but the rye would make up the deficiency. She calculated that taking rye and corn together, they could eat a little less than a pint of grain a day and still make their supply last to the first of May. By that time the alewives would run, and there would be green things growing, and Uncle Josiah might arrive with new supplies.

But two or three days on this ration convinced her that it was not enough. If she and Joel ate each a third of the day's allotment, Polly was not satisfied with her share. Their dwindling store of potatoes would not last — unless they used those meant for seed. Mima had days when she thought often of Mrs. Forbes watching her children starve up on the Kennebeck. She had nights when she dreamed that she and Joel and Polly were starving in a fireless cabin, with the cold pressing in and crushing them.

But she did not tell Joel her fears. Sometimes he asked how their supplies held out. From the buttery or the cellar she would call to him: 'Oh, we've plenty. We'll be fine.'

Her mother came again on the eleventh of January, and this time she decided to stay on. 'Snow's too deep for me to come traipsing 'way up here again,' she said. 'And anyway, I can take the heft of the work off your hands. Susie can do for them at home.' Mima was glad to see her; but she begrudged every mouthful her mother ate.

One day, a week later, Jess brought Sis with him when he came to replenish the supply of firewood. The deep snow made it impossible for the children to reach their cabin, so school was interrupted and Sis found her occupation gone. Joel on his crutches hobbled out-of-doors where the snow was packed down, to talk with Jess while he worked; and Sis and Mima and Mrs. Robbins talked of babies. Mima was very tired, and Mrs. Robbins thought she was near her time.

'It can't come too soon to suit me, either,' she told Sis. 'And I guess Mima's tired of waiting too.'

'I wish we were going to have one,' Sis confessed. 'Everybody else has had a baby this year, or they're going to. Jess and I feel kind of out of it.'

Mrs. Robbins chuckled. 'Maybe you've been trying too hard,' she suggested. 'Grass never grows on a well-trod path.'

Mima smiled, and Sis colored. 'Well, we do want one pretty soon,' she confessed.

'You'll be coming in fresh, give you time,' the older woman predicted. 'But don't go having a baby in the winter, the way Mima's doing.' She said: 'Now with sheep, we manage it for them a sight better. We fix it so they'll drop their lambs along April or May, and the lambs have all summer to get a start. But human beings have more sense for sheep than they have for themselves. The winter's no time to have babies; but nobody ever stops to think of that in June.'

'Summer'd be worse,' Mima declared. 'I'd hate to have a little new baby when it was hot, and fly time too. If you covered him up he'd roast, and if you didn't, the flies'd eat him alive. I'll choose to have mine winters.'

'Well,' Mrs. Robbins admitted, 'this is one time you're going to have your d'ruthers. If you go another three days I'll be surprised.'

Mima did not go even one more day. Jess and Sis went home at dusk. They were early abed, but Mima woke in the night, and when she was sure, she went out and stirred up the fire and herself filled the kettles. Mrs. Robbins heard her and came down from the garret, and they consulted quietly together. The bedroom was far enough from the fire to be cold, but Mrs. Robbins brought down the straw tick from the bed in the garret and made up a bed on the cabin floor. The leaping fire gave light enough. Joel waked, but they bade him stay where he was.

'Keep the bed warm,' Mrs. Robbins told him. 'You're going to have company by and by.'

The new baby arrived at the crack of dawn, and with so little confusion that Polly slept undisturbed. 'It's a boy, just the way I said it would be!' Mrs. Robbins triumphantly announced. 'Here, Joel, you hold him while I 'tend to her. Keep that blanket around him.'

Mima, her senses clouded, asked drowsily from where she lay in the other room: 'Has he got a broken leg?'

Her mother answered her. 'I should say not! He's as handsome a young one as I ever see. He'll weigh all of ten pounds, Mima. What you going to call him?'

'Peter,' Mima said. 'After Joel's father.'

Joel, still in bed, holding the bundle in his arms, called in a gleeful tone: 'Say, Mima, it's some different, having a son!'

13

JANUARY was a month of bitter cold, with day after day of iron-gray skies and blustering winds out of the west and northwest; and the wind at night was bitter, scouring up snow fragments and pelting them against the cabin walls. December had piled snow three or four feet deep around the cabin; these January winds carved it and drifted it. Mima, waking in the night to nurse her baby, heard great trees cracking in the frost's grip; and she held Peter close and warm against her breast, between her and Joel so that their two bodies kept him warm. Sometimes on the coldest nights, Polly came in with them, and they packed tight together, four in a bed, while the cold stole in like serpents. No matter how the fire leaped and roared during the day, after it was banked for the night the house chilled quickly. The great chimney with its wide flue sucked air out, and cold air came in through every crack and cranny, and in the morning they could discover the crevices through which the cold had leaked in by white patches of frost crystals around them. They might have kept up the fire all night; but Mima would not yet consent that Joel should do anything which required him to lay aside his crutches, and she herself had to lie abed a few days after Peter was born, and though Mrs. Robbins stayed on with them during this interval, she slept in the garret and flatly refused to descend to mend the fire.

The cold complicated the business of living. The moose meat had to be thawed in a pail of water for hours before it could be used; and potatoes froze in the cellar, so that Joel was afraid those he had saved for seed would be ruined. Mima could not tend her rabbit snares, and Mrs. Robbins would not; but Jess once or twice brought them rabbits he had caught. Mima had kept the white skins of those she had captured during the winter, curing them; and she spent this period of her own inactivity working them soft and cutting them into strips to weave a warm sleeping bag for Peter like that she had made for Polly.

Except that she begrudged every mouthful the older woman ate, Mima enjoyed her mother's long stay with them, and so did Joel; and when after the fifth day Mima began to sit up a while, the three of them might stay after supper in the firelight, talking quietly of many things.

Also they had now visitors enough, coming to see the new baby. Mima's father tramped up from Seven-Tree Pond the second day after it was born, and he said: 'Well, Ma, your job's done. When you coming home?'

'I aim to keep Mima abed a week or two.'

'Two weeks?' He chuckled. 'Hell's afire! You used to have yours and git up and git breakfast for the two of us the next morning!'

'More shame to you for letting me,' she retorted. 'I aim to see to't Mima has it some easier. She's been working too hard anyway. She needs the rest and all the strength she's got, with that young moose to feed!'

He stroked Mima's head with his hand in a strong affection. 'Guess womenfolks ain't what they used to be!' he said; but there was a twinkle in his eyes.

*　*　*　*　*

Mima for a few days was glad enough to lie quiet and be waited on; but as her strength returned, she became impatient to be mistress of her house again, and it was a relief to her when her mother finally decided to go home. It was almost two months since Joel broke his leg the second time; and he had discarded his crutches and now used a cane, but he moved cautiously about the house, and he was as careful as Mima wished him to be. Mrs. Robbins before she left warned him not to go jumping and stomping around, and tripping over things and falling down.

'But I guess your leg'll get strong all the quicker if you use it,' she admitted. 'Only don't put a strain on it. Jess'll keep coming to tend the wood and feed the sheep. You want to act like you was still a cripple, Joel, even if you don't feel like one.'

Joel said he would. 'I don't want to be laid up again,' he admitted; and Mima promised to keep him quiet.

When her mother was gone, she clung to Joel happily. 'Oh, it feels good to be alone with you again, Joel!' she told him. 'Just us and our children. That's all the world I want.'

'We'd have been hard put to it without your mother, this last two-three weeks.'

'I know, but we don't need her now.' Mima added: 'Besides, she ate so much; and we're going to need every bite we've got.' She laughed at herself. 'I guess that's pretty mean of me, to say that; but I don't want Polly and Peter to go hungry, Joel.'

He said: 'They won't. I'll manage, now't I can get around.'

She told him, smiling: 'You couldn't grow corn in the snow, Joel, even if you had two good legs! You're pretty wonderful to me, but you can't do that!' She sighed contentedly. 'Just the same, it's a relief to have you up and around.'

'I can do a lot more than your mother thinks I can.'

She said, her eyes thoughtful: 'You know, it's funny what a difference a house makes to a woman, the way she feels about her own house, or being in someone else's. When we first came up here, we all lived together in the old house, all of us and

David's family too, the first winter; and as long as I lived there, whenever I went anywhere else I was just visiting. Then when I went to live at the Royal Mess, it was like visiting to go back to Father's house. I used to start back up the river to the Royal Mess, and think I was going home.

'And now this is home, and when I'm away from it I want to get back to it, and when I'm in it, I don't want any other people here, only us. Having my own mother here was like she was a stranger. I didn't feel like I knew her, hardly.'

'I know how you mean,' he assented. 'Take Jason and Matt and me. I lived with Matt and Jason till there wasn't anything we didn't know about each other. But now we're all kind of — well, shy, when we get together. I guess that's because we all know that there's the biggest part of the other one's life we don't fit into any more at all.'

'I'm that way with Mother,' she agreed. 'Kind of shy.' She laughed comfortably. 'I'm never really myself except when I'm alone this way with you.' She smiled at him. 'It takes two of us to make one of us now, Joel.'

He touched her shoulder. 'Four of us, Mima. And more to come, some day.'

'Lots more,' she promised him.

Before the end of the month, she was herself again, happy in the comfortable routine of their lives of which Peter was now a part, even though she could not long forget that their provisions were low. Joel delighted to watch her nursing the baby. 'One thing sure, he'll never go hungry,' he said. 'You're a good heifer, Mima.'

She looked down at the small head pressed against her breast, and terror touched her, and she looked up at Joel and said in a low tone: 'I could nurse Polly too, Joel. If I had to.'

'You won't have to. We'll have plenty.'

'There's all of February and March and April ahead,' she reminded him. 'And the rabbits are getting scarce, and what moose meat we've got left isn't hardly fit to eat, and we can't live on just meat anyhow. Polly eats more than you and me put together, Joel; and she has to have bread and pudding and all.'

'We'll go kill some fresh meat — Jess and me — as soon as I can travel.'

'You're not going off on snowshoes this winter and break your leg again and maybe never get home.' She held Peter closer. 'We'll stay here together, Joel, whatever comes.'

She watched from day to day, with jealous eyes, the steady shrinkage of their store of grain, portioning it out as carefully as if it were gold. After her mother was gone, she found that her calculations would have to be made afresh; and she did this, measuring the corn and rye a cupful at a time. The result was alarming. Her mother had been unwilling to stint Mima, or baby Polly; and what might have been a month's scant supply had been consumed in the fortnight of her stay here. Mima still clung in her thoughts to the first of May as the day to which their stores must carry them. Sometimes, lying awake at night, she wondered why she was so sure that if they could manage till then they would be all right. Certainly there would be no new crops coming to fruition for another two months after May arrived. It would not even be possible to plant anything till mid-May or the first of June. But there would be fiddle-heads uncurling in the flowed-lands, and the alewives would be running, and there would be at least the blessed certainty that winter had loosed its grip on them. With all the world coming to life about them, certainly they would not starve.

But April and May were far away, for this was only February, not yet a week gone. She counted twenty-three more days in February and thirty-one in March and thirty in April; and on every one of those days Polly would be hungry, and so would Joel, and so would she. She was always hungry now, never quite satisfied, never free from the faint but persistent desire for something — anything — to eat. Mima, while except in the spring of the year after the barn burned she had never been thin, was always lean and hard-muscled as a boy, with only enough surplus flesh to round her legs and arms, her flanks and shoulders. But now she began to feel her ribs near the surface and she could see the muscles play in her arms as she did her household tasks. Joel spoke of it one day admiringly.

'You look fit and fine,' he said. 'Like you were facing into a strong wind.'

She told him she felt fine, and she did; but she was thinner every day. What she ate might have been enough for her, but not for Peter too. He alone of them all never went hungry; and Mima, holding him close while he nursed, felt in this fact a fierce, triumphant pride.

She thought sometimes that her days would be easier if their enemy were more tangible; if it were possible to meet him face to face in definite and final combat, to win or lose. But their enemy was within themselves; their own hunger, with the inexorable passing days for allies, nibbled away at their resources, was never satisfied, sapped their strength, pressed upon them crushingly. And in the other cabins the same enemy was at work; in none of them was any bountiful supply. No one had food to spare. The long privation and the common danger made each household draw in upon itself, each husbanding its own small store. No scrap was thrown away; and Mima began to look for ways to supplement their supplies. Their moose meat, smoked in the fall, frozen through the winter, still held out; but it was either half-spoiled or dry and tasteless. Joel said one day that he might butcher one of the sheep in the fold by the brook, but Mima would not hear of it.

'They'll drop their lambs in April or May,' she reminded him. 'One apiece and maybe two. You kill one now and you're maybe killing two or three. We'll keep 'em through.'

'They're thin as a picked fishbone, anyway,' he admitted. 'No meat on 'em.'

She smiled and said: 'We're kind of fined down ourselves, Joel, if it comes to that. Your shirt would go around you twice, and my dresses are as loose as if Mother hadn't took them in after Peter came.' She added soberly: 'And there's two months and more to go till May.'

He said urgently: 'Spring'll be here before you know it, Mima.'

She spoke in a carefully casual tone. 'Joel, we're about out of potatoes, only the ones for seed. Do you think if we cut off the seed ends and the eyes and ate the rest, they'd grow all right?' She added: 'I remember the winter Father's barn burned, David dug up his potatoes after he'd planted them, and cut off all but the eyes to eat, and they grew.'

'We can if we're put to it,' he agreed; and he said: 'Matt's Sally was telling me once, one year down in Warren they took the under bark off the birch logs they had for firewood and they used to gnaw at it. She said it gave you a full feeling, only it kind of tied you up after a while.'

'We could try mixing a little of it with our meal,' she suggested. 'It'd make the corn go farther. We'll try it ourselves first, and if it don't hurt us we can give Polly some.'

'You'd better not eat it,' he decided. 'With Peter to feed. I'll give it a try.'

He did so. There were some birch logs in their pile. He stripped off the white outer bark; then scraped away the inner bark, brown and dry. It had little fibre, and he was able to pound it into a coarse powder of the texture of meal. They boiled it into a sort of mush and mixed cornmeal with it and added a little moose tallow for flavoring, and Joel ate it and declared it tasted well enough. Mima watched him fearfully, but he showed no immediate ill effects; and after Joel had continued to eat the mixture for a day or two, he proposed to try it on Polly. But Mima would not consent.

'We won't do that till we're put to it,' she decided. 'It might make her sick — even if it don't hurt you.' Joel declared he liked the flavor, so she continued to mix the ground-up bark with meal and make a mush for him.

Polly began to lose some weight, despite the milk that came

up from Seven-Tree Pond whenever there was any way to send it; but she seemed well. The days plodded wearily and there was snow and snow. Joel's leg was better all the time; but for the first three weeks of February Jess still came every day or two or three, to work up the wood for their fire. Mima kept Joel from using snowshoes, since they were always apt to slide or twist; and it was for the present she who tended the sheep in their fold. Even for that short journey webs were necessary; and she had a path well beaten down. She tried to prevent Joel's handling the heavy logs Jess fitted for them, but his leg improved from day to day and he did more and more.

* * * * *

One morning late in February, Jess after his axe work was done came in and sat down, talking at random in some apparent embarrassment, till Mima laughed and asked him: 'Come on, Jess, what is it you're trying to get up the gumption to say?'

'Why, I be'n wondering how Joel's leg was,' he confessed.

Joel said heartily: 'Good as ever, only Mima's bound to baby me — as if two babies wasn't enough for her to take care of. Why?'

'Well, Johnny Butler was up to see me yesterday,' Jess explained. 'He's took Lucy and the children down to Thomaston.' Mima looked at him in a sharp attention, and he read her thought and explained: 'No, it ain't that. They've got as much to eat as anybody has. But there's some sort of a church meeting down there, and Mis' Robbins is kind of running it. A minister named Isaac Case, he's got everybody worked up about religion, and Mis' Robbins wanted Lucy to hear him preach a few times; so she sent word to Johnny to fetch Lucy and all the young ones down there.'

'Those four babies!' Mima protested; and somewhere in the back of her mind she thought of Mrs. Forbes with her four children, no shelter, no fire, in the forests far up the Kennebeck. watching her babies starve and die.

Jess nodded. 'They made the trip all right,' he declared. 'Johnny and Lucy dragged them on hand sleds. There's a beaten track from Warren the rest of the way.' And he explained: 'But Johnny doesn't want anything to do with the meetings, so he come back and he wants I should go over to the Madomock with him.' He added: 'And I was thinking, if you could get along without me, or maybe if Jason would come over and give you a hand, I'd go along.'

'Go ahead,' Joel said strongly. 'I'll manage fine.'

'I can leave Sis with my folks,' Jess explained. 'And a piece of fresh moose meat would eat good to me. Ours that we smoked last fall hasn't kept so good. Has yours?'

'Not so good,' Joel admitted with a grin. 'It stinks us out even to boil it. That hot weather in November must have started it.'

'But we can eat it,' Mima said. 'And it hasn't hurt us.'

Joel asked her: 'What do you think, Mima? Think I'd be all right to go?'

She wanted to say no, to protest that Joel was not yet able to handle the wood. She looked at him, and he spoke, but not to insist.

'I'll do whatever you say, Mima,' he told her. 'I feel fit to do any job that needs doing, and if it was me alone I'd risk it. But if I do get laid up again, the hard part would come on you.' He grinned. 'I'd just set easy another two-three months and let you wait on me. So I'll do whatever you say. If you want Jess to stay here, say so.'

Her instinct was to protect him, but she knew his own helplessness irked him, knew how he hated having Jess do his chores. In the end she nodded slowly. 'You go ahead, Jess,' she said. 'We'll manage. What Joel can't 'tend to, I can. I'm as strong as ever now.' She added: 'But you see to't you bring us some meat! I could eat a moose myself, if I had one.'

Jess promised to bring back a loaded sled. 'We'll kill all we can, and take some more men over to haul the meat home,' he said; and next morning he and Johnny set out. They came across Round Pond. The day was sunny and fine, the trees heavy with snow that had fallen in the night. Mima had gone to pull down hay for the sheep. The hay was piled on the poles which roofed their fold, and they had eaten up into the pile from below, nuzzling through between the poles. When she forked some into the pen for them now she discovered this. 'Well, you'll just have yourselves to blame if you run short,' she told them. 'There was enough to last you if you weren't such greedy guts!' They baa-ed at her inanely, and she heard the sled coming. The men were ascending the line of the brook, and Mima went to see them pass and to wish them good hunting. They were in tandem, with a line to haul the sled; and Jess was in the lead, breaking trail. Johnny, since Lucy was not at home, had let his beard grow these two or three days and it was gray across his cheek and chin. She watched them follow the meandering brook till they disappeared into the woods beyond the clearing before she turned back to the house again.

'Well, they've started,' she told Joel. 'Funny for Johnny's hair to turn gray and him so young.'

'A black-haired man, it goes that way sometimes,' he reminded her, and smiled and said: 'Maybe Lucy's nagged him gray-headed. She gives him fits sometimes.'

'Jess was breaking trail,' she remarked. 'He'll take his turn where the going's easy, every time; but he'll let Johnny do it when they begin to climb.'

'Jess does his share,' he assured her.

She laughed. 'But he'll always work it so his share's the easiest, or the one he wants to do.' She began to clean up the breakfast dishes, decided she would not tell Joel that the sheep had been stealing their own hay. He had enough to worry about, without sheep. So long as he had been helpless, he had not begun to lose weight, but now as he did more and more work, she could see his flesh shrink away. His cheeks were flat, and the line of his chin was clean cut, with no fulness below it. If she dropped her arm around his waist it was as hard as the trunk of a tree in her embrace. She thought he looked fine; but during that week while they waited for the return of the hunters, something disturbed his digestion. He was helpless for an hour one night with stomach cramps, and she decided this was from eating birch bark, and refused to feed it to him any more.

* * * * *

They looked forward to the return of the hunters, thinking how good fresh meat would taste; but when Jess and Johnny did come back, they were empty-handed, frostbitten, half-starved. All that day of their return, a northwest storm had blown, some snow falling, some scoured up by the wind; and the two men drifted before it like cattle. They came to the door at first dark, and Mima heard the clack of snowshoes and opened to them. They kicked off their webs and came in and dropped down like men half-dead; and Joel and Mima warmed them and presently fed them till they began to be themselves again, before there was any talk at all save necessary words.

Jess answered the question they had not asked. 'No,' he said. 'No luck. We didn't find a yard, and not hardly any tracks. I guess the folks from Broad Bay have been up that way, drove 'em all north.'

'I've heard wolves over there three-four times this winter,' Mima remembered. 'The wolves might have pushed the moose right out of the country.'

Joel said heartily: 'Well, you're home. That's something, this weather. You'd best stay the night here. It's wicked cold, and this wind and all. No sense in going on.'

'I've about done my stint for one day,' Jess confessed. 'It's been rough going all week, matter of that. We didn't take much along in the way of grub, looking to find plenty; but there wasn't a track of anything anywhere only a few rabbits, and we didn't stay in one place long enough to snare any of them.' He was

eating wolfishly, gnawing at a strip of tainted meat which Mima
had seared over the fire; and he reflected: 'I'd like to see Sis
tonight, but she's staying with the folks, and that looks like a
long pull, the way I feel right now.'

Johnny wearily commented: 'No s-sense my going home.
Lucy's not there.' He sat back, his hunger dulled.

Mima asked him: 'Did you hear Mr. Case preach while you
were down in Thomaston with them?'

'No,' he admitted. 'But they say he's p-powerful. P-Preaches
election and reprobation. He c-came from Harpswell. He's
been p-preaching down there the last year. He's a B-Baptist;
so Mis' Robbins sent for him. She's about the only B-Baptist
in these parts, I guess. He p-preached at her house the first
Sunday.' Johnny grinned sleepily. 'He m-must be quite a
t-talker,' he said. 'M-Mily got c-conviction that first day. Phin
told me she took it hard!' He added: 'Soon as the ice goes out,
Mr. Case says he's going to have a b-baptizing; but M-Mily
wants to have her baby first. It's due in April.'

Mima thought it was like Mily to react to Mr. Case's exhorta-
tions. Probably he was a young, handsome man. She wondered
how long it would be before she could hear Mily's name without feeling this cold grip on her heart. 'Well, you don't have to
go on home tonight, if no one's there,' she said.

'No, ma'am,' he agreed. 'And I'd thank ye k-kindly to keep
me till m-morning. I'm real sorry we didn't bring home a nice
saddle of m-moose m-meat for you.' His eyelids drooped. He
was almost too tired and sleepy to stutter.

Joel reflected: 'I know within a mile of where half the moose
in the country have gone, I reckon.' He spoke to Mima. 'Up
where the river forks, you take the west fork and it fetches you
into as thick a swamp hole as you'll find anywhere around. Old
I'm Davis told me most winters there's so many moose trails
beaten down through there it's like roads in a town.'

'We see one track on the other side of the Madomock, heading
north,' Jess agreed. 'That moose was going through three-

four feet of snow and his belly didn't even touch. If I'd got a sight at him, we'd have et hearty, but we followed the track right onto two miles and then it come on dark and in the morning the wind had filled the track in so you couldn't tell where to look for it.' He suggested: 'Say we have a try up-river when the snow settles some.'

'Joel can't travel, not on that leg of his,' Mima protested.

'Bother you any while I was gone?' Jess asked.

'Not to mention,' Joel assured him. 'It's a little shorter than the other, I guess. Seems like I come down harder on that foot.'

Mima had noticed that little hitch in Joel's gait, had thought it was no more than a limp from the pain of the knitting bones; and her eyes suddenly burned with sorrowing that Joel's fine body which she loved should in any part be marred. 'It will be right when it's all well, Joel,' she predicted; and then she said: 'There, Jess, look at Johnny! He's asleep a'ready. You and him want to go up in the garret? There's a straw tick there.'

'We'll bed on the floor here,' Jess decided. 'It's plenty soft to suit me. I aim to keep the fire going all night. Seems like I've been cold as long as I want to be.'

In the morning they were early away. 'We'll get Ma to give us breakfast,' Jess explained. 'Johnny wants to make it to Thomaston today, and you've fed us your share.' He grinned. 'I'll bring you some of our smoked moose to make it up to you if you want.'

Joel laughed and said: 'I'd full as soon have a piece of your wore-out moccasins, Jess. They'd be tenderer — and more to 'em, too!'

When they were gone, he told Mima: 'Well, we could have used the meat if they'd got any. But they had a hard drill and nothing to show for it. The only thing is, Jess being away has put me on my feet again. It's a relief to me to be doing again.'

She knew this was true, had seen the change in him as he found his leg equal to its work. During the next few days she watched him, without letting him know she did so, to see if that hitch in his gait began to disappear. It did not, but presently she ceased to notice it. He was as vigorous as ever. He kept a space shovelled clear of snow around the door of the house and as far as the woodpile, so that he could go out to use the axe or to carry wood. The snow he had shovelled out of this small area rose as high as the top of the door on every side. Their world was thus constricted, except that Mima, and Joel when he insisted he was fit for it, kept a trail beaten to the sheep fold, and he went every day to portion out the dwindling supply of hay to the bleating creatures.

February ended. Mima spoke of it — a day too soon. 'There's an extra day in February, this year,' Joel reminded her.

She begrudged that one additional day, that extra food that must be found; but she would not tell him so. The birch bark had disagreed with him, so they no longer used it; but it had helped them make some slight saving. 'And I don't mind so much now,' she told him. 'The days are getting longer all the time. We'll make out. Pretty soon the buds will begin to swell, and I can boil them and make sauce. And we've got enough corn to last till April anyway, using it the way we do. I feel like I ate more than my share, Joel; but Peter's hungry all the time — and so am I.'

He said quietly: 'You have a right to be.' He took her in his arms, and she pressed against him, looking up at him, smiling up at him.

'Are we always going to feel this way about each other, Joel?' she whispered, and she saw his eyes darken in a way she knew, and watched his lips come down to hers.

*　*　*　*　*

On the afternoon of the fifth of March, Jess brought word that the new minister down the river, Elder Isaac Case, was coming Sunday to hold a meeting at Philip Robbins' house.

'They say he's a powerful preacher,' Jess declared. 'Repent

or be damned, he tells 'em. He's been down in Thomaston since the end of January, and there ain't enough sin left down there to butter parsnips. Every time he opens his mouth, three sinners fall in and come out saved!' He grinned. 'He's run out of folks to work on, there, so he's coming up to give us a going over.'

Joel laughed; but Mima did not. 'Maybe it ain't so funny as you think,' she protested. 'And even if it was, it wouldn't be funny to the ones he's helped. You hadn't ought to go laughing at it.'

'That's so,' Jess assented. 'I didn't go to laugh, but it struck me funny.' He said thoughtfully: 'Queer how a thing like that goes. I hadn't thought he was funny till I said he was a powerful preacher and saw Joel kind of grin, and that made me laugh too.'

'I grinned because I was thinking he must be almighty powerful to bring Mily to grace,' Joel explained. 'You mind Johnny Butler told us he did.'

'Well, she can stand it,' Jess assented. 'Her and Phin are coming up tonight to Lucy's, bringing Lucy home. Anyway, Mima, Ma wanted I should let you all know, up here, so if you wanted to come.'

'We might,' Mima agreed. 'If the going ain't too bad.' She wondered whether Mily would seem changed.

'The going's good,' Jess assured her. 'There's a crust making. Dave and Rich and me were figuring to start next week, see if we can find some moose up-river. The snow's hardened up enough so's it will hold you up all right with webs; and a sled with wide runners goes good. I'm going on over to see Matt and Jason, see if they're a mind to go.'

'We need some fresh meat bad,' Joel agreed. 'I wish I could go along and give you a hand.'

Mima said: 'Tell Ma we'll come if the weather's anyways decent, Jess. We can take the young ones down on the sled, give Peter his first ride.'

Jess went on to do his errand with Jason and with Matt; and an hour later when Mima stepped outside for a pail of snow to melt, she heard his snowshoes as he cut straight across the pond from Matt's to his own home. There was in the sound none of that tight squeak which comes when snow kernels are ground together in bitter cold weather; and the night in fact was mild and the stars were blurred by a warm haze. Coming indoors again, she said:

'There's a feel of spring in the air, Joel.'

'It's coming,' he assented. 'We've got a downhill pull from now on. You can see the sun marching. It's rising further north every morning.'

She was busy with supper, moving to and fro. Peter murmured in the box under the loom where he spent most of his days; and small Polly tended him with elaborate conversation, and many reassurances, bidding him not cry when his burblings were as amiable as possible, wiping off bubbles when he blew them, scolding him for nothing so that she might forgive and comfort him again. Joel watched them, smiling.

'He's giving her a time, to hear her talk,' he said. 'You'd think she was a mother with ten squalling brats around.'

'She plays with him all day long,' Mima agreed. 'When she's not letting on to be his mother, she's pretending to be a baby herself, and I have to cuddle her and rock her to sleep and put her to bed and all.' She smiled to herself. 'This morning when you were down feeding the sheep, she was bound she'd nurse, and she was so cute about it I let her.'

'You remind me of Sally Partridge and Alibeus,' he chuckled. 'The time he was so cute about it! But don't do that, Mima. Polly can eat anything, and Peter can't. He needs all you've got to give him.'

'Can't I sometimes, Joel?' she pleaded. Her eyes were softly shadowed. 'I have plenty — and she's getting real thin. I hate having her hungry.'

'Think she is hungry? She doesn't make a fuss about it.'

'That's because I give her a piece of bread or something every little while to sort of spoil her appetite. Eating a piece between meals, she don't want so much mealtimes.' And she said: 'I hope we can go down Sunday, Joel. We've been shut in since November, not hardly going anywhere. If we can once get out and around, it will make it seem more like the end of winter.'

'We'll have a try at it, anyway,' he promised. 'If the snow's good, we can manage.'

'I'd kind of like to hear some preaching, too,' Mima confessed. 'It will be the first in Sterlingtown, Joel — only Mr. Urquhart, and he didn't act like a preacher. It will seem kind of good to sort of go to church again.'

'If Elder Case did a stint on Mily, he must be good.' He said: 'We ought to have a church up here. I never went, much, since I was a boy; but a time like this winter, I've thought it would help some, take our minds off our worrying.' He added: 'Sis didn't keep her school going long; but with a church and a school, the first thing anybody knew we'd have a town.'

'She couldn't keep the school going, with the snow so deep and all. The young ones couldn't get around. She'll get it started again, come spring.'

He nodded, smiling a little, his arm around her. 'Come spring!' he repeated. 'We're always saying that. Winter's a hard time; but once the ice goes out, and the snow settles, and the robins come, and the land's full of birds, and things are growing, you forget about it.'

'It's like waking up after bad dreams,' she agreed. 'Things that look black at night just disappear in the morning — or in the spring.'

* * * * *

The shovelled space between the door and the woodpile caught the morning sun, and the high snow walls shut off any but a strong wind; so small Polly, well bundled, sometimes played out there for a while before dinner. Next morning she was there, Mima and Joel indoors; but the day was mild and Mima had left the door open, and she heard some sound toward the pond. She stepped to the door to listen, and told Joel over her shoulder: 'Someone's coming.' The snow walls were so high she could not see over them; but after a moment Phin Butler appeared on the high ground above the house, against the sky. She called a greeting, glad to see him; and Joel came to the door as Phin climbed the snow wall and slid down inside, grasping Mima's hand and then Joel's.

They stood a moment so, and Phin kicked off his webs. Mima thought there was a change in him. He held his head higher. It no longer drooped forward, and his neck no longer jerked when he spoke, as though he expelled each word with an effort. Joel bade him in; and they went indoors, and Joel put a log on the fire. 'We heard you and Mily were coming up for the meeting,' he said.

Phin looked at Mima. 'We didn't come for that,' he said. 'Mily was bound she'd come.' He was speaking to Mima. 'She wants to see you,' he said.

Mima felt a stiffening in her like fear. 'I guess we'll go to the meeting,' she told him assentingly.

He shook his head. 'No, ma'am,' he explained, 'she wanted to see you, the both of you, before.'

Joel asked in sharp surprise: 'What for?'

Phin did not answer directly. 'I thought you might make it to Lucy's,' he explained. 'She's there. She'd have come herself, but she's pretty heavy. It wore her down, getting that far.' He added: 'She wanted to know could you come see her this morning?'

Mima clutched at any excuse to avoid this encounter. 'I can't leave the babies.'

Phin said: 'I'd stay with them.' And he spoke almost urgently. 'I wish if you could go,' he said. 'She wants it, and I like her to have what she wants.' He hesitated, and his head rose, and he said proudly: 'Mily's some changed, Mima, since Elder Case come to Thomaston. She's all right. Her and me get along fine, and she's been real good to Pa and Ma.'

Joel clapped the other's shoulder hearteningly, feeling the emotion in the man. 'Why — let's go, Mima,' he said. 'Phin can stay here. Do you good to get out of the house.'

'I doubt if your foot will stand it,' she protested, still shrinking from this encounter.

He laughed. 'Sho, my leg's as good as it's ever going to be.'

So Mima was overborne, and she and Joel presently set out, leaving Phin to mind the babies here. While they crossed the knoll and descended to the pond, she watched Joel, fearful some harm might come to him; but on the level of the pond the going was easier. Joel was exhilarated by this sudden taste of freedom. He began to sing, and broke off and said: 'First time I've been farther from the house than the brook, since I broke my leg, Mima. It feels good.'

'I've stayed pretty close my own self,' she reminded him.

'Taking care of me.' He said gently: 'Mima, I don't say much, but I think a lot. I know how it's been for you — and never a word out of you, never anything but cheerfulness.'

'There's been times I didn't feel cheerful.'

'You never let me see it. You've done a hard stint. I know it. I'll be the rest of my life making it up to you.'

They came to the head of the river and moved down toward Seven-Tree Pond. It was warm enough so that her own exertions made Mima breathe a little quickly and perspire; and the blood racing through her veins made her want to run. 'I feel like a spring lamb,' she declared. 'I want to skip!'

'I'll race you,' he challenged.

'No and you'll not! Besides,' she added, 'if we start running we'll work up an appetite — and eat ourselves out of house and home when we get back, and have to starve from now on.'

Her words sobered him too. 'Next year I'm going to plant

enough corn to feed the whole town,' he said, and laughed and added: 'If it looks like a freeze I'll bring it in the house and sleep with it to keep it warm.'

'I've started cutting up the seed potatoes,' she confessed. 'I can get a lot off of them and still keep the seed ends for planting.'

They emerged into Seven-Tree Pond and started across toward the Mill Stream. 'Wonder what Mily wants to see us for?' Joel asked. 'Phin was queer about it.'

'Probably just sociable,' Mima said. It required all the courage she could muster to go on to face this interview. She had learned during the winter to forget Mily for days at a time; and the old hurt was easing. She wondered whether Phin was right in thinking they would find Mily changed; and she wondered whether she would ever ask Joel whether what Mily said that day by the riverbank was true, and knew she would not. Mily's word might be literally true; but literal truth was sometimes the darkest lie. Whatever the truth might be, Mily had never had any real part of Joel; and Mima knew this with a sure knowledge not to be shaken by any testimony.

Yet she dreaded facing Mily now, seeing the other woman heavy with that baby soon to be born. Johnny said it would be an April baby, but Johnny might be wrong. Phin said Mily was near her time; and this was March and that day when Joel spent an hour alone with Mily in the cabin up the river fell in June. Mima had to drive herself to each forward step toward where Mily waited. Joel was talking beside her, and she heard herself answer him, but she did not know what she said, nor hear his words.

They crossed Seven-Tree Pond and came to the shore, and started to ascend toward the mill. Johnny's house was back from the stream a few rods on a knoll there; but the beaten track through the snow followed the water side. Mima remembered the day she first came here, now almost eight years ago; and she looked toward the ledge where she had stood that day. Then she saw someone coming to meet them; saw that this was Mily, without snowshoes, trudging through the snow.

They met her above the gorge ten or fifteen feet deep through which the Mill Stream ran. Mily stopped as they came near, and waited, her hand at her throat; and Mima saw how big she was, and her shadowed eyes. But she saw too, before they spoke, a difference in Mily. Her eyes were as blue, her hair as bright; but she was a woman now.

They came to where she stood, Mima in the lead; but Joel was the first to speak. 'Well, glad to see you, Mily. We left Phin to mind the babies. You look good.'

But Mily was not looking at him. She faced Mima, and Mima thought there was something beseeching in her eyes. She looked from Mima to Joel; and Mima said through lips dry with terror, not knowing what was to come: 'Phin said you wanted to see us.'

Mily nodded. She asked in a low tone: 'You all right, are you? You and Joel?'

'Yes,' said Mima strongly. 'We're all right and always will be.'

'You're thin.'

'We've made out. Joel's leg's as good as ever.' She asked challengingly: 'What did you have to say?'

Mily said quietly: 'I wanted to tell you, I lied to you, that day, Mima.'

Mima tried to speak and could not. Joel, puzzled, perceiving that there was here something hidden from him, stood wondering by. To Mima it seemed that the world was roaring all about her, that a great song like shouting filled the air.

'I was crazy mad,' Mily said. 'I wanted to have you believe it. I'm sorry now. I wanted to tell you I lied.'

Joel demanded: 'Lied about what, Mily?'

Mily faced him bravely. 'About you and me, Joel. I told her this was your baby I'm carrying.'

He stared at her in a blank astonishment. 'Mine?' he echoed.

His cheek reddened with anger. 'Why, damn you!' But then his expression changed. He looked at Mima, asked in a different tone: 'When did you tell her that?'

'The day you came to get Phin to sign the petition.' Mily's lips were trembling. Mima suddenly took the other woman in her arms.

'It's all right, Mily,' she said. 'You're real good to tell me now. I know how hard it is for you to do it. But you didn't do any harm.'

'I wanted to. I'd have done harm enough if it had been anybody but you.'

Mima said, smiling: 'Well, it was me.'

Joel spoke to her. 'Mima, come home.' She looked at him, and saw his eyes, and a warm flood filled her from head to foot. He touched her arm compellingly. She turned away. Mily spoke behind them, in a slow wonder.

'You didn't even ask him, did you, Mima?' she said.

Mima could not speak. Joel told Mily quietly: 'She's waited on me hand and foot all winter, if you want to know. Four months of it. She's done the chores, and tended me, and kept cheerful herself, and half-starved, and had a baby.' His voice rose a little, his anger returning. 'You go back to the house, Mily. We're going home.'

Mily said: 'I guess you've got a right to blame me plenty!'

Joel shook his head. 'No,' he said. 'I'd already forgot about you, Mily. Mima — you come home.'

They left Mily there and turned down to the pond together, walking side by side. There were no words in Mima. Her world was full, completed now. But Joel said at last, evenly and steadily:

'You've had that in your mind all winter.'

'I never believed it.'

'You never would believe it,' he assented understandingly. 'You wouldn't let yourself. But you couldn't help knowing it might be true, the kind I was.'

'I knew it might be true,' she confessed.

'Then how could you go on taking care of me, the way you did?'

Her eyes met his. 'I guess you know,' she said.

'I guess I do,' he assented. His hand touched hers, and their eyes held. They needed no more words.

14

Spring was weeks away, but spring was here. The morning proved to be sunny and fine, and with no wind it was warm enough. Mima, as they prepared to go down to her father's for the meeting, was full of a rich happiness. Joel set the hand sled on the snow outside the shovelled space by the door, and he put a drag rope on it. From the house down to the pond the sled would need to be held back and guided down the path. Mima bundled Peter in the pouch of plaited twists of rabbit skin which she had made to keep him warm, and wrapped him snug and tied him on the sled; but Polly, gleeful with excitement, stoutly refused to be tied on.

'No, no, Polly sit!' she insisted, and she did, on the tail of the sled, her chubby legs straight forward. When they were ready, Joel banked the fire and they set out. Mima took the drag rope to hold the sled back, refusing to risk Joel's falling; and he went ahead down to the pond, guiding the sled along the path while Polly screamed with delight and bobbed hard to make the sled go faster. They came out on the level all laughing, even Peter gurgling in his bonds; and Mima joined Joel on the towrope and they pushed on across the pond. The going was good enough, the sun was warm; and Mima said:

'Another month and there'll begin to be open water around the shores, Joel, and in the river; and six weeks from now the river'll be open and maybe the pond too, and buds swelling. It won't be no time.'

'You can smell spring in the air today, all right,' he agreed. Across the pond, he led the way ashore. 'I don't want to risk hitting a spring hole in the river,' he reminded her. 'And anyway, it's more fun going through the woods.'

They were the first to arrive at Philip's house. Elder Case would come with Ez Bowen, tramping up from Warren. 'I don't know as he'll get here till afternoon,' Mrs. Robbins said. 'He's going to stay the night.'

'Jess didn't say when he'd be,' Mima remembered. 'I don't know where I got the idea it was this morning.'

'I'm full as well pleased to have a visit with you.' Mrs. Robbins was helping unbundle Peter, and Sue had taken Polly in charge, and Philip and Joel and Jacob were standing by the fire, watching, laughing at the women and the babies. Mrs. Robbins said to Joel: 'Got so you can get around again, have you?'

'Good as ever,' he assured her. 'Only that leg's just a hair shorter than the other.'

She chuckled. 'You'll get used to that!' She brought Peter in her arms nearer the fire, looking down at him. 'You'll spend the rest of your life,' she said, 'getting used to having little things the matter with you. None of them amount to much, but every once in a while you'll notice there'll be something you don't want to do any more.'

Philip came to stand beside her, considering his new grandson, poking a big finger at the youngster, making strange sounds that were meant to be seductive. Mrs. Robbins said sharply: 'Stop it! You'll make his eyes toe in.'

Philip chuckled. 'You said that when Dave was a baby, and

every one after,' he reminded her. 'But I kept a-doing it, and they ain't any of them cross-eyed that I can see.'

Joel, watching them together, said in surprise and in amusement too: 'Say, I've just realized something — just noticed something!' He came to Mima, put his arm around her. 'See those two old folks over there?' he demanded, pointing at her father and mother. She nodded, looking up at him, wondering what was coming. 'Well, they feel about each other just the way you and I do,' he declared.

Mima smiled; and Mrs. Robbins demanded: 'Why wouldn't we, I sh'd like to know!'

'I didn't go to laugh about it,' Joel assured her, suddenly gentle. 'I just — hadn't realized it before. I thought that was one way people changed, getting older.'

Mrs. Robbins looked down at the baby in her arms, sleepy now, beginning to close his eyes. She swayed a little to and fro, and her voice fell low and lower as though she sang a lullaby to him. 'It's only on the outside that people change, Joel,' she said. 'It's only on the parts that show. Inside, they stay the same. Take this little young one.' She rocked Peter in her arms. 'He don't know the meaning of it, yet; but he'll learn fast for a while, and he'll think he's smarter than his pappy and his mammy put together, before you know it. Then he'll grow up — but he won't ever grow older inside, after that.'

Philip, beside her, said: 'The thing is, Joel, if you marry the right one, you never get over it.' Mima, watching them together, was warmly happy. 'It keeps you feeling like a young buck, long as you live, just having her around.'

Mrs. Robbins nodded, assenting. 'And a woman's the same,' she said, 'when the man's the right one.' She met Mima's eyes. 'I don't mean on the outside,' she repeated. 'Men get gray-haired, or maybe bald, and they get crow's feet around their eyes, and they thicken up some around the belly; and women lose their shapes having babies, and they kind of spread out and settle down. The flesh and blood part of them gets older, and looks it.

'But the inside part of them goes right on feeling anywhere from eighteen to twenty-four or five.' Her voice was like a low song. 'He's asleep with his fist in his mouth,' she said, watching Peter in her arms.

'Want me to take him?'

'No, I like the feel of him,' she said, and she went on: 'I think sometimes getting old is like a candle burning down. A young one grows up and the first thing he knows he's in love and marrying; and you can see something new in his eyes, deep and strong. That's like a candle when first you light it, standing up so straight and white and slim and fine; and the flame's real pretty to look at.

'But the candle burns on. Maybe it melts crooked, but the flame stays just the same shape and brightness. Maybe if the wind blows, the flame flutters some; but when the wind stops, the flame's just the same again. The candle keeps a-burning, and the tallow runs down the sides of it, and it gets all lumpy and out of shape like a woman after she's had babies for twenty years, or a man that likes his victuals.

'But the flame still burns bright and pretty. The candle gets shorter and stumpier till there ain't hardly anything left of it; but the flame's still there, burning bright, clear and brave and fine, right down to the very end.'

She met their eyes. 'That's the way it is with the right kind of people,' she said. 'Rheumatism can cripple them and tie them up in knots, or the outside of them can change other ways so you'd hardly know them to look at them. But their insides don't change. The flame in them keeps burning clear and fine. If you just look at the flame and not the candle, you'll see it never does change — until one day the candle burns down, and all of a sudden the flame gets small and then it's gone.' She said: 'I'll put the young one on my bed, Mima.'

Mima felt Joel at her side. She looked up at him, and his hand touched her shoulder. She laid her hand on his there. Mrs. Robbins had gone into the bedroom. Philip said quietly from where he stood: 'Your ma's a fine woman, Mima.' He asked: 'How's your corn holding out, Joel? You're looking pretty thin, the both of you.'

Mima watched Joel as he answered, proud that he held his head so high. 'We're all right,' he said. 'We'll be fine, come spring.'

THE END

Postscript

THE historical novel usually concerns itself with persons who have made a major imprint on their times and on the minds of posterity; with generals and statesmen and kings and queens. But for every general there were ten thousand soldiers, and for every king there were subjects. An historical novel may as justly deal with the lives of people who were important not individually but in the mass.

The attempt in this book has been to tell the story of the founding of a small Maine town, by ordinary people, in what was then an ordinary way. It was the way in which towns were founded from the Atlantic seaboard west to the great plains, by stripping off the forest and putting the land to work. The people in this book were not individually as important as George Washington; the town they founded was not as important as New York. But people like them made this country, and towns like this one were and are the soil in which this country's roots are grounded.

This is an historical novel in the sense that most of the major incidents here related actually happened, and that every person named in this book actually lived and wore the name he here wears. The single exception is the girl named Fanny. There were two such girls — see the footnote on page 38 of Sibley's

History of Union — but their names are not known. Some slight liberties have been taken with dates. Josiah Robbins came to Sterlingtown in 1785, not in 1783. A drowning tragedy which suggested the one here used occurred in 1793, and Joel Adams rescued the only feminine survivor. The episode of the Forbes family starving in the wilderness occurred in 1784, not in 1783 as stated in the book.

This book ends on March 7, 1784; but the people in it lived on. Philip Robbins died in 1816 at the age of eighty-six, and Mrs. Robbins died a year before him. When he died, he was survived by six children, fifty-one grandchildren, eighty-five great-grandchildren, and five great-great-grandchildren. Of all his descendants, only three of his children had died before him, and only fifteen grandchildren — a commentary on the sturdiness of their physical inheritance.

Joel Adams was a member of the first board of selectmen, and he served the town in that or some other capacity almost every year of his life thereafter. He and Mima had ten children. Peter, whose birth is recorded in this book, died when he was nine years old; but at least seven of their children grew to maturity, and there is no record of the death of the other two. The youngest son, Joel, became a Methodist minister; Polly married a minister; and several of Joel's grandchildren occupied pulpits. Joel died in 1830, at the age of seventy-seven, but Mima outlived him fourteen years, and was eighty-seven when she died.

Most of the characters in the book had large families and lived long; but Joel's sister who married Jess had only one child, and she and the baby both died in 1790, less than ten years after her marriage. Of the others, Ezra Bowen and Experience had eleven children, of whom two died young. Experience died in childbirth when she was about fifty. Johnny and Lucy Butler had twelve children. Three died as babies. Lucy lived to be eighty-two years old. Phin Butler and Mily had ten children, of whom seven grew to maturity. Both Phin and Mily lived to be over ninety. Rich and Bet had eleven children, David and Bess had twelve, Jason Ware and Polly had eight.

Matt Hawes kept a diary which is a source book constantly referred to in Sibley's history of the town. He and Sally had nineteen children, including two pairs of twins; but only nine of their nineteen children lived to maturity. Eight of the others did not pass their first birthday. Sally died in 1801, aged about fifty.

When this town of Union was incorporated in 1786, there were nineteen families and seventy-five inhabitants. In 1790, there were about 200 inhabitants. The population doubled every ten years till 1810, then increased more slowly to a peak of 1970 in 1850. In 1860 it was 1958. Since then it has steadily decreased. The population in 1930 was 1060.

The spelling of place names is taken from contemporary records and documents. Biguyduce, sometimes called Major-bagaduce or Penobscot, is now, of course, Castine. Sibley's *History of Union* furnished the skeleton of this book and many of the incidents, but much of the material has been drawn from Eaton's *Thomaston* and his *Annals of Warren*; from Locke's *Camden*; from Williamson's *History of Maine* and Williamson's *Belfast*; and from early histories of towns along the Kennebec and the Atlantic seaboard north of Boothbay.

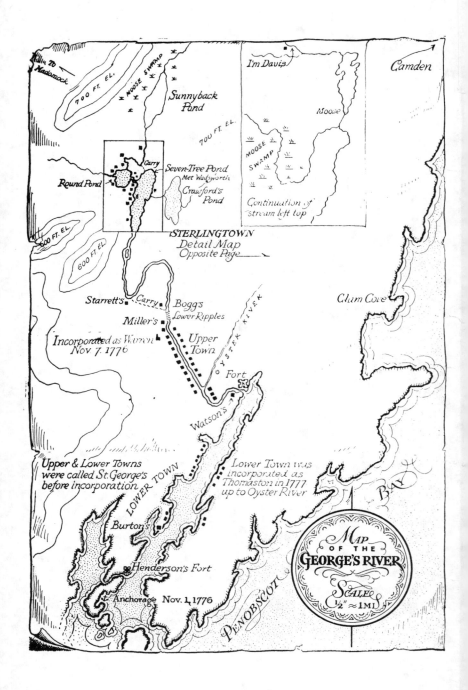

TO Medomock

700 FT. EL.

MOOSE SWAMP

Sunnyback Pond

700 FT. EL.

Im Davis

Camden

Moose

MOOSE SWAMP

Carry

Seven-Tree Pond
Net Wadsworth

Crawford's Pond

Continuation of stream left top

Round Pond

700 FT. EL.

600 FT. EL.

STERLINGTOWN
Detail Map
Opposite Page

Starrett's   Carry   Bogg's
                      Lower Ripples

Miller's

Incorporated as Warren
Nov 7. 1776

Upper Town

OYSTER RIVER

Fort

Clam Cove

Watson's

Upper & Lower Towns
were called St George's
before incorporation

LOWER TOWN

Lower Town was
incorporated as
Thomaston in 1777
up to Oyster River

Burton's

Henderson's Fort

Anchorage   Nov. 1, 1776

PENOBSCOT   BAY

MAP
OF THE
GEORGE'S RIVER
SCALE
½" ≈ 1 MI